# STRATEGIC MANAGEMENT DYNAMICS

# STRATEGIC MANAGEMENT DYNAMICS

## Kim Warren

*London Business School*

John Wiley & Sons, Ltd

Copyright © 2008    Kim Warren

Published by    John Wiley & Sons, Ltd
                    The Atrium, Southern Gate, Chichester,
                    West Sussex PO19 8SQ, England
                    Telephone +44 (0) 1243 779777

Email (for orders and customer service enquiries): cs-books@wiley.co.uk
Visit our Home Page on www.wiley.com

Reprinted with corrections September 2008

*Other Wiley Editorial Offices*

John Wiley & Sons Inc., 111 River Street, Hoboken, NJ 07030, USA

Jossey-Bass, 989 Market Street, San Francisco, CA 94103-1741, USA

Wiley-VCH Verlag GmbH, Boschstr. 12, D-69469 Weinheim, Germany

John Wiley & Sons Australia Ltd, 42 McDougall Street, Milton, Queensland 4064, Australia

John Wiley & Sons (Asia) Pte Ltd, 2 Clementi Loop #02-01, Jin Xing Distripark, Singapore 129809

John Wiley & Sons Canada Ltd, 6045 Freemont Blvd, Mississauga, ONT, L5R 4J3

Wiley also publishes its books in a variety of electronic formats. Some content that appears in print may not be available in electronic books.

*Library of Congress Cataloging-in-Publication Data*

Warren, Kim.
   Strategic management dynamics / Kim Warren.
      p. cm.
   Includes bibliographical references and index.
   ISBN 978-0-470-06067-4
1. Strategic planning.  2. Strategic planning–Case studies.  3. Strategic planning–Problems, exercises, etc.  I. Title.
   HD30.28.W3735 2008
   658.4′012–dc22                        2007034464

A catalogue record for this book is available from the British Library

ISBN: 978-0-470-06067-4

Typeset by Thomson Digital, New Delhi, India
Printed and bound in Great Britain by Scotprint, Haddington, East Lothian

To Christina, without whose patience, support and hard work
this book would not have been possible.

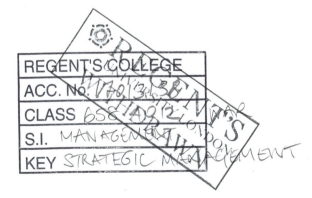

# CONTENTS

# PREFACE

This book takes a somewhat different path from other strategy textbooks, largely because it starts from a slightly different point. The purpose of designing and implementing strategy is to improve performance *over time*. In corporate settings, shareholders value the likely stream of future cash flows, rather than profitability ratios. Simply put, investors will prefer a company generating 12% returns when cost of capital is 8% over a company generating 15% if the first company is growing substantially and the second is not. No matter how sustainable the second company's superior profitability may be, whether due to finding an attractive industry situation or establishing a hard-to-imitate advantage, its lack of growth limits its value.

This overriding imperative to improve performance over time is not limited to the strategic management of corporate entities. It applies equally to public service and voluntary organizations, although they may focus on achieving some other quantifiable purpose rather than creating financial value. Functional parts of organizations also face the requirement to improve performance over time, such as improving service quality, accelerating product development or reducing staff turnover.

To move forward from this concern with performance over time requires a rigorous and quantitative causal explanation for the direction and rate at which performance is changing. This analysis quickly identifies that accumulating resources are the ultimate cause of current performance—customers drive revenue; capacity and staff drive costs, for example. Any desire to estimate how performance will change must therefore depend on how those tangible resources will change.

The complicating issue is that accumulation and depletion of resources do not follow the straightforward form of causality we usually hope to discover. The quantity of each resource at any particular time reflects the organization's entire history, its customer base today, for example, being precisely the sum of every customer ever won, minus every customer ever lost. This has serious implications. If performance depends on factors that have been built up and sustained throughout the past, it cannot be explained by the current values of other factors today—price or marketing spend, for example—no matter how persuasive the correlation results.

The accumulating asset-stock, or resource, is the fundamental component without which no explanation of performance can be accurate. Its principal consequence is that each organization is on a trajectory into the future that has been steered by its previous strategies and decisions. Our quest is to find adjustments to those strategies and decisions that will redirect that trajectory onto a better path. Even when it is possible to achieve step-changes in performance, reliable growth thereafter is still required.

The time-based behavior of accumulating resources and other asset-stocks lies at the heart of a method called system dynamics. This method also captures the next stage in the causal logic—showing *why* resources are being won and lost. These flow rates of resources are fundamental to why performance is changing over time. If there are no flows, then resources don't change, and if resources don't change then other things being equal performance remains the same. Rates of change in resources reflect management decisions and certain external factors, such as competitors' efforts or limited availability of those resources. Crucially, however, as the strategy field has long known, the rate at which resources can be acquired depends strongly on the quantities already in place. This gives rise to interdependence relationships, the capture and quantification of which generates the organization's basic operating system—its core "strategic architecture."

This is the point to which Chapters 1 through 4 of this book progresses. Although the resulting frameworks cover only a mundane set of simple, tangible resources, they already provide valuable explanations for the performance of real organizations over time. Later chapters add to this the intangible factors and capabilities of the strategy field's "resource-based view" of performance,[1] along with competitive and other mechanisms.

While linking resources to performance over time may be somewhat unfamiliar, it nevertheless connects to recognized strategy frameworks and tools. Since strategy is concerned with the acquisition and retention of customers, for example, Chapter 3 shows how the value curve[2] can be a valuable tool for explaining those flows. Owning and acquiring resources are the principal costs incurred by most organizations, so the make-up of the value chain[3] can be more accurately assessed if these separate

---

[1] See for example Barney J. (2002) *Gaining and Sustaining Competitive Advantage*. 2nd edn, Pearson Education, Upper Saddle River, NJ, Chapter 5.

[2] Kim, C. and Mauborgne, R. (1999) Creating New Market Space, *Harvard Business Review*, **77**(1), (January–February), 83–93.

[3] Porter, M. (1980) *Competitive Strategy*, Free Press, New York, Chapter 2.

elements are made explicit. Chapter 4 explains how balanced scorecards[4] can be more robust if built on foundations of a strong causal explanation for performance, which the strategic architecture provides. It is not even necessary to desert our attachment to spreadsheet views of performance. Properly organized, the logic of causality that lies behind an organization's strategic architecture and performance over time can readily be presented in spreadsheet form. However, there are better forms for displaying and working with an integrated picture of performance than the static, isolated tables and charts to which management is usually limited. The book is supported by a simple software tool that enables this improved display of strategic architecture and performance.[5]

The book is intended to be useful in either of two ways. First, individual chapters together with the supporting learning materials can readily be used to supplement existing courses, not just in strategy, but in marketing, entrepreneurship, voluntary sector and public service management and other subjects. The book can also be used as the basis for a full course that focuses on management's imperative to develop and implement strategies that improve performance over time.

Since examination and analysis of performance over time is both unfamiliar and intuitively challenging, simulation-based learning is essential to its appreciation. While we can be told the principles of riding a bike in endless detail, it is not until we climb on and fall off that we learn to manage its dynamics. For most managers, that painful learning takes place on the job, and with other people's money! The frameworks in these chapters are therefore supported by a variety of simulation-based exercises. These include some substantial computer-based business games[6], suitable for class instruction and for distance learning. In particular, a complete and detailed example familiar to all audiences—a low-fare airline—is built up from chapter to chapter. Instructors can therefore make use of well-known case studies from the industry, as well as enriching their classes with the extensive business game provided for this setting.

---

[4] Kaplan, R. and Norton, D. (1996) *The Balanced Scorecard*, Harvard Business School Press, Boston MA.

[5] "**my**strategy™" available from www.strategydynamics.com.

[6] These games are known as "microworlds", after Seymour Pappert, *Mindstorms*, (1980), Basic Books, New York.

**A note on case examples:**

Examples of companies or organizations that appear to be well managed—or sometimes badly managed—are very common in business books. However, exemplary cases at one point in time can readily become failures in later years, and failures can be turned around. In this book, short examples are used to illustrate good or poor practices or performance on a particular issue, in particular circumstances, and at particular times.

Organizations and their situations change constantly—executives come and go, competitors alter their strategies, new market challenges arise, and many organizations simply forget good practices they once employed. It is even possible for a practice that is good for an organization under one set of circumstances to become bad for it when things change. For these reasons, do not read more into the examples reported in this book than they deserve. Certainly do not conclude that "Company X did well by doing Y, so that must be right for us too." Each example should be considered in its own context.

# ACKNOWLEDGEMENTS

The complete list of people who have helped nurture the ideas in this book in one way or another would make a new chapter on its own. However special thanks must go to John Morecroft for opening up this box of magic for me, and to Rod Brown, Jan Polak, Suresh Mistry, Lars Finskud, Maurice Glucksman and Vittorio Raimondi for working with the ideas in their early, ill-formed manifestations. Amongst many others who have provided encouragement and guidance are David Exelby, David Lane, John Voyer, Jeff Trailer, Shayne Gary and Scott Rockart. Thanks also go to those who have contributed content in various places, including Aldo Zagonel, Drew Jones, Jack Homer and their colleagues, and to others who have granted permission to include their work.

The book builds on the powerful foundations laid down by Professor Jay Forrester half a century ago, and extended by the great work of John Sterman and many other outstanding professionals who have shown how the dynamics of some of the most challenging real-world issues can be understood and tackled. I would like to thank all of these colleagues for paving the way to this point, and for their generous help and guidance. I am also grateful for the encouragement of the International System Dynamics Society in its granting of the 2005 J.W. Forrester Award for my previous book "Competitive Strategy Dynamics," as well as for the constant stream of stimulating ideas that flow around that community.

Like all teachers, I have learned a great deal from the very many outstanding students it has been my privilege to teach, especially from their experiences in applying the book's ideas to an amazing diversity of cases—everything from funeral homes to satellite firms, oyster farming to football clubs. Students *will* go and use ideas for purposes for which they were never intended, which is where many extensions of the frameworks in this book came from!

My wife and partner, Christina Spencer, deserves a very special mention. The wide range of learning resources supporting this book is due to many years of persistence and hard, skilled work on her part. So you have Christina to thank for the value of anything you learn from using the book and its supporting materials.

Lastly, I would like to thank Steve Hardman and the team at John Wiley & Sons, Ltd, Chichester, who have been just a delight to work with and who have done what I hope you will agree is a great job in producing this work.

# HOW TO USE THIS BOOK

*Strategic Management Dynamics* is primarily designed as a textbook for introductory courses in strategic management. However, it can be used—in whole or in part—in other types of course, as well as for independent study.

The basic appreciation of how firms and organizations function covered in the early chapters can support foundation courses in business and management, designed to give students a clear context for understanding how functional courses relate to each other. Elsewhere, in MBA and similar programs, the book provides powerful, rigorous frameworks applicable to functional or topic-oriented classes, such as marketing and sales, human resource management, product development, operations management, entrepreneurship and innovation.

Its rigorous, integrated perspective on how the major functions and departments of an organization work together over time also provide a useful basis for a business management and strategy course within specialist Masters' and professional courses in such subjects as finance, marketing, accounting, information systems, and technology management.

## INDEPENDENT STUDY

This book will be useful for anyone wishing to develop their understanding of business and strategy, both newcomers to strategy and those wishing to update their prior knowledge. This may be particularly important to professionals—consultants, analysts and members of strategy teams—who need to keep their skills up to date.

For those who have previously studied strategic management—perhaps as part of an MBA degree or other professional course—the book extends many of the concepts and frameworks in the field in ways that make them more precise, reliable and usable. These contributions arise from its relentless focus on quantified explanations for what is happening to performance in any situation and why, making possible confident, sound choices on "what to do, when and how much" to make substantial and sustained improvements to that performance. The book's own underlying principles and frameworks are powerful and reliable in their own right, as well as supporting existing strategy frameworks. Strategy curriculums other than those used recently at London Business School and a few other leading institutions will not have covered these principles or frameworks.

The study plan is simple—read and review each chapter in turn, making sure to refer back to any concepts developed earlier in the book. Go through the "suggested questions and exercises" at the end of the chapter, answering the questions from memory before checking your answers by looking back into the text. Some of the exercises cannot be validated without instructor advice, although studying similar examples from other parts of the book will give a good sense of how accurately each exercise has been done.

Finally, make use of the online resources available. It is not possible to develop a sound understanding of how decisions and other factors influence an organization's performance over time without actually *experiencing* those connections—in detail and repeatedly. Using the online resources will soon show that even small changes in policy and decisions can cause considerable variations in performance. Simply assuring oneself that the principles have been understood will not be adequate and the simulation exercises should be explored in some depth.

# INTRODUCTORY STRATEGY COURSES

Depending on the number and length of classes available, an introductory course based on this book might use only the early chapters, especially the first four, or include some or all of the topics in later chapters. It is possible to design a strategy course on the basis of one chapter per class (where each class is taken to be approximately three hours, or a pair of 90-minute sessions). If more time is available, the most extensive chapter topics, such as rivalry (Chapter 7), can be spread over more sessions. However, the wide scope and depth of the book's frameworks and exercises mean that instructors will probably wish to focus on certain sections of later chapters, rather than attempt to cover the entire content.

In general, the activities making up a typical half-day of instruction consist of:

*Pre-class work*

- Assignment of preparatory questions for students to consider, typically in the context of specific cases or common examples (see for example the suggested exercises at the end of each chapter).
- Preparatory reading of the selected chapter or sections of the book, with pre-assigned questions or exercises for the students to prepare.

*Class time*

- Review the results from students' group-based simulation exercises from the *previous* class.
- Review the framework(s) on which this class is focused, including review of the assigned student work.
- Demonstrate and discuss the insights arising from the simulation(s) supporting the frameworks for this class, especially focusing on how those insights can be extended to diverse situations.
- Specify the group exercise(s) based on the same simulation(s), for discussion in the following class. (Note: the simulations supporting this book are mostly small exercises, taking less than an hour to explore, not to be confused with the large, complex strategy simulations often used in capstone courses.)

*Between-class student activity*

- Since it is not possible to fully appreciate how strategic performance behaves over time without experiencing those dynamics, it is strongly recommended that students be assigned exercises between classes that utilize the simulation-based resources noted at various points throughout the book.

## CASE STUDIES

Although real-world organizations would generally have access to most of the information needed to carry out the analysis described in the book's frameworks, virtually no existing strategy case studies provide that depth of information. The choice of low-fare airlines as the cumulative example that runs through the book is heavily motivated by the existence of many good cases on such firms and the public availability of much of the required data. Otherwise, the book relies on synthetic cases—examples illustrative of organizations in various sectors.

Case studies can, however, be used as background reading for a class and to explore other issues and concepts. For example, any reasonably detailed case on the launch of a consumer brand would provide a useful context for a class discussing the strategic architecture of such a product outlined in Chapter 4. In addition, instructors can invite class discussion about how the book's frameworks *would* apply to cases, and what data would be necessary in practice to undertake the detailed analysis. For example, the rivalry frameworks can be discussed in relation to case studies about games machines from Nintendo, Sony and Microsoft.

# ADDING ELEMENTS TO EXISTING STRATEGY COURSES

Instructors currently using other strategy textbooks will find that key sections of this book provide important additional content. If only certain chapters are to be assigned, students can be directed to DeskTop Editions available from Wiley.

The key element to employ is the set of principles from Chapters 1–4 that explain how performance over time reflects accumulating and interdependent resources. This naturally fits in the part of a strategy course that deals with internal analysis of organizations, often with a focus on resources and capabilities. Note, however, the important relationship between the established resource-based view of competitive advantage (RBV) and the somewhat different view of resources and performance explained in Chapter 2. At a minimum, Chapter 3 alone can be used, which explains the quantitative implications for performance arising from accumulating resources. A second point on which this book can contribute strongly is in the area of competitive dynamics.

Finally, the book and its supporting learning materials—especially the many small simulations—provide a sound appreciation of how strategy is guided by the policies and decisions made by management as time passes. This makes a powerful contribution to discussions regarding the implementation of strategy, as distinct from the focus of many strategy frameworks on strategy formulation.

# FUNCTIONAL OR TOPIC-BASED COURSES

The early chapters of this book offer simple frameworks for the development of isolated organizational resources—customers, staff, and so on—before developing progressively more detailed models for how these different resources are developed and sustained. Instructors in marketing and sales, human resources, product development, and operations management will therefore find a collection of frameworks that add important concepts to their courses. These can be identified by reviewing the book in its entirety, noting examples and frameworks that relate specifically to the functional course in question. It is then possible to select just those elements required from the book's online resources and exercises.

The book makes a particularly strong contribution to courses in entrepreneurship, focusing as it does on the development, integration and sustaining of basic resources. Experience with students using its frameworks for this context suggests that these add considerable confidence to the resulting business plans for new ventures. Indeed, the launches of many such ventures have been substantially revised and enhanced as a result of this scrutiny, whilst others that do not promise a viable future have been abandoned. Chapters 1–4 provide the essential elements for this purpose.

# SPECIALIST MASTERS' COURSES IN BUSINESS-RELATED TOPICS

The book provides a useful foundation for instructors wishing to offer a core course in business and management as part of Masters' programs in specialist subjects. It offers distinct frameworks for understanding how key functional elements of a business operate—customer acquisition, staffing, product development, and so on—as well as showing how these elements combine in determining performance. It also discusses how firms interact with competitive and other external forces.

To use the book in this way, follow the general guidance above regarding its use in an introductory strategy course.

# ONLINE LEARNING MATERIALS

*Strategic Management Dynamics* is supported by a rich variety of learning materials. These include in particular many small models that run in the **my**strategy™[1] mapping and modeling software, and business simulation games that provide short but rich learning opportunities for groups and individuals. Worksheets are also provided to support each chapter—they are most easily used in software form. The availability of such materials is noted at the relevant points. Finally, a range of online class presentations covering the major topics in each chapter will be developed and offered both for individual instruction and for use in class by instructors.

Many of the learning materials above are available at no charge. For a detailed and up-to-date listing, see www.strategydynamics.com/smdresources and, for instructors only, www.wiley.com/go/smd.

---

[1] "**my**strategy" is a registered trademark of Global Strategy Dynamics Ltd.

# CHAPTER 1

# PERFORMANCE THROUGH TIME

## KEY ISSUES

- ✪ Business value reflects future earnings.
- ✪ The management imperative: building performance into the future.
- ✪ Nonfinancial performance measures, especially in public service and voluntary organizations.
- ✪ Appropriate objectives: achievable, but developing the full opportunity.
- ✪ Inappropriate performance measures: ratios, market share, percentage growth rates.
- ✪ Multiple and conflicting objectives.
- ✪ Choosing appropriate timescales, depending on the issue of concern.
- ✪ Functional challenges and choice of objectives.
- ✪ Implications for information needs.

Worksheet 1: Performance Objectives over Time.

This chapter makes connections to the following concepts: economic profit, free cash flow, value based management, sustained competitive advantage.

## THE PERFORMANCE IMPERATIVE

Before trying to develop tools and frameworks for understanding and improving strategic performance of firms and other organizations, it is helpful to clarify the question we need answered—that is, what exactly *is* the "performance" that we want to improve? Popular writing on strategy, whether in management journals or books, avoids this question entirely and moves directly on to offering recipes, frameworks, checklists and general advice. Yet it will be difficult to have confidence in such advice if it is not clear what outcomes are expected, or how exactly the recommended actions lead to those outcomes.

## FINANCIAL PERFORMANCE

Strategy textbooks, which are largely devoted to commercial business situations, generally take some indicator of financial performance as the measure of concern. The large financial values involved in the commercial sector create an understandable incentive for academics, consultants and executives to develop strategy tools for such cases. However, as a result, the strategy concerns of public sector, voluntary, and other not-for-profit organizations are somewhat neglected. Ideally, we need tools and frameworks that are helpful to management in all cases, not just for business. Furthermore, many strategic issues in corporate situations, while they will ultimately affect financial performance, primarily concern nonfinancial issues: poor marketplace reputation, rapid loss of staff, business lost to competitors, and so on. Nevertheless, since the financial performance of firms is helpfully clear, as well as highly valued, we will start with these concerns before widening the question to encompass other kinds of objectives.

A wide range of financial measures are featured in firms' reporting, controls and objectives, but the overriding concern with the interests of investors has led to the choice of one specific measure—economic profit—as the basis for assessing performance for any particular time period. The rationale for this choice is extensively explained in other textbooks, so it will only be summarized briefly here.[1]

Two elements of profit must be distinguished. First is the "normal" profit that investors would expect to receive for the use of their capital, given the level of risk they are taking on by investing in a particular type of business. This leaves a second element, the "economic profit", which is the surplus that remains after the costs of *all* inputs (including the cost of capital) have been paid out, so:

*Economic profit = operating profit* minus *taxes* minus *cost of capital*

This has become more than just a theoretical concept, with economic profit or the closely related "economic value added" (EVA) being adopted as a management tool by many large corporations.[2,3]

An exclusive focus on current profit poses a rather obvious problem. We can nearly always boost profits *now*, by simple changes such as pushing up prices or cutting expenditure, although shareholders will not thank us for these actions if we damage *future* profits. Historical and current profits are therefore only relevant insofar as they provide important clues to what profits will likely be in the coming years. This severely limits the value of any strategy approaches or frameworks based on explanations for profitability in a single period, no matter how persuasive the statistical significance of those explanations.

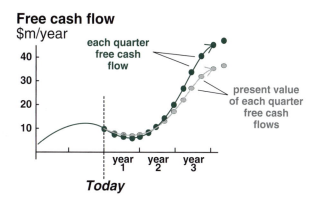

**Figure 1.1: Future free cash flows and their present value.**

The money available to distribute to shareholders in future years will be the cash flow generated by the company's operations, minus any additional capital input required to make that operating cash flow possible. So another measure that receives attention is "free cash flow." Current period profits include an allowance for writing off the past expenditure on fixed assets, known as depreciation. This depreciation needs to be added back and replaced by the actual expenditures on fixed and working capital. This results in the following measure of a firm's free cash flow:

*Free cash flow = operating profit + depreciation − taxes − change in fixed and working capital*

The value of a firm to its investors reflects the expected stream of all *future* free cash flows,[4] but is not simply the sum of these amounts. Cash received today and in the near term is valued more highly than the cash that may be received far in the future, due to the increasing uncertainty involved and the fact that the money invested has alternative uses. Each period's cash flow is therefore discounted by the firm's cost of capital to arrive at its "present value" (Figure 1.1), and the firm's total value is the sum of all those values out into the future.[5]

To evaluate a firm's strategy, we therefore need a way to estimate the *future trajectory* of cash flows, not just a single period. Furthermore, since strategic management concerns *improvements* in performance, we need a way to estimate what impact on that cash flow trajectory may arise from any actions or decisions we may be considering. Such changes may be relatively minor, such as a price reduction intended to accelerate sales growth, or major, such as the acquisition of another substantial business.

In Figure 1.2, Strategy B should be preferred because it delivers a greater total discounted present value than Strategy A, even though it involves lower cash flows in year one.[6] Outcome B could, for example, arise from entering a new market or

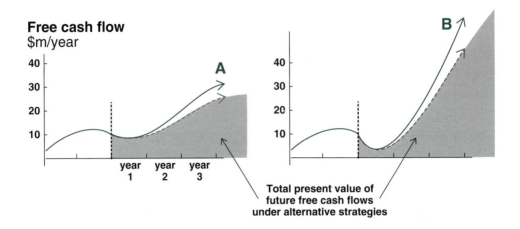

**Figure 1.2:  Total value of a firm under alternative strategies.**

launching a new product, either of which would incur short-term costs but with the prospect of enabling additional growth thereafter. Management will, of course, face the challenge of convincing investors to share their confidence in option B!

The principles outlined to this point provide the overriding focus for this book:

**Strategic management is about building and sustaining
performance into the future.**

This is not a novel idea in the strategy field, but goes back to seminal work in the 1950s by Edith Penrose,[7] who pointed out that superior profitability is neither interesting in itself, nor sustainable in any but the most exceptional circumstances. Rather, management should be concerned with growing future economic profit.[8]

To illustrate the idea that shareholders value future cash flows, even if money has to be invested in the short term, Figure 1.3 shows the profit history for Amazon.com.

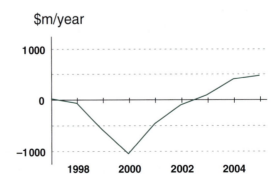

**Figure 1.3:  Profit history at Amazon.com.**

In the years up to 2001, the company repeatedly delivered only losses (and heavily negative cash flows). Investors nevertheless ascribed value to the firm because of the prospects that profits would arise in due course. Indeed, those early losses were often greater than investors had previously expected, yet they still valued the company positively since each new level of loss arose from additional spending to develop ever more sources of sales and thus future cash flows. (Note that this is not a story many firms can credibly copy, since few face the burgeoning new opportunities that Amazon.com enjoyed.)

> From this point on, we will assume that the appropriate translation between operating profit, economic profit, and free cash flows can be properly carried out by finance professionals. Our task in developing and evaluating strategy is to provide a confident estimate of what those top-level profits are likely to be. We will therefore generally refer to operating profit or cash flow when discussing the financial performance of commercial firms.

## NONFINANCIAL PERFORMANCE OBJECTIVES

The purely financial view implied by this approach to valuing firms need not be inconsistent with other objectives, or with concerns for wider issues, such as social responsibility. Indeed, lack of attention to such issues can easily create problems that ultimately damage long-term profits and business value.

Management often sets targets for measures that are not expressed in financial terms—customer growth, market share, staff numbers, and so on. Some companies even set aims for intangible measures, such as reputation. This is not to say that they ignore bottom-line financial performance. Rather, they focus on these other factors because they *drive* financial performance. Investors, analysts and other outside commentators also pay attention to firms' performance on such measures, so nonfinancial aims and progress towards them are often made quite public. Airlines report passenger volumes, cellphone operators report on subscriber numbers, fast-moving consumer goods (FMCG) firms report market shares, and so on.

Skype, the voice-over Internet protocol (VoIP) telephony service, is a well known situation where management and outsiders alike watched progress with keen interest. As Figure 1.4 shows, attention focused on the quarterly growth in the number of registered users. Having registered subscribers is not especially

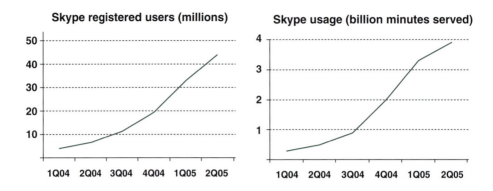

**Figure 1.4: Early growth in registered users of Skype VoIP, and usage of the service.**
Source: Company reports.

useful, however, unless they are *using* the service, so a secondary indicator is actual usage. As at the end of the second quarter, 2005 (2Q05), management might have been somewhat disappointed to see that usage growth had dipped below growth in user numbers. However, it is possible that VoIP, like other new technologies, won the keenest users first, so this was not necessarily a cause for concern. These nonfinancial indicators do not make financial performance unimportant, of course, and Skype seeks to earn revenues from add-on services, such as "Skype-in" and "Skype-out", which connect calls in from, and out to, normal phones.

## PERFORMANCE CONCERNS IN NONCOMMERCIAL SETTINGS

Nonfinancial performance aims are understandably common in public sector, voluntary, and nongovernmental organizations (NGOs). One such case concerns the increasing prevalence and cost of diabetes in affluent societies.[9] In the United States, for example, the number of people with diabetes more than doubled between 1980 and 2003, from 5.8 million to 13.8 million (Figure 1.5).

Now there *is* a financial objective in this case: to limit the cost of treating diabetes and the various unpleasant illnesses that it can cause. The total costs of diabetes in the United States in 2002 were estimated at $132 billion, with $92 billion of that amount in direct medical expenditures and the other $40 billion in indirect costs due to disability and premature mortality.[10] But since those costs flow strongly from the number of people with the complaint, it is entirely reasonable that attention should focus on this nonfinancial indicator.

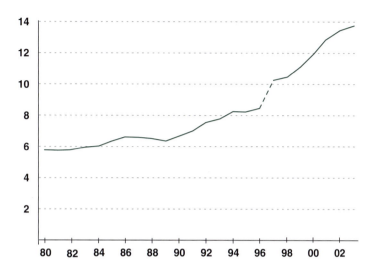

**Figure 1.5: Prevalence of diabetes in the United States (millions).**
Source: This chart gives numbers of diagnosed cases – total cases are approximately 25% higher. Reproduced by permission of the US Centers for Disease Control and Prevention (change in measurement between 1996 and 1997).

# THE MANAGEMENT CHALLENGE: IMPROVING FUTURE PERFORMANCE

We have established that the time path of future performance is central to the concerns of investors in commercial firms, as well as to stakeholders in public policy and nongovernmental organizations. Disappointment with strategic performance defined in these terms is widespread,[11] so it is important to examine the issue in more detail. There are three distinct, but related questions lying behind the issue of how businesses and other organizations perform through time:

● **Why** has our historical performance followed the time path that it has?
● **Where** will the path of future performance take us if we carry on as we are?
● **How** can we improve that future performance?

The first question may not be relevant in every case—a new venture start-up has no history, for example. However, in most cases, history is highly relevant to the likely trajectory of future performance. To see why these three questions are important, and how widely they vary in character between different situations, consider the example of Amazon.com in more detail.

Amazon.com is an outstanding growth story, as the company expanded from the online sale of books by offering an increasingly wide range of other

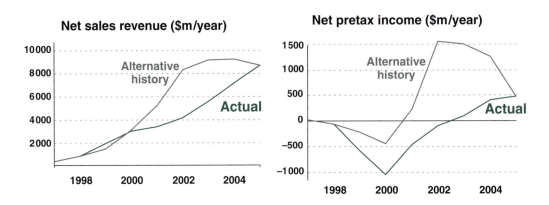

**Figure 1.6:** **A hypothetical alternative sales and profit history of Amazon.com.**

high-value/small-size consumer goods. Since its founding in 1994, the company has promised and delivered growth in its business although, as explained above, it took until 2002 to translate increasing sales volume and revenue into profitability.

So how do our three questions apply to Amazon.com?

*Why has our historical performance followed the time-path that it has?* Sales have grown strongly as consumer uptake of online purchasing has spread and as Amazon.com has extended its product range and entered new geographic markets. Earnings have bounced back from heavy losses into positive profitability, as early expenditure generated the sales growth and gross profits to more than cover the continuing costs of serving customers' demand.

However, the company's development need not have followed the same path, even if it ended up at the same point in 2005. Figure 1.6 compares the company's actual record with an alternative, fictional history. In this other world, the answers to our first question would be quite different. The company might conceivably have grown its revenues still more strongly between 1999 and 2002 than it actually did, due to an even faster penetration of online shopping by consumers or extension of its product range and services. From 2002 to 2005, sales growth could have slowed and reversed, perhaps due to saturation of the potential market, the emergence of strong competitors, or a slowdown in the company's expansion of its offerings. The alternative income line is more worrying still, and explanations might include reduced margins due to competitive activity, poor cost control, or deliberate increases in spending in an effort to restart growth.

*Where will the path of future performance take us if we carry on as we are?* This second question shows the importance of answering the first. The two alternative histories *must* imply very different prospects for the future, even though the 2005 endpoint is identical. Figure 1.7 extends the time horizon beyond 2005, and offers a plausible

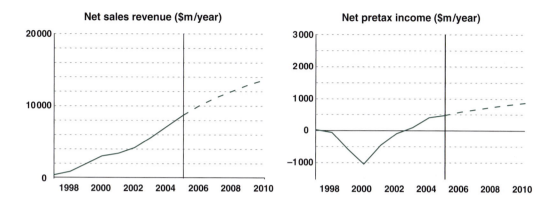

**Figure 1.7: Plausible sales and profit prospects for Amazon.com, reflecting its actual history to 2005.**

future for Amazon.com's sales and profits, given the company's actual history. Sales continue to grow for much the same reasons they have in the past—more consumer use of online shopping and extended coverage by the company of product and geographic markets. As a result, profits continue to grow.

But the answer to "where might we be heading?" would likely be very different, had the alternative history occurred (Figure 1.8). Now we are worried that the slowdown in sales could become a serious downturn, especially if the recent history had reflected progress by powerful rivals. If this were to come about, the profit forecast could be very disappointing, with the company slipping into losses as it struggles to contain costs that it has built up to support a growing sales rate.

*How can we improve that future performance?* Amazon.com's actual history to 2005 offers encouraging prospects for sales and profit growth thereafter, so in reality,

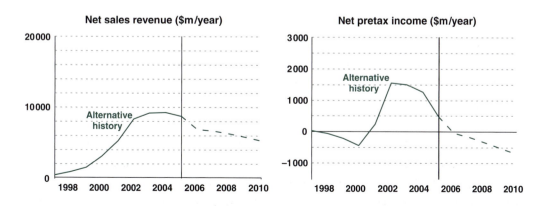

**Figure 1.8: Sales and profit prospects for Amazon.com reflecting a fictional alternative history.**

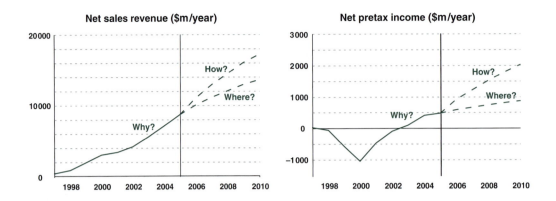

**Figure 1.9:** Plausible improvements to sales and profit prospects for Amazon.com, given its actual performance history.

answers to this third question focus on pushing growth just a little faster, while not risking damage to the business system that supported its performance to date. Perhaps further product and service development would drive additional growth, and this could plausibly lead to still higher profits (Figure 1.9).

The answers to this third question would have appeared very different if the company had reached 2005 by the alternative path (see Figure 1.10). Instead of asking how the firm might safely push for even faster growth, it would instead be worrying about how to stop sales revenue slipping backwards, and then how to restart growth. Such a turn-round would likely be costly, so the time path of recovery might well show an even worse profit performance in the next year or two than the "do nothing" projection.

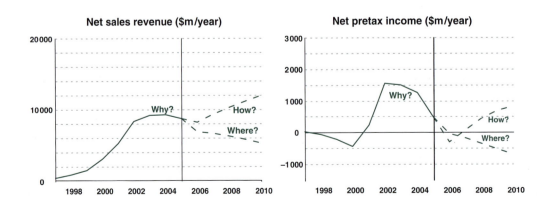

**Figure 1.10:** Desired sales and profits improvements for Amazon.com, following an alternative history.

## SETTING APPROPRIATE OBJECTIVES

Failing to understand these three questions of performance through time can make it difficult for management to determine an appropriate performance goal. Two types of errors are common. Objectives may be set that are completely beyond the scope of the business to accomplish. Alternatively, management may significantly underestimate performance that might be possible, if it were to pursue policies that would allow the business to fulfill its potential.

Figure 1.11 shows overly ambitious targets for an international group in the IT and communications industry that was intent on capitalizing on the emerging opportunity for integrating mobile communications with corporate information systems. The opportunity was genuine, very large, and developing rapidly, driven by new technology and the efforts of some large competitors. Top management set a target of multiplying the business fourfold in four years. Unfortunately, this required three times the number of technical specialists that the company had in its sales and customer support teams. Very few such people existed in the industry and they were in high demand. It would take at least two years to develop existing staff, and the business was declining rather than growing. The goal was entirely unrealistic.

It is important not to confuse this error with the setting of "stretching" goals, which can energize an organization toward what may appear a daunting ambition.[12]

---

**Doing it right: history matters!**

There is often a reluctance to examine the history of an organization's performance—immediate results naturally get the most attention, followed perhaps by concern with the medium to long term. But there are two key reasons for examining history.

- performance reflects how complex business systems interact, so history contains considerable information about these relationships that has important implications for what may happen in future
- much of the future is *already determined* by occurrences in the past, so the trajectory of performance over recent history has important implications for what is about to happen in the short to medium term

**No amount of analysis of current business, financial numbers or ratios alone, at whatever level of detail, can tell us how the company's future performance will develop.**

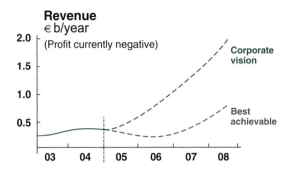

**Figure 1.11: Revenue growth aims in a new market for an IT/communications firm.**

Companies frequently establish a future vision and most standard strategy texts offer examples of vision or mission statements that set the tone for an organization's progress toward outstanding achievements. However, that is not what is being described here, which is a specific financial target that clearly cannot be hit due to the basic physics of the business system. Setting targets like this destroys credibility in any vision that management may articulate, undermining, rather than assisting in its achievement.

The contrasting case in Figure 1.12 concerns the credit card business of an East European bank. The firm had an overall corporate goal to achieve 15 % annual growth in profits. Given the attractive opportunity in the market, it set a "stretch goal" of 22 % growth. On examination, it became clear that the opportunity was already many times greater than this bank or its rivals had appreciated. None had

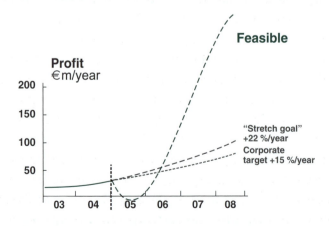

**Figure 1.12: Profit growth opportunity for the East European credit card business of a major bank.**

assembled the resources or capacity to develop the opportunity nor had they under-taken the necessary marketing to capture the potential. This division could readily multiply profits by many times over the next few years, provided that it immediately committed sufficient resources.

## INAPPROPRIATE PERFORMANCE MEASURES

### FINANCIAL RATIOS

This chapter's initial explanation of investors' financial concerns emphasized the importance of the future stream of cash flows, rather than any particular ratios at a point in time. It also pointed out that financial ratios can be easily manipulated in the short term, to the detriment of future profits. In general, then, when looking at strategy, management should be giving higher priority to how profits will grow over time, rather than to these ratios.

This is *not* to say that financial ratios are unimportant. If they are not healthy, or cannot be expected to move to healthy levels, then management will not be able to deliver on its strategy goals. Nevertheless, we argue strongly that management should switch from being driven by financial ratios to taking control of the absolute scale of financial results.

This implies that profit margin, return on capital or any other financial ratio should *never* be chosen as the metric on these performance-over-time charts. In-stead, the charts should be populated with absolute values of profits or revenues (e.g. $m/month), or with absolute values of business activity, such as sales volume (e.g. 1000 units/month) or factors that drive that activity. In many businesses, customer numbers are an obvious choice. Certain sectors have rather particular business drivers. Construction companies, for example, need to anticipate the number of future projects and oil companies focus on how their oil reserves will change as existing fields are depleted and new discoveries are made.

Care is needed, though, if the strategy focus is on revenue growth or its drivers. This implicitly assumes that the costly supply side of the business will be fine—that it will be soundly developed to be affordable and sufficient to win and support revenue aspirations. If this might not be the case then attention should probably be moved to the revenue *and* cost prospects, i.e. to likely profit results.

In nonbusiness cases, too, a natural starting place is with likely future activity rate, or with the factor that drives that activity—e.g. the number of diabetes suffer-ers mentioned above, which drives activity rates for various medical services. Volun-tary organizations supporting disadvantaged groups will focus on the likely future rate of demand for their services, driven by the number of people served. Police and armed forces will be concerned with the likely rates of criminal or hostile activity and therefore with the numbers of criminals or enemy forces driving those rates.

Again, this is not to say that financial viability is unimportant or that financial ratios should not be tracked to ensure an organization's viability. However, this is not the strategic focus—an organization's financial health should serve its purpose, rather than being its master.

## MARKET SHARE

In some industries, management is focused—sometimes seemingly obsessed—with market share. There are a number of problems with this measure as a basis for strategy. First there is the rather simple point that you will enjoy larger sales with 25 % of a $100 million/year market than with 50 % of a market that is only $20million/year in total.

Secondly, market share is merely a coincidental ratio between sales and the total market, so a company has no decision levers that connect directly to this ratio. It is *sales* that any decisions or policies will affect—by winning customers and persuading them to buy more. The same applies to your competitors, so when you track market share, you are mixing up the consequences of both your own choices and those of your rivals.

Thirdly, seemingly small movements in market share can disguise big underlying changes. This may delude management into thinking nothing much is happening and that nothing much *can* happen. In the case of a mature pain-relief product, market shares were changing very little while, in relation to the company's sales rate, many new customers were acquired and others lost. A new focus on reducing customer loss rates highlighted the potential for real sales growth that the company had not seen for years. Market share did increase as a result of developing a clear picture of how sales might grow, but no amount of attention to this ratio, or the tiny fractions by which it had changed from year to year, revealed anything useful about what the company should do.

A competitor's achievements or failings also contain important information—such as successful acquisition of new customers or the failure of a marketing campaign to boost customer purchases. Your market share may have gone up or down by a percentage point or two during a particular year, while a large competitor has lost 20 % and a new rival has won a significant share. Both those changes contain much more useful information than the marginal shift in your own situation. Your strategy should incorporate learning from the things that the new rival is doing and avoiding whatever difficulties the loser experienced.

## PERCENTAGE GROWTH RATES

The growth rate for a market or business is another common indicator that can be highly misleading. Again there is the simple observation that 10% growth in a $100m market is more actual business than 50% growth in a $10m market.

The limited relevance of this percentage measure is highlighted particularly as new markets emerge or new businesses develop. At some point in their history, Skype and Amazon.com alike probably hit a level for their customer base that was three times the previous year, so their growth rates were 200% per year. However, this percentage contains no useful information. Absolute numbers, on the other hand, are critical—specifically, the number of new customers and their future revenue potential.

When markets are developing, market growth rates and market share measures both mislead management into ignoring the *potential* customers, sales and profits that will become available as this potential develops. This has led to the sound suggestion that "opportunity share" is a better issue to track.[13] Skype's market share of the 2005 VoIP telephony demand was much less significant to its future prospects than was the fraction of potential demand that it had captured.

The importance of opportunity share is not limited to new technology industries. In 2004, the Chinese insurance market was worth 150bn yuan ($18bn) and growing at a reasonable, if not spectacular, rate. As China opens its markets to foreign participation, large insurance companies are scrambling to grab a share, often by acquiring local distributors. The real prize, however, lies with the vast numbers of customers who are currently uninsured but likely to become available as income levels rise. Ill-advised attention to current market share is leading some to sign up poor quality business, where salespeople move from firm to firm, taking their clients' business with them.

## BENCHMARKS

Something of an industry has grown up for research organizations that survey firms in a sector and sell back to them anonymous performance rankings for all the firms on various measures. Individual companies can then compare their performance on a specific issue with "benchmarks"—the best performance to be found among their competitors.

Benchmarking may help to ensure firms are with the pace on key measures of operating performance, like quality levels and productivity. This may be fine when you are comparing like with like, for example car makers with similar product ranges, but it can be dangerous when firms are operating with significant differences.

One oil company participated in a benchmarking study that included comparisons of maintenance spending. This company's expenditure per unit of production was somewhat greater than the "best in class", and the gap represented huge potential savings. Sure enough, by pursuing this benchmark, costs were reduced and profits boosted—for a while. Five years later, the company's equipment was in such a poor state that breakdowns and emergency repairs soared. There were even worries about safety being compromised. Spending had to be raised far above the original rates just to stop things from continuing to decline. Even if you are comparing yourself with similar competitors, the danger is that the allegedly best-in-class competitor may itself be making a mistake.

## MULTIPLE AND CONFLICTING OBJECTIVES

Most organizations discover that it can be risky to focus on one performance measure alone. Pursuing profit growth might be achieved at the expense of losing sales and market share, if it is achieved by raising prices, which could lead to losing customers. Consequently, many companies have an eye on both profits and sales volume (or less advisedly, market share). Conversely, some companies focus on market share believing that profitability will follow. This assumption received strong support from research in the 1960s and 1970s, which seemed to show that firms with higher market shares were typically more profitable than firms with less. This encouraged many companies to pursue increased share at almost any cost, neglecting the true reasons why larger firms were more profitable. While the correlation may have been statistically significant, it did not follow that market share *caused* profitability. More successful firms generally had better strategies and management of their operations, resulting in both growing sales volume *and* profitability.

Few firms today pursue profitability or sales growth alone—or any other single measure. Most pursue a balance between these two items, and often more, recognizing that it would be foolish to ignore the factors necessary for the sustained health of the business. Those factors often include "soft" issues, such as reputation, service quality or product appeal. The observation that firms need to track and manage performance on multiple dimensions has led to the widespread adoption of "balanced scorecard" systems,[14] which lay out a range of mutually consistent performance measures covering customer-related, organizational, financial and operational factors.

In practice, organizations cannot avoid simultaneously tracking several measures. Therefore, our analysis of strategy dynamics will always track multiple measures, even when it starts from a single primary indicator of how performance is changing into the future. This will enable management to see how conflicting aims are changing in relation to each other, and to make appropriate trade-offs continually as the future unfolds.

## TIMESCALES

Most examples of performance challenges discussed so far have played out over recognizably strategic timescales—several years at least. However, not all strategic situations have such long-term horizons.

The example of Skype already illustrates a situation that is evolving rapidly. For the organization to simply watch progress from year to year would be far too casual. "Strategic" does not equal "slow!" Even though concern is with future performance, short-term conditions and events can have a big impact on longer term outcomes.

> **An issue, decision, opportunity or challenge is "strategic" if it is likely to significantly alter the trajectory of future performance.**

Take the case of a pharmaceuticals company facing an attack by its largest competitor. The general manager of this €250 m/year business unit discovered he had four weeks to prepare for a major competitive onslaught. Why the urgency, and why is this short episode strategically important?

The market in question is travel vaccines, so sales build strongly during the pre-vacation period of May through June. There are five to six major diseases covered by the available vaccines, such as hepatitis A and B and typhoid. The market in the region where this attack is about to break out is worth approximately €500 m/year and is growing.

This company has 50 % of the market, and the major rival has about one-third, with the rest being served by smaller firms. Both of the large companies have an almost complete range of vaccines, except that this firm has the only vaccine approved for one major disease, a product that generates €50 m/year of the company's revenue and one-third of its profits.

The threat arises as the major rival announces its own alternative—a near-identical molecule that has just been approved. Doctors are delighted, because the competitor has a track record of undercutting on price by at least 15 %. The competitor's salesforce of 50 is excited, because they have long suffered resistance from doctors due to this gap in their product range. Their company inundates the medical journals and doctors' surgeries with advertizing and promotional literature. One year ago, this same rival successfully stole 40 % of the company's sales on another product within three months of a similar launch.

While this situation will play out over a few months, it is *still* a strategic issue. Losing a substantial fraction of this critical market threatens the cash flow that supports the salesforce, R&D and marketing expenditure. Failure will demoralize the company's salesforce, and encourage many to leave—most likely to the competitor! The company has historically sustained higher prices by offering better customer support, but this is costly, and the price premium that funds this service is threatened by the competitor's low-price positioning. Overall, this single episode could be the start of an unstoppable decline for the whole division. Figure 1.13 shows two versions of this division's short-term sales.

As things turned out, this company was able to fend off the attack by its competitor without even having to reduce prices. The defense included exploiting inaccuracies in the competitor's claims for its product, loading the doctors' inventory with their own product, and undermining the morale of the competitor's salesforce and their commitment to the new product.

Even though many organizations operate in environments that move quickly, senior management is still surprisingly committed to annual planning systems that have no capacity to respond to such rapid changes.[15] Budgets are set, say, in December for the coming 12 months and managers are held to those numbers regardless of unforeseen events. This results in errors of two kinds. As the year progresses, unforeseen difficulties arise—a competitor launches a better product for example—but the company still carries on as though the original sales target for the year was correct. Alternatively, things may turn out better than expected—perhaps customer adoption accelerates well ahead of forecast—but sales and marketing budgets that were chosen on much more cautious assumptions are immovable.

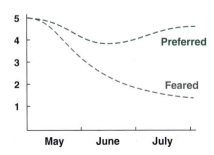

**Figure 1.13: Sales projections for pharmaceuticals firm facing new threat—000 packs per month.**

# PERFORMANCE AIMS IN DIFFERENT CONTEXTS

The Amazon.com example features the pleasant challenge of sustaining growth that is already strong. Not all organizations are so fortunate as to be concerned only with how quickly they can keep growing.

## STABILITY

Many firms, particularly in developed economies, operate in markets that long ago went "ex-growth", with every customer who might be interested in taking the product or service already doing so. Examples include utilities such as power or water supply, fast-moving consumer goods (FMCG) such as cleaning materials or food and drink products, and well-established services such as hairdressing.

There is a difficult balance to achieve in such cases. On the one hand, operating in a low-growth or no-growth market is not sufficient reason to assume that no growth is possible. On the other hand, efforts to pursue growth that are not realistically attainable can be badly damaging.

One possibility for driving growth in mature markets is to challenge the reasons that are assumed to be preventing growth. This occurred in the cinema industry in the 1970s. Until then, it had been widely assumed that movie going was doomed by the growth of TV and other home entertainment. Investment by film studios led to a stream of new, big-budget movies, and cinema operators developed much-improved cinemas, which brought the industry back into growth.

Even if the industry is irretrievably mature, growth in sales and profits can often be taken from competitors or substitutes (products that serve the same customer need, without being directly competing products). Firms in such markets are often satisfied to take small points of market share from their competitors and, if sustained over a long enough period, such creeping progress can indeed lead to a significant change.

However, more substantial performance may be possible, as the earlier example of the pain-relief product shows. For this brand, simply slowing the churn rate among consumers would allow sales to grow, which could be achieved with a more focused marketing strategy than previously employed. As a result, the renewed sales growth could be initiated with a *reduced* marketing budget, leading to a disproportionate increase in profits (Figure 1.14).

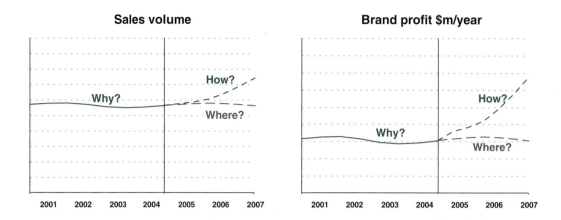

**Figure 1.14: Profit opportunity for a product in the low-growth painkiller market. (Actual data are confidential.)**

While it is important to seek opportunities for profitable growth in low growth industries, it is also essential to avoid pursuing growth that will damage the business. One company that encountered this danger at least once in its history is McDonald's (see box).

In spite of declaring a *lower* target for earnings growth, the net income of McDonald's actually rose from $893 m in 2002 to $1 471 m in 2003 and $2 279 in 2004. Nor did it take long for investors to recognize the realism of this new strategic focus. The stock price, which had fallen from over $29 to $15 by the end of 2002, recovered to $24 by the end of 2003 and climbed to $34 by late 2005. All of these activities occurred during a time of immense pressure on the company from public concern with the health effects of its products.

Blockbuster Inc., the global rental store chain for in-home movies and games, also has to sustain performance in mature markets. The company boasts more than 9 000 stores throughout the Americas, Europe, Asia and Australia. It built its business by renting videos during the boom in consumer purchases of video recorders in the 1990s. Although it has since moved on to renting out DVD films and video games, it is constantly threatened by substitutes for its service, such as the increasingly wide range of movie transmissions by cable and satellite TV, or postal distribution of rental DVDs from the likes of Netflix and Amazon.com.

## THE GROWTH-TO-MATURITY TRANSITION

The contrast between the strategic imperative facing firms in high-growth markets and those in more mature sectors comes into sharp focus when industries

> **Extract from letter to McDonald's Shareholders from the Chairman and CEO, included in 2002 Financial Results**
>
> *... Over the past several years, McDonald's has lost momentum ... and lost what it takes to make customers feel special. We have struggled to grow our business in the face of weak and uncertain economic conditions around the world. The result has been disappointing financial performance. This is not acceptable.*
>
> *It didn't take me long to realize that some difficult—albeit necessary—decisions had to be made. To start, we are **targeting a lower earnings growth** rate. Given the nature and size of our business, **the prior earnings per share growth target in the 10 percent to 15 percent range is no longer realistic**. Yet, we are committed to returning the Company to reliable, sustainable annual sales and earnings per share growth. We also have decided to lower our capital expenditures compared with recent years until we achieve significant improvements in sales, margins and returns at our 30 000 existing McDonald's restaurants. ... McDonald's is in transition from a company that emphasizes "adding restaurants to customers" to one that emphasizes "adding customers to restaurants."*
>
> (Bold type added for emphasis.)

move rapidly from growth to maturity. Management has to switch from driving exploitation of the emerging opportunity to conserving what has been accomplished and extracting sustainable value into the future.

The cellphone industry exhibits this transition clearly. As markets developed, cellphone operating companies engaged in a race to sign up new subscribers, offering generous handset subsidies and reseller incentives. However, as penetration of cellphone ownership approached 100%, marketing strategies began to demonstrate a significant shift.

First, operating companies tried to persuade subscribers to switch from competitors' services to their own. It did not take long, though, for cellphone operators to realize that stealing each others' customers was ultimately a zero-sum game. With the costs of signing up a new subscriber often more than the full-year income that each might generate, with usage charges falling and with churn rates (the fraction of customers leaving each year) hitting 25% or more, the financial case for such ferocious competitive efforts quickly became marginal. Most recently, then, the marketing efforts of major operators such as Vodafone and Verizon Wireless have changed once again. They now focus on raising usage by existing subscribers, both for phone calls and for additional services, rather than on enticing subscribers to switch.

Not all companies recognize this need to change strategy as growth slows. The dotcom boom of the late 1990s saw many casualties of this error, one example being Exodus Inc.,[16] a provider of Web site hosting and related services (Figure 1.15).

The company persisted in employing large numbers of people and spending large amounts of money despite industry research showing that the remaining potential for its services was approaching zero. The cooling love affair with everything e-based in 2000 saw the demise of some of its main customers and this, combined with the company's relative inattention to supporting its *existing* customers, raised customer churn to a rate that matched its win rate. The cost of pursuing unachievable growth quickly overwhelmed the company's revenues, leading to a collapse in earnings, and the bankruptcy that ended its existence as an independent entity.

The United Kingdom satellite broadcasting company, British Sky Broadcasting PLC (BSkyB, see www.sky.com), is another firm facing the challenge of this growth-to-maturity transition. As its name implies, the company broadcasts digital TV from satellite, and offers a very wide range of channels for viewers who subscribe to its service. The uptake of this service grew strongly from 4.5 million at the end of 2000 to 8 million at the end of 2005 (Figure 1.16). With a total of 26 million homes, the market appeared still to offer ample opportunity for further growth, especially since, unlike in the United States, penetration of cable TV was low (3.8 million) and showing little growth. The company therefore committed to still higher penetration, promising investors that it would acquire 10 million subscribers by 2010.

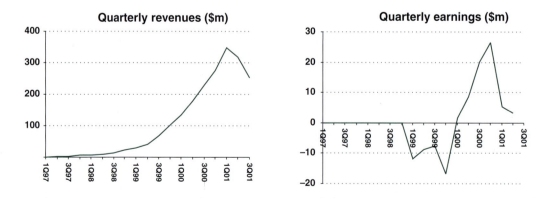

**Figure 1.15: Revenue and earnings history for Exodus Inc. 1997–2001.**

Unfortunately, reaching this objective presented a number of challenges. First, 2005 saw the strongest growth yet in penetration of "Freeview" services—digital TV broadcast direct-to-home (DTH) from terrestrial transmitters, provided free of charge, though with a limited range of channels. Viewers of this service hit 4.6 million in 2005, an increase of over 1.5 million from the previous year. At the same time, churn rates amongst Sky's own subscribers continued rising, exceeding 11 % or nearly 0.9 million per year. Nevertheless, the company persisted in its growth efforts, with costly increases in marketing spend and discounting of its services. The curious feature of this situation is that no one actually asked the company to make the promise in the first place.

Notice that Figure 1.16, like the chart for the vaccine's sales above, shows two alternative outcomes—a "preferred" projection, which reflects how management would like to see the future turn out, and a "feared" view of what might happen if things do not work out. This pair of projections is not simply a comparison between high and low growth. Notice, for example, that the feared future starts out on much the same trajectory as the preferred. Rather, each projection depicts a coherent story of plausible events. In this case, the preferred forecast arises if viewers are slow to take-up the Freeview alternative, leaving plenty of potential for Sky to win new subscribers. In the feared alternative, take-up of Freeview is rapid, so although Sky initially keeps winning new subscribers who really want the full range of channels, the remaining potential quickly drops, so that the rate of new subscribers soon approaches zero.

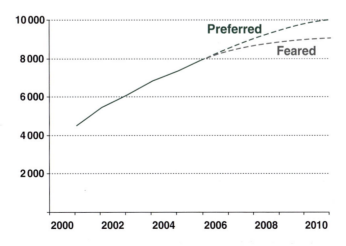

Figure 1.16: Subscribers to BSkyB at year end.

## DECLINE

Other firms find themselves facing conditions that are still more challenging than mere maturity in their industry—some sectors experience inexorable decline. The people who head such organizations are rarely recognized with the heroic status accorded to leaders of exciting growth businesses. Yet any success they achieve is no less important to their investors, and often requires considerable skill and determination.

A current example concerns the switch from photo-film to digital cameras. According to PMA Marketing Research, consumer photographic print volumes in the United States fell from about 30 billion in 2000 to less than 19 billion by 2005, as uptake of digital cameras made the use of traditional photo film increasingly obsolete. Retail travel stores face a tough time as travelers switch to the online purchase of holidays and other travel, and newspapers face declining advertizing revenues as advertizers switch marketing budgets to online channels. Not all such challenges are driven by changes in technology, however. Firms in the European defense industry faced dramatic falls in demand for military hardware following the collapse of the former Soviet Union.

The pain of industry decline need not, however, be equally shared by all. Strong strategic management enables businesses to thrive at the expense of their competitors. Even as the switch to digital photography began to bite between 2000 and 2003, Kodak's arch rival Fuji captured market share, worsening Kodak's difficulties. In the European defense industry, BAE Systems PLC saw revenues rise between 2000 and 2004 from £12.2bn to £13.5bn as its strategy took business away from weaker rivals. In many cases industries see widespread rationalization as those weaker participants close down or sell out to the stronger survivors. This is further evidence that there can be substantial strategic opportunity in apparently difficult industry conditions.

We should not leave the issue of performance in declining situations without a word about organizations whose purpose is in effective to *accelerate* decline, even to the point of putting themselves out of business. Many voluntary organizations aim to eliminate some hardship or problem, such as reducing homelessness, drug use or domestic violence. "Success" for such organizations would mean achieving zero rates for their key indicators of harm, at which point the organization's purpose would cease.

Many public sector and nongovernmental organizations also recognize success in terms of eliminating the need for their work. In December 2005, the United Nations (UN) was able to announce the conclusion of one of its largest missions ever to eliminate civil conflict, as it planned the withdrawal from Sierra Leone of the last of its peacekeepers—a force that had once numbered 17500.[17] The force had been deployed in 1999 to restore government control and to disarm and demobilize fighters. The UN's intervention was prompted by a further escalation in an eight-year conflict that had killed 20 000 and left thousands more badly injured. Essentially, the "performance objective" was to reduce to zero the rate of deaths and injuries (Figure 1.17).

Note that this chart again makes explicit both a preferred and feared future from the point in time at which the situation is being assessed, each of which reflects a plausible story of how the future may develop.

Fulfilling those aims had not been without difficulties. In early 2000, more than 700 UN peacekeepers were abducted and later that year 11 British troops were taken hostage by the militia group, the West Side Boys. This event, however, prompted a sweeping rescue operation that all but eliminated that militia, sending a powerful signal that the UN force was serious about its intent. Over the subsequent five years, 72 000 combatants were disarmed and demobilized, and over 30 000 arms were destroyed. By 2002, the major conflict was effectively over, with virtually no casualties being reported.

# FUNCTIONAL PERFORMANCE OBJECTIVES

Concern with improving performance over time is not limited to organizations' overall strategic aims, but may also arise on issues concerning just a part of the organization—staffing, marketing, product development, information systems, etc. Success in these specific functional areas may support a wider improvement in overall performance, but they often deserve attention in their own right.

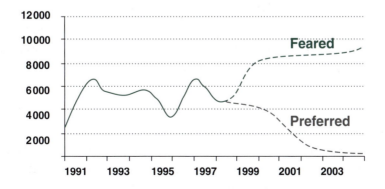

**Figure 1.17: The estimated number of deaths and serious injuries from civil conflict in Sierra Leone.**

Among the cases we have already discussed are some that naturally present challenges for the sales and marketing functions—growth in subscribers for BSkyB and sales for the painkiller, for example. In others, sales and marketing clearly have a major role to play, such as McDonald's recovery in earnings. Time charts for sales volume and revenue are an essential starting point for any strategy intended to improve these performance indicators. In many cases, this may be the major focus for improving profits, provided we can be confident that the cost elements are well managed.

---

**Doing it right: properly defining a performance challenge as a time chart**

If a chart of performance over time is to provide a strong foundation for subsequent analysis and development of strategy, it is important that it is constructed properly

- Include a clear numerical scale (sales volume, profit, customers, etc.).
- Specify the timescale over which the situation is expected to play out (e.g. eight quarters, 12 years, etc.).
- Include as much history as may be important to explain the current situation (last four quarters, last three years, etc.).
- Show the *time path*—how much and how fast the situation has changed over the past, and may change into the future.
- Include information for this time path with as much frequency as is necessary to display important changes—it is not good enough to show only annual numbers, for example, if profit or anything that has driven that profit has changed substantially from quarter to quarter or month to month.
- Show alternative futures, especially contrasting what may feasibly happen if the strategy is poor or the issue is not dealt with well, versus what might realistically be expected if a strong strategy is pursued or the issue is handled well.

---

Sales growth is not always an appropriate aim, and in some cases can even be a major error. As the Exodus Inc. case illustrates, many organizations may be better advised to hold on to good quality business—larger, high-value customers who generate high rates of gross profit, while being readily supported by affordable sales and service capacity—rather than scavenging for any growth they can find, regardless of whether it can be translated into profitable business.

Even when sales growth is the correct objective, it can be a mistake to leave *all* such problems at the door of the salesforce or marketing department. A number of failings in other functional areas of the business can compromise sales success—poor product quality or lack of capacity in production and distribution can undermine otherwise successful sales effort. It is also important to remember that sales growth is not only the result of what has been won, but reflects what has been lost too. Poor service quality can cause customers to leave, including even such apparently trivial issues as poor management of cash receivables (collecting money that customers owe) in the accounting function.

## STAFF CHALLENGES

The earlier telecom company example has already shown how staffing difficulties alone can undermine achievement of otherwise quite plausible objectives. That company needed to develop a strategy to initiate and sustain rapid growth in the specialist staff it required. Staffing challenges are common sources of difficulty, and can be quite difficult to solve. A sound strategy for staff development can be particularly tough when business relies on highly skilled people, such as in consulting companies, law firms and other professional service organizations.

One mid-size law firm had grown successfully, providing specialist services to medium- to large-sized companies. Its reputation with the clients it had won over previous years was such that it was constantly being asked to do more for those clients, so had little need to seek new ones. The firm found itself losing talented people, which made it increasingly difficult to serve its clients' rising demands (Figure 1.18). Staff losses were concentrated amongst lawyers with 5–10 years' experience. This amplified the problem, since this group carried the burden of leading the work for client projects. Shortages at this level threatened the firm's ability to undertake work that had been sold by partners, or to complete that work to a high standard. This risked damaging established client relationships, ultimately threatening a fall in the firm's revenues, rather than furthering the growth it sought.

Ironically, the cause of this trouble was the firm's growth in the four to five years before 2003. A large number of young lawyers joined during this time and quickly progressed through to senior partner positions by winning new client relationships. They were well rewarded, so had no reason to move on at that time.

Exit interviews with the lawyers who were leaving suggested two problems. First, they were overburdened with the increasing volume of work coming from clients. Normally, such professionals put up with this pressure for the promise of substantial rewards when they achieve partner level. However, the second reason given was

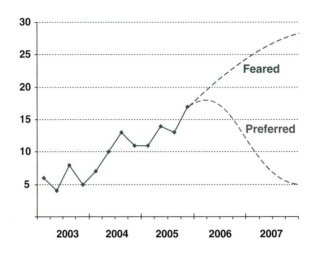

**Figure 1.18: Quarterly staff losses at a mid-size law firm.**

that they faced the prospect of being stuck at their grade, with limited opportunities to progress to partnership themselves. With little chance of progress, these talented people were choosing to pursue their careers elsewhere, leaving those who had joined the firm earlier and had reached more senior positions to cope with the client work themselves, which increased further the work pressure.

To take a more positive example, progressive improvements in staffing issues can be powerful drivers of performance. Not many people may know of Yum! Brands Inc.(www.yum.com), but they do know of the Kentucky Fried Chicken, Pizza Hut, and Taco Bell chains the company owns. Spun off from PepsiCo in 1997, Yum!'s management appreciated that treating its franchisees and staff well was vital if those people were to keep customers happy. By 2005, US restaurant employees were on average staying 12 months with the company, far longer than is typical for the industry.

Not all staff challenges are about obtaining the resources needed to drive growth. It is not often appreciated that a management hierarchy is a powerful system for "breeding" growth. As young people are brought in at junior ranks, others expect to be promoted to middle management. Existing middle managers hope for senior positions and ambitious senior people want the top jobs. Since there can be many times more people at any level than at the level above, only a small fraction can expect a promotion in any year.

For example, if there are 1 000 juniors and 100 middle managers, of which only 20 per year are leaving or being promoted, then only 2 % of juniors can hope for promotion in any year. There are only two solutions to this problem—either the organization must be growing (just 5 % growth per year means that 7 % of juniors can be promoted in this example), or else senior people must be moved out to make space for juniors. The flatter the organization, and the wider the span of control from one level of seniority to the next level, the more serious this issue becomes.

Certain additional factors can worsen this need to speed up the turnover of staff. In 2004, one large United States financial institution had the laudable aim to increase the proportion of people-of-color and disadvantaged staff amongst its senior management from 60, or 6% of that rank, to 200 by 2008 (Figure 1.19). Turnover amongst senior people was running at less than 5% per annum, and there were few experienced minority staff in the pipeline, so unless something else could be changed, the entirely well-intentioned objective could not possibly be met. This would be very serious for the company's reputation, causing potentially considerable damage to its *future* hiring needs, and even to its business revenues.

Incidentally, this challenge is dwarfed by that facing some South African businesses, where regulations require representation among all management grades for people-of-color to reach levels representative of the population as a whole within just a few years.

### The special case of zero targets

Functional issues, like the overall objectives of certain noncommercial organizations, sometimes make it appropriate to "aim for zero." One example that has transformed business performance in many manufacturing industries is the pursuit of zero defects—"the only acceptable rate of product failure is zero, so wherever we are starting from, that is the target, and we will hit it by (date)." However, manufacturing is not the only setting in which zero may be an appropriate aim. Call center operations may aim for zero unanswered calls, and accounting departments may aim for zero errors.

Yet care is needed to avoid setting a zero target when this is not advisable, even though one may think it would be. It is not good in most cases to have zero staff turnover, either for organizations or for the staff who work for them. New ideas need to be brought in, people need to develop in ways the organization cannot fulfill, and so on.

Lastly, zero targets will frequently conflict with other performance aims. Whilst it may be highly desirable for a call center never to fail to answer a call, this may only be achievable at an unacceptably high cost.

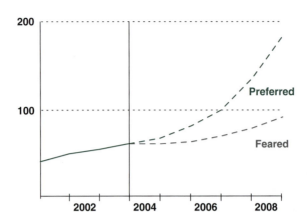

**Figure 1.19: Number of minority staff amongst senior management at a large financial institution.**

## PRODUCT DEVELOPMENT

Major drugs companies provide a good example of how serious time-based challenges can be in research and development programs (R&D). These firms have grown to their present scale over several decades, on the back of a stream of major drug discoveries—highly effective treatments for widespread and costly ailments, such as heart disease, stomach ulcers, and depression. These so-called "blockbuster" drugs, with annual sales of $1bn, are so critical that firms pursue enormous R&D investments in an effort to discover more such drugs. The imperative to discover big revenue products is intensified by the limited patent life for drugs, which means that high prices and revenues can only be sustained for a limited number of years before sales are decimated by low-price generic products—essentially the same product, but without the brand name.

For these firms, the performance over time of concern is the rate of new product introductions that offer a high potential revenue stream. Unfortunately, having successfully developed drugs to treat the most widespread complaints through the 1980s and 1990s, companies are left only with complaints that are suffered by fewer people in developed economies, or more complex complaints for which wonder drugs are harder to find.

Controversially, the last large-scale opportunities for disease treatment are concentrated among the populations of the world's poorest countries. This has led to accusations that drug firms are ignoring the needs of the poor due to their inability to pay the high prices needed to justify the large R&D costs involved. In other industries, firms have found ways of serving the poor profitably,[18] an aim that many pharmaceuticals firms also pursue

## CAPACITY

Time-based challenges frequently arise in the building of capacity, whether for production, distribution or service.

Retailers of all kinds face this challenge—"capacity" in their case consisting of retail stores. We have already seen in McDonald's an example of such a company running out of good quality locations where they can expect strong incremental sales. Supermarket chains such as Wal-Mart in the United States, Tesco in the United Kingdom or Japan's Daiei also used up the best locations long ago and must work hard for new opportunities, either developing novel retail formats that can reach smaller markets, or else switching to emerging markets.

Manufacturing capacity can also pose strategic challenges. Roche Diagnostics is a major global producer of blood test meters for diabetics, under the Accu-Chek brand (www.accu-chek.com). As explained earlier, numbers of people with this disease are very large and growing quickly, although only a fraction of these are severe enough to need blood meters. During 2004–5, the company introduced two new products, which it hoped would extend the brand's uptake amongst meter users. In addition, the company's existing meter users would likely want the new products, since machines typically last just three years, and users are naturally interested in having the latest model. Since nothing exactly similar had occurred in the market before, at least on such a scale, the company faced great uncertainty regarding the likely rate of uptake for the meters, and therefore the capacity required to fulfill that demand (Figure 1.20).

Neither the replacement rate amongst existing Accu-Chek users nor the penetration rate among new users could be known exactly before the launch. The problem was exacerbated by uncertainty as to whether the two new products should

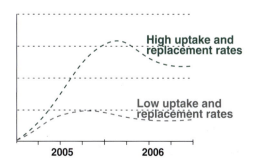

High uptake and replacement rates

Low uptake and replacement rates

2005    2006

**Figure 1.20: Capacity requirement for Roche Diagnostics' new model blood test meters (actual data are confidential).**

be launched simultaneously and at the same time in many countries, or staggered over several quarters and different geographic markets.

This uncertainty posed a tricky question about how much production capacity to build for the new products—should initial capacity be sufficient to fulfill the highest likely rate of uptake, or be limited, leaving further expansion to be deferred until uptake rates became clear? If the latter course were adopted, what might be the value of potential sales that would be lost through inability to supply? Furthermore, what competitive risk might this pose that sales might be taken by the company's arch-rival, Johnson & Johnson, and other competitors?

Firms facing similar decisions risk making a subtle, but important strategic error. The business case for building higher or lower levels of capacity may take reasonable account of the medium-term trade-off between the higher cost of building plenty of capacity versus the loss of sales and profits from building too little. However, this is not the end of the story, since underprovision creates a serious strategic threat—in this case, the risk of medical advisors, retailers *and* end users all switching their allegiance to rival products. This would threaten not only immediate sales, but longer term business too. Yet such consequences are rarely factored adequately into such decisions for fear of missing quarterly earnings targets.

Another example requiring a strategy for capacity growth, this time from a public policy perspective, concerns the provision of biodiesel—an environmentally attractive alternative to diesel produced from petroleum. Although diesel is not a popular fuel for cars in the United States, it is widely used in Europe and elsewhere, and could potentially switch a large fraction of overall fuel consumption onto renewable sources. (Note, however, that if this shift were to occur on a large scale it would introduce a new problem, since the grain required to fill a large vehicle's tank would alternatively feed a person for many months.) Oil from crops, such as rape seed, and even old cooking oil, can easily be converted to motor diesel. It is already technically feasible for mid-scale diesel users, such as taxi firms, to operate their own small conversion plants.[19]

Since the technology is feasible and environmental benefits are so clear, why has this system of biodiesel production not swept the industry? Unfortunately, powerful forces are holding back growth in capacity. First, whilst purchase and use of a conversion plant may make economic sense at a particular point in time, fuel prices are volatile, driven both by the global supply–demand for petroleum and the short-term supply–demand balance for particular fuels. Unless tax policy is heavily skewed in favor of the new product, this uncertainty will likely continue, which makes investment in conversion facilities risky. The constraint on capacity is worsened by the impact of the same uncertainties for farmers who may be considering switching acreage on their farms to oil-producing crops. While they might see a good price for such crops in one particular year, these farmers cannot be sure when they are sowing crops that the same conditions will apply when it comes to harvest time. This adds further to the uncertainty facing firms wondering whether to install conversion capacity.

Equivalent issues apply to the addition of crop-based ethanol to gasoline in the United States and other markets.

For a government committed to raising the adoption of biofuel, a time chart of "the issue" would feature the historic growth in capacity (*why* have we come to be in the present situation), the likely future of capacity growth under current policies (*where* will we get to if we continue as we are), and an alternative higher growth aspiration (*how* we can drive growth at a higher rate, and to a higher level).

Functional challenges often need to be examined over short timescales. In fashion retailing, for example, the success of new product introductions is fundamental to the appeal of a store's overall product range. One such company operated a fast-test policy, in which it would test new product lines in selected stores for just two to three weeks before deciding whether to order large quantities for the whole chain. The company took on a new senior executive with much experience in the sector, who made a number of changes, such as reallocating floor space amongst product categories, and switching key product ranges to new suppliers because of better supply prices. Within weeks of these changes, the fraction of test products making the transition from trial to the core product range had fallen from 0.8 to 0.6 (Figure 1.21).

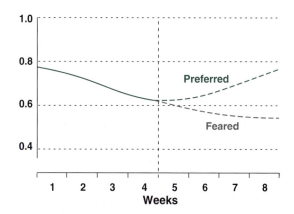

**Figure 1.21: The fraction of fashion chain products successful enough to be added to the core product range.**

The company faced a tough decision. It could try to reverse the changes, although it could not be certain which were most harmful, or whether some might, on their own, have been successful. They could also not be certain that all the original suppliers would be able to respond.

Again, though, why is such a short-term issue "strategic"? This seemingly isolated error hits several parts of the business. First, in addition to failing in the eyes of consumers, the changes led to the loss of other staff in the buying and merchandising group. Without these people, the company could not be certain of reestablishing good performance on this important issue. The reduced appeal of products sourced under the new arrangements also meant that those items that *did* make it to the core range suffered a faster fall-off in sales. Consequently, while discounted products previously featured little in the company's stores, these came to represent a large fraction of both floor space and sales. Having previously been known for its high-appeal clothing, on which it could sustain high margins, consumers quickly came to associate the company with cheap goods at discount prices, making it difficult to reverse the changes. The particular market segment this company served is viciously competitive, with several similar chains fighting it out in most shopping areas. This company's loss of position was quickly captured by rivals. Finally, if these problems were to continue for any length of time, they would make many of the stores uneconomic, resulting in closure and further loss of revenue and profit.

## SUPPORT FUNCTIONS

A focus on performance over time is also a good starting point for functional departments whose primary role is to support other groups. Common examples arise in departments that provide information systems and finance/accounting services.

Sometimes such groups are run as profit centers—"selling" their services to other departments, to generate revenue, and managing their resources (largely people and equipment) to deliver adequate service at sufficiently low cost to make a "profit." In other cases, these services are outsourced to independent firms, such as EDS Inc., CSC Inc. or providers from low-cost economies such as India, China or Eastern Europe.

When these functions are operated wholly or partly inhouse, their leadership is concerned with future levels of activity and providing the necessary resources to serve that activity. A starting point for establishing and running their strategy will be a time chart of projected activity rates and capacity, measured perhaps in full-time equivalent people, or person-hours per month.

Simply running the service for their customers is not the whole story for internal service functions. Such groups have the equivalent of a company's "product range."

This means they have to be concerned with product development, i.e. creating new services that the business may require. They may also offer project-based services to other parts of the business, creating the equivalent of an internal consultancy group. All such tasks add to the "demand" on their capacity, and ensuring that these tasks will be well implemented requires a time chart of expected future project numbers and the labor requirement these will bring.

Customer satisfaction is another factor that internal service functions share with businesses. In the case of business customers, poor service can lead to such customers deciding to switch to competitors. This is not necessarily so easy for internal users of service functions, but service department management is nonetheless keen to keep service quality high. Any drop can result in removal of support by their users for any spending they may need to make, and in extreme cases, poor service quality can drive internal customers to seek service from third-party suppliers—the equivalent of "losing customers." It is therefore vital for management of these service departments to track service quality over time.

# INFORMATION NEEDS

An important implication of the time-based start point for functional objectives concerns the availability of the necessary information, especially when attention is focused on the time path of what is happening. Companies need to know: *why* have we come to be in our current situation?

Most companies can readily provide historic information on sales, revenue, costs or profits. Organizations are often less well informed, though, about important functional factors. The law firm suffering rising staff turnover described above is a rare case of a business that could lay its hands immediately on the staff loss numbers, quarter by quarter, not just for the firm as a whole but for any specific group. More often, while management may be aware that staff losses are increasing and that something needs to be done, it does not have such information routinely available and regularly scrutinized.

To illustrate the point, consider an example from the mutual fund industry, where highly skilled investment analysts and fund managers are vital. (These are the people who decide to invest or disinvest money in particular stocks, bonds or other investments.) Yet in the case of one such large firm, there was no routine tracking of staff movements. Consequently, when staffing was identified as the major issue constraining its future prospects, the only way to identify the seriousness of the challenge was to retrieve and analyse old payroll records from its archives.

Later chapters will expand on this issue of information needs, but for now it is sufficient to note that top-level performance factors need to be tracked, over time, their likely future trajectory needs to be assessed, and feasible improvements estimated. Moreover, this needs to be done with accurate, quantified measures—even for soft factors like service quality—and displayed and scrutinized in the form of frequently updated time charts.

## CASE EXAMPLE: PERFORMANCE OF RYANAIR, THE LOW-FARE AIRLINE

The diagnosis of performance dynamics can best be understood by following a single example through the various stages of the analysis, starting with the principle of focusing on performance through time. The case developed through this chapter and later ones concerns the European low-fare airline Ryanair (www.ryanair.com). This case has been chosen for three reasons. First, it is a clear business model with which readers will be familiar. Secondly, very similar businesses operate in all regions of the world, and continue to be started, so the analysis can be readily replicated for similar airlines in North America, Asia, or other parts of the world. Finally, this business and others like it are well documented, with long histories of published data on key factors needed to complete the analysis.

Figure 1.22 shows the history of Ryanair's sales volume, revenue and profit, and two alternative futures. (This analysis examines profit at the level of earnings before interest, tax, depreciation and amortization(EBITDA).) The measure of sales volume is *passenger-journeys booked* (millions)—a key indicator reported by all airlines. This sales volume drives revenue, both through the fares paid for flights and various ancillary revenues, such as inflight food and drink sales and ground transportation. Profit arises from this sales revenue, minus the airline's costs, including those for aircraft, staff and marketing, as well as other costs driven by operating airports and routes.

The charts observe some important rules. There is a clear definition of each item, e.g. "passenger-journeys booked," not just "passengers." There is a specific scale on each item, and a clear timescale over which performance is examined. As in the earlier examples, the two alternative futures are not simply "best" versus "worst" cases. Each arises from a specific story of the future.

- In the preferred future, Ryanair continues to be able to find large numbers of new airports, between which enough passengers wish to fly for many additional routes to be economically viable. It remains sufficiently stronger

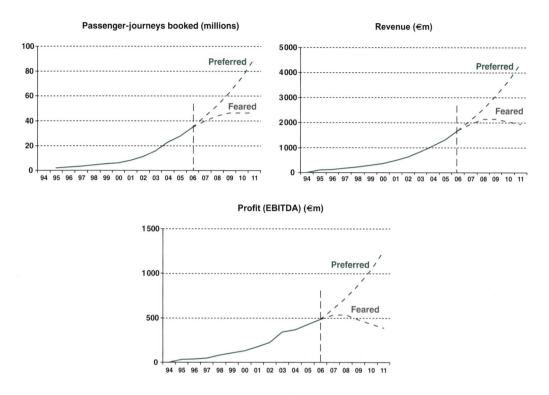

**Figure 1.22: Historic and potential performance for Ryanair.**

than competitors that it can fill its aircraft on those routes without excessively low fares, and continues to be highly efficient in delivering its service.

● In the feared future, it becomes increasingly difficult to find routes that are popular enough to deliver sufficient passenger volumes. Competitors capture many potential new routes before Ryanair can develop them itself, and competitive pressure on existing services hits passenger volumes and puts downward pressure on average fares. Although the airline continues to be operationally efficient, this is not sufficient to make-up for the slowdown and reversal of sales growth, leading to reduced profits.

Chapter 2 will also discuss this case example, and show how to trace out a causal analysis of these sales and profits time paths. Chapters 3 and 4 will then examine how the underlying resources of the airline have developed up to 2006, how they may develop into the future, and the interdependencies that explain why performance has progressed as it has, and might develop into the future. Later sections of the book will add to this core analysis by examining how competitive rivalry works, and show how to deal with important attributes of the business (e.g. the varying levels of demand on different routes) and "soft" issues, such as reputation.

### Summary of Chapter 1

Investors in commercial businesses are concerned with the likely future growth in free cash flow, rather than with current financial ratios.

Investors and executives alike share a concern *to improve performance over time.* The same applies to stakeholders in voluntary organizations, public policy and other noncommercial cases, although the key performance measure may not be financial.

The history of performance up to now is important because it determines the trajectory on which future performance is heading.

Three key questions need to be answered in order to develop and sustain a sound strategy (Figure 1.23):

(1)  *Why* has our performance to date followed the path that it has?

(2)  *Where* is that performance heading into the future under likely conditions and current strategy?

(3)  *How* can strategy be changed to improve that future performance path?

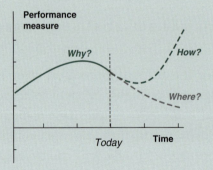

**Figure 1.23: Three generic questions about performance over time.**

Absolute values should be adopted as the top-level aims—cash flow, sales, customers—rather than ratios. Multiple measures may need to be pursued e.g. profit *and* sales, even though they may conflict.

Performance aims need to recognize the reality of the context in which an organization finds itself—e.g. a growing market versus maturity or decline. Decline may even be an objective for organizations whose purpose is to eliminate harm.

Large departments or functions of an organization may have challenges to "improve performance over time," as well as the organization as a whole.

# SUGGESTED QUESTIONS AND EXERCISES

1. What are shareholders expecting when they invest money in a company?
2. What are the advantages and disadvantages of looking at market share and other ratios for a company when assessing its strategy?
3. Why can the percentage growth rate of a company's sales be a poor indicator of how well it is performing?
4. What are the three key questions concerning an organization's performance over time that management needs to answer? Under what circumstances might one of these questions not be relevant?
5. Give examples of nonfinancial measures that might be tracked by three different companies to indicate successful progress in their strategy.
6. Give examples of nonfinancial measures that might be tracked by three different noncommercial organizations to indicate successful progress in their strategy.
7. Give examples of nonfinancial measures that might be tracked by three different departments within a company to indicate successful progress in their strategy in a particular functional area.
8. Select an organization for which good information is publicly available (e.g. from case studies, newspapers or journals, or the Web). Use Worksheet 1, below, to sketch a time chart of both their historic and plausible future performance on one principal measure, observing all the rules for constructing such charts. Add a second time chart for a supporting indicator that might be important to track because it is fundamental to achieving progress on the principal measure.

# USING WORKSHEET 1

A worksheet that can be used for the first stage of a strategy dynamics analysis is provided below.

Following the guidance provided in this chapter, the larger chart on the left can be completed with a time chart for the principal measure of performance of concern, whether that is an overall outcome (e.g. sales, profits or quantity of service delivered), or an indicator of functional performance (e.g. staff turnover, new product development rate, or error rate).

The smaller chart on the right is optional, and can be used to display some important supporting indicator to the principal objective, such as sales volume, which will enable a revenue or profit objective.

It is important to observe the discipline required to make these objectives usable:

1.  Specify a numerical scale for each chart, sufficient to include the hoped-for upper value of the principal objective. For example, if profits have grown over the last three years from $-$$2.5 million to $+$$3.4 million, and you hope by five years in the future to reach $10 million, then the vertical scale should run from $-$$3 million to $+$ $10 million

2.  Define the timescale and time periods over which the objectives are to be achieved—to continue this example, the timescale runs from year $-3$ to year $+5$, or, if you are doing this in 2007, from 2004 to 2012.

3.  The vertical dashed line on each chart shows "today", and this point in time should be specified: 2007 in this example. Include as much history for each chart as is necessary to give a clear picture of why today's values have come about (not relevant for new ventures).

4.  Include both a "preferred" future, for the most positive scenario—external conditions are favourable and your management of the situation is successful— and a "feared" future that might result if conditions are challenging and the company is less successful than hoped.

5.  Use the table at the bottom of the page to record the numerical values for each objective, both as they stand today and that you hope to reach by the end of the timescale on the charts. You can also usefully write these values on the charts.

# WORKSHEET 1: PERFORMANCE OBJECTIVES OVER TIME

**Principal objective:** .........................

**Supporting objective:** .........................

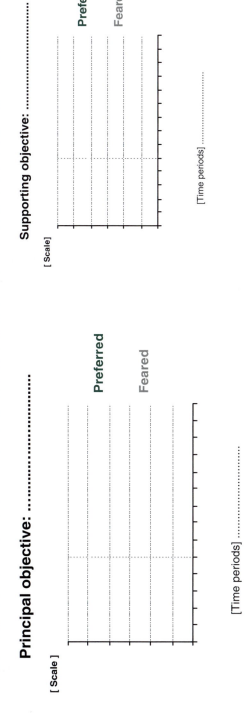

## SUMMARY

Insert values in the table below to show today's value for the principal and supporting measure, and preferred and feared future values at a target date.

|  | Today date .............. | Future date .............. | |
|---|---|---|---|
|  |  | Preferred | |
| **Principal objective** ............. | | *Feared* | |
|  |  | Preferred | |
| **Supporting objective** ............. | | *Feared* | |

# NOTES

1. Many strategy textbooks explain the rationale for the choice of financial performance measures. See, for example, Grant, R.M. (2005) *Contemporary Strategy Analysis*, 5th edn, Blackwell, Oxford, pp. 37–57. For a more extensive discussion of the theoretical foundations underlying economic profit, see Barney, J. (2007) *Gaining and Sustaining Competitive Advantage*, 3rd edn, Prentice Hall, Upper Saddle River NJ, Chapter 2.

2. For a clear, non-technical explanation of EVA, see Ehrbar, A. (1998) *EVA: The Real Key to Creating Wealth*, Wiley, Chichester.

3. Martin, J.D. and Petty, J.W. (2000) *Value-based Management*, Harvard Business School Press, Boston MA.

4. For an eloquent explanation of why free cash flow should be of overriding concern to investors, rather than reported profits, see the letter to shareholders that opens the 2004 Annual Report from Amazon.com (http://phx.corporate-ir.net/phoenix.zhtml?c=97664&p=irol-reportsAnnual).

5. For an explanation of the principles of valuation, see Copeland, T., Koller, T. and Murrin, J. (2005) *Valuation—Measuring and Managing the Value of Companies*, 4th edn, Wiley, Chichester.

6. Rappaport, A. (2006) Ten ways to create shareholder value. *Harvard Business Review*, **84**(9), 66–77.

7. Penrose, E.T. (1959) *The Theory of the Growth of the Firm*, Oxford University Press, Oxford.

8. This perspective has been reviewed in Rugman, A.M. and Verbeke, A. (2002) Edith Penrose's contribution to the resource-based view of strategic management. *Strategic Management Journal*, **23**(8), 769–780.

9. I am grateful to Drew Jones of the Sustainability Institute and his colleagues for contributing this example.

10. Jones, A.P., Homer, J.B., Murphy, D.L., et al. (2006) Understanding diabetes: population dynamics through simulation modeling and experimentation. *American Journal of Public Health*, **96**(3), 488–494.

11. See, for example, Mankins, M.C. and Steele, R.C. (2005) Turning great strategy into great performance. *Harvard Business Review*, **8**(7), 64–73.

12. Collins, J. and Porras, J. (1996) Building your company's vision, *Harvard Business Review*, **75**(5), 65–72. Enhanced edition available, February 2000, from Harvard Business Online: http://harvardbusinessonline.hsbp.harvard.edu.

13. Hamel, G. and Prahalad, C.K. (1994) *Competing for the Future*, Harvard Business School Press, Boston MA, Chapter 2.

14. Kaplan, R. and Norton, D. (1996) *The Balanced Scorecard*, Harvard Business School Press, Boston MA. See also www.balancedscorecard.org.

15. Mankins, M.C. and Steele, R. (2006) Stop making plans: start making decisions, *Harvard Business Review*, **84**(1), 76–84.

16. I am indebted to Vitorrio Raimondi of Vanguard Strategy Ltd. for this example (see www.vanguardstrategy.com).

17. See www.irinnews.org.

18. Prahalad, C.K. and Hammond, A. (2002) Serving the World's poor, profitably. *Harvard Business Review*, **80**(9), 48–57.

19. I am grateful to Mike Chmielewski for this example.

# CHAPTER 2

# RESOURCES DRIVE PERFORMANCE

## KEY ISSUES

- ✪ The need for rigorous causal explanations of performance.
- ✪ From performance outcomes to the resources that drive demand and supply, revenue and costs.
- ✪ Measures of performance for a whole time period versus quantities of resources at an instant in time.
- ✪ Critical importance of tracking numbers over time, including nonbusiness cases and functional challenges.
- ✪ From understanding history to estimating future performance—market-based and resource-based explanations and forecasts.
- ✪ Strategy dynamics and the resource-based view of strategy.
- ✪ Identifying, specifying and measuring resources—and definitions for resources and capabilities.

Worksheet 2: Resources Driving Performance.

This chapter makes connections to the following strategy concepts: value curve, value chain, the resource-based view, generic strategies, industry forces, vision and mission.

Chapter 1 explained the principle that management should focus on improving performance into the future, and introduced the three key questions—*why* the organization has performed as it has over its recent history, *where* that performance will likely go if current policies continue, and *how* management might improve that trajectory. Answering these questions requires development of a sound explanation for what *causes* that performance—in other words a "theory."

Theory has something of a bad name amongst executives. Believing (correctly!) that management is a practical profession, many see theoretical concepts to be the opposite of what should concern them. They also have good reason to be skeptical about theory, given its patchy record when it comes to providing good advice for organizations. Consequently, few theories are used by management or consulting firms for designing strategy or making strategic decisions.[1]

## THEORY—"WHAT CAUSES WHAT AND HOW"

Yet theory *is* important and not a complex concept—a theory is simply an explanation for *what causes what, and how.*[2] Without such an explanation, there can be little confidence in the likely effect of any strategy we develop or decisions we might take. In Figure 2.1, the "what" we believe to be the cause is at the left, the "what" that is the effect we need explained is at the right, and the "how" is the set of causal mechanisms that sits between cause and effect.

The basic purpose of management research is to discover the mechanisms that connect the causes over which management might be able to exert some control—price, for example—with the effects that they want to influence—such as profitability. Whether they like it or not, decision makers use theory all the time, even if it is only their own private beliefs about why things happen and the likely impact of their decisions.

Theory is powerful when it fulfills three criteria—being *general* (works in a wide variety of situations) *useful* (tells us something we can affect) and *true*. The last point is a reminder to be skeptical about supposed "rules" of successful strategy that might seem to make sense, but are not in fact reliable, such as "the first firm to enter a new market will always beat firms who follow later." This would be a general rule, and useful, but is unfortunately not true.

For various reasons, confirming the soundness of management theory is far from easy. In the physical sciences, researchers can often undertake controlled experiments—holding everything constant except the one cause–effect relationship they want to test. This is rarely possible for management, because many factors are beyond their control, e.g. competitors' price levels or customers' changing preferences. Investors and other stakeholders may also be unhappy with the possible risks of experimenting with their organizations. Nevertheless, there is a strong case for at least *some* experimentation—as is commonly done for new product launches—and

Figure 2.1: Theory as "what causes what and how."

certain companies that value strongly the sound understanding of "what causes what and how" use experimentation to inform their analysis.[3] These companies include credit card company CapitalOne, the Marriott hotel chain, the Boston Red Sox and Amazon.com.

A second difficulty facing management research is ambiguity about the *causal mechanisms* that lie between the suspected cause and its effect; an ambiguity that often arises because many causal mechanisms involve people making choices. We might want to see, for example, if increased spending on research leads to better profits by analyzing these factors across a large sample of firms. Yet people within those firms make decisions about the products to develop and launch and customers decide if they like those products and are willing to pay a good price. Not only is there a complex causal chain with many branches, but most of those chains include human behaviors that are unlikely to be uniform or consistent over time.

Faced with the difficulty of observing directly the causal mechanisms that operate in business and the problems in making controlled experiments, research often seeks to confirm hypotheses (tentative theories or suppositions provisionally adopted to explain certain facts, and to guide investigation) by collecting large quantities of data on possible causes and effects, and then looking for statistical correlation between them. Unfortunately, the ambiguity and complexity of the causal mechanisms involved is often so severe, and so difficult to trace in practice, that even a strong correlation between cause and effect is not sufficient to offer more than suggestive support for a particular hypothesis. One consequence of this is that there are hundreds of research papers published annually, all claiming to have found a relationship between firm profitability and a host of plausible causes. As Professor Clayton Christensen of Harvard Business School has remarked, we can often say little more than the business equivalent of "most flying things have feathers and flap their wings." Attempts to design flying machines based on that statistically significant observation were not notably successful!

To make some headway in tackling this causal ambiguity and complexity, it is helpful to identify parts of the explanation for performance where concrete causal connections can be stated confidently. Therefore, this chapter begins the process of tracing the causal connections that ends up at certain performance outcomes, a journey that will be largely completed in Chapters 3 and 4. Whether the outcome of concern is financial or nonfinancial, or a combination of both, the process is the same. For reasons explained in Chapter 1, the concern is often with future profits or cash flows, but whether this or some other measure is the focus, the key issue concerns how performance is *changing through time.*

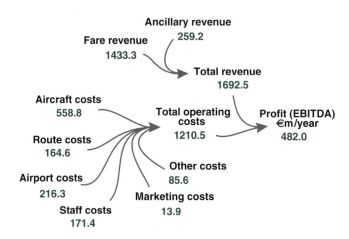

**Figure 2.2: Causal structure of Ryanair profits for year ended March 2006.**

Figure 2.2 picks up the example of Ryanair introduced in Chapter 1 and shows the firm's income statement for year ended (y/e) March 2006 in causal form. Profit (and this analysis examines profit at the level of EBITDA: earnings before interest, tax, depreciation and amortization) results from the revenue the company received from the fares that passengers paid, and from other items, minus its operating costs. These are split into some major categories—staff costs, the costs of operating aircraft, airport operations and routes—plus marketing and other costs. The causal relationships here are clear:

- profits = total revenue minus operating costs
- total revenue = fare revenue plus ancillary revenue
- operating costs = aircraft costs plus route costs plus airport costs plus staff costs plus marketing costs plus other costs

If that causal explanation for profits is accurate for y/e March 2006, and the business has been conducting the same activity in the past, it was also accurate for every previous year. It is therefore possible to join up time charts of those items in the same way, as shown in Figure 2.3. Each chart in this figure portrays the historic values for the item named.

Although this diagram may be an unfamiliar view of a company's income statement, it is just showing in a graphical, causal layout the same data we normally see in spreadsheet form (Table 2.1).

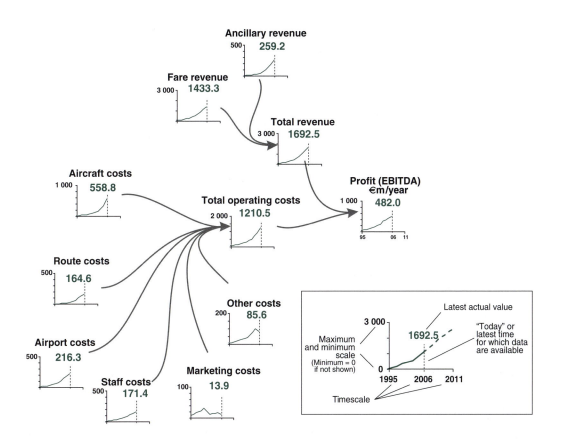

**Figure 2.3: Explanation for Ryanair profit history to 2006.**

Since the remainder of this book will rely heavily on diagrams such as Figure 2.3, it is important to be clear about their features. The box at the lower right of the diagram gives a detailed legend for the time charts in the figure. As for the performance charts in Chapter 1, every item includes a specific, quantified scale on the vertical axis, and a specific timescale on the horizontal axis. The current value "today"—usually the latest time for which data are known—is highlighted as the green value, just above a vertical dotted line for the time at which it applies. The time path of historical data is shown as the solid green line —. Later charts will be adding forecasts, which will be denoted by a dashed green line - - -.

It is also important to be clear about what is meant by the connecting arrows in these charts. Word-and-arrow diagrams are common throughout books on management and strategy and usually imply some kind of causal relationship between the factors that are linked by arrows. Often, such implied relationships encompass a whole chain of causality, with all the ambiguity and complexity discussed above. In this book, every such link will have the more localized and precise meaning that

## TABLE 2.1: RYANAIR'S SUMMARY HISTORIC INCOME STATEMENT

| | 1995 | 1996 | 1997 | 1998 | 1999 | 2000 | 2001 | 2002 | 2003 | 2004 | 2005 | 2006 |
|---|---|---|---|---|---|---|---|---|---|---|---|---|
| **Total operating revenue** | **102.9** | **130.2** | **173.2** | **231.9** | **295.8** | **370.1** | **487.4** | **624.1** | **842.5** | **1074.2** | **1319.0** | **1692.5** |
| of which: | | | | | | | | | | | | |
| Fare revenues | 91.5 | 115.7 | 152.8 | 203.8 | 258.9 | 330.5 | 437.4 | 551.0 | 732.0 | 924.6 | 1128.1 | 1433.3 |
| Ancilliary revenue | 11.4 | 14.5 | 20.4 | 28.1 | 36.9 | 39.9 | 50.0 | 73.1 | 110.6 | 149.7 | 190.9 | 259.2 |
| **Total operating costs** (excluding depreciation) | **69.3** | **90.8** | **124.7** | **149.7** | **191.7** | **242.0** | **314.2** | **402.1** | **502.2** | **708.1** | **891.6** | **1210.5** |
| of which: | | | | | | | | | | | | |
| Total aircraft related costs | 18.2 | 23.8 | 32.7 | 39.3 | 51.4 | 60.7 | 90.9 | 134.3 | 158.6 | 229.9 | 336.7 | 558.8 |
| Route charges | 7.0 | 9.2 | 12.6 | 15.1 | 20.8 | 26.3 | 35.7 | 46.7 | 68.4 | 110.3 | 135.7 | 164.6 |
| Airport & handling charges | 11.1 | 14.6 | 20.0 | 24.0 | 29.0 | 43.1 | 66.3 | 84.9 | 108.0 | 147.2 | 178.4 | 216.3 |
| Staff costs | 14.2 | 18.6 | 25.5 | 30.7 | 39.8 | 48.5 | 61.2 | 78.2 | 93.1 | 126.6 | 141.7 | 171.4 |
| Marketing and distribution costs | 9.6 | 12.6 | 17.3 | 20.8 | 24.6 | 32.1 | 21.5 | 12.4 | 14.6 | 16.1 | 19.6 | 13.9 |
| Other | 9.2 | 12.1 | 16.6 | 19.9 | 26.0 | 31.3 | 38.6 | 45.6 | 59.5 | 78.0 | 79.5 | 85.6 |
| **Profit (EBITDA)** | **33.6** | **39.4** | **48.5** | **82.2** | **104.1** | **128.1** | **173.2** | **222.0** | **340.3** | **366.1** | **427.4** | **482.0** |

"'A' can be calculated or estimated from the values of 'B' and 'C' at each point in time." Figure 2.3 follows this rule—it displays the relationships in the company's income statements in a graphical, time-based form. These relationships hardly merit the term "theory," being simply the conventions by which we determine a company's profits, but they are nevertheless rigorous and reliable.

# FROM PERFORMANCE TO RESOURCES

To this point, analysis of historic performance has not departed from normal practice, except for the addition of time charts for the revenue, cost and profit items. Analysis needs to go further, however, and seek explanations for why revenue has followed the path that it has and why the individual cost items have developed as they have. Conventionally, revenue would be "explained" in terms of market size and the company's market share:

*Ryanair's revenue = size of air travel market multiplied by Ryanair's market share*

This is not, however, a causal explanation so much as an arithmetical observation. It could equally be stated the other way round, i.e. *market share = Ryanair revenues* divided by *market size*. The reality is that *customers* drive revenue and management activity and decisions act to win and retain customers.

Similarly, costs are sometimes "explained" in terms of the company's success in reducing the percentage of revenue expended on each item. So, for example:

*Ryanair staff cost = Revenues multiplied by the percentage of revenue spent on staff*

Again, this can equally be expressed another way: *staff-cost-percentage = staff cost* divided by *revenue* multiplied by 100. While management frequently seek to contain such percentage cost ratios, the reality is that *staff numbers* drive the cost of staff, and management controls those costs significantly by hiring and firing staff.

To achieve a true explanation for profit over time requires working back from the P&L account along the causal chain until we encounter factors that management can influence.

## SALES REVENUE

For Ryanair, revenue results from the number of passenger-journeys sold, multiplied by the average price paid by customers for those journeys. This is certainly true of the revenue from passenger fares, but is also largely true of the additional ancillary revenue, since that income comes almost entirely from items sold to passengers. There is a small difference between journeys booked and the number of passengers actually carried, since some 7% of people do not show up for the trips for which they have booked and paid.

The number of journeys purchased depends, in turn, on the number of customers who use Ryanair, and the frequency with which they buy tickets from the company. Among those customers will be a substantial number who are regular travelers with the airline, as well as less frequent users. There will also be just a few who use it so infrequently that they cannot be regarded as part of the regular customer base, but these are very few in number, and contribute little to the journeys and revenues of the airline.

These relationships are laid out in Figure 2.4. Like most airlines, Ryanair regularly publishes data on "passengers flown," but the number reported is strictly *passenger-journeys*, not passengers. It is not known, therefore, whether the 34.8 million journeys bought in 2006 came from 17.4 million people traveling on average twice during the year, or from 3.48 million people traveling 10 times each—these two alternatives are not the same, and the difference is important. If the first explanation were true, then the company has achieved a very high penetration of all people who may want to travel, and might be advised to focus on persuading them to travel more often. If the second explanation is correct, then it has an enthusiastic, if much smaller, band of customers, and would do better to focus on attracting more such people. For understandable reasons of commercial sensitivity, Ryanair does not publish this detail, so the data on journey frequency and passenger numbers in Figure 2.4 are illustrative.

Note that Figure 2.4 strictly observes the rules highlighted earlier, with every causal arrow meaning that each item can be estimated from those that are linked to it—in this case a simple multiplication of pairs of items.

The box shown around *customers* also has a specific meaning. It signifies that customers are a particular kind of element—a "resource" that builds over time, or

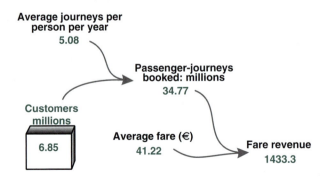

**Figure 2.4: Ryanair sales revenue, driven by customers, travel frequency and fares: year ended March 2006 (illustrative for customers and travel frequency).**

accumulates. This is quite different from the nature of the other items. A passenger-journey that happens today, for example, is a purely transitory event, quite distinct from a journey that took place last month or last year. The customer base today, on the other hand, includes many of the same people who were part of that customer base last month or last year, and many of those who will be part of the customer base one month or one year in the future. Such variables are known as "resources," or more technically as "asset-stocks," since they can be thought of as assets that are collected—or stocked—over time. These resources or asset-stocks will be of central importance to understanding how performance changes over time.

For now, note that Figure 2.4 introduces a fundamental principle, that:

### customers drive sales

A similar principle applies in noncommercial situations, even though the focus may not be on the financial income received from customers who pay money for goods and services. In voluntary organizations, for example, demand is driven by the number of beneficiaries the organization serves. In public services too, there is often a population driving demand for services, whether that be the number of children who need schooling, criminals committing crimes that require policing, or sick people needing healthcare.

Notice too that this principle extends the view of the organization's system beyond the boundaries of what it "owns." Nevertheless, there is a degree of reliability about customers or clients that makes them an integral part of the organization's business system. Indeed, customers can be a more reliable part of the system than employees who are paid to be there. McDonald's, for example, can expect its average employee to remain for just a few months, whereas many customers have been loyal users for many years.

One further qualification needs adding to the principle that "customers drive sales." Where firms supply durable products, such as washing machines or cars, sales volume and revenue arise from the *winning* of the customer, rather from holding the customer into the future. This point will be explained in more detail in Chapter 4.

Figure 2.4 is far from complete, even as an explanation for sales revenue alone. The number of transactions each customer makes each year depends on a number of further factors, including:

- price
- the range of destinations offered
- service frequency and quality

and how all of these compare with what competitors offer and what customers expect.

Lastly, Ryanair can only win customers and the journeys they wish to take to the extent that those customers *want* that service. Various general market conditions are therefore relevant, including:

- the overall propensity of consumers to travel by air
- the impact of general economic conditions on demand—e.g. a general fall in consumer incomes may reduce their travel frequency
- fundamental changes, such as population growth and changing behavior due to fashion or technology

Both the internal and external causal relationships have been added in Figure 2.5. Note that the range of routes appears as another resource, or asset-stock since, like the customer base, it has been built over many years, by adding new routes to the network and discontinuing others. This figure and similar diagrams for other firms can be described as a "resource-driven" explanation for sales revenue, in contrast with explanations based on estimates of market size and share.

The causal links shown in Figure 2.5 observe the rule that every item is "explained by" those that connect into it. However, unlike the strict arithmetical relationships in earlier charts, the links into *average journeys per person per year* indicate that we can estimate (rather than compute) this number from knowing the routes offered, fare, service quality, and so on. Understanding the relative influence of these factors under different circumstances and for different customer groups is of fundamental importance since it allows firms to design their products or services, direct their marketing efforts, and manage their pricing in ways that can make a considerable difference to sales rates and hence to revenues and profits. This element of the system that drives a firm's profits lies at the heart of the analytic methods practiced by

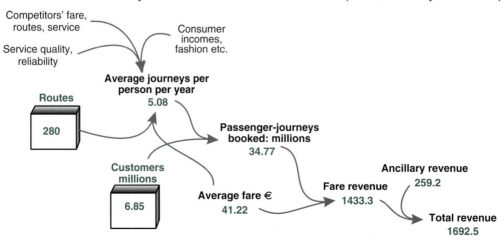

**Figure 2.5: An extended explanation of Ryanair's sales revenue.**

Amazon.com, CapitalOne and others mentioned earlier in this chapter, enabling them to extract considerable value from deep analysis.

### "Lookup" relationships

It is not always possible to define the relationship between a causal factor and its consequence in a simple mathematical relationship, as we did for *revenue = passenger-journeys* multiplied by *fare*. However such relationships can often be displayed graphically. For example, an airline may have a good understanding of how often the average customer will fly with it, at different levels of fare it might charge. Figure 2.6 allows us to "look up" this journey frequency, with the assumption that services, choice of destinations and other factors are fixed (and setting aside the additional complications caused by airlines' yield management systems, which vary the price as bookings fill up).

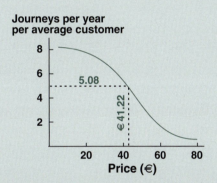

**Figure 2.6: An illustrative "lookup chart" for travel frequency versus price.**

Such lookup charts are not restricted to estimating how price affects demand from current customers. They can be used to display a wide variety of other cause–effect relationships:

- how availability for a consumer product changes (fraction of customers who can find it) as the number of retail outlets increases

- how staff turnover changes (staff leaving per week) as work pressure rises

- how maximum factory output changes as product range increases

The most common complicating factor when using lookup charts is that there may be several items affecting the same factor. A supplier of a consumer product may wish to know what fraction of consumers can obtain the product that it has worked so hard to promote. Knowing how many stores stock that product will likely give it a good estimate of this fractional availability. Average journey frequency for customers using an airline, on the other hand, reflects multiple factors (Figure 2.5). However, if you have a clear product or service proposition, you may nevertheless be able to estimate a lookup chart for purchase rate versus price by assuming those other factors are fixed. In effect, you would be saying "We know that this set of things we offer is what people want, so the only remaining question is how often they will buy as price varies." It may also be possible to estimate such a chart for "normal" values of other factors and scale that estimate up or down. Therefore, Figure 2.6 could include several curves, each of which shows how journey frequency varies as the choice of destinations increases.

To show how such lookup relationships link to explaining performance over time, Figure 2.7 shows a company that considers increasing its product range, with the belief that this will increase customers' purchase rate. It started, in month 0, offering only 1500 products, and achieved a purchase rate of 8.0 transactions per customer per year. It started increasing its range from month 6, and at first saw the purchase rate increase quickly as its customers more often found what they wanted amongst the increasing variety available. As more products were added, however, the purchase rate increase slowed, until by month 12, the company was offering 5000 products, but only achieving a purchase rate of 12 transactions per customer per year. This was not affordable since products are costly to stock, and many items sold too slowly to be worthwhile. From month 18, then, the company rationalized its product range to just 3000 items, but still achieved a purchase rate of 11.4 transactions per customer per year.

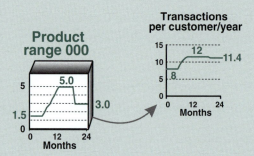

Figure 2.7: Customers' purchase rate versus product range (illustrative).

In this case, the variable "transactions per customer per year" does not contain an arithmetic equation that defines how this value varies with product range, e.g. *transactions per customer per year = product range * 5 / 1000.* Instead, the company's information over the first 12 months suggests that it can "look up" what the purchase rate might be for any product range it offers. This is shown in Figure 2.8 below. The table that defines the relationship between product range and purchase rate is shown at left, with the "lookup chart" version of the same relationship alongside. Finally, on the right is the performance over time of the company's actual experience that results from its choices of product range over the 24-month period. Note that the lookup chart also shows what might be expected if the company offered a smaller product range.

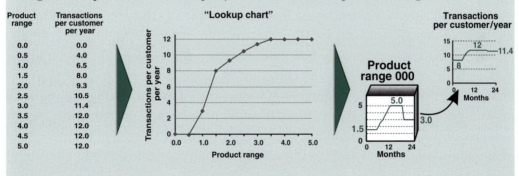

| Product range | Transactions per customer per year |
|---|---|
| 0.0 | 0.0 |
| 0.5 | 4.0 |
| 1.0 | 6.5 |
| 1.5 | 8.0 |
| 2.0 | 9.3 |
| 2.5 | 10.5 |
| 3.0 | 11.4 |
| 3.5 | 12.0 |
| 4.0 | 12.0 |
| 4.5 | 12.0 |
| 5.0 | 12.0 |

**Figure 2.8:** The data and chart from which purchase rate can be "looked up."[†]

## LIMITATIONS TO THIS EXPLANATION FOR SALES

Although the analysis to this point has highlighted the importance of working back along a rigorous chain of "what causes what," we do not escape entirely the problem of causal ambiguity. The factors determining customers' travel frequency are numerous and their relative importance is complex. However, we can localize that uncertainty to a specific point in the causal explanation for profits. The other causal links are simple arithmetic, so efforts to explain why profit is changing can focus on the specific sources of uncertainty.

---

[†] Spreadsheet software is not well suited to displaying the relationships between variables as they change through time. The structures and models used throughout this book were created in a simple software package, **my**strategy™, which can be obtained from www.strategydynamics.com/ **my**strategy. ("**my**strategy" is a registered trademark of Global Strategy Dynamics Ltd.)

Furthermore, few businesses are able to offer as simple a customer proposition as that provided by Ryanair, and the unavoidable complexity in other cases extends the analysis required. Amazon.com, for example, must serve customers who are far from uniform, either in what they buy or their purchase motivations. Some buy often, while others rarely do. Some use the service to purchase books alone, some mostly DVDs, and others buy items from various product categories. Some customers are strongly attracted to the lowest available price, while others are motivated by the choices available or the convenience of home delivery. A more complete explanation of Amazon's sales revenue would therefore divide customers and product groups into distinct segments, making it necessary to replicate the kind of structure in Figure 2.5 for each combination of customer group and segment group.

The final limitation is critically important but is fortunately addressable. The variables in Figure 2.5 above, apart from the number of customers and routes, are the total or average amounts for the whole year, from April 2005 to March 2006—total journeys taken or average fare paid. However, the number of routes and customers (if it were declared by the company) is stated *at the year end*. We therefore have an inconsistency. If the number of customers increased during the year, as it certainly did, then the year-end quantity would have been higher than this average number of 6.85 million. Similarly, the number of routes offered at the end of the year was also higher, at 330, than the average during the year of 279.5.

### The value curve, demand and segmentation

As we develop this book's approach to designing and delivering strategy, it will be helpful to show where common strategy approaches fit in. The value curve is a simple tool for understanding the relative importance to customers of benefits offered by alternative providers.[4] This framework plots product ratings or service characteristics that are important to capturing sales in a market, a process that can be useful for various purposes, including:

- Identifying what combinations of benefits may be attractive to different customer groups (e.g. in airlines or hotels, the contrasting priorities for business customers vs. leisure customers).

- Developing a new combination of benefits that may be more generally attractive to customers than is currently offered by existing firms (e.g. the introduction of simple-to-use cellphones with basic functions only, to take advantage of the overcomplexity of many previous products).

While using the value curve in such general terms can help in assessing opportunities, our need is rather more detailed—i.e. to break apart the different factors involved in the causal chain leading to sales. Consequently, it is necessary to distinguish the various points at which such performance ratings actually affect customer behavior. The structure shown so far for Ryanair has identified a specific behavior of concern, that is, customers' journey frequency. This behavior is influenced by the mix of benefits offered by the airline. Furthermore, those benefits are of differing importance to different customer segments.

Figure 2.9 illustrates the distinct balance of preferences for leisure travelers and for business travelers, and compares these with what Ryanair may be seen to offer. Low price, for example, is important for leisure travelers. Business people, on the other hand, may be less concerned with low price—they may be able to find a cheaper flight, but add-on services, such as lounge facilities or flexible tickets, may be more important. The total journeys sold by the airline will be the sum of the journeys sold to business and leisure customer segments.

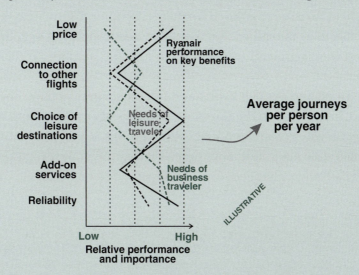

**Figure 2.9: Value curve needs of two customer types and their impact on purchase behavior for Ryanair.**
Source: A reproduction of an s-curve from W. Chan Kim, Renee A. Mauborgne (2002) Charting Your Company's Future, *Harvard Business Review* **80** (6).

A more sophisticated approach to ranking combinations of product attributes is "conjoint analysis," which is widely used in marketing. The method is based on the fact that the relative values of attributes considered jointly can better be measured than when considered in isolation.[5]

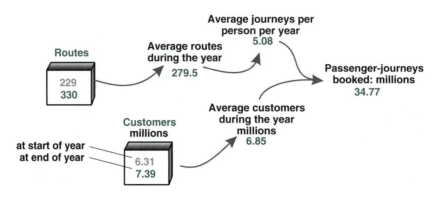

**Figure 2.10: Passenger-journeys reflect changing numbers of customers and routes.**

Note that the purchase rate is not the only component of demand—as shown in Figure 2.5, the *number* of customers is also fundamentally important. It is therefore also necessary to assess how factors included in the value curve drive the acquisition of customers, an issue examined further in Chapter 3. Other cases may require still more factors to be explained. For a retailer, sales reflect not only the number of customers and their purchase frequency, but also the number of items bought on each occasion.

A more accurate and explicit explanation of passenger-journeys booked is given by Figure 2.10, in which both the start/end numbers of customers and routes as well as the average for the year are denoted. Although this is a more accurate causal explanation, it could be made still more precise if it were known exactly how numbers of routes and customers changed during the year. (See box below.)

---

**Doing it right: time periods versus instants in time**

Many companies track growth in their customer base and some even declare the number publicly at the end of each reporting period, such as subscribers for cable TV or cellphone companies. Most companies need to be careful about the distinction between total activity *over the period as a whole*, e.g. sales volume or average purchase rate, and the *opening and closing* numbers of customers who give rise to those totals or averages. This is a familiar distinction because it has always been necessary when looking at the cash *flows* that have come in or gone out during the year versus the cash *amounts* at the start and end of the year. It is also an important distinction because it has implications for other items, such as interest income

In order to work out a company's interest income, we cannot just take the cash at the start or end of the year, since the quantity of cash will have changed throughout the year. In Figure 2.11, a company starts with $100m in cash, and with interest of 6%/year, would be earning $1.5m/quarter—except that by year end it has cash of $200m, so its rate of interest earned will have risen from $1.5m at the start of the first quarter to $3m by the year end. If cash has grown steadily over that period, it will have reached $125m by the end of the first quarter, so interest earned in that quarter will be 6% of the quarterly average cash level ($112.5m), i.e. $1.69m.

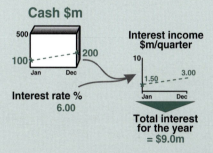

**Figure 2.11: Tracking interest income as cash levels rise.**

But what if cash levels had *not* grown in a straight line during the year? Figure 2.12 shows a scenario in which much higher levels of cash had been held at various times during the year. The average cash level is therefore far higher than the simple average of the start and end amounts and the interest earned is also more.

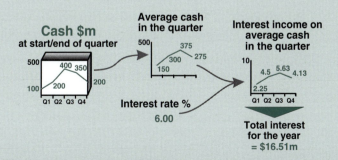

**Figure 2.12: Tracking interest income as cash levels change from quarter to quarter.**

None of this will be new or puzzling for accountants, since it is the fundamental difference between what is reported in a company's income/cash flow statements versus the balance sheet. However, accountants are not the only professionals who need to appreciate this difference between period start/end values for resources (cash, in this case), and the consequences of those resources changing *during* a period. Some simple changes to this example demonstrate how important the same principle becomes when looking at other resources. Figure 2.13 shows the implications for total annual revenue when we change from recording numbers of customers at start and end of a year to tracking changes in the customer base each quarter.

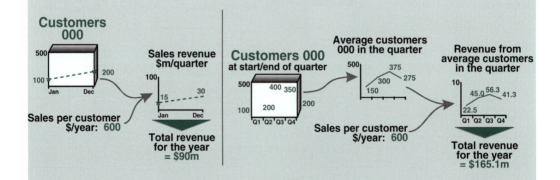

**Figure 2.13: Tracking sales revenue as customer numbers change.**

Even this magnification of the timescale may not be enough, depending on how rapidly things are changing, and how accurate our understanding of revenues needs to be. Just as cash levels may move up and down *within* a quarter—indeed, from day to day—so may numbers of customers. The more quickly things are changing, and the more precise the analysis needs to be, the shorter the time periods for which data must be collected and assessed. The time periods must be short enough that the *change* in the resource level during each period is small, relative to the *quantity* of the resource at the start of the period.

Our causal explanation for performance must therefore be extended. Not only do "customers drive revenue," but:

**customers drive revenues over time**

## OPERATING COSTS

Efforts to assess and forecast business performance generally pay close attention to cost ratios and it is common for management to control costs by setting ratio limits—"labor cost must not exceed X% of sales revenue," for example. However, this is a crude form of control that clearly falls down in many cases.

If a retailer were to control labor costs strictly by capping the percentage of revenue that can be spent on service staff, then a decline in sales would cut the spending available for service. This would cut the number of service people, which would likely damage the service experienced by the few remaining customers, leading to still further sales loss. Such crude rules of thumb are therefore often overridden by executive common sense. Ratio-based controls are especially inappropriate for deciding on many truly important factors, such as what product range to offer, how much capacity to operate, or how many staff to employ.

### Generic strategies: cost leadership, differentiation and focus

An extreme simplification of the value curve connects back to a long-established view of strategic choice—generic strategies.[6] This concept developed from statistical analysis of business performance across many firms and industries that suggested profitability correlates with market share—the greater a firm's market share in its industry, the more profitable the firm could be. However, further investigation suggested that high profitability could be achieved with rather low market shares—it was in the middle-size zone that profitability suffered most.

It seemed that industry leaders' strong profitability reflected cost advantages that smaller firms simply could not match, such as economies of scale in manufacturing and marketing. In some industries, it appeared that being the *cheapest* supplier might be the only way to succeed—on the value curve diagram described above, then, price would be the only factor to consider. Consequently, total attention to reducing costs would be imperative, so rivalry would take place amongst the largest firms, each of whom would strive to identify every possible cent of cost saving they might achieve. Remnants of this philosophy can still be seen in some commodity industries, such as the manufacturing of steel, cement or bulk petrochemicals.

Profitable *smaller* firms could not match those advantages of scale, so they must have been relying on other sources of advantage. They managed to put together some combination of product features, quality and service support, for which customers were willing to pay more than the costs of providing them—i.e. a set of benefits that could be compared on the value curve with those offered by competitors or valued by customers.

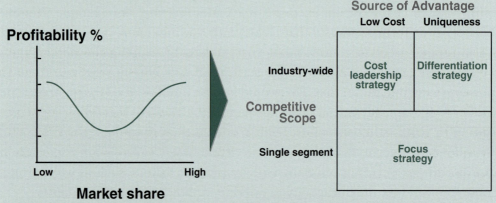

**Figure 2.14: Profitability, market share and generic strategies.**
Source: Porter, M.E., *Competitive Strategy* (1980), Free Press.

Since it often proved difficult to sustain either cost advantage or differentiation across all segments of a market, a third generic strategy was identified, namely a focus on the specific needs of particular customer groups. This strategy choice could be further subdivided into a cost-led focus for price-driven customers and a differentiation-led focus for customers who valued other factors.

Ryanair's reported results conveniently show the resources that drive its operating costs. Its aircraft are costly to operate and its staff must be paid. Substantial costs are also incurred due to the number of airports it serves and the number of routes it operates. (An airline can operate more routes than it has airports by flying to multiple destinations from each.) Figure 2.15 shows how *staff costs* reflect the *average number of staff employed* and the *average cost per person* during the year ended March 2006. As was

**Figure 2.15: Staff numbers drive staff costs.**

the case for customer numbers, this figure also shows the reported number of staff at the start and end of the year and the average number of staff would be more accurate if numbers were available for more numerous points in time during the year.

**Doing it right: time periods versus instants in time (continued)**

An earlier box explained the important distinction between the number of customers at start and end of a period, and the total or average values of items that reflect how that number changed during the period. Exactly the same distinction arises in the case of costly resources and the various items that depend on their quantity. A further adaptation to the cash and interest example used earlier shows how a company's changing staff numbers between the start and end of a year impact total salary costs for the whole year (Figure 2.16).

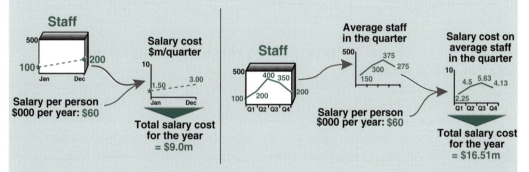

**Figure 2.16: Tracking salary costs as staff numbers change.**

Cost is not the only item that depends on such changing resource quantities. The work output of those staff may be of interest, e.g. the total number of sales calls a salesforce can make during a period, or the number of customer enquiries a call center can handle. Similarly, production capacity—another resource whose quantity may be defined at the start and end of a period—determines how much output a manufacturing company can produce and the amount of energy it consumes during a period.

Our causal explanation for performance must therefore be extended. Not only do "customers drive revenue and other resources drive costs," but:

**customers drive revenue *over time***

and

**other resources drive costs *over time*.**

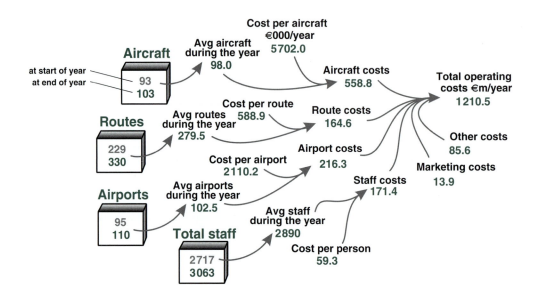

**Figure 2.17: Ryanair's internal resources and operating costs: year ended March 2006.**

Figure 2.17 extends this principle to the other major resources required for Ryanair to provide its services and adds marketing spend and other costs to arrive at a complete explanation for the company's operating costs.

This figure raises a subtle but important point regarding what drives costs. The *cost per aircraft,* for example, is indeed the total reported aircraft costs divided by the average number in place during the year. However, those costs are split between the fixed costs that arise from the aircraft existing, such as lease costs and insurance,[7] and the variable costs of flying them—mostly fuel and maintenance. To determine cost per aircraft would require identifying the number of flying hours that occurred, and fuel consumption per hour. Flying hours would then depend on the number of routes served, the service frequency and distance of those routes. Figure 2.17 assumes that Ryanair, as a highly effective operator, ensures a high and steady aircraft utilization and that the costs of operating those aircraft can be totaled and averaged across the fleet. While sufficient for a strategic assessment, this would not be adequate for a detailed operational analysis of the company's performance from month to month.

Similar issues arise with airport costs, some of which are incurred simply by having a presence at each location, while others, such as handling charges, depend on the frequency of aircraft arrivals and departures. Staff costs, in contrast, are mostly fixed by the number of people employed, rather than being dependent on the business activity rates.

Although it is true that "resources drive costs," and that such costs may dominate in many businesses and noncommercial organizations, three additional cost categories must be noted.

- If a business buys raw materials, which it then sells, either after transforming them into further products or simply retailing or reselling them as they are, it incurs a "cost of goods sold." This is deducted from sales revenue, giving rise to a "gross profit" from which operating costs (largely resource driven) are deducted to arrive at operating profit. Figure 2.18 below illustrates this for Amazon.com.
- Certain other costs result directly from management choices to spend money, rather than being incurred as a result of owning resources. Examples include marketing expenditure and training. There is still a link to resources, however, since these spending decisions reflect a desire to build resources—customers and staff skills respectively. A more complete statement of principle, then, is that:

### Building and holding resources drive costs.

- Many of the costs of building resources feature in companies' income statements, but large capital assets, such as physical production capacity, vehicles, or computer equipment, may instead be treated as capital spend.

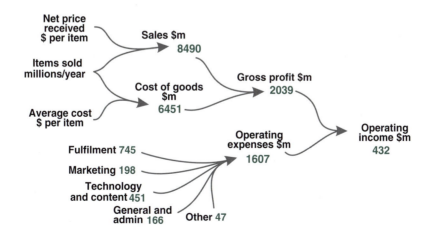

Figure 2.18: Amazon.com gross profit, operating costs and operating income for the year to December 2005.

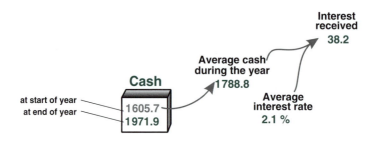

Figure 2.19: Cash (or debt) levels drive interest income (or cost).

## CASH, DEBT AND INTEREST

One final type of resource we must note is the company's cash (or debt), which drives interest income (or expense). This has not been included in the analysis of Ryanair's performance because the profit number explained is *earnings before interest tax depreciation and amortization (EBITDA)*. A company's cash and debt position and the resulting interest income and cost are clearly important, however, so Figure 2.19 shows how Ryanair's cash changed between April 2005 and March 2006, and the resulting interest income. Note again that the average cash and average interest rate are approximations and could only be calculated exactly with information on how cash and interest rates changed on a daily basis throughout the year.

## SUMMARY CAUSAL STRUCTURE FOR SALES AND PROFITS

Figure 2.20 summarizes the causal analysis of Ryanair's profit history. Note that these charts show all data from 1995 to 2006, but offer numerical values (in green) only for the year ended 2006. All the resource items on the left are the quantities in place at the end of March 2006 (estimated in the case of customers), while all other items for revenues and costs are the total or average over the whole year.

(Online learning materials are available to support this example, see paragraph on p.xxi.)

## ESTIMATING FUTURE PERFORMANCE

### A STANDARD FORECASTING APPROACH

Given the overriding importance in corporate settings of future sales and profits, the process by which these items are estimated is critical, both for investors wanting

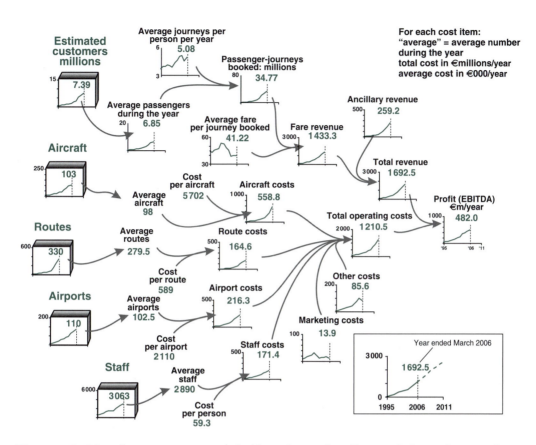

**Figure 2.20: Summary causal structure for Ryanair's sales and profit history to March 2006.**
Source: Porter, M.E., *Competitive Strategy* (1980), Free Press.

### Resources and value-chain analysis

Value-chain analysis is a common tool for strategy development, used to identify where value is added as a product or service is put together, marketed and sold by a company. It is sometimes used qualitatively, to identify where management priorities should be focused, or where specific policies aim to create competitive advantage.

When used quantitatively, the analysis can be carried out in various ways, for example, by asking what happens to each $100 received by a firm, or what happens to the cash value of each unit produced. It is important to note, though, that the cost and value added by a single firm is usually just one stage in a complex supply chain system. Consider for example the purchase of a $30 book from a bookstore.

Figure 2.21 illustrates where that $30 could go. The bookstore pays the publisher, say, $20, so retains $10 to cover its own costs of $8.50 and leave a profit margin of $1.50. The publisher has to purchase paper and other goods and services for say $12.00, leaving it with $8.00 to cover its own costs of $6.50 and leave a profit also of $1.50. Value-chain analysis looks inside that $6.50 of costs and asks where *that* money goes. These distinct cost elements are detailed on the right.

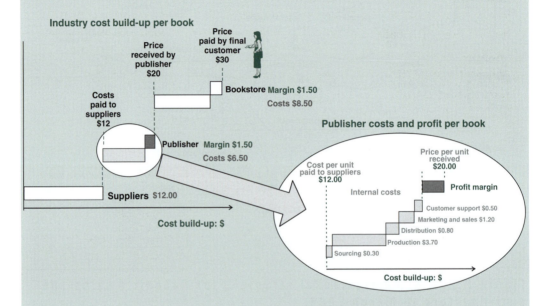

**Figure 2.21: Illustrative value-system for book supply and publisher's value chain.**

There are some difficulties in carrying out this analysis. How, for example, should cost items be treated that occur only once for the publication of a particular title, such as editing, layout and cover design? What about the cost of marketing and sales effort that drives overall sales, rather than being specific to each book sold? These issues are dealt with by standard methods of cost and management accounting.

Strategy development can gain a certain amount of insight from this level of value-chain analysis. For example, a publisher could consider how the cost structure might differ between books sold through stores versus those sold through online retailers, using this information to evaluate priorities between these channels. Companies can also evaluate the potential benefits from changing the balance of effort between different stages—a manufacturing company might decide to spend more on improved production, for example, to make products more reliable and save on customer support.

It is also necessary, though, to look at the *total* value build-up for the firm, in addition to this per-unit analysis. Figure 2.22 therefore looks at the total costs and profits of the company in $ millions, and separates out the costs of support activities, such as information systems and administrative overhead.[8] Some judgment is again required with this firm-level view of value added. For example, a firm's marketing costs may include expenditure on advertizing placed through different media. Strictly speaking, this is a bought-in cost rather than an internal cost of the company, but it would be misleading to leave this cost out of the analysis of the company's own value chain.

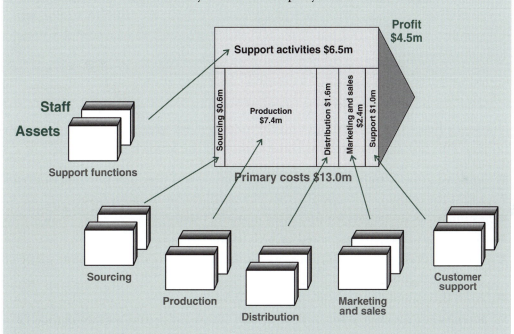

**Figure 2.22: Resources drive value-chain costs—publishing company illustration.**

The important connection to the resource-based analysis is shown in Figure 2.22, where each value-chain cost is largely driven by the assets and staff deployed in those activities. This is not the full story, however, and still leaves questions.

First, firms make different choices about what to do themselves, rather than buying in from third parties. For example, dedicated logistics firms can often distribute goods more effectively and at lower cost than many firms could do themselves. The assets and staff needed to enable this "value-chain" activity, along with the costs of those resources, therefore reside in a third-party supplier, rather than in the firm itself.

Secondly—and critically—costs are not driven solely by the *existence* of physical assets and staff, but also by *building* those resources. In extreme cases, such resource-building activities are vast and account for a very large fraction of a company's cost structure. A pharmaceutical firm's R&D expenditure, for example, which drives additions to its product range, is a large fraction of total costs. This issue limits the insight obtained from value-chain analysis, since such costs have little or no relation to current revenues, which are generated from current products that exist due to *past* expenditures.

to assess a firm's future earnings and for management wishing to set performance targets. This task typically follows some version of the following approach:[9]

- forecast growth and thus future size of the markets in which the firm operates
- assess the impact of competitive activity on likely future price levels
- estimate, or set targets for increases in market share
- from these, calculate expected growth in the firm's sales turnover
- forecast, or set targets for, improvements in the fraction of revenue spent on purchased goods
- from this calculate the firm's gross profit on sales
- forecast, or set targets for operating cost ratios (sales and marketing, distribution, product development, training, financial administration, etc.)
- from the expected price trends and these cost ratios, project operating profit margins (*operating profit* divided by *sales*)
- using the forecast for sales turnover, and estimates or targets for gross margins, cost ratios and operating profit margins, calculate projected operating profits

In addition, estimates are needed for any investments the firm needs to make in order to deliver the growth in sales and improvements in margins and cost ratios, such as increased capacity or improved IT systems. The capital required comes at a

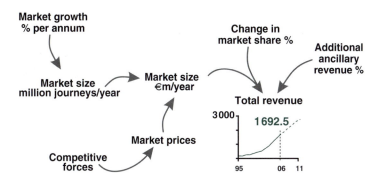

**Figure 2.23: Market-based forecasting for Ryanair sales.**

cost, which is deducted from the firm's operating profits to arrive at its "economic profit," as explained in Chapter 1.

Applying this approach for Ryanair requires starting with the history of the total size of the air travel market (millions of passenger-journeys per year) in the region it serves, and forecasting likely growth in demand for air travel in future years. This would be multiplied by the company's historic and hoped-for future market share (Figure 2.23), to arrive at a forecast for its revenue from passenger fares. Then, a forecast for ancillary revenues would be added, assuming these are a continuing percentage of fare revenues, to arrive at forecasted total revenues.

In practice, this process is more complex than it might appear. For example, there is the question of which "market" is the appropriate basis to start from—the total air travel market in Europe, or only that served by low-fare carriers, assuming those carriers can be definitively identified from other airlines? Then, there is the question of where the boundaries of that market lie. Does it include, for example, flights from Italy to Turkey or Israel, and if Ryanair starts to operate across those boundaries does the whole analysis have to be recreated to reflect this newly increased scope? Other cases bring up further complications. Ryanair offers one service—flying people from point to point. Amazon.com, on the other hand, diversified from selling books alone, adding music, software, games and household goods, so the kind of analysis in Figure 2.23 would have to be repeated for each product market, and the results added together.

Not only is it important to work out the market size and probable growth rate, but likely price levels must also be estimated in order to produce a revenue forecast. Analysts typically consider the impact of "competitive forces" when working out likely price trends.[10] These forces include:

- Activities of *competitors*: both the direct rivalry between near-identical companies—Ryanair versus easyJet versus Air Berlin, for example—as well as with less similar competitors such as Lufthansa, Iberia or American Airlines, to the extent that those companies operate at all on Ryanair routes.

- The risk that new entrants are attracted by the profits they believe they can make in an industry, and that they will exert further downward pressure on the market shares of existing competitors and the prices they can charge—there has been a high rate of new low-fare airlines starting up in recent years, and no sign of such new entry ceasing.

- Availability and appeal of *substitutes*, i.e. goods and services that, while not precisely the same as those sold by the company, nevertheless offer the customer similar benefits—e.g. traveling by train or car, or even (for business travel at any rate) videoconferencing.

- The buying power of *customers* to drive prices down by switching between competing suppliers, if the product is sufficiently costly to make it worth while to do so—with this process being easy in the case of air travel, falling prices are only to be expected.

- The power of *suppliers* to command high prices, which will be greater if they are few in number, or if their goods are unique and/or of critical importance to the industry they supply—major airports are an important example in air travel and low fare airlines work hard to find cheaper, secondary locations.

### A problem with market-growth based forecasting

Chapter 1 noted that focusing on percentage growth rates in market size ignores the issue of market *potential* and is therefore a poor basis for setting performance objectives. This chapter's outline of how market growth is used to develop a sales forecast exposes a further problem with the implied theory, namely that market growth and changes in market share explain sales. This mindset makes the error of taking market size as an independent variable—something "out there" that we can have a piece of if we do a good job of serving its needs. In many cases, however, market size is not independent, but is itself subject to companies' actions and decisions.

Chapter 1 pointed out that the market for VoIP is the size it is today in large part because Skype created it. Skype is far from alone in having created the very market it serves. There was no market for worldwide 24-hour TV news until CNN offered the service, and the growth of "market demand" since its launch has been determined by the company's own success in extending its service through hotels and other worldwide locations.

Not only is the current market *size* often a reflection of what companies provide, but so too is its *growth rate*. The air travel market today is the size it is in large part because of what SouthWest in the United States, and Ryanair and easyJet in Europe offer. Every time these companies open a service between two new destinations, large numbers of people start to travel those routes who did not do so before. The market's growth rate largely reflects the rate at which such firms have been able to extend their services.

In the case of Amazon.com, between 1997, 1998 and 1999, the company's net sales grew from $148m to $610m to $1640m—year-on-year growth of 312% and 169% respectively. However, had the calendar years happened to fall rather differently, its growth might have been 240% and 190%, or some other combination of remarkably large numbers. Management would have gained little insight from forecasts of "market growth in online book sales" since they were responsible for bringing it about.

Having estimated likely sales revenue, the usual next step is to forecast (or for management, set targets for) reductions in the cost of goods the company buys. For Ryanair, key items are the costs of aircraft and fuel, but also include airport handling charges and other purchased services. For manufacturing companies, this includes the cost of raw materials or components needed to make their products, and for retailers, the prices paid to product suppliers. In such cases, deducting these costs from revenues leads to the company's gross profit on sales.

Lastly, the forecasting process looks at operating cost ratios and any future scope for improving these ratios. Figure 2.24 shows historic and anticipated improvements in Ryanair's ratios for airport and staff costs. The illustration assumes that the company will be able to reduce airport costs as a fraction of revenue—perhaps due to scheduling more flights per week through each airport—but will need to sustain

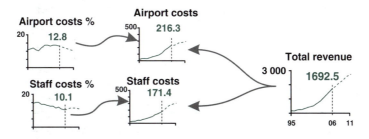

**Figure 2.24: Changes in Ryanair cost ratios.**

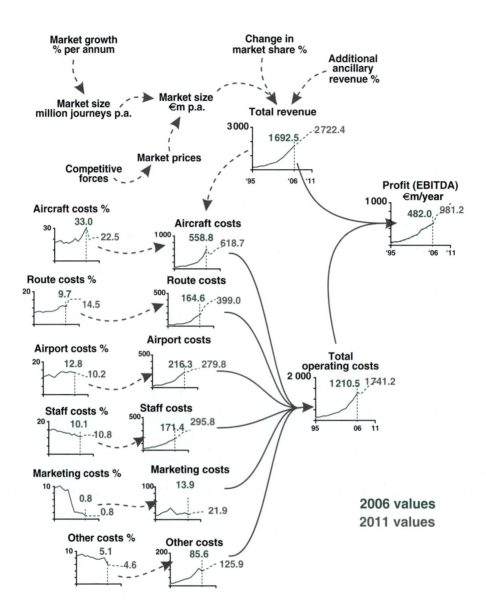

**Figure 2.25: Market growth and ratio-driven explanations for Ryanair sales and profits history, and a plausible forecast to 2011.**

the percentage of revenue spent on staff, to ensure continuing service levels. Similar calculations can be made for costs of routes, aircraft, marketing and other items. To make these forecasts more accurate, each cost might be separated into elements associated with fares and ancillary revenues.

Combining these assessments produces an integrated picture of the company's sales and profits, as shown in Figure 2.25. The solid links show the direct relationship between items in the P&L account, while dashed links indicate the relationships to factors and ratios explaining the sales and costs. Note that the analysis should in practice be extended to include the capital investment needed to enable the sales growth and cost improvements, and thus arrive at the firm's economic profit.

The logic of this process for forecasting revenues, costs and profit margins relies on some fundamental assumptions:

- that the markets in which the company operates are growing of their own accord, independent of the actions of the company or others serving that market
- that competitive forces dominate the prices companies can charge, and therefore, the profitability they can achieve

Translating this into a simple theory of cause and effect produces the view shown in Figure 2.26. This is referred to as the "structure-conduct-performance paradigm" since it asserts that markets' structural conditions limit what management is able to do (their conduct) to build sales and profitability (performance). This can be useful for management, since it may help them choose markets, or segments of those markets, where growth prospects are strong and competitive forces not severe. This is often described as the strategic choice of "where to compete," to which are added decisions about "how to compete," i.e. what products and services to offer and how to provide them.

The structure-conduct-performance paradigm has provided the bedrock for understanding business performance for decades, and the competitive-forces perspective derived from it has dominated approaches to strategy analysis since the 1980s. However, more recent research suggests that industry conditions are not a good predictor of business performance. Work by Rumelt[11] showed that business unit factors (i.e. characteristics and choices of businesses themselves) accounted for more of the variance in profitability among firms than did "industry conditions" (i.e. characteristics of the industries in which firms operate). McGahan and Porter[12] responded to this paper with an alternative analysis, which suggested a stronger role for industry conditions in explaining profitability variance, but nevertheless acknowledged the dominance of business unit factors.

**Figure 2.26: How market and competitive conditions determine management scope to build sales and profitability.**

The debate about the relative importance of industry conditions versus business factors continues and although some papers identify an important role for industry conditions,[13] it is now generally accepted that the decisions of business executives have a larger influence on performance than do industry conditions. In managerial terms, this implies that it is possible to deliver strong performance in industries with tough competitive conditions—consider the airline industry where competitive forces are notoriously hostile—and to perform badly in industries where competitive forces are benign. A further reason for paying attention to organizations themselves is that industry conditions are not entirely independent factors, but can be influenced—sometimes strongly—by what firms do. Businesses often succeed in placing barriers that make it difficult for others to enter their industry, whether by acquiring critical resources, or developing powerful capabilities that others find difficult to copy.

## "Five forces" and profitability

The assessment of how pressure from competitors, customers, suppliers, new entrants and substitute products and services affect the scope for profitability in any industry has come to be very widely used, and is commonly referred to simply as "the five forces approach." It should be noted, though, that the basic question this approach seeks to answer is somewhat different from the question of performance over time explained in Chapter 1. Rather, five-forces analysis provides an explanation for the profitability (return on sales or on capital employed) of an industry and its variability amongst the firms that operate within the industry. In Figure 2.27, for example, firms in industry A achieve relatively high profitability, and there is a wide variance in the profitability of different firms within the industry. Industry B, on the other hand, typically generates lower profitability and with much less variance between firms.

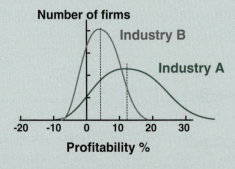

Figure 2.27: Illustrating profit variance between two industries.

So why do firms in industry B not simply switch to industry A? The principal problem is that different industries require firms to have different resources and capabilities, so it is hardly helpful to tell a struggling airline, for example, that profitability is higher in pharmaceuticals.

Then why do investors continue to hold shares of companies in industry B, rather than invest in companies operating in industry A? As explained in Chapter 1, investors look for earnings *growth* when deciding where to invest. The earnings of firms in industry B already reflect the tough forces at work, and investors will already have taken that into account when deciding what companies in the industry are worth. It is therefore possible for investors to *increase* investment in low profitability industries if they expect conditions to become more favorable, resulting in rising stock prices for industry B. Conversely, they may decide that competitive conditions in industry A are becoming more difficult and *reduce* their investment, resulting in falling stock prices.

Extensive discussions of how industry forces operate, their impact on business performance, and implications for analyzing and developing strategy can be found in most strategy textbooks.[14] While recognizing the rationale for the process described above and its theoretical foundations, the approach adopted here takes a somewhat different path for two principal reasons.

First, there is the ambiguity of causality discussed earlier in this chapter, which results from the sheer number of factors involved, the number of steps along the causal chain, and the uncertainties involved in anticipating human behavioral responses. For management to build sales in a market segment, for example, it must identify customers, develop products, build the capacity to produce, supply and support those products, train people, market effectively to win and retain customers, and price and promote those products to win potential customers' purchases. Even if all this causality is understood, the eventual success of these activities together still depends on how effectively the firm carries them out compared to its rivals. There can therefore be little confidence in the relationships among any of the industry-level drivers—numbers of competitors, size of customers, market growth rates—and the sales and profitability outcomes for companies.

The second reason is that the standard approach does not pay appropriate attention to the choices actually available to management. There is much more management can do to build a strong business system than to alter the competitive structure of the markets in which they operate. Nor does management have much freedom in practice to make fundamental changes to where it competes.

Achieving profitability in the airline industry is endemically difficult, due to exactly those competitive forces mentioned above, but the management of Delta Airlines, for instance, does not have any practical option to switch to another industry where competition is less intense. Even switching between segments *within* industries can be difficult, as shown by the disappointing experience of full-service airlines that have tried to serve the low-fare segment.

## A RESOURCE-BASED APPROACH TO ESTIMATING FUTURE PERFORMANCE

The explanation developed earlier for Ryanair's performance through 2006 demonstrated the dominant causal explanation—that resources drive revenue and costs, and hence explain profits. That has been true throughout the company's history and it will continue to be true into the future.

Figure 2.28 shows a plausible future for Ryanair's fare revenues, driven by aspirations for growth in the total number of customers using the airline, plus assumptions about journey frequency and fares. Note that this causal explanation does not escape the need to assess the effect of competitive pressures, which encompass both the frequency with which customers will choose to travel with this airline and the fares they are willing to pay. However, as noted when seeking explanations for historical revenues, customers' willingness to choose this company is also due to its own success in offering the routes and service they want. Outstanding development of its strategic business system explains why this company has been and will likely continue to grow profits strongly in an endemically challenging industry.

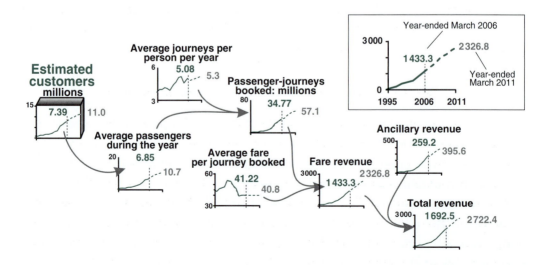

**Figure 2.28: A customer-driven forecast to 2011 for Ryanair revenues.**

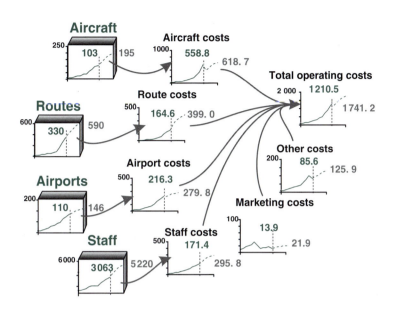

**Figure 2.29: A resource-driven forecast to 2011 for Ryanair's operating costs.**

Adopting the same principle for the airline's costly resources leads to the plausible projection for operating costs shown in Figure 2.29. If the company is to serve the number of customers anticipated in Figure 2.28 above, then it will have to extend the number of airports to reach those customers, offer more routes between those airports to attract their travel choice, add planes, and hire additional staff.

Combining the anticipated revenues from Figure 2.28 and costs from Figure 2.29 leads to the same profit forecast as in Figure 2.25, above. The important difference, however, is that this new explanation has been constructed from assessing the number of resources that must be built, rather than from assumptions about percentage growth rates, market share and cost ratios.

### Resources *are* important: a model of milk production

"A popular economic journal published the research of a noted economist who had developed a very sophisticated econometric model designed to predict milk production in the United States. The model contained a raft of macroeconomic variables woven together in a set of complex equations. But nowhere in that model did cows appear. If one asks how milk is actually generated, one discovers that cows are absolutely essential to the process. Thinking operationally about milk production, one would focus first on cows, then on the rhythms associated with farmers' decisions to increase and decrease herd size, the relations governing milk productivity per cow, and so on."[15]

## RESOURCE-BASED DEMAND AND COST DRIVERS IN NONCOMMERCIAL SETTINGS

The principles adopted in the Ryanair analysis can be readily applied to non-commercial cases too, such as voluntary groups, public services and nongovernmental organizations (NGOs). Consider the Motor Neurone Disease Association (www. mndassociation.org), a voluntary organization working to deliver the support needed by people living with MND (plwMND)—of whom there are over 3000 sufferers in the United Kingdom.[16,17] In addition to supporting medical research into MND, the association offers a range of services to people affected by MND, including a helpline, 14 care centers, equipment loan service, plus support, advice and information from 21 regional care advisors, and a befriending service from over 300 association visitors. Six regionally based volunteer development coordinators support additional volunteer and fundraising activity through a network of 95 branches.

MNDA's primary objective is to achieve a high level and quality of support. A similarity with business cases is that the "demand" for its support is driven by "customers", i.e. the number of plwMND who are registered with the organization. The principal resources that determine how much support MNDA can give are the

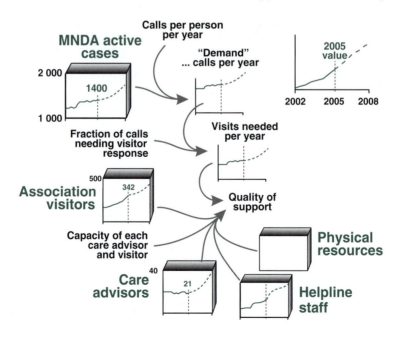

**Figure 2.30:** Demand for MNDA services is driven by the number of people with MND, and capacity is determined by the number of care assistants and visitors.

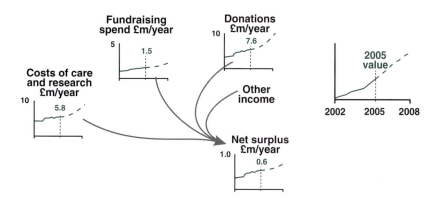

**Figure 2.31: Income and costs for the Motor Neurone Disease Association.**

care advisers and visitors, plus the staff and physical resources associated with the helpline (Figure 2.30).

Although MNDA is not concerned with profit, it does have to work within its financial means, so costs must be covered by donations and legacies. Raising these funds requires some spending, even though volunteers raise considerable amounts of cash. Thus, the association's financial surplus or deficit (Figure 2.31) is the difference between income raised and the costs of both raising those funds and providing support to plwMND.

MNDA's income from donations is driven by the number of donors, most of whom are regular givers and therefore constitute another resource. Fundraisers also bring in income from the general public, and encourage giving from regular donors (Figure 2.32). Both sources of donations are boosted by money spent on promoting the association's aims.

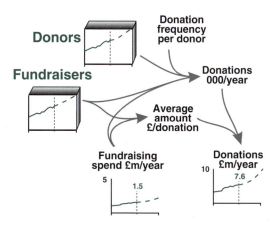

**Figure 2.32: Donors and fundraisers drive income for MNDA.**

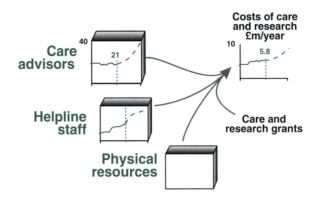

**Figure 2.33:** Staff and other resources drive costs for MNDA.

Apart from fundraising expenditure, the association's costs are largely determined by its staff and physical assets, plus financial grants to research projects (Figure 2.33). Note that the association visitors are volunteers, so do not drive significant continuing costs, although there is a cost for training them.

Figure 2.34 unites these pieces of the resource-based explanation for MNDA's performance, and can be used to sketch its prospects. A number of challenges

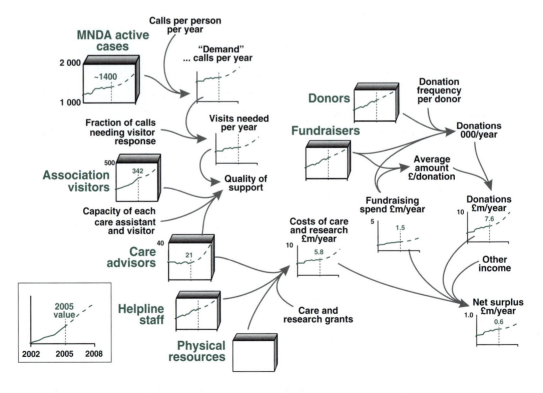

**Figure 2.34:** Resources drive performance—overall summary for MNDA.

facing the association could change its future substantially, and thus alter the time path of both its resources and performance outcomes.

First, it is estimated that only half of the people registered with MNDA actually use its services. If the inactive cases were to become active cases quickly, the help-line could be overloaded, leading to long delays for callers' needs to be resolved. If that bottleneck were removed, demands on the care assistants and visitors would escalate, and their ability to deliver quality care would be compromised. It takes time, however, to find and train these carers, and a further lead time as new staff learn processes, e.g. liaising with health service providers. All this requires a faster rate of fundraising, so more volunteers would be needed, and either the number of donors and/or their donation rate must increase. This would be challenging, since MND is something of an "orphan" affliction, and does not receive the public attention of high-profile diseases such as cancer.

Secondly, the association is facing a likely rapid increase in demand, since the number of plwMND is rising as life expectancy and medical treatments of other ailments improve. This, plus the untapped population of people served by MNDA, indicates that rapid growth is needed in all the supply-side resources.

## SUMMARIZING THIS RESOURCE-DRIVEN PERSPECTIVE ON PERFORMANCE

Figure 2.35 summarizes how the resource-based approach to understanding and projecting performance—an approach that will be developed in later chapters—contrasts with the widely used market-based approach. Both diagrams are highly simplified representations of the detailed *and extensive* analysis that is actually conducted. To be properly used, the market-based approach requires extensive research

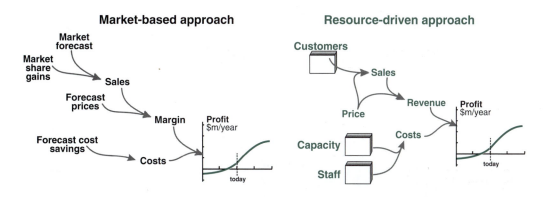

**Figure 2.35:** Contrasting the market-based and resource-driven approach to understanding performance.

into the impact of economic conditions on market demand, the effect of competitive forces price levels and changes in market share, and the price elasticity of demand. The resource-based perspective, too, will be expanded to incorporate these important exogenous factors. In particular, close attention will be given to where customers come from and go to, both for the business itself and for the whole market. It will also examine how staff, capacity, products, distribution channels and other resources are developed and sustained, some of which will also be subject to external constraints and competitive conditions, e.g. availability of staff and channels.

### Strategy, vision, purpose, mission and goals

Many strategy textbooks explain that organizations should set out a vision or mission or define a clear organizational purpose as the basis for engaging their people in building that future.[18] Managerial articles also discuss the issue and recommend approaches for defining, developing and communicating these concepts to people throughout an organization.[19]

Although it is easier for people to work towards an organization's aims if they understand them, there are many views as to what form an organization's vision should take, and the distinction with mission or purpose is not precisely specified in a generally agreed form. It is, however, accepted that vision and mission are more than a single, quantitative target or goal, such as "getting to 10 million customers by 2008." Vision, mission and purpose are often more qualitative and inspirational, for example, "we will be seen to be the leading firm in our industry."

All approaches to establishing a company vision may be helpful in different ways, but the approach described here offers particular, quantitative support. If we take a vision to be a realistic, attractive future for the organization, then we can bring such a vision into sharper focus if we specify key numbers to describe that future. For an existing organization, the causal structure shows the logical relationship between performance and underlying resources. It is therefore possible to clarify a vision in terms such as:

- by [date] we aim to be serving XXX customers, who will be giving us XXX amount of business

- to achieve this, we will need to have developed the following products and services—XXX

- we will need XXX people, working in the following functions—XXX

- we will have built XXX capacity in XXX locations

- on the XXX revenue we will make, we believe we can achieve XXX margin, and the costs of XXX for our people, capacity and other resources should enable us to make profit of XXX

Importantly, we are offering not only a specification of the *destination*, but also of the *path* by which that destination might be reached. It is most unlikely, of course, either that those precise numbers will be reached or that they will be reached by exactly the path we specify. This simply requires that the vision be continually updated in the light of successes or difficulties that emerge as time passes.

To some degree, this quantification of our path into the future can be viewed as little more than a longer term version of an operating budget for the coming financial year. However, as will be seen, each line of this vision has important implications for the rate at which key parts of the organization must develop. If we can specify the number of people needed to support our future scale of business, for example, both in total and by each key function, then we can estimate the rate at which those people must be acquired. If that staffing requires experience to be built, then we can also understand how rapidly people must be developed, and both hiring and development rates can be adjusted to reflect likely staff turnover.

Later chapters will also show how this approach to vision can ensure that the scale of each goal is consistent with others, and how that vision can be extended to bring clarity to important issues that are often left in general terms, such as market reputation and staff satisfaction.

## RESOURCE DRIVERS FOR FUNCTIONAL OBJECTIVES

Ryanair and MNDA are examples of whole organization strategy issues. However, the principles they demonstrate are also directly applicable to functional strategies and challenges.

Chapter 1 discussed the case of a law firm, concerned at the loss of its experienced lawyers. As in the Ryanair and MNDA cases, working back along the causal chain explains what has been happening:

- staff losses depend on work pressure, and on the chance of promotion to partner
- work pressure depends on the quantity of work to be done, divided by the number of lawyers available to do it—pressure that shows up in the number of hours per week each lawyer bills to clients
- the total quantity of work to be done comes from the number of projects each quarter and the average workload of each project
- the number of projects each quarter comes from the number of clients and the average projects per client per quarter

These relationships are shown in Figure 2.36. The "performance objective" is to keep the loss rate of lawyers down—hopefully to less than 10 per quarter. The figure shows how "demand" comes from the resource of *clients* and how "supply" comes from the number of lawyers. The balance between this demand and supply is shown in the chart for *billable hours per lawyer.*

The second cause of staff loss is also traced back to a balance between supply and demand—in this case the demand for partners to manage client relationships and the number of partners available to do this task. As growth in client numbers slowed, few new partners were required. The increasing work demanded from those clients also reduced the need for another key partner task—client acquisition. For these reasons, fewer new partners have been appointed from

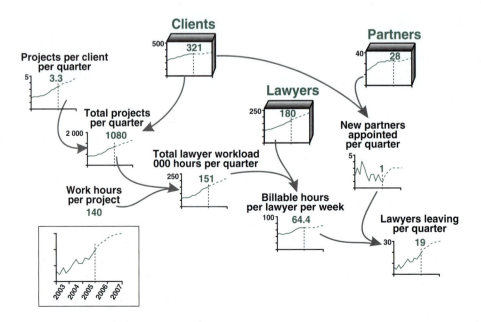

Figure 2.36: Resources driving staff losses at law firm.

among the lawyers, contributing further to the increasing numbers who have been leaving.

This is just one example of a huge range of functional challenges, such as:

- accelerating the quantity and quality of products emerging from a product development function
- improving the quality of customer support provided by a service delivery organization
- maintaining the reliability of assets in a company dependent on capital equipment
- ensuring that information systems contribute to improved operational effectiveness

# THE RESOURCE-BASED VIEW OF STRATEGY

As mentioned earlier, the strategy field recognizes the strong influence of firm characteristics and choices on performance, in addition to the forces impacting on the firm from its industry and competitive environment. This recognition is encompassed in the so-called "resource-based view" of strategy (RBV).[20] Although recent interest in the topic dates from the mid-1980s,[21] the fundamental importance of firm resources can be traced back nearly half a century.[22]

Since this chapter has emphasized that resources drive performance, it might be thought that this principle and RBV are one and the same. As will be explained shortly, this is not the case, although as the resource-driven approach is developed in later chapters, it will connect to some of the key principles in RBV.

Barney 2002[23] (Chapter 5) provides an eloquent explanation of RBV and its implications for strategic management, together with comprehensive coverage of the supporting literature. He explains that resources are "…all assets, capabilities, competencies, organizational processes, firm attributes, information, knowledge, and so forth that are controlled by a firm and that enable the firm to conceive of and implement strategies designed to improve its efficiency and effectiveness." This source also describes how such resources can be grouped into financial, physical, human and organizational categories. Managerial explanations of how evaluating resources can be used in strategy can be found in certain articles,[24] as well as in the widely used strategy textbooks listed earlier in this chapter, for example Grant (2005), Chapter 5.

Management often blames any shortfall between the strategic aims of organizations and their actual performance on "inadequate resources."[25] It may seem self-evident that resources are important to performance, but RBV claims that the connection is not so simple. Since many resources are readily available—cash can be borrowed, production capacity can be bought, staff can be hired—most resources cannot give rise to superior performance. Any firm that gains an advantage by owning such factors is simply copied by competitors, who eliminate that advantage. The RBV therefore asserts that any resource can *only* contribute to sustained advantage if it is valuable, rare, hard to imitate, and supported by other organizational procedures—the so-called "VRIO criteria." These considerations can be investigated in more detail by asking the following questions:

- How *durable* is the resource? A resource that decays, deteriorates or becomes obsolete quickly is not likely to provide sustainable advantage. Plant wears out, staff skills decline, and investors' enthusiasm to fund an enterprise may fade away. Even if the resource itself doesn't change (e.g. a product's functionality, or standards of service in retailing), it may effectively be nondurable because of the progress of technology or rising customer expectations.

- How *mobile* or *tradeable* is the resource? Many resources, while important to effective operation of the business, are so easily acquired or moved between firms that they seem unlikely to provide sustainable advantage. Resources are particularly mobile if they can be bought and sold, i.e. if they are "tradeable." Equipment suppliers may be keen to sell the latest technology to your rivals as well as yourselves, customer lists can be purchased, and staff can be attracted by better salaries. Resources may also move between firms for other reasons than price. Employees move for a better lifestyle or environment, and suppliers of important inputs may favour rivals who operate in more attractive end markets.

- How *replicable* is the resource? Many resources can be easily copied by rivals, and thus offer little scope for competitive advantage. A firm can add new items to its product range, and boost its market share for a short time, but if the product is easily copied (e.g. a new mortgage product from a retail bank), the benefit will be short lived.

- Can the resource be *substituted*? Even if your business cannot buy or copy its competitors' resources, you may still be able to challenge them by using a different resource that fulfills a similar purpose. A common example is the use of alternative distribution channels (e.g. telephone ordering or Web sites) to overcome lack of access to retailers. Dell's spectacular advance in its early years of selling PCs through a direct-to-customer sales system is a celebrated example of making competitors' resources obsolete, i.e. IBM and Compaq's then powerful access to retailers and resellers.

## The "resource-allocation" myth of management

It has been common to think of management controlling strategy by "allocating" the scarce resources at their disposal. The image conjured up is of some general in battle sending battalions and equipment to various parts of the battlefield. In reality, the only resource that can generally be allocated is cash—if funds are not unlimited, should more be spent on marketing, on training, or on research? Sometimes, capacity can be allocated—should we produce more red widgets or blue widgets—but most other resources are simply not so characterless that they can be deployed at will in different roles. It may be helpful if spare accountants could be redeployed in the product support department when customer complaints increase, but the fact is that they will not be helpful because they don't have the necessary skills. Nor is it meaningful in most cases to talk of taking our products and "allocating" them to different customers or markets.

As Chapter 3 will show, the true management challenge is to *build and sustain resources*, not allocate them.

This dismissal of simple tangible resources in the quest for explanations of firm performance has caused RBV to focus on more subtle and complex factors, notably intangible resources, capabilities (or competences), knowledge and processes. Again, extensive discussion of these factors can be found in the strategy textbooks listed earlier, but the concepts can be summarized as follows.

Intangible resources include items such as reputation, staff morale and brand. Management consulting firm McKinsey & Co., for example, has a strong reputation, built up over many decades, for its ability to tackle the most challenging problems confronting the largest and most complex organizations. This reputation has undoubtedly enabled the firm to keep winning high-value contracts with large corporations in every industry throughout the world. All kinds of other organizations realize that staff morale and motivation are key to improving productivity, but are also essential to effectiveness in sales, customer service and other key functions. Brands are regarded as an additional intangible resource, and the contribution of strong brands to firms' profitability and growth—from Coca-Cola to BMW to Starbucks—is self-evident. So important are powerful brands known to be that an entire industry has developed around putting a value on brands themselves, as distinct from the organizations that own them.[26]

There is wide divergence as to what exactly is meant by organizations' capabilities and competences. Barney (2002) for example, defines capabilities as tangible and intangible assets that enable a firm to take advantage of other resources, while Grant

(2005) describes a capability as the capacity to undertake a particular productive activity. It is perhaps simplest to think of capabilities as concerning *activities* the organization is good at *doing*, as opposed to those *things* it *has*. The building of capabilities has certainly become recognized as a vital component of good strategy.[27] The concept has spawned some popular notions, including the idea of an organization's "core competences"[28]—those unique capabilities that lie at the heart of what a business succeeds at and that find expression in its range of products and services. Some have seen the issue almost as a subfield of RBV, referring to it as a "competence-based view" of strategy.[29] Interest has particularly focused on "dynamic capabilities"—the ability of firms consistently to identify and exploit new opportunities.[30] Incidentally, the distinction between capability and competence is now generally accepted to be semantic and the terms are often used interchangeably.

Knowledge management is a logical extension of the resource- and capability-based views of firm performance, and concerns the way in which organizations collect and share what they have learned on a whole spectrum of subjects and processes, then exploit that knowledge to build performance.[31] The idea has become so popular that it has generated a large number of managerial articles and books,[32] leading to the knowledge-based view becoming a recognized subtopic within RBV.[33] A key distinction made in this perspective is between what an organization *knows about*, which largely concerns information in various forms, and its *knowhow*, which concerns skills at getting things done. Such knowhow consists of processes, procedures and organizational routines—the ways in which important activities are carried out. If an organization repeatedly carries out the same activity, it would be surprising to find individuals or teams being left to make-up a new way of doing that activity on each occasion. Instead, organizations establish a regular, reliable series of steps to be followed. Taken to the extreme, firms such as McDonald's fine tune processes to such a degree that everything from checking inventory to cleaning the fryers to sorting the garbage is documented in detail, enabling them not only to ensure consistency in everything they do, but also to share those processes with franchisees so that they too can achieve that consistency.

## DIFFICULTIES IN APPLYING THE RESOURCE-BASED VIEW

It is hard to dispute the notion that resources, capabilities and knowledge are vital elements of a strongly performing organization, but applying the approach in practice raises difficulties. Chief among these is that most of the items identified are abstract and qualitative in nature. Efforts to work with them can therefore fall into semantic discussions about an organization's intangible resources or capabilities, conclusions about which tend to reflect the views and influence of those individuals who are involved in the discussion. This is hardly a firm, professional foundation on which to build confident strategy, with clear implementation ability and probable outcomes. Nor is it easy to steer strategy and performance into the future, since assessing any improvement in these factors will also be judgmental. When, for example, do we know that an organization's product development capability has improved from four out of 10 to six, or that our distribution network rates three compared with the industry leader's seven?

For a theory of performance to be widely applicable, reliable and useful, any analysis should be replicable, regardless of who carries it out, provided they follow the prescribed method. In contrast, evaluations of resources and capabilities often get no further than a list of items rated on some abstract scale (e.g. 1 = weak, 10 = strong), organized into charts or grids that imply more specificity and confidence than the underlying data justifies.

A key source of this ambiguity lies in RBV's assertion that tangible resources, such as cash, capacity, and staff are of little relevance to performance, since competitors can copy or buy them, or use substitute resources. This implies that such tangible factors cannot be "strategic" resources, so should be ignored in the analysis. To contribute to sustained advantage, it is claimed, any resource must be valuable, rare, hard to imitate, and supported by other organizational procedures—the VRIO criteria, mentioned above.

In contrast, the approach developed here argues that, since organizations' performance in any period is directly and unavoidably dependent on resources that do *not* fulfill the VRIO criteria—customers drive revenue, while staff and capacity directly drive costs, for example—an adequate resource-based model of performance *must* include such factors. This is not to say that VRIO factors are unimportant, but they can only affect performance through their influence on the simple, tangible resources that constitute the core business system.

There are even cases that question whether VRIO resources are always required. There is nothing unknown or mysterious about how Southwest, Ryanair or McDonald's function. The two airlines pursue a completely transparent strategy, even signaling ahead how they intend to develop further. And as mentioned already, just about every detail of McDonald's operations is actually written down and passed around in its franchise manuals! Furthermore, large numbers of executives have gained experience in these companies during their long periods of success, and are deeply familiar with their inner workings. Why, then, have such individuals who have left those firms with that knowledge not been able to replicate their success?

The RBV responds to this challenge by claiming that the true key to success in such cases lies in some still more abstract advantages amongst the high-level capabilities of the senior management. But this leads into a tautological minefield—such organizations are successful because they are capable, but the only way we know they are capable is because of their success!

The strategy dynamics approach developed in the remainder of this book therefore departs from RBV in three principal ways:

- First, it will not bypass the tangible factors that comprise the heart of any business or organization, but make them explicit, quantify them and connect them to the organization's performance outcomes. It will *include* intangible factors, capabilities, knowledge and so on, but their influence will be captured through the impact they have on developing and retaining the tangible factors that directly drive performance.

- Secondly, strategy dynamics will not limit the analysis to resources that are "owned or controlled" by the organization. To influence performance, an organization need only have somewhat reliable access to the resources it needs—by which we mean "if it is there today, it is likely to be there tomorrow." One crucial consequence of this, noted earlier, is that "customers" become part of the business system, even though they are certainly not owned or controlled. Very many organizations perform as they do only because customers are reliable—newspaper readers and TV viewers remain customers of particular organizations for many years, and sports clubs and banks are among a select class of businesses who can expect a relationship with their customers to last longer than those customers' marriages! Other external resources will also be reliable in many cases, such as suppliers and finance providers.

- The third departure from RBV is that the strategy dynamics approach will make explicit the nature of "complementarity" amongst resources, both tangible and intangible. The RBV does recognize that complementarity amongst resources is important, i.e. how effectively they work together—strong awareness for a brand is of little value without the distribution channels to generate sales, a technologically advanced product will not penetrate a market without the skilled staff to produce it reliably and efficiently, and so on. However, we will add to this general principle a reliable approach to specifying how these inter-relationships work and quantifying the impact they have on organizational performance and development. The way complementary resources operate is crucial to answering the key question of why performance *through time* progresses as it does.

This last consideration explains why some firms are able to sustain a competitive lead, even when their business model is entirely explicit. Once resources have started building, and come to constitute a strongly self-supporting system, any new competitor can only overtake them by assembling the same resources, of a similar scale, *and* making their self-reinforcing growth run at a faster rate. That is not to say that such an enterprise can never be beaten. Management may inadvertently damage the system it runs, for example by pursuing growth beyond the system's feasible limits, as the letter to McDonald's shareholders in Chapter 1 illustrates. Competitors can also identify and assemble a different, superior system of resources that is capable of stronger growth and performance than the established firm. Even so, the superior performance is derived from the effectiveness of the whole *system*, not from some particular magic factor.

## DEFINITIONS

Terminology can be one final difficulty in using the resource-based view for our purpose of presenting a rigorous structural analysis of an organization. If resources are, in Barney's words "... all assets, capabilities, competencies, organizational processes, firm attributes, information, knowledge, and so forth," then we do not have a term for those items that are not capabilities, competences or processes. In particular, we need an expression for those simple, tangible factors that comprise the core of the organization's system. "Assets" is not really suitable, since it is generally associated with inanimate objects, such as plant and equipment.

Extensive experience in applying the method developed in this book has led to a terminology that minimizes ambiguity and enables consistent, replicable analysis, while staying as close as possible to language in common use. Throughout this book, the following terminology will be used:

- "Resources" will be reserved for those things or people that an organization has, or to which it has reasonably reliable access—i.e. excluding capabilities, competences and processes.
- "Capabilities" (or "competences") will refer to those activities that an organization *does*.

We will not make much reference to "processes," but to the extent that these arise, they will be taken to be groups of actions that get things done. We will also need some language to help distinguish different kinds of resource, in particular to separate out hard factors from soft.

- "Tangible resources" will refer to items that can be seen, touched, bought or sold—customers, products, capacity, staff and cash, and certain other items discussed below.
- "Attributes" will refer to characteristics or qualities of resources that are important to their impact on the organization's performance—e.g. customer value, staff experience, product functionality.
- "Intangible resources" will refer to *soft factors* that cannot be seen, touched, bought or sold—many of these concern the feelings of people on important issues, for example, staff morale, trust, reputation, investor confidence, and some negative factors, such as staff stress and customer-annoyance. Other categories of intangible resources deal with information-related items, such as data, knowledge and technology, and some forms of quality (see chapter 9).

We do not escape ambiguity entirely. For example, "knowledge" may be intangible, or may be manifest in documentation that is tangible, or as patents that can be bought or sold. However, such cases are few, and provided that they are specified at the point where they are used, this small uncertainty will not obstruct understanding or impede progress.

# IDENTIFYING, SPECIFYING AND MEASURING TANGIBLE RESOURCES

Having explained and demonstrated the link from tangible resources to revenues, costs and profits (or other performance outcomes), some guidance is needed regarding how to identify resource items for any particular case.

A checklist of tangible resources to start from is as follows:

- customers
- products
- production capacity
- staff
- cash

We have already seen some of these items in the Ryanair case—where *products* = routes served, and *capacity* = aircraft, but more rigorous specifications are needed if analysis is going to be reliable and repeatable. If most organizations exist to provide the necessary "supply" to meet some form of "demand," then resources can be sought on each side of this supply–demand relationship.

## DEMAND-SIDE RESOURCES

The most obvious resource on the demand side of the relationship is "customers"—the people or organizations who have the requirement for the goods or services the organization provides. They may come with various different names in different businesses—consumers, subscribers or clients, for example. Store-based retailers have a direct relationship with a clear population of customers—consumers in their case. Many business-to-business companies also have direct relationships with a single population of customers. Law firms, consulting companies and other professional service firms have direct relationships with immediate customers ("clients" in their terminology). However, there can be some complications—two in particular stand out.

First, customers often come in multiple varieties. Suppliers of telecoms and utilities such as water or power may have consumers *and* business customers. Airlines and

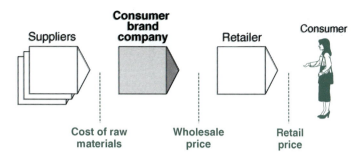

**Figure 2.37: Supply chain for consumer goods.**

hotels serve some mix of leisure travelers and business customers. Such customer segmentation will be looked at in Chapter 3.

Secondly, a company may supply one set of customers, who then have their own customers, who may in turn have further customers. Of these, only the first group is strictly the company's "customer"—i.e. the organization that takes the company's products in exchange for payment. Nevertheless, the other parties downstream in the chain are critical to explaining the quantity of the company's sales. If your customer does not have its own customers, then you do not sell your product.

Take, for example, a consumer brands business, such as Coca-Cola or Proctor & Gamble. Their direct customers are retailers, such as Wal-Mart, and those retailers' customers are personal consumers. The supply chain is shown in Figure 2.37.

If such a company wants to explain its sales, then, simply knowing how many direct "customers" there are (i.e. retailers) will not be sufficient. It will only receive sales if consumers also exist who want its products. The demand-side architecture, then, needs to show the quantity of both retailers *and* consumers. In Figure 2.38, *retailers* stock the brand in their stores, offering it to *consumers*. Five thousand stores happen to make the brand available to 72% of consumers, so only this fraction can actually buy the product. Sales volume depends on both resources—*retailers* and *consumers*. (Incidentally, *stores* are also a resource—an attribute of each *retailer*. Later chapters will explain how to deal with such resource-attributes.)

Note the quite fundamental difference between Figure 2.37, which shows how product flows along a supply chain, and Figure 2.38, which enables the value of each variable to be calculated from the factors on which it depends. For a company supplying consumer products through retailers, this causality would be modified in the short term by changes in retailers' inventory levels, but over the longer term this set of causal relationships is a close explanation for the volume of sales.

For the consumer brand company, retailers are its true "customers," but they are an intermediary in the indirect relationship with consumers. Such intermediaries arise frequently, as the examples in Table 2.2 illustrate.

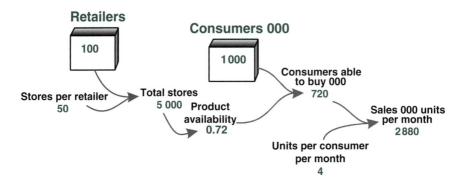

**Figure 2.38: Demand-side architecture for a consumer brand company. (Online learning materials are available to support this example, see p.xxi.)**

The last two examples are cases where more than one intermediary stands between the company and the end user of its products. Intel, for example, sells its processors to PC manufacturers (sometimes called "original equipment manufacturers" or OEMs), who in turn sell PCs to retailers and other resellers. Those resellers in turn sell the PCs, perhaps with added services, to consumers and businesses. The sales volume of Intel processors must reflect the number of OEMs making PCs with Intel chips in them, the number of retailers and resellers stocking or supplying Intel-based PC models, and the number of end users who prefer Intel-powered PCs over machines with other manufacturers' chips. These three resources are strongly interdependent—retailers will favor Intel-based PCs if that is what end users want, and OEMs will make Intel-based PCs if that is what retailers order.

## TABLE 2.2: INTERMEDIARIES FOR VARIOUS TYPES OF COMPANY

| Company type | Intermediaries | | End users |
|---|---|---|---|
| Consumer brands | Retailers | | Consumer |
| Car manufacturer | Dealers | | Consumers (car-buyers) |
| Office-product manufacturer | Distributors | | Business users |
| Power producer | Power distribution companies | | Consumers and firms |
| Hotel chain | Travel agents | | Guests |
| Plastics manufacturer | Plastics product producers | Retailers | Consumers |
| Computer hardware producer | Computer manufacturers | Computer retailers | Computer user |

**SWOT analysis—Strengths, Weaknesses, Opportunities and Threats**

Although strategy professionals now regard SWOT analysis as an outdated and simplistic approach, it remains the tool that most ordinary managers think of first when asked how they would go about assessing their strategy. It is therefore appropriate to explain how a resource appraisal lends clarity to any assessment of firm's "SWOT." This four-part checklist splits naturally into two halves:

- Opportunities and threats are features of *the external environment*, mostly competitors and other external pressures. These external factors are more properly dealt with by two formal methods—the "five forces" framework discussed above, and analysis of political, economic, social, and technological forces, which will be discussed in later chapters.
- Strengths and weaknesses are features of *the firm itself*, relative to existing and potential competitors and other external forces.

Since this second pair of topics focuses on the firm, these are the key topics that have the closest connection with a resource-based approach. Strengths and weaknesses are evaluated in terms of the resources and capabilities that the firm has, or needs, for its system to work, in the context of the external conditions in which it participates (Table 2.3).

**TABLE 2.3: STRENGTHS AND WEAKNESSES AS THE PRESENCE OR ABSENCE OF RESOURCES AND CAPABILITIES**

| Strengths | Weaknesses |
|---|---|
| Resource and capabilities with one or more of the following characteristics: | Resource and capabilities with one or more of the following characteristics: |
| a. greater quantity | a. smaller quantity |
| b. higher quality | b. lower quality |
| c. slower rate, or lower risk of loss | c. faster rate, or higher risk of loss |
| d. faster rate of acquisition | d. lower rate of acquisition |
| e. support for the acquisition and retention of other resources | e. lack of support for other resources |
| … compared with actual or potential rivals. | … compared with actual or potential rivals. |

A more rigorous approach to assessing strengths and weaknesses, then, is to carry out the quantified, fact-based analysis of resources introduced earlier in this chapter. In addition to the tangible resources discussed earlier, a sound assessment of strengths and weaknesses should also consider intangible factors and capabilities.

## DEMAND-SIDE RESOURCES IN PUBLIC SERVICES AND VOLUNTARY ORGANIZATIONS

Although public services and voluntary organizations may not sell products or services, they too experience "demand" from individuals or groups who fulfill a role analogous to that played by a company's customers (Table 2.4). The MNDA example above includes the people with MND who generate the demand for its support services. Voluntary organizations frequently serve a population of beneficiaries, each of whom exhibit a rate of demand for the organization's service.

Other cases are not so clear cut. Amnesty International exists to defend the human rights of people throughout the world, but does not receive direct demand for its services from those individuals. It also works to highlight abuses of those rights by specific countries or groups within countries. The demand for its service is therefore not directly related to an identifiable population of specific individuals. Nevertheless, there is a broad relationship between the size of the relevant population—people suffering abuse—and the overall requirement for Amnesty's activities. This case also highlights a further common feature of voluntary organizations—namely that the potential demand for their activity may grossly exceed their capacity to respond.

Some voluntary organizations have other purposes than to provide services to beneficiaries. In medicine, certain entities exist to fund medical research. For these,

## TABLE 2.4: RESOURCES DRIVING DEMAND IN PUBLIC SERVICE AND VOLUNTARY CASES

| Organization | Resource driving demand |
| --- | --- |
| AIDS charity | AIDS sufferers |
| Medical research charity | Research teams |
| Police force | Criminals |
| School | Children of school age |

demand arises from the teams carrying out research in their chosen field, a number that they create by accepting proposals from research teams.

Many public services exist to serve the needs of a defined group of beneficiaries. As noted earlier, schools serve the demand for education generated by the number of children of school age, and social services meet the demands of numbers of people requiring different kinds of welfare support.

## MULTIPLE DEMAND-SIDE RESOURCES

Although customers, clients or beneficiaries are a near-universal category of demand-driving resources, a few organizations can only thrive if they serve well the needs of two distinct groups. Newspapers and other media companies must offer content to meet the demands of readers, viewers or subscribers, but must also offer space to meet the needs of advertizers.

The online auction company eBay provides a further intriguing example. Although the sellers who use its services to dispose of their goods pay for the service, it must also serve the needs of buyers. The rate of transactions through eBay's system is strongly determined by the numbers of both buyers and sellers. This case is complicated by the fact that some users are both buyers and sellers and that both buyers and sellers come and go. However, a large number of people are confident enough in the service that they would use it on any occasion when they have a specific need to buy or sell something.

## SPECIAL CASES

It may seem self-evident that every business must have customers if it is to receive payment for its goods or services, but surprisingly that is not in fact the case—at least it need not have *identifiable* customers. Much of the world's demand for crude oil, minerals and agricultural products is not sold by specific producers to specific customers, but is traded through commodity markets. In such cases, the producing company may have no idea who ultimately receives the specific materials that they originally produced.

Some organizations deal with customers so infrequently that they may feel the relationship is quite transitory, rather than being true resources. Consumers buy furniture or other durable goods only once every five or 10 years and have no particular need for any relationship with the supplier from which they last bought. In such cases, the resource is best described as an "installed base," though strictly that describes the goods themselves, rather than the people who own them. Such companies attempt to have a relationship with the buyers of their goods, but it is often only possible when there are intervening opportunities for contact, e.g., servicing for motor vehicles. Of course, the producer's true customers are generally the retailers or dealers who resell their products so, like the consumable brand mentioned above, these intermediaries are a key resource. In some industries, this installed base generates virtually no continuing sales until the next time the owner wishes to replace or upgrade the product—washing machines and furniture, for instance. In other cases, the installed base continues to generate a separate flow of sales, either from service (e.g. cars, elevators or aircraft engines) or from "consumables" (e.g. ink for printers or games for games consoles). Chapter 4 will clarify this distinction further.

Construction and consulting companies face a similar problem. They only have an active relationship with specific customers for the period when they are undertaking a construction project or consulting assignment. For these companies, *current projects in progress* are a key resource. Since projects occur infrequently, such companies often attempt to create longer lasting relationships that continue between active projects—much more feasible than keeping in touch with millions of washing machine owners who buy once every 10 years!

## SUPPLY-SIDE RESOURCES

### CAPACITY

All organizations need some form of capacity if they are to deliver products or services. The clearest cases are manufacturing companies, whose factories or plants can produce a maximum rate of output. Car producers' assembly plants can make-up to a certain number of vehicles per month, oil refineries produce up to some limit of gallons per hour, and so on.

Capacity can come in other forms, depending on the industry. Retailers have stores and shelf space, airlines have aircraft and seats, and online providers have computers and the transaction rate that those computers can handle. In some industries, capacity actually consists of people—lawyers in law firms, engineers in construction companies, repair staff for vehicle breakdown organizations, or call-handling staff in call centers. This phenomenon of people-as-capacity is a particular feature of many public services and voluntary organizations. Police forces have officers, schools have teachers, welfare services have case managers, and aid charities have the field staff that delivers their support to beneficiaries.

Care may be needed when defining capacity. It is easy, for example, to view underground oil reserves as the capacity of an oil firm. Those reserves are certainly a vital supply-side resource, but the firm's capacity to *produce* oil depends on the number of wells and related equipment it has in place to extract that oil.

## STAFF

Organizations need staff to undertake the various functions that have to be fulfilled. We could identify the total number of staff and assume that the organization can fulfill the demand it needs to serve, provided that this total is sufficient. However, this will rarely be adequate, because organizations can be heavily dependent on certain groups of staff who are difficult to find, develop or retain. It is necessary in most cases to identify separately the number of staff in specific groups.

### Look out for surprising staff dependencies

Sometimes an organization's dependency on staff does not arise in the most obvious parts of the organization. One chemical company found itself in severe difficulties because it had too few people in its technical support team. Not only were those scientists lacking within the company, but very few were available throughout the industry, and its major competitor DuPont employed most of those. It would take at least five years to rebuild the group's numbers and expertise to even adequate levels, during which time the company's product performance in the eyes of customers would continue to fall behind that of its rival. No quantity of sales people or production staff would compensate for this shortfall and no feasible pricing discounts would persuade customers to buy inferior products.

How had this company got itself into this position? By responding to pressure "from Wall Street" to hit the same low cost ratios as its larger competitor, an objective that could not possibly be achieved without cutting these critical staff and other essential resources.

We have just mentioned the staff that actually *is* the "production capacity" for some organizations. Many companies with physical capacity also need operational staff—car makers need assembly workers, airlines need pilots and cabin crew, restaurants need waiters and waitresses. Some companies also have specialist staff that, though they do not actually operate the production capacity, are closely associated with it, such as production engineers who work to improve the efficiency and reliability of the production process. It is therefore helpful when thinking about staff to check that everyone associated with the organization's "capacity" resource has been covered.

There are usually various categories of staff to fulfill functions in marketing, sales and customer support. Most companies have a salesforce in some form, though they may give them different titles, such as "business development executives." Marketing staff develop and deliver the organization's communications to actual and potential customers. Other customer-related functions may include frontline staff or service groups, such as helpline staff. Other specific examples include maintenance engineers (e.g. for elevator service companies) and the specialist staff who configure computer hardware and software for firms who supply companies with IT equipment.

Some companies are heavily dependent on groups of staff to develop their product-range resource. Research staff undertake the fundamental innovation of new products, but the effort does not end there. People are also needed to continue the development of existing products and to test their appeal amongst customers. There are also accounting staff to process the organization's financial transactions and run its management and statutory reporting routines, human-resource staff to deal with hiring, training and so on.

### Doing it right: When more detail is too much

This section has shown how different categories of staff may be involved in any particular case. Fortunately, it is rarely necessary when evaluating an organization's strategy to delve into the detailed numbers of every group. It is often safe to assume that many functions can develop at whatever rate is required for any plausible future the organization may pursue. Accounting staff may be essential for processing the organization's transactions, for example, but this may not be strategically significant if we can be sure that the necessary people can be found. Generally, strategically critical staff groups will be associated with one or more of the organization's nonpeople resources—groups such as sales staff (essential for winning and retaining customers), service staff or engineers (for supporting customers), or technical specialists (for developing products and services).

In many cases, then, it is sufficient to identify the number of people in just a few critical groups, and encompass the remainder in "other staff." Beware, though, as highlighted above, that strategic constraints can arise in some surprising places. Ensuring that staff development structures can deliver the number and quality of people required is one of the major challenges in delivering strategic performance.

Just because a company outsources some activities to third-party suppliers does not necessarily mean it can ignore the need for staff. Many oil companies, under pressure to reduce costs, have slimmed down their engineering staff over the last 15–20 years. They have increasingly relied on contractors to meet their needs, but since the whole industry reduced its hiring, those contractors also find themselves short of the required experience. Some utilities firms have reduced maintenance and replacement of equipment to meet short-term financial targets. When they eventually have to replace their worn-out equipment, they should not be surprised if they find that their suppliers do not have capacity or people to provide it.

A topical example concerns the nuclear industry. When nuclear power gained an unfortunately poor image in the 1970s and 1980s, many countries slowed or stopped their development of nuclear power stations. Now, with the recent alarm over global warming, nuclear power has resurfaced as an option that generates no emissions of greenhouse gases (though other concerns remain). In the intervening decades very few young engineers have enrolled in nuclear engineering courses—indeed few such courses even exist. So, if society *does* accept the building of such power stations once again, there will be a severe shortage of people who know how to do it and a long delay in creating such skills.

## PRODUCT OR SERVICE RANGE

In addition to capacity and staff, all organizations have some range of products or services that they provide. Retailers have thousands of product items featured on their shelves, and the consumer goods companies who supply them have the range of brands they hope those retailers will offer to consumers. Deciding that range's width should be of major importance—too small, and the company will miss out on potentially large groups of consumers: too many, and the sales they achieve may be fragmented among so many products that none makes enough money to justify the marketing and sales support required. Similar considerations arise with the model ranges offered by firms such as car and motorbike producers and computer manufacturers.

Certain industries have their own special form of product range. For airlines, this product range consists of the routes served, and for a TV or radio channel, it is the range of programs broadcast. Public service and voluntary organizations often provide services, rather than products, but these too can be identified and specified. This step is important, because the provision of each service has implications for the numbers and requisite skills of people needed to deliver those services to clients.

Some organizations may not have a specific product range, but offer products that are made uniquely for each customer. House builders construct unique properties for clients, large construction contractors design and construct each project from scratch, and much of the work of law firms is specific to each case. Even in these cases, though, there can be benefit from identifying standardized products and services. House builders can reduce costs by replicating standard designs, perhaps with some small cosmetic features to make each building appear different. If construction contractors can achieve enough repeat business it may be possible for them to develop standardized designs—or at least standardized components of those designs. Law firms, too, can often benefit from identifying the types of work at which they excel and focusing on both developing and promoting that special expertise.

## CASH

Although not directly associated with "supply" of products and services to customers, cash is an important resource that enables the other supply-side resources to be developed. It is important to note that cash has a negative sibling—debt—that drives the cost of interest payments.

Yet despite cash featuring in the list of resources for all businesses, it is not always essential to include it in the analysis of their performance to date, nor in the development of future strategies. If the impact of strategy makes the difference between cash flow being satisfactory and growing strongly, then it will not constrain the company's ability to implement that strategy. With huge cash reserves, there is for example no cash constraint on Ryanair's strategic development. There are, of course, situations where cash levels cannot be ignored, including:

- when the organization is in financial difficulties
- when the strategy requires costly initiatives
- when the organization concerned is a new venture, which has access to only a limited pool of potential cash to fund its development

---

**Important: most resources can be used without being "consumed"**

Fortunately, most resources continue to perform their role in the business system as it generates output and profits, without being "used up" in the process. In most cases, similar quantities of staff and capacity will be available tomorrow as were there today. Cash is the obvious exception, having to be spent in order to create new capacity or to pay staff. One other exception arises in so-called "extractive" industries—oil and gas, minerals and mining—where the reserves or deposits a company controls constitute a resource that will be used up as it is extracted and sold.

## SUPPLIERS

It might seem puzzling that, of all the resources on the supply side of an organization, "suppliers" themselves are not listed as a universally important factor. While suppliers are, of course, an essential part of most organization's business system, the same question arises for cash—is the organization's strategic development significantly dependent on being able to access suppliers? Although most businesses struggle to win and retain their customers, most do not find the same difficulty acquiring the suppliers they need. Indeed, the problem can sometimes be in choosing among the many potential suppliers who would love to provide the goods and services needed.

Supply can be a constraint in certain circumstances, usually where the physical source itself is limited. This can occur with certain natural raw materials, and where an important new product is in short supply because capacity needs to be expanded. However, the problem in these circumstances is often that the number of suppliers is very limited, perhaps to just one provider. An interesting special case concerns industries that depend on talented, independent individuals—publishers need authors, film producers need stars, sports clubs need players, etc.

## SPECIFYING AND QUANTIFYING RESOURCES

Table 2.5 summarizes how the most common categories of tangible resources might appear for certain businesses. The list includes two items—intermediaries and cash—that may need to be added in a significant number of cases.

### TABLE 2.5: THE MOST COMMON TANGIBLE RESOURCES IN STRATEGY ANALYSIS

|  | Tangible resource | Coffee shop chain | Law firm | Start-up airline | Consumer brand |
|---|---|---|---|---|---|
| Demand-side | **Customers** | Consumers | Clients | Customers | Consumers |
|  | *Intermediaries* |  |  |  | *Retailers* |
| Supply-side | **Capacity** | Stores | Professional staff | Aircraft |  |
|  | **Staff** | People |  | Service staff | Salesforce |
|  | **Product range** | Products | Legal services | Routes offered | Brands offered |
|  | ***Cash*** |  |  | *Cash* |  |

(Italic indicates additional resources that may be important in some cases)

While this table provides a useful checklist in most situations, special cases such as those mentioned earlier may need adjustments or additions to the list, for example:

- commodity producers who have no identifiable customers
- durables suppliers who do not have a population of repeating customers, but a resource in the form of an installed base
- organizations such as newspapers who must serve two entirely different types of customer (not just different segments)
- service providers whose capacity consists of staff
- IT-dependent organizations for which information systems capacity may be a strategically critical resource

Given a clear and explicit list of the tangible resources driving sales and costs (and comparable measures in public policy and other not-for-profit cases), quantifying them should not be problematic in most cases. *Customers* are simply numbers of people or organizations, *staff* are clearly numbers of people, and so on. A few complications can arise, however.

The Ryanair example already raised the issue that some customers buy from a company so infrequently that they are not in any real sense reliable enough to be counted as part of "our" group of customers. Even when customers have actual accounts with a company, it is not certain that an account holder is a customer in any real sense, as many banks know from the large number of dormant accounts they have.

Complications also arise when customers are organizations who cover multiple points of purchase or delivery. Retail chains are a common example, any one of which may own numbers of individual stores. In such cases, stores are an "attribute" of each company, and should feature as a separate resource from the companies that own them. A specific dynamic framework for assessing this resource/attribute relationship will be explained in Chapters 5–7 of this book. When a customer organization has a number of subsidiaries, the best guideline is to treat these as separate customers if they are independent in their choice of supplier, but to treat them as a single customer when supplier choice is centralized.

The size of the product range may also raise questions of definition. Is BMW's product range simply the main models—the 3-series, the 5-series, and so on—or does every submodel within these groups count as a separate "product"? Does a quarter pounder with cheese count as a separate product from one without cheese? The guidance here is first to choose the level of detail that is sufficient to answer the issue of concern, and secondly to record that definition clearly so others understand the basis on which any analysis is carried out.

> **Doing it right: give resources their proper names**
>
> If the list of resources for a situation is to be useful for explaining performance and developing strategy, each will need to be used to calculate other items, so must be properly defined. The most important guideline for this purpose is to **specify a measurement for any resource in its own physical terms**, and do not use some proxy instead. "Staff" are people—do not use their cost as a substitute for this simple number. "Customers" are people or organizations—do not use sales or market share as a substitute. "Product range" consists of numbers of actual products or services—do not use ambiguous terms such as "value propositions" instead. Not only will it prove hard to quantify resources that are defined in abstract or proxy terms, but it will be difficult to calculate or estimate their impact on other parts of the system.

The occasional exception to the rule of naming resources purely in terms of their physical form concerns "capacity." It is often possible to maintain the rule—an airline's aircraft, a retailer's stores, a logistics firm's vehicles, or a manufacturer's machines, are examples of capacity whose units are all easily stated. In many cases, however, capacity arises from a complex mix of physical items and activities that result in defining and measuring "capacity" in terms of potential output—e.g. the production rate of an oil firm or the transaction rate of IT systems.

The units used to measure most resources are relatively simple—numbers of items (customers, people, dollars). Capacity needs to be treated carefully, however. There are usually identifiable "things" involved—machines, stores, computers, phones—and these values should be specified. However, capacity itself is measured in terms of how much supply can be delivered per time period. Examples of capacity include:

- oil company: output in barrels per day
- car manufacturer: number of vehicles that can be produced per hour
- consulting firm: projects that can be completed per month
- Starbucks: customers that can be served per hour
- police force: incidents that can be responded to daily

Often, this available capacity is dependent on more than one item of physical capacity. For example, a retailer's capacity (customer transactions per day) is determined by the physical floor space of its stores, the number of people replenishing shelves, and the number of checkouts available to process consumers' purchases. If management focuses on how these multiple assets are developing to grow capacity, then it would be necessary to quantify these items separately and examine how they are changing over time. If, on the other hand, the concern is about ensuring the organization has a sound system for balanced growth among customer demand, product range, capacity and cash flow, then it may be sufficient to treat capacity as a single aggregate resource, such as "maximum customers per hour."

This chapter explained the important dependence of organizations' performance upon the tangible resources it owns or can access. The next chapter will explain a crucial feature of these resources—their tendency to accumulate and deplete over time—without which no confident explanation of performance is possible.

### Summary of Chapter 2

To develop a strategy for achieving improved future performance we need a rigorous, unambiguous and quantified explanation for what causes an organization's performance.

Working back from the performance measure, through the logical explanation of revenue and costs, leads to the tangible resources that drive demand, and to the costly resources that comprise the organization's ability to supply that demand. Equivalent causal logic explains the performance of public service and voluntary organizations, as well as functional performance.

If that causal logic works to explain today's performance, and if the organization engaged in the same activities in the past in the same manner, time charts for every item in that causal chain can be linked to provide a complete explanation of the organization's performance history.

Market size, growth rates, market share and cost ratios do not constitute causal explanations for sales and profits, nor for other performance outcomes. Rather, the causal path from performance ultimately encounters "resources" that build over time, resulting in a resource-based explanation for performance (Figure 2.39).

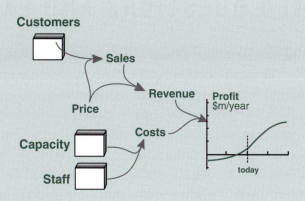

**Figure 2.39: Summary of resource-based approach to understanding performance.**

While performance and other measures often relate to what has occurred over a whole period of time, these resources are recorded at moments in time, especially at the end of reporting periods. Consequently, accurate explanations for performance depend on knowing what has happened to the quantity of relevant resources *during* that time period.

If performance depended on the past growth of resources, then it will continue to do so into the future, so forecasting future performance requires estimating the quantities of resources that will have to be built in order to deliver that performance. This principle is as applicable to public service, voluntary and functional performance issues as it is to business profits.

While related to the resource-based view of strategy, strategy dynamics pays more attention to simple tangible factors—customers, staff, capacity, products—to defining and measuring these items, and to tracking how they change over time. Intangible factors and capabilities can only impact on performance outcomes by influencing the development of these tangible resources.

It is not always necessary to include or specify every category of tangible resource involved in a situation if some are not significant in influencing performance issues. However, it *is* always important that any resources considered are properly specified and measured.

# SUGGESTED QUESTIONS AND EXERCISES

1.  When showing the structure of causal relationships determining how an organization's performance depends on various items, what is the guiding principle for ensuring that causal connections are valid?

2.  Select a company for which good information is publicly available (e.g. from case studies, newspapers or journals, or the Web). Be careful to choose a company that is well focused on just a single activity, rather than having differing businesses under its control—e.g. Starbucks rather than Wal-Mart. Sketch out the causal structure of its profit-and-loss statement, including relevant data for the latest available reporting period, as illustrated by Figure 2.2.

3.  What kind of resource drives sales for most businesses? What are the main categories of resources that may be involved in driving costs in a business?

4.  Returning to the sample company chosen above, use the supporting table in Worksheet 2, below, to list and define the key resources driving sales and profits. You may need to include items you know to be important, even if the scale of those resources is not reported by the company.

5.  What are the advantages of showing time charts of profit-and-loss items and other indicators in a connected structure such as Figure 2.3, as compared with a simple table of the same data?

6.  Why is it important to be careful when including performance measures for a reporting period on the same causal diagram as period-end values for cash, customers, staff and other resources?

7.  According to the resource-based view (RBV), what are the key characteristics a resource must possess if it is to contribute to sustainable competitive advantage?

8.  What challenges face management in using RBV to assess performance and develop future strategy?

9.  Returning to your sample company, what factors are important to its success in winning sales to customers? Construct a value curve diagram for those measures, including how well the company rates against the needs of one or more groups of customers, similar to Figure 2.9.

10. What are the key assumptions or targets used conventionally in estimating a company's future profits? Estimate a reasonable forecast for your sample company this way. (If you are using the same company as for the Chapter 1 exercise, this forecast will hopefully match the chart from Worksheet 1!)

11. Use Worksheet 2 to sketch out a resource-driven explanation for this performance forecast, as shown in Figures 2.28 and 2.29. You are likely to be missing data for

key items in this structure, in which case make reasonable illustrative estimates for what their values might be, as has been done for customers, journey-frequency and journeys booked in the Ryanair case from this chapter.

Alternatively, select a noncommercial case for the exercises on this page.

# USING WORKSHEET 2

A worksheet is provided below that can be used for stage 2 of a strategy dynamics analysis, and a supporting table for the current and future scale of resources that lie behind performance today and at some future date.

1. Copy the time chart of the overall performance objective from Worksheet 1 (end of Chapter 1) into the "principal objective" chart on Worksheet 2. Remember to copy the scale and timescale, not just using a rough sketch.
2. If Worksheet 1 had a supporting objective, copy this to another of the charts on Worksheet 2.
3. Following the disciplined rule of causal analysis—that it should be possible to calculate or estimate each item from those that connect into it—work back from right to left, linking items that explain the outcomes in the objectives. For each, observe the rules:

   - include an unambiguous title for the item
   - include a numerical scale on the Y-axis
   - make sure the timescale matches that of the principal objective

4. For each item, insert above the "today" line, the current value for that item—its actual value if known, or your best estimate if unknown. Include an (E) on any estimated value. **It is preferable to enter an estimate than leave no indication at all of what the number might be.**
5. For each item, add at the right-hand end the value that will be reached by the future end date—i.e. what each item will need to reach if the performance objective is to be achieved. Use the supporting table, "resources driving performance" that follows Worksheet 2 to specify each item and note its scale, both today and at some future time.
6. Sketch the historical values of each item on the chart and its likely future values. If appropriate, include both a "preferred" and "feared" future, as explained in Chapter 1.
7. Carry out the same steps 3 to 6 for the resources at the left of the chart, connecting these also into the causal explanation of the principal objective.

## TIPS

- You may not need all the items on this chart—simply leave others blank.
- Alternatively, you may need to add further items by hand.
- Some items may be constant (i.e. not changing over time)—either add these as separate items on the chart, or use one of the time charts and insert only its constant value, with no time chart
- Worksheet 2 may be easier to work with if it is photocopied to a larger size.
- The **my**strategy software is a more flexible and powerful method for completing the causal analysis of Worksheet 2, and also offers the basis for developing the further stages of analysis that will follow in later chapters. The **my**strategy software version of Worksheet 2 is available, see p. xxi.
- For team-based work, this entire process can be readily carried out on a large whiteboard. The result can then be copied so everyone has a record of the result (a digital camera can be helpful for this purpose), or else put into the **my**strategy software.

# WORKSHEET 2: RESOURCES DRIVING PERFORMANCE

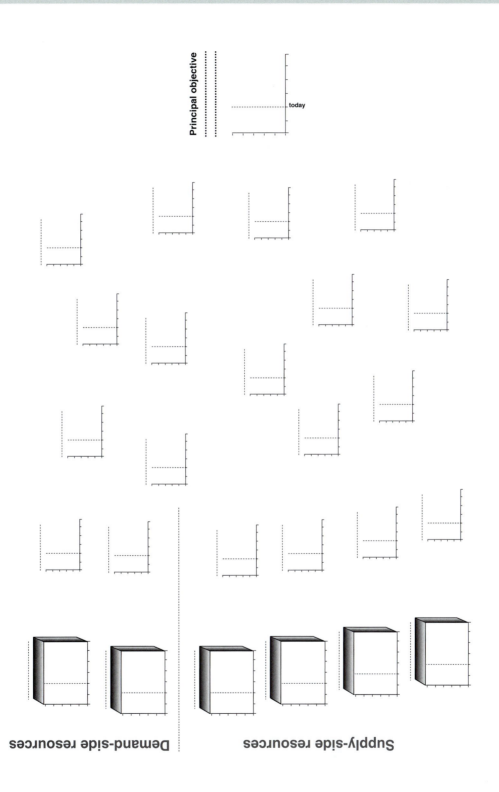

Principal objective

today

Demand-side resources

Supply-side resources

# WORKSHEET 2 (CONTINUED): RESOURCES DRIVING PERFORMANCE

| Tangible resource | Measure | Quantity Now<br>Date .............. | Quantity needed<br>By date ............. |
|---|---|---|---|
| **Demand-side** | | | |
| **Customers** | | | |
| Intermediaries | | | |
| **Supply-side** | | | |
| **Capacity** | | | |
| **Staff** | | | |
| **Product range** | | | |
| Cash | | | |

# NOTES

1.  Coyne, K.P. and Subramaniam, S. (1996) Bringing discipline to strategy. *The McKinsey Quarterly*, **4**, 14–25.

2.  Christensen, C. and Raynor, M. (2003) Why hard-nosed executives should care about management theory. *Harvard Business Review*, **81** (9), 66–75.

3.  Davenport, Thomas H. (2006) Competing on analytics. *Harvard Business Review*, **84**(1), 98–107.

4.  Adapted from Kim, C. and Mauborgne, R. (1999) Creating new market space. *Harvard Business Review*, **77**(1), 83–93.

5.  Although some marketing textbooks provide a brief description of conjoint analysis, a more detailed explanation can be found in Bakken, D. and Frazier, C.L. (2006) Conjoint analysis: understanding consumer decision making, in *The Handbook of Market Research: Do's and Don'ts* (Eds R. Grover and M. Vriens), Sage, London, Chapter 15. A rich source of further information, including the technicalities of how it is carried out and where it can be applied can be found at www.conjointpage.com.

6.  Porter, M. (1980) *Competitive Strategy*, Free Press, New York, Chapter 1.

7.  Note that Ryanair owns most of its aircraft, rather than leasing them. The major cost is for depreciation and, since this analysis is for earnings before interest, tax and depreciation, this cost element is not included. For 2006, the total cost of depreciation and amortization was €112.9m, most of which directly reflects the number of aircraft owned.

8.  Adapted from Porter, M. (1985) *Competitive Advantage*, Free Press, New York, Chapter 2.

9.  See, for example, Martin, J.D. and Petty, J.W. (2000) *Value Based Management*, Harvard Business School Press, Cambridge MA, Chapter 4, and Copeland, T., Koller, T. and Murrin, J. (2000) *Valuation—Measuring and Managing the Value of Companies*, 4th edn, John Wiley & Sons, Ltd, Chichester.

10. Porter, M. (1980) *Competitive Strategy*, Free Press, New York, Chapter 1.

11. Rumelt, R. (1991) How much does industry matter? *Strategic Management Journal*, **12**, 167–185.

12. McGahan, A. and Porter, M. (1997) How much does industry matter, really? *Strategic Management Journal* (summer special issue), **18**, 15–30.

13. Hawawin, G., Subramanian, V. and Verdin, P. (2003) Is performance driven by industry or firm-specific factors? A new look at the evidence. *Strategic Management Journal*, **24**, 1–16.

14. Grant, R. (2005) *Contemporary Strategy Analysis*, Blackwell, Oxford, Chapter 3. Hitt, M., Ireland, D. and Hoskisson, R. (2001) *Strategic Management: Competitiveness and Globalization*, 4th edn, South-Western/Thomson, Cincinatti, Chapter 2; McGee, J., Thomas, H. and Wilson, D. (2005) *Strategy, Analysis and Practice*, McGraw-Hill, Maidenhead, Chapters 3 and 5; Barney, J. and Hesterley, W. (2006) *Strategic Management and Competitive Advantage*, Pearson, Upper Saddle River, NJ, Chapter 2; Johnson, G., Scholes, K. and Whittington, R. (2005) *Exploring Corporate Strategy*, 7th edn, Prentice Hall, Harlow, Chapter 2.

15. Richmond, B. (1993) Systems thinking: critical thinking skills for the 1990s and beyond. *System Dynamics Review*, **9**(2), 113–133.

16. I am grateful to Suresh Mistry of SDS Ltd. (www.strategydynamicssolutions. com) and to Kirstone Knox, CEO of MNDA (www.mndassociation.org) for this case example.

17. Motor neurone disease, also known as amyotrophic lateral sclerosis or ALS, is a degenerative affliction of the nervous system that generally results in death within a few years of diagnosis. Similar support groups exist in other countries such as the ALS Association (United States) (www.alsa.org).

18. See, for example, Grant, R. (2005), *Contemporary Strategy Analysis*, 5th edn, Blackwell, Oxford, Chapter 2; De Wit, B. and Meyer, R. (2004) *Strategy: Process, Content, Context*, 3rd edn, Thomson, London, Chapter 11; Hitt, M., Ireland, D. and Hoskisson, R. (2001) *Strategic Management: Competitiveness and Globalization*, 4th edn, South-Western/Thomson, Cincinatti, Chapter 1.

19. See, for example, Collins, J. and Porras, J. (1996) Building your company's vision. *Harvard Business Review*, **75**(5), 65–72. (Enhanced edition available, February 2000, from Harvard Business Online, http://harvardbusinessonline.hbsp.harvard.edu.)

20. See Montgomery, C.A. (1995) (ed.) *Resource-based and Evolutionary Theories of the Firm*, Kluwer, Boston MA; Foss, N.J. (1997) (Ed) *Resources, Firms and Strategies*, Oxford University Press, Oxford. These provide extensive discussions of the development of the resource-based view in the academic community.

21. Wernerfelt, B. (1984) A resource-based view of the firm. *Strategic Management Journal*, **5**, 171–180.

22. Penrose, E.T. (1959) *The Theory of the Growth of the Firm*, Oxford University Press, Oxford; Amit, R. and Schoemaker, P. (1993) Strategic assets and organizational rent, *Strategic Management Journal*, **14**(1), 33–46.

23. Barney, J. (2002) *Gaining and Sustaining Competitive Advantage*, 2nd edn, Pearson, Upper Saddle River, NJ.

24. Collis, D. and Montgomery, C. (1995) Competing on resources: strategy in the 1990s. *Harvard Business Review*, **73**(4), 118–128.

25. Mankins, M. and Steele, R. (2005) Turning great strategy into great performance. *Harvard Business Review*, **83**(7), 64–73.

26. See, for example, the extensive research on brand valuation carried out by Interbrand, part of the Omnicom Group (www.interbrand.com/studies.asp).

27. Stalk, G. Jr., Evans, P. and Schulman, L. (1992) Competing on capabilities: The new rules of corporate strategy. *Harvard Business Review* (March–April), 57–59; Ulrich, D. and Smallwood, N. (2004) Capitalizing on capabilities. *Harvard Business Review*, **82**(6), 119–127.

28. Prahalad, C.K. and Hamel, G. (1990) The core competence of the corporation. *Harvard Business Review*, **68**(3), 79–91.

29. Sanchez, R. and Heene, A. (1997) Reinventing strategic management: new theory and practice for competence-based competition. *European Management Journal*, **15**(3), 303–317.

30. Teece, D.J., Pisano, G. and Shuen, A. (1997) Dynamic capabilities and strategic management. *Strategic Management Journal*, **18**(7), 509–533; Eisenhardt, K.M. and Martin, J.A. (2000) Dynamic capabilities: what are they? *Strategic Management Journal*, **21**(10/11), 1105–1121, and other articles in this 2000 special edition of the *Strategic Management Journal* on the evolution of firm capabilities; Winter, S. (2003) Understanding dynamic capabilities. *Strategic Management Journal*, **24**(10), 91–95.

31. March, J.G. (1991) Exploration and exploitation in organizational learning. *Organization Science*, **2**, 71–87.

32. See, for example, Morten, T., Hansen, N. and Tierney, T. (1999) What's your strategy for managing knowledge? *Harvard Business Review*, **77**(2), 106–116 and Krogh, G. von, Ichijo, K. and Nonaka, I. (2000) *Enabling Knowledge Creation: How to Unlock the Mystery of Tacit Knowledge and Release the Power of Innovation*. Oxford University Press, Oxford.

33. Grant, R.M. (1996) Towards a knowledge-based theory of the firm, *Strategic Management Journal*, **17**(winter special issue), 109–122.

# CHAPTER 3

# RESOURCE ACCUMULATION

## KEY ISSUES

✪ The inescapable and critical behavior of resources—building up and draining away over time.

✪ Understanding the math of how resource flow rates determine resource levels.

✪ Seeking explanations for what causes the rate at which resources are won and lost.

✪ "Causal ambiguity"—understanding causes—and how accumulating resources devalue correlation analysis.

✪ Resource accumulation and constantly changing value-chain structures.

✪ Dealing with important details, including segmentation, and one-time changes in resource levels.

Worksheet 3: Resource Inflows and Outflows.

This chapter makes connections to the following strategy concepts: value curve, value chain, asset-stock accumulation and causal ambiguity.

Chapter 1 explained the importance of focusing on how organizational performance changes over time, and Chapter 2 showed how to trace the causal logic that explains this performance, until that chain reaches the underlying resources determining demand and capacity, revenue and costs. For a simple company, this reasoning might identify that:

- *profit per month* is explained by revenue minus costs
- *revenue per month* is explained by units sold multiplied by price
- *units sold per month* is explained by customers (a resource) multiplied by average units bought per customer per month
- *total costs* are explained by the sum of specific costs, such as salaries, production costs, and research costs
- *staff costs per month* is explained by *staff* (another resource) multiplied by average cost per person per month ... and similarly for other costly resources.

The next question that arises in this causal logical is, "What determines the quantity of *customers* and *staff* (and every other resource) at any time?" It is at this point that the unique characteristic of resources and other "asset-stocks" comes into play. All the causal relationships discussed in Chapter 2 come in the form of:

X is some function of Y, Z, W etc. or

If we know the value of Y, Z, W etc. at a particular time, then we can calculate or estimate the value of X at that time.

Ideally, we want this explanation to be well understood and sufficiently stable that it has largely been true throughout the historical period we are considering and is likely to remain true for the future time horizon we want to anticipate. The math of such relationships is:

$$X(t) = fn\ [Y(t),\ Z(t),\ W(t),\ \ldots]$$

Asset-stocks, in contrast, do not obey any such relationship. Their verbal explanation is:

The quantity of X today is the total amount of X that has ever been added, minus the quantity that has ever been lost.[1]

It is important to be clear about what this means:

- The number of customers you have today is not "explained by" anything else—not by the prices charged, products offered, marketing dollars spent or sales effort expended. The number of customers is *precisely* the sum of every customer ever won, minus every customer that left, since the day your business started. It is those gains and losses that are explained by your price, products, marketing and sales effort, not the quantity of customers itself.
- The number of staff you have today is not explained by the salaries you pay, the career prospects you offer, or the attractiveness of your work locations. That number is precisely the sum of every person you ever hired, minus every person who ever left or was fired. It is those gains and losses of staff that are explained by your salaries, career prospects, and so on.
- The number of products offered today is the sum of all the products ever launched, minus every product discontinued.
- The capacity you have today is the sum of all the capacity ever added, minus all the capacity ever shut down.
- The amount of cash you have today is the sum of all the cash that ever came into the business, minus all cash ever spent.

This raises the significant problem that we cannot do anything unless we know the entire history of every resource since day one. Fortunately, we can cope with this problem, by working out what has happened since some previous point in time. In particular:

> If we know how much of resource X we had at the start of any period, and how much X was added or lost during the period, then we know precisely how much X we will have at the end of the period—and that quantity will then be how much X there is to start the next period.

The math of this explanation is quite different from the expression above, as follows:

$$X(t + 1) = X(t) +/- \Delta X(t . . t + 1)$$

Where "$\Delta$" means "change in …" and "$(t . . t + 1)$" means "between time $t$ and time $t + 1$". Chapter 2 already explained the important distinction between items that are measured at *points in time*, such as cash, customers, capacity, staff (i.e. asset-stocks), and items whose values are reported for *periods of time*, such as sales, costs, profits. It also explained how, if the quantity of a resource has changed during a period, calculating any item that depends on that resource can only be done accurately if repeated sufficiently often during the period to reflect those changes.

A similar principle applies to calculating the quantity of a resource—we can only know what the change in "X" has been between $t$ and $t + 1$ in the equation above if we know how quickly it has been added to or lost during the intervening period. If we start the year with 100 customers, and add five per month, we will end the year with 160 customers, but if we add five in January, three in February, seven in March and lose two in April, we will need to know every month's change in order to calculate the year-end number.

It is important to appreciate just how fundamental asset-stocks are to understanding and directing organizations' performance. As noted in Chapter 2, the possession of feathers and flapping wings may be common among things that fly, but understanding of flight made little progress until the properties of aerofoils were discovered. This single component makes air passing over a wing move faster than air passing underneath, so the air on top is less dense. The wing is therefore subject to more pressure from below than from above, and experiences lift upwards. As far as winged flying things are concerned, it is the aerofoil (not feathers or flapping wings) that is the single vital component without which it is *impossible* to explain performance, whether of a plane, bird, insect or tree seed. It is also impossible to anticipate the behavior of any new wing or change of design without understanding how that component functions.

The accumulating asset-stock is as fundamental to the behavior of business and other organizations as the aerofoil is to the behavior of winged objects. The math of each asset-stock's accumulation is vital to calculating performance, and without that component, only rough approximations are possible. It is also only possible to anticipate performance for a new or changed organization with any accuracy if the math of the accumulating asset-stocks is included in the analysis.

Returning to the idea that theory is an explanation of "what causes what, and how," the equation above is the core theory that lies at the heart of how business and other organizations perform.

> The rate of gain and loss for any resource over time explains the quantity of that resource at any time, and it does so by accumulating.

This second principle can be added to our emerging theory of performance:

1. **Performance depends on resources, and**
2. **Resources accumulate and deplete**

To complete the picture, we will also need to explain what causes those rates of gain and loss for each resource—a question addressed later in this chapter.

# WINNING AND KEEPING RESOURCES: "BATHTUB BEHAVIOR"

Since firms' performance derives directly from the resources that are available at any time, the challenge for managers is *how to build and maintain the quantity* of each resource. To help understand this problem, a resource can be thought of as behaving like water in a bathtub or tank. The inflow rate is the measure of how quickly water is flowing in through the faucet and the outflow rate measures how quickly water is running away through the drainhole.

In just the same way, resources are built by the *flow* of new resource into the stock - for example, winning customers *adds to* a customer base; recruiting new people *increases* our employee resource; promoting our products and services *raises* awareness among potential customers; training our staff *enhances* their level of skill. At the same time, resources are lost through misfortune, mistakes or the actions of others; customers are *lost* to competitors; resignations *reduce* our employee base; consumers' loss of interest *cuts* a brand's awareness, and discontinuing a product *reduces* our product range. Such losses can be thought of as resources "flowing" out of the tank.

This defining characteristic of resources—that they build and deplete over time, so-called "asset-stock accumulation"—is well-known to be critical to strategic

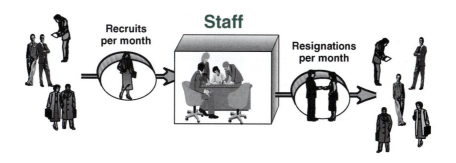

**Figure 3.1: Building, and losing, the staff resource.**

performance. This idea is captured for a staff resource in Figure 3.1. The "tank" in the middle holds the number of staff we have right now. To the left is the outside world, where there are many people, some of whom might become future staff. The big "pipe" flowing into the tank has a pump on it (the oval symbol) that drives *how fast* that stock of staff is being added. On the right, another pump on a pipe flowing out of the stock determines how fast we are losing staff, so they join other people in the outside world who include our former employees.

This picture begins to show why the firm's history is so important. Since people have been pumped into and out of the tank for many months or years, the number in place right now *must* reflect all of that history. The level of resource we have today is on a trajectory through time, reflecting how well we have been building it (and holding on to it!) in the past. This not only explains why the business is in its present state, but also determines its current trajectory into the immediate future. Unless recruitment rates and resignations vary quite randomly from month to month, which is rare, the number of staff will be changing in some direction that is likely to continue if those rates are sustained.

The behavior of this process (known mathematically as "integration") is intuitively tricky to estimate over time, but is in fact quite familiar. You probably have a bank account and know more or less how much money was in it at the end of last month. You have some idea how much will be added to it during this month, whether from salary or other sources, and how much you will have to pay out of it. You therefore can work out what will be left at the end of the month.

Figure 3.2 shows this idea, and the numbers illustrate another valuable point. If the inflows and outflows differ then you know exactly how *fast* the resource is changing—if the numbers in this figure continue through time, you will have $1 050 at the end of next month, $1 100 at the end of the month after, and so on. It is also easy to work out what will happen if your rent goes up from $200 to $300/month. If this illustration makes sense to you, it seems you already know how to "integrate" resources over time, even if you didn't realize it.

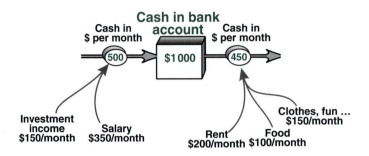

**Figure 3.2: Drivers of flows into and out of your bank account.**

The simple principle captured in Figures 3.1 and 3.2 is a graphical representation of the deeply fundamental principle that the amount of any resource right now is the sum of everything ever added, minus everything ever lost. This is not a matter of opinion, nor a result of surveys, research or statistical analysis. It is more even than a "theory"—it just IS the way the world works, and is mathematically unavoidable. There is no other explanation for the amount of cash in your account besides the historical sum of payments in and out.

# DEFINING AND MEASURING RESOURCES AND THEIR FLOWS

We were careful in Chapter 2 to ensure that the causal connections were arithmetically accurate, for example, that *quantity sold per month* was equal to *customers* multiplied by *quantity per customer per month*. It is equally important that the units of resources and flows are accurately defined. This is simple, though:

> **Whatever the units by which a resource is measured, the inflows and outflows are always measured in the same units *per time period*.**

There is never any exception to this rule. Table 3.1 lists the major types of resource, the units by which they are measured, typical inflows and outflows for each, and the units for measuring those flows.

The only judgment to be made about the correct units for resource flow rates concerns the choice of time period—should it be *people per week, per month,* or *per year*? Chapter 2 explained that analysis should be done on time periods that are short enough for change during any period to be relatively small, compared with the overall scale of the situation. The guiding principle is that the time period should match that chosen for the causal explanation of performance. So if, for example, you are looking at how profits have been changing from quarter to quarter, then

**TABLE 3.1: MEASURING INFLOWS AND OUTFLOWS FOR VARIOUS RESOURCES**

| Resource | Units | Inflows and outflows | Units of inflows and outflows |
|---|---|---|---|
| **cash** | $ | cash received<br>cash spent | $ per month |
| **staff** | people | recruitment<br>resignations<br>dismissals | people per month |
| **customers** | people or companies | new customers won<br>customers ceasing to trade with us | people per year or companies per year |
| **product range** | products | products launched<br>products discontinued | products per year |
| **plant capacity** | tons/day | new plant purchases<br>plant closures | 'tons/day' per year |

customer gains and losses should be measured in *customers per quarter*. If you are in a faster moving business and want to understand why sales rates change substantially from week to week, then you need information on weekly sales, and your measure of customer flows should be *customers won per week* and *customers lost per week*.

The last item in Table 3.1 shows a complication that arises in certain cases—when a resource itself includes time. Production capacity for, say, a cement or steel producer

**Doing it right: depicting resources, flows and factors that drive them**

To continue an accurate causal explanation of performance, it is important to maintain the discipline of depicting correctly "what causes what," just as we did with the causal connections in Chapter 2. Since the current quantity of a resource is "caused by" whatever we had at the start of a period, plus what was added, minus what was lost, it cannot be caused by anything else. The diagram in Figure 3.3 must therefore be wrong—the marketing spend of $5 000 per month cannot explain the number of 1 015 customers at the end of the month. It is missing all three of the numbers needed to work out that quantity (the number at the start of the month, and the numbers gained and lost), and the causal link from *marketing spend* to *customers* is meaningless.

The correct causal structure is shown in Figure 3.4. The "stock and flow" structure includes all the values needed to explain the end-of-month number of
customers. It also shows the causal link that "marketing spend of $5000 per
month has won 20 customers during the month."

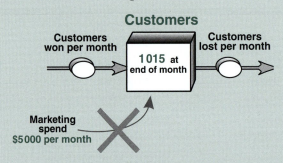

**Figure 3.3:** Incorrect depiction of how resource quantities are
caused.*

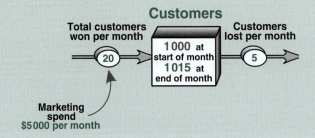

**Figure 3.4:** Accurate causal structure of resource-and-flow
relationships.

There is a further reason why marketing spend cannot explain the number
of customers—five customers have been lost during the month—and that
cannot be due to marketing (it requires especially bad advertizing to positively drive away customers who were previously happy with a product or
service). There must therefore be some other explanation for the customer
losses.

---

* Links such as are shown in Figure 3.3 sometimes appear in simulation models, but their function
is purely to set the *initial* value for the resource (1000 customers in this case), after which all values
for later time periods are calculated from the in- and outflows.

is measured in "tons/day." If we *change* capacity by adding new equipment or closing a plant, the result is an inflow or outflow of a certain number of "tons/day this year." This is a one-off inflow, a feature that will be discussed further at the end of this chapter, but continuous changes in flow rates may also occur. The production rate for an oil field is measured in "barrels per day", but as a field is drained, its production rate typically falls. This decline would therefore be measured in "barrels per day, per year."

# RESOURCE FLOWS CHANGE OVER TIME

Figures 3.2 to 3.4 have only looked at the relationship between a resource and its flow rates for a single period, but if we are to understand how performance varies continuously over time, then it is necessary also to understand what is happening to resource levels over time. Consequently, we need to understand the relationship between resources and their flow rates from period to period. Before looking at the complexities of real cases, some simple illustrations will clarify the principles involved. Figure 3.5 shows sales for some product, driven by customers who buy at a steady rate of seven units per month. The business starts with 100 customers, and wins five new customers per month, ending the year with 160 customers. Sales start the year at the rate of 700 units per month, and end the year at 1 120 units per month (160 customers * 7 units per customer per month).

Notice an important consequence of what the accumulating stock of customers does in this situation—the *constant* customer win rate results in a *rising* number of customers and an increasing rate of sales. This is a general property of accumulating resources:

> **Constant flow rates cause changing resource levels, and therefore changes in performance.**

Typically, management decisions and policies, such as marketing spend or pricing, impact the flow rates into and out of a resource. So this nonlinear relationship between the flow rate and the resource it is filling can make it difficult to estimate

---

**Beware sloppy language on "rates" and "levels"**

Such is the general lack of awareness about the important distinction between stocks and flows of resources that most of us casually misuse language. We talk, for example, about the "level" of government borrowing, when it is in fact a rate—its units are $billions *per year*. The "level" in this case is the level of government debt, whose units are $billions. We talk about the "level" of profit, when profit is in fact a rate, with units of $millions per year. Conversely, we talk about the "rate" of unemployment, when unemployment is a level—units being people, not people *per year.*

Does this matter? It does if the confusion causes us to mistake the consequences of our decisions. If you are worried about the *level* of debt on your credit card, for example, and you do not appreciate the distinction between levels and rates, you might imagine that cutting your "level" of spending would reduce your debt. But up to a certain point it won't—reducing the *rate* of spending would merely slow the rate at which your debt is rising!

Similarly, a company concerned with falling sales revenue might mistakenly think that reducing the "level" of customer churn would lead to increasing sales. But customer churn is the *rate* of customer losses (units being customers per month), and sales revenue will continue falling until that rate is less than the rate of customer acquisition.

The confusion also matters on bigger issues. Governments are to varying degrees committed to reducing the "level" of greenhouse gas emissions, in the belief that this will "tackle" global warming. It won't. Greenhouse gas emissions are a *rate* (units are billions of tons per year) that is adding to the *level* of those gases in the atmosphere. As long as the emission rate exceeds the absorption rate of the planet's biosphere, any reduction in emissions is merely slowing the rate at which that level is rising. If you are filling a bathtub with a fire hose, turning the hose down by a few percent is not going to stop your house from flooding!

This has important implications for how management decides on objectives. If you fear that your credit card debt is too high, the only appropriate objective is for your spending rate to be cut to less than your repayments, minus interest charges. The company with falling revenue must aim for the rate of customer churn to be less than its rate of customer acquisition. And if governments believe high levels of greenhouse gases to be dangerous, then the only appropriate aim is for the rate of emissions to fall below the planet's absorption rate, which is a very large cut indeed. If greenhouse gas levels really are a problem it is grossly dishonest, if politically convenient, to tell the general public that minor cuts in their use of hydrocarbon fuels will actually "reduce" global warming

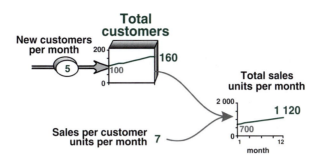

**Figure 3.5: Constant customer acquisition drives rising sales.**

what will happen to the level of that resource and the performance it drives. This estimation becomes particularly difficult when, as is common, more than one resource flow is involved. Customers may be lost as well as won, so this overall win rate of five customers per month could easily be the *net* result of winning 10 and losing 5 each month, winning 20 and losing 15, or even winning 100 and losing 95. These alternative situations are not equivalent! A company experiencing the last of these cases will have some serious problems:

- it requires effort and cash to win customers, so a high rate of customer churn will be costly
- the large number of customers being lost will likely damage the company's reputation
- if there is a finite number of potential customers, the company risks running out of customers

Now consider what happens when a customer flow rate is not constant but changes over time. In Figure 3.6, the business is winning 20 customers per month, and initially losing only 12/month. However, as each month passes, this loss rate increases, rising in successive months to 14, 16, 18, and so on, until by the end of month 12, customers are leaving at the rate of 36 per month.

We have a straight-line trend on customer losses, and a constant win rate, but the stock of customers follows a curving path through time, peaking at 120 during month five (when 20 customers are won and another 20 are lost), then decreasing ever more rapidly until the year ends with only 64 customers in place.

## A "SPREADSHEET" VIEW OF RESOURCE ACCUMULATION

Although the situation shown in Figure 3.6 may seem an unfamiliar way of looking at business performance, it simply re-presents what could equally be shown in a spreadsheet. Table 3.2 shows the causal logic and calculation sequence:

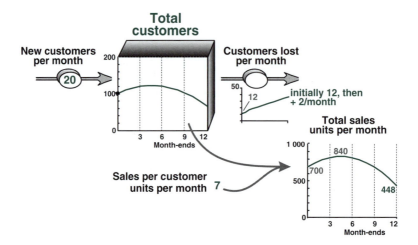

**Figure 3.6: How changing customer losses affect customer numbers and sales. (Online learning materials are available to support this example, see p.xxi.)**

- the resources available at the start of each month (*customers*) determine the performance rate (*total sales*)
- resources added and lost during the month (*new customers* and *customers lost*) determine the resources that will be available at the start of next month

## TABLE 3.2: CUSTOMER FLOW RATES DETERMINE MONTHLY CUSTOMER NUMBERS AND SALES RATES

| Month-end | 0 | 1 | 2 | 3 | 4 | 5 | 6 | 7 | 8 | 9 | 10 | 11 | 12 |
|---|---|---|---|---|---|---|---|---|---|---|---|---|---|
| Total customers | 100 | 108 | 114 | 118 | 120 | 120 | 118 | 114 | 108 | 100 | 90 | 78 | 64 |
| New customers per month | 20 | 20 | 20 | 20 | 20 | 20 | 20 | 20 | 20 | 20 | 20 | 20 | 20 |
| Customers lost per month | 12 | 14 | 16 | 18 | 20 | 22 | 24 | 26 | 28 | 30 | 32 | 34 | 36 |
| Sales per customer per month | 7 | 7 | 7 | 7 | 7 | 7 | 7 | 7 | 7 | 7 | 7 | 7 | 7 |
| Total sales units per month | 700 | 756 | 798 | 826 | 840 | 840 | 826 | 798 | 756 | 700 | 630 | 546 | 448 |
| Average sales last month | | 728 | 777 | 812 | 833 | 840 | 833 | 812 | 777 | 728 | 665 | 588 | 497 |

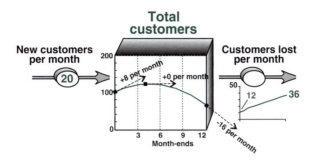

**Figure 3.7:** Customer flow rates determine the trajectory on which the customer base is heading.

The spreadsheet also adds an extra line for *average sales last month*. As discussed in Chapter 2, when factors are changing over time, taking periodic calculations will become increasingly accurate as the time between those snapshots shortens. In this example, monthly periods lead to an error of just a few percentage points in the exact rate of monthly sales. This is likely close enough for explaining why the sales rate has followed its historic path. It is also probably sufficient accuracy for estimating what might happen to future sales, given the uncertainties that typically surround any forecasting.

Note that the resource flow rates here—*new customers* and *customers lost per month*— are telling us the *trajectory* on which the business is heading at the start of each period (Figure 3.7). At the start, the customer win rate of 20/month and losses of 12/month mean that the customer base is heading upwards by a net +8 per month. By month 4, customer losses match the win rate, so there is no net change in the customer base. By month 12, customer losses of 36/month are way faster than the win rate of 20, so into the *next* month (month 13), the net change will be −16/month.

It is worth reemphasizing an important implication of this structure:

### It is vital to know, separately, resource inflows and outflows.

Here, winning 20 customers and losing 12 is *not* the same as winning 100 and losing 92! And this distinction is likely to prove important in relation to other resources also. For example, for many years it was taken as normal for staff in the fast food sector to turn over quickly, with the average person staying for just a few months of temporary employment. Work methods and training systems were designed to get new staff productive as quickly as possible. However, certain less well defined aspects of staff performance, such as the quality of customer service, come with experience. Consequently, Starbucks always has enjoyed a significant advantage with a staff employment system that succeeded in retaining staff for much longer periods—typically well over 12 months. Not only were the costs of hiring and training reduced, but the quality of customers' experience was also enhanced.[2]

# PRACTICAL EXAMPLES OF THE IMPORTANCE OF RESOURCE FLOWS

## BMW MINI

After their acquisition of the defunct British carmaker MG-Rover, BMW in 2001 launched an updated version of the Mini. Although reminiscent of the 1960s classic, the car was a decidedly sophisticated vehicle, with BMW's level of engineering and quality. Sales, it was hoped, might hit 100 000 units per year.

But by 2005, sales had reached around 200 000 units, and the Mini had achieved almost cult status, even in the United States, in spite of a price tag at least 20% higher than other prestige small cars. Furthermore, well over half of mini owners went on to buy another BMW—though not necessarily another Mini—a remarkably high loyalty rate. Loyalty and repurchase on this scale are to be welcomed, but it is worth reflecting on what this implies for acquisition of new customers.

Figure 3.8 illustrates a plausible scenario in which first-time Mini buyers keep their car for two years, so the resource in the center is the stock of people who own Minis less than two years old. (An additional stock of used car owners, not shown, is filled by the right-hand flow of new vehicles being sold.) The time charts on the architecture show how the numbers up to 2005 work out if 20% of new vehicle buyers repurchase a Mini. As can be seen in the bottom left chart, the number of

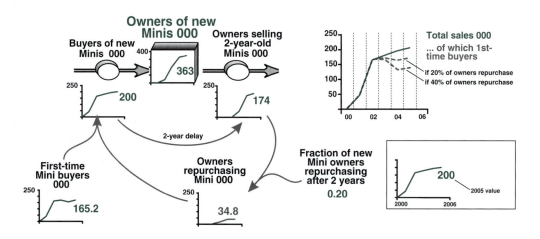

**Figure 3.8: Illustrative sales of BMW Minis to first-time and repurchasing buyers—2001 to 2006.**

*first-time buyers* would actually have fallen in 2004 if this 20% repurchase fraction were correct. The more detailed chart at right goes on to show how total new vehicle sales would have split between *first-time buyers* and *owners repurchasing*, for repurchase rates of 20% and 40%. If as many as 40% of owners had repurchased a Mini after two years, the number of first-time buyers would have fallen from 157 200 to just 125 000 between 2003 and 2004 (a rather extreme and unlikely case).

Note, as always, that this figure follows the causal discipline that every item can be estimated arithmetically from those linked to it.

This distinction between first-time and repeat buyers is important for BMW's marketing policy. People who have previously owned a vehicle understand deeply what it is like, both practically and emotionally, whereas those who have not can only trust the reputation they hear from others and the very limited experience of a test drive. The emphasis of marketing messages and the communications channels for reaching each group are thus quite different—BMW may even be able to communicate directly with existing owners.

There is also a possible concern that the car may only appeal to a very small group of potential customers, and that sooner or later that potential will be exhausted. The higher the proportion of sales that come from repurchase by existing owners, the lower that implied limit is, and the stronger the evidence that this saturation point is being approached. Then there is the question of the relative effort and spending to put onto each source of new sales. BMW could, in principle, promote the car *only* to existing owners, so that those customers dominate future sales. Not that the company would in practice make such a choice—BMW has arguably the strongest record of any volume car producer in building what might be termed "incipient" demand among people who would love to own one of their vehicles, but are not yet able to afford one.

(Online learning materials are available to support this example, see p.xxi.)

## LAW FIRM STAFF TURNOVER

The problem discussed in Chapter 2, concerning staff turnover in a law firm is more clearly understood if the staffing story is laid out properly, complete with inflows and outflows (Figure 3.9). While the only data this figure adds, compared with Figure 2.36, is the hiring rate chart at left, it also adds the important feature that all the values around this staff resource are now joined up in a mathematically rigorous way—the three flows of *new lawyers*, *lawyers-to-partner*, and *lawyers leaving per quarter* are absolutely consistent over every quarter with the net change in the stock of *lawyers*.

(Online learning materials are available to support this example, see p. xxi.)

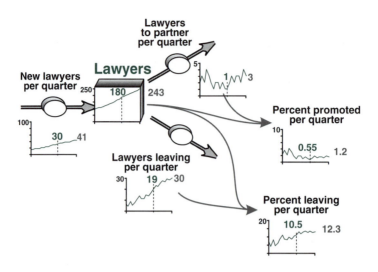

**Figure 3.9: Staff flows at the law firm with a staffing challenge.**

## BRANDED PAIN-RELIEF PRODUCT[3]

Chapter 1 mentioned the case of a branded product in the mature market for over-the-counter pain relief drugs in the United States. Despite some growth in customers for this brand (Figure 3.10), market share was declining because their average purchase rate was falling. Close examination of consumer behavior discovered that, far from the stability that the low market growth rate implied, buyers of pain-relief

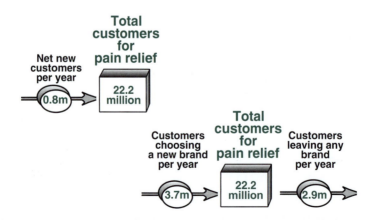

**Figure 3.10: Apparent and actual change in customers for a United States brand of pain relief pills. (Data disguised for confidentiality.)**

products were actually churning quite quickly, with nearly 13% switching their preferred product each year. The consumer churn for this specific brand was comparable to these rates for the market as a whole. Consequently, although net change in consumer numbers and sales was very small, the scope for improving the situation was considerable. Rather than trying still harder to capture sales from the market leader, attention was shifted to retaining specific consumer groups who were leaving most rapidly. The falling average purchase rate per consumer was explained by the fact that consumers being won were lower volume buyers than those being lost.

Further analysis identified that customer churn could readily be reduced by two percentage points a year, comparable to the best performing competitor, an improvement worth over $1 million per year in extra sales, and a significant increase in market share. Better still, this could be achieved with a *lower* marketing spend than previously, since there was less competitive marketing activity directed at the consumer group that was being lost. As at summer 2006, the brand's performance was well ahead of this estimated gain.

## UNITED STATES WELFARE TO WORK[4]

In August 1996, Bill Clinton signed a law requiring states to encourage welfare recipients into work—a policy that came to be known as workfare. This policy included limiting families to just five years of federal money, together with incentives

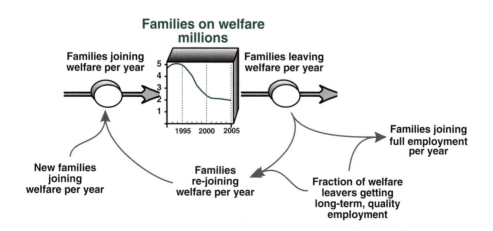

**Figure 3.11: Reduction in United States families on welfare—1992 to 2005.**
Source: United States Dept of Health and Human Services

for states to shrink their welfare caseloads. This step change in policy triggered some significant changes in states' approaches to welfare, including the requirement for applicants to try job searches, assistance in finding child care, and subsidized travel to work.

While the policy remains controversial and problems of poverty remain, the next decade saw welfare caseloads fall by 60% from 5 million to 2 million families (Figure 3.11). An important objective for many states was to achieve long-term, quality employment for claimants, with the intent of helping people into careers, not just low-grade temporary jobs. New York State, for example, was able to see employment among single mothers increase from 40% to over 60% in just five years.[5]

## OTHER RESOURCE FLOW CHALLENGES

Flow rate challenges can arise in relation to any resource, in any organizational context:

- A confectionery company featured a range of products roughly twice that of the market leader, Mars, although most of those products achieved sales rates that were uneconomically low. How had this situation come about? In an effort to compete, the company had introduced new products over many years in the belief that this would capture additional customer segments and confectionery-consuming occasions. Unfortunately, although most new product introductions (the flow of *products introduced per year* to the *product range* resource) achieved reasonable sales volumes, a large fraction of these sales came from cannibalization of existing products. Reluctant to discontinue any product for fear of seeing total sales fall, the company allowed the product range to widen inexorably, requiring its limited marketing budget to be spread too thinly, and making it difficult for its salesforce to talk persuasively with retailers. The problem could only be fixed by rationalizing its range (increasing *products discontinued per year*) and refocusing its marketing and sales effort.

- As the world's largest provider of Internet services, AOL showed spectacular growth in its early years, hitting 10 million subscribers by 1997 and 34 million by 2002. Given the inexorable growth in PC penetration worldwide, and the public's apparently insatiable appetite for online services, even this vast subscriber base might not have been the limit to the company's scale. However, its early growth was dominated by uptake in the United States of standard telephone modems, for which AOL offered the simplest and widest service. As broadband services quickly multiplied and penetrated United States households, AOL found itself trapped by reliance on its large dialup subscriber base. If it left subscribers alone, they would become increasingly dissatisfied and leave, but if it encouraged them to switch to broadband, they would likely shop around for alternatives. In any case, AOL made lower margins on those services. With multiple competitors emerging for supply of connections for online services and for provision of online advertizing, the company found every part of its business model under threat. Subscriber churn became unstoppable, reaching as much as 3% per month, and by 2005, subscriber numbers had fallen to less than 27 million. Its "bathtub" was draining fast, and there was little sign of an inflow that might run fast enough to refill it.

- Many companies wish to make their internal IT service departments more accountable and commercial by rendering them partly independent, sometimes even spinning off the group into a separate company. One utility company took this step with a 120-member IT department, but before doing so, helped the group develop a strategy for its future independence. A serious issue in this review concerned staff turnover, which had been running at 5–7% for as long as anyone could remember. Staff therefore typically had 15–20 years of employment experience with this company. Since innovative behavior would be required for a commercially competitive organization in this fast-moving industry, management recognized that turnover would have to accelerate. At the same time, growth opportunities meant that total staff numbers would also need to rise. These implications proved especially challenging for the group's HR function, who would see the rate of hiring and training multiply fivefold in just two years as the organization speeded up its development.

- Oil and gas production companies—indeed all firms concerned with extracting natural resources—constantly struggle to achieve new discoveries at least as fast as they deplete reserves they have already discovered. The resource in question is "proven reserves" (in millions of barrels, cubic feet, tons, etc, as appropriate), the inflow is "new reserves discovered per year" and the outflow is "production rate per year." Looking at the oil industry as a whole, the rate of new discoveries in recent years appears to be failing to keep up with the production rate, resulting in the global level of proven reserves falling for the first time since the industry's birth.

- A most unfortunate example of resources, gains and losses concerned a security services firm, which explained that its annual numbers were the same for all three items in Figure 3.7! Each year it won a hundred customers, had a hundred on its books, and lost a hundred! While this situation may seem bizarre, the process by which it came about is hardly unusual. One month the firm loses a key customer, so revenues and profits are down. Top management demands that "something be done!"—i.e. cut costs and replace the customer. The general manager gears up the sales effort and manages to replace the lost customer. He cuts staff to reduce costs and bring profits back on target. With the new client coming on board, these staff cuts damage service quality, so next month two customers leave … revenues and profits are down again, and the demand comes through once more—"Do something about sales and costs!" … so the manager seeks more new customers, and cuts some more staff. Eventually, client turnover reaches very high rates, and both sales and service staff are working frantically to keep the business going. The solution in this case was to stop selling business! Switching management and staff effort onto service delivery rebuilt quality for remaining clients and stopped the high rates of client churn. This solution, although resulting in a drop in sales revenue, did not cause a drop in profits. Much of the new business was won by offering contract prices so low as to be unprofitable, and the company was also able to cut its sales costs.

# RESOURCE BUILDING IN RYANAIR

Chapters 1 and 2 introduced the performance history and prospects of the low-fare airline Ryanair and showed how that performance reflected the company's tangible resources—customers, aircraft, routes, airports and staff. The analysis can now be extended to incorporate the principle introduced in this chapter, by showing how resource flows have varied over time to bring about today's levels, and how they will need to develop in the future in order to deliver the company's hoped-for performance. Table 3.3 lists the company's resources and quantities as of March 2006, and required by 2011, if the desired sales and profit growth are to be achieved.[6]

## TABLE 3.3: RESOURCES AND FLOWS FOR RYANAIR

| Resource | Quantity in 2006 | Required by 2011 | Inflows and outflows |
|---|---|---|---|
| Customers (millions) | 7.39' | 11.0 | Customers won per year customers lost per year |
| Staff | 3063 | 5220 | Hiring resignations dismissals |
| Aircraft | 103 | 195 | New aircraft bought aircraft sold |
| Routes | 330 | 590 | Routes opened and closed |
| Airports served | 110 | 146 | Airports added and left |

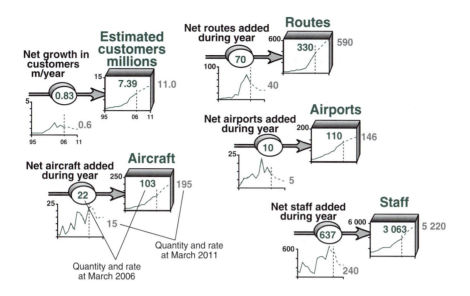

**Figure 3.12: Net flow rates for Ryanair's tangible resources— 1995 to 2011.**

Figure 3.12 shows *net* growth in these resources since 1995 and the flow rates required to hit the plausible projected scale by 2011. Understanding how perform- ance has developed to date, and assessing future potential, ideally requires informa- tion on both the inflow and outflow for each resource. This detail is not available to outsiders—for example, we do not know how many staff were hired, dismissed or resigned—although it would be available to management. However, to illustrate the value of this more detailed information, Figure 3.13 shows these separate flows for two resources: routes, where actual additions and closures *are* reported, and cus- tomers, where as explained in Chapter 2, we are using illustrative data.

Ryanair has been opening and closing routes in recent years, behavior that may seem puzzling for such a successful company in the industry. However, closures are an unavoidable consequence of the extremely rapid growth of the company's route network. If it is adding 100 or more routes each year, a small fraction of those will inevitably fall short of the passenger-journey volumes required to be economic.

The numbers of customers were estimated in Chapter 2 from known passenger- journey numbers and assumptions about travel frequency. Figure 3.13 further assumes that 10 % of customers choose to stop using the airline each year.

Note that once again, the math of these structures is essentially simple, and can be readily shown in spreadsheet form (Table 3.4), but it is easier to see the connec- tions and resulting changes over time in the format of Figure 3.13.

(Online learning materials are available to support this example, see p. xxi.)

TABLE 3.4: **SPREADSHEET DEPICTION OF CHANGE IN RYANAIR'S ROUTES—1995 TO 2011**

| Year | 95 | 96 | 97 | 98 | 99 | 00 | 01 | 02 | 03 | 04 | 05 | 06 | 07 | 08 | 09 | 10 | 11 |
|---|---|---|---|---|---|---|---|---|---|---|---|---|---|---|---|---|---|
| Routes as at March each year | 9 | 9 | 12 | 20 | 26 | 35 | 42 | 55 | 75 | 140 | 219 | 320 | 390 | 450 | 500 | 540 | 580 |
| Routes added in coming year | 0 | 3 | 8 | 6 | 9 | 7 | 14 | 20 | 76 | 84 | 116 | 93 | 88 | 82 | 76 | 79 | |
| Routes closed in coming year | 0 | 0 | 0 | 0 | 0 | 0 | 1 | 0 | 11 | 5 | 15 | 23 | 28 | 32 | 36 | 39 | |
| Net change in routes | 0 | 3 | 8 | 6 | 9 | 7 | 13 | 20 | 65 | 79 | 101 | 70 | 60 | 50 | 40 | 40 | |

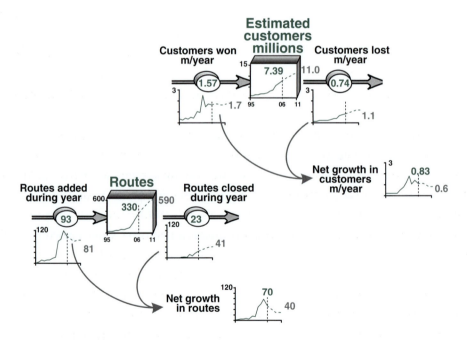

**Figure 3.13:** Inflows and outflows determining Ryanair's customers (illustrative) and routes—1995 to 2011.

# WHAT DRIVES RESOURCE FLOWS?

Our pursuit of a rigorous causal explanation for performance has identified that (a) performance depends on resource levels and (b) resource levels depend on inflows and outflows. The next question that arises, then, is "what drives those flows of resources?" Three main categories of item determine the rate at which any resource is running at any point in time:

- management decisions
- external factors
- existing levels of one or more resources

The third of these issues is the principal mechanism involved in the living, interacting system that is a functioning organization. It raises important issues and gives rise to some complexity, so will be dealt with in detail in Chapter 4. This section will therefore focus on the impact of management decisions and external influences.

## MANAGEMENT DECISIONS

Some resource flows are determined directly by management, for example, how many additional vehicles are required by a transportation firm. Unless there was suddenly a worldwide shortage of the particular vehicle type required, that decision will simply happen. Similarly, many companies can decide how many operational staff to hire, and can also fire staff, provided they observe any employment legislation regulating lay offs.

Others' decisions may be desired, but may be moderated by other factors. The law firm featured in Figure 3.9 could wish to hire 30–40 lawyers a year, but its success depends on the availability of newly qualifying lawyers with particular skills, on the efforts of any competitors to hire those same people, and on the firm's reputation as an employer. In spite of these moderating influences, management can nevertheless have reasonable confidence in getting what they want, unless conditions change. A rather larger law firm than featured above regularly received about 300 applicants each year, to whom it would offer 100 positions, and expect to hire 50. In one particular year, however, it merged with another firm and changed its name. It was surprised when, the next year, applications fell to only 80, not due to any problems with the newly merged firm, but simply because the young graduating lawyers did not recognize the new firm's name among the list of recruiters!

Other decisions have more unpredictable impacts on resource flows, the most substantial example being customer acquisition. While management may have a desire to add 50 customers in any year, their mechanisms for achieving such growth are remote from the decisions of customers themselves, strongly moderated by factors outside management's control, and thus highly uncertain. Marketing spend may build awareness and understanding among possible customers, price changes may alter those customers' perceptions of value, and sales effort may be sized to

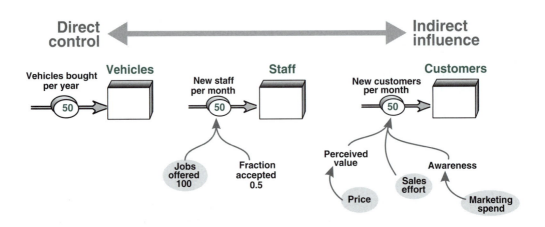

**Figure 3.14:** **Varied uncertainty regarding how management decisions affect resource flows.**

target a known number of possibilities. However, whether these factors will bring in 50, 10 or 100 new customers—or none at all—is rarely certain.

Figure 3.14 illustrates this spectrum of certainty about what influences resource flow rates. One final issue to bear in mind on these indirect influences is that often a number of choices impact on the resource flow, so identifying the separate contribution of each can be challenging.

## EXTERNAL FACTORS

In addition to those factors over which management has some influence, other issues may be under someone else's control or independent of any organized influence. Competitors' decisions and policies, usually on very similar items as our own management, impact on some of the same issues that we ourselves would like to influence—marketing, price and sales effort for example. Indeed, competitors' influence appears to rise as our own control reduces. There is not much a rival can do to stop us buying the vehicles we need and only a limited possibility of preventing us hiring the people we want.

Socioeconomic factors, such as demographic change, unemployment or consumers' disposable income are issues about which neither we nor rivals have much influence. There may also be little possibility to alter fundamental preferences among customers, intermediaries, staff, investors or other stakeholders. As noted above, AOL experienced devastating customer losses simply because so many better, cheaper alternatives arose for people to obtain the services for which they previously paid AOL significant prices. The company did not suffer defeat at the hands of a particular competitor's superior strategy or policies—its business model had simply become obsolete.

# CHANGING STATE VERSUS CHANGING ACTIVITY

These first two categories of items influencing resource flow rates (management decisions and exogenous factors) may seem familiar, since they match the factors discussed in Chapter 2 that influence customers' purchase rates. When considering "animate" resources, notably customers and staff, there are broadly two types of influence we wish to have:

- **persuading people to do some activity at a greater or lesser rate**
- **persuading people to move into or out of some resource—or to remain in their present state**

As Table 3.5 shows, similar considerations apply to animate resources in voluntary and public policy cases.

These influences can readily be represented graphically, as shown in Figure 3.15.

This structure turns out to be extremely widespread; indeed it is so common that it may be regarded as a generic tool in dynamic performance analysis. Looking back at some of the cases discussed earlier illustrates how it provides a focus for organizations' strategic challenges. Ryanair's principal concern is to win new customers, and secondarily, to persuade them to fly more often. There is little evidence of a

**TABLE 3.5: DESIRED INFLUENCES—CHANGE ACTIVITY RATES VERSUS SWITCHING BETWEEN STATES**

| Resource | Desired change in activity | Desired movement into a resource | Desired choice to remain in a resource |
|---|---|---|---|
| Customers | buy more of our product | become our customer | do not cease to be our customer |
| Staff | be more productive | become our employee | do not resign |
| Donors to voluntary group | give more | become a donor | do not cease to be a donor |
| Criminals | commit fewer crimes | "go straight" | remain an honest citizen |

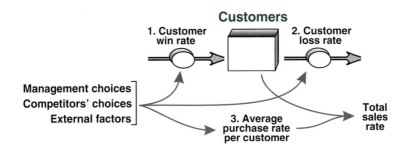

**Figure 3.15: Generic structure for the influences on three types of customer behavior.**

problem with customer retention. Reviving sales for the painkiller required the focus to switch from customer acquisition to retention, especially as the customers being lost were those purchasing at a higher than average rate. The marketing issue was not significantly concerned with persuading any customer group to consume more pills. The law firm's concern is with persuading lawyers not to leave the firm. It is not always a matter of *choosing which* of the three behaviors to drive, so much as deciding the *balance between* those choices. BMW mini sales, for example, require separate attention to new customer acquisition and to retention of existing owners when they replace their vehicle. Since a car is a durable product, there is no equivalent behavior to the "purchase frequency" that applies to airline flights or consumable goods—if a car owner makes a repeat purchase of the same type of vehicle, this event is a simultaneous outflow and inflow.

Ryanair's business growth provides a good illustration of how these three behaviors combine to determine business sales rate. The volume of business (*passenger-journeys booked*) depends on the current number of active customers and their average travel frequency, and the number of active customers depends on the history of customers won and lost. Chapter 2 showed how the value curve framework can provide an approximate explanation for customers' travel frequency. However, as noted in Table 3.5, purchase rate is not the only customer behavior driven by price, service and other features—similar issues drive win and loss rates too. So Figure 3.16 shows how the value curve approach can be extended to deal with the whole structure of customer acquisition, retention and purchase frequency. Note that the single largest influence on new-customer acquisition arises simply from opening new airports to reach new potential customers, but the value curve factors then determine how well that potential is developed.

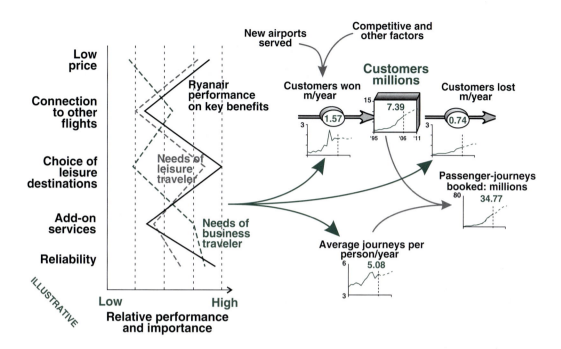

**Figure 3.16:** Value curve influences on Ryanair customers' three behaviors.

# SEGMENTATION

Chapter 2 explained why it may be necessary to identify and quantify separately how different customer segments contribute to total demand—distinguishing between leisure and business travelers, for example. Purchase rates are not the only important behavior where such segments may differ, however. They are also likely to vary in their tendency to become customers in the first place, or to cease being customers if the company does not offer what they want.

If purchase rate were the only issue on which behavior differed, then any change in what is offered—price, for example—would merely move the company's sales and profits to a new level, and growth or decline would continue on the same trajectory as before. However, the distinct behaviors of customer segments when it comes to flow rates also have implications for performance over time. This mechanism can be illustrated by comparing two situations (Table 3.6). In case A, a company has 1000 customers and its customer base is growing at 10% per year. In case B, the company also has 1000 customers, growing at 10% a year, but that customer base consists of two segments. Segment 1 has 200 customers, growing at 30% a year, and segment 2 has 800 customers growing at 5% a year.

**TABLE 3.6: TWO CASES OF CUSTOMER DEVELOPMENT, INITIALLY GROWING AT EQUAL RATES**

| Resource | A: Single Segment | B: Two segments | | |
|---|---|---|---|---|
| | | Segment 1 | Segment 2 | Total |
| Initial customers | 1 000 | 200 | 800 | 1 000 |
| Growth rate per year | 10 % | 30 % | 5 % | 10 % |

Figure 3.17 shows the development of these two cases. Although starting out with exactly the same growth rate overall—100 new customers per year—the one-segment case grows to only 2 594 customers after 10 years, while the two-segment case grows to 4 060. This should not be too surprising. After all, a customer base of 1 000 growing at 10% would in any case be overtaken at some point by another market of just 200 growing at 30%. In Figure 3.17, this event is about to occur just after year 10, at which time Segment 1 of case B, at 2 757 customers, is just behind the total customers

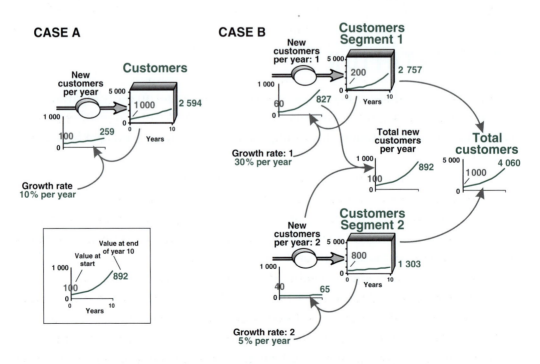

**Figure 3.17: Development of a single segment market (left) versus two-segment market (right) with same initial growth.**

in case A (2594). However, if management initially *thinks* that it is operating case A, when the situation in fact reflects case B, they will badly mistake how the future will turn out.

It might be good news that our slow-growing market actually consists of segments that, when considered together, will grow faster. In reality, though, the potential *size* of those segments, and of the total market, will be limited. Consequently, case B will also run out of potential faster than case A.

# CAUSAL AMBIGUITY AND PROBLEMS WITH CORRELATION

The notion that resources, or "asset-stocks," accumulate has long been recognized in the strategy field. The most widely cited article that considers how this phenomenon affects strategy and performance dates back to 1989.[7] This article introduces the bathtub metaphor, explained earlier in this chapter, and concludes that "a key dimension of strategy formulation may be identified as the task of making appropriate choices about strategic expenditure … with a view to accumulating required resources and skills." It points out that the difficulty competitors face in imitating resources can provide competitive advantage to any firm that already has those resources, and identifies four specific problems that a competitor will face:

- *Time compression diseconomies.* In layman's terms, this simply means that it takes time to accumulate resources. For example, no matter how aggressively a new competitor might seek to copy the branch network of McDonald's or Starbucks, it will take years, or perhaps decades to match the sheer scale of that resource. Putting in double the effort does not halve the time required. This is arguably the single dominant reason why we do not require, as the resource-based view of strategy (RBV) implies, abstract and indefinable "strategic" resources and capabilities in order to explain the long-term leadership of organizations whose business model is entirely transparent. No matter how brilliant you or I may be at developing fast food products and offering them to the public, it will take a very long time to find and acquire the great retail locations needed to capture customers and build sales. Likewise, unless Ryanair or Southwest airlines falter, there is no possibility of you or I overtaking them in their chosen market.
- *Asset mass efficiencies.* To put this phrase into common parlance, "the more you have, the faster you can get more." There is little mystery to this process, which can extend across the whole panoply of resources, and exactly how it operates will be explained in Chapter 4. For now, consider these questions. If you

happened to own a great retail store unit, would you rather offer it to Starbucks or to me, a complete unknown in the coffee store market? If you operated a small airport in some underserved part of the United States, would you try to get Southwest to start flights into your city, or me, who has no track record in the airline industry? If you are a highly skilled business professional, are you more likely to join the leading global consultancy McKinsey & Co, or an unknown consulting firm? As Dierickx and Cool point out, a company with a large stock of R&D knowhow is better placed to make further innovations than those with little prior knowledge. This is *not* to say that such leading firms can never be beaten. For various organizational reasons, firms that ought to have an innovation advantage can fail to achieve it, e.g. overcommitment to what has already been developed. It is also possible for competitors to bypass a leader's dominant resource ownership by using a substitute resource, as explained in Chapter 2.

- *Interconnectedness of asset-stocks.* In other words, building a particular resource depends on other resources already in place. Taking McKinsey once more—major organizations in global industries seek advice from this firm because they know it employs the brightest business analysis brains available, and the brightest young business brains join the firm because it serves the most important clients in global industries. This interdependence goes further. Those great brains can only do such great work because the firm has built up a powerful knowledge base of information and insight about major firms in important worldwide industries—that could only be built because McKinsey has long experience of working with that elite category of clients. This interconnectedness is crucial to explaining the performance of sector-beating firms, and will be explained in detail in the next chapter.

- *Asset erosion.* Many tangible and intangible assets deteriorate unless effort and expenditure are committed to maintaining them, i.e. resources suffer outflows. Physical plant wears out, staff skills become obsolete, attractive products lose their appeal, and brand customer loyalty decays. This threatens the competitive advantage that a firm can enjoy from its superior resources, a challenge that can vary widely for different firms in the same industry. A survey of brand managers in the beer industry, for example, estimated that decay rates for consumer brand loyalty could be as high as 50 % per year for novel, niche products, or as low as 5 % per year, for products such as Budweiser or Guinness—rather similar in magnitude to the mortality rate of their consumers! This is important because it is the *stock* of resources that provides todays advantage—physical capacity and brand loyalty, for example—not the flows, such as production output or advertizing spend.

- *Causal ambiguity.* It can be hard to determine, even for the firm that owns a resource, why exactly it accumulates and depletes at certain rates. Those rates that simply reflect management's decisions (the leftmost category in Figure 3.13) are not problematic, but the problem escalates as we move further towards the types of resource where management decisions are more distant from the resource flow and where competitive and other factors become influential. As Chapter 2 explained, much of the causality of performance outcomes may be simply arithmetical, back to the point where resources drive sales and costs. This chapter has shown that the current value of each resource is not just influenced by, but *totally* determined by resource flows over time. Explaining what causes those resource flows, then, is often where causal ambiguity is focused.

Asset-stock accumulation has a further important implication for the ability to discover causality, however. To illustrate the significance of this problem, and how it arises, consider a simple manufacturing company that wants to understand whether it should spend more or less money on marketing. It looks at its recent history and sees the patterns for marketing and operating profit shown in Figure 3.18.

The charts reflect the following history:

- The company was originally dissatisfied with its low and stagnant profits up to month six.
- A new head of marketing arrived, who persuaded the company to increase its marketing spend from month seven. This increase in expenditure immediately led to lower profits, as the increase in sales was insufficient to cover the extra cost, although profits started to recover over the following nine months.

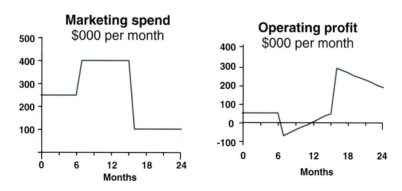

**Figure 3.18: Two-year history of marketing expenditures and profits at a simple manufacturing company.**

- In month 15, the head of finance lost patience with the situation, pointing out that the company had seen a total loss of profits over those nine months of more than half a million dollars, compared with what they could have expected from just pursuing the original low rate of marketing. He even doubted that the previous rate of marketing was necessary.
- The CEO agreed, so the company cut its marketing spend sharply from month 16. Sure enough, profits jumped as the savings in marketing spend were far greater than the value of lost sales. The head of finance was clearly correct, and pointed out to his colleagues that he had made the company over $1.5 million of additional profit over the 12 months since his recommendation, compared with the original low profit rate.

The head of marketing was feeling somewhat dejected about this. Convinced that she was right to raise marketing spend, she commissioned some industry research. The company was one of 50 near-identical firms and fortunately information on monthly marketing spend and profits was available for all of its competitors.

Figure 3.19 shows two results from comparing operating profit with marketing spend for this large sample of companies. The left-hand chart shows how operating profits in any month compare with marketing spend in the same month. The head of marketing was not at all happy with this finding, which suggested that profits were *negatively* correlated with marketing spend. On reflection, she was not too surprised, since marketing would surely take some time to have its effect, so its most significant impact in any month would be an immediate increase in cost.

Perhaps operating profits would increase some months *after* marketing is spent? She looked at how competitors' marketing spend compared with operating profits

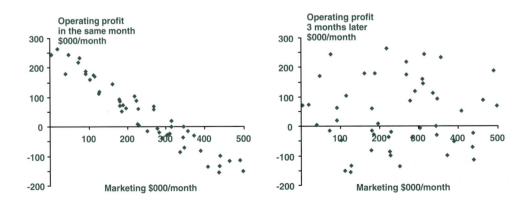

**Figure 3.19: Operating profits versus marketing spend for a large sample of simple manufacturing firms.**

three months later (right-hand chart in Figure 3.19). Disappointingly, there still seemed to be no positive correlation between marketing spend and profits—but at least the negative relationship had disappeared.

Figure 3.20 shows what was actually happening with this firm. It is a very simple business:

*operating profit = revenue − production costs − marketing spend − overhead*
*sales revenue = customers * sales per customer * unit price*
*production cost = sales in units * variable cost per unit + fixed production cost*
*customers today = customers last month + customers won − customers lost*
*sales per customer = base sales per customer + marketing spend * sales increase per marketing $*
*customers lost = five per month*
*customers won per month = marketing spend * customers won per marketing $*

If the business structure is very simple, why could the head of marketing not discover any correlation between marketing spend and profits? The problem lies at the flow-to-stock boundary. As the detail in Figure 3.21 shows, there is no obvious relationship between the number of customers in any month and the win rate of customers in that same month—nor should we be particularly surprised at the lack of such a relationship, since *today's* number of customers reflects the entire *history* of customer gains and losses.

If the head of marketing had been able to discover this data for her competitors, she would have discovered the correlation in Figure 3.22, i.e. no meaningful correlation at all.

This has profound implications that need to be recognized when seeking to explain performance outcomes:

**It is unsafe to seek correlation between possible causal factors and performance outcomes if any accumulating stock exists between that cause and outcome.**

**It is meaningless to seek correlation between asset-stocks and the flow rates that determine them.**

There *is* a correlation that the head of marketing could have implemented, which would have supported her case for higher marketing spend, namely the relationship between marketing spend and the subsequent *change* in operating profit (Figure 3.23).

This works because the profit increase reflects the *increase* in customers, i.e. the flow rate rather than the stock. Yet an important question remains. What is the

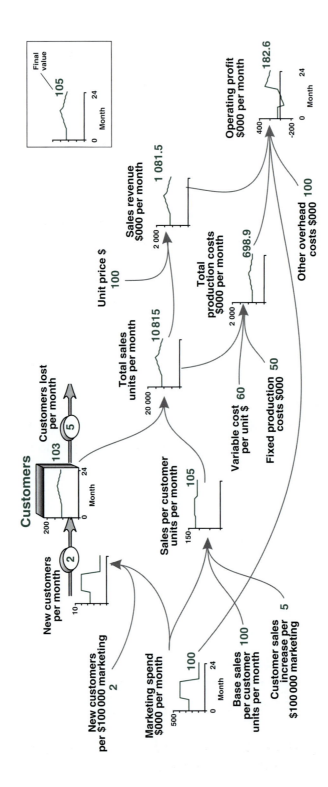

Figure 3.20: The causal structure and history of marketing and profits for the simple manufacturing firm.

**Figure 3.21: Detail of the manufacturing company's customers and current win and loss rates.**

value of the relationship in Figure 3.22 that might be confirmed using correlation methods, when the actual causal structure in Figure 3.19, and the relationships it contains are *entirely* determined? There is no ambiguity in that structure, so it provides precise explanations for the company's performance at all times.

This reasoning suggests where the origins of causal ambiguity may truly lie. It is not so much that asset-stock accumulation itself causes uncertainty—as we have seen, it is about as certain a causal mechanism as it is possible to imagine. Rather it is (a) that accumulation is not properly incorporated in hypothetical causal relationships, and (b) that the causes of resource flows are ambiguous. As Figure 3.15 shows, many factors are involved in driving the customer win rate and, though not shown in that figure, similar uncertainty surrounds the causes of customer loss rates. It therefore *is* safe—and important—to use correlation to identify the relative importance of factors determining how quickly resources are filling and draining.

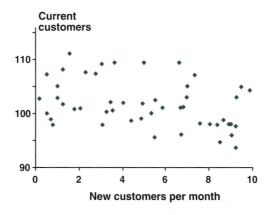

**Figure 3.22: Customers versus customer win rate across a large sample of simple manufacturing firms.**

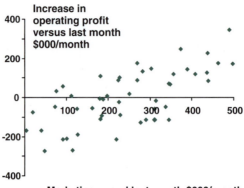

**Figure 3.23: Operating profit increase versus pervious month's marketing spend for simple manufacturing firms.**

We can focus further on where causal ambiguity arises. It is quite clear, for example, what causes cash flows to arise, products to be launched or discontinued, and physical capacity to be added or lost, i.e. all flows of inanimate assets. It is not as clear why customers are won or lost, why staff choose to join or leave us, or investors give or withdraw their support.

### Causal ambiguity is concentrated on the behavioral choices of customers, staff and other stakeholders.

It is therefore not quite accurate to locate causal ambiguity exclusively at the inflows and outflows of customers, staff and other groups of people. As the Ryanair structure illustrates, outcomes also depend on customers' purchase rate. In other circumstances, output may also depend on staff productivity. This takes us back to the two distinct behaviors of customers, staff, and so on, that must be understood: their decision to *change state* and their choice of *activity rate*.

Later chapters will also show that intangible factors such as reputation and morale have an important influence on performance—factors that again concern how people behave. It is the existence of *people* in the system that principally distinguishes business and other social systems from the deterministic behavior of manufacturing and other systems that are dominated by inanimate, physical elements.

Causal mechanisms may also be complicated by threshold effects that render the relationship between cause and effect highly nonlinear. Such thresholds can arise on both a resource's inflows and outflows. Many consumers have long liked the idea of flat-screen TV, but found the available products to be beyond their affordable range and not sufficiently functional. (One consumer magazine in 1998 commented that a certain model was not much use as a TV, but made a pretty good room heater!) Improvements in the technology and reductions in price still did not win over consumers until both reached thresholds of acceptability, at which point sales escalated sharply. Such threshold effects clearly make life difficult for researchers seeking to explain business performance, but pose very practical and serious challenges for management too, who may be taken by surprise when seemingly insignificant issues lead to sudden changes for which they are unprepared.

These and other sources of causal ambiguity are sometimes said to result in extreme complexity, and used to justify rejecting efforts to work out the best course of action. With this view, management can only learn from experience (and not much, even then), and there is little point in seeking theory about what causes what and how. However, there *are* patterns in behaviors of people, especially averaged across large groups, which make it possible for management to make choices with a substantial degree of certainty as to how those groups will behave. If this were not so, as the infinite complexity advocates would have us believe, McDonald's would have no idea how many staff would arrive for work tomorrow, Ryanair would have no idea how many customers were likely to buy flights on a new route, and Wal-Mart would have no idea what would happen to sales if it doubled its prices. While not completely certain, the important behaviors of customers, staff and other groups are sufficiently understandable in practice for a great many decisions to be made with reasonable confidence in the likely outcomes.

# RESOURCES, FLOWS AND VALUE-CHAIN ANALYSIS

Chapter 2 showed how resources dominate the cost structure of firms and therefore constitute the main factors determining the shape of an organization's value chain. Costs are not merely incurred by the existence of resources, however, but also arise from the acquisition and development of resources—hiring and training staff, marketing winning customers, developing products, etc. This implies that the distribution of the various costs within the cash flows of a business will vary from time to time, depending on which resources are growing or declining.

This phenomenon can be illustrated using another simplified business with the following profile (Table 3.7)

**TABLE 3.7: AN ILLUSTRATIVE PROFILE OF A MANUFACTURING FIRM**

| | | |
|---|---|---|
| Customers | Initially 80 | Lose five per month, win two per month per $100 000 marketing |
| Sales per customer | 80 units per month, plus 25 units per month per $100 000 marketing | |
| Unit price | $120 | |
| Sourcing costs | $7 per unit | |
| Production costs | $100 000 fixed cost, plus $25 raw materials cost per unit[8] | |
| Distribution costs | $1 000 per customer, plus $5 per unit | |
| Sales and marketing spend | Initially $100 000 per month | |
| Service staff | Initially 16 | Hire or lose one person per five customers |
| Service costs | $5 000 per person per month | $20 000 hiring + training per person |
| Overhead cost | Fixed at $100 000 per month | |

Table 3.8 gives the initial monthly profit statement for this company and Figure 3.24 shows its value-chain diagram.

The business appears to be in good shape, with a healthy 23.5 % operating profit margin on sales of just over $1 million per month. However, its sales and marketing spend of $100 000 per month means it is winning only two customers per month, while losing five. Consequently, its business is shrinking, and by month six, revenues are down to $781 200, and profits are just 12.6 % of revenue at $98 330. Its value chain now looks very different, both in scale and make-up (Figure 3.25).

This situation clearly cannot continue, so in month seven, the company makes a major increase in sales and marketing spend. Given the strong response of its customers to sales and marketing effort indicated in Table 3.7, this substantially increases current sales, but also changes the make-up of the value chain once more.

Rather than continue to show the company's value chain at particular points in time, Figure 3.26 shows the dynamics of its costs and profits over an 18-month

**TABLE 3.8: ILLUSTRATIVE EXAMPLE OF A MANUFACTURING FIRM'S INITIAL PROFIT STATEMENT**

| Sales | 8400 units per month | |
|---|---|---|
| | *$000 per month* | *Percent* |
| **Revenue $000** | 1008.0 | 100.0 |
| Sourcing cost | 58.8 | 5.83 |
| Production costs | 310.0 | 30.75 |
| Distribution costs | 122.0 | 12.10 |
| Sales and marketing spend | 100.0 | 9.92 |
| Service costs | 80.0 | 7.94 |
| Overhead cost | 100.0 | 9.92 |
| **Total costs** | 770.8 | 76.47 |
| **Operating profit** | 237.2 | 23.53 |

episode, but with costs and profits on the vertical axis and time along the horizontal axis. The large increase in sales and marketing spend in month seven clearly transforms the company's financial shape, both in absolute cash values and in fractional terms. Crucially, it not only changes the current cost and profit figures; it also changes the *trajectory* on which the company is heading. The value chain continues to change out to the end of the 18 months.

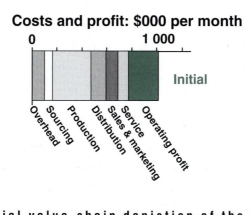

Figure 3.24: Initial value-chain depiction of the manufacturing firm's profit statement.

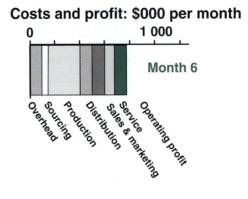

**Figure 3.25:** Value chain of the manufacturing firm after six months of decline.

This case demonstrates an important principle:

**The make-up of a company's value chain is likely to be changing, both as market and competitive conditions change and as management respond in order to improve future profits**

Examining an organization's value chain at any particular point in time may offer limited guidance for assessing its ability to build future performance.

(Online learning materials are available to support this example, see p.xxi.)

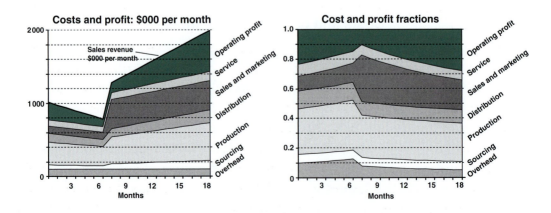

**Figure 3.26:** Changing shape of value chain for the manufacturing firm: absolute values and fractions of revenue.

## RESOURCE LEVELS AND FLOWS IN THE VALUE CHAIN

It was remarked earlier that most costs in a firm's value chain, other than raw materials, are driven either by *having* those resources (staff, capacity and other assets), or by *building* them (winning customers, hiring staff, developing products). This latest example illustrates the point. The firm's production costs include a large fixed element that would be driven by its capacity and production staff (i.e. resources), while its marketing costs are driven by the need to win customers (i.e. a resource flow). Its service function, however, shows how costs reflect both *ownership* and *growth* of a resource.

In this example, every five customers require the support of one service person. When the business is stable, both the number of service people and the cost of employing them remain constant. As the business starts, its 80 customers need 16 service staff, but since the number of customers is declining, that number falls (Figure 3.27). However, because the number of staff is proportional to the number of customers, and their purchase rate is also constant, the fraction of revenue consumed by the cost of service support is constant, at just under 8%—service staff are assumed to be lost at no cost, perhaps through normal turnover. When in month seven, management decides to increase marketing and sales effort, more customers start to be won than lost (eight versus five), so more service staff have to be taken on at the rate of 0.6 per month, or roughly one person every 2.5 weeks. This introduces an increase in total service department costs, due to the cost of hiring and training each new person (the upper section in the *service cost* charts in Figure 3.27). This would raise the fraction of revenue spent on service, were it not for the immediate jump in revenue caused by the increased marketing and sales spend. Revenue increases sharply in month seven, by a larger proportion than the increase in service costs, so the service cost *percentage* actually drops to about 6% of revenue, even allowing for the additional cost of hiring. As the business grows beyond month seven, the hiring rate and its cost remain constant and the cost of *having* a growing service team grows, but since sales also grow the percentage of revenue spent on service gradually declines.

Figure 3.28 provides a similar picture of changing cost and profit fractions for Amazon.com, from 1997 to 2005. Prior to 2003, total costs exceeded revenue and the company reported large losses. In 2000, for example, costs were nearly 140% of revenues. Only in the last three years have operating profits been achieved.

The mix of costs in Amazon.com's value chain has changed markedly as the company's growth in sales has overtaken its heavy investments of the early years. Yet the mix continues to change. Research and development may appear to be a relatively small percentage of revenue, but actually increased from 4.1% to 5.3% between 2004 and 2005, or from $283m to $451m. Had Amazon.com kept this spend unchanged, it could have delivered nearly $600m of profits in 2005, rather than the $428m it actually

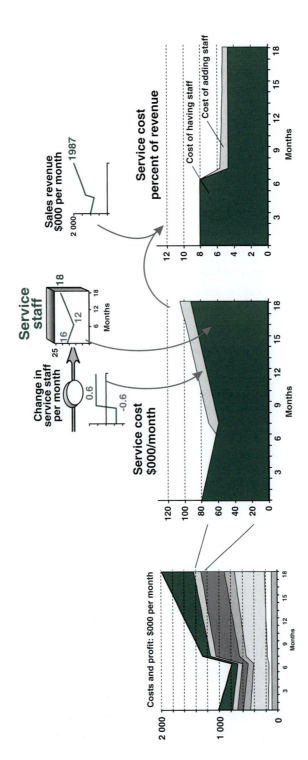

Figure 3.27: Changing costs of having and adding service staff, as the manufacturing business changes.

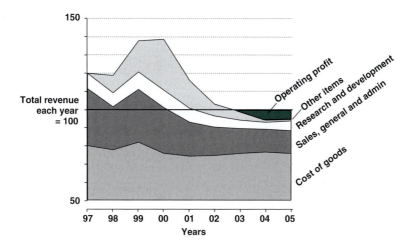

**Figure 3.28:** Amazon.com costs and profits as percentages of net revenue: 1997–2005.

delivered. Did the company lose control of its research and development costs? That is unlikely. More probable is that this increase was deliberate and intended to drive further innovation in its services, which will increase its revenues and profits in future years, leading to yet more changes in the make-up of its value chain.

# ADDING "LUMPS" OF RESOURCE

The accumulation principle has an important consequence for the behavior of resources over time. A step change in a flow rate does *not* cause a step change in the quantity of resource. It causes a change in the *trajectory* for the resource's growth or decline over time. In Figure 3.26, for example, the step change in service staff hiring does not result in a step change in staff numbers, but merely a change from a declining to a growing trend.

Growing resources continuously in this manner may not always be sufficient. Organizations sometimes need to make step shifts in resource levels, either to correct some imbalance in the system or to initiate other changes. Raising finance or launching a new range of products are actions intended to increase resource levels quickly. In other cases, resource may be *lost* quickly, either by accident (for example, when a whole team of staff leave at once) or deliberately (e.g. when a firm closes a whole group of unattractive customer accounts). Such changes are captured with the same stock-and-flow structure, but show up as a *pulse* on the flow, which causes a *step* in the stock.

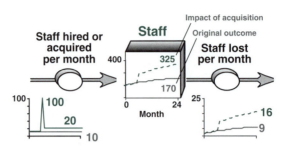

**Figure 3.29: Intended growth in staff from acquiring a similar sized organization.**

To see how this works, Figure 3.29 shows an organization trying to grow a key group of 100 staff at about 5 % per month (grey line). Its hiring of 10 each month is partly countered by an attrition rate of 5 %, or initially five people per month. As the staff group grows, however, this 5 % rate becomes an increasingly large number, so looking out to month 24, the organization can expect about 170 staff, of which about nine are lost each month.

In month six, the organization doubles in size by acquiring a similar business. The green line shows this pulse of 100 new staff, and the associated step increase in staff numbers. Thereafter, the organization doubles its previous hiring rate, so as to continue its growth. If it did not, the 5 % attrition rate would now be greater than 10 per month and the staff numbers would decline.

This approach to the capture or loss of "pulses" of resource shows that acquisitions, mergers and joint ventures are simply ways to make step increases to a number of resources simultaneously. This organization may also have acquired some additional customers, more capacity and significant additional products, for example. Complications often arise, however, because significant events such as this can affect the entire business and upset whatever balance previously existed. This kind of upset may be deliberate or accidental.

- Deliberate upset arises when the acquiring firm sees an opportunity to follow the deal with an immediate rationalization of surplus resources (typically staff, product range or fixed assets).
- In accidental cases, the acquiring organization fully intends to sustain the now larger pools of resource, such as staff, distributors or customers. However, since people are involved, and may not be pleased with the new situation, unintended outflows may be triggered.

Figure 3.30 shows what happens to the staff numbers in this example if the acquisition results in staff attrition rising from 5 % to 10 % per month. Far

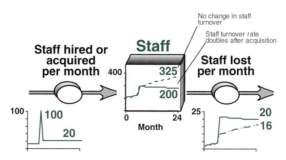

**Figure 3.30:** Impact of increased staff losses following acquisition of a similar sized organization.

from growing, the number of staff actually declines, in spite of the faster hiring rate.

Mergers of professional service firms are particularly vulnerable to this kind of difficulty for several reasons. First, people *are* their capacity, so any loss of staff hits their ability to both win clients and business and to deliver the required service. Secondly, clients often have relationships with particular individuals in the firm, especially with senior partners, so unhappy staff that leave can take clients with them. Thirdly, staff carry much of the organizational knowledge—there is a limit to how much knowledge can be captured in information systems. So staff losses damage the organization's ability not only to do the *quantity* of work required, but also to do it effectively and efficiently.

The acquisition by IT consultants Cap Gemini of accounting firm Ernst & Young's consulting business in May 2000 proved problematic. Complicated by changes the company was also making to how it organized its customer service operations, the company struggled to retain and integrate staff, pushing its North American operations into losses. An example of more successful management of this kind of merger was the 2002 IBM acquisition of the worldwide consulting business of accountants PricewaterhouseCoopers (PwC). The PwC business became available because of controversy about conflicts between the auditing and consulting services of the global accounting firms. Although PwC had not been accused of serious misconduct, clients had been shocked by the involvement of auditors/consultants Arthur Andersen in the collapse of energy giant Enron, causing 149 large clients to cease using PwC's services. IBM was already the largest worldwide provider of business and information technology services, with 150 000 staff and turnover of $35 billion. By acquiring the 30 000 staff of PwC consulting and $5bn of revenue, IBM intended to consolidate its ability, in its words "to deliver business value to clients through the integration of technology and business process insight."[9] In spite of integration difficulties, IBM was able to retain nearly all of PwC's

1 100 partners, plus most of the other 30 000 PwC employees. Furthermore, it was able to retake 99 of the 149 accounts that PwC had recently lost.[10]

## Summary of Chapter 3

Having identified that resources are a dominant factor "causing" performance outcomes over time, it is critical to know what causes the quantity of any resource to be at a given level at a particular time.

It has long been understood that resources fill up, and drain away. Consequently, the level of any resource today is the level it was yesterday, plus or minus any amount that has flowed in or out in the meantime. Today's resource level is therefore totally, and exclusively, explained by its history of gains and losses. This is an absolutely fundamental feature of how the world works and is entirely different from the instantaneous causality that occurs among other factors.

The units for resource flow rates are *always* the units of the resource itself, per time period—e.g. products launched per year, customers won per month, staff resigning per week. It is not sufficient merely to know the net increase or decrease in any resource—we need to know the gains and losses separately. Adding 10 customers or staff is not the same as adding 100 and losing 90.

Since resource flow rates are so critical to how performance changes over time, it is vital to understand what *drives* those resource flow rates. Some resource flow rates are directly under management control—e.g. adding capacity, launching new products, or spending money. Other resource flow rates depend on how people behave, and can therefore only be influenced somewhat by management decisions.

The existence of multiple segments of customers, staff, and so on, has an important impact on how the aggregate resource develops over time and must therefore often be identified and assessed.

Two distinct categories of behavior are important for people-based resources—their decision to change state (becoming a customer or ceasing to be, joining our staff or resigning), and their choice of activity rate (buying more or less often, working with more or less effort). Similar causal factors may drive both types of behavior, but to different degrees.

"Causal ambiguity" describes the problem of understanding how performance outcomes reflect the multifarious factors that could plausibly give rise to those outcomes. Since much of the causal structure of organizations' performance is logically simple, this ambiguity is mostly located at points where these two types of behavior arise.

The accumulating behavior of resources severely damages the ability of correlation methods to confirm hypotheses regarding the causes of organizations' performance. It is unsafe to use such methods in almost any situation where an accumulating resource exists between the suspected "cause" and the outcome we wish to understand.

Costs result from both *having* resources and by efforts to *build* those resources. The changing balance between these two elements, together with the need for different amounts of various resource types as an organization develops result in a constantly changing balance between its various costs. Consequently, static value-chain analysis is of limited value.

It is sometimes necessary to add resources in "lumps," rather than smoothly over time—a purpose often achieved through mergers or acquisitions. However, such events may unbalance a situation, giving rise to difficult consequences.

# SUGGESTED QUESTIONS AND EXERCISES

1.  What is the defining characteristic of resources, and why is this feature of such fundamental importance?

2.  An insurance company has 100 000 policyholders, 20 % of whom do not renew their policies each year. How many policyholders will the company have by the end of year five if it does not sell any new policies?[11]

3.  What is wrong with this sentence? "The level of sales this month is better than last month, and substantially ahead of the level needed to meet our budget for the year."

4.  Why is it important to identify separately the inflows and outflows for a resource?

5.  The insurance company above has 50 sales agents, each of whom sells 200 policies per year. How many policyholders will the company now have at the end of year five if, again, 20 % of policyholders do not renew? (Assume that only those policyholders in place at the start of each year fail to renew, and not any of those that the sales agents win during the same year.) How many agents would the company need in order to end up with the same number of policyholders with which it started (100 000)?

6.  The company has a target to reach 150 000 policyholders by the end of year 5. How many sales agents will it need to hit that target, assuming each sells at the same rate of 200 policies per year, and that 20 % of customers each year do not renew?

7.  For the sample company you identified for the Chapter 2 exercises, identify one or more resource flows that are directly under management control (i.e. whatever management wants will happen for sure), one or more where they can be somewhat confident that their desired resource flows will happen, and one or more resource flows that are heavily influenced by factors outside management control.

8.  For the same sample company, identify (a) an activity that it would prefer to have customers or staff do more of, (b) a decision to change state that the company would prefer those customers or staff to take, and (c) a decision to change state that the company would prefer those customers or staff *not* to take.

9.  Under what circumstances should management be careful about using correlation methods to discover the impact of a particular decision on company performance?

10. Why should management be careful about drawing conclusions from a one-off comparison of its cost structure (value chain) with that of its competitors?

11. For each of the resources in the sample company selected in Chapter 2, use Worksheet 3, below, to identify how its inflows and outflows have changed the quantity of that resource over time, and how that quantity might change into the future, given realistic targets for its win rate and loss rate.

# USING WORKSHEET 3

A worksheet is provided below that can be used for stage 3 of a strategy dynamics analysis. The same timescales of history and future periods should be maintained as for the performance measure in Worksheet 1 and the causal explanation of performance laid out in Worksheet 2.

Worksheet 3 should be used separately for each resource identified in Worksheet 2, as follows:

1.  Copy the time chart for the selected resource on Worksheet 2 into the resource-stock in the middle of Worksheet 3.
2.  Identify and name, precisely, the inflow and outflow that are adding to this stock of resource and depleting it, e.g. customers won, customers lost, staff hired and fired.
3.  Include in the label for each item the correct units, e.g. customers won *per quarter*, or staff lost *per month*.
4.  Fill in the time chart for each resource flow *making sure that the math is correct!* If necessary, use the simple table at the bottom of the page to make sure this is accurate.

The result should be a set of charts similar to those shown for Ryanair in Figures 3.11 and 3.12.

If you find yourself dealing with a resource for which there is more than one inflow or outflow, use the extended version of Worksheet 3b.

## TIPS

- You may not have data separately for inflow and outflow of a particular resource. In this case, complete the net flow chart only, but still make sure the math is accurate. (Do, however, attempt to identify the inflows and outflows separately, if at all possible.)
- The **my**strategy software is a more flexible and powerful method for completing the inflow and outflow analyses of Worksheet 3, and includes a special function to "derive" missing data. For example, if you know how many staff have been in place over 12 separate months, and how many have been hired, you can derive the missing loss rate. The **my**strategy software version of Worksheet 3 is available online, see p. xxi.

# WORKSHEET 3: RESOURCE INFLOWS AND OUTFLOWS

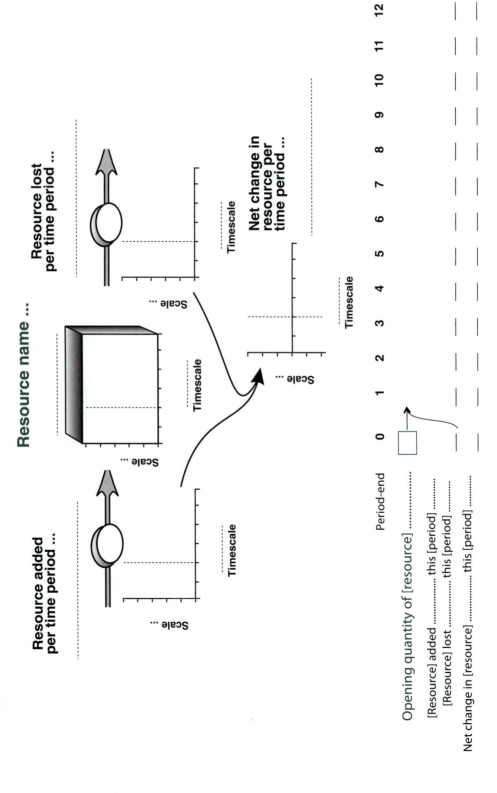

# WORKSHEET 3B: MULTIPLE RESOURCE INFLOWS AND OUTFLOWS

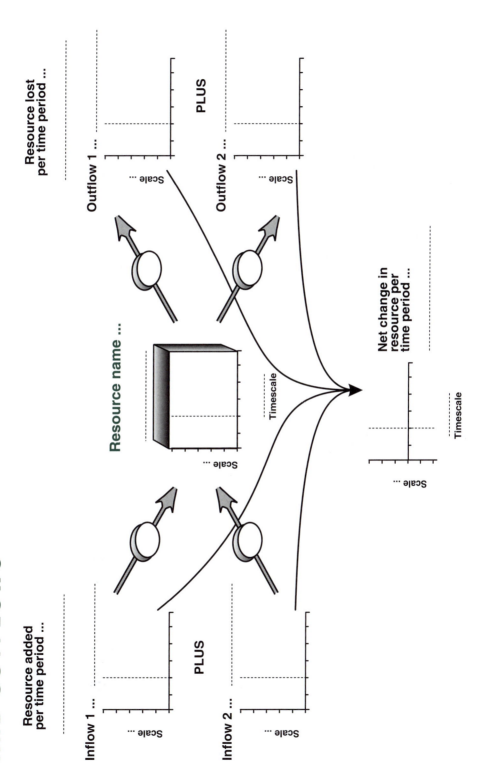

# NOTES

1.  This principle lies at the heart of a method known as system dynamics. See Forrester, J. (1961) *Industrial Dynamics*, Pegasus Communications, Waltham, MA; Sterman, J. (2000) *Business Dynamics*, Irwin/McGraw-Hill, New York.

2.  Moon, Y. and Quelch, J. (2003) *Starbucks: Delivering Customer Service.* Harvard Business School Publishing, Boston, MA.

3.  I am grateful to Lars Finskud of Vanguard Strategy Ltd for this example (www. vanguardstrategy.com).

4.  I am grateful to Aldo Zagonel-Santos and his colleagues for information on this case.

5.  Pataki, G.E. and Wing, B.J. (2002) *Welfare Reform in New York State: Effects on Work, Family Composition and Child Poverty.* New York State Office of Temporary and Disability Assistance, New York.

6.  Ryanair has a habit of achieving surprising growth rates and commentators in 2006 point out that there is plenty of potential to achieve much greater scale by 2011 than these illustrative targets imply, for example by extending operations further into Eastern Europe, the Middle East and Africa.

7.  Dierickx, I. and Cool, K. (1989) Asset stock accumulation and sustainability of competitive advantage. *Management Science,* **35**, 1504–1511.

8.  Chapter 2 explained how value-chain analysis considers the value added to the cost of raw materials but here, for simplicity of presentation, this is included within the production cost of the business.

9.  See http://news.earthweb.com/bus-news/article.php/1436271.

10. This story and the learning IBM extracted from it are reviewed extensively in Reger, S. (2006) *Can Two Rights Make a Wrong*, Prentice Hall, Upper Saddle River, NJ.

11. Online learning materials to support this example are available for instructors, see p. xxi.

# CHAPTER 4

# THE STRATEGIC ARCHITECTURE

---

## KEY ISSUES

- ✪ Complementary resources: why growth depends on existing and potential resources.
- ✪ How interdependence causes feedback that can both drive growth and constrain it.
- ✪ Mapping the interactions amongst resources to complete the "strategic architecture" that drives organizations' performance over time.
- ✪ How different organizations in related industries exhibit common core architectures.
- ✪ The causes of discontinuities and tipping points.
- ✪ Using strategic architectures with other strategy tools.

Worksheet 4: Drivers of Resource Win and Loss rates.

Worksheet 5: The Core Strategic Architecture.

This chapter makes connections to the following frameworks and concepts: the Bass diffusion model, tipping points, issue tree analysis, value drivers, balanced scorecard, strategy maps.

---

Our attempts to explain how organizations' performance changes over time has so far identified that current performance depends on resources, external factors and certain management choices (Chapter 2), and that the current level of each resource depends on historic rates of gain and loss that cause them to accumulate and deplete (Chapter 3). We are left needing to explain what causes those resources to grow or decline at their particular rates. Chapter 3 started to explore this question, identifying that some of the same factors causing current performance are also involved in resource flow rates: price causes customers to be won and lost, for example, as well as affecting how much current customers buy, and working conditions cause staff to leave us, as well as determining the productivity of staff currently in place.

This is an incomplete answer, however, because some of those causal factors themselves need to be explained—what causes working conditions to be attractive, for example—and because it leaves out other factors that must be important, such as competition. To complete the picture, it is necessary to return to the discipline adopted in Chapter 2, and step back along the logical chain of causality, to see what lies at the start of that chain. Carrying out this next step reveals that:

Three categories of factor determine the rate at which any resource increases or declines:

- management decisions
- competitive and other external factors
- the existing levels of resources already in place

Chapter 3 already showed that some resource flows simply *are* management decisions—adding capacity or borrowing cash, for example. Other decisions may only have partial influence on flows, in combination with other factors. Figure 3.16 in Chapter 3 showed the "value curve" items determining airline Ryanair's ability to win customers, to retain customers and to persuade customers to fly frequently. Those value curve items included fares, choice of destinations, range of add-on services, and reliability. The three categories of factor influencing resource flow rates can be illustrated by focusing on just one part of this structure—the winning of new customers—and tracing the causality back through these items.

## MANAGEMENT DECISIONS

It is no surprise that price plays an important role in the ability of a low-fare airline to attract new customers. Figure 4.1 shows the history of the company's average fares from 1995 to 2006, and its estimated customer win rate over that period. Of course, other factors have also played a major role in determining that win rate, especially its opening of new routes to gain access to new potential customers. However, had its price followed a different path, perhaps sustaining its highest level of something over €50 per flight, its customer win rate would certainly have been different. Critically, that also means the company would have a different *quantity* of regular customers today, and very different revenues and profits, even if all other factors had remained unchanged.

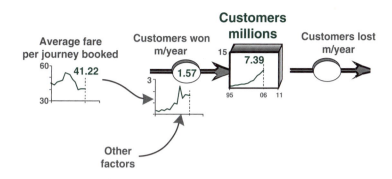

**Figure 4.1: Ryanair's choice of price levels drives its customer win rate.**

## COMPETITIVE FACTORS

Customers are likely to be attracted to any service offering lower fares, but Ryanair may not be alone in offering much cheaper flights. Also, the full-service airlines have not ignored the threat from low-fare rivals, and have themselves lowered prices. So although Ryanair's low prices have led to its winning new customers, this success has also required that those prices be as attractive as its competitors. This particular company is very aggressive in its pricing, so although detailed data are not available on competitor fares for comparable routes and services, it is reasonable to expect that Ryanair has maintained a price advantage over most of its history. Figure 4.2 illustrates the fare differential versus competitors, as well as how the company's own fares might have worked to drive its customer win rate.

Similar structures would depict competitive comparisons on other issues of importance to would-be customers, such as choice of destinations and range of services.

# INTERDEPENDENCE: RESOURCE FLOWS DEPEND ON EXISTING RESOURCE LEVELS

The third category of factors driving the inflow and outflow of resources is of such importance that it deserves extended attention. Chapter 2 explained the reasons why resources are important to performance (where "performance" concerns sales and profits), but pointed out that explanations of performance cannot ignore resources that are neither rare nor difficult for other organizations to imitate. One criterion in the resource-based view of strategy for determining whether resources are important

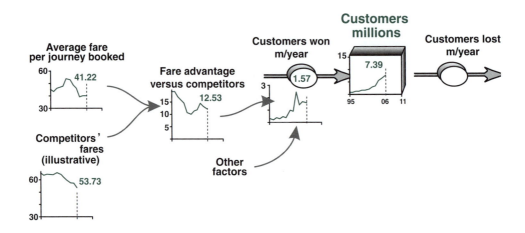

**Figure 4.2: Competitors' price levels also influence Ryanair's customer win rate.**

was not, however, examined at that point—namely the extent to which they are complementary, i.e. work well together.[1,2] This issue is critical and quite familiar to management. It is clearly not sufficient, for example, for a company to have products its customers might value if it does not have the sales capability to bring those products to their attention, and it may lead to trouble for a company to win customers if it lacks the physical capacity to produce the volume of product they need.

Chapter 3 explained further the unique characteristics of accumulating asset-stocks[3] (including resources) and some of the resulting consequences. Two features of accumulating resources' role in determining performance, however, remain unexplored. First, there is the tendency of certain resources to be easier to acquire when there is already a substantial quantity in place—so-called "asset-mass efficiency." Secondly, there is the issue that asset-stocks are interconnected. If we trace back the causal logic of why a resource flow is running at a certain rate at a particular time, both of these features can be identified.

## Growth of a resource may depend on its own current level.

The simplest mechanism by which resource flows depend on existing resource levels is when that dependency is on the same resource. The most common examples concern word-of-mouth effects, when existing customers recommend products or services to others. This becomes apparent if, when we want to know what has caused the total customer win rate during a certain period, we find that a fraction of those new customers were influenced by recommendations they received. The rate of those recommendations must reflect the number of *existing* customers.

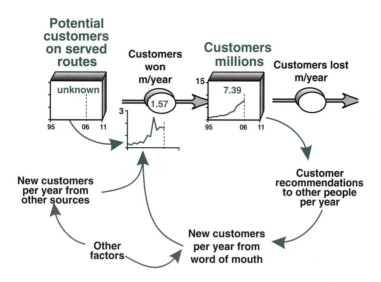

**Figure 4.3:** Part of Ryanair's customer win rate is caused by recommendations from existing customers.

Figure 4.3 demonstrates this causal chain for Ryanair's customer growth. Note that for this causal mechanism to function, other factors also must be satisfactory (e.g. attractive fares). For completeness, the picture must also include customers won from other sources.

Note that in this figure and others that follow, our aim is to *explain the flow rate*, and that tracing back along the green causal links ends up back at one or more *existing resource levels.*

Such self-dependency between resources and their own growth rate can apply to resources other than customers. It is common, for example, for people who enjoy their jobs to recommend that their friends seek employment with the same organization. Nor need such mechanisms rely on active communication between existing resources and those who may be won. Airport operators who welcome requests by Ryanair to start services from their airport need not have had conversations with existing airports served by the company, because they can readily see the passenger traffic the airline brings.

### Resource growth may depend on the existing levels of other resources.

The final part of the causal explanation for resource flow rates completes both the key mechanism in the resource-based view of strategy and performance—that resources should be "complementary"—and the interconnectedness that features among accumulating asset-stocks. If we trace back what causes the current rate of

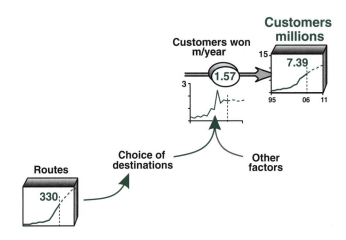

**Figure 4.4: Ryanair's customer win rate depends on the number of routes it operates.**

any particular resource flow, we frequently find at the start of that causal chain the existing level of *other* resources.

Figure 4.4 shows that Ryanair's customer win rate depends in part on the choice of destinations available, which in turn depends on the number of routes the airline operates. The choice of destinations available to a particular individual at a location is not a simple function of the number of routes, since many more destinations are offered from some locations (such as Dublin), than from others (Oslo, for example). Nevertheless, adding destinations clearly increases the number of people who may fly with the airline. Ryanair needs to consider whether adding a particular route will attract enough new customers to be commercially viable.

Note that the dependency here traces back to *routes* rather than *airports*. This is because the airline has many options to add further routes among the network of airports it already operates. Its decision to add a new route is therefore separate from, but enabled by, any earlier decision to add another airport to its network—another case of a resource *flow rate* (opening new routes) depending on the *existing* stock of resources (airports served and routes already offered).

### Loss of a resource depends on its own current level and may depend on the level of other resources.

Customers are lost for many reasons, including the activities of competitors. However, before blaming outside forces, it is useful to check that the organization has not brought about its own loss of this important resource. Frequently, the ability to retain a resource depends directly on the adequacy of other resources, the most common mechanism being when poor service quality reflects inadequate numbers

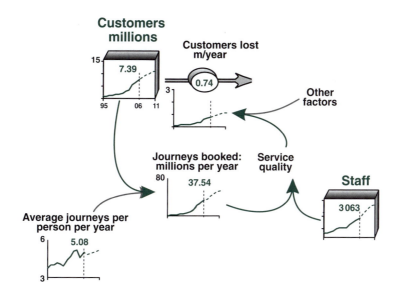

**Figure 4.5: Ryanair's customer loss rate depends on the current number of customers and staff.[4]**

of staff. Figure 4.5 demonstrates how this mechanism would work for Ryanair. We have estimated that the airline might have over 7 million customers, making over 37 million journeys per year. Those journeys create demands on airline staff, especially for check-in and inflight service. If there are too few service staff, customers will experience poor service—delayed check-in, late departures, and so on—which will cause a fraction of those customers to decide not to use the airline again in the future. The stock of customers is then reduced by this loss rate.

This structure is common in many situations and has important properties:

- We do not say here that the customer loss rate *may* depend on the current number of customers—it *does* depend on that number. At the most basic level, a company can only lose customers that it has. If the number approaches zero, no customers are lost due to poor service or for any other reason.
- There is a threshold for staff capacity to cope with customer demand. The approximately 3 063 staff may be able to handle 35 million passenger-journeys per year, but not 40 million. Provided that customer numbers remain below about 7 million, service quality is fine, and losses due to poor service are negligible; if customer numbers cross that threshold, staff become increasingly unable to cope, and loss rates escalate. Thresholds of this kind are a further obstacle to discovering the causes of organizations' performance, and add further to the limited value of correlation methods for such purposes discussed in Chapter 3.

● This structure is self-correcting. If poor service drives customers away, customer numbers and journeys booked will drop, until a level is reached at which staff capacity is once again sufficient. Happily, customer service is satisfactory once again, although the reason for that good news may not be so welcome. This phenomenon seems remarkably common in real-world cases. This raises the intriguing question as to whether management is commonly satisfied with limited growth caused by their own choice to provide inadequate resources, even when considerably greater growth potential exists.

Structures similar to Figure 4.5 account for other causes of customer loss. The number of aircraft limits the frequency of flights that can be offered, so any attempt to offer more than that frequency will result in delays and cancellations. Those problems will affect a fraction of current customers, who may then decide not to use the airline again. Unlike the capacity of service staff, there may be no threshold in this case. Customers are affected by delays, even if the aircraft is half empty, so losses could continue down to very low numbers of customers.

Figure 4.6 brings together the mechanisms discussed above to depict some of the major mechanisms likely to account for Ryanair's gains and losses of customers, and extends the data from actual historical values to plausible future trajectories. The diagram shows how the growth of resources outlined in Chapter 2

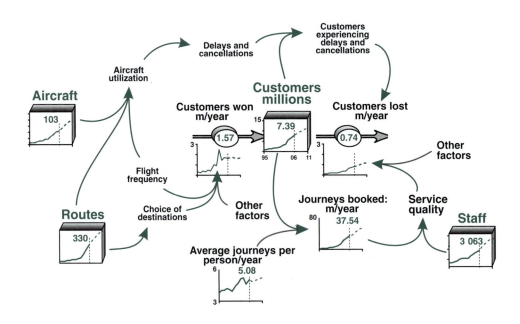

**Figure 4.6:** How Ryanair's customer win and loss rates depend on the existing level of certain resources.

(Figure 2.29) come together to hit the "preferred" sales projection in terms of *journeys booked.*

The green causal chains in Figures 4.3 to 4.6 show the critical principle that accounts for interdependency and complementarity among resources:

**The current *rate* at which any resource is won or lost frequently depends on the existing *level* of other resources and of that resource itself.**

The main exceptions to this mechanism arise when a resource flow depends solely on a management decision, e.g. adding capacity, as described in Chapter 3.

**A simple exercise where word-of-mouth feedback interacts with capacity constraints**

The interaction between self-reinforcing growth amongst customers and constraints imposed by limited capacity can be explored in a simple model concerning an illustrative new cellphone business, as shown in Figure 4.7.

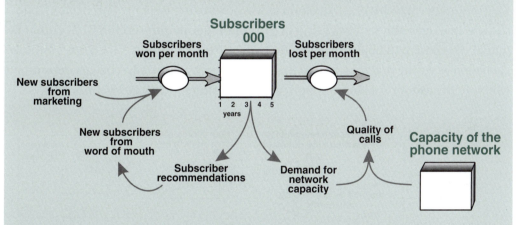

**Figure 4.7: Structure for growth of an illustrative cellphone business with network capacity constraints.**

The business has a simple income statement, with revenue from new subscribers as well as calls made by existing subscribers, and costs driven by marketing, capacity and the acquisition of new subscribers. Even so, the model illustrates the challenge of trying to optimize profit growth by balancing customer acquisition with increases in investment.

(Online learning materials are available to support this example, see p.xxi.)

Dell Computers is a case that illustrates the potential for service capacity to damage an otherwise powerful business growth system. Long admired as a seemingly unstoppable leader in PC supply, with its ultra-efficient production systems and direct-supply logistics,[5] the company lost its top rating for customer service after moving much of its call center support to offshore locations and employing large numbers of part-time staff. As Michael Dell put it, "The team was managing cost instead of managing service and quality."[6] Fixing this problem required hiring literally thousands of staff, at a cost of over $100 million per year.

## THE IMPACT OF POTENTIAL RESOURCES

The final dependency of resource flows concerns resources that have not been visible up to now, namely *potential* resources. Organizations are often constrained in their ability to develop because they run out of potential—they cannot find more customers who are not already buying from them or their competitors, or key staff in their industry prove to be scarce. In Figure 4.8, advertizing is attracting a potential market of 500 000 customers. An advertizing spend of $2 million per month is needed to reach all potential consumers, and this reach declines as less advertizing is spent. This decline is not a straight line, however, so advertizing of $1 million per month reaches 61 % of that potential. Of those potential customers that advertizing reaches, 5 % become customers each month. As the potential is used up, however, even a large advertizing commitment can only attract ever smaller numbers, and the customer win rate declines

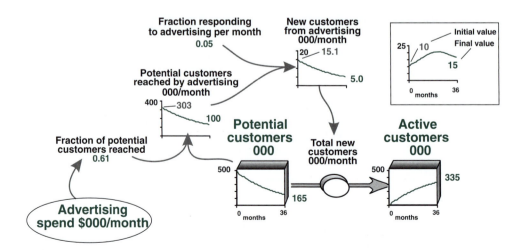

Figure 4.8: Declining customer win rate as a potential population is used up.

Eventually, the potential market is so small that advertizing is completely ineffective. One might wonder, then, why companies such as Coca-Cola or Heinz continue heavily advertizing products that seem to have used up their market. These cases feature several mechanisms not captured in Figure 4.8. First, customers tend to lose interest in products and slip back out of the *actual customers* stock. Second, there are often competing products, and therefore a third place for consumers to be—in the competitors' stock. Then there is a constant feed of new consumers as each new year, groups of consumers start to buy the kind of product these companies offer. Finally, there may be potential to persuade active customers to purchase more of the product.

How potential customers constrain growth is somewhat complicated in Ryanair's case, because the company itself adds constantly to that potential by its rapid opening of new routes. If it were to stop adding new routes, its success in winning potential customers on routes already served would soon have captured just about every customer who might like to fly, and its growth would be seriously limited. Given that our aim is to be able to calculate or estimate the customer win rate, we cannot fulfill this aim if analysis does not take into account this number of potential customers (the green link in Figure 4.9). Only in situations where the potential is so vast that any likely win rate will not significantly alter that potential can the potential customers resource be ignored.

Ryanair's actual growth is so significant because every newly opened route brings with it a new population of potential customers—the company is constantly refilling the left-hand stock in Figure 4.9. The potential is also being refilled by underlying growth in both the desire of consumers to fly and their ability to do so as incomes and free time increase. In some cases, growth in this potential can be extremely

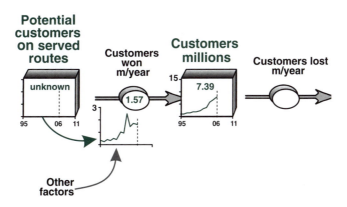

**Figure 4.9: How Ryanair's customer win rate is constrained by the limited number of potential customers.**

rapid, even without any action by the business. Growth in demand for cellphones in China, for example, has been fueled by a rapid increase in the number of potential subscribers, as incomes rise. Demand for many software products and online services is enabled by increasing numbers of potential customers as PC ownership and broadband access rise.

Chapter 2 highlighted the need for executives to focus less on market share, and more on "opportunity share"—how much of the feasible potential for their products or services they have developed and captured, and how quickly they can capture the maximum share of the remaining potential. Such attention to what might be possible can sometimes yield surprising results. For example, Professor C.K. Prahalad has examined the possibility for companies to alleviate poverty in low-income economies, yet do so profitably.[7,8]

Limited potential among customers is not the only constraint to growth that organizations face. Limited potential staff can also cause difficulties. Such limitations may be quite local. One company that decided to locate a customer service call center in a town with high unemployment found itself well able to staff its operations—until success in growing its business required so many new staff that it could not hire enough people in that locality. Ultimately, it had to open a second call center elsewhere.

On the other hand, limited staff potential can be a global problem. The Royal Dutch/Shell oil company wanted to restore its reputation in exploration and production in 2005. After a controversy over its reporting of oil reserves, it announced a drive to hire 1000 experienced petroleum engineers. Following many years of underrecruitment in the industry, combined with young graduates choosing other careers, all oil companies faced both a shortage of such staff and an aging workforce, the average age rising to 48. Industry commentators and rival companies alike expected that the company would find it extremely difficult to find so many experienced staff. Note that, in this case, the company is regarding as potential staff those who currently work for competitors, a feature that can readily give rise to a "war for talent" within an industry.[9] This issue will be examined further in Chapters 5–7.

This section has added the third principle to the emerging theory of performance:

1. **Performance depends on resources.**
2. **Resources accumulate and deplete.**
3. **Resource accumulation and depletion depend on existing resource levels.**

Statements 1 and 3 need to be extended somewhat to recognize that both current performance and current resource accumulation and depletion rates also depend on (a) management decisions regarding key factors under their control, such as price, and (b) exogenous factors, such as competitors' decisions and market conditions. This allows us to formalize the principles as follows:

> Performance, $P$, at time $t$ is a function of the quantity of resources $R_1$ to $R_n$, discretionary management choices, $M$, and exogenous factors, $E$, at that time.

$$P(t) = f[R_1(t), .. R_n(t), M(t), E(t)] \tag{1}$$

> The current quantity of each resource $R_i$ at time $t$ is its level at time $t$-$1$ plus or minus any resource flows that have occurred between $t$-$1$ and $t$.

$$R_i(t) = R_i(t-1) +/- \Delta R_i(t-1 .. t) \tag{2}$$

> The change in quantity of $R_i$ between time $t$-$1$ and time $t$ is a function of the quantity of resources $R_1$ to $R_n$ at time $t$-$1$, including that of resource $R_i$ itself, on management choices, $M$, and on exogenous factors $E$ at that time.

$$\Delta R_i(t-1 .. t) = f[R_1(t-1),.. R_n(t-1), M(t-1), E(t-1)] \tag{3}$$

(Note that for this set of equations to be accurate, the time period must be sufficiently short for the change $\Delta R_i(t$-$1 .. t)$ to be small, relative to the scale of resource $R_i$. Since our purpose is to explain performance *today*, we must explain resource quantities today, which depend on those quantities *yesterday*. It is equally true that resource quantities *tomorrow* will be equal to the quantities today plus or minus the rate at which they are currently changing, i.e. $-R_i(t+1) = R_i(t) +/- \Delta R_i(t .. t+1)$.)

## THE BASS DIFFUSION MODEL

A particularly useful framework arises when the saturation of a limited opportunity combines with word-of-mouth communication between already active customers and potential customers. The mechanism explaining how customers "diffuse" from potential to active was identified and specified in a 1969 article by Professor Frank Bass,[10] hence the framework's title. Although initially focused on how durable products become adopted, i.e. products that last a long time after their initial purchase before being replaced, the principle can be widened to deal with both consumable and durable products.

As in Figure 4.8, advertizing is the direct factor under the discretion of management for attracting potential customers. In addition, potential customers are persuaded to buy a product by talking to or observing actual customers. Consider a market with the following characteristics:

- Potential customers = 500 000 (Initial customers or owners = 0.)
- Advertizing required to reach all potential customers = $2 million per month (lower spending reaches a progressively smaller fraction of potential customers).
- Maximum contacts per month between potential and actual customers = two times per month. Up to that point, contact frequency per potential customer reflects the proportion of the total population who are already actual customers.
- Two percent of potential customers reached by advertizing become new customers each month (a lower fraction than the 5% assumed in Figure 4.8).
- Five percent of potential customers who come into contact with actual customers become new customers each month.

Figure 4.10 shows how customers in this market develop, going through what is known as "S-shaped growth," because the chart of active customers looks like an elongated "S." Initially, advertizing is the only factor driving the customer win rate, as there are no active customers for potential customers to talk with or observe. As potential customers are used up, advertizing effectiveness declines as before, but now potential customers are also made aware of the product by contact with active

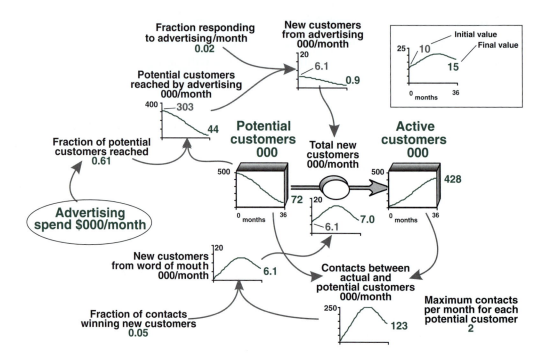

**Figure 4.10:** The Bass diffusion model of new product uptake. (Online learning materials are available to support this example, see p.xxi.)

customers. While the active customer base is growing fast and the potential is still large, this word-of-mouth effect wins customers increasingly fast. Eventually, however, so few potential customers remain that this rate also declines, even though there is a large number of active customers. The word-of-mouth win rate also starts to decline, along with the advertizing-driven win rate.

Exactly what pattern of customer win rate this model exhibits over time depends heavily on several factors—the size of the potential market, the relationship between advertizing spend and potential customers reached, the contact frequency between active and potential customers, and the fractions of people contacted who are converted into active customers. What makes this model especially useful is that, unlike other forecasting techniques, it is able to anticipate a reversal of sales. This occurs in month 19, when *total new customers* hits a peak of nearly 16 000 per month. It is therefore possible to assess the impact of *changing* advertizing rates as the product's uptake develops. It might make sense, for example, to start with heavy advertizing to get some active customers quickly, then cut back on advertizing and allow the word-of-mouth mechanism to do the work of winning new customers. (Online learning materials are available to support this example, see p.xxi.)

## CONSUMABLE VERSUS DURABLE PRODUCTS

Chapter 2 noted the need to be careful about the principle that *customers drive sales*, since for durable products, sales volume and revenue arise from the winning of the customer, rather from holding the customer into the future. The stock of active customers is then an "installed base" of product owners, who may not generate any continuing sales revenue at all until the next time they replace the product. In contrast to highly durable products, such as cookers, other products are semi-durable — they are replaced relatively frequently, but not repeatedly consumed, e.g. sports shoes. Figure 4.11 shows how sales and revenues play out over 36 months for durable, semi-durable and consumable products with the characteristics in Table 4.1.

**TABLE 4.1: CHARACTERISTICS OF ILLUSTRATIVE DURABLE, SEMI-DURABLE AND CONSUMABLE PRODUCTS**

|  | Durable | Semi-durable | Consumable |
|---|---|---|---|
| Fraction of customers repurchasing per month | Zero | 0.1 | 1.0 |
| Implied repurchase frequency | Never | 10 months | monthly |
| Unit price | $1 000 | $100 | $10 |

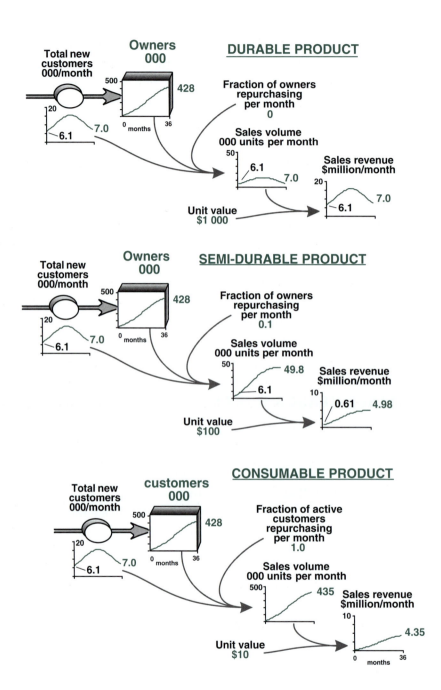

Figure 4.11: Sales outcomes from durable, semi-durable and consumable products in the Bass framework.

There are two details of this comparison to note. First, the durable product is "never" replaced. This extreme case is not realistic for actual products of course, since all wear out eventually. However, it approaches reality for very long-lived products, such as swimming pools. Second, the repurchase frequency for the semi-durable product is not shown as a simple delay in which, for example, people buy the product today and repurchase in exactly 10 months. Rather, 10 % of owners repurchase each month, even from the start. A fixed-delay scenario would produce slightly different results.

Note that cases where the sale of durable products is followed by the sale of consumables that customers subsequently require, operate somewhat differently than the situations distinguished in Figure 4.11. Companies that provide printers and ink cartridges or elevators and elevator service enjoy two separate streams of revenue. The first comes from the durable product (printer or elevator), and will follow the durables model above, while the second (ink or elevator service) follows the consumables model. While such companies would clearly like the consumables revenue to share the installed base of *owners* arising from the durables sale, this cannot always be guaranteed, as demonstrated by the sale of compatible ink cartridges by competing companies. In elevator service, manufacturing companies can often capture continuing revenue by servicing rivals' elevators—Schindler maintaining Otis elevators, for example.

The Bass Diffusion model can be found in numerous real-world situations, and can be extended in many ways to capture the richness of more complex situations than discussed here. For example, the potential customer stock can be divided between "early adopters"—customers who are particularly keen to try new products and respond strongly both to advertizing and to observing other early adopters with the product—and late adopters or followers who only respond when products are well established. There may indeed be several categories of potential customer, each of which responds at a different rate.[11] The model can also be extended to deal with complex issues, such as pricing, product functionality, R&D investments and the timing of new product introductions.[12]

# FEEDBACK EFFECTS ARISING FROM INTERDEPENDENCE

The dependence of resource flow rates on the current levels of existing resources gives rise to a critically important phenomenon: feedback. Feedback comes in two different flavors:

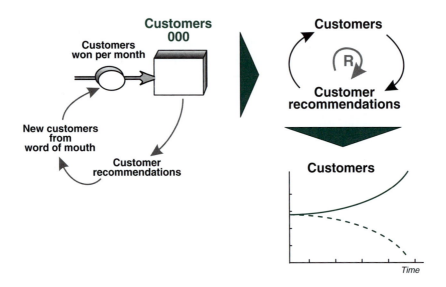

**Figure 4.12: Illustrative reinforcing feedback depiction of word of mouth, and its claimed behaviors.**

- "reinforcing" feedback, in which an initial change in a resource has consequences that continue to push change in the same direction—if the initial change is upwards, then further growth follows
- "balancing" feedback, in which an initial change in a resource has consequences that act to counter that change

We have seen examples of both these kinds of feedback already, in the example of growth for a cellphone business (Figure 4.7). Figure 4.12 offers a generalized depiction of the left-hand section of that model, where word-of-mouth feedback drives growth. Rather than make the *customers* resource explicit, the feedback diagram traces a simplified picture of "what causes what," and adds the "R" in the center to indicate that this feedback loop reinforces its own change. If customers start to increase, more recommendations result, which increases the number of customers further. If it were a true reinforcing structure, a decline in customers would initiate an accelerating decline, as shown in the dashed line of the time chart.

Similarly, the right-hand section of the cellphone subscribers' model can be generalized as shown in Figure 4.13. The feedback loop at right suggests that growth in customers leads to poorer service quality, which causes customers to be lost, countering—or "balancing"—the initial growth. If the situation starts with more customers than its capacity can handle, the system triggers decline (dashed line in the time chart), until the system comes into balance. Since the system behavior

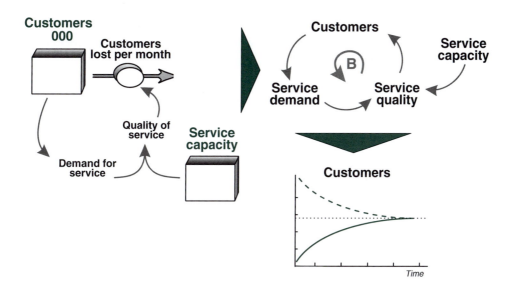

**Figure 4.13: Illustrative balancing feedback depiction of capacity constraints, and its goal-seeking behavior.**

appears to seek out a balance between customer numbers and service capacity, its behavior is referred to as "goal seeking."

Combining these simplified causal loops in various ways enables a quick depiction of many complex situations, resulting in causal loop diagrams (CLDs) of management challenges. Examining these CLDs over a wide variety of cases has identified a number of common structures or "archetypes," which show characteristic behaviors, such as limits-to-growth and success-to-the-successful, in which an organization with an initial advantage accrues further advantages that exacerbate its leadership.

Causal loop analysis based on these principles has become popularized in an approach to problem structuring known as "systems thinking."[13] It is also established as a professional process for mapping problem situations as a precursor to building system dynamics simulation models.[14]

Whilst systems thinking is a quick and powerful means of gaining a qualitative overview of many challenges facing organizations, care is needed in applying the approach. First, the behaviors of the underlying feedback loops are not quite as simple as they seem. In Figure 4.12, for example, while the self-reinforcing growth behavior of the causal loop is quite feasible, there is not any mechanism for the structure to decline. Fewer customers may indeed lead to fewer recommendations, but that implies slower *growth*, not decline. Similarly, the causal loop in Figure 4.13

includes no mechanism for growth, so it cannot exhibit the behavior shown in the solid line of the time chart. Both of these CLDs lack important additional causal mechanisms if they are to produce the behaviors shown. Second, being a qualitative approach, it can be difficult to retain a clear connection between the structures that emerge and the *quantitative* behavior of performance over time that management is seeking to understand and control.

# THE STRATEGIC ARCHITECTURE

Having established the main considerations concerning the drivers of resource inflow and outflow rates, we are now in a position to add these principles to those from earlier chapters in order to assemble a complete diagnosis of a business system. To do this, we will start with a simple case concerning the launch and growth of a consumer brand, such as a premium coffee product. This case will not concern itself with production or distribution issues, but solely with the sale of products into stores and the capture of consumer interest in the brand. For this, three resources are involved:

- consumers, of whom there are 3 million potentially available
- retail stores, of which there are 20 000 potentially available
- the salesforce, which starts at zero

Management has three controls over this situation:

- advertizing spend, to capture consumers' interest
- salesforce hiring
- wholesale price (i.e. the price charged to stores, who add a percentage mark-up to set the retail price to consumers)

After four years of sales and marketing efforts from its initial launch, the brand's sales and profit statement is as shown in Table 4.2.

The following paragraphs outline the analysis that explains how the product arrived at this position.

### 1. Performance depends on resources

The history of the brand's relatively unsuccessful profit growth is shown in Figure 4.14. Constant advertizing of $500 000 per month, and sales effort that built up over the first two years, were unable to drive sales growth quickly enough to generate gross profits that would recover those sales and advertizing costs until well into the third year. Even after this breakeven point was reached, sales growth slowed

> **TABLE 4.2: SALES AND PROFIT STATEMENT FOR A CONSUMER BRAND**
>
> | | | |
> |---|---|---|
> | Consumers interested 000 | 1 448 | |
> | Consumption per person (constant) | 0.8 | units/month |
> | Salesforce | 50 | |
> | Stores stocking the brand | 5 682 | |
> | Product availability | 0.60 | fraction of consumers able to find the product |
> | Sales volume | 691 | 000 units per month |
> | | $000/month | |
> | Sales revenue | 6 220 | . . . at a wholesale price of $9.00 |
> | Product cost | (4 838) | . . . at a unit cost of $7.00 |
> | Gross profit | 1 382 | |
> | Advertizing spend | (500) | |
> | Salesforce cost | (250) | . . . at $5 000 per person per month |
> | Brand profit | 632 | |
>
> *Note: rounding of values causes small discrepancies.*

and by month 48 is nearly flat. It will take some years more before the losses of the product's launch period are recovered. The product's sales history is explained in Figure 4.15.

Although the number of interested consumers increased relatively well at first, the product was in very few stores. Only after the number of stores stocking the brand started to grow did availability rise to levels that enabled most consumers to purchase the product. The principle that "resources drive performance" is rather simple here:

- sales depend on consumers and stores
- costs depend on the number of sales people

## 2. Resources accumulate and deplete

Figure 4.16 shows the brand's history of resource development. After an initial rapid acquisition of consumers, growth has been slow. Note that the

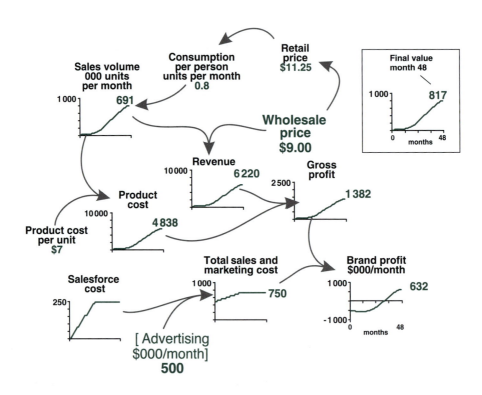

Figure 4.14:  Slow development of profits for a consumer product.

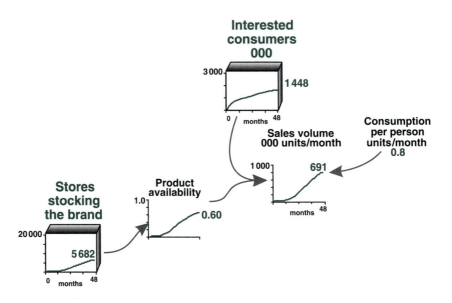

Figure 4.15:  Sales growth for the consumer product reflects consumer interest and availability in stores.

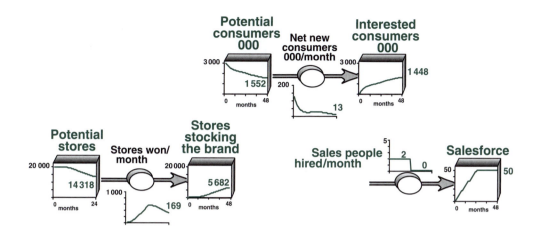

Figure 4.16: Resource development for the consumer brand.

flow is the *net* change in numbers of interested consumers, and it will be important to identify whether consumers have been lost at the same time as others have been won. Indeed, it may be that the brand's advertizing has done a fine job of winning consumers, only to see them quickly forgetting it again.

After a slow start, the store acquisition rate picked up quite well, but started to slow again halfway through the four-year period. Although growth continued, it was at a progressively slower rate. The salesforce grew simply in line with the hiring rate until it had reached 50 people.

### 3. Resource growth depends on the current level of existing resources and management decisions

In this illustrative case there are no direct competitive or exogenous forces to worry about—consumers are won from a fragmented market. This would not be true in a real market for premium coffee, where specific competitor reaction would be substantial. Apart from the direct lever of salesforce hiring, the other management decision that affects resource growth is advertizing (Figure 4.17).

Initially, this advertizing is the main factor driving consumers to become interested in the product.[15] However, its success is enhanced, constrained or negated by four distinct influences from current resource levels. The causal chain for each of these can be traced in Figure 4.17.

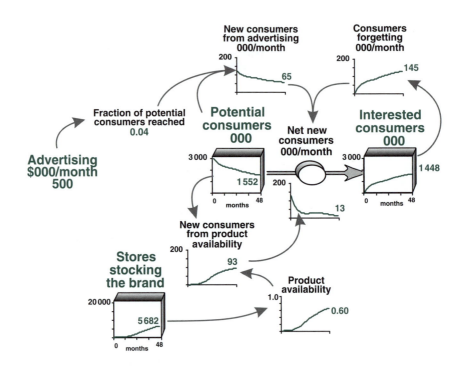

**Figure 4.17: Current resource levels determine growth of consumers interested in the brand.**

- As people become interested in the product, the falling number of potential consumers who remain to be won constrains the advertizing-driven win rate, which therefore declines.

- As the number of stores increases, the product's availability in those stores raises the consumer win rate. However, this win rate is constrained by the falling number of potential consumers. The rising number of stores sustains this source of growth in spite of the diminishing potential, although this win rate would ultimately start to decline.

- A fraction of consumers forget the brand each month, so as more consumers become interested, this fraction represents an increasingly large number of lost consumers, partly negating the two growth drivers.

Note that in this case, there is not believed to be a significant word-of-mouth feedback effect from the existing number of interested consumers driving further consumer acquisition.

Figure 4.18 shows how stores are won and highlights four dependencies on existing resource levels:

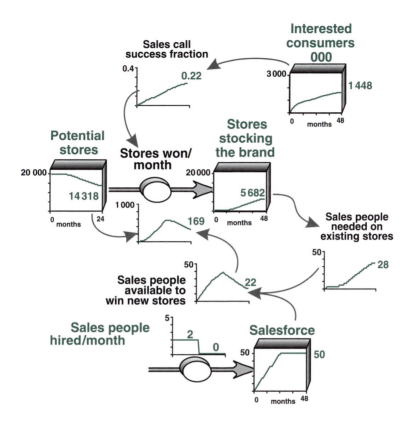

**Figure 4.18:** Current resource levels determine growth of stores stocking the brand.

- Stores can only be won if called on by sales people, so the size of the salesforce is clearly a direct driver of this win rate.
- Those calls will only be successful if a sufficient number of consumers are interested in the product to make it likely that stores will achieve significant retail sales. Therefore, the number of interested consumers constrains growth of stores.
- As more stores are captured, sales people have to spend more time maintaining relationships with those stores, leaving less time for winning new relationships. Therefore, the existing stock of stores also constrains the win rate.
- The remaining stock of potential stores remains sufficiently large that it does not significantly constrain the number of stores sales people can call upon, although the salesforce's success declines somewhat since the most promising prospects are pursued first.

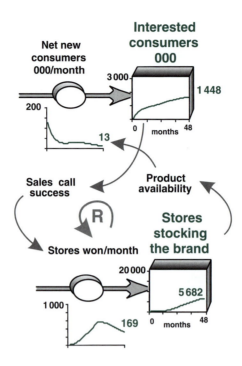

**Figure 4.19:** **Reinforcing feedback between a brand's stores and consumers.**

This illustrative example demonstrates the principle of resource interdependence:

- the consumer win rate is enhanced by the number of stores at any time (lower section of Figure 4.17)
- the acquisition of stores depends on the level of consumer interest (upper section of 4.18)

Figure 4.19 extracts these causal mechanisms. The reinforcing growth that arises from this interdependence can be confirmed by tracing the consequences of any positive value for either of the two win rates—for consumers or stores. Winning more consumers increases the fraction of sales calls that are successful, raising the store win rate, which increases product availability, which raises the win rate of new consumers once again.

Note the warning mentioned earlier regarding reinforcing feedback. A decline in either of these resource win rates does *not* result in a decline in either resource, nor in the system as a whole, since there is no mechanism in this structure for either resource to be lost. A fall in the consumer win rate still results in an increase in the *number* of consumers, and hence increases in sales call success. Even a one-off fall in consumer numbers still leaves a positive contribution to sales call success, so store numbers would increase, raising product availability and enhancing the win rate of consumers.

While the power of such reinforcing feedback mechanisms to drive growth is limited, this complementarity among resources is fundamental to the power of business systems to develop and sustain themselves. Consequently, there is little possibility of explaining business performance unless such mechanisms are included in the analysis. Having established the basic concept of interdependence in the functioning of an organization's system, two important implications become apparent:

1. **Some minimum input is required to achieve any positive performance.**
2. **There is a limit to the sustainable performance that can be extracted from a finite set of resources (although this limit may be exceeded temporarily).**

In the scenario summarized in Figure 4.20, management has tried to minimize the cost of the brand's launch by limiting the advertizing spend to only $300 000 per month. Although some consumers are interested in the product, growth has been very slow and has reached a very low level. Even with the same sales effort, stores have not been won in significant numbers, because the low consumer interest promised too little value to the stores for them to stock the product. As a result, sales volume

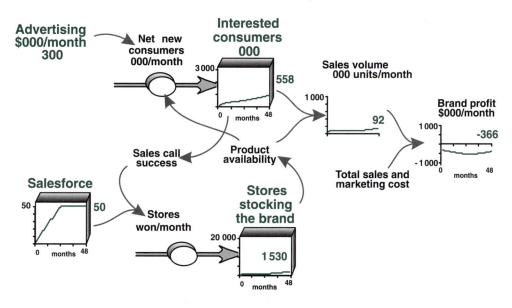

**Figure 4.20:** Brand performance fails to be achieved, due to insufficient input.

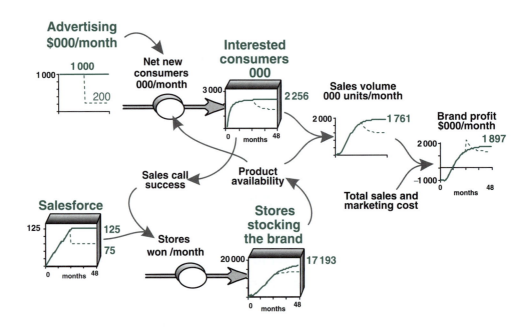

**Figure 4.21: Maximum limit to performance that can be extracted from the brand's finite resources.**

grows at only a very low rate, generating insufficient gross profit to cover the reduced costs. Although it appears that performance is heading towards positive profit rates, the consumer-forgetting rate will ensure that point will take years to reach, if ever. (For online learning materials to support this example, see p. xxi.)

Figure 4.21 (solid lines) shows a much more attractive result, in which heavy advertizing and growth of a larger salesforce pushes consumers and stores to high levels, resulting in strong sales volume and profit. However, most of the opportunity has now been used up, with most consumers captured and most stores stocking the product. Pushing advertizing higher, or adding more sales people, is at or near a point where the extra cost of more spending does not result in any further increase in profits, as Table 4.3 demonstrates for rising rates of advertizing spend.

Varying both advertising and salesforce may generate some slightly higher profit rate, but there will be an absolute limit that cannot be exceeded—at least not sustainably. The dashed line in Figure 4.21 shows a strategy of cutting both advertising and salesforce after the brand has reached nearly its full potential. The monthly savings amount to $800 000 from advertizing and $250 000 from the salesforce, but these total savings of $1 050 000 are immediately wiped out as consumer numbers fall sharply. This loss, combined with poor success of winning new stores, leads to a lower ultimate profit outcome.

**TABLE 4.3: ULTIMATE BRAND PROFIT AS ADVERTIZING SPEND INCREASES, FOR THE SALESFORCE PLAN IN FIGURE 4.21**

| | | | | | |
|---|---|---|---|---|---|
| Advertizing spend: $000/month | 800 | 1000 | 1200 | 1400 | 1600 |
| Interested consumers 000 | 2045 | 2256 | 2450 | 2587 | 2661 |
| Incremental consumers for +$200 000 advertizing spend 000 | | 211 | 194 | 137 | 74 |
| Brand profit in month 48: $000/month | 1757 | 1897 | 2005 | 2020 | 1938 |

Examining real organizations' performance suggests that errors arise frequently from ignoring these two fundamental features of finite resource systems. It seems that numerous business opportunities that were perfectly worthwhile end up failing because they never received the initial input that could have pushed them over the viability threshold. Many other cases arise where management commits far more resources and expenditure than is worthwhile, in a determined effort to push more performance out of the system than it can deliver. Finally, yet other cases feature underperformance that results from cost cutting that is intended to boost profits but that instead damages the system, destroying more profitability than the cost saving provides.

### Exploring the consumer brand model

You can explore these interactions between consumers and stores in the Brand Management Microworld. (This is available from www.strategydynamics.com. Note that the market parameters and relationships differ somewhat from the model developed in this chapter.) This PC simulation gives control over price, advertizing and salesforce, and offers extensive information in the form of tables, reports and time charts. The game includes a number of management challenges, such as stimulating an underdeveloped brand, and turning round a business that is in decline. Figure 4.22 provides a sample screenshot of the game.

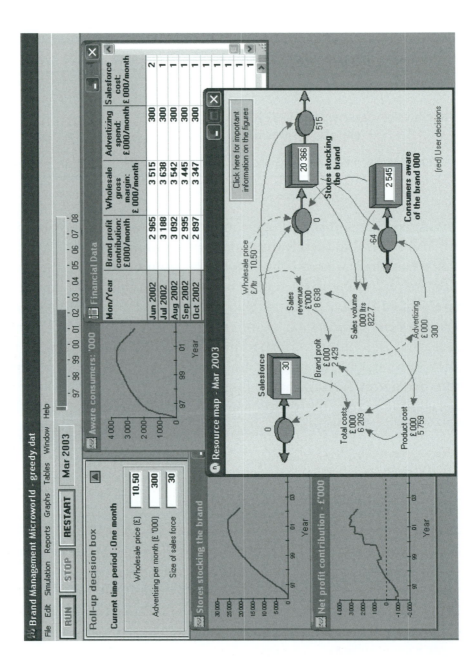

Figure 4.22: Screenshot of the Brand Management Microworld PC game.

## A "SPREADSHEET" VIEW OF THE STRATEGIC ARCHITECTURE

Chapter 3 explained how resource accumulation can be understood in familiar spreadsheet language (Table 3.2). From this foundation, it is possible to develop a standard spreadsheet layout that mimics the logic of a strategic architecture and the three underlying equations. The start point is to note first that we need to explain resource flow rates, because they determine where the business is heading next period, and second, that the factors at the origin of what causes those flow rates are current resource levels, management decisions and external factors. Since it is the resource levels that will be changed, put those at the top of the spreadsheet, followed by the management decisions and other factors. Next, calculate the performance values. Finally, calculate the resource flow rates at the bottom as the *last* items required to enable the next period to be started.

Table 4.4 shows how this is applied to the brand architecture, with the values at the beginning and end of month 48. Note first that the data reported on the diagrams above are all taken at the final instant of the 48th month. As explained in Chapter 2, the exact value of the various performance numbers for month 48 are some average of the opening and closing values. For example, at the start of month 48, revenue is made at the rate of $6 014 000/month, and by the end of the month, at a rate of $6 224 000/month. The monthly steps of this model are small enough to take the average of these two values safely as an accurate figure for the actual revenue made during the month.

Some examples of how causality runs through this structure are shown to the left and right of the month 48 column:

- *Resources, decisions and external factors drive performance*: e.g. the dotted black connections show that sales volume depends on the resource of interested consumers, the availability of the product due to the stores resource, and on consumers' consumption rate.
- *Resources accumulate and deplete*: e.g. the solid green lines show that the number of interested consumers at the start of month 49 (end of month 48) is given by the number at the start of month 48, plus the number of new consumers won since the start of that month. Similarly, the number of *potential* consumers is reduced by the same number. The dashed green links show the same logic for stores.
- *Resource flow rates depend on existing resources, decisions and external factors*: e.g. the rate of new consumers depends partly on the number of stores making the brand visible, and on the reach of advertizing spend, which is limited by the remaining stock of potential consumers. Note that this same logic carries on from the start of month 49 to determine how things will be in future periods.

**TABLE 4.4: A "SPREADSHEET" VIEW OF THE BRAND STRATEGIC ARCHITECTURE IN MONTH 48**

| | Start of Month 48 | Start of Month 49 | | Units |
|---|---|---|---|---|
| **RESOURCES** | | | | |
| Stores stocking the brand | 5 509 | 5 682 | | stores |
| Interested consumers | 1 435 | 1 448 | the future | 000 people |
| Salesforce | 50 | 50 | | people |
| Remaining potential stores | 14 491 | 14 318 | | stores |
| Remaining potential consumers | 1 565 | 1 552 | | 000 people |
| **DECISIONS** | | | | |
| Advertising spend | 500 | 500 | | $000/month |
| Salesforce hired per month | 0 | 0 | | people/month |
| Wholesale price | 9.00 | 9.00 | | $/unit |
| **EXTERNAL AND CONSTANT FACTORS** | | | | |
| Total consumers | 3 000 | 3 000 | | 000 |
| Total stores | 5 000 | 5 000 | | number |
| Fraction of consumers forgetting | 0.1 | 0.1 | | fraction/month |
| Consumption per person | 0.8 | 0.8 | | units/month per person |
| Product costs | 7.00 | 7.00 | | $/unit |
| Maximum stores per sales person | 200 | 200 | | stores/person |
| Maximum new store call rate per person | 50 | 50 | | stores/person per month |
| Cost per sales person | 5.0 | 5.0 | | $000/person per month |
| **PERFORMANCE RESULTS** | | | | |
| Product availability | 0.582 | 0.597 | | fraction |
| **Sales volume** | **668.2** | **691.5** | | 000 units per month |
| Sales revenue | 6 014 | 6 224 | | $000/month |
| Product costs | 4 677 | 4 840 | | |
| **Gross profit** | **1 336** | **1 383** | | |
| Advertising spend | 500 | 500 | | |
| Salesforce cost | 250 | 250 | | |
| Total sales and marketing costs | 750 | 750 | | |
| **Brand profit** | **586** | **633** | | |
| **CAUSAL CHAIN AMONGST RESOURCES** | | | | |
| **Consumer win rate** | | | | |
| Product availability | 0.582 | 0.597 | | fraction |
| New consumers from availability | 91 | 93 | | 000/month |
| Fraction of unawares reached by advertising | 0.04 | 0.04 | | fraction |
| New consumers from advertising | 66 | 65 | | 000/month |
| Consumers forgetting | 143 | 145 | | 000/month |
| **Net consumers won** | 13 | 13 | | 000/month |
| **Stores win rate** | | | | |
| Sales people needed on existing stores | 27.5 | 28.4 | | full-time equivalent people |
| Sales people available on new stores | 22.5 | 21.6 | | full-time equivalent people |
| New stores called on per person calling | 36.2 | 36 | | stores per person per month |
| Fraction of sales calls successful | 0.213 | 0.218 | | fraction |
| **Net stores won** | 173 | 169 | | stores per month |

The principal observation that we should focus on from this spreadsheet view of strategy—albeit for this very simple business—is of paramount importance:

### It's all about the flow rates

Put simply, if the flow rates here were zero, and we changed nothing else, nothing would change from month to month. If we *did* change something else, and later reversed that decision, performance would revert to where it was. This is why re-source flow rates are of such importance. They are the factors that determine our path into the future, and it is the influence of management's decisions and choices on flow rates that *change* that trajectory. If we don't change decisions, and nothing else changes, then the trajectory carries on in its present direction.

It rapidly becomes impractical to show all the interdependencies in this table, which is one of the principal problems with relying on spreadsheet thinking and analysis to carry out more than the most trivial of performance analyses. You *could* construct a monster spreadsheet for a complex business, but you can draw out a clear causal structure, including performance over time, with tools better suited to the task. This is not the only problem in using spreadsheet thinking for strategy. Others include:[16]

- *Fragmentary planning.* Plans are frequently put together by function, with the bottom lines of each being extracted to arrive at a "complete" analysis. With no formal means of capturing interdependency a coherent plan is hard to achieve.
- *Inconsistency with the past.* Plans for the future make hidden assumptions that things are going to work quite differently than they have done until now—sales success is going to jump, service problems drop, and so on, with no rationale as to why such shifts should occur. It may certainly be possible for an improved *trajectory* to start, but not a discontinuous shift.
- *Fragmented and implicit assumptions.* Plans are full of assumptions—about how customers will react to new marketing efforts, how staff will improve perform-ance with training etc.—yet those assumptions are not evident, and cannot be seen from a spreadsheet table. Often, having not worked through the causal logic in detail, even the author is unaware of the implicit assumptions behind her estimates.
- *Neglect of competitive and other external effects.* With no structure to incorporate the impact of competitor behavior or changes in customer preferences, spread-sheet performance projections simply bury such effects in assumptions about changes in market share. Chapters 5–7 will deal with this issue in some detail.
- *Top-down: bottom-up disconnects.* Spreadsheet analysis is the customary "business case" for plans and proposals. With only linear spreadsheet models to refer-ence, people jump to conclusions. Promoters make optimistic assumptions, and skeptics challenge the analysis. Without a fact-based causal logic available, views are reconciled by some political or social process.

## THE BRAND ARCHITECTURE AND MANAGEMENT TEAM CONTROL PANEL

Figure 4.21 offers a high-level summary of the resources, interdependencies and management policies driving performance of the consumer brand—a picture that can be thought of as a summary "strategic architecture" of the business. The full architecture would include all the detail of Figures 4.14, 4.18 and 4.19 and would be rather more extensive than can conveniently be displayed on a single regular page.

While there can be value in displaying the full detail on a single figure, depicting both the summary and the subdivided elements offers advantages. Figure 4.21 provides a summary picture that the whole management team can understand and discuss quickly. However, that team will likely consist of people with specific responsibilities—the financial controller trying to help make profits out of the product's sales, the head of marketing seeking to build consumer interest, and the head of sales trying to win and retain stores.

The more detailed diagrams for each major section of the architecture are of specific value to each of these individuals, showing what is hindering or contributing to success in their own part of the system. Crucially, the diagrams also show how their success relies on others, and thus become a tool for truly shared understanding and decision making. They would know, for example, when advertizing has achieved its purpose of winning maximum realistic consumer interest, and how much additional spending is needed to sustain that level. They would also know how many sales people would likely win stores at certain rates, and how many are needed to maintain those stores' loyalty to stocking the brand once it has penetrated the market. They also would share an understanding of the trade-off between spending to sustain consumers and stores and keeping the resulting costs down in order to deliver strong profits.

Therefore, the strategic architecture helps answer, from month to month, the three questions introduced in Chapter 1—why are we performing as we are, where is our performance going under current policies, and how can we adjust strategy and decisions to improve those prospects? The summary architecture provides a powerful "control panel" for the business, each chart of which can be readily populated with the next month's data point. The summary can be displayed on the wall of the management team's main meeting room, and the detailed subsections on the walls of each department head's office.

We need only add in the third key management lever—price—(which we have held constant in the assessment above) to see that the answers to these questions might become quite complex, even for what is a rather simple business structure. In reality, this team would have several more dimensions of complexity to consider, such as the behaviors of different consumer groups, their aims and performance in different store categories, and the impact on the brand's performance of rival products. Yet each of these issues can be handled by replicating or extending the brand's core strategic architecture in various ways, allowing the team near-total understanding and control over performance.

## THE STRATEGIC ARCHITECTURE FOR AN AIRLINE AND OTHER EXAMPLES

Figure 4.6 showed the principal dependencies of Ryanair's customer base growth on its other resources—routes, aircraft and staff—plus the dependency on the current level of that customer base itself. This is the most involved piece of the company's strategic architecture, since most other parts are under direct management control. Figure 4.23 summarizes the relationships in the strategic architecture for an airline by adding these other elements to the structure around the customer base. (Online learning materials are available to support this example, see p.xxi.)

The items highlighted in green are the key choices that constitute management's strategy, and determine the airline's performance (together, of course, with competitors' choices on the same issues and other exogenous factors). These items include:

● adding airports gives access to additional potential customers and increases the number of routes that could feasibly be served
● opening new routes expands the choice of destinations to which customers from any location can travel

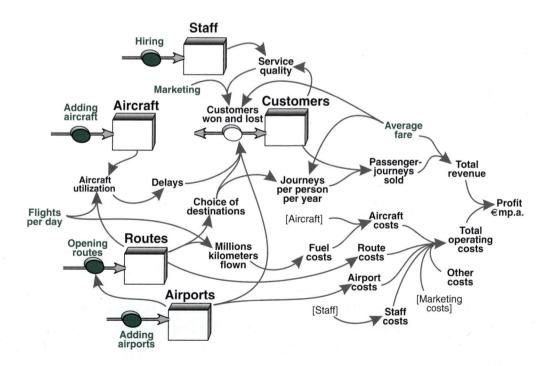

**Figure 4.23: The core strategic architecture for an airline.**

- expanding the number of flights per day, together with increased numbers of routes, increases the utilization of the aircraft fleet
- adding aircraft keeps that utilization down to levels that minimize delays
- choices on fare levels and marketing are the key controls of customer acquisition and retention, as well as the frequency with which customers travel
- hiring decisions provide the staff numbers needed to ensure customers are not lost through poor service

When populated with time chart data, Figure 4.23 becomes, like the brand architecture, a summary control panel for the business. It can be subdivided into more detailed sections, focusing, for example, on customer acquisition, on airport and route expansion, on fleet operations and on financial performance. Management does not *have to* use such diagrams. The teams that head Ryanair and Southwest Airlines have these relationships clear in their heads, and are quite capable of making good strategic and operational decisions without the need for such a picture. Yet that is a key advantage of operating an essentially simple business model, targeting a clear customer group with a highly simplified service and a single compelling value proposition, delivered by an equally simple infrastructure and capacity model. Few companies of any scale manage to find and develop such a large enterprise without encountering greater complexity, at which point it becomes increasingly difficult for any individual or team to keep everything in their heads and to understand and manage the complexity.

### Try out strategy with the LoFare Airline Microworld[17]

Some of the issues raised by the airline architecture can be explored with the LoFare Airline Microworld, which gives control over pricing, marketing, fleet and route development (see Figure 4.24). This PC game provides extensive information in the form of tables, reports and time charts. The market's development is not hardwired into the game, but develops as your enterprise succeeds in stimulating demand by offering services on increasing numbers of routes. The game includes a number of management challenges, such as the struggle to overtake rival low-cost operators who are pursuing the same growth opportunity as you.

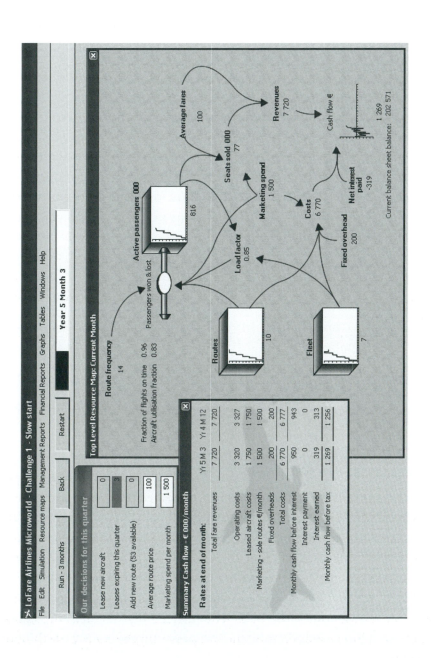

Figure 4.24: Screenshot of the LoFare Airline Microworld.

**"Where to compete? How to compete?"**

These architectures for the brand and airline demonstrate an approach to *implementing* strategy. In each case, management has implicitly already made the two major choices in *developing* strategy:

"Where to compete?" is an important choice, since it defines the types and number of potential customers to be pursued. Chapter 2 explained how the value curve can clarify the particular needs of separate customer types, so that the company can design its service proposition to most closely meet the needs of one or more groups. For the airline, the simple segmentation is between business travelers and leisure travelers. However, Ryanair has also made other choices about where to compete. It does not offer long-haul services, for example, where its highly efficient ground operations would be of less competitive value than on short-to-medium haul routes.

Management in the consumer brand case has also made implicit choices about where to compete. The brand's characteristics make it appealing to a potential audience of three million consumers who share particular characteristics and preferences. In addition, the brand is being pushed through a large number of stores, starting with the largest. In practice, such a company would also have to choose among different categories of retailers, from the large multiples like Wal-Mart to the specialist and smaller independent stores.

"How to compete?" is a separate question, but one that must be answered in the context of the choice about where to compete. The value curve is quite explicit about this point also, in regard to Ryanair (Figure 3.16). The company will compete by offering the lowest possible prices between the largest possible range of destinations, and deliver these profitably by relying on ultra-cheap airports, implementing simple operational methods and driving down costs. The proposition is also clear about what it will *not* offer—services between main city airports, flight connections and many other services. Even the simple brand architecture implies some clear choices on how to compete. Although a premium product, it is aimed to be attractive to a broad market segment, rather than targeting a select niche or being sold through a narrow category of retail stores.

## GENERIC INDUSTRY ARCHITECTURES

While the case example developed through Chapters 2–4 has focused on the performance of one specific company, Ryanair, the architecture developed is essentially the same for any passenger airline. For less focused airlines than Ryanair or Southwest, the architecture would feature added complexity caused by issues such as multiple customer groups, short-haul versus long-haul services, multiple aircraft types and so on. Nevertheless, it is not the *structure* of the business system that gives rise to widely differing outward characteristics and performance among companies—it is the set of *choices and policies* used to direct the strategy of that structure. Choices include decisions about which customer segments and needs to serve, the exact proposition of products and services to offer, which channels to employ, which activities to undertake within the company and which to outsource.[18]

It is rare for companies to radically revise the strategic architecture of an industry, and notable when they do. Often such revision involves removing the need for some key resource, such as intermediaries from the system, as illustrated by Dell's bypassing of retailers and the emergence of direct-to-consumer sale of insurance, banking and other services. Of course, the radical technological change introduced by the Internet has also spawned new business architectures, but even there common structural opportunities have been identified by several companies—eBay is not the only online exchange and Amazon.com is not the only online supplier of books and DVDs. Several enterprises have created systems such as Elance to enable service providers to bid for projects posted by would-be clients for their services (www.elance.com).

To illustrate, Figures 4.25 and 4.26 show summary architectures for a car manufacturer and magazine producer respectively. The car firm's sale of vehicles depends on the appeal of its product range, the intensity and effectiveness of its marketing, the number of dealers to reach potential car buyers, and competitive prices offered by its models' value proposition. It can only sell as many vehicles as it has the capacity and production staff to produce, and these resources are two dominant drivers of cost (apart from the cost of raw materials and components).

The magazine producer enjoys revenue both from sale of its editions and from sale of page space to advertizers. It has an advertizing salesforce to promote that revenue source, and journalists to produce its content, in addition to other groups of staff not shown. It has to balance the temptation to fill the magazine with advertizing space with the need to ensure a good proportion of content to keep each edition attractive to readers.

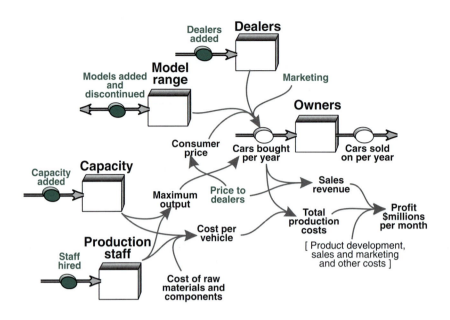

Figure 4.25: The core strategic architecture for car manufacturer.

Each of these architectures can, like the airline structure, be applied with little modification to many firms in the same industry. Indeed, with little more change, they also apply to closely adjacent industries. A producer of motorcycles, buses, or even earth-moving equipment will not look substantially different from the car

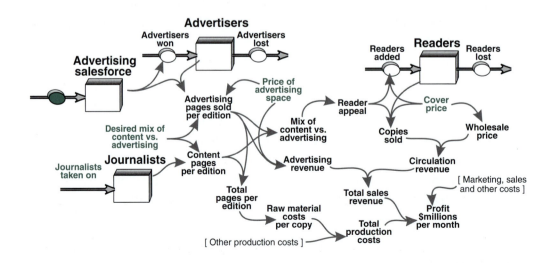

Figure 4.26: The core strategic architecture for a magazine.

manufacturer. Even a TV channel shares many features of its architecture with that of the magazine, such as the possibility of revenue from advertizers and from viewers and the need to balance content with advertizing. Other common architectures will feature later in this chapter, as well as in Chapters 5–10.

## HOW MARKETS EMERGE

Mutual dependency between supply and demand does not operate only at the level of individual companies, as shown in the sample business architectures above, but also determines the development of entire markets or industries. The clearest cases concern simple buyer/seller markets, such as that operated by eBay. This service clearly requires the existence of both a population of sellers to provide goods for the marketplace, and another population of buyers to create the demand for those goods. But what determines the rate at which a market might grow?

One case that illustrates how the resulting market dynamics might be assessed concerns the emergence of iMode Web-browsing service for cellphones in Japan. Unlike the United States or Europe at that time, PC penetration in households was limited, and Japanese language browsing facilities were poor. As shown in Figure 4.27, new subscribers flocked to the new offering, subscribing to iMode cellphone services and choosing compatible handsets. This clearly offered providers of many consumer services a great opportunity to capture those consumers by developing Web sites compatible with iMode.

Or did it? Just as clearly, the development of iMode-enabled Web sites made the iMode attractive to potential subscribers, who then sought out cellphone

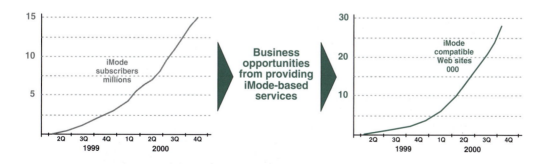

**Figure 4.27: Subscriber growth drives Web site development for Japan's iMode service.**
Source: NTT-DoCoMo: see www.nttdocomo.com/services/imode/.

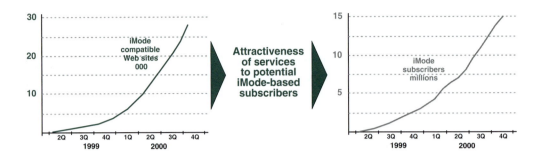

**Figure 4.28:** Web site development drives subscriber growth for Japan's iMode service.

subscriptions and handsets that would allow them to enjoy the new related benefits (Figure 4.28).

So which was it? The answer is: both. The uptake rate of iMode subscriptions reflected the number of Web sites that offered the services, *and* the development rate of Web sites reflected the number of subscribers. Figure 4.29 shows the system in this case.

But while the mechanics of this situation may be clear enough, how might we estimate the *rate* at which the system is changing? On both sides of the equation we

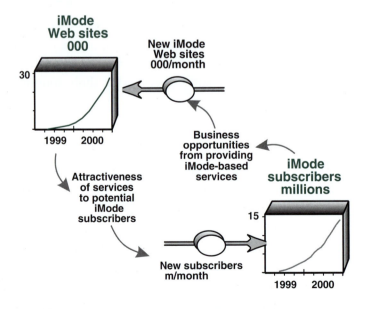

**Figure 4.29:** The core architecture capturing mutually dependent growth of Japan's iMode service.

need to consider both the potential, and the feasible rate at which that potential might be developed. In any month, a number of cellphone subscribers were likely to renew their subscriptions, of which we could estimate a fraction that would choose an iMode service. Given the size of that fraction in the third quarter of 1999, for example, and increases in the range of iMode Web sites available, we could estimate the fraction, and hence the number, likely to choose iMode in Q4. To this number could be added the rate of first-time subscribers and the proportion of those who would choose the service, perhaps informed by a Bass diffusion approach to the word-of-mouth effect.

On the other side of the equation, we could examine the number of service providers starting iMode-compatible services in the third quarter of 1999, by sector (restaurants, cinemas, airlines, etc.). This gives the fraction of each sector adding iMode facilities each month, and another Bass model of uptake would give an estimate of the number of new sites in Q4.

This story stands in stark contrast to the hoped-for launch of WAP services in Europe at around the same time. In contrast to Japan, domestic PC penetration was already high among those interested in browsing the Web. The fraction of cellphone subscribers wanting to choose a WAP enabled phone when renewing their subscription would therefore be limited. Service providers already enjoyed a good stream of interest from their existing Web sites, so saw little incremental benefit from adding WAP compatibility. The initiative was also hampered by the fact that the facility did not work well with then-current technological capabilities of 2G cellphone services. Even by 2006, when cellphone Web browsing had become slick, and little tailoring of Web sites was required, usage was still limited relative to at-home activity.

Similar principles can be applied to the emergence of other markets. Insurance companies long ago relied upon salaried salesforces to sell their products to consumers. New entrants wishing to sell into this market could not afford the large salesforce needed, so required independent sales people, but unfortunately those people mostly worked for the established firms. However, competitive pressures pushed some incumbents into releasing their employed sales staff, who were pleased to offer their private clients products not only from their former employers but also from the new entrants. As the possibility of making a living by selling insurance from multiple suppliers became more evident, more sales people saw this as an alternative to salaried employment, and the number of independent financial advisors grew. Ultimately, a market emerged in the selling of insurance products between the insurance company providers and the independent resellers.

## TIPPING POINTS: REINFORCING FEEDBACK, THRESHOLDS, AND DISCONTINUITIES

The idea of "tipping points," where modest change in a situation can suddenly tip over into rapid growth, has become popular in recent years, as examples have emerged of explosive growth in markets and in organizations' perform-ance.[19] Care is needed, however, to be clear about what exactly is causing any such phenomenon.

Note first that reinforcing feedback itself does *not* represent a tipping point. If customer numbers for a product or service grow from 10 to 50 to 250 to 1 250 in suc-cessive quarters, the quarter-on-quarter growth multiple is constant. The numbers may look impressive, but there is no tipping point (see comment on percentage rates of change in Chapter 1). If the quarterly numbers go from 10 to 50 to 200 to 600, the growth still looks impressive, but the multiple is actually declining each quarter. The cases where tipping points are observed concern situations in which previously mod-est growth rates suddenly escalate. At least four mechanisms can bring this about.

Segmentation is the first possible cause of tipping points. Chapter 3 explained how an average growth rate for a market can disguise a combination of a large, low-growth segment and a small (at least initially), high-growth segment. As the smaller segment overtakes the larger, it can appear that the overall market has suddenly switched from low growth to high.

The second common cause of tipping points arises from the role of key groups in a population, sometimes known as role models or key opinion leaders. While a few "ordinary" members of a population are the only people seen to be customers or followers of whatever behavior is of interest, few others will take any notice. How-ever, when key individuals do so, other members of the general population suddenly want to join. Medical practitioners can be (thankfully, we may feel!) a conservative community, reluctant to change medications or procedures they know to be reliable. When, however, they see that experts in a particular therapeutic area are endorsing some new treatment, uptake can escalate sharply. Similar mechanisms clearly operate in many fashion-based businesses, which explains the effort such organizations go to in order to gain celebrity endorsement.

A third situation in which tipping points can arise is where win and loss rates are both strong and almost evenly matched, but where the win rate itself is increasing modestly. In Figure 4.30, a small customer base of 100 is churning over at a high rate of 49/month, but is also growing at 50 % per month, due, for example, to strong word of mouth from the few customers that are not immediately leaving. Many people looking at the stock of customers in this case would agree that there appears

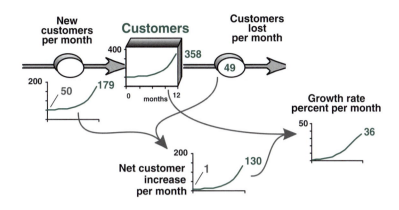

**Figure 4.30:** Tipping point in customer growth as win rate overtakes losses.

to have been a tipping point, and locate that point perhaps some time during the third quarter. However, all that has happened is that a strong growth mechanism is gradually escaping from a counter-effect that is not growing to the same extent.

The last type of situation in which tipping points can occur was mentioned briefly in Chapter 3, namely when "thresholds" are crossed. In Figure 4.31, a product's

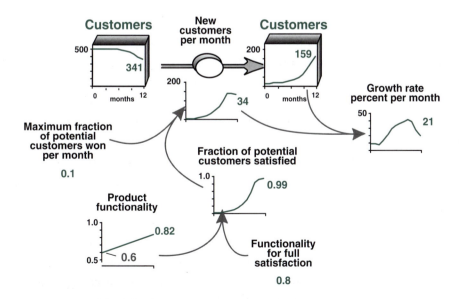

**Figure 4.31:** Tipping point in customer growth as threshold of acceptability is crossed.

functionality is being steadily improved by the company's product development efforts (similar to the kind of rating given by consumer magazines to electronics products). While the product's rating is well below 80%, few people are sufficiently satisfied to want it, but as it approaches that rating, the fraction of potential interested customers rises sharply.

There are still constraints on the fractional rate of uptake. The company may, for example, need time to develop distribution, or its marketing may reach only a fraction of possible customers. In the case of durable products, uptake is often constrained by customers' normal frequency for replacing such products. Like the previous tipping point mechanism in Figure 4.30, observation suggests a sudden shift in the trajectory for customer numbers in quarter three, although the percentage growth rate clearly rises rather earlier. So note the warnings regarding excessive attention to percentages discussed in Chapter 1. In month six, for example, there is growth of 35% on a current number of 23 customers, while in month 11, the customer base of 123 is growing at "only" 29%.

Thresholds of this kind may arise in regard to issues such as the acceptability of a product or service, its availability or price. They are rarely clear cut—i.e. at $100 no one is interested, while at $99 everyone is—but span a range, For example, only 1% might be interested at $120 and rise increasingly to 50% at $100, and approach 99% at $80. In this example, this effect is handled with a "lookup" relationship, explained in Chapter 2, between functionality and customer satisfaction.

Threshold effects can arise with resources other than customers. A company's attractiveness as an employer can remain modest while it is small and not apparently doing anything special, so it struggles hard to find the staff it wants. As it becomes noticed more—as, for example, happened with Google in the early 2000s—would-be employees multiply rapidly until the company is receiving a veritable tidal wave of applications from highly qualified and motivated applicants. Similar phenomena can also arise at the level of entire industries. One peculiar example in recent years concerns the increase in applications for would-be pathologists as the visibility and romance (!) of the job has been built up strongly by popular TV series.

Note that tipping points can also be negative and unhelpful. In the case of customer losses, a rising rate of service problems may be tolerated up to a point, but once those problems exceed a threshold of acceptability, customer churn can escalate. Similar issues arise with staff—work pressure is tolerable up to a point, but then gets too much for many staff and fractional attrition rates jump.

(Online learning materials are available to support these two tipping point examples, see p.xxi.)

# THE STRATEGIC ARCHITECTURE AND OTHER APPROACHES TO MAPPING STRATEGY

A number of other approaches exist for decomposing business performance to identify where strategy should be changed in order to bring about improvements. This section will briefly explain some of these and the connection with the resource-based architectures that form the core of the strategy dynamics approach.

## ISSUE-TREE ANALYSIS

The issue-tree approach is widely used in consulting firms to identify early on in a project where investigation of a client's business challenge should focus. The approach fits into a typical project process as shown in Figure 4.32.

Starting from a statement of the problem that the study intends to solve, the issue tree itself should be a rigorous causal chain explaining why that problem exists. This brings the process very close to the causal analysis of performance described in Chapter 2. The factors at each stage in an issue tree should be "mutually exclusive, and collectively exhaustive" (MECE).

- *mutually exclusive* means that no two statements should overlap in describing all or part of the same thing
- *collectively exhaustive* means that, taken together, all the statements should cover all possibilities

In the simple example in Figure 4.33, a company is concerned that its profit growth is slowing. Its sales growth is still strong, so its profit margins *must* be reducing. Since its sales growth is still strong and it is winning customers more quickly, those

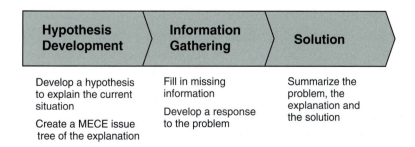

**Figure 4.32: Simplified consulting project process.**

**Figure 4.33: An issue tree explaining a company's slowing profit growth.**

new customers *must* be fewer than previously. Prices are still strong, production and other costs are under control, but service costs are rising faster than sales, which are also explained by the smaller size of customers.

There is clearly a connection between issue trees and the strategic architectures generated by the strategy dynamics approach. An issue tree could simply summarize the relationships between key changes that are seen to be taking place when a strategic architecture is inspected. The causal structure for Ryanair's profit history in Figure 2.20, for example, shows fare revenues continuing to grow strongly, even though average fares dropped significantly. Passenger-journeys, therefore, *must* have grown faster to compensate for this decline. However, the strategic architecture contributes three features that issue-tree analysis frequently misses:

1.  The fundamental difference between "A causes B" and "A accumulates and depletes," i.e. the resource accumulation issue. If a company's customer base was stable, it would be easy to conclude that this factor is OK and move on to other questions, without spotting that customer win and loss rates were both rising.
2.  The often long timescales over which causality plays out, due to the accumulation process. A company finding itself short of experienced engineers, for example, may be experiencing little turnover among those it has, but its shortage is traceable back to hiring it did not do 5–10 years ago. Similar considerations will arise when working out solutions to a problem—as the telecoms example in Chapter 1 demonstrated, actions taken to address a shortage of key staff today may only contribute business benefits in the future.
3.  The interdependence and feedback that arise from "the quantity of B drives the rate at which A is growing." This has the quite severe consequence that the

same observation can be a good thing under one set of conditions, and a bad thing under others. It might be thought, for example, that winning customers is always good—but if you cannot supply the product or service support those customers want, it can become a bad thing.

Finally, issue-tree analysis is, as its name implies, primarily concerned with helping deal with an "issue," i.e. a problem to be solved or an opportunity to be taken. While a strategic architecture is a powerful tool for such one-off studies, it is also effective for continuous management of the business from month to month and year to year.

## VALUE DRIVER ANALYSIS

Value driver analysis is closely related to the issue-tree view of problem solving, and is a major theme in the value-based management approach to controlling business performance.[20] The philosophy behind this view is that, if we can identify the key factors on which profitability ultimately depends, these must be the "value drivers" for the business. Management can then set targets for those factors and put systems in place for monitoring and control, confident that any improvement will result in increasing profitability.

In Figure 4.34, prices drive operating margins, cash profit, operating cash flow and ultimately, business value. Inventories drive changes in working capital, which is an investment that reduces operating cash flow, once again affecting business value. This example encompasses factors that impact on investment requirements, as well as on the cash profit outcomes that has been the focus of our attention thus far.

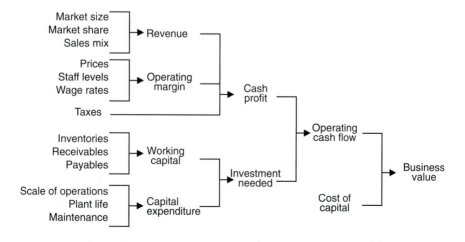

Figure 4.34: Example of value driver analysis.

Given this logical "MECE" causal structure, management can identify where it may be possible to intervene to drive up the value of the business. If we can improve market share (while everything else stays in its current healthy state), then market share, revenues, cash profit, operating cash flow, and business value will all improve. Less obviously, if we can extend the life of our plant, then capital expenditures can be lower, again improving operating cash flow and business value.

Again, there are clearly connections with the strategic architectures that emerge from the strategy dynamics approach. To populate such a value driver tree with time-based information extracted from a strategic architecture would require two extensions. First, working capital levels would need to be identified. Three items—inventories, receivables and payables—are all asset-stocks, and their change over time will relate to such issues as customer growth, changes in product range, terms of trade with suppliers and customers, and the effectiveness of management control. Secondly, the capital expenditure required would be driven by changes in the production capacity resource. Plant life and maintenance are issues related to the productivity and reliability of equipment, an issue that will be dealt with in Chapters 5–7. The only remaining item is the company's cost of capital, an important issue concerning the financial structure of the business, beyond the scope of our concern with the operating performance of the business.

Value driver analysis is widely used as the basis for identifying strategic priorities and for setting performance targets that go beyond the high-level measures of profit and return on capital. Like issue-tree analysis, however, it does not deal with the implications of accumulating factors, and it again has difficulty dealing appropriately with long lead-time factors. Note also that typically value driver analysis resorts to market forecasts and market share estimates to arrive at revenue projections, rather than the specifics of customer numbers and size.

A further difficulty arises from the omission of interdependence and feedback. At the heart of value driver analysis is the assumption that total value can be subdivided down into more detail until we know how much value is created by each separate element of the business. Interdependence invalidates this assumption. As noted under issue-tree analysis above, changes that may be good under one set of conditions (for example, winning customers) may be bad under others. Similarly, a change that "adds value" in one situation can destroy value in other circumstances. It is the *system* that creates value, not individual components of the system. Nevertheless, value driver analysis has moved many organizations beyond a simple focus on "growing sales and controlling costs" to identify powerful options for performance improvement.

## BALANCED SCORECARD

The balanced scorecard has transformed the way in which many types of organization track and steer their performance, and is now a popular tool among large companies.[21] The method recognizes that management needs to track a range of measures if it is to be in good health and sustain strong performance, so includes measures in four categories:

- financial: e.g. revenue growth, margins, profitability, return on capital
- customers: e.g. satisfaction, retention, market share and share of business
- internal processes: e.g. delivery systems, service response and new product introductions
- learning and growth: e.g. employee expertise and staff development

The balanced scorecard offers important advances over traditional reporting approaches, both in recognizing the interconnectedness within the business and the importance of measuring and managing soft issues. Increased training of support staff about a company's products, for example, will improve sales effectiveness, which will, in turn, improve sales and margins. Yet a particular challenge arises in assembling a balanced scorecard for a business—the choice of exactly which factors are important in each of the four domains and what measures to adopt to monitor and control them. An example shows how a strategic architecture can form the basis for identifying metrics for the four domains.

Figure 4.35 shows a core strategic architecture for a consulting firm. It makes one particular simplification in treating all professional staff as a single resource, rather than the several distinct levels of experience and seniority that exist in reality. This feature will be explained in Chapters 5–7. It also adds an intangible factor in *staff expertise*—Chapters 8–10 will show how to deal with intangible resources of this kind. If the strategic architecture for this firm were populated throughout with time chart data, as it should be, it can provide the rigorous, integrated numerical measures that a sound balanced scorecard requires. Measures for the financial domain of the scorecard can clearly be extracted from the revenue, cost and profit region of the architecture, and several more financial measures would be tracked than are included in this limited picture. The customer domain can extract data and movements in customer-related measures from the top section of the architecture, safe in the knowledge that those measures are entirely coherent in their causal relationships.

The architecture needs to be expanded somewhat to properly populate the scorecard domain concerned with internal processes, but the figure illustrates how

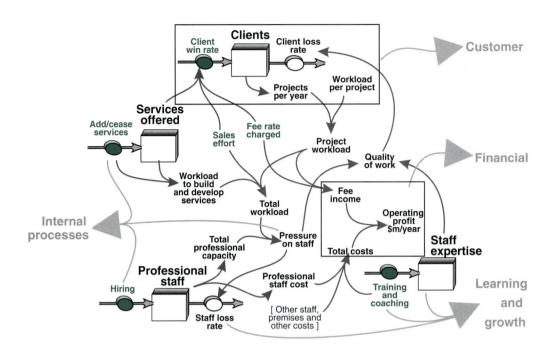

**Figure 4.35: Extracting balanced scorecard measures for a consulting firm.**

processes concerned with service development, hiring and the management of staff pressure can be extracted from separate locations in the architecture. Finally, learning and growth measures should be tracking training and coaching inputs to staff expertise, as well as the experience gained from staff involvement in current projects (not shown). Note also the need to track factors that may be undermining expertise, such as staff losses—a mechanism of "organizational forgetting" as opposed to the more common focus on organizational learning alone.

The most important contributions that a sound architecture can make to a balanced scorecard view of performance are exactly those on which issue tree and value driver methods are limited. It highlights the need to focus on rates of change—in this example, these are clients won and lost, staff hired and lost, services added, and input to staff expertise. While many company scorecards include such items, they are often not comprehensive in this coverage and do not give them sufficient priority.

An architecture highlights and quantifies interdependence and may even call into question the appropriateness of certain targets. In Table 4.5, for example, the firm is pleased to have exceeded its target for winning new clients, but its staff are overloaded and risk delivering poor work, so was it wise to set this client acquisition

| TABLE 4.5: QUARTERLY BALANCED SCORECARD REPORT FOR THE CONSULTING FIRM, WITH ILLUSTRATIVE VALUES | | | |
|---|---|---|---|
| **Strategic objectives** | **Target** | **Actual** | **Variance %** |
| **Financial** | | | |
| F1: Fee income $millions | 15.0 | 15.6 | +4 |
| F2: Fee rate $/staff-day | 800 | 820 | +2.5 |
| F3: Staff cost $millions | 10.0 | 10.0 | – |
| F4: Profit $millions | 5.0 | 5.6 | +12 |
| Etc. (more financial metrics in practice) | | | |
| **Customer** | | | |
| C1: Clients | 60 | 59 | −1 |
| C2: Clients won | 8 | 10 | +2 |
| C3: Clients lost | 5 | 8 | +3 |
| C4: New projects | 70 | 75 | +5 |
| **Internal processes** | | | |
| I1: Pressure on staff | 0.95 | 1.1 | +0.15 |
| I3: Staff hired | 25 | 15 | −10 |
| I3: New services added | 3 | 4 | 1 |
| **Learning and growth** | | | |
| L1: Staff loss percentage | 15 | 16 | +1 |
| L2: Training days per person | 3 | 3.5 | +0.5 |
| L3: Staff expertise assessment | 0.85 | 0.87 | +0.02 |
| | | | Areas of concern |

target in the first place? Another difficulty with the balanced scorecard is how to manage lead times. For example, if the hiring target had been met, would it have alleviated pressure? Possibly not, because having new staff actually diverts established staff from their current workload. It might take a quarter or two for new hires to contribute more than they subtract from the organization's capacity to deal with client projects. Yet, taking a longer term perspective, this hiring cannot be slowed for many quarters or the organization will in five years' time find itself with a shortfall in the availability of staff with five years' experience.

One last observation on balanced scorecards—at least as they are commonly implemented—is that they pay too little attention to external factors. Merely adding market share to the customer domain in this example is quite inadequate, for reasons explained in Chapter 1. Most companies should be tracking the availability of potential customers and their success in both winning and retaining those customers, relative to competitors. This is not always easy, although in many industries relative competitive performance on various measures is available. Even in cases where it is not, a marketing function that is doing its job should know the competitive make-up of its market, and sales people are often quite well aware of customers they and their competitors are winning and losing. If this is not the case, the question arises as to how they know where to direct their efforts. In the consultancy case above, just as in the law firm example from Chapter 3, competitive issues also arise in relation to staffing—success at hiring new professionals, loss of staff to other firms and so on. A balanced scorecard for any organization that competes for particular staff should also include measures of this important performance driver.

Chapters 5–7 will have more to say on the topic of rivalry for customers, staff and other scarce resources.

## STRATEGY MAPS

An evolution of the balanced scorecard has been the development of Strategy Maps,[22] which add a sense of causality to the four domains.

Figure 4.36 offers a strategic architecture for a simple consumer insurance company. The success of its salesforce in selling new policies depends on the balance between the risk the company is willing to accept (taking only the safest customers reduces the success rate) and on the premium charged (higher premiums reduce their success). The annual premiums paid by these policyholders are the source of the company's premium income—its revenue. In practice, those premiums are invested to provide an additional income stream not shown here. The higher the risk level the company accepts, the larger the proportion of policyholders who make claims, which drives the total rate of claims received. A higher risk level may also lead to a larger proportion of claims being rejected, which is not popular with policyholders. The company's ability to deal with claims from policyholders depends on having

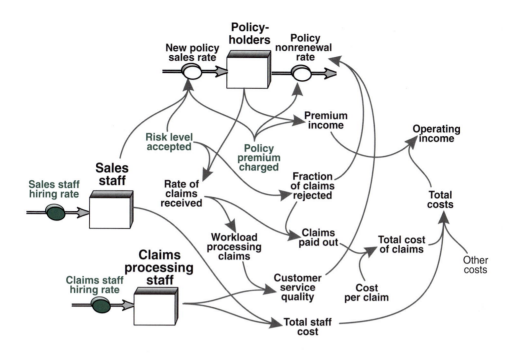

**Figure 4.36:** **A strategic architecture for a simple consumer insurance company.**

enough people to process those claims; otherwise customer service suffers, which again risks driving policyholders away.

This example also includes a number of simplifications and omissions. It does not, for example, capture the size of policies and the resulting impact on premium income or size of claims, nor does it show the need for claims assessors (although that activity may be outsourced). In many developed markets, of course, this kind of product is increasingly sold direct by phone or over the Web, but personal sales models persist in less developed markets.

Importantly, premium income, risk level and claims rates all reflect the *history* of the company's decisions, although this simple architecture does not show exactly why this is the case. Imagine that the company had long pursued a strategy of accepting only low-risk customers, charging low premiums and experiencing a low rate of claims. It then switches to a strategy of accepting high-risk customers, charging higher premiums and accepting a higher claim rate. From the moment of that change, the stock of policyholders continues to reflect the low-risk history for many years, as the previous population is gradually replaced. Premium income would therefore not jump to a new high rate but would move upwards over some years. At the same time, the claim rate and fraction of claims rejected would also gradually transition from low to high rates, with important implications for the company's service capacity. The risk, premium income and claim rate are all *attributes* of the population of policyholders, an important issue that will be addressed in Chapters 5–7.

This company may face a number of opportunities for improving performance in addition to adding higher risk customers. It might wish to improve the speed of customer response and quality of service by enhancing its claims processing systems and instilling a new customer-oriented culture among its staff. It may wish to reduce errors in claims processing by improved training and staff retention. Or it may wish to reduce the rate of nonrenewal by policyholders by adding customer retention to the responsibilities of its salesforce, maintaining the view that time spent on customer retention is more effective than the same time spent on customer acquisition. A strategy map for such a strategy shift is shown in Figure 4.37.

This strategy map adds important dimensions to the architecture in Figure 4.36 in identifying *activities* to be undertaken and *processes* that need modification in order to implement the change. It also addresses subtle issues of culture and attitude. At the same time, the architecture adds important dimensions to the strategy map, including the ability to *locate* exactly where in the business system each initiative will act (reduced errors in claims handling will reduce the policyholder outflow, for

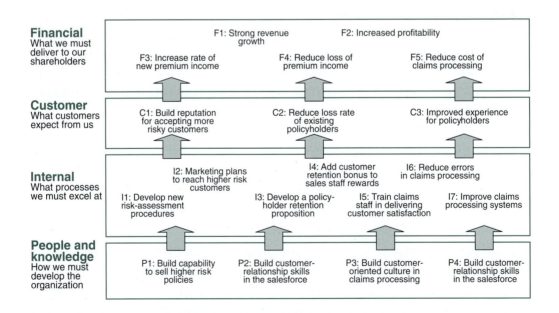

Figure 4.37: A strategy map for performance improvements in a simple consumer insurance company.

example), and *quantify* the probable impact of that change. This quantification goes beyond putting a single number on the benefit, such as "reducing the error rate from 4% to 1% should cut customer losses from 400/year to 50/year," by displaying the time profile over which the improvement can be expected to occur. This means we can see how quickly revenues and profits will change, not just the before-versus-after comparison. Furthermore, the rigorous numerical causality of the strategic architecture ensures that any interactions among the initiatives are captured and quantified, ensuring that benefits are not double counted, e.g. the impact of *both* reduced errors *and* salesforce effort on reducing customer losses.

---

### Summary of Chapter 4

Earlier chapters have identified that performance depends on the resources available, on certain key management decisions, and on competitive and other external factors. These same items also determine how quickly resources grow and how effectively they are retained. The items on which the *development* of any resource depends may be the *existing level* of that resource itself, and quantity of *potential* resource that is available.

The interaction between existing and potential customer resources gives rise to the characteristic S-shaped pattern of growth as markets emerge, develop and mature. The Bass diffusion model captures this pattern for new technology products, and can be adapted to reflect the behavior of many kinds of market. For consumable products, the stock of customers drives revenue, whilst for durables revenue reflects the customer acquisition rate.

Powerful reinforcing feedback can arise when resources drive their own growth or the growth of other resources. Conversely, balancing feedback that extinguishes growth can arise when limited resources prevent others from developing, often as an unintended result of management policy. Extensive study of the many feedback structures in an organization gives rise to causal loop diagrams that provide a qualitative explanation for performance.

Completing the interactions amongst tangible resources, management decisions and external factors gives rise to a quantified diagram of performance that forms the core of a "strategic architecture" for an organization. Intangible, competitive and external factors will add to this core architecture in Chapters 5–10. Enterprises engaged in similar activities share common architecture structures, with performance differences arising from the wide range of choices available to management regarding the specific characteristics of resources they choose to develop within the general structure, and the policies they adopt to do so.

Mutual interdependence between demand-side and supply-side resources explains the rate of development of entire markets, as well as individual companies. Discontinuities can arise in the development of resources for a number of reasons, giving rise to "tipping points" where growth or decline can suddenly accelerate.

Other approaches to mapping performance are in widespread use. Issue-tree analysis traces the fundamental causes of challenges that an organization may be facing. Value-based management relies on identifying the factors that drive financial value. The balanced scorecard and strategy maps are closely related approaches for controlling strategy that emphasize the need to target, monitor and respond to customer-related measures, internal processes and the organization's learning and growth. These methods can all be informed by strategy dynamics analysis, which handles interdependencies within the business system, as well as the lead times involved in resource development. Otherwise, there is the risk that hitting a target can be good under one set of circumstances at one time but problematic in other situations and at other times.

# SUGGESTED QUESTIONS AND EXERCISES

1. What are the three categories of factor determining the rate at which any resource develops?

2. Explain why it may be important to know the quantity of a potential resource, and to know how that potential is changing.

3. List the three principles that together explain how an organization's performance is changing over time.

4. What are the principal mechanisms captured by the Bass diffusion model of market development, and how does each mechanism affect the market's growth rate over time?

5. Explain the differences between the way in which revenues arise for durable, consumable and semi-durable products. Give two examples of each product type.

6. What are the two main forms of feedback that arise amongst resources, and what characteristic patterns of performance over time arise from each?

7. State the two implications for performance that arise when a business system depends on developing finite quantities of potential resources.

8. How should a spreadsheet be organized to follow the logical causality of an organization's strategic architecture?

9. For the sample company you identified for the exercises in Chapters 2 and 3, follow the instructions on the next pages for Worksheets 4 and 5 to develop a core strategic architecture of your case.

10. Follow the steps recommended in Chapters 2–4 to construct outline architectures (no data) for one or more of the following examples:
    (a) a retail chain, such as Starbucks
    (b) a company manufacturing and servicing elevators
    (c) an online dating agency
    (d) a voluntary organization providing medical centers in locations that have no alternative provision.

# USING WORKSHEETS 4 AND 5

Worksheets for stages 4 and 5 of a strategy dynamics analysis are provided below. Stages 1 through 3 should already have been completed, including (a) in Worksheet 1 a clear chart of how one or more performance measures have been changing over time (b) in Worksheet 2 a causal chain from performance back to tangible resources, and (c) in Worksheet 3, repeated for each resource, diagrams showing how resources are accumulating and depleting.

# WORKSHEET 4

This worksheet lays out the causal connections that explain why a resource is changing as it is. It is not required for resources whose changes are simply decided by management choice, such as adding or closing capacity or launching new products (see Figure 3.14). The process is demonstrated in detail for Ryanair's customer base in Figures 4.1 to 4.9.

Worksheet 4 is likely to be necessary in most cases to explain why customers, and possibly staff, are being won and lost. For each such resource:

- copy the resource and its inflow and outflow from Worksheet 3 into the structure in the middle of Worksheet 4
- connect factors that directly drive the resource's inflow, e.g. product appeal, contact with existing customers
- work back along the causal chain from each item until reaching either a decision (e.g. price) or a resource (e.g. product range, existing customers)
- it may be necessary to add the potential resource to the left if this constrains the inflow rate
- complete the same process to lay out the explanations for the resource's outflows

## TIPS

- It may be necessary to complete Worksheet 4 for more than one customer group, or for hiring or retention of more than one staff group.
- The **my**strategy software is a more flexible and powerful method for completing the inflow and outflow analysis of Worksheet 4. The **my**strategy software version of Worksheet 4 is available, see paragraph about online learning materials on p.xxi.

# WORKSHEET 5

This worksheet combines Worksheets 1 through 4. Its purpose is to generate the core strategic architecture, as illustrated in the full picture of the consumer brand from this chapter shown in Figure 4.38, following Worksheet 5.

- Copy the causal structure that explains how resources drive performance from Worksheet 2 into the right-hand side of Worksheet 5.
- For resources to the left of the diagram whose flows are simply decided upon by management, add those flows and decisions.
- For resources whose flows are caused by more complex mechanisms, add the causal structure you have just developed on Worksheet 4. It may be necessary to add potential resources to the left of a resource if that potential constrains its growth.
- Check that all interdependencies between resource flows and existing resources or decisions are captured. You should be confident that you can explain why every resource has behaved as it has over time from other items on the architecture, and hence explain how overall performance has come about.

## TIPS

- It is likely that analysis will become more complex than this regular page-size template can accommodate. Use larger paper to develop more extensive diagrams.
- It is especially effective if teams work together to generate the strategic architecture on a wall board, capturing the result with a digital camera.
- The resulting diagram can be simplified by (a) summarizing a high-level view, as has been done for the consumer brand in Figures 4.20 and 4.21 and (b) keeping detail of major sectors of the architecture on separate diagrams, as in Figures 4.14, 4.17 and 4.18.
- Alternatively, the **my**strategy software is a more flexible and powerful method for completing Worksheet 5. The **my**strategy software version of Worksheet 5 is available, see paragraph about online learning materials on p.xxi.

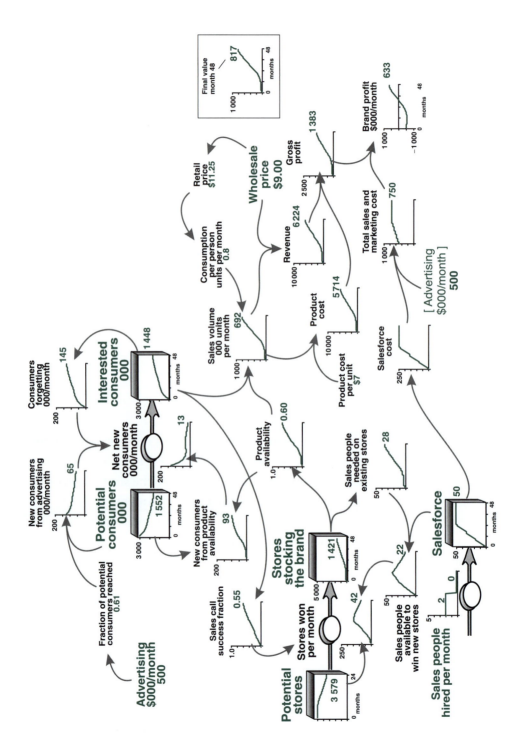

Figure 4.38: Strategic architecture for the consumer brand.

# WORKSHEET 4: DRIVERS OF RESOURCE WIN RATES AND LOSS RATES

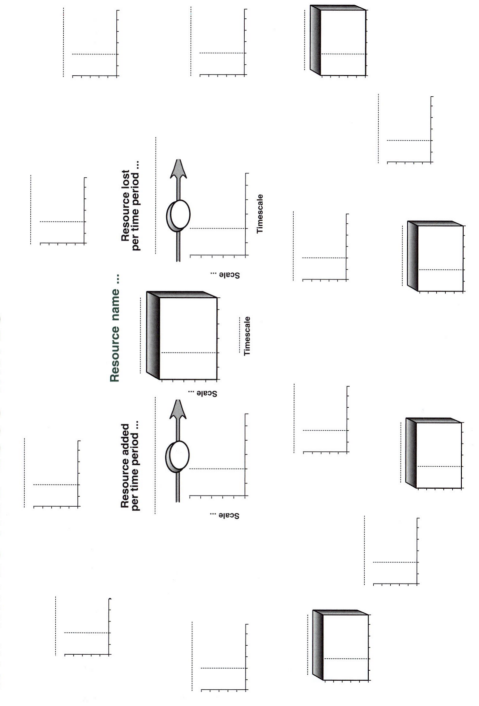

# WORKSHEET 5: THE CORE STRATEGIC ARCHITECTURE

Work back from the performance outcome.
Add causal links, naming each item in turn.
Use as many items as needed.
Add additional factors and constants by hand.
Quantify and add time charts (illustrative if needed).
Highlight management controls.

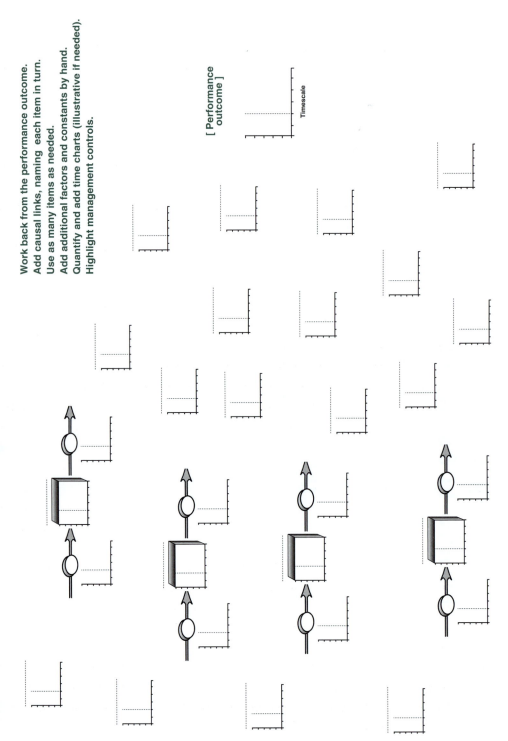

[ Performance outcome ]

Timescale

# NOTES

1. Grant, R. (2005) *Contemporary Strategy Analysis*, Blackwell, Oxford, Chapter 5.
2. Barney, J.B. (2002) *Gaining and Sustaining Competitive Advantage*, 2nd edn, Pearsons Education, Upper Saddle River, NJ, Chapter 5.
3. Dierickx, I. and Cool, K. (1989) Asset stock accumulation and sustainability of competitive advantage. *Management Science*, **35**, 1504–1511.
4. The passenger-journeys booked in Figure 4.5 are the year-end rates, reflecting the estimated year-end number of customers rather than the average number reported in Chapter 2.
5. See case study: Rivkin, J. and Porter, M. (1999) *Matching Dell*, Harvard Business School Publishing, Boston, MA.
6. Kirkpatrick, D. (2006) Dell under siege. *Fortune*, **18** September 2006, pp. 34–39.
7. Prahalad, C.K. (2005) *The Fortune at the Bottom of the Pyramid: Eradicating Poverty Through Profits*, Wharton School Publishing, Upper Saddle River, NJ.
8. Prahalad, C.K. and Hammond, A. (2002) Serving the world's poor profitably. *Harvard Business Review*, **80**(9), 48–57.
9. See Michaels, E., Handfield-Jones, H. and Axelrod, E. (2001) *The War for Talent*, McKinsey & Co., New York; Axelrod, E., Handfield-Jones, H. and Welsh, T. (2001) The war for talent: part 2, *McKinsey Quarterly*, **2**, pp. 9–12; Pfeffer, J. (2001) Fighting the war for talent is hazardous to your organization's health, *Organizational Dynamics*, **29**(4), 248–259.
10. Bass, F. (1969) A new product growth model for consumer durables. *Management Science*, **15**, 215–227.
11. This perspective is examined in detail in Moore, G.A. (1999) *Crossing the Chasm, Marketing and Selling High-tech Products to Mainstream Customers*, HarperCollins, New York.
12. See, for example, Milling, P.M. (2002) Understanding and managing innovation processes, *System Dynamics Review*, **18**(1), 73–86.
13. Senge, P. (1990) *The Fifth Discipline*, Doubleday, New York.
14. Sterman, J.D. (2000) *Business Dynamics: Systems Thinking and Modeling for a Complex World*, Irwin/McGraw-Hill, Boston, MA.
15. This two-stage representation of customer acquisition is a considerable simplification of reality in such cases. In practice customer development goes through multiple stages of awareness and interest, a process that will be examined in detail in Chapter 6.

16.  I am indebted to Alan Graham of PA Consulting for his observations on these issues.

17.  The "LoFare Airline Microworld" is available from www.strategydynamics.com.

18.  Markides, C. (2000) *All the Right Moves*, Harvard Business School Press, Boston, MA.

19.  See, for example, Gladwell, M. (2001) *The Tipping Point*, Abacus, London and Kim, W.C. and Mauborgne, R. (2003) Tipping point leadership, *Harvard Business Review*, **81**(3), 60–69.

20.  Martin, J.D. and Petty, J.W. (2000) *Value Based Management*, Harvard Business School Press, Boston, MA.

21.  Kaplan, R. and Norton, D. (1996) *The Balanced Scorecard*, Harvard Business School Press, Boston, MA. See also www.balancedscorecard.org.

22.  Kaplan, R. and Norton, D. (2004) *Strategy Maps*, Harvard Business School Press, Boston, MA.

# CHAPTER 5
# RESOURCE ATTRIBUTES

## KEY ISSUES

- ✪ The attributes possessed by resources that describe their quality and determine their contribution to performance.
- ✪ Understanding how those attributes improve and deteriorate as resources are added or lost.
- ✪ Implications for developing human resources, product range and other functional issues.
- ✪ Using the quality-distribution of resources to decide where to compete and where to focus efforts at improving performance.
- ✪ Situations when resources bring with them the potential to access others.
- ✪ The importance of competitive structure in an industry and using attributes to undermine competitors.

Worksheet 6a: Resource Attribute Analysis

Worksheet 6b: Resource with Multiple Attributes

Worksheet 6c: Primary Resource Brings Access to Potential Secondary Resource.

This chapter makes connections to the concepts of: human capital, skills and competency audits, marketing channels, industry consolidation, corporate turnround and rejuvenation.

Chapters 1–4 of this book assumed for simplicity that resources were uniform. Customers all purchased at the same rate, staff all possessed the same skills, and products were equally appealing. However, some customers buy more than others, staff have varying levels of skill, and products differ in their appeal to customers. Moreover, adding and losing customers, staff or products means that these important characteristics, like the resources themselves, are changing over time. A realistic explanation of performance in most situations therefore requires that these characteristics be included in the analysis and planning of strategy.

# QUALITY OF TANGIBLE RESOURCES

Most tangible resources have some quality or characteristic that affects their impact on the business system and its performance. These qualities are referred to as "attributes" (Table 5.1).

The scale and development of attributes have important implications for other resources and for performance. A fitness club might, for example, receive $100 000/month in membership fees from 500 members paying $200/month. Another club might receive the same income but from 1000 members paying $100/month. The members of the two clubs will have quite different expectations regarding the stand-ard and range of facilities offered, and will expect different levels of service, which implies differences in both the number and experience of staff.

The importance of this difference in customer quality can be demonstrated by extending the manufacturing company example from Chapter 3 (Tables 3.7 and 3.8). In its initial state, the company had 80 customers each buying 105 units per month, to give total sales of 8 400 units per month. It could, however, receive the same sales volume from three times as many customers (240), each of whom buys one-third of the quantity, or 35 units per month (Table 5.2).

The company's revenue is identical, and most of its costs do not change. But its distribution costs and service costs are both higher, though not in direct proportion to the number of customers. Table 5.2 shows the impact on the company's profits if distribution costs double to serve three times the number of customers, and if service costs increase by 50 %.

## TABLE 5.1: EXAMPLES OF ATTRIBUTES OF TANGIBLE RESOURCES

| Tangible resource | Measure for the resource | Attribute | Measure for the attribute |
|---|---|---|---|
| Customers | People or companies | Sales value | $/month per customer |
| Staff | People | Experience | Years per person |
| Products | Number | Customer appeal | Rating 0–1 for each product |
| Distributors | Companies | Potential end-customers | End-customers per distributor |
| Equipment | Units | Reliability | Failures per unit per year |

These financial consequences of the differing customer quality also reflect our principle that "resources drive performance" (Chapter 2). The distribution costs are higher because more delivery vehicles and staff are needed, and the service costs are higher because more service personnel are required. Those additional resources are only required because of the larger number and lower quality of customers.

The issue of customer quality differences also adds to the list of reasons given in Chapter 1 for being wary of market share as a performance indicator or objective. This company may have the same market share regardless of whether it has few large customers or many small ones, but its current performance is quite different. Its potential future performance will differ too, if its lower cash flows in the latter case limit its ability to invest in growth.

## TABLE 5.2: AN ILLUSTRATIVE MANUFACTURING FIRM WITH DIFFERING CUSTOMER QUALITY

|  | Few, large customers | | Many, small customers | |
|---|---|---|---|---|
| Customers | | 80 | | 240 |
| Sales per customer | | 105 | | 35 |
| Sales | | 8 400 units per month<br>*$000 per month* | | 8 400 units per month<br>*$000 per month* |
| Revenue $000 | | 1008.0 | | 1008.0 |
| *Sourcing cost* | 58.8 | | 58.8 | |
| *Production costs* | 310.0 | | 310.0 | |
| *Distribution costs* | 122.0 | | 244.0 | |
| *Sales and marketing spend* | 100.0 | | 100.0 | |
| *Service costs* | 80.0 | | 120.0 | |
| *Overhead cost* | 100.0 | | 100.0 | |
| Total costs | | 770.8 | | 932.8 |
| Operating profit | | 237.2 | | 75.2 |

Chapter 2 explained that firms in the same or similar industries feature resources that are quite characteristic of those industries. Retailers have stores and oil companies have reserves, for example. These industry-specific resources also have important attributes. Each store in a retailer's portfolio gives access to a certain number of consumers; each oil field has a certain volume of oil reserves, and so on (Table 5.3).

Resources in public service and voluntary organizations also carry important attributes. In policing, criminals differ in the frequency and seriousness of the offences they commit. Schools differ in the learning abilities of their students. Voluntary organizations are often concerned with the value of their donors; some deliberately choose to focus on a few rich individuals, whilst others adopt a policy of "every little helps" and seek donations, no matter how small, from as many people as possible. Table 5.4 offers some further examples.

Such attribute differences can complicate policy, and give rise to unintended consequences. In the United States, for example, care for the terminally ill is funded on the basis of a fixed rate per patient-day. This puts providers of care in the difficult position of favoring patients with relatively simple needs for palliative relief, rather than those with more complex needs, such as cancer sufferers.[1]

The key point to note from all these examples and others that follow is that:

**Resources have quantifiable attributes that must be known and managed to ensure the organization's system is effective and to drive performance.**

## TABLE 5.3: EXAMPLES OF INDUSTRY-SPECIFIC RESOURCE ATTRIBUTES

| Industry | Tangible resource | Measure for the resource | Attribute | Measure for the attribute |
|---|---|---|---|---|
| Retailer | Stores | Number | Consumers reached | People per store |
| Oil company | Fields | Number | Oil reserves | Barrels, millions per field |
| Media company | Advertizers | Companies | Advertizing spend | $000 per month per advertizer |
| Utility firm | Equipment | Items | Reliability | Failures per unit per year |
| Contracting company | Current projects | Number | Workload | Workload per project |

## TABLE 5.4: EXAMPLES OF RESOURCE ATTRIBUTES IN PUBLIC SERVICE AND VOLUNTARY ORGANIZATIONS

| Sector | Tangible resource | Measure for the resource | Attribute | Measure for the attribute |
|---|---|---|---|---|
| Healthcare | Cancer patients | Number | Drug requirement | Units per month per patient |
| Waste disposal | Consumers | Households | Refuse generation | Volume per week per household |
| Sport | Players | People | Performance | Various, e.g. yards carried, home-runs hit, etc. per player |
| Business school | Students | People | Prior business experience | Years per student |

# RESOURCES AND ATTRIBUTE "CO-FLOWS"

It is challenging to understand and manage changes in attributes and the consequences of those changes. If the second of the fitness clubs described at the start of this chapter wished to move away from its low-price positioning to attract higher-paying members, all its other resources have to be changed. Equipment and facilities need to be improved, and staff either replaced or retrained. This will be costly, so membership fees may need to rise somewhat before the full improvement program is complete. The original members may not be happy about this, and may start to leave, so the club will need to seek new members willing to pay higher fees. However, this may be difficult before the improvements have been completed.

This simple example illustrates once again that strategy must recognize and cope with change *over time*, so needs a method for quantifying both scale and speed of progress. Now though, we must not only evaluate change in key resources, but also in the quality of those resources.

Table 5.5 looks at how the customer base and sales for the manufacturing firm in Table 5.2 would evolve if it started with the larger number (240) of small customers (each buying 35 units per month), and set out to win larger customers, each buying 105 units per month. Its customer base increases, but its total sales

**TABLE 5.5: ADDING LARGER CUSTOMERS TO THE MANUFACTURING FIRM'S CUSTOMER BASE**

| Start of month . . . | 1 | 2 | 3 | . . . | 22 | 23 | 24 | end |
|---|---|---|---|---|---|---|---|---|
| Customers | 240 | 245 | 250 | | 345 | 350 | 355 | 360 |
| New customers per month | 5 | 5 | 5 | | 5 | 5 | 5 | 5 |
| New sales per new customer *units per month* | 105 | 105 | 105 | | 105 | 105 | 105 | 105 |
| Increase in total sales rate | 525 | 525 | 525 | | 525 | 525 | 525 | 525 |
| Total sales units per month | 8400 | 8925 | 9450 | | 19425 | 19950 | 20475 | 21000 |
| Average sales per customer *units per month* | 35.00 | 36.43 | 37.80 | | 56.30 | 57.00 | 57.68 | 58.33 |

rise still faster, and over two years the average customer size increases from 35 units/month to more than 58. It does not actually end up with 355 customers each buying at this higher average rate, of course. Instead it has the original 240 buying at the low rate and an additional 120 customers buying at the higher rate.

This change in customer quality can be depicted in rigorous time chart form, as shown in Figure 5.1. As in earlier chapters, the causal arrows reflect specific relationships:

*New sales each month = new customers per month multiplied by new sales per new customer*
*Average sales per customer = total sales per month divided by customers*

In Figure 5.1, the attribute *Total sales per month* is shown as a resource, in parallel with the *Customers* resource. This is because, like customers, it accumulates and would deplete if customers were lost. In other words, *sales per month* is something that "flows with" customers, so the way this relationship is displayed is referred to as a "co-flow" structure.

There are two potentially confusing features of this structure to clarify. First, the attribute of *Total sales: units per month* is increased by the arrival of new sales from newly won customers. The units of this increase are therefore "units per month, per month," so the phrase *New sales each month: units per month* is used to avoid confusion.

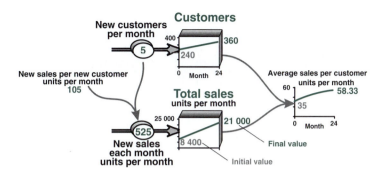

**Figure 5.1: Depicting changing customer quality as larger customers are won.**

The second puzzle is why the attribute resource is given as *total sales*. If we want to track the average customer quality, why does the lower resource not contain *average sales per customer*? The reason is that it is much easier to make the math work out if the lower resource contains the total sales, rather than the average per customer.

Extending the bathtub analogy of resource-accumulation introduced in Chapter 3 may help clarify why this should be so. Imagine that the resource itself is the amount of water in a bath. The quality of interest is the temperature of that water. If you want a warmer bath, you can add hot water. How much warmer it gets depends on how much heat the added water brings with it. The initial temperature is the initial quantity of heat divided by the amount of water that shares it, and the final temperature is the new quantity of heat divided amongst the new, larger quantity of water. Unlike our manufacturing firm, however, the water does not stay divided into two separate amounts, one of which is hot and the other cool, but gets mixed up so that the whole bathtub reaches a similar temperature.

Note that the chart for *average sales per customer* is a curve of gradually decreasing slope, even though the resource of *Customers* and the co-flow resource of *Total sales* are both straight lines. A look at Table 5.5 will confirm this observation. In the first month, the five new customers raised the average sales per customer from 35.0 to 36.43 units per month—an increase of 1.43. In the final month, the same increase of five customers only raised the average from 57.68 to 58.33—an increase of just 0.65. This is because the higher the *average sales per customer* becomes, the less this average can be increased by adding more customers of the same higher quality. If better customers were added indefinitely, the average could never exceed the 105 units per month each new customer brings, any more than the temperature of your bath could ever exceed that of the hot water you are adding.

**Doing it right: some attributes may "break the rules" on defining resources**

Surely the additional resource in Figure 5.1 is breaking the rules that were so carefully laid down in Chapter 2 regarding what is or is not a resource? That chapter asserted that variables such as sales, revenue, costs and profits are *not* resources. Since their units are "XXX per time period" they are instead flows of orders or money. That rule remains important, but the attribute resource in Figure 5.1 is being used to describe the quality of the customers, not as a resource in its own right. Figure 5.2 shows the calculation of *total sales* and *revenue from customers, average sales per customer* and *unit price*—a structure that follows exactly the rules laid down in Chapter 2. It also shows that the customer attribute of *Total sales* is exactly the same chart with the same numbers as appear in the causal explanation for revenue.

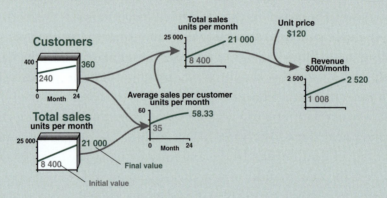

**Figure 5.2: Customer sales attribute matches the firm's sales volume.**

Adding larger customers is just one way to increase the average size of the customer base. An alternative is to remove smaller customers. Consider what might be done if the company's initial 240 customers who are buying an average of 35 units per month actually consisted of 120 buying 50/month, and another 120 buying 20/month. The company could allow the smaller customers to be lost, leaving itself with a customer base increasingly dominated by larger customers. If five smaller customers were to go each month, the company would end up after 24 months with *only* the 120 customers buying 50 units/month (Figure 5.3—online learning materials are available to support this example, see p.xxi).

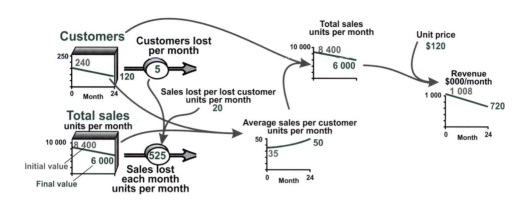

**Figure 5.3: Improving average customer quality by losing smaller customers.**

Although the company improves its average customer quality by this mechanism, it does of course suffer a fall in total sales. Consequently, it could end up making lower profits in spite of the better quality of its customers, depending on how much it can reduce costs as customer numbers fall.

## UNEQUAL QUALITY OF INDIVIDUAL RESOURCE ITEMS

In reality, a company's customers are most unlikely to be all equal in size, or to be clustered in two groups of identical small customers and large customers. There is generally a size distribution, ranging from large to small. In Figure 5.4, the company has such a range of customer sizes, with the largest buying 90 units per month and the smallest 8.5. The chart can be used to look up the sales rate of any customer in size order; for example, the 67th largest customer generates sales of 46.8 units per month (see Chapter 2 for further explanation about lookup charts).

Rather than wait for smaller customers to be lost, a company discovering an uneconomic "tail" in its customer base may well decide to undertake a one-off rationalization. Smaller customers may be passed on to resellers to deal with, or simply discontinued. If this particular company were to close the smallest half of its customer base at once, it would lose the sales volume indicated by the shaded area to the right of Figure 5.4. In total, this amounts to approximately 1 900 units per month of the company's total sales of 8 400.

Such harsh measures should be taken with care, even if smaller customers are unprofitable. It is vital that all the costs that make them unprofitable really are

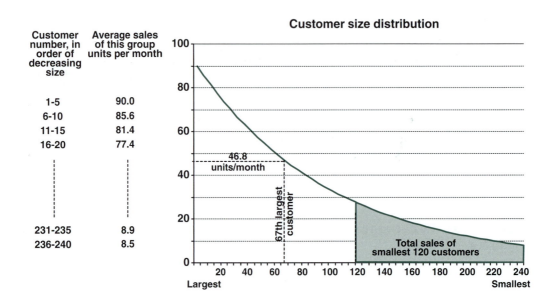

| Customer number, in order of decreasing size | Average sales of this group units per month |
| --- | --- |
| 1-5 | 90.0 |
| 6-10 | 85.6 |
| 11-15 | 81.4 |
| 16-20 | 77.4 |
| ⋮ | ⋮ |
| 231-235 | 8.9 |
| 236-240 | 8.5 |

**Figure 5.4: Improving average customer quality by losing smaller customers.**

eliminated, or else the company can end up with a smaller business and profits that are lower rather than higher. There is also the risk of damage to the company's reputation from turning customers away. Nevertheless, deciding on the scale of customers that will be served is an essential part of the strategic question of "where to compete." If this choice is not made explicitly, and reviewed periodically, an organization's business mix can drift into a customer-profile that is inadvisable, even if it was not intended.

### "Lumpy" resources and implications for attributes

Firms in certain industries face particular challenges when their acquisition of resources comes in large lumps, rather than a more or less steady stream. Contract-based industries are often subject to this phenomenon where the winning of a large project brings with it the attribute of a substantial workload that must be worked off as the project progresses. Larger firms have some advantage in such sectors, since running a number of projects in parallel means that the arrival of a new one does not represent too large a proportion of additional work. In contrast, a smaller firm with, say, two projects currently under way will face a substantial challenge to gear up its capacity if they win a third.

One such example concerns the medium-sized law firm mentioned in Chapters 1 and 3. This organization wished to grow and break into the select group of larger firms by bidding against them for major contracts, such as the legal issues involved in corporate acquisitions. Although it had some success in this effort, each project brought such heavy workloads that certain groups of lawyers with particular skills found themselves overloaded for long periods. This left the firm unable to support the steady stream of smaller contracts, causing annoyance amongst the majority of clients who provided the bulk of its work.

## A LIMITATION OF THIS APPROACH TO RESOURCE QUALITY

The simple framework in Figures 5.1–5.3 deals only with changes to the *average* quality of customers. It does not capture specific changes within that average. For example, an increase in average customer size may arise either from winning many new customers that are slightly larger than average or from winning just a few very large customers. The difference between these two cases is lost in the averaging, but may have substantial implications. As soon as the specific sales rate for a newly won customer is added to the overall resource, that value is lost in the averaging that takes place across the entire population. Similarly, the loss of a customer takes with it the specific sales rate of that customer, not just the average for the whole customer base. This loss of detail is avoided with a method known as agent-based modeling, in which behaviors of a whole population are made up of the individual behaviors of individual "agents"—customers, staff, companies, etc.[2]

It is often important to retain these customer-specific details, not just for planning sales activity towards particular customers, but also for understanding the dynamics of the business as a whole. It would be entirely possible, for example, for this company's sales rate to arise from a wide variety of different customer size distributions, rather than the smoothly declining curve shown in Figure 5.4. Whilst the framework provides a good overview of the situation and how it is changing over time, it is often necessary to support it with a customer-by-customer record of sales rates, how those customer-specific sales rates are changing, and the scope for further improvement. Most companies have access to the data needed for such detailed analysis, at least as regards customers with whom they deal directly. It becomes more challenging, however, when very large numbers of customers are involved (e.g. for many retailers) or when there are intermediaries between the company and the ultimate consumers of its products (e.g. firms who produce and market fast-moving consumer goods).

Similar considerations will apply when qualities of other resources are aggregated in this way.

- The average productivity of a salesforce reflects the specific success rate of individual people within the team. This may be distributed rather evenly, or there may be a few "stars" whose performance is very different from the average of their colleagues. The impact on total sales of losing a sales person thus depends on exactly who leaves.
- The average failure rate of a large number of items of equipment may reflect a broadly even failure rate across the entire population, or may be distorted by especially high rates for a few particularly unreliable units. The impact of maintenance efforts or spending on replacement will therefore depend on exactly which items are dealt with.
- Crime rates in a city reflect the number of criminals and the average frequency of the crimes they commit. However, there may be a small number of especially active villains, the detection and removal of whom make a disproportionate contribution to reducing the overall crime rate.

The key point to note here is that:

**Treating any resource as a uniform population with average attributes loses detail that may be important.**

If the details of individual resource items are important to evaluating a strategic issue, it may be desirable to carry out analysis of each discrete event. For example, a retail bank concerned at the falling profitability due to the growth of online banking wanted to rationalize its branch network. Each branch had its own characteristic number of customers, and different towns and city areas had numbers of branches serving overlapping populations of consumers and business users. The impact of alternative closure plans could only be evaluated by estimating the impact of closing each branch, including the transfer of customers to other branches and the loss of others to competitors.

## THREE MECHANISMS THAT CHANGE ATTRIBUTES

We have looked at how adding larger customers and removing smaller ones can raise the average size of a firm's customer base. To these mechanisms must be added a third—raising the size of customers that remain with the organization over time. This may arise if the customers themselves increase their purchase rate—perhaps consumers increase their demand for your product, or in the case of business-to-business firms, customers' own business may grow. Where customers are shared with competitors, it may also be possible to raise average sales by capturing a larger share of business with each customer.

Taken together, these are the only three mechanisms that can cause a change in average size of customers, or more generally, a change in quality of any attribute. Changes in quality are not always in a positive direction, of course—large customers may be lost, new customers may be smaller than those we already supply, and existing customers may decline. Table 5.6a summarizes the mechanisms that raise or lower average customer size, and Table 5.6b translates these into generic mechanisms for any resource.

### TABLE 5.6a: MECHANISMS RAISING OR LOWERING AVERAGE SIZE OF CUSTOMER

| Increase average customer size | Decrease average customer size |
|---|---|
| Add larger customers | Lose larger customers |
| Lose smaller customers | Add smaller customers |
| Increase sales to existing customers | Suffer a fall in sales to existing customers |

### TABLE 5.6b: MECHANISMS RAISING OR LOWERING QUALITY OF ANY RESOURCE

| Improve average quality | Decrease average quality |
|---|---|
| Add better quality resource items | Lose better quality resource items |
| Lose lower quality resource items | Add lower quality resource items |
| Improve average quality of existing resource items | Suffer a fall in average quality of existing resource items |

### Extending the bathtub analogy

The three mechanisms of resource improvement can be understood by extending the idea that resources act like water in a bathtub. As already noted in this chapter, the attribute of interest for people taking a bath is the temperature of the water. If this is too cold, you have two options: add hot water (equivalent to adding bigger customers), or using a heater—of appropriate safety design! —to warm up the existing water (equivalent to increasing the business you do with existing customers). The third option, of losing smaller customers, cannot be done with real bath water, but would imply finding cold drops among the hot and taking them away.

## APPLYING THE ATTRIBUTE PRINCIPLE TO STAFF RESOURCES

Customers are a convenient resource to illustrate the principles of changing resource attributes, since they are of obvious concern in most commercial cases. However, other resources also have important characteristics that contribute to organizations' performance, especially through their influence on how others parts of the strategic architecture develop.

People have many characteristics, but two that impact powerfully on their contribution to the performance of organizations are skills and experience.[3] At the simplest level are the basic task skills needed to do routine jobs, such as food preparation in fast-food outlets, or document processing in banking. Organizations are often highly explicit about such skills, documenting exactly what tasks people need to be able to do, providing detailed training on exactly how to do them, and giving recognition to those who have demonstrated their mastery, for example through a badge system.

In Figure 5.5, a call center manager has 80 staff, each of whom needs to have a number of skills if they are to deal adequately with customers' enquiries. Ideally, each person would be able to respond to the full range of 20 issues that may arise from customers' calls, but that ideal is hard to achieve because of staff turnover, which is running at five per month. Initially, the average person knows how to answer 12 of the maximum 20 issues.

New staff have none of the necessary skills (only cold water is available to add to this particular bathtub!), so training is provided, both to give new staff some basic skills, and to increase the skills of existing staff. Staff also forget the skills that they were trained in, because some customer issues arise too infrequently for them to be reinforced through practice. In the base case (dashed lines) there is no staff turnover, and no hiring, so all the training builds skills amongst existing staff. Improvement slows to a standstill because improvements become increasingly overtaken by the forgetting rate (the hotter the water in the bathtub becomes, the faster it cools down). In the second case (solid line and bold text values), staff turnover adds to the rate at which skills are lost (warm water is lost, to be replaced by the cold water of unskilled staff). By the end of the 24 months, training is adding 120 units of skill to the population, but 40 of these are being lost with people leaving (four people per month with 10 skills each) and 80 are being forgotten (10 % of the 803 that remain by that time).

This simple structure is able to replicate a wide range of realistic behaviors for staff numbers and average skill levels, including, for example, the diluting effect that arises when staff groups grow without adequate training, and the improvement

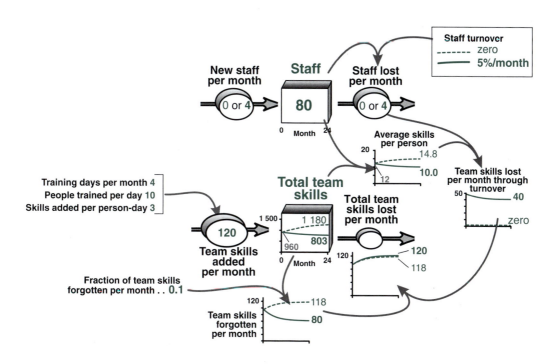

**Figure 5.5: Skill building and losses in a call center with and without staff turnover.**

in average skill that can arise if lower skilled individuals are removed from a mixed-ability group. (Online learning materials are available to support this example, see p.xxi.)

---

### Doing it right: put the total attribute in the parallel resource

This chapter already explained (after Figure 5.1) why the lower resource with its co-flows of attributes added and lost should contain the *total* quantity of the attribute—total team skills in Figure 5.5—rather than the average, e.g. skills per person. This can give rise to some seemingly strange features in the attribute stock. The units for *total team skills* in this case are "people skills" because the total of 960 skills at the start will contain the nine skills of person A, plus the seven skills of person B, the 10 skills of person C, and so on.

Note also that each skill may not be equally held by all individuals—all 80 people may have skill X, 20 people have skill Y, but no one at all has skill Z.

This latter situation can create paradoxical outcomes. Since unskilled individuals may need guidance or cause errors that their skilled colleagues have to correct, their departure may actually *increase* the capacity of a team to cope with the demands that are placed on them. The team's true capacity is not given by the total number of people, but is reduced by the number who have to spend time dealing with the demands caused by unskilled colleagues. One case where this can arise is when hospitals use nurses from employment agencies to cover shortages of full-time staff. Although such staff are competent at general nursing skills, they may not be familiar with particular routines in the department where they are posted. Permanent nursing staff then have to explain things to the temps, rather than get on with their own work.

To work out the impact of the demands of the unskilled people on the capacity of an entire group therefore requires the numbers of skilled and unskilled people to be separately identified. The group's capacity is then given by:

*(total skilled staff minus skilled staff supporting unskilled) * capacity per skilled person*
*plus:*
*unskilled staff * capacity per unskilled person.*
*where:*
*skilled staff supporting unskilled = unskilled staff * skilled staff needed per unskilled*

This example of staff skills demonstrates the key point that:

> **There are only three ways to improve the quality of a resource—
> win better quality items, remove poorer quality items, or raise
> the quality of existing items.**

## IMPLICATIONS FOR PERFORMANCE ARISING FROM CHANGING LEVELS OF STAFF SKILL

Management is concerned about skill levels because of their ultimate impact on performance. Since the skills in this case concern customer support, the quality of that support is vulnerable to any shortfall in *either* the number of staff *or* their skills. If there are too few staff, calls will go unanswered, and if skill levels are too low some of the calls that are answered may not be responded to adequately. Either outcome will disappoint customers and a fraction of those who are disappointed will be lost.

In Figure 5.6, the business starts with 200 000 customers (at right), who make an average of one call per month to the call center. The initial 80 staff are enough to answer all incoming calls, and their skill level is high enough to ensure that virtually no customer calls are badly handled. The training rate of 7.5 days per month is sufficient both to maintain skills amongst existing staff and to train up the few new staff who arrive to replace the 5 %/month of people who leave.

About 5 000 new customers are won per month, which increases the rate of calls received. The call center hires an additional two staff per month, which raises capacity in line with growth of customers and call volume.

The call center thus continues to have enough capacity for staff to pick up the phone to every caller. In the first case (dashed lines) training continues at the rate of 7.5 days per month. Even the small number of additional new staff progressively dilutes the center's skill level. Although all calls continue to be answered, an increasing proportion of customers' enquiries are not dealt with properly. Even assuming that only a fraction of disappointed customers leave each month (20 % in this illustration) the loss rate rises until, by month 24, the business is losing as many customers as it wins. This is in spite of the fact that it has plenty of capacity to actually answer calls: 320 000/month versus a call rate of 270 000. If this example is carried forward beyond month 24, the loss rate continues to escalate, leading to a real decline in customers.

In the second case (solid lines, and bold text figures for the month 24 situation), the center manager raises the training time at a rate sufficient to ensure that the additional new staff are also trained. Average skill levels are maintained, customer enquiries are handled well, and virtually none of those customers is lost.

This numerical approach to estimating how skills are developing may appear rather mechanistic for an issue that is somewhat intangible and hard to define. However, specifying skill requirements and auditing organizations' skills or competencies is now a common practice,[4,5] and many consultancy organizations offer support for such assessments.[6] Furthermore, such audits are not limited to the routine task skills of operating-level staff, but are also applied to middle and senior management roles.[7] Table 5.7 illustrates a typical management competency matrix, with the competencies themselves listed down the left and the level of each competency across the top. Note that this horizontal axis is measuring the *level* of competency, so that any individual may expect to develop across the grid as their experience develops.

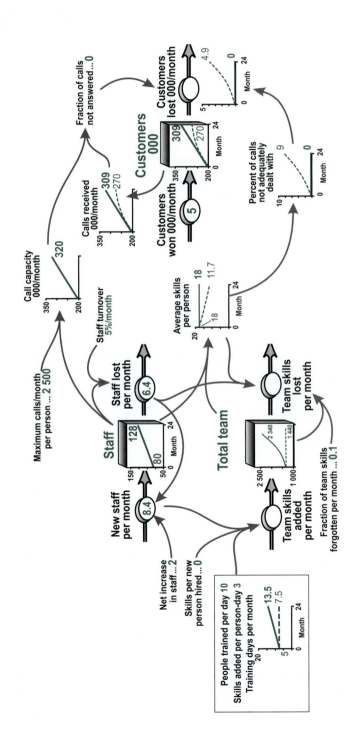

Figure 5.6: Customer losses arising from the dilution of skills amongst call center staff.

TABLE 5.7: ILLUSTRATIVE COMPETENCY MATRIX FOR MANAGEMENT

| | Entry | | Competent | | Mastery |
|---|---|---|---|---|---|
| | 1 | 2 | 3 | 4 | 5 |
| **Delivery** | | | | | |
| Delivering results | | | | | |
| Perseverance | | | | | |
| Target orientation | | | | | |
| **People-related** | | | | | |
| Team working | | | | | |
| People development | | | | | |
| Organizational awareness | | | | | |
| Change management | | | | | |
| **Intellectual** | | | | | |
| Analysis and problem solving | | | | | |
| Expertise development | | | | | |
| Knowledge sharing | | | | | |
| **Strategic** | | | | | |
| Customer orientation | | | | | |
| Market awareness | | | | | |
| Strategic focus | | | | | |

Adding up the assessment of these competencies across an entire cadre of management gives an integrated picture of skill levels covering the principal domains of ability that an organization needs from its executives. To gain value from such competency assessment for the continuing development of skills (rather than a one-time audit) requires consistent and regular application. If this is achieved, it is a relatively straightforward, if substantial, exercise to capture the staff/skills co-flow structure in Figure 5.5 for each identified skill. This understanding can then be used for a variety of purposes, such as providing the correct focus for assessing new hires, prioritizing training efforts, or identifying the impact of promotions or lateral job moves amongst management.

## STAFF EXPERIENCE

Not all staff skills can be made quite as explicit as is shown in Figures 5.5 and 5.6. In many cases, management simply understands that "experience" is important and that people perform better with more of this experience. This perspective implicitly assumes that tacit skills develop through time from exposure to the challenges of an individual's career. More experience is better—but only to a limited degree, since there may be limits to how much an individual can improve with additional experience.

Changes in experience levels can be captured by making some small adjustments to the staff/skills co-flow structure above. First, whereas skills are raised by training, experience is increased simply by the passing of time—each year that a person remains in their role adds one year to their experience. Second, experience is not "forgotten"—that extra year is added to their experience and is never lost. This is not to say that the implicit skills that come with experience are immortal; they are not, which is one reason why performance may not increase indefinitely as experience rises. Total experience for any group at any time is therefore given by:

$$
\begin{aligned}
\textit{Total experience today (person-years)} = &\ \textit{Total experience last year} \\
&+ \textit{staff hired * experience per person hired} \\
&+ \textit{staff remaining from last year * 1} \\
&- \textit{staff lost * average experience per person lost}
\end{aligned}
$$

This structure can pose challenges of many kinds, whether an organization is growing quickly, stable in size, or shrinking.

The challenge for a rapidly growing organization is to achieve the rising numbers of people it needs, whilst ensuring that there is sufficient experience to keep the enterprise functioning properly. In Figure 5.7, a 50-strong organization must hire enough people to grow at just 20% per year, and also to replace those lost through staff turnover. Initial experience averages five years, but new hires bring no new experience with them. Staff leaving the organization have the same experience as the average.

In the first case (dashed line and light text for year five values), staff turnover is a modest 10% per year. Even this modest rate of staff turnover leads to falling experience levels, since in each year the population contains three people in every 12 with no experience. For every 10 people leaving in the first year, 50 person-years of experience go with them, to be replaced with one more year for every person in the

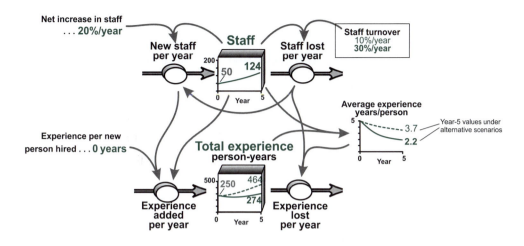

**Figure 5.7: Loss of experience in a fast-growing organization.**

population. Note that, although only 40 of the opening number of staff remain by the end of year one, some additional experience is lost by people who leave part-way through the year, and some more is added by newcomers who join early in the year. With 20 % growth, average experience can only be sustained at five years per person if there is zero staff turnover.

It is not uncommon for fast-growing organizations to experience much faster staff turnover than 10 % each year, so the second scenario in Figure 5.7 (solid lines, bold text for year five values) shows the impact of 30 % turnover. Average experience now plunges to just 2.2 years. The challenge becomes still more serious if those people who leave have more than average experience, as may occur if such organizations are targeted by competitors looking for scarce talent in a rapidly developing industry. If the organization shown here were to lose people who have been around two years longer than average, experience levels amongst those who remain would drop to barely one year.

Two further points should be noted. First, this problem is not limited to the growth pains of entrepreneurial small firms, but can also arise for fast-growing groups within more established organizations. It can also arise when growth is limited, but rapid staff attrition is driven by powerful forces. A particularly tragic example concerns the impact of AIDS on companies' experience base in countries where the disease is prevalent. In South Africa, for example, the challenge is so serious that it has led to pressure for public companies to spell out how AIDS is affecting their business, markets and workers, and show how they are fighting it.[8]

Second, it can become impossible for such groups to develop any significant capability. Capability arises from the combination of skilled people and the processes and procedures, both explicit and tacit, that they develop by working together. (This issue will be addressed in detail in Chapters 8–10.) With so little collective experience, there is little opportunity for effective processes and procedures to develop, and a high chance of any that *are* developed being lost. No one knows how to do things effectively, so constant, wasteful reinvention occurs.

Quite opposite issues arise in mature organizations where staff numbers are static or falling. With few alternative career prospects, turnover amongst staff is limited, so there is little scope for hiring to bring in new blood. In Figure 5.8, an organization develops over 20 years, starting with 200 staff of 15 years' average experience. Staff turnover is initially low, at about 4% per year. As the organization tries to reduce costs, staff numbers are reduced by 5% per year.

In the first scenario (dashed lines and light text) staff with 10 years' experience are hired only in sufficient numbers to replace natural attrition. Experience levels climb as incumbent staff age, until after 20 years the organization reaches an average of nearly 28 years' experience. It may seem a good thing to have highly experienced staff, but this situation may well imply that the average person is in his or her 50s. Now, whilst it is unreasonable (and in some jurisdictions illegal) to discriminate against older employees, this situation brings real threats to the organization's performance. With so little replacement of staff, the bulk of the population will be heading towards retirement within 10–15 years, at which point the business will face a collapse in staff numbers. This is beginning to occur in Figure 5.8, as natural staff turnover rises to 9.7% per year.

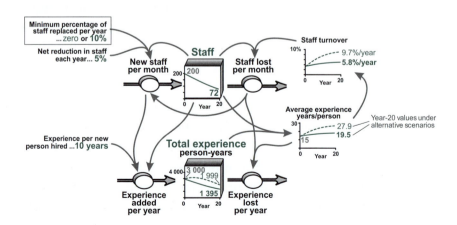

**Figure 5.8: Aging staff in a shrinking organization, and the effect of forced hiring and turnover.**

(Online learning materials are available to support this example, see p.xxi.)

Such problems currently afflict a number of industries. After nearly two decades of under-hiring by oil firms, for example, the industry finds the average petroleum engineer is approaching 50 years of age (see www.uh.edu/ednews/2006/waco/200602/20060215engineers.html). In privatized European utilities firms, pressures from industry regulators to cut prices has put such pressure on industry costs that power companies have shed engineers without replacing them, as have water and gas companies. In these industries too, the average age is climbing. With limited job opportunities, few new graduates will be available when these industries finally have no choice but to replace aging staff who retire.

Public services and voluntary organizations are also vulnerable to such dynamics. With low turnover amongst nurses, for example, some countries needed only to encourage a rather low rate of training for new nurses. As the existing population of nurses aged, turnover gradually increased leaving health services with severe shortages that could only be filled by hiring staff from developing countries—countries that could least afford to lose people with these important skills.

The only way to avoid the challenges arising from over-aging of staff is to enforce some minimum rate of new hiring, which may entail forced attrition amongst existing staff if this is permitted. In the second scenario of Figure 5.8, the business makes sure to hire at a rate that adds at least 10 % of new staff to the group, and asks enough existing staff to leave in order to make space for these new arrivals. This ensures that experience levels do not climb above an average of 20 years. Such a policy should, of course, be implemented only in ways that are consistent with the ethical treatment of employees and any relevant legislation.

## STRATEGY AND HUMAN CAPITAL

There is of course much more complexity and subtlety in the contribution of people to organizational performance than simply their numbers, skills and experience. To be effective, organizations need people with commitment and motivation. These features combine with processes and procedures to determine productivity of different groups. People generally must collaborate in order to achieve what the organization needs, collaboration that reflects the culture and style of leadership and management at all levels. In addition, when operating in fast-changing conditions, as many organizations do, they may need people to be adaptable and innovative. Note, though, that not all groups or organizations require the "constant reinvention" sometimes advocated in popular management articles. Many situations call for people who are both able and willing to follow stable, well-defined procedures for many years.

Clearly, staff and the ways in which they are organized, rewarded and managed are critical to performance, which makes the development of effective human resource policies and practices most important.[9] Human resources and human capital are therefore widely acknowledged in the strategy field to be vital; indeed, it is sometimes claimed that people may be the only truly sustainable source of competitive advantage.[10]

Suggestions as to how these issues should be treated in considering firm strategy vary significantly.[11] The term "human capital" may be used variously to refer to the knowledge and skills of a firm's entire workforce, or—moving some way from the people themselves—the productive services that they offer to the organizations for whom they work. The phrase implies that human resources might be valued and added to a company's assets on the balance sheet, although this is not feasible in practice because people are not "owned" by the organization they work for, cannot usually be bought or sold by employers, and have a tendency to leave of their own volition. Attempts to ascribe a proportion of the value a company creates to its human assets will also fail since, as pointed out in earlier chapters, it is the entire system that creates value, not any isolated element.

Nevertheless, there is one sense in which "accounting" for human resources may be useful, and to which the strategy dynamics approach offers a contribution. Since companies frequently claim that people "are our most important assets," it is entirely reasonable to expect those assets to be properly accounted for, just as is done for cash. Earlier chapters have recognized that staff obey the stock-and-flow structure in just the same way as any other resource.

Human resource accounting has been a recognized practice, if not widespread, for many years, and stems from the appreciation that important human resource decisions involving hiring, training, compensation, and so on, are often made with little information about the costs and benefits involved.[12] Measuring the costs of recruiting, hiring, rewarding and training employees allows management to evaluate training programs, productivity investments, and policies towards promotions, transfers, layoffs, and so on.

The approach illustrated in Figure 5.5 takes a somewhat different, albeit complementary perspective, in that it "accounts" for people and their skills *in their own terms*, not simply by reference to the financial costs, benefits and values involved. Table 5.8 demonstrates a conventional spreadsheet format for this approach, replicating data for the early months of Figure 5.6.

TABLE 5.8: ACCOUNTING FOR MONTHLY CHANGES IN STAFF NUMBERS AND SKILLS

| Start of month . . . | 1 | 2 | 3 | |
|---|---|---|---|---|
| **Staff** | 80 | 82 | 84 | 86 |
| New staff per month | 6 | 6.1 | 6.2 | 6.3 |
| Staff lost per month | 4 | 4.1 | 4.2 | 4.3 |
| **Total team skills** | 1440 | 1449 | 1457 | 1463 |
| Fraction of team skills lost per month 10% | | | | |
| Decrease in total team skills per month | 216 | 217 | 219 | 219 |
| Increase in total team skills per month | 225 | 225 | 225 | 225 |
| Average skills per person | 18.0 | 17.7 | 17.3 | 17.0 |
| Training days per month | 7.5 | | | |
| People trained per day | 10 | | | |
| Skills added per person-day | 3 | | | |

These data can readily be connected with the corresponding financials, such as the cost per new hire, cost per training day, salary cost per person, and so on. Furthermore, the financial benefits in terms of the impact on sales that arises from these changes in numbers and skills of people can also be articulated, as explained in Chapter 2. Note that the approach offers the additional contribution of making clear the likely connection between the *timing* of hiring, training and other interventions and the changing trajectory of revenues and costs that will result. It thus makes a strong contribution to assessing strategy, not just evaluating the cost/benefit trade-off from distinct decisions, since it lays out how those most important assets—people and their skills—are developed and sustained over time.

With only the basic elements of staff numbers, skills and experience to work with, it is only possible to make a limited start towards the goal of clarifying the connection between human resources and strategic performance. Further progress will require the formulation of broader organizational capabilities, which will need to reflect both the skills of people and the processes and procedures at their disposal. This will be covered in Chapters 8–10.

## ATTRIBUTE DYNAMICS FOR PHYSICAL RESOURCES

Many organizations rely heavily on physical assets for their operations—the production equipment of manufacturing companies, the distribution equipment for utilities firms, furniture and fittings in restaurants, hotels and hospitals, and so on. Such equipment may have important attributes that describe their contribution to total capacity. For example, each vehicle in a distribution firm can move a certain quantity of freight-miles each day.

Another important feature of physical assets, however, is their state of repair. Nearly all such items wear out, with a range of undesirable consequences. In restaurants and hotels, worn out furniture damages customers' perceptions of quality; in process industries, deteriorating equipment can lead to a fall in throughput; and in many industries, aging equipment becomes unreliable, leading to increasing failure rates.

Organizations that rely on physical assets therefore have a tricky balance to achieve. On the one hand, they need to keep equipment sufficiently young and well-maintained to perform well. On the other hand, they need to minimize the cash they spend on maintaining equipment and on replacing items that are in an especially poor state.

In Figure 5.9, a utility company is concerned with a group of increasingly unreliable units of equipment (e.g. pumps for a water supplier, power switches in an electricity distribution firm). There are 5 000 of these units, which are initially quite reliable with only 5 % failing in any year. In an effort to contain costs, management has limited spending on both maintenance and replacement. It has been spending $5m/year on replacing the worst of its units, sufficient to upgrade 100 units per year. It has also been spending $5m/year on maintenance, sufficient to maintain each unit on average once every three years. Units deteriorate evermore rapidly as the time between each maintenance event increases (beyond a minimum of six months).

The attribute of concern here is reliability, specified in terms of the failure frequency per unit—strictly its "unreliability." New units bring with them a low number of failures per year. Unreliable units that are replaced take with them their high failure rate. Since it is the worst units that are replaced, they take with them five times the average failure rate of the entire population of units. (Note that this constant multiple is a substantial simplification.) The total number of failures per year is added to by the rising failure rate of all existing units.

With the failure rate increasing rapidly, management is concerned with how badly the situation could deteriorate if current spending plans continue. As each year passes, existing units are giving rise to 250 new failures per year, and the few reliable new units are bringing only two additional failures per year (100 units with

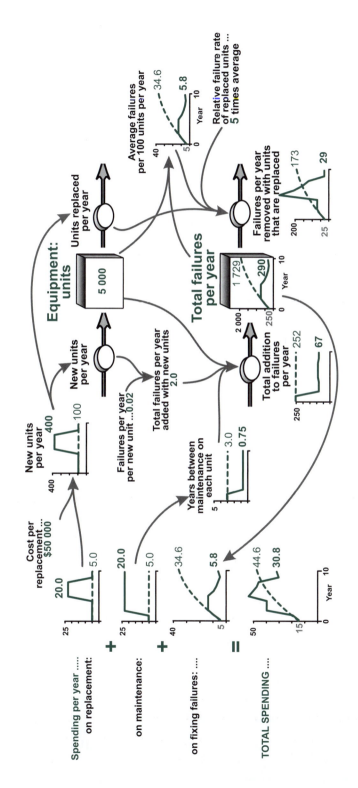

a failure rate of 2%/year). Continuing this strategy will lead to an ever escalating failure rate (dashed lines and light text for values at year 10 in Figure 5.9). Although the costs of maintenance and replacement remain low, the company has to spend increasingly on fixing the rising number of failures. The problem only slows in its growth because the few units that are replaced are so unreliable that removing them nearly balances the high rate of new failures.

The question for management concerns how much to spend on maintenance and replacement, and what this might do to future failure rates and total costs. In the strategy shown (solid lines and bold text), they choose in year two to increase sharply the spending on maintenance, reducing the average time between maintenance events from three years to 0.75 years. This increases total spending to about $39m/year, but at least the failure rate is not getting worse, and the previous strategy would, in any case, lead to similar costs by about year seven—as well as risking damage to the firm's reputation with customers.

Although reliability is prevented from getting worse after year two, management is still dissatisfied with the high rate of failures of approximately 680/year. They therefore embark on a program of equipment replacement, and for years four to eight raise the rate of replacement from 100 to 400 units per year. This is very costly, but drops total failures to under 300/year, at which point, the replacement program is cut back once more. Costs more or less stabilize at $30.8m/year. (Online learning materials are available to support this example, see p.xxi.)

A number of issues are illustrated by this example, with important implications for strategy:

- First, note that this strategy is concerned with the *cost* side of the firm's profit and loss, rather than its revenues. For firms in mature, capital-intensive industries, this is a substantial and challenging part of their strategy, especially if the scope for revenue growth is limited—not many people in developed economies are starting to express a new demand for water, for example.
- Second, such situations exhibit long timescales between changes in strategy and the performance consequences. In this case, it took five years before the initial increase in maintenance spending was outweighed by the savings in cost of failures.
- This can give rise to unfortunate consequences. It is always tempting to cut back on current costs so as to hit short-term profit goals and "meet investor expectations." However, tomorrow's investors will not be pleased to inherit a business that is in bad shape and quickly getting worse.

The main counter to this imbalance of incentives arises from dissatisfaction amongst customers, who may punish suppliers, if they are able to, by leaving for alternative providers. You can always tell, for example, when a hotel or restaurant chain is in trouble from the increasingly dilapidated state of its outlets. In some industries, such punishment by customers is not possible —there is not generally an alternative power grid or water network for consumers to choose. Consequently, such industries are often regulated, with targets for prices *and* for reliability being imposed by regulators on the firms involved. Regulators, too, can misunderstand the balance between these factors—in one market, for example, water companies' investment plans approved by the regulator were sufficient to replace their assets once every 250 years!

## DEPRECIATION

The fact that equipment and other assets deteriorate is recognized in financial terms through depreciation. A newly purchased item brings with it its initial cost, which gets added to the total current value of the organization's fixed assets. Thereafter, as each year passes, some of that initial value is deducted from the total and charged to the profit and loss account as a notional cost of doing business in that year. If the item is sold, it is removed from the stock of assets, along with its remaining value.

Some items depreciate slowly—heavy equipment in utilities, process industries and so on can last 10 years or more. Other items depreciate more quickly, such as computer equipment or retail store fittings. This depreciation can be captured readily in the resource attribute co-flow structure, with the units themselves being held in the upper resource-stock and the total current value in the lower attribute. To do this accurately would require each different type of asset to be handled separately, and in practice this offers little value for strategy development and strategic management that cannot be obtained directly from normal accounting approaches to assets, value and depreciation.

# THE RESOURCE QUALITY CURVE

A useful device for understanding and working with resource attributes is the "quality curve," which lays out the quality profile of individual elements within a certain type of resource. This method works by showing the contribution of each item— each customer, product, employee, etc.—to some measure of quality that is of interest. It is an adaptation of Figure 5.4, which showed the size-distribution of a firm's customer base.

Figure 5.10 shows an example of such a quality curve. It is constructed by showing first the revenue from a company's largest customer, then adding the revenue from

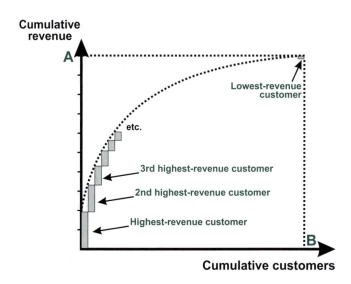

**Figure 5.10:** The resource quality curve, e.g. customers' contribution to total revenue.

the second largest, the third largest, and so on. At the far right is shown the very small revenue contributed from the company's smallest customer. The average revenue per customer is given by dividing the total revenue, A, by the total number of customers, B.

The key principle to note is that:

> **Individual items within a resource may vary in quality, and that variation can have important implications.**

The size profile of a customer base can vary widely, from a quite balanced distribution, where customers differ little in size, to highly skewed, where the few largest customers dominate the company's revenue and a long "tail" of small customers contribute very little (Figure 5.11). Such differences can arise from features of the market the firm serves, or result from a deliberate policy choice by management. A balanced distribution, for example, may reflect a decision to target customers within a certain size band. One insurance company developed a real-estate insurance product aimed at households in the second quartile of income (i.e. 25% of households earn more, and 50% earn less). The income distribution within this band is not especially wide, so the largest customers' policies were not many times larger than the smallest. Conversely, a skewed distribution could result if, for example, management decided to move from a history of serving smaller customers by chasing a few large deals.

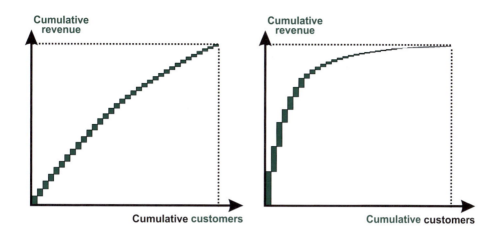

**Figure 5.11:** Balanced versus skewed distribution of customer quality.

Most companies would benefit from knowing the shape of this curve, and from having an explicit policy detailing how they wish it to develop, covering the three classes of change highlighted earlier—adding (or losing) larger customers, losing (or adding) smaller customers, and seeking to grow existing customers.

It can be valuable to develop equivalent quality curves for other resources too, with appropriate choice of measure for the quality indicator on the vertical axis. Examples include the productivity of individual employees in a team, market-reach of distributors, numbers of customers attracted by separate products in a product range, and reliability of individual items of equipment.

Similar pictures can be helpful in voluntary organizations and the public sector, for example the varying contribution of funds from donors to charitable organizations or political parties, the rates of illegal activity committed by criminals, and so on. In the case of the Motor Neurone Disease Association discussed in Chapter 2, analysis of the volunteers who visited the Association's members to provide help and comfort discovered that this resource was highly skewed. A small fraction of visitors were highly active, supporting large numbers of people, whilst the majority were making very few visits to small numbers of members. This distribution reflected the way in which the volunteers were managed, as well as their personal circumstances. With some turnover amongst volunteers, and a significant cost involved in their training, the Association needed to focus on developing volunteers who were willing and able to visit members quite frequently. At the same time, it was recognized that very few volunteers would be able to contribute the highest rates of activity, so attention focused on growing the number of volunteers in the middle band.

## MANAGING THE CUSTOMER QUALITY PROFILE

Before deciding how to drive change in the quality profile of a customer base, it is important to note that:

**Customer *size* is not the same as customer *value*.**

It is therefore necessary to distinguish the *scale* of customers in terms of their contribution to sales volume or revenue from their *value* in terms of profitability. This ordering of customers by profitability may not match the size-order for various reasons:

- larger customers may press for lower prices, so although their size is large, the profit margin on their purchases is low

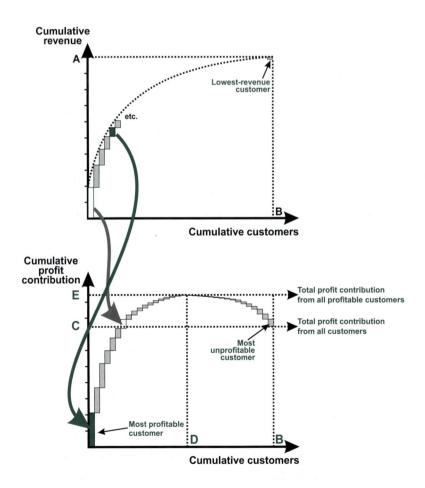

**Figure 5.12: Customer quality differs when considering value rather than size.**

- larger customers may expect higher levels of service, which incurs more cost and again depresses profitability
- larger customers can be more complex to serve, again raising cost and reducing profitability.

Figure 5.12 illustrates this link from a size distribution to profit distribution, where the white customer is the largest but not the most profitable and the green customer is the most profitable but not the largest. Note that the lower curve for profit distribution turns down at the right-hand end if there are any unprofitable customers, i.e. these loss-makers "add" negative profits to the cumulative positive profits earned by the profitable customers to the left of "D."

### Doing it right: take care with cost allocations

The analysis in Figure 5.12 can be very sensitive to exactly how costs are allocated. Note that the vertical axis is "profit *contribution*," not simply "profit," to recognize that some costs are not driven by specific customers but are incurred across the customer base (e.g. the cost of the sales vice-president or the customer-information systems). Closing customers between "D" and "B" will not remove the need for these kinds of cost. It is therefore important to know by how much total costs will actually be cut if such a rationalization is to be carried out. Similar caution is needed if the curve is constructed, say, to assess the profit contributions of individual products in a product range. Many shared costs will not be eliminated if the product range is reduced.

It is tempting to interpret this curve as saying simply close down unprofitable customers to the right of "D" and profits will jump from "C" to "E." However, in addition to complications arising from the allocation of costs (see box), there are several further reasons to investigate before taking such simple actions.

- An individual customer may not remain at a fixed point on the curve—it may be possible to develop loss-making customers so that they move over to the left of "D." Banks, for example, recognize this when they accept young adults as customers in the knowledge that they will become profitable as they mature and enjoy rising incomes. It remains important, however, to be disciplined about this issue, checking periodically that promising but unprofitable customers genuinely *are* moving to the left, rather than simply accepting optimistic assertions that this will occur.

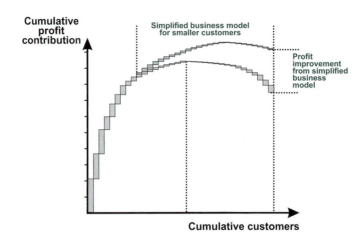

**Figure 5.13: Enhanced profitability curve resulting from a simplified service to smaller customers.**

- Customers may be linked. To continue the banking example, the bank may well be incurring losses in serving that same young customer, but it would be careless to close their account and risk upsetting their millionaire parents!
- Finally, it is often possible to challenge fundamentally why the curve is the shape it is. There may be simplified and cheaper ways to serve smaller customers that enable viable profits to be made that could not be obtained with the full-service business model required by larger customers (see Figure 5.13). Such differential service models are common in many industries, from telecoms and IT support to industrial equipment supply—indeed customers may be divided into several bands, rather than just large versus small.

## USING THE CUSTOMER QUALITY CURVE FOR CHOOSING WHERE TO COMPETE

In addition to assessing the quality curve for their own organization, management may also be able to estimate its shape for the market as a whole. They can then make an explicit choice about where on the curve to compete. This question is not solely about selecting customer segments that may have different needs, as explained with the discussion of the value curve in Chapter 2. It also includes selection of what scale of customers to choose from the range of sizes available. Rather than scramble for the biggest (in terms of potential sales volume or revenue), firms should consider the merits of targeting somewhat lesser customers who may have less power to demand lower prices or high support, and who may be relatively neglected by competitors.

Not only is the selection of priorities on this customer quality curve important for enhancing profitability, it can also have important implications for the wider strategic architecture of the organization. If, for example, a business expected to enjoy substantial growth in numbers of mid-range customers, rather than the slower growth that may be possible if it focused only on the largest, that choice would alter the required size and experience of its sales team. It could also have important consequences for the scaling of customer service operations or (in the case of product-supply companies) their logistics resources in the form of warehousing or vehicles. The choice may even call into question what activities the firm should do itself, rather than outsource to others. A limited organization with a large potential number of smaller customers may decide that it cannot undertake sales and support efforts itself and work instead through agents or resellers.

It was noted earlier that using a single attribute resource alongside a tangible resource may lose the detail of how resource quality is distributed within a population, captured by the quality curves described above. One way to achieve some of the benefits of quality curve analysis without excessive complexity is to divide the resource into segments; for example, looking at numbers of customers that generate small average sales versus large. Analysis can then focus on how quickly small customers are being won, lost or developed into large ones, and on how quickly large customers are being won, lost, or declining to become small ones.

If it is sufficiently valuable, the customer base could be divided into more segments, each defined in terms of a range of sales or profit contribution, and the dynamics of each monitored and managed.

## THE QUALITY CURVE FOR OTHER RESOURCES

The quality curve can also be usefully assessed for resources other than customers. It can often be enlightening to assess the contributions to sales and profits from individual products in a product range. This may be a relatively simple exercise where products are few in number and serve a simple business, for example menu items for a restaurant chain or individual routes in an airline's network. It can become considerably more complex when the product range is large, complex and highly interdependent. Discontinuing products in a supermarket or home improvement chain, for example, must be done with care if those products are fundamental to why customers visit the stores in the first place or support the sales of other products.

Employees within a team or function may also exhibit a quality profile. Telephone sales teams sometimes employ a ranking system to reward the most successful members and to inspire competitive behavior amongst the team as a whole. Naturally, such rankings are also used to suggest to the lower performers that their talents may be better employed elsewhere.

A further example concerns the "negative" attribute case of equipment failures described in Figure 5.9. The illustration simply assumed that there would always be a substantial number of units that were five times more unreliable than the average. In practice, individual units have their own risk of failure, and the profile may range between being relatively even, with little spread in breakdown rates across all units, or heavily skewed by a small number of highly unreliable units. The latter case will require capital expenditure to replace just the few worst units, whereas failures that are more widely dispersed across the population will require a similarly widespread expenditure on maintenance, which may take longer to have an impact and require more staff resource to achieve.

# ATTRIBUTES THAT BRING ACCESS TO OTHER POTENTIAL RESOURCES

Certain resources bring with them access to *other* potential resources that must then be converted into an active part of the business. Those potential resources are themselves attributes of the first resource. For these purposes, we will describe the first resource as "primary," and the resource to which it brings access will be termed "secondary." This terminology does *not* imply any importance—both may be vital to the organization's performance.

## RETAIL STORES GIVE ACCESS TO POTENTIAL CONSUMERS

This is perhaps the most visible example to the general public of a case where a resource (stores) is expanded so as to give access to a separate resource (consumers). We can see daily the opening of new outlets for Starbucks, Wal-Mart, IKEA, etc., and many of us change our shopping habits when an appealing new retail store appears in our neighborhood. Behind this expansion lie highly sophisticated procedures for assessing the likely sales and profitability of each new unit. For units in high streets or shopping malls, retailers will assess the numbers of people using the area, the likely numbers passing different possible units within the area, and their likely capture rate for passing consumers. For destination shopping—cinemas, home improvement stores, restaurants—they will appraise the number and profile of consumers living within a likely catchment area of a new location, that area being defined not in terms of simple distance (people living within five miles) but in terms of drive-time (people living within 15 minutes).

This case raises the important issue that gaining access to *potential* customers is not the same as actually *winning* those customers. Having opened a new store, a retailer must of course offer products and services that its target consumers want and at prices that represent good value. It also illustrates a vital consideration in all cases where resources are expanded in order to reach others—how far to push that expansion. Early in the expansion of a retail chain, every new store can be opened in a locality that is new for that chain, and where there are large numbers of potential consumers. As expansion continues, however, two things change:

- locations for new stores offer access only to smaller numbers of consumers
- each new store's catchment area is increasingly likely to overlap with that of existing units, so any sales it attracts may only arise by taking sales from neighbors.

In Figure 5.14, an initially successful retailer is expanding its network of stores over a 10-year period. With its first stores able to reach 20000 consumers who each spend

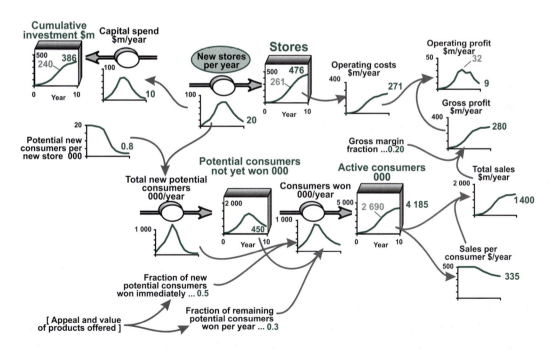

Figure 5.14: Sales and profits of a retailer exceeding the viable potential for store numbers.

$500/year on its goods, management believes there is potential for over 200 stores reaching up to five million consumers. For the first five years, plans go well, but as expansion passes the target number of stores, consumer numbers and sales fall short of expectations. Nevertheless, with each new store seeming to win enough consumers to be worthwhile, and sales continuing to grow, the company presses on with expansion. (Online learning materials are available to support this example, see p.xxi.)

Unfortunately, hidden beneath the reasonable top-line indicators there is a sharp fall in the true number of new consumers won with each new opening, and new stores increasingly succeed only by taking sales from established stores. Furthermore, the later consumers turn out to spend less with the stores than those captured from around the initial locations. The costs of operating these later stores, whilst lower than the costs of the earlier stores, is not covered by the incremental revenues and gross profit from the sharply reducing rate of new consumers, and profits go into decline.

Had this company cut its expansion rate when the additional numbers of consumers with each new store dropped sharply (e.g. as shown in grey text about half way through its expansion in year six), it would have attracted most of the potential market, kept profits at $32m/year, and only had to invest $240million of capital rather than the $385million it eventually spent.

In fact, the firm's performance with this capped expansion would have been still better. Note (bottom of Figure 5.14) that each store captures about half of its potential consumers as soon as it opens, but continues to win more of the remaining potential in each following year. Consequently, this business would continue to grow active consumers, sales and profits even after it stops expanding at 261 stores, reaching over $70million in operating profits by year 10 (not shown in this Figure).

Strategic management of market saturation with expansion of a retail business can be explored in the White Label Restaurants Microworld business simulation game available from www.strategydynamics.com. In addition to this issue, the microworld includes the impact of product development on expanding market potential, the pressure to accelerate progress when a competitor is pursuing the same opportunity, and the need to satisfy investors' requirements in order to attract the capital to continue expansion.

The framework in Figure 5.14, has further important implications for the strategic question of "where to compete?" In this case, as in many real-world situations, management has become focused on taking all the available potential. Not only is it impossible to serve this potential profitably, but the efforts to do so lead to further difficulties. These include damage to the firm's reputation in the market as it is seen to operate second-rate units, diversion of management attention onto solving the problem they themselves created, damage to investor confidence, and poor morale amongst middle- and front-line management. It is worth recalling the comment in McDonalds' 2002 letter to shareholders reported in Chapter 1, that the business was *"in transition from a company that emphasizes 'adding restaurants to customers' to one that emphasizes 'adding customers to restaurants'."*

This is not to say that management should give up at the first sign of having "used up" their business opportunity. It is often possible to find ways of profitably serving smaller markets. Second, many retail chains have expanded the potential market, and thus lifted the ceiling on viable growth by extending the range of products and services offered in the same space. Many have also developed slimmed-down units, offering limited product-ranges and incurring much reduced operating costs precisely to enable them to reach smaller local markets. These principles can readily be adopted with suitable adjustment by businesses in other industries.

## BUSINESSES USING AGENTS, WHOLESALERS, RESELLERS OR DISTRIBUTORS

Chapter 2 explained that many organizations have "intermediaries," in addition to end-customers. At that point in our discussion, these two types of resource were treated quite separately, but they are in fact closely linked, since each additional distributor gives access to a certain number of potential end-customers. 3M Inc, for example, has long made use of distributors to sell its ranges of industrial consumables, such as abrasives, adhesives and cleaning products to business customers of all kinds. Since many such customers are quite small (e.g. car repairers), it was not practical for a large organization to deal directly with each. Distributors, on the other hand, could do so economically, by avoiding the complexities and overheads of a large organization and by providing a wide range of products from a variety of suppliers.

Companies who rely on such intermediaries face important strategic decisions about how best to use them. They may need to consider whether to rely on these organizations totally, or deal directly with some end-customers themselves. This brings with it the potential for serious conflict between the intermediary, who wishes to control the customer relationship, and the supplier, who may want to develop a direct relationship.[13] The advent of Internet-based trading has sharpened this dilemma by making it possible for many companies to deal directly with customers who could previously be reached only through wholesalers or distributors.

## ORIGINAL EQUIPMENT MANUFACTURERS

An example of original equipment manufacturers (OEMs) (whose customers produce a range of final products into which the OEM's product may be incorporated) concerns suppliers of car subsystems, such as air conditioning or braking systems, who engage in fierce rivalry to have their particular systems incorporated in car makers' model ranges. Intel and AMD are engaged in similar battles to have their processor chips incorporated in the computer models of PC manufacturers.

Another intriguing example concerns the continuing competition for the supply of operating systems for cellphones.[*] In the early years of cellphone production, manufacturers developed simple software themselves to operate their handsets. However, as the required functionality increased, this investment became unsustainable for individual producers.

Formed in 1998 as a joint venture between four manufacturers of wireless communication and computing devices—Nokia, Ericsson, Motorola and Psion—a business called Symbian inherited the software division of UK company Psion Ltd and set out to create an industry standard operating system for "smartphones." These devices add to regular phones the functionality of personal digital assistants (PDAs), especially the ability to synchronize data on contacts, appointments, and so on, with users' PCs. These operating systems now enable a considerably wider range of functions, often developed by independent application developers. In trying to stay ahead of its main rival Microsoft, Symbian sought to capture each handset manufacturer as a licensee for its operating system. Each such producer releases a number of handset models each year, so as each manufacturer is won, Symbian gains access to a stream of new handset releases.

## NEW PRODUCTS GIVE ACCESS TO POTENTIAL NEW CUSTOMERS

In the car industry, manufacturers occasionally identify new classes of vehicle that meet previously unserved needs of car buyers, for example people-carriers, sport

---

[*] I am grateful to Andrie de Vries for his work on this case.

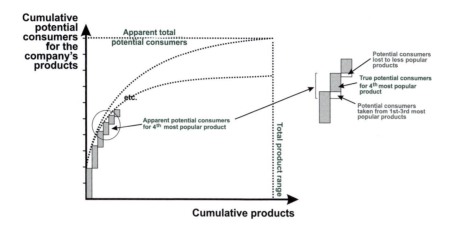

**Figure 5.15: Cannibalization amongst individual products in a confectionery product range.**

utility vehicles (SUVs), and hybrid-engine vehicles. Each such new product brings access to the population of potential customers who might desire that type of vehicle, but the company still has to create good vehicles and promote them effectively in order to turn those potential customers into actual buyers.

Just as the retail store chain in Figure 5.14 overextended its expansion, it is easy to overextend a product range. This is what happened with the confectionery company mentioned in Chapter 3 that tried to outperform market leader Mars by offering a wider range of products. Figure 5.15 illustrates what was happening in that case. If the company added up the numbers of consumers who enjoyed each product, it may have believed its overall product range could capture the total number of consumers given by the upper curve. However, as the detail at right for product 4 illustrates, each later product was cannibalizing potential consumers from stronger products, and was in turn losing some of its own potential consumers to less popular products. Overall, the product range only addressed the smaller number of consumers given by the lower curve. Indeed, the weakest products attracted virtually no *additional* consumers at all—their apparently worthwhile sales volume only arose from capturing sales that would otherwise have gone to the strongest products.

This phenomenon of overextended product ranges is widespread in consumer goods, and has led to companies in the sector and the consultants who advise them developing substantial programs for slimming down a brand portfolio.[14] Companies in other sectors would do well to see if they also have added too many products without cutting back on weaker items in the range.

**Beware self-inflicted damage**

Remarkably, certain firms pursue policies that appear purposefully designed to make life difficult for themselves. A famously innovative global manufacturing firm offers a range of consumable products that it sells to very large numbers of mostly small- to medium-sized business customers. The company controls salesforce costs via strict headcount limits, whilst at the same time driving the organization to introduce new products as rapidly as possible. Whenever a new product arrives, therefore, the salesforce has no choice but to give up promoting established, profitable products to free up time for the new item. Whilst the company largely avoids the danger illustrated in Figure 5.15 of supporting too many products that cannibalize each other, the result is a constant churn of perfectly successful products and very short product lives. Market after market is sacrificed to competitors who gratefully accept the gift!

# RESOURCES CARRYING MULTIPLE ATTRIBUTES

Sometimes it is necessary to track more than one characteristic of a value resource; for example, both the skills and experience of staff, both the sales and service support needs of customers, and so on. Where customers are concerned, this is a further important element in firms' decisions regarding the part of their market in which they wish to compete. It will have consequences not only for the demand and revenue element of performance, but also for various elements on the supply side (required product performance, service support needs, etc.) and resulting costs.

The financial services industry offers a number of examples where customers carry several important characteristics. In Figure 5.16, for example, a large bank starts with 1.8m consumer loans, each of $4000 value, for which it charged interest of 8% p.a. when the loans were granted. Enquiries for new loans are driven by marketing spend of $5m/month, with higher interest rates resulting in a lower fraction of enquiries being converted into actual sales of new loans. Initially, this rate of new lending matches the number of loans repaid after a 24-month loan period. This is an example of an important and widespread issue:

**Resources may have more than one attribute that determines their contribution to performance.**

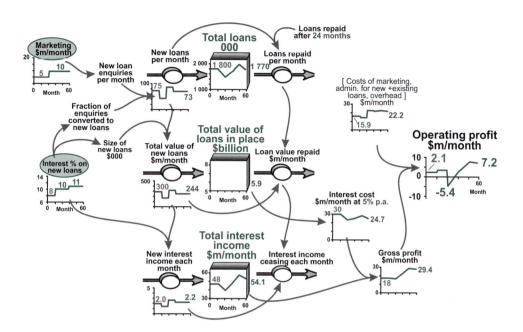

**Figure 5.16:** Impact of marketing and interest rates on value and interest income for a bank's loans.

Each new loan brings with it two key attributes—its value, and the monthly interest income received. The *total* value of loans in place starts at $7.2 billion (1.8m loans of $4000 each), and *total* monthly interest income starts at $48/month. (Note that this interest income is a further example of a factor that is not strictly a resource, but is used to indicate the attribute of the loans.) In practice there is a third important attribute in such cases—the probability that the borrower would default in any month. This would result in an additional outflow from each resource in this picture; i.e. the loss of loans, their value, and the interest income that was previously being received. (Online learning materials are available to support this example, see p.xxi.)

The company initially makes a gross profit of $18m/month on the difference between interest received and what this money costs the firm (5 % p.a.) In addition to its marketing costs and $2m/month in overhead, the bank incurs the following costs:

- responding to initial customer enquiries ($10)
- setting up loans that are granted ($50)
- administering existing loans, e.g. providing statements and answering enquiries ($2/month per loan).

The bank has two main options for managing its performance:

- Increasing its marketing spend will raise costs but bring in more enquiries, a fraction of which will convert to actual new loans.

- Raising the interest on new loans will reduce the fraction of enquiries that are converted, reduce the average size of loan consumers take on, but raise the monthly interest received per $ lent.

After 12 months, the bank raises the interest rate charged on new loans from 8% to 10% in an effort to improve margins. However, fewer loans are granted, and of a smaller size, so the total number and value of loans in place starts to decline. Total monthly interest income also declines, but at a slower proportional rate due to the higher interest being charged on the new loans. Consequently, gross profit barely changes—it actually declines very slightly in the chart near bottom-right— and savings in the cost of taking on fewer new loans result in a small improvement in operating profit.

To counter the loss of new loan inflows, the bank doubles its marketing spend in month 24, causing a higher rate of new enquiries, and reversing the decline in total loan volumes, value and interest income. Operating profit is sharply reduced by the extra marketing spend, but starts growing as new interest income is earned.

With this success, the bank is tempted into pushing interest rates up once more, to 11% in month 36. This again reduces the proportion of enquiries that are converted, and the size of each loan, but the higher interest rate causes gross profit and operating income to continue rising.

With no changes in policy, it might be expected that the trajectory of improved performance would continue after month 36. However, in month 48 there is a sudden reversal in growth, caused by a jump in the loan repayment rate. The cause of this is that the higher rate of new loans in month 24, triggered by the decision to double marketing spend, is now due to be repaid.

Several large organizations in the financial services industry have in recent years adopted a strongly analysis-driven approach to product development, market segmentation, marketing and pricing. CapitalOne, for example, caused great disruption in the credit card industry through the 1990s by spotting the opportunity to configure products to match the needs and price-tolerance of distinct segments of users.[15] Such detailed targeting requires a highly segmented analysis of the impact of policy changes on the dynamics of all customer segments and products.

# RESOURCE ATTRIBUTES AND PERFORMANCE AT RYANAIR

For a low-fare airline, several resources have attributes that are important to the company's performance. Customer service staff have skills, and aircraft bring seat capacity and fuel efficiency. However, two resource attributes are critical:

- the number of journeys each passenger is likely to make each year
- the number of potential passengers to which each new route gives access.

The first of these follows the same pattern as the model of customers and sales in Figures 5.1 to 5.3. Figure 5.17 shows this structure with two alternative scenarios for the future. (Since these data are not disclosed by the company, the figure shows illustrative numbers.)

The base case (green) shows the business forecasts out to 2011 that appear in Chapter 2, Figure 2.28. The second scenario shows the combined impact of three pessimistic assumptions. (Online learning materials are available to support this example, see p.xxi.)

- customer losses of 15% per year rather than 10%, with those lost customers taking with them the journeys they would have made
- a reduced journey frequency for customers who will be won in future, compared with the past
- slower growth in journey frequency by existing passengers.

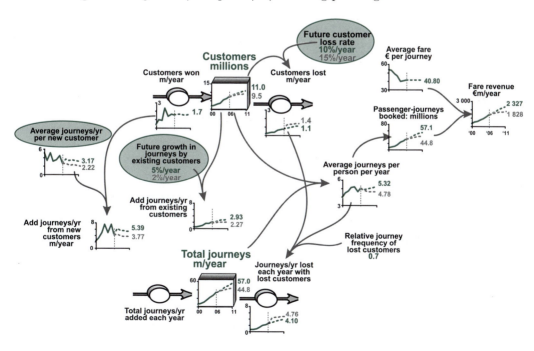

**Figure 5.17: Impact of higher customer churn and lower travel frequency on future Ryanair sales.**

Taken together, these three factors substantially reduce the number of customers who will regularly use the airline by 2011, and cut sharply the otherwise healthy growth in passenger-journeys and revenues.

In the case of route development (Figure 5.18), the base case forecast assumes a relatively high rate of closures, rising to 41 routes being closed in the final year. With a more optimistic assumption that closures can be kept down to just one-third of this rate, the route network grows to 690, rather than 590. However, closing routes because they attract too few sales implies that the number of customers lost is far less than the average across the network as a whole. Indeed if, as shown in Figure 5.18, the closed routes are just one-fifth as busy as the average, then the impact on total customer numbers is very small. If this relationship between low-activity routes and customer numbers turned out to be accurate, then the company may well decide that these routes are not worth operating and close them down.

Note that Figure 5.17 is a more accurate and explicit causal explanation for how the opening of new routes increases airline customer numbers than the simplified structure in Chapter 3 (Figure 3.16).

The structure in Figure 5.18 hides an important feature, namely that opening new routes brings access to *potential* customers, who then have to be won in a similar fashion to the retail stores case in Figure 5.14. If the airline does not offer attractive fares or flight schedules, those potential customers will remain dormant rather than becoming active and contributing to its sales.

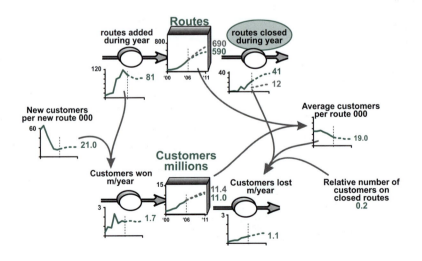

**Figure 5.18: Impact of future route closures on Ryanair customer numbers (illustrative).**

A further reason for making explicit this pool of potential customers (as well as other potential resources) is that this potential can be subject to significant exogenous forces. These forces are commonly assessed under four headings—political, economic, social and technological issues—leading to the approach being termed PEST analysis.

Quantifying the impact of exogenous factors will be examined in more detail in the next chapter. For now, Figure 5.19 illustrates how Ryanair's future route expansion could interact with the attribute of the potential customer pool to influence the number of customers using the airline. The base case future (green dashed lines) corresponds to previous projections in Chapter 2, in which the potential customer base was not made explicit; that is, it was assumed that all potential customers instantly became active users of the airline. However, in Figure 5.19, this assumption is removed, and the airline instead acquires only 70% of the potential whenever it starts a new route.

In the alternate future (grey dashed lines), two things change:

- After opening a new route and winning 70% of the potential customers this event brings, the company continues to capture one-fifth of the remaining potential in each subsequent year. This pulls more customers out of the potential state into the active stock.

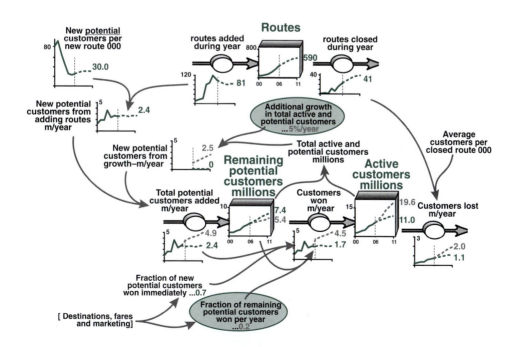

**Figure 5.19: Implications for Ryanair customer numbers arising from a growing potential (illustrative).**

- Additional growth occurs in the total number of customers (potential + active) who are available to the airline, growth that may arise for example from faster economic development in the new regions the airline serves compared with the West European routes that have dominated its business to date.

Socioeconomic growth drivers effectively "refill" the potential stock of customers, which the company's continuing successful service provision captures and converts into active customers. Were it not for this additional growth, the company's continued capture of the potential customers on its routes would deplete the stock of *remaining potential customers* much more quickly.

Taken together, these two new mechanisms substantially raise the company's growth rate and scale by 2011.

# OTHER USES OF THE RESOURCE ATTRIBUTE CONCEPT

## ATTRIBUTES IN NONCOMMERCIAL CASES

Resource attributes pose challenges for managers of noncommercial organizations, just as they do for business executives—clients, beneficiaries and other demand-side resources bring with them the service demands they place on the organization, staff bring skills and experience, and so on. A particular issue for many not-for-profit organizations concerns the raising of funds, often from the giving of individual donors.

In Figure 5.20, a charitable organization wishes to increase the income it receives from the regular giving of individuals. The *total giving* (at bottom right) is an attribute of the donors who support the organization. As for customer sales in commercial cases, there are three separate levers to improve this outcome—win more donors, keep more of those that we have, and get those donors to give more. Winning new donors is achieved by focusing the efforts of fundraisers on calling prospective donors. At the same time, however, existing donors must be called, both to ensure they continue supporting the organization and to increase the amount they give each quarter. This poses a difficult question about how best to allocate the efforts of those fundraisers (at top left).

The amount each donor gives each quarter is likely to be less than the maximum amount they *could* give, if sufficiently motivated by the good outcomes of the organization's work. Each donor thus brings a potential for giving, and a part of fundraisers' efforts in calling existing donors is to win more of this potential. The organization therefore has a second issue on which to choose (middle left) — whether to seek new donors who may not be able to give much money but who are numerous and easily won, or seek richer individuals who can potentially give more

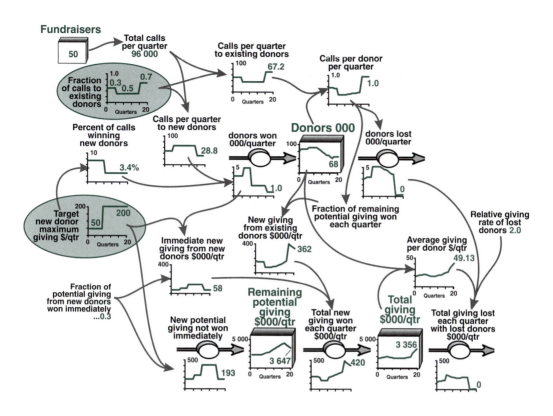

**Figure 5.20: Improving the rate of giving by donors to a charitable organization.**

money but who are few in number and harder to win. (In practice, there is much more activity around fundraising than this simple question of making calls, including advertising, mail campaigns and public relations efforts.)

The scenario in Figure 5.20 plays out the organization's fundraising strategy over five years, or 20 quarters. There are initially 80 000 donors, each giving $20/quarter, but with the potential to give $50. Total giving amounts to $1.6m/quarter, but could be $4m if those donors could be persuaded to give the maximum amount possible.

- For the first year, fundraisers' time is split equally between calling potential new donors and calling existing donors, both to make sure of their continued support and to capture more of their potential giving. The winning of new donors and the capture of more giving from existing donors slightly exceeds the loss of giving from donors who leave, so total giving slowly increases.

- In the second year, the organization tries to make faster progress by switching effort away from existing donors and on to winning more new donors, targeting the same category of individuals who could give up to $50/quarter. It is successful in capturing new people, but these gains are wiped out by the increased loss of existing donors who are neglected and slower progress in winning more of their potential giving. Total giving therefore declines.

- In the third year, the organization moves its focus onto wealthier potential donors, targeting those who could potentially give $200/quarter. The success rate of these calls is much lower than when lower-value donors were being pursued, so far fewer new donors are won each month. However, each person won brings with them more immediate giving, plus greater potential for more giving in the future. Nevertheless, this rate of new giving is not sufficient to counter the loss of neglected donors. This situation continues through year four, with total donors declining, little change in actual giving, but strong growth in the potential giving that could be won from the new, more wealthy donors.

- In year five, the organization realizes that there is a large potential for more giving from the existing donors, who now include a substantial proportion of wealthier individuals. Fundraisers' efforts are therefore switched onto retaining donors and seeking more of their potential giving. Donor losses are reduced to near zero, and there is a sharp increase in the rate of giving from existing donors, resulting in strong growth of the organization's income, to over $3.3m/quarter (bottom right).

Note that this strategy could not be sustained indefinitely, since a point would arise at which most of each donor's potential giving had been captured. Effort would then need to switch back onto acquiring new donors. A further general point to note from this example is that the organization's choice regarding which category of new donors to pursue is closely analogous to the question commercial organizations face regarding "where to compete." It may also be worthwhile to examine the "quality curve" of donors, stacking up the giving of each individual to see whether it is highly skewed towards a few large donors or more uniform. As in commercial cases, it is advisable to be conscious of this profile and to make deliberate choices about where on the curve to focus fundraising efforts.

(Online learning materials are available to support this example, see p.xxi.)

## STRATEGIC RECOVERY

Chapter 4 described how an organization's set of resources are linked, both to sustain each other and to generate performance, the resulting picture being described as its "strategic architecture." Mostly we are concerned with relatively low-stress situations where management wishes to drive faster growth, avoid possible constraints, or reverse declining performance. Improvements can often be achieved with revisions to strategy that result in gradual changes in the quantity or quality of resources and strengthening the mutual dependency between them.

Occasionally, however, organizations find themselves in crisis, with resources and revenues in sharp decline and financial losses that are worsening so fast as to threaten their survival. In such cases, drastic action is unavoidable, and a number of components must come together to avoid insolvency, including stabilizing the immediate situation, new leadership and organization, gaining support of investors and lenders, tight cash management and elimination of surplus assets.[16]

This crisis handling approach also includes the important issue of refocusing the organization's strategy. Research suggests that successful recovery may simply reflect cut-backs to reduce costs—firing staff, closing facilities, and so on.[17] However, measures for identifying that strategic refocusing has taken place are not easy to specify, and it is in any case likely that the scale, speed and subsequent performance following strategic recovery is more substantial when refocusing is included. It is also possible that strategic refocusing is not sufficiently understood that it features strongly in recovery situations.

The final reason for looking at refocusing is because it may avert a crisis in the first place.[18] Figure 5.21 shows alternative paths that management of organizations wishing to rejuvenate themselves might pursue.[19] The reasoning behind this framework highlights the difficulty of moving directly from a complex, moribund state directly to a still complex but successful condition (dashed path) without first going through the stage of simplifying business activity. This removal of complexity is important as a means to help mobilize the organization once again.

Simplification may involve shutting down business activities that show no prospect of performing—closing uneconomic facilities, terminating products that

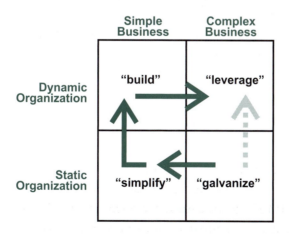

**Figure 5.21: Alternative paths to rejuvenating a mature business.**
Source: Baden-Fuller, C. and Stopford, J. (1992), *Rejuvenating the Mature Business*, Routledge, London.

cannot be sold at a healthy margin, withdrawing from markets where no prospect exists for achieving profitable sales, and so on. However, dangers arise both from indiscriminate cost cutting and blind termination of unprofitable activity. First, cutting costs may inflict further damage on the ability of the business to sustain itself, for example, cutting sales effort. Second, unprofitable business may contain within itself the core of a potentially powerful enterprise.

### Strategic recovery and turnround generally require the simultaneous rationalization of multiple resources.

A case that illustrates these points concerns an investment fund company facing sharply declining profits after the stock market reversal in 2000/1. This company gives private investors the opportunity to invest in pools of shares, rather than in individual companies. Investors buy units in one of the company's funds on the advice of an investment broker, or invest indirectly through pensions and insurances. The funds range from safe, low-return investments, for example government bonds or corporate debt, to high-risk but potentially high-return funds investing, for example, in high-tech sectors or emerging economies.

Emboldened by the strong stock market conditions of the late 1990s, this company, like many others, grew substantially, adding more funds, investing in more equities across many industries and geographic regions. It also started marketing its wide variety of funds directly to the public, in the hope that many ordinary folk were becoming investors for the first time and would pull demand for the company's funds through the increasing number of brokers with whom it was dealing. To support this expansion, they had hired many more fund managers—the clever individuals who choose where to invest the capital in each fund. To help these experts, the company had taken on many analysts whose task was to assess the likely performance of companies in which each fund's capital was invested.

This expansionist strategy appeared to be working during the years of strong stock market growth, but these conditions disguised a number of problems. In a similar fashion to the confectionery company products described above, the new funds were attracting little new real business. Many of the new brokers being dealt with were small, and the end-customers were investing only small amounts. The increasing numbers of brokers and investors and their transactions still needed to be administered, so overhead costs increased substantially. Many of the newly launched funds were not performing well, so investors were seeing no increase, or even a decrease, in their value. This had arisen because the increasing diversity of stocks in which the funds were invested meant that neither the fund managers nor the analysts who advised them understood the investments well enough to make good decisions. This was exacerbated by the "war for talent" in the market for these experts, which had led the company to both overpay and to be insufficiently careful about the quality of that talent.

The company thus found itself with a poor "quality curve" for every one of its resources (Figure 5.22); too small investors and brokers, an over extended range of investment funds many of which were performing badly, invested in too diverse a range of stocks, managed by large numbers of staff that included many underperforming people. These problems became apparent in 2000/1 when stock market conditions collapsed following the bursting of the "dot-com" bubble, and led to a reversal of business growth and rapid deterioration of profitability.

It is important to highlight two distinct features of this crisis. The first and most obvious problem was falling sales and profitability. This led management to a range of common crisis reactions, such as cutting its back-office staff (i.e. the people who actually made sure investors transactions were properly handled), deferring IT investments that would simplify processes and reduce costs, cutting staff training, travel budgets, employment benefits, and so on. Whilst some of these actions may have been advisable, they did nothing to address the second, more fundamental problem. The "system" had for some time been in a state that would accelerate its own demise—as every resource declined in quality, it undermined the ability of other parts of the system to perform. For example, the worse the performance of the smaller funds, the more investors deserted the company's products, and the more brokers ceased recommending its funds to other investors. This self-reinforcing collapse had already been occurring, but had not been visible because it was hidden by the strong performance of the core business.

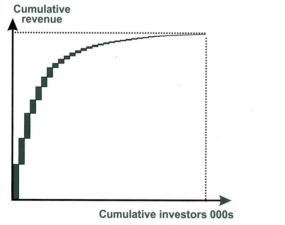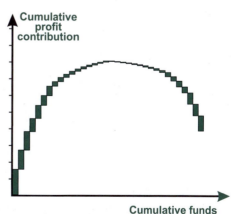

**Figure 5.22: Examples of poor resource quality curves for the fund management company.**

Fortunately, the firm's main investment funds were still performing as well as any in the market, given investment conditions at the time, and were widely held by investors. Many of the most marginal customers had already disinvested and the remainder included many valuable clients, accessed through high-performing brokers. Some excellent professionals remained with the firm, sustaining its capabilities in fund management, marketing, sales and customer support. Reassuringly, the firm's reputation was holding up, and morale was remarkably buoyant, thanks to good leadership. Better still, the best quality resources were tightly coupled—the best people were looking after the best clients, holding the best products, managed by more of the best people.

This good news made it possible for the senior team to devise a comprehensive program of rationalization back towards a solid core of business that would function well and provide a platform for renewed growth when more favorable conditions returned. The recovery (Figure 5.23) went as follows:

1. The poorly performing funds were identified and closed; that is, the product range was substantially rationalized. This was not entirely straightforward, since investors' capital had to be switched into alternative funds.

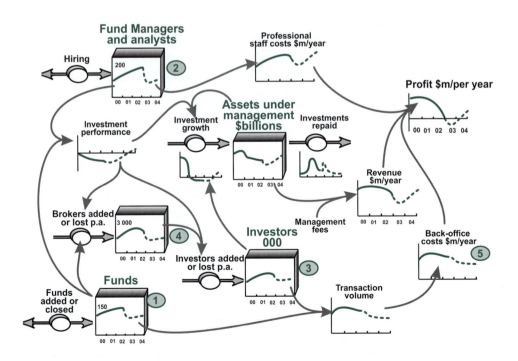

**Figure 5.23: The recovery path for the troubled fund management firm.**

2. This much narrower range of products would require fewer professionals, but to protect morale the plan included the transfer of some investment funds along with the associated staff to rival companies who were more successful in certain classes of investment.

3. Some remaining low-value clients had to be rationalized, some of whom departed with the cutting of the marginal products. For the rest, efforts were made to make them more worthwhile, for example consolidating several small investments into one, and simplifying service support.

4. The company stopped dealing with many smaller brokers who had in any case brought in mostly low-value clients.

5. With reduced support and transactional activity in the business, back-office costs could be reduced, but only *after* the business had been safely simplified.

Further important side benefits of this rationalization soon appeared. Simply removing the complexity reduced the pressure on back-office administration, leading to more reliable service. This boosted the firm's reputation with investors and brokers, and the product rationalization was turned into a further reputation advantage by explaining how closing down under-performing funds was actually in investors' best interests.

After the crisis was averted, the team was able to use the architecture as a living control panel, on which they could track each month's progress towards their better future, making adjustments if things worked out better or worse than expected. Like many firms today, they already employed a balanced scorecard system to track many of these factors (see Chapter 4)—data that could be dropped straight onto the architecture.

## LESSONS FOR STRATEGIC RECOVERY

Many features of this situation are to be found in firms struggling to escape financial troubles. Difficulties often originate in historical developments undertaken in more favorable trading conditions. Fortunately, this very heritage may offer the chance of strategic recovery.

First, as firms scramble to win growth opportunities, they may rush to capture every possible new customer. In the process, much poor-quality business is signed up, which only becomes apparent when market conditions deteriorate. Unfortunately, it's a tough management decision to shut down customers at exactly the time when an organization seems to need every one they can get, which is why the decision must be linked to a coherent plan for improving other resources in parallel.

Whilst sales are booming, novel products and services can proliferate fast, and no one sees any need to check if the last great idea was successful. This can leave companies with slow-moving products, and rationalizing these provides the second opportunity.

Regrettably, the corollary of bringing business back to a sustainable core is a reduction in the staff needed to run a slimmer business. But by not acting, everyone is put at risk—and a strategically sound rebasing of the business is going to be substantially less troubling than the, unfortunately common, practice of indiscriminate and repetitive cuts that do little to fix the real problem.

This case example illustrates a further general point:

> **Strategic recovery and turnround generally result in businesses or organizations that are smaller, but more capable of performing.**

## PRODUCT FUNCTIONALITY

The development of product features is another context where an adaptation of the quality-curve concept can be valuable. When introducing new products and services, firms race to provide sufficient functionality to make them useful enough for customers to buy. As usage rises, suppliers compete by "improving" their products—increasing functionality by adding to the sheer number of features included (Figure 5.24). In effect, functionality for such products and services lies behind the user benefits captured by the value curve of reasons why customers choose the product and stick with it rather than switching to rival products (see Chapters 2 and 3).

### TABLE 5.9: BASIC AND EXTENDED BENEFITS FOR SELECTED PRODUCTS AND SERVICES

| Product/service | Basic benefits | Extended benefits |
|---|---|---|
| Cellphones | Reliable calling, number store | Voicemail, three-way calls, games |
| Word-processing software | Text editing, spell checking, auto-save | Mail merge, outlining, revision tracking |
| IT services | Data-processing outsourcing, application development | Business process redesign, strategy development |

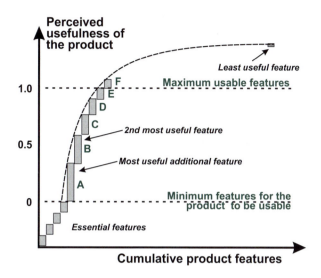

**Figure 5.24:** Increasing usefulness of products as the number of features is increased.

If a supplier stops participating in this improvement process, their once exemplary product becomes merely average, and then obsolete. They are left behind, not because their offering has actually become worse, but because customers' expectations have risen (Table 5.9). This happens because users become accustomed to what is currently offered, and because suppliers try constantly to rise above their rivals by offering more. The cellphone industry is a powerful illustration of how this race can develop into desperation as firms explore every possible avenue for providing more reasons for customers to take their products and services.[20] This process eventually runs out of momentum.

> **There is a limit to how many features customers can benefit from and there comes a point where adding a new feature does nothing useful for the majority of users.**

Nevertheless, firms continue to add features in their efforts to be seen to offer superior products, often well beyond what is useful to customers, a phenomenon known as "feature fatigue."[21] Consumer electronic devices and office software both illustrate how far this process can be pushed—both product categories now offering functionality that is far beyond the ability of most customers to use or even understand.

This development of product functionality, the raising of customer expectations and the inevitable limits that the process faces need to be understood if the evolution of sales and profitability over product life cycles are to be managed. The steps in the process are as follows:

1.  Identify the list of features, elements or functions that combine to make the product or service useful, starting with those without which no users would be interested, and ending with those that are merely "nice to have."
2.  Assess the overall usefulness that customers would perceive from a product or service possessing a smaller or larger set of these features (Figure 5.24). This perceived usefulness will vary between different individual customers. It may be necessary to repeat the exercise across several contrasting customer segments, each with their own characteristic mix of needs (e.g. business users versus young consumers, in the case of cellphones).
3.  Identify the features of your own product and service, and so place yourself on the customers' scale of usefulness relative to competing suppliers. Competing products may not offer the same range of incremental features; that is, you may offer features A, B, D and E, whilst a competing product offers A, B, C and F. (This step is well demonstrated by the ubiquitous rating tables published by consumer magazines on products and services as diverse as cars, game-machine software and air travel.)
4.  Estimate the rate at which you and competitors are advancing the features offered, and assess how customers are changing their view of the usefulness of the product or service.
5.  Use this picture of comparative features and perceived usefulness to evaluate the pace of product development that you should be adopting. Customers typically do not view features and usefulness in isolation from price. Their view of product usefulness should therefore be compared with pricing to assess the value for money that rival products are felt to offer.

In Figure 5.25, market research for a consumer electronic product indicates that without a minimum of four specific features no one will find the product useful. Product development efforts make progress in raising the product's features, resulting in a useable product after one year. During year two, added features make the product more appealing so the product's sales rate escalates. By year four, the product has been made about as useful as can be to likely customers, and uptake slows down.

Note that several additional factors may be involved:

•   The price must be sufficiently attractive, awareness must be built with marketing, and the product must be available for customers to find.

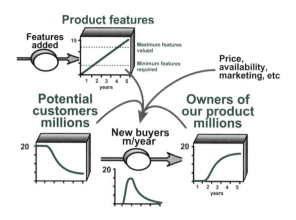

**Figure 5.25: Impact of increasing product functionality on product uptake.**

- There will likely be a diffusion effect, with uptake being accelerated by word of mouth from existing customers, and increasingly limited by the declining pool of potential customers who do not yet own the product (see explanation of the Bass diffusion framework in Chapter 4).
- Sales may well continue after all potential customers have been captured, due to continuing sales of replacement and upgrade products (see explanation of durable products in Chapter 4).

### Disruptive technologies and the innovator's dilemma

It is tempting for companies with a successful stream of products to continue pursuing the process described above time after time, with each new release of a product raising functionality so as to appeal to more and more customers and fulfill more and more of their needs. However, this can leave them vulnerable to innovations that may at first seem to be no threat, but which emerge to overtake the established product type so comprehensively as to make them obsolete.[22] Well-known historical examples are numerous: gas lighting for homes and streets became obsolete as electric lighting developed, propeller engines for aircraft reached a limit to performance that jet engines could surpass, and some readers may remember the Sony Walkman—a small portable tape-cassette player that allowed users to listen to 100 hours of music whilst on the move, provided they could carry 100 tape cassettes!

A further feature of disruptive technologies is that they may underperform established products on one dimension, but offer alternative advantages that are sufficiently persuasive as to capture customers in spite of the disadvantage. It is these alternative advantages that often "disrupt" the product development for the old technology that was previously progressing in a quite satisfactory manner. In computer storage technologies, for example, it is common for each new solution initially to have less capacity than the one it replaced, but to be smaller, lighter, or with fewer moving parts (or none). In other cases, the initial disadvantage is price—new technology often starts with a cost disadvantage, since it has not yet received the benefits of production engineering and scale enjoyed by the technology it will ultimately replace. However, as its uptake grows, cumulating sales and investment by producers drives down unit costs until it becomes price competitive with the old technology, as well as functionally superior.

This trade-off between alternative product benefits of established versus new technologies can be assessed using the value curve approach introduced in Chapter 2. Note in particular that a step-change in one of the benefits on that curve may not just win sales to existing customers, but trigger the capture of new customers and alter retention rates, as explained in Chapter 3 (e.g. Figure 3.16).

The dilemma for established product providers is whether and when to switch to the disruptive technology themselves—if they can. A company that has built massive scale and driven down cost in the old technology will have grown sales and strong cash flows from that product. Why would they deliberately accelerate the replacement of those sales and cash flows by introducing a product that will cannibalize them? The answer is often that if they don't do it themselves, others will do it to them. Difficulties arise when the threatening technology is one in which the incumbent firms have no significant capability.

An intriguing sector that currently illustrates the principles of disruptive technology and the disadvantage of incumbent suppliers is energy supply. Hydrocarbon-based technology has been pushed to high levels of efficiency and functionality, so that much of our lifestyle is enabled by products that just work, at reasonable cost, whether those are domestic gas boilers or large-scale power stations. Solar cell generation of power has generally been grossly uncompetitive on a cents-per-kilowatt-hour basis. Nevertheless, in certain applications, such as remote locations requiring modest power, the technology offers alternative advantages (no need for access to a power grid or gas supply) that outweigh the basic cost disadvantage. Like all micro-electronic technologies, however, solar cell performance has been driven upwards; that is, the fraction of potentially available energy that is captured, and the unit cost driven down. The technology is thus inexorably pushing into more and more application areas previously dominated by fossil-fuel based solutions— Figure 5.26. Note that few if any of the firms that historically enjoyed technology advantages and the resulting profitability in the old solutions have any capability in the new one. Similar considerations apply to other technologies, such as wind power and geothermal energy sources.

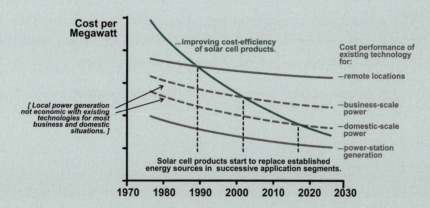

**Figure 5.26: Improving performance of solar cells progressively substitutes existing power generation sectors [illustrative].**

The important contribution of the dynamics framework to understanding this process of technology disruption is that it enables the scale and speed of substitution to be anticipated and worked on. It combines with the effects caused by political, economic and social factors to have considerable implications for the emergence, maturity and demise of entire product markets and industries, an issue that will be examined further in Chapter 6.

## UNDERMINING COMPETITORS

It is almost axiomatic that strategy is about beating competitors. Much of the language—competitive advantage, deterring new rivals, first-mover advantage, etc.—hints at this adversarial perspective. Many popular books play to analogies of military strategy with a sense of almost war-like behavior, discussing both the strategic brilliance and leadership of great historic figures.[23] It is important not to push this analogy too far, however, since military strategy is dominated by geographical considerations that have no useful counterpart in most business situations. Also, warfare most often involves just two sides in a conflict whereas competitive industries usually concern several rivals.

Chapter 2 explained how a long-established view of strategy focuses on the impact that competitive forces have on industry profitability. Those forces include not just current, direct competitors, but customers' buying power, suppliers' control of key inputs, and pressure from substitute products and new competitors.

**The competitive fragmentation of an industry is changed by the entry of new firms and the exit of others, and has powerful effects on prices, costs and profitability.**

Firms can try to manipulate those forces to improve competitive conditions in various ways. Two of these aims are:

1. encouraging current competitors to leave the industry
2. deterring possible new entrants from starting up in the industry.

Many jurisdictions include regulations that forbid "anti-competitive" behavior, such as contract terms that restrict customers' freedom of choice, or cutting prices below cost to drive rivals out of business and deter new entrants. Nevertheless, there is much scope to make life difficult for competitors in ways that are not illegal. These can be understood by considering an industry-level picture of how competitive conditions change over time.

In Figure 5.27, the left-hand column displays the fragmentation of an industry by showing how its total revenue is accounted for by stacking up the revenue of each competitor. The industry's growth is attracting new competitors. In the scenario on the left, our own business grows little, both because those new entrants absorb the industry's growth and because we are less successful than some of the original competitors in driving our own growth. The implications of the competitive-forces view are, first, that these changes make it harder to sustain prices and second, that cost efficiency improvements are competed away by still greater pressure on prices.

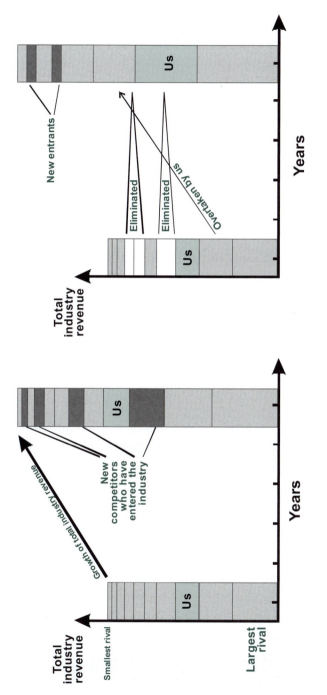

Figure 5.27: Alternative dynamics of the competitive structure of a growing market.

Average profitability therefore suffers, and we suffer more from this process than others who develop more successfully. Importantly, there is no assumption that either new entrants or the original competitors are positively profitable at all. Indeed, the first situation illustrated in Figure 5.27 could well result in many firms, or even the industry as a whole, being unprofitable for many years. From this scenario arises the suggestion that we, as original participants in the industry, would benefit if we could "deter" new entrants.

The scenario on the right depicts the same overall industry growth, but this time with fewer new entrants. In addition, some of the original competitors have exited the industry, leaving more space for us and the remaining firms to grow. Not only has this benefited our growth, but it (1) reduces the tendency amongst the smaller number of firms to compete away prices and margins in a desperate attempt to capture increasing sales; and (2) enables remaining firms to extract efficiency savings more quickly. Finally, we have been more successful in developing our own business and overtaken the previous number two competitor.

This has an important implication for competitive strategy, namely that it is valuable to select and act against *specific* competitors, rather than trying simply to be better than everyone across the market. The latter approach has several disadvantages.

- Taking on all competitors at once can be very costly. Any effort that is spread across the entire market has to be of a commensurate scale, so trying to underprice, outmarket, outsell and outservice all competitors will inevitably incur considerable cost.
- Efforts dissipated across the whole industry will likely have less impact than efforts focused on specific parts of the market or against specific competitors.
- Such industry-wide competitive efforts will attract retaliation from all competitors, risking great damage to our own business.
- Our efforts will be highly visible, exacerbating the very competitive conditions that make it difficult to sustain profitability, for example by triggering price wars, escalating advertizing commitments or starting a war for talent.

Taken together, these considerations mean that such indiscriminate competitive efforts simply don't work, or else take so long and at such great cost that the business pursuing them suffers along with all the others.

**Selecting specific competitors to attack is more advisable than indiscriminate efforts, even to the extent of seeking their total elimination.**

To select the most promising competitor to attack and identify how to do so requires a deep understanding of individual rivals. In their efforts to cut out unnecessary overheads, many companies lack the resources to build-up even the most basic competitor intelligence. Given the value potentially at stake from even modest progress against rivals, this is a false economy.

A range of methods is available for competitor appraisal.[24] These involve assessing their strengths and weaknesses in some way—comparable to parts of the SWOT approach from Chapter 2 that management might use to assess its own business. Most such competitor analysis frameworks are qualitative and high-level, and quite inadequate for designing and implementing specific competitive campaigns. A more rigorous approach builds on two principles:

1. A competitor operating in our own industry will likely have both a similar set of resources and a similar architecture for organizing them to ourselves. Competitors may differ in which exact segments they serve, which exact set of products and services they offer, and so on, but the elements will be largely the same. Even where they differ (e.g. outsourcing certain activities that we do ourselves) many of the remaining parts of their resource system will be similar to our own.

2. Like us, a competitor will have a range of "quality" for each of its resources— larger and smaller customers, products that perform well and not so well, stronger and weaker sales people, and so on.

If we can understand how our own business performs, we should be able to evaluate the performance of any competitor—and therein lies the opportunity to damage that performance at little risk to ourselves.

To illustrate how this can be done, consider the real case of a mid-scale, mid-market restaurant chain, developing fast in a promising market, but number two to a long-established market leader. Although operating only 120 restaurants compared with the leader's 300+, it was generating nearly as much profit, due to a recent history of finding great locations and developing better products than the leader. With a good understanding of the profit contribution profile of its own restaurants, it was able to estimate the equivalent profile for the competitor (Figure 5.28).

Making this estimation of the competitor's performance was especially easy in this case—without resorting to illegal espionage! The profit of a restaurant is simply given by the revenue that comes from customer numbers and prices, minus its costs, which are dominated by numbers of staff and the ownership cost of the real estate. Prices are on the menu, customers can be counted, and their typical meal purchases can be observed. Staff numbers can be counted, and the costs of real estate are in the public domain. The resulting estimation was not exact, but close enough to know roughly how much profit was coming from each of the competitor's units.

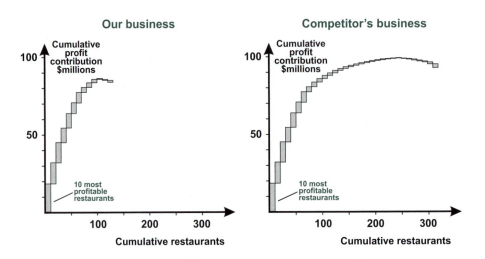

**Figure 5.28:** Comparable profit contribution curves for two mid-market restaurant chains.

Armed with this information, selecting the point of attack was relatively simple. Trying to damage their most profitable units would be difficult—they were clearly popular with their local consumers, were operated well, and received plenty of attention from headquarters' management. Any attack on these would certainly have been noticed, and vigorously defended.

Attacking unprofitable units was pointless, as the competitor would not be concerned or damaged by their loss. The appropriate targets were the restaurants contributing profits in the mid-range. A random selection of these moderately profitable units consisted of individual locations that were geographically dispersed and supervised by different regional managers within the competitor's management structure. Consequently, attacks on this random selection were not noticed, provided that the tactics were subtle. So what should those tactics be, bearing in mind that they are *local*; that is, conducted by specific units in our business against neighboring units of the competitor?

- Most importantly, the tactics should *not* be led by price cuts. Price reductions significant enough to be noticed by customers hit profit margins hard. They must also be promoted to consumers if they are to work, which would make them highly visible to the competitor.
- Promotions that offer extra value for customers are less costly, and more difficult to retaliate against. Those promotions were not blanketed across the locality served by each of the attacker's units, but were selectively targeted at specific neighborhoods from which the competing restaurant drew its customers.

- The next principle is to address every item on consumers' value curve—service quality, the environment and product quality. The local tactics therefore included ensuring that restaurants were oversupplied with staff, that the best food preparation staff were deployed and that the quality and maintenance of the customer environment were as good as possible.
- Finally, the units leading the attack were allocated the best unit managers—those who were most skilled at motivating staff, at ensuring high quality of product and service, and at befriending customers.

Taken together, these tactics took away a substantial proportion of the revenue from the competitor's units that were targeted, at which point their own policies started to act against them. With lower revenue, their management tried to sustain profits by cutting costs, especially staffing levels, which further damaged consumers' experience. With the targeted restaurants becoming rather quiet, they became increasingly unappealing and lost still more consumers. Eventually, the targeted units moved into losses or marginal profits, following which they were neglected by management until they were closed.

Repeating these tactics across a selection of mid-profit outlets inflicted disproportionate damage to the competitor's overall profits. In Figure 5.29, eliminating the profitability of just 11 units hits the competitor's profits by 12%, a process that could be accomplished in as little as six months. Repeating this principle over two to three years, dealing in all with 70–80 of the competitor's units did such damage that they started to experience further problems.

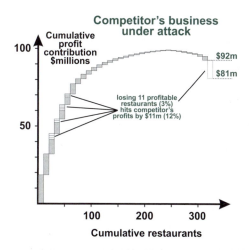

**Figure 5.29: Targeting selected units does disproportionate damage to a restaurant competitor's profits.**

- The pressure to sustain profits drove them into system-wide policies that did further damage, such as price discounting and cuts in staffing, marketing budgets, product development and maintenance, all of which undermined critical resources in their strategic architecture.
- The competitor's management started to lose motivation and commitment, and many left for better opportunities—often with the attacker!
- The confidence of investors was damaged—in this particular case, the business was one of several similar operations operated by the competitor's corporate owners—so requests for capital were turned down, making it impossible for the rival to match the high quality new units that were being added to the aggressor's business.

In this case, the competitor left the industry after just a few years of the competitive strategy being implemented, selling most of its remaining viable restaurants to the one-time number two, who was left with a dominant position.

The general conclusion that can be drawn from this example is that:

**It is often possible and valuable to understand the quality profile of competitors' businesses as the basis for focused attack.**

Not all situations make it so simple for management to develop focused competitive tactics. More commonly, it is necessary to learn about the competitor's source of profitability from customers, rather than from distribution outlets as in the restaurant case.

The business banking division of a major bank did not know which competitors were making how much profit from which customers. However, the bank knew from its own experience the likely value of the banking services for any customer of any size in any sector. It could then make a reasonable estimate of the profit a competitor might be receiving from a similar customer of a similar size in the same sector. From this initial estimate, management could make adjustments if they had reason to believe for example that the competitor made better margins or had some cost disadvantage. The bank's customer-relationship managers were also able, over a period, to approach customers with whom they did not deal and find out which bank provided its services.

Other considerations in such targeted competitive strategies include:

- *Choosing which competitor offers the best target.* Small rivals are not necessarily easy to take on, and in any case may offer little benefit from being defeated. On the other hand, bigger stronger competitors can have powerful resources to defend with or retaliate. Often it can be best to choose a mid-ranking rival, but the key criteria should be (1) that their defeat offers a significant improvement to competitive conditions overall and (2) that a tactical campaign can be devised that is feasible and minimizes the risk of retaliation. In another restaurant industry case, a new competitor tried taking on McDonalds in an important country market. They were destroyed in just 18 months by very similar tactics to those described above—the only difference being that all their units were attacked at once. The original plan was never feasible, and a waste of time and money.

- *Deciding whether to be open or covert about the attack.* In the restaurant case, secrecy was important because, had the competitor been aware of the plan, it could have looked out for those units that were under attack and responded locally with sufficient effort to prevent the loss of business. With the covert and seemingly random scatter of attacks it simply appeared that once-successful units were gradually failing for no apparent cause other than generally disappointing performance in the market. In the business banking case, it was also important that the plan not be disclosed, because the target of the attack was of comparable size and power to the attacker. In other cases, it can be appropriate to be open about the attack if it helps the competitor decide early on to admit defeat and withdraw.

- *Choosing which resources to use as the basis for a competitive attack.* The quality curve can sometimes be constructed, for example, for the profit contribution a competitor enjoys from the individual products in its product range. The attack can then focus on products that are weak, even though they contribute significantly to the competitor's performance—perhaps a product that is becoming obsolete or that is poorly supported. In the car industry, US manufacturers have repeatedly been picked off by European and Japanese producers who offered superior models in product segments that were seen as secondary, such as compact cars, performance saloons and hybrid vehicles. The result was, as management pundit Tom Peters has remarked, that the US auto industry has been "nibbled to death," piece by piece over four decades.

- *Deciding on the effort to devote to deterring new entrants.* At the time of the warfare described above in the restaurant market, several would-be competitors had announced development plans that in total would have added over 700 new units in the market over five years. These plans were encouraged by the market's growth, and by the winning company's very success. Had that number of units actually been opened, virtually all of those competitors would have lost money and failed, and done considerable damage to the eventual victor. Too many firms thought that running restaurant chains was easy, not understanding the complexity of product development, staff training, operating procedures, sourcing and logistics, and real-estate development. Open communications were used, such as industry magazines and conferences, to clarify the difficulty of building a successful business and demonstrate just how powerful was the winner's system of resources. The implicit message was "Sure, we are successful, but do not for a minute imagine you can match us—and be sure that we will destroy you if you try!" On reflection, many of the would-be entrants decided that the challenge looked just too difficult, and abandoned their plans. Less than half of the announced new units were ever opened.

It is worth emphasizing once more that:

**It is vital in competitive battles to observe legal prohibitions on anticompetitive behavior.**

Competition regulators in general believe that larger numbers of competitors inevitably improve conditions for customers by driving down prices and driving up quality and service.[25] Whilst this is debatable—the pressure to drive down prices can make it impossible for competitors to invest in improved products and service quality, and with large numbers of small competitors it is impossible for any to obtain the benefits of scale and learning that drive down costs—it does mean that regulators strongly favor removal of entry barriers and disapprove of attacks on specific competitors. Nevertheless, there is much that can be done without falling foul of such legal constraints. There is nothing illegal about a company choosing where to direct its sales effort, which products to promote or how to allocate its customer support.

# INCORPORATING ATTRIBUTE ANALYSIS IN STRATEGY DEVELOPMENT

Chapter 4 showed a number of examples of generic architectures for firms in certain industries—for example, fast-moving consumer products, airlines, vehicle manufacturers, professional firms, insurance companies and media companies. All these architectures have the advantage of capturing, on a single page, the

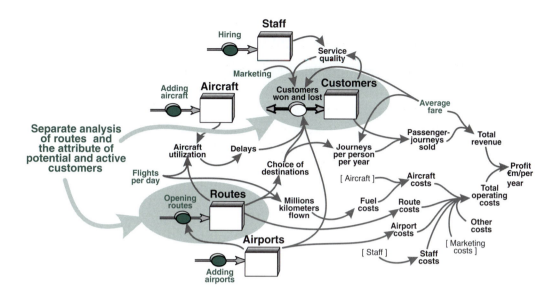

**Figure 5.30:** Extracting summary attribute data to include in the strategic architecture for an airline.

essence of how the business works and relating that system to its performance. The development of usable architectures of this form, complete with data for each element, as described in Chapters 1–4, can be a substantial and complex task. Not only are the diagrams and detailed data generally extensive, but it may be necessary to segment customers or assess the dynamics of distinct groups of staff.

It is not therefore advisable to try to incorporate the analysis of resource attributes into that overall picture. Fortunately, it is also not generally necessary. The analyses illustrated in this chapter, many of which have been taken from real cases, can be carried out in isolation and only the high-level results incorporated back into the overall architecture. In rescuing the fund management company from decline, for example, some six distinct attribute analyses were required across the customer base and product range. Each of these was carried out alone, although it was necessary to check consistency between them, for example a certain cut in the number of funds would require a certain cut in fund managers, and would likely result in an estimated loss of customers and fee income.

Figure 5.30 shows the core architecture for an airline from Chapter 4 (Figure 4.23) and highlights how the summary information on numbers of routes and customers can be picked up from detailed attribute analysis such as Figure 5.19.

**Summary of Chapter 5**

Resources carry important qualities, known as "attributes," for example customer profitability, staff skills, equipment reliability. These strongly affect their contribution to performance and to developing and sustaining other resources. Attributes are themselves resources, accumulating and depleting over time. These qualities "flow with" gains and losses of the resource itself, resulting in a structure known as a "co-flow."

The average level of an attribute is improved by three mechanisms—adding resources of higher quality (e.g. hiring skilled staff), losing resources of lower quality (losing unskilled staff), or directly improving the quality of existing resources (training staff). Attributes can be thought of as being like the temperature of water in a bathtub or tank, which changes with the quantity of hot water added, cold water lost or heating applied to the water.

Attribute changes associated with staff skills and experience are an important element of organizations' "human capital," recognized as being a powerful component of strategy.

Some attributes are negative, such as the failure rate of equipment, and must be minimized by adding resources with *less* of this undesirable quality, removing items with more of it, or slowing its increase.

The individual items within a single type of resource differ in quality—larger and smaller customers, more and less experienced staff and so on. The dynamics framework loses this detail in averaging out the quality of such resources, although this can be dealt with partially by analyzing the dynamics of segments within the population, for example how numbers of small and large customers are changing.

The distribution of quality within a specific resource can be understood by constructing a "quality-curve" chart of cumulative quality versus cumulative resource items, for example profit contribution versus customers, experience versus staff. This provides important information to aid management decision making about where to compete, and where to focus resource-improvement efforts.

Certain attributes actually consist of the access that they bring to other resources, for example the number of consumers reached by each unit of a retail store chain. Such resources are only potentially available, however, and must still be captured—in the case of customers, by offering and promoting attractive products, services and value.

Some resources carry more than one important attribute, for example bank loans have a loan amount, an interest rate and a risk of default. Strategy choices about where to compete make important trade-offs amongst such attributes—accepting higher-risk customers implies charging higher interest rates to allow for a greater proportion of bad debts.

Key attributes in the airline industry include the potential customers who are made available by opening new routes and the travel frequency of different customers.

The principles of resource attributes and the quality curve are equally important in noncommercial cases, for example the giving of donors to charitable organizations or the sickness rate of patients in a hospital's catchment area.

Recovering a business in trouble may require rationalizing several resources, the aim being to get the system back to a core of better-quality resources that, though smaller, is capable of both generating positive performance and developing into the future.

Products carry an attribute of functionality, which must hit a minimum threshold before being acceptable to potential customers, but may reach a maximum level beyond which few customers find additional features valuable.

Truly *competitive* strategy requires strong understanding of competitors and choices about which to attack—industry-wide efforts to outperform everyone, on everything, in all parts of the market generally achieve little. It is often possible to estimate the quality profile of competitors' resources, and use this knowledge to undermine their business performance, though care must be taken not to infringe legal and ethical constraints on competitive behavior.

# SUGGESTED QUESTIONS AND EXERCISES

1. Why are the qualities or attributes of tangible resources important to understand and to measure?

2. How can the metaphor for a resource of water flowing into and out of a tank or bathtub be extended to understand how resource attributes change over time?

3. What are the three ways in which the average quality of a tangible resource can be changed? In each case, what happens to the *quantity* of the tangible resource itself?

4. Why is the framework that links the attribute resource and its flows with the tangible resource and its flows referred to as a "co-flow" structure?

5. Why is the quantity for the attribute measured as the *total* resource (e.g. total sales from customers or total skills of all staff), rather than the *average* (e.g. sales per customer or skills per person)? What rule about tangible resources does this measurement seem to break in certain cases, and why is that OK?

6. Why is it sometimes important to look at the *distribution* of quality within a population of customers, staff, products, etc., not just the average? Sketch an illustrative quality curve (accurate data not expected) for a resource attribute involved in a case with which you are familiar.

7. Identify a case in which one resource is acquired in order to gain access to a second resource, e.g. retailer seeking stores to gain access to consumers, product suppliers seeking distributors to gain access to end-customers. Sketch the structure, or use Worksheet 6c (below) to specify how these factors are linked in your case. What choice does this raise for management when deciding to develop this tangible resource?

8. Identify a case in which a tangible resource has more than one attribute, e.g. bank loans with loan amount *and* interest rate. Sketch the structure, or use Worksheet 6b to specify how these factors are linked in your case. What choices does the organization have to make when deciding to develop this tangible resource?

9. Return to the example case you developed in answer to the questions for Chapters 1–4 (or pick another case for which you have good information). Identify any key attributes associated with one or more of the organization's tangible resources, then use Worksheet 6a, 6b or 6c below to lay out the relationship between each resource and its attribute(s).

10. Faced with an organization whose performance is bad and getting worse, what is the main purpose of rationalizing poor quality elements from several of its resources?

11. Why is it important to understand the competitive structure of an industry (i.e. how many competitors of what sizes account for its total revenues)? What should companies know about the resources of their customers? How can this knowledge be used to defeat competitors?

# USING WORKSHEETS 6a, 6b AND 6c

The following pages offer blank templates for dealing with resource attributes. These may be used in two situations:

1. To assess and improve a single tangible resource (e.g. improving customer profitability, raising the level of staff skills, or improving the quality of a product range).
2. As part of a wider analysis to understand and improve an organization's overall performance, within which raising the quality of one or more resources may be important.

Before starting with any of these worksheets, specify the timescale over which the situation is to be examined, including any history. Observe the disciplines of naming the resources, flows and other factors accurately, and ensuring that the units of measurement and the arithmetic relationships between the various elements are properly worked out. If real data are not available, use careful estimates instead, but again, stick to the rules!

## WORKSHEET 6a: RESOURCE ATTRIBUTE ANALYSIS

(See Figures 5.1, 5.3, 5.5 and 5.9 for examples.) Specify clearly the resource and its quality attribute that you wish to analyse. Follow the numbered steps on the worksheet.

1. Enter the information for the tangible resource and its flows in the upper stock, i.e. the history and likely future for the quantity of the resource itself, and its win rate and loss rate. (You may be able to copy this from Worksheet 3, if the work has already been done.)
2. Enter the history and anticipated future for the *average* quantity of the attribute in the middle chart.
3. From this data on the average quantity and the total tangible resource, calculate the *total* attribute quantity in the lower stock.
4. Enter, or estimate, the history and future for the average quality of new tangible resource that has been, and will be added, i.e. the average amount of attribute that each new resource item brings with it.

5.  Calculate the rate at which this adds total resource to the lower attribute.
6.  Enter or estimate the average quality of resource that has been, and will be, lost in the chart on the right.
7.  Calculate the rate at which this removes total resource from the attribute.

Finally, check arithmetically that the total resource attribute in the lower stock is consistent with the accumulation and depletion of its inflows and outflows. If the math has been done properly, the history of these data should be mutually consistent. If the data for the *future* are inconsistent, then check whether the expected future resource quality is realistic (e.g. we hope to improve average customer revenue, but cannot win large customers fast enough, or lose enough small customers to meet our aims).

This framework and its math are most easily done with the **my**strategy software version of Worksheet 6a, see paragraph about online learning materials on p.xxi.

## WORKSHEET 6b: RESOURCE WITH MULTIPLE ATTRIBUTES

This worksheet is used when a resource has more than one important quality, for example staff with experience *and* salary, bank loans with loan amount *and* interest rate. (See Figure 5.16 for example.) Repeat the process for Worksheet 6a for each attribute.

Note that the worksheet offers two attributes below the main resource, and a third attribute above it, though it is rarely necessary to assess more than two attributes.

This framework and its math are most easily done with the **my**strategy model of Worksheet 6b, see p.xxi.

## WORKSHEET 6c: PRIMARY RESOURCE BRINGS ACCESS TO POTENTIAL SECONDARY RESOURCE

This worksheet is used when adding a primary resource brings access to a second potential resource, for example adding distributors to access potential end customers, adding stores to reach consumers, adding airline routes to reach potential passengers (see Figures 5.14 and 5.19 for examples). The following steps adapt those for Worksheet 6a.

1.  Enter the information for the tangible resource and its flows in the upper stock, i.e. the history and likely future for the quantity of the resource itself, and its win rate and loss rate. (You may be able to copy this from Worksheet 3, if the work has already been done.)

2. Enter the history and anticipated future for the *average inactive potential* of the secondary resource in chart 2 (e.g. potential passengers per airline route who are not yet using the airline).

3. From these data on the average quantity and the total tangible resource, calculate the *total inactive potential* secondary resource in the lower-left stock (e.g. the total potential passengers who could be using any of the airline's routes, but are not yet doing so).

4. Enter the history and anticipated future for the *average active* quantity of the secondary resource in chart 4 (e.g. active passengers per airline route).

5. From these data on the average quantity and the total tangible resource, calculate the *total active* secondary resource in the lower-right stock (e.g. the total active passengers using any of the airline's routes).

6. Enter the history of new secondary resource that is converted from the potential to active state per year (e.g. the total number of new passengers who start using the airline each year—this win rate will be driven by such factors as marketing, price and reputation, as explained in Chapter 3).

7. Enter, or estimate, the history and future for the average quantity of new potential secondary resource that has been, and will be, added (e.g. the new potential passengers that are reached by each new airline route).

8. Calculate the rate at which this adds total potential to the secondary resource (e.g. the total new potential passengers per year who are reached by the opening of all new routes in the same year).

Note that the loss of a primary resource (e.g. closing an airline route) now takes with it the loss of *both* inactive potential (passengers who could use the airline on that route but do not) *and* active secondary resource (passengers who do currently use the airline on that route). So:

9. Enter or estimate the average *active* secondary resource that has been, and will be lost with each primary resource that is lost in chart 9.

10. Calculate the rate at which this removes total active resource from the lower-right stock (chart 10).

11. Enter or estimate the average *inactive potential* secondary resource that has been, and will go with each primary resource that is lost in chart 11.

12. Calculate the rate at which this removes total active resource from the lower-left stock (chart 12).

This framework and its math is most easily done with the **my**strategy model of Worksheet 6c, see paragraph about online learning materials on p.xxi.

# WORKSHEET 6a: RESOURCE ATTRIBUTE ANALYSIS

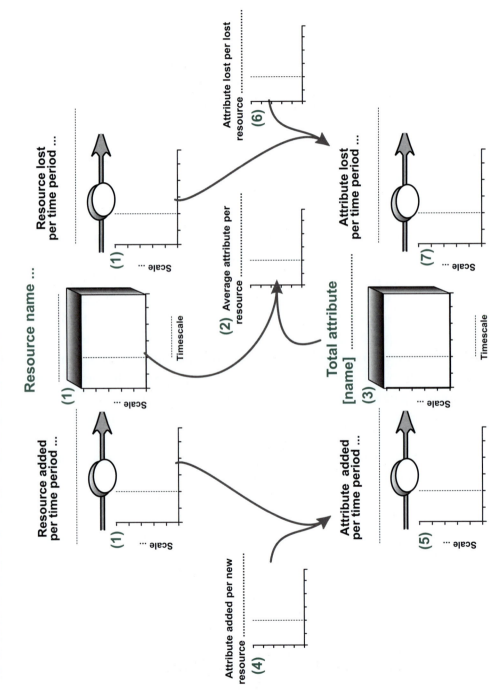

# WORKSHEET 6b: RESOURCE WITH MULTIPLE ATTRIBUTES

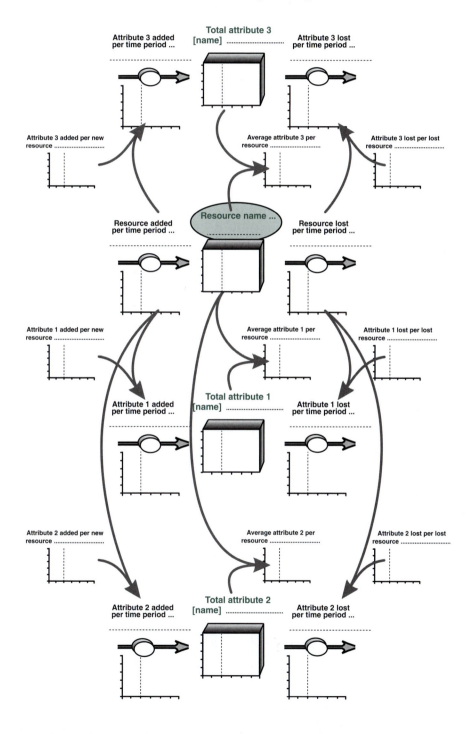

# WORKSHEET 6c: PRIMARY RESOURCE BRINGS ACCESS TO POTENTIAL SECONDARY RESOURCE

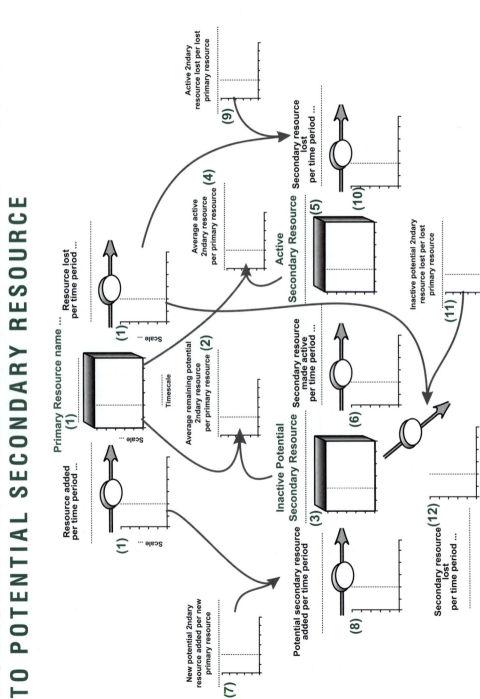

# NOTES

1.  I am grateful to Professor Brad Killaly of the Merage School of Business, University of California, Irvine for bringing this example to my attention.

2.  Agent-based modeling is explained, together with examples of its application to strategic management issues, in Macal, C.M. (2007) *Managing Business Complexity: Discovering Strategic Solutions with Agent-based Modeling and Simulation*, Oxford University Press, New York.

3.  Gratton, L. (1999) People processes as a source of competitive advantage, in *Strategic Human Resource Management* (Eds Gratton, L., Hope Hailey, V., Stiles, P. and Truss, C.), Sage, London, Chapter 9.

4.  Hayton, G. and Loveder, P. (1992) *How To Do a Skills Analysis and Skills Audit*, TAFE National Centre for Research and Development Ltd, Leabrook, South Australia.

5.  Tovey, L. (1994) Competency assessment: A strategic approach—part II. *Executive Development*, **7**(1), 16–19.

6.  See www.ambridge.com/services/audits/skills-audits for a typical example of such services.

7.  Watkins, C. (2006) Filling the empty chair. *Hay Group Newsletter*, **1**, 3.

8.  *The Economist* (2002) Strategic caring: Firms strategise about AIDS, 3 October.

9.  See Pfeffer, J. (1994) *Competitive Advantage Through People: Unleashing the Power of the Work Force*, Harvard Business School Press, Cambridge, MA, and Ulrich, D. (1998) A new mandate for human resources, *Harvard Business Review*, **76**(1) (January–February), 124–134.

10. Snell, S.A. and Youndt, M.A. (1995) Human resource management and firm performance: Testing a contingency model of executive controls. *Journal of Management*, **21**, 711–737.

11. Grant, R. (2005) *Contemporary Strategy Analysis*, Blackwell, Oxford, p.145; Hitt, M., Ireland, D. and Hoskisson, R. (2001) *Strategic Management: Competitiveness and Globalization*, 4th edn, South-Western/Thomson, Cincinatti, p.501; Johnson, G., Scholes, K. and Whittington, R. (2005) *Exploring Corporate Strategy*, 7th edn, Prentice Hall, Harlow, p.118.

12. See Sackman, S., Flamholtz, E. and Bullen, M. (1989) Human resource accounting: a state-of-the art review. *Journal of Accounting Literature*, **8**, 235–264; Flamholtz, E. (1999) *Human Resource Accounting, Advances in Concepts, Methods and Applications*, 3rd edn, Springer, Berlin.

13. The issue of how to choose and configure marketing channels that include intermediaries is dealt with in standard marketing texts, such as Doyle, P. and Stern, P. (2006) *Marketing Management and Strategy* (4th edn), Pearson, Harlow, Chapter 11. More detailed treatment of the management of marketing channels is given in, for example, Coughlan, A., Anderson, E., Stern, L. and El-Ansary, A. (2006) *Marketing Channels* (7th edn), Prentice Hall, Harlow and Kasturi Rangan, V. (2006) *Transforming Your Go-to-Market Strategy*, Harvard Business School Press, Cambridge, MA.

14. See, for example, Bahadur, N., Landry, E. and Treppo, S. (2006) How to slim down a brand portfolio. Strategy+Business Resilience Report, **44**, 14–16. Also available at www.strategy-business.com/resiliencereport.

15. A rich variety of case studies explain both some of the methods of CapitalOne and the development of its strategy, for example Pfeifer, P. (1996) *Capital One Financial Corporation: Response Modeling*, Darden Business Publishing, Charlottesville, VA and Anand, B., Rukstad, M. and Paige, C. (2000) *Capital One Financial Corp*, Harvard Business School Publishing, Cambridge, MA.

16. See, for example, Slatter, S. and Lovett, D. (2004) *Corporate Recovery: Managing Companies in Distress*, Beard Books, Washington, DC.

17. Barker III, V.L. and M Duhaime, I. (1997) Strategic change in the turnaround process: theory and empirical evidence. *Strategic Management Journal*, **18**(1), 13–38.

18. See Luffman, G.A., Kenny, B., Lea, E. and Sanderson, S. (1996) *Strategic Management: An Analytical Introduction*, Blackwell, Oxford, Chapter 15.

19. Baden-Fuller, C. and Stopford, J. (1992) *Rejuvenating the Mature Business*, Routledge, London.

20. *The Economist* (2002) Snap happy: can multimedia messaging live up to the mobile industry's hype?, 25 April.

21. Rust, R., Thompson, D. and Hamilton, R. (2006) Defeating feature fatigue. *Harvard Business Review*, **84**(2), 98–107.

22. See Christensen, C.M. (1995) Disruptive technologies: Catching the wave. *Harvard Business Review*, **75**(1), (January–February), 43–53. Two books expand on these ideas: Christensen, C.M. (1997) *The Innovator's Dilemma*, Harvard Business School Press Boston, MA, and Christensen, C.M. and Raynor, M.E (2003) *The Innovator's Solution*, Harvard Business School Press, Boston, MA. See explanation of disruptvie technology at http://en.wikipedia.org/wiki/Disruptive_technology.

23. Examples include the sixth-century BC Chinese military treatise by Sun Tzu (1983) *The Art of War*, Delacorte Press, New York; Jay, A. (1996) *Management*

*and Machiavelli* (revised edn), Pfeiffer, San Francisco, CA, which draws on the sixteenth-century work of Niccolo Machiavelli, then a diplomat in the pay of the Republic of Florence; Kurke, L.B. (2004) *The Wisdom of Alexander The Great: Enduring Leadership Lessons From The Man Who Created An Empire*, Amacom, New York; Suchet, A. (2004) *Napoléon et le Management*, Tallandier, Paris.

24. Common methods for assessing competitors are explained in Fleisher, C.S. and Bensoussan, B.E. (2003) *Strategic and Competitive Analysis*, Pearson, Upper Saddle River, NJ.

25. See for example US Federal Trade Commission, *Promoting Competition, Protecting Consumers: A Plain English Guide to Antitrust Laws*, available at www. ftc.gov/bc/compguide/index.htm and the European Union, *Mission of the Directorate-General for Competition*, available at http://ec.europa.eu/comm/dgs/ competition/mission/. For information on the role of the Japanese Fair Trade Commission, see www.jftc.go.jp/e-page/aboutjftc/role_index.html.

CHAPTER 6

# RESOURCE DEVELOPMENT

## KEY ISSUES

- ✪ Recognizing that resources contribute differently to an organization as they move through different stages.
- ✪ The importance of knowing and controlling the rates at which resources develop—customers, staff, products and assets.
- ✪ Resources that deteriorate rather than improve as they develop.
- ✪ Attracting and reaching potential customers and staff before they become active.
- ✪ The exceedingly long-term consequences of strategic decisions on developing resources.
- ✪ Assessing the impact of external factors as they drive resource development in innovation and industry emergence.
- ✪ The continuing contribution of staff and customers after they leave the business.
- ✪ Resource development in noncommercial cases.
- ✪ How resource development connects with the organization's core strategic architecture.

Worksheet 7a: Staff Development

Worksheet 7b: Customer Development

Worksheet 7c: Product Development

Worksheet 7d: Asset Life Cycle

Worksheet 8: Impact of Political, Economic, Social and Technological factors (PEST)

Worksheet 9: Experience Curve Cost Reduction.

This chapter makes connections to the following frameworks and concepts: staff hierarchies, R&D pipelines, the "AIDA" framework and other models of customer development, sales pipeline, "PEST" analysis of political, economic, social and technological factors, the experience curve of cost reduction and dynamics of industry innovation.

# RESOURCE DEVELOPMENT WITHIN THE ORGANIZATION

In explaining the link between resources and performance, Chapters 1–4 made some simplifying assumptions, notably (1) that elements of a particular resource were alike and (2) that resources could be simply won and lost. Chapter 5 dealt with the first of these simplifications, and showed how to deal with the varying qualities, or attributes that resources carry. In this chapter we will look at a more realistic picture of how resources are won and lost, with the observation that *resources may develop along a series of states.* The simplest cases concern resources that develop from state to state *within* an organization, such as staff being promoted up through levels of seniority. Development paths may also extend outside the organization, such as the growing awareness and interest of potential customers, and the continued influence of former customers.

## STAFF DEVELOPMENT

The promotion of staff from junior to senior positions provides a clear example of a resource (people) moving from state to state (junior to senior) in many organizations. Chapter 3 already introduced such a case with the law firm concerned about the rising rate of attrition amongst its lawyers (Figure 3.9). A more accurate treatment of the problem is shown in Figure 6.1, which depicts how lawyers are hired and promoted to partner along a simple two-stage chain. (There may of course be more than two levels of staff in an organization or department, but this case concerns just two main levels.) This figure shows both the issue of concern—the rising lawyer attrition at the bottom of the diagram—and the reduced rate of promoting lawyers to partner that has been one cause of the problem.

   (Online learning materials are available to support this example, see p.xxi.)

   Chapter 3 explained how the math in stock-and-flow relationships is vital to the quest for a rigorous causal explanation of performance, and emphasized in particular the mathematical identity between the quantity of a resource at any point in time and the cumulative history of all resource gains minus all resource losses. The same principle applies equally to each state in a developing resource chain. Here, the number of 180 lawyers below the partner level is entirely explained by the firm's history of all lawyers who were ever hired, promoted

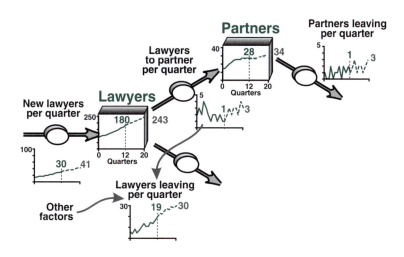

**Figure 6.1: Two-level staff chain in a law firm.**

and lost. Similarly, the number of 28 partners at quarter 12 is precisely explained by the sum of all lawyers ever promoted to partnership minus all partners who ever left. There could in practice be a third flow affecting partner numbers—experienced people who are hired directly into the partner grade, rather than being promoted up through the firm—but that has not been happening in this particular firm.

This stage-by-stage development of staff and other resources has important implications for strategy, since it extends the timescale over which cause and effect are separated. In this case, for example, no more than 4% of lawyers have ever been promoted in any quarter (in quarter three, when four were promoted out of a population of 107). This means that a newly hired lawyer cannot expect to be promoted to partner in less than 25 quarters, or about six years. More recently, the expected delay between being hired and promoted has extended still further, which as explained in Chapter 3 is one of the major reasons lawyers are leaving. An important consequence of this delay is that promotion rates in any year are in part dependent on the number of lawyers hired many years previously—if the firm hired no new lawyers six years ago, then there will be no lawyers today with six years' experience. If this resulted in a shortage of partners today, and if this shortage were to cut the firm's ability to win work from clients, the resulting performance reduction would have been caused by the firm's hiring failure six years previously.

### Doing it right: working the numbers out along the chain

Given the simple arithmetic relationship between stocks and flows of resources, it is not difficult to ensure that the numbers in resource chains such as Figure 6.1 are accurate—a task that is essential! Table 6.1 shows how the numbers change from quarter 12 to 14.

- The number of 190 lawyers at the start of quarter 13 is given by the 180 in place at the start of quarter 12, plus the 30 hired during the quarter, minus both the 19 who leave and the one who is promoted.
- The 28 partners at the start of quarter 13 is given by the 28 in place at the start of quarter 12, plus the one person promoted into the partner grade, minus the one person who leaves.

Looking at staff movements and other resource changes over extended timescales such as in Figure 6.1 is important for evaluating and developing strategy. However, it can also be useful to carry out simple calculations such as Table 6.1 for just one or two periods, to ensure that everyone involved understands how short-term changes will work out and what needs to be done to keep resources developing as required.

## TABLE 6.1: WORKING OUT STAFF MOVEMENTS FROM QUARTER TO QUARTER IN THE LAW FIRM

| Start of quarter | Lawyers hired | Lawyers | Lawyers leaving | Lawyers promoted | Partners | Partners leaving |
|---|---|---|---|---|---|---|
| 12 | 30 ⊕ | 180 ⊖ | 19 ⊖ | 1 ⊕ | 28 ⊖ | 1 |
| 13 | 32 | 190 | 23 | 2 | 28 | 2 |
| 14 | 30 | 197 | 19 | 1 | 28 | 1 |

Note that the values shown for the resource flows in Figure 6.1 give the numbers of people who will move during the coming quarter (following the principles explained in Chapter 3).

Like all the math in the strategy dynamics approach, spreadsheet computations such as Table 6.1 can easily be used for this simple analysis. However, it is easier to see how the numbers and flows interact over time using the **my**strategy mapping and modeling software.

This simple two-stage model of staff development is readily extended to three or more levels of seniority. It can usefully be applied to particular groups of staff, or repeated across departments to provide a picture of how an organization's entire human resource structure is developing. The structure can give rise to a variety of practical challenges, ranging from situations where staff development is too slow, to others where it is too fast.

Chapter 5 already explained how fast growth and/or rapid staff turnover can severely limit an organization's ability to develop staff experience. This can lead to further difficulties if organizations need experience developed among junior levels in order to feed more senior positions. Problems can even arise when neither growth nor attrition is especially high—it is only necessary for the required promotion rates to be high *relative to* the availability of developing juniors.

Chapter 1 introduced the case of a well-known bank that in 2003 set itself the worthy goal of increasing the representation of disadvantaged minorities among its senior management from about 6 % to 20 % by 2008. The bank had about 1 000 senior staff in total, of whom 60 were from the identified minority groups. To aid in this goal, the bank already had a program to identify and support junior staff who were felt to have the potential for senior positions. Typically, these senior-potential staff could be promoted into senior ranks about four years after first being identified. Figure 6.2 shows the staff pipeline—for minority-group staff only—with its recent history and likely future. The green lines show the likely outcome if current rates of identification, promotion and attrition were to continue. The consequences of these continuing rates were way short of management's aim, because the staff development rates were too slow, and attrition rates too high.

(Online learning materials are available to support this example, see p.xxi.)

Management therefore considered what it could do to improve the outcome (the gray lines for each rate in Figure 6.2). With luck and effort, they might identify 25 % of juniors with senior potential each year, and promote one-third of those already identified into senior positions, rather than a quarter. They might also hope to improve staff retention, with attrition cut from 35 % to 30 % per year for juniors and from 25 % to 20 % amongst seniors and senior-potential staff. Even with these improvements, however, the company would, by 2008, be barely half way to its target.

At first sight, this was puzzling. The aspiration seemed realistic, requiring merely an increase of three percentage points each year in minority representation among senior staff. However, adding three percentage points to a current level of 5 % is a *60 % increase* in actual numbers in the first year. There was simply no way to make

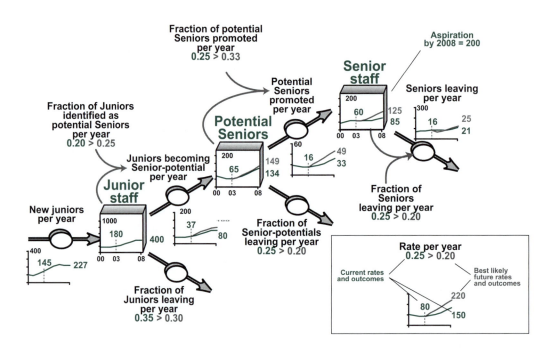

**Figure 6.2:** **Aspiration to increase minority-representation amongst senior management at a large bank.**

this kind of step-increase. Indeed, no plausible improvements to staff development or retention could take the company anywhere close to the goals management had set.

Chapter 1 described two classes of error that arise in setting performance goals for organizations—either grossly undershooting the potential of a situation, or aiming for outcomes that are impossible. At that point, we were discussing the issue at the level of the strategic performance of organizations as a whole. Here we have an example that is concerned with a single functional issue, though one that management undoubtedly felt to be of strategic importance. Whilst the aim was entirely well intentioned, the basic physics of the system meant it could never be achieved.

A further question that arises is why management set the goal in the first place. No one was asking them to hit the 20% representation figure, although they were probably being sensitive to pressure from various lobbying groups. Several dangerous consequences arise. Having set an impossible goal, management is now setting themselves up for serious criticism of their inevitable failure to reach it. In striving to reach this goal they will likely make decisions that are damaging, both to the organization and its people, such as promoting potentially capable people before they have enough experience, and setting *them* up to fail also. Furthermore, employees themselves may respond in ways that are unhelpful. Other minority-group staff who see good people fail may either feel that expectations being placed on them are too high, or else blame management for cynicism in their policy—either way, attrition among minority groups may rise rather than fall. Finally, good people who are outside of the identified groups will likely believe that the organization offers them few prospects and leave. All of these consequences run the further risk of damaging the organization's ability to hire the total number of people it needs in the first place.

## WHEN STAFF DEVELOP TOO QUICKLY

Many senior executives express concern at the difficulty of finding enough of the people they need and the challenging war for talent into which they are drawn. Yet it is easy to overlook the converse problem, namely that, as mentioned briefly in Chapter 1, staff hierarchies are in effect powerful "breeding machines" for management.

Consider the case of a rapidly growing company starting and developing a number of different retail businesses over about 10 years. Groups of stores within each chain are managed and controlled by area managers, who report to a few regional vice-presidents, who report in turn to a head of store operations. Whilst each business is growing, there is a continuing need for more area managers, and thus a good prospect of promotion for store managers. There is also a continuing need for regional VPs, and thus opportunities for area managers to be promoted. The problem arises as growth opportunities for the chain slow down. With no need for more area managers and regional VPs, promotion rates fall sharply. If, for example, each area manager looks after 20 stores, and stays in-post for five years, there is on average only a one in 100 chance of any store manager being promoted in any year.

The problem is reduced if the organization invents new retail store formats and starts to grow more new businesses. A manager in a mature business can then be offered an equivalent position or a more senior post in one of the new businesses. However, this process too will eventually run out, and the organization will need to look at alternative policies to open up promotion opportunities for its staff. This is one reason for the seemingly perverse policy adopted by certain professional organizations known as 'up or out.'

Under an up-or-out policy, staff at any level *must* seek promotion after a certain number of years in their current grade. If they succeed in winning promotion, all well and good. If they fail, they are asked to leave. This seemingly aggressive policy is intended specifically to tackle the problem caused when an organization's likely growth simply cannot provide space sufficiently quickly for the people coming up through the lower grades. Such opportunities are essential in order to motivate the high work rates and ambition on which such organizations depend. It is also essential to clear out lower grades so that new generations of eager youngsters can be brought in and the organization's intellectual horsepower refreshed. There are risks in such policies, however, especially the destruction of any loyalty to the organization. The best exponents of the practice therefore devote considerable effort and expense to ensuring those people who are asked to leave are well supported, especially in finding good positions outside the firm, often with its own customers. This is turned to advantage when those former employees, or alumni, favor their former employer with work.

This problem extends out beyond the boundaries of the firm itself, both backwards into the student-pool from which such firms hire, and forwards into the alumni population, an issue that will be examined further later in this chapter.

## PRODUCT DEVELOPMENT

Another situation in which resources develop through stages largely within the organization itself concerns product development. Typical stages may include:

- idea generation, making use of diverse sources including basic R&D, competitors' products, customer focus groups or direct requests, employee suggestions, and so on
- initial screening, where the basic technological feasibility and market potential are assessed
- technical development, which includes the product's initial specification and testing
- commercial evaluation, including market research, assessment of likely sales volumes, prices and revenues, and detailed estimation of production costs and capital investment
- final development, when the product itself takes the form that customers will actually see, and the details of the production process are specified
- product launch, when marketing and sales activity start, sales are generated and product is shipped.

The exact stages involved and the activities that occur in each vary considerably from industry to industry. It is also common for companies to run stages in parallel in order to collapse the time between initial idea and product launch—for example, production engineering running in parallel with final product design and market testing.[1]

In many cases, firms can be rather sure that a product idea entering the process will go all the way through to launch, and even commercial success. Many new cellphone models, for example, have been successful when they are simply a development of a family that has repeatedly been popular in the marketplace before. At the other extreme, some industries feature a very large fallout indeed between initial ideas and ultimately successful products. Pharmaceutical companies, for example, routinely examine thousands of molecules for every drug that actually achieves commercial success.

The product development process often raises strategically important questions. Increasing the proportion of products at one stage of the pipeline that are carried through to the next will clearly increase the resources required at that next stage. This demand for resources may divert effort from other parts of the process, and alter the likelihood of each product's later success—doubling the rate at which products enter technical development may well not result in double the rate of successful product launches.

Successful product development increasingly relies on close integration with other parts of the business.[2] It requires the understanding of customer needs, which depends on close collaboration with the sales and marketing functions. If this is achieved, companies add a powerful mechanism whereby current resources (customers) accelerate the development of other resources (products).

The technical R&D element of the product development process summarized above brings challenges of its own, including effective planning and management of the technical personnel required, demonstrable contributions to current business performance as well as to future products, and maintaining a spirit of inquiry under pressures for cost containment and efficiency.

Much of the product development activity summarized above takes place a long time before any actual sales are made to real customers—another issue that makes tracing causality from management choices to performance outcomes challenging. Even in sectors that are not especially technologically challenging, a new product development today may well take some years before it has been designed, its production process developed, customer interest tested, and the product finally launched. The costs involved can be substantial, so it is important for management to have a sense of the value of their R&D pipeline and of the technologies that lie behind it.[3]

Figure 6.3 illustrates a staged resource structure for such a product development process. New ideas enter the process at the bottom left, and progress up the chain. At each stage, a product may fail and fall out towards the bottom right. There is a

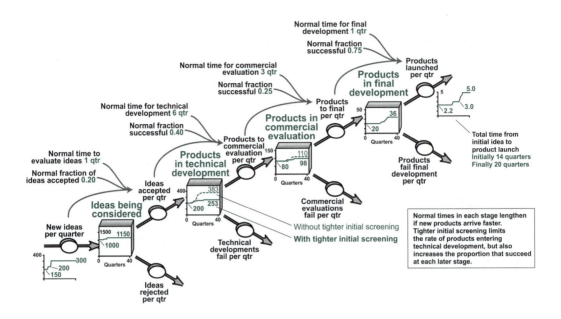

**Figure 6.3:** Dynamics of a product development process with increase in initial ideas.

fractional probability of each product making it from one stage to the next, and each development stage requires some time to work on a product idea. The total time for a product to pass through development is 14 quarters or 3½ years, provided that the rate of new ideas and products passing between stages is within the limits that staff in each stage can handle.

(Online learning materials are available to support this example, see p.xxi.)

### Doing it right: pipelines must contain the same "stuff," and stocks and flows must be properly defined

The resources flowing up the chain in Figures 6.1 and 6.2 are all "people," and those flowing up the chain in Figure 6.3 are all "products." This is the general principle that resource development pipelines *must* contain the same kind of resource in every stock and in every flow between those stocks. We do not have, for example, "research staff" in the first stage of Figure 6.3 and "product" in the second stage.

Note too that some of the stages listed above in the description of typical product development steps actually describe the *transitions* from stage to stage (i.e. the flow rates) rather than the stocks themselves. Idea generation, for example, is a flow of new ideas into a stock that has not yet been screened, and screening results inflows that push each idea either into technical development or else out of the system as a reject. Technical development, on the other hand, is a state in which a product resides for some time, as is commercial evaluation and final development. If the progress of product development is to be quantified, then, it is important to describe each state and each flow rate accurately. So, when using resource development chains, be sure to define precisely each *state* on which the resource can be; that is, the stocks, and the *flow rates* between each state.

After quarter four, management take steps to increase the rate of new product ideas entering the process from 150 to 200 per quarter. Although the technical development staff are able to cope with the faster arrival of new ideas, products reach the later stages faster than those teams can handle, and the total process lengthens by 1.5 quarters. More new products are launched, but slightly later than before.

After quarter eight, a further initiative raises the rate of new ideas to 300 per quarter. Management recognizes that this could throw much more work into technical development than the group can handle (dashed lines), a problem that would also feed through to later stages. Consequently, a tighter screening process is introduced at the same time. This cuts sharply the number of ideas that would otherwise flow into technical development. It would be expected also to cut the flow of work into later stages, but the tighter screening increases the quality of new product ideas, so more make it through at each stage. As a result, the increase in new product launch rate (5.0 per quarter versus 2.2 originally) is proportionately greater than the increase in the rate of new ideas. However, this comes with a penalty of longer development times overall (20 quarters versus 14) due to the higher workload—a problem that could be tackled by increasing staffing selectively on the stages where work pressure becomes most severe.

Product development processes raise important strategic questions, both in their own right and in connection to the organization's wider strategy. The example above has already illustrated the issue of balancing rapid generation of new ideas with an adequately resourced system for progressing and testing those ideas. It also raised the conflict between letting many ideas pass each stage to maximize the final number that may succeed versus imposing tight criteria at each stage in order to ensure that limited development effort can be focused on the few most promising ideas.

These policy choices have important implications for the development and deployment of technical staff and others involved in the process. If the increased rate of new ideas in Figure 6.3 had not been more tightly screened, for example, many more people would have been needed in technical development, and somewhat more in commercial evaluation. Given the problems described in the previous section regarding the dynamics of staff development, few organizations are able to react quickly to such rapid changes in staff requirements.

Management may therefore need to be careful in mandating a change to the normal steady flow of activity in such product development processes. The general point to take away from this observation is that:

**An unfortunate characteristic of stagewise resource chains is that small disturbances can escalate sharply as resources move along the chain.**

There are several further issues to note regarding this model of product development dynamics:

- *It is not necessarily advisable to drive for "more products, faster."* If new products appear frequently, customers may defer purchasing the current product in the expectation that another will be released soon—and may defer buying *that* one because they expect a still better product after that. Companies therefore need to pace new product releases to ensure the maximum overall progress in winning and retaining customers.

- *The chain does not end with the launch of a product.* A newly launched product may succeed and become established, or it may fail in the market and be withdrawn. Technical and commercial development may well continue for products that are already on the market—that is, that have previously left the development chain. Indeed, there is often no hard and fast point at which a product is "complete" and ready to launch. As explained in Chapter 5, companies often have a choice regarding how much functionality to build into products that are launched— less functionality may enable the stages of Figure 6.3 to be shortened, but limit the product's initial appeal. After launch, additional functionality may be added to extend the product's market reach. It can then become a matter of semantics as to when an upgrade is just an improvement to an existing product, and when it is effectively a "new" product.

- *Similar stages may apply to service products.* Although the process above is most easily recognizable for physical products, equivalent steps may arise in bringing a new service to market. Training companies and business schools undertake initial design and commercial evaluation for new programs, followed by detailed design before the program is launched. Consultancy companies seek opportunities for new advisory services they can offer to clients, and will undertake development efforts—often with existing clients who have a high level of trust in their advisor—before seeking to sell the service more widely. Television production companies develop and test new program concepts and series, and may undertake a single-program trial to evaluate a program's potential before a more extensive launch.

- *Parallel development compresses, but complicates the process.* As can be seen, waiting for each stage of development to be finished before the next starts results in a quite lengthy delay between an original idea and a product actually being launched. Consequently, companies seek to run parts of the process in parallel, for example by carrying out some parts of the commercial evaluation whilst the product is still in technical development. Running such processes entirely in parallel is rarely possible. It may not be feasible for example to complete a full commercial assessment until a reasonably complete prototype emerges from technical development.

- *"Failed" products may not leave the system.* The four outflows of product ideas in Figure 6.3 imply that failures are simply lost. In practice this is rarely the case. The pharmaceuticals industry is a major illustration of why failed products should be retained. With the increasing difficulty and expense of developing new drugs, many companies in the industry are searching their archives of previously rejected products to identify any that may have useful properties for medical purposes other than the one for which they were originally developed.[4] A well-known example concerns thalidomide, a drug that reached notoriety in the 1960s for the distressing effect it had on unborn babies after being given to their pregnant mothers to alleviate morning sickness. However, the drug has useful properties and is now being developed for the treatment of various forms of cancer. A major advantage of this rejuvenation of old products is that they have often gone through much of the product development process in relation to their original purpose, thus reducing the time and cost of renewed development.

- *The principle applies to other issues than new products.* Many organizations seek innovations across their entire range of business processes. Each new idea still needs to be screened, developed and tested before being implemented, so will go through a number of stages similar to some of those in Figure 6.3. In addition, ideas need not all be large scale. A celebrated exponent of widespread innovation is the Toyota car company whose process is reckoned to have generated over a million ideas since the 1970s, over 80% of which have been implemented.[5]

## ASSET LIFE STAGES

Equipment and other fixed assets constitute another class of resource that may move through recognizable stages. Management of physical assets is a somewhat neglected issue in strategy, even in operations management. Yet for many companies, the value involved is considerable—a typical utility company, for example, could have tangible assets worth five times the company's annual turnover or more. For such organizations, the renewal and maintenance of physical assets is a dominant component of its business strategy. This is not simply due to the sheer scale of financial value and expenditure involved; the consequences of success or failure on the issue reaches out into the market, through the impact on customers' experience and hence on the company's reputation. A company that manages the issue well may also achieve superior performance overall, enabling it to develop both organically and by acquiring others.

Chapter 5 discussed how physical assets deteriorate, often by becoming increasingly unreliable. It treated any particular type of asset as a single population, and averaged out its reliability across all units. Chapter 5 also pointed out that the *distribution* of asset quality has important implications for asset management strategy, whether quality is rather uniform across all units, or heavily skewed by a few particularly poor units.

The distribution of asset quality does not arise by chance but instead reflects the history of their acquisition and aging. This can lead to recognizable stages in the life of an individual unit, for example:

- Whilst new units are "bedding in," even small problems in their manufacture can give rise to undesirable failure rates, despite suppliers' best efforts to ensure this does not arise.
- Units may then enter a long period when they are highly reliable, provided they are properly maintained. For motor vehicles, this period of high reliability may last many years, depending on mileage, whilst for many industrial items, 10–20 years of reliable life is common.

- Maintenance staff or users may then notice an increasing occurrence of failures—not sufficient to make the product unusable, but inconvenient and costly nevertheless. Regular maintenance is not sufficient to prevent this higher failure rate of older units. The unit may be described as "degrading." For cars and industrial assets this stage may last several more years.
- Finally, the unit becomes so unreliable that it is frequently breaking down, often seriously so, causing considerable inconvenience and cost.

Although industrial cases provide the clearest examples of this aging chain, with the important impact on reliability that arises from the process, similar stages can be observed with buildings and with key assets in other industries, such as refrigeration equipment in data centers, vehicles in logistics firms, food preparation equipment in catering and the quality of fittings in restaurants, hotels and leisure outlets. To use the following framework in other cases, it is only necessary to review and define the life stages appropriate to the particular situation of concern, and identify how many units reside in each stage.

Note that certain intangible "assets" also degrade over time. Information technology systems (as distinct from the hardware on which they run) effectively become less useful, even though the code of which they consist remains the same or even improves, because the business needs that the systems serve are moving forward. Similar decline applies to business processes and technologies.

Strategic management of an asset base includes a number of policy options—for example, how frequently to undertake routine maintenance, when to replace a unit completely, and when to refurbish a unit. Refurbishment involves taking the unit out of service, replacing worn-out parts and effectively restoring it to an as-new state. Depending on the asset involved, this may be possible only with units that are not too seriously dilapidated, and may only restore the unit to a partial state of as-new health.[6]

Table 6.2 shows an illustrative population of equipment units in a regulated power-supply firm, distributed amongst the four states defined above, with the number of years a unit stays in each state and the corresponding failure rate.[7]

Given this initial mix of assets and reliability, total failures occur at the rate of 900 per year (0.9 per 100 assets per year), each such event costing $20 000 in repair effort and related costs. The company receives a fee for each unit of power it supplies to customers in its region, but a penalty charge is deducted from this fee for any failures in its system that inconvenience its customers. (This situation reflects a particular regulatory regime, which may differ between countries.)

**TABLE 6.2:  CHARACTERISTICS OF ASSETS IN EACH LIFE STAGE OF AN ILLUSTRATIVE COMPANY**

|  | Bedding-in | Reliable | Degenerating | Unreliable |
|---|---|---|---|---|
| Number of assets (000) initially in each stage | 5 | 60 | 30 | 5 |
| Time in this stage (with normal maintenance) | 1 year | 20 years | 10 years | Until replaced |
| Failures per year per 100 assets | 1.0 | 0.5 | 1.0 | 5.0 |

Even with perfect maintenance, this population of assets inevitably flows towards the unreliable state, so unreliable assets must be replaced with new, at a cost of $50 000 each. Degenerating units can be taken out of service and refurbished, making them as-new at a cost of $20 000 each. Maintenance spend ensures that reliable and degenerating units remain in those states for the longest possible time. Any shortfall in this optimum maintenance spend shortens each unit's life, resulting in an increasingly unreliable network.

Figure 6.4 shows a long time horizon for the company's assets. The business starts with a relatively poor asset base that continues to deteriorate for the first five years:

- maintenance spending on reliable assets is not sufficient to keep this number at its initial level
- maintenance and refurbishment of degenerating units are not sufficient in total to prevent a rapid flow of units into the unreliable state
- spend on new equipment is insufficient to prevent the number of unreliable units growing quickly
- the total rate of failures is growing, driven especially by the rising number of unreliable units, and price penalties are reducing the company's revenue
- falling revenue and rising operating costs are causing a rapid decline in the company's net cash flow.

(Online learning materials are available to support this example, see p.xxi.)

The strategic question here is where to intervene with changed spending rates, and how those spending rates should change as time passes, so as to both reestablish and sustain an acceptably low failure rate whilst at the same time producing acceptable and sustainable cash flow. The strategy depicted is as follows:

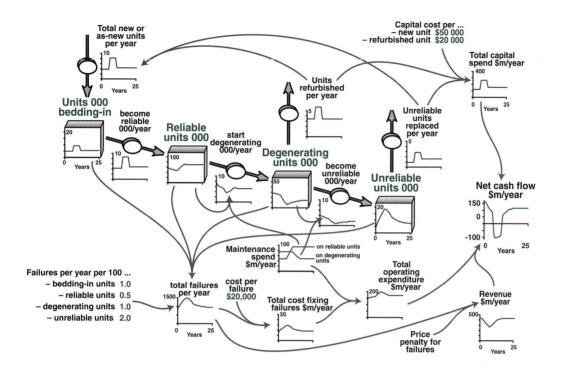

**Figure 6.4: Recovery strategy for a deteriorating asset base in a power supply firm.**

- From years 5–10, the company undertakes a major investment program to replace many of its unreliable units.
- Over the same period, most of the degenerating units are refurbished. This not only reduces their contribution to the overall failure rate, but also cuts drastically the pool of degenerating units that subsequently become unreliable. The number of unreliable units therefore continues to decline even after the replacement program is cut back from year 10.
- To prevent the number of degenerating units rising too quickly once again, maintenance of reliable units is progressively increased—a switch of spending away from the declining number of degenerating units. The rate of reliable units starting to degenerate does rise, simply because of the greater number of reliable units in existence, but not sufficiently to allow much increase in the population of degenerating units.
- Over the later years, the continuing fall in unreliable units allows a slight reduction in overall failure rates, though this is partly countered by a small increase in degenerating units.

- After the replacement and refurbishment programs are ended, and maintenance is reallocated onto reliable units, falling failure rates reduce the price penalty on the company, allowing net cash flow to recover to a healthy and sustainable rate. (Note that this illustration does not include the cost of capital. Over the five-year period of higher replacement and refurbishment, the company invests over $500m more than it would have done, had its original investment rate continued. The interest cost of this additional investment would reduce the ultimate improvement in cash flow, but the result is still preferable to the original performance.)

In practice, the asset base for such a company would be made up of a variety of asset-types—switches, transformers, cables, etc. Each of these asset types would have its own characteristics of aging rate, maintenance requirement and contribution to failures, and each require its own strategy for reaching and sustaining an adequately reliable performance level. The aging chain in Figure 6.4 would thus need to be repeated across each type of asset, and the resulting performance added up across all the types of asset involved.

---

**Doing it right: resources in development must be "MECE"**

The resource development chains in this section each encompass the entire population of the resources involved.

The law-firm chain includes all lawyers in the firm, partners and others, the product chain covers all products undergoing development, and the utility firm model includes all of the firm's units of equipment. This illustrates an important principle that is essential to making sure the performance outcomes are numerically accurate—the stages in the chain must be "MECE," mutually exclusive and collectively exhaustive; that is, each unit of resource must be in one of the chain's stages and *only* one.

- The lawyers in Figure 6.1 are either regular lawyers in the lower stock or partners, but not both.
- The products in Figure 6.3 are either in unscreened ideas *or* in technical development *or* in commercial development *or* in final development.
- The utility firm's assets are either bedding-in *or* reliable *or* degenerating *or* unreliable.

This principle can require some care. It is important to label each state carefully to avoid any uncertainty as to the state in which any resource unit resides. It may also be necessary to clarify any exclusions—for example, the product development chain stops when products are actually launched, and therefore excludes products that were previously developed.

There can be complications when a resource unit is participating in two or more development processes. As noted above, firms sometimes try to compress the product development cycle by working in parallel on technical development and commercial evaluation. Depending on the complexity of the situation and the potential impact of specific decisions, it may thus be necessary to construct linked development models. As far as one department is concerned, products have either not started development, are in the initial technical development stage, or are in final development. But the commercial department needs a chain taking a different view, with products either being not yet in commercial development or actively being worked on. These two separate chains must still conform to the MECE rule.

## FURTHER IMPLICATIONS OF RESOURCE DEVELOPMENT

### ATTRIBUTES CARRIED FROM STATE TO STATE

Chapter 5 explained how resources carry attributes with them when won by, or lost from an organization. Resources also carry attributes with them as they develop from stage to stage. A common case concerns staff experience, which for simplicity can be measured in years. Figure 6.5 shows a three-level staff structure, with junior staff being hired with no experience. Thereafter, three distinct mechanisms raise or lower experience:

- junior staff add one year of experience for each year they remain in that grade
- each junior person lost reduces the total experience of the group by taking with them the number of years' experience they have
- each junior person promoted also reduces the total experience of the group by taking with them the number of years' experience they have, but this is added to the experience of the middle management group.

Note, as explained in Chapter 5, that the stock of *total juniors' experience* is expressed in person-years, so the average person's experience is given by dividing this total by the actual number of *juniors*.

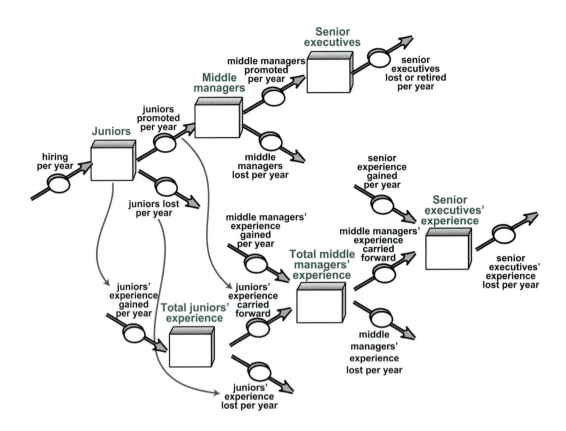

**Figure 6.5: Staff carry experience with them as they develop within an organization.**

The same three mechanisms operate on the middle management group, with the addition of an inflow to experience brought by the newly promoted juniors (causal links not shown for clarity). The same mechanisms apply once again for senior executives, except that there is no onward promotion.

The quantitative implications that arise when resources develop and carry their attributes with them can be readily computed, provided that the procedures of Chapter 5 are properly combined with those for resource development explained in this chapter. This kind of analysis is useful in a variety of situations. For example, an organization facing the imminent retirement of a large fraction of its experienced senior management can anticipate the likely impact of accelerated promotion from its middle grade to fill the senior vacancies. The resulting reduction in experience amongst senior management is just one important consequence. Others include the unavoidable loss of experience amongst middle managers, reduced losses from that level as middle managers see promotion prospects improving, and concern about adequate experience amongst juniors who will be needed to replace the promoted middle managers.

Attributes are carried forward by other types of resource as they develop through the system. Products, for example, are often developed because it is believed they could appeal to an estimated number of potential customers. This potential is the attribute that the product carries with it as it progresses through development. Management must take this attribute into account when prioritizing the product development pipeline. When faced with limited R&D resources, for example, should priority focus on products with a large potential market, but limited probability of success, or on a larger number of products, each with a smaller potential market but higher likelihood of success? The pharmaceuticals industry once again provides dramatic examples of this issue. Each product is targeted at a certain therapeutic use, for which there is a known population of sufferers. As mentioned in Chapter 1, the industry's problem is that the companies' pipelines are increasingly lacking in drugs that carry a large potential pool of patients with them from stage to stage along the development process.

## ADDING ALREADY DEVELOPED RESOURCES

If there is too little resource in early stages of a pipeline to feed the developed resource an organization needs, a common solution is to bring in already-developed resource from outside. Drugs companies, for example, often buy or licence part-developed drugs from competitors, or even acquire whole companies in order to access a promising pipeline of drugs in development.

Companies frequently hire middle or senior managers if they find they lack the internal staff to fill the positions that are needed. Figure 6.6 shows (highlighted) the mechanism by which this direct hiring of seniors adds to the other mechanisms that change the accumulated experience of the senior population. This quick fix needs to be used with care, however. The quality of external hires is not readily known. Sheer years of experience is not a reliable guarantee of true capability—hence the considerable demand for the services of head-hunters who claim to ensure that quality. Bringing in new senior staff can also disrupt the other flows. Middle managers may feel devalued, leading to faster loss of both people and experience from that level. Consequently, the organization may find a still greater scarcity of suitable internal talent when next it is seeking senior candidates. So beware:

**Introducing staff at senior levels can have damaging impacts on organizations, so needs careful planning and implementation.**

When numbers of senior staff are relatively small, there is little new insight to be gained from quantifying the flows of people and experience depicted in Figure 6.6.

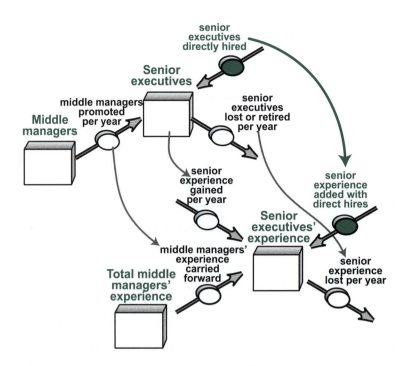

**Figure 6.6: Direct hiring of senior staff adds to the mechanisms driving senior experience.**

However, for larger organizations it is valuable to be explicit about both numbers and experience of middle and senior staff, to track the dynamics of their development and to anticipate likely changes over many years into the future. It should also be noted that Figures 6.5 and 6.6 have, for simplicity, illustrated the principles purely on the basis of years' experience. As Chapter 5 explained (Table 5.7), a more relevant assessment of management quality can be arrived at by use of a competency matrix. Not only does this tool provide a profile of the current population; it can also provide a focus for the numbers and characteristics required of external hires brought into middle or senior positions.

# DEVELOPING RESOURCES BEYOND THE ORGANIZATION'S BOUNDARIES

The examples of resource development explained thus far in this chapter have concerned resources developing within the organization—staff, products and (developing negatively) fixed assets. However, some resources develop through stages before they become part of the organization's activity, and may continue to play a role after they leave.

## THE CUSTOMER CHOICE PIPELINE

The development of resources prior to becoming an active part of the business system was already introduced with the consideration of potential customers in Chapter 4 (see Figures 4.8–4.10). In practice, there may be more going on in this precapture stage and the details can be very important. It is very rare, in practice, for customers to be simply switched from "potential" to "active" as implied in Chapter 4. Most often, customers must be moved through a number of stages. This process has long been recognized in the marketing field, and has been developed into a wide variety of models.[8]

One of the simplest early models of customer development, affectionately known as "AIDA" depicts the winning of customers as working through four stages: gaining their attention, attracting their interest, stimulating desire and finally motivating them into action to purchase the product. Later developments included the "hierarchy of effect model"[9]—awareness, knowledge, liking, preference, conviction and purchase—and the "low involvement model,"[10] in which purchase may be somewhat spontaneous, leaving positive interest and attitudes to emerge later.

In all such models, however, customers move amongst various stages, some of which do not involve any purchase or any active participation with the product whatever. In spite of this noninvolvement, it is often important to understand these states and how customers move between them. First, companies spend considerable sums on marketing activities in order to bring customers through those stages, prior to enjoying any sales revenue from them. Second, there can be interactions involving inactive customers that have important effects on customer acquisition and retention. Many people, for example, have positive attitudes towards BMW cars, even though they have never owned or even driven one, which has a positive influence on the attitudes of other nonowners. Conversely, many people have negative attitudes towards fuel-inefficient SUVs, again despite having no actual experience of them, which impacts negatively on the attitudes of other nonowners.

Figure 6.7 shows a customer-development chain depicting a product launch over 36 months for a mass-market fast-moving consumer brand, such as a coffee product. The marketing challenge is to move consumers up through a series of stages until they hopefully become loyal buyers of the product. Since each flow represents numbers of consumers changing their state of mind each month, marketing

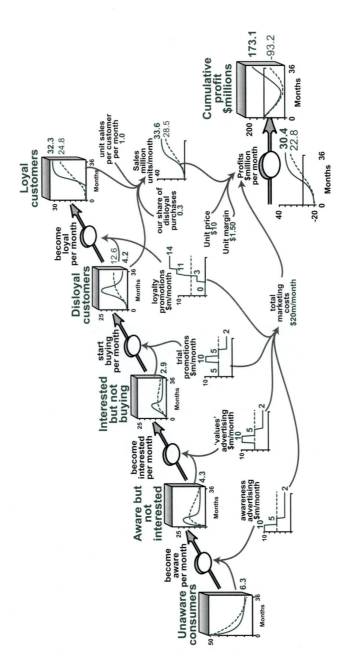

**Figure 6.7: Phasing marketing spend priorities to accelerate profit growth for a consumer brand.**

Source: Finskud, L. (2004) *Competing for Choice*, Vola Press, UK. Reproduced by permission of Lars Finskud.

is ultimately trying to alter their choice regarding product purchase—hence the framework's description as a "choice pipeline."[11]

In this illustration, market research suggests there may be 50 million potential consumers for the product, who need to be won by marketing and promotional spending. This particular chain combines the "interest" and "desire" stages of the AIDA framework into a single population of interested consumers. However, it splits active customers between those who are loyal and disloyal. "Loyal" consumers are those who would always purchase the brand when they need this kind of product—"Disloyals" share their purchases between this brand and its competitors.

Management has a total marketing budget of $20million/month to divide across four categories of spending: (1) advertizing to build awareness; (2) advertizing to communicate the brand's "values" and win consumers' interest; (3) promotions to persuade interested consumers to add the brand to those they purchase; and (4) loyalty promotions to persuade consumers to purchase this brand and no other. In the base case (dashed lines), the budget is allocated evenly across all four activities in every month. It takes a long time for the early advertizing at the front end of the chain to bring consumers within reach of the promotion spending that will persuade them to actually buy the product. Consequently, sales are slow to take off, so the brand does not break even until month 20, and by month 36 has failed to pay back the investment in its own marketing—cumulative profits are still negative.

In the better case (solid lines), management first prioritizes awareness advertizing, followed by values advertizing in the first year. This pumps up numbers of aware and interested consumers more quickly than in the base case. So when spending is swung towards promotional activity after month 12, it is much more effective. Thereafter, spending at the front of the chain can be cut—since few disinterested people remain to be communicated with—and is increasingly focused on capturing active customers and winning their loyalty. Total active consumers (disloyal plus loyal) climb to roughly the same number as in the base case, 37 million, but a larger proportion are loyal. Furthermore, the total between about months 18 and 30 is considerably greater than before, resulting in a large increase in profitability during that period and helping the brand easily pay back its investment by month 36.

(Online learning materials are available to support this example, see p.xxi.)

As with resource chains already discussed in this chapter, the five states in this chain are "MECE." Any individual consumer must be in one, and only one of the stocks, so careful definition of each stage is needed. The second stage is "aware but not interested," for example, because "aware" alone describes consumers in all the stages except the first.

Figure 6.7 simplifies considerably the way in which marketing communications work.[12] It is most unlikely, for example, that roughly comparable spending on four types of marketing would be advisable in any real case. In addition:

- Each type of marketing will have some impact on more than a single flow of customers, e.g. values advertizing will contribute to awareness as well as making people interested.
- Multiple consumer segments will certainly exist, each of which exhibit different responses to the communication, different purchase rates, and so on.
- The chain does not show all possible movements, e.g. the possibility of consumers moving directly into upper levels of the chain with spontaneous purchase, following the low-involvement model mentioned earlier.
- Unlike the situation described in Chapter 4, this illustration assumes that the product is fully available in stores from the start.

Even so, this model illustrates important issues.

> **Allocating fixed marketing spend to different activities over time is never optimal, especially when circumstances are changing quickly.**

It is still more inadvisable to allocate spending on the basis of certain fractions of sales revenue. In the early months of no revenue, the company would spend nothing and therefore generate nothing.

The illustration shows again that:

> **Performance in any period depends on the whole history of previous decisions.**

The sharp growth in disloyal customers in the middle year, for example, reflects strongly the peak in values advertizing from months seven to 12. Had that peak not happened, then the large stock of interested consumers by month 12 would not have been available for the subsequent peak in trial promotion spend to exploit.

The model can also show further principles. For example, as noted above it is most unlikely that a fixed rate of total spending (here, $20m/month) would be

### Take care about "delays"!

Managers understand perfectly well that delays occur between events in their world or the decisions they take and the impact these have on performance results. This understanding is not, however, entirely accurate.

Looking back to the math of the causal mechanisms explained in Chapter 4, it can be seen that all the regular causal links operate instantaneously—e.g. sales volume today, multiplied by price today equals revenue today. Furthermore, the flow-to-stock causality is also instantaneous—the moment a new customer is captured, the number of customers increases by one. There is thus no delayed causality whatever in Figure 6.7.

There is no mechanism in the real world (aside from the weird phenomena in quantum physics!) for cause and effect ever to be separated in time. *Apparent* delays can only arise if something is stored from one moment to another, which is precisely what resources or stocks actually do. The item stored may be physical. There is a delay, for example, between your order for a new car and its delivery, because your vehicle moves from stage to stage through the production and distribution system. There are also information delays, for example between the time you place the order and its effect on the person (or computer) who initiates your car's production. Much improvement to performance has of course been made in all kinds of organizations by reducing both kinds of delay. Whether physical or informational, such delays are termed "pipeline" delays because something—a physical "something" or information—acts as though it has entered a pipe, and taken some time to move along the pipe before popping out at the other end.

Whilst this may seem a fussy and disputable point, it is important because we often act as though such pipeline delays are occurring when instead there is an accumulation process going on. In Figure 6.7, it may *look like* there is a delay between the increased promotion spending in month 13 and the resulting increase in number of active consumers, but *from the moment the spending is increased*, consumers are pumped faster into the disloyal stock.

anywhere near the optimal policy. In this model, for example, breakeven can be achieved as early as month 13 and cumulative profits reach $500 million if spending rates are doubled in the early period and cut back to just $10m/month in the third year.

The model can also show the principle highlighted in Chapter 4 that:

### A minimum "input" is needed to make a business system perform at all.

Had this brand invested only, say, $5 million per month, it would never have hit sales rates sufficient to pay for its own marketing, no matter how that small sum was allocated. In Chapter 4, this failure reflected the inadequate self-reinforcement between consumers and stores. Here, however, the failure arises from a different mechanism, hidden in the detail of the consumer flow rates.

Figure 6.8 gives more information about the flows around disloyal and loyal customers. It shows that, whilst some consumers are being pumped up the chain by the brand's promotion spending, others are slipping back down the chain. This could arise for a number of reasons, such as being attracted to competing products, changes in price or availability, or ceasing to find the brand's values sufficiently interesting to continue being loyal, or buying it at all. With insufficient marketing spend overall,

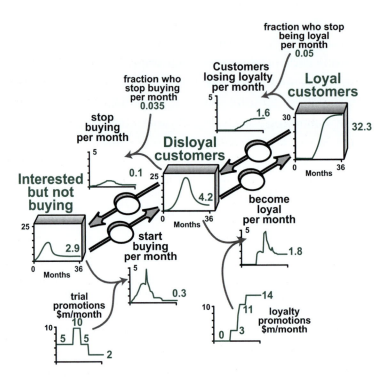

Figure 6.8: Forward and backward flows of consumers for a brand.

these backflow rates negate the small forward flows of consumers as soon as numbers in the upper stages become significant. These backflows also explain why companies continue to advertize products everyone knows about. There are always factors at work that push customers back down these pipelines, so continued effort is nearly always required in order to keep customers up at the top of the chain.

Further important implications emerge from this additional detail regarding customer development:

- Marketing mechanisms contribute to slowing the backflows of customers, as well as driving the forward flows, a clear example being loyalty promotions that help hold on to loyal customers as well as making them loyal in the first place.
- It is vital to identify correctly the states in which customers reside, and what movements take place amongst those states. If, for example, people buy on impulse, with no prior interest in the product, then a new state needs to be shown such as "recent spontaneous buyers," together with flows into that state from either unaware or aware. From this new state, additional outflows may be needed that show people moving into the other states on this chain.
- Figure 6.8 also highlights vital data to track—as noted in previous chapters:

### Managing performance is all about the flow rates!

Here, we can expect 32.5 m loyal customers in month 37 (32.3, plus 1.8, minus 1.6) and 4.2 m disloyal customers (4.2 + 0.3 − 0.1 − 1.8 + 1.6). But it is not enough to know merely that there are currently 4.2 m disloyals. Nor is it sufficient to know that there will be zero net change in that number next month. All four of the flows that are building and depleting that stock are important.

- It is important also to know what is driving those flows. This figure simply states that 5 % of loyal customers cease to be loyal each month—it does not explain why. Some of those factors will be outside our control, e.g. a competitor's price-reduction, and some we may be able to influence.
- To all of this must be added additional impacts of marketing efforts—especially persuading customers to favour this product more often and to buy more frequently. The model shown here has a constant fraction of disloyal customers buying the brand, and a constant overall purchase rate.

It is normal practice for customer research to ask customers whether they are aware, interested, and so on, but rarely asks further vital questions such as—"Have you recently *become* interested?" or "Have you recently *ceased* being a loyal customer?" Recall from Chapter 3 the important insight regarding the pain-relief product that arose simply from identifying separately the number of new and lapsing users of the product each year. The same principle applies to all stages of the choice pipeline. Since customer flows such as those illustrated in Figure 6.8 *must* be taking place to some degree in virtually every case, and decisions on marketing, pricing, and so on, operate by influencing those flows, then the question arises as to how companies can make those decisions without knowing each of those numbers.

> **It is not possible to make sound decisions about resource development without knowing the flows, in both directions, of resources moving along a chain.**

When choice pipeline analysis is conducted in practice, then, it is frequently necessary to suspend work whilst new research is conducted to answer such vital questions. Furthermore, a company will only be able to *continue* making well-informed marketing choices if they continue to monitor and use these data.

Clearly, the kind of analysis illustrated above is extensive, complex and time-consuming, and it is costly to obtain the research required for it to be well-informed. This will only be worthwhile when the potential value is high—that is, when there are large numbers of potential customers, purchase rates are high, and/or the unit value of the product or service is substantial. Nevertheless, there is much that can be done with this perspective, even for smaller organizations and lower-value cases.

- Simply laying out the probable structure of customer states and the flows between them can help clarify what management is *trying* to do, even if there are 10 data to show how successful those efforts have been.
- The diagram also provokes questions that management can usefully ask. Chapter 3 mentioned the problem that customers may have "gone" even though they continue to exist on the company's customer database. One commonly useful question to ask, then, is which customers on the database continue to be real, which have become dormant, and which have effectively been lost.
- The diagram offers a rigorous picture of the situation that can be widely shared. Not only will this clarify for people outside the team what is supposed to be happening, but it will also stimulate new ideas and insights to bring it about.

## USING THE CHOICE PIPELINE IN OTHER SECTORS

Although Figures 6.7 and 6.8 have focused on the case of a mass-market, fast-moving consumer product, the principles can be adapted to many other situations. In professional service businesses, such as consulting companies or law firms, clients must generally still be brought through awareness and understanding of the provider's service before they can be expected to buy it. Many established business-to-business (B2B) providers have little problem with the early stages in the chain—most significant business customers, for example, are aware of alternative telecoms providers and are sufficiently well informed about the services available to be interested in some providers and not in others. In such sectors, then, the challenge focuses on the upper stages, with selling efforts focused on changing a customer's interest level sufficiently that they are prepared to make a potentially risky move in switching suppliers. This is not true of all B2B products and services—novel offerings will require marketing efforts at the front end of the chain.

Choice pipelines also arise in the voluntary and public service sectors. There is widespread ignorance in many countries amongst those who may gain from welfare benefits, for example, of what those benefits are or how to obtain them. There have even been cases where government agencies, in an effort to minimize their costs, budget for their expenditure in the full knowledge that uptake will be far less than 100%, and make no efforts to increase that uptake. Whether intentional or not, the under claiming of welfare benefits frequently results in voluntary organizations having to provide marketing and advisory services to potential claimants. Voluntary organizations themselves often face the same problem—that the people they wish to help do not know of their existence or of their services.

Firms who are small relative to the market in which they operate face a challenge in stimulating any awareness or interest at all. They have a particular need to identify a clear part of the wider customer population where they stand some chance of initiating movement up the choice pipeline. For this purpose, common market segmentation tools are helpful, for example segmenting both the different customer *groups* who may be served and the specific *needs* that one or more groups may have.[13]

## FURTHER CONNECTIONS AND DEVELOPMENTS OF THE CHOICE PIPELINE

The choice pipeline may often need to be used in conjunction with other approaches and frameworks. The value curve, introduced in Chapters 2 and 3, offers a simple diagnosis of customer benefits that the second stage of advertizing—winning customers' interest—must communicate. When there is an identifiable separate stage of "desire," as distinct from mere "interest," products may rely on emotional, rather than purely functional values. Those values continue to feature in the later stages of the chain, when customers decide to buy or be loyal to the product. The simple value curve tool does not generally deal adequately with such subtleties, and more sophisticated customer research methods are needed.

## ADDING WORD-OF-MOUTH AND OTHER FEEDBACK MECHANISMS

Chapter 4 explained the Bass diffusion model, in which word-of-mouth com-munication between potential customers and already active customers added to advertizing in encouraging people to become customers. The choice pipeline offers several routes by which that interaction may operate. Existing customers may make other people aware, make them interested, or encourage them to buy a product (Figure 6.9). Still more interactions are possible, such as interested customers mak-ing others aware, even though they do not themselves buy the product, and loyal customers persuading others to become loyal.

It is rarely possible or affordable to carry out research in sufficient detail to identify all these mechanisms separately from the impact of the various marketing efforts. Furthermore, whilst all these processes are occurring, still further factors are influ-encing the pipeline, such as competitor efforts to capture customers. Nevertheless, it is valuable at least to be conscious that these mechanisms are at work. Not only can it offer plausible explanations for dynamics that are not precisely accounted for by numerical analysis, but it can also suggest activities or policies to improve strategic performance. It is common, for example, for firms in many B2B industries to attend conferences in order to make potential customers aware of their services and capabilities. Such events are almost purpose-made to accomplish the kinds of choice stimulation shown in Figure 6.9. Companies can sometimes radically raise

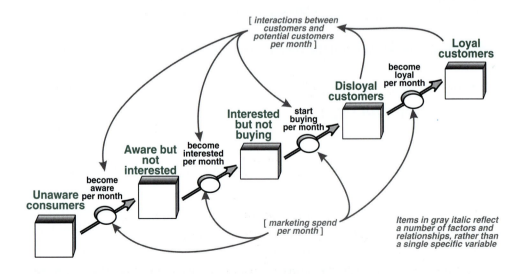

**Figure 6.9: Word of mouth adds to the impact of marketing in pushing customers along the choice pipeline.**

the effectiveness of such events by being quite explicit beforehand as to the purpose or purposes for which each event is to be used—which customer segments are to be targeted, with which information about what services. Furthermore, the identifiable group of aware and potentially interested customers created by the activity becomes a high-quality target list for subsequent promotion and sales efforts.

### Take care with the sales funnel

The choice pipeline appears similar to the sales pipeline commonly used in salesforce management, except that sales pipeline analysis generally focuses on the upper stages of the pipeline. It is an extremely widespread and important tool for salesforce planning and management.[14] Explanations of how this tool works often describe the sales process as operating like a "funnel," with very large numbers of potential customers at the top narrowing down to a very small number of eventual sales (Figure 6.10). Not only are customers at each stage identified and quantified, but the probability that each will result in a sale is also estimated, together with the potential value of the sale. Definitions of the exact stages involved vary considerably, depending on the situation and the sophistication of the organization using the tool.

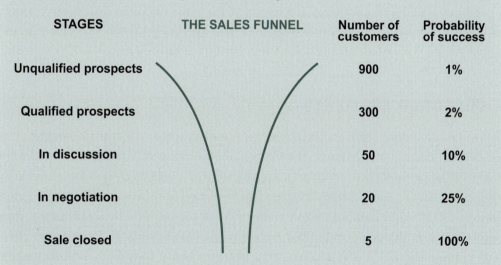

| STAGES | THE SALES FUNNEL | Number of customers | Probability of success |
|---|---|---|---|
| Unqualified prospects | | 900 | 1% |
| Qualified prospects | | 300 | 2% |
| In discussion | | 50 | 10% |
| In negotiation | | 20 | 25% |
| Sale closed | | 5 | 100% |

**Figure 6.10: Examples of stages in the sales funnel, the conceptual basis for sales pipeline management.**

(Note: There is not necessarily a correspondence between the relative numbers of customers in each stage and the probabilities of success, e.g. in this example, 1% probability amongst the 900 unqualified prospects implies that this population may ultimately generate nine actual sales, rather than the five sales that have actually been recently closed.)

The funnel is a poor analogy, however. Everything entering the top of a funnel emerges from the bottom. This is not the case for sales prospects, which can stop at certain stages, move back up the funnel, or be lost from it completely. The ambiguity can result in confusion between states in which customers reside (e.g. a qualified prospect) and movements of customers between those states (e.g. an initial approach).

A more accurate analogy is of customers being moved by sales efforts up a series of tanks on a hillside, and being likely both to flow back down from tank to tank, or to flow out of the side altogether. Every stock on that picture connects to a specific state of mind for the customer (e.g. "I have been approached by this supplier," or "I am in negotiation with this supplier"), and every flow corresponds to a specific *change* in the customer's state of mind ("I have just become informed about what this supplier offers," or "I have just decided to reject this supplier"). The analogy also makes explicit the distinction between forward and backward flows of customers—as noted in Chapter 3, there is a big difference between approaching 100 prospects and losing none, and approaching 500 and losing 400!

## CUSTOMER SEGMENTS

It is often valuable to replicate the choice pipeline to capture the contrasting dynamics of distinct customer segments. For Coca-Cola for example, there are considerable differences between how teenagers are distributed along the pipeline's stages and how parents of young children are distributed. There are also big differences between males and females within each of these segments. The dynamics of these segments also differ considerably between the sub-brands the company offers, and there are cross-flows of consumers between these brands as well as to/from competing products. This has important implications not only for advertizing and promotion efforts, but also for issues such as product packaging and distribution. The complexity of the multiple dimensions involved in this case is considerable, but the value at stake makes it worthwhile for the company to adopt rigorous pipeline-based analysis and the market research needed to deploy that analysis in planning and implementing its global brand marketing.

A clear demonstration of the value of choice-pipeline analysis for distinct customer segments arose in the case of pregnancy testing products. These are of interest to two distinct groups—couples wanting to have children, and women, often young and single, who do not. The choice pipeline was adapted to capture the distribution of each group of customers separately, resulting in quite different packaging styles for each segment. Retail distribution also differed, with one packaging style featuring in the maternity section of retail stores and the other in the birth-control section.

Another special feature arose in this case. The pipeline often addresses a relatively stable overall population of actual and potential customers—mostly the same people are buying the type of product or service this year as last. In this case, the potential customer-pool is transient, only being potentially interested in the product-type for a short window of time. Similar conditions apply in other cases, such as for providers of wedding products or funeral services. The temporary availability of potential customers in such cases introduces unique challenges in winning awareness and interest quickly before the need is passed.

## EARLY, MIDDLE AND LATE ADOPTERS

A common characteristic on which customers differ is their willingness to adopt new products and services. A few consumers, for example, are always keen to get hold of the latest gizmos, whilst others take them up only once they are convinced the product does something useful for them, and a further group of laggards only buy long after the majority has done so.[15] The same phenomenon arises in certain B2B cases, when some companies are keen to try a new business product or service whilst others prefer to wait, out of caution or concern for cost. Many large organizations, for example, stayed with the Microsoft Windows 2000 operating system for many years after Windows XP became available.

It may be possible to identify clear differences between several groups, each progressively more cautious and therefore slower in its uptake (Figure 6.11). This framework needs to be developed, however, because customers are not as tidy in their behavior as the figure suggests. People who are inclined to be innovators will not necessarily all purchase within the first period. Nor will people inclined to be early adopters all wait until innovators have bought and make their own purchases in the second distinct period.

(Note that the total number of customers in each group is given by the area of each segment: total early majority customers = early majority customers buying per year multiplied by the years over which they buy.)

Companies are sometimes disappointed when the enthusiastic take-up of early adopters fails to be followed by a flood of purchases by the larger majority

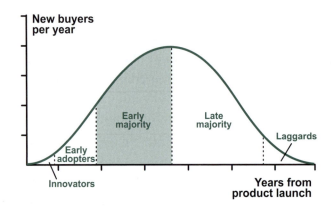

**Figure 6.11:** Adoption rates and timing for different customer groups.

of customers, a challenge known as "crossing the chasm."[16] Chapter 3 already explained how the existence of two customer segments with different growth rates leads to a different rate of total growth than a single segment of the same total size that initially grows at the same average rate. A development of this principle using the choice pipeline shows how the "chasm" between early adoption and widespread uptake might fail to be crossed.

In Figure 6.12, a company is launching a consumer electronic product for which it believes there are one million potential customers. After six months, it has sold some 40 000 units and—given the large potential market—it expects the rate to continue growing strongly. It is also about to reach breakeven, with gross profit on sales nearly covering total marketing costs of $0.9 million per month. Immediately after this point, however, sales growth slows dramatically, and the product struggles to do much more than break even.

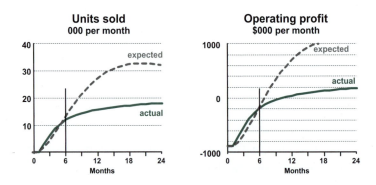

**Figure 6.12:** Disappointing sales and profits following early growth for a consumer electronic product.

The company has been misled by the existence of just two distinct segments—"early adopters" and a "late majority," each of which develops up its own choice pipeline. Being a durable product rather than a consumable (see Chapter 4), the last stock of consumers represents the installed base of product owners, rather than the disloyal/loyal split that applies in the case of consumables. Owners replace or upgrade their product occasionally, and some discard it altogether. The two groups behave very differently, not only in their responsiveness to the marketing they receive, but also in the frequency with which they upgrade the product and the rate at which they discard it. Table 6.3 shows how these two groups differ, and compares them with the characteristics of the uniform market that the company thinks it may be serving—that is, the market that would generate the higher performance outcomes in Figure 6.12.

Figure 6.13 displays the true dynamics of the upper part of the customer chain, splitting out the initial purchasing and ownership of the two groups, the respective replacement rates, total sales and profits. Early adopters arrive quickly at the top of the choice pipeline, contributing strong sales with their initial purchases. They are also quickly used up so this uptake soon drops away. However, they continue to drive significant sales with their frequent replacement purchases.

**TABLE 6.3: CHARACTERISTICS OF A UNIFORM MARKET FOR AN ELECTRONICS PRODUCT VS. A MARKET SPLIT BETWEEN EARLY ADOPTERS AND THE LATE MAJORITY**

|  | Uniform market | | Segmented market | |
|---|---|---|---|---|
|  |  | | Early adopters | The majority |
| Percentage becoming aware per $100000 of mass marketing | 2% | | 5% | 1% |
| Percentage of awares becoming interested per $100000 of values marketing | 5% | | 10% | 2% |
| Percentage of interested people buying per $100000 of promotion spending | 5% | | 20% | 3% |
| Fraction of owners replacing or upgrading each month | 2% | | 10% | 1% |
| Fraction of owners discarding the product completely each month | 2% | | 3% | 1% |

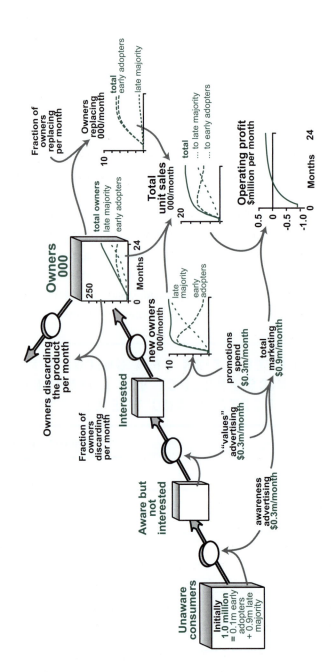

Figure 6.13: Limited take-up of late majority consumers slows growth for a consumer electronic product.

Meanwhile, the late majority is much slower to take-up the product, although they continue to do so at a steadily increasing rate. The total number of late majority owners therefore continues to grow through the end of the period, and their modest repurchase rate also sustains sales. Note that, by month 24, the actual number of early adopters owning the product has started to fall away, as they discard this product and move on to the next hot item.

This stalling of uptake for a new product can be overcome by a powerful mechanism introduced in Chapter 4—word-of-mouth feedback—creating an extension of the Bass diffusion model. There may well be feedback from those early adopters who own the product and those who do not. ("All the cool kids have got an iPod, so I want one too because I am a cool kid.") The chasm-crossing process, however, requires feedback between early adopter owners and late majority people who do not yet own the product. ("All the cool kids own an iPod, and I am into music, so looks like I might find it useful too."). Note that this is not strictly speaking a feedback mechanism, since the user base is not connecting back to its own development rate, but to the development of a separate group.

Figure 6.14 shows the impact on sales and profits if ownership by early adopters is able to double the development rates for the late majority. The actual uplift to those development rates in any month is proportional to the fraction of early adopters who own the product.

(Online learning materials are available to support this example, see p.xxi.)

### The "aging" process

Many of the examples discussed above make an important simplifying assumption—that the overall population of actual and potential customers is stable—but this is often not the case. Customers often "age" at the same time as they move along the choice pipeline. The significance of aging may be relatively minor in cases where products appeal to large numbers of people across many years of their life. But the more transient the need, the more important it becomes to include numerical assessment of aging, both as it brings new potential customers within reach and as it moves them out of reach.

An intriguing example concerns the recent tribulations of Barbie, the fashion doll, who has delighted children for many decades. Although a few adults retain an active affection with Barbie and her friends, most children move

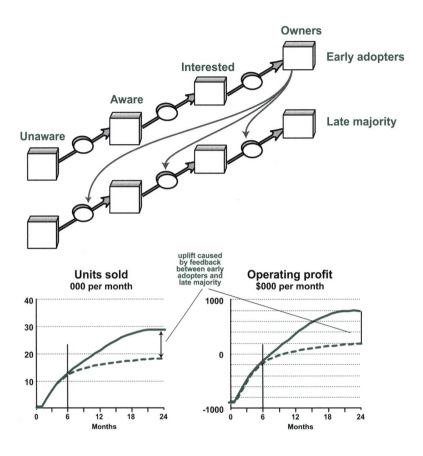

**Figure 6.14: Impact of early adopters raising the development rate for late majority consumers.**

on to other interests at some time during their teenage years. Barbie therefore faces a continuous need to attract awareness, interest and custom from each year's cohort of new children. The Walt Disney Company realized in 2001 that it possessed certain advantages in capturing a large part of the same market. It had a ready-made cast of characters in its "princesses" (Snow-White, Cinderella, etc.). They already had considerable awareness and understanding amongst the potential customers for dolls, and those customers would actually *pay* to be marketed to when they viewed the movies. The princesses had the further advantage of catching children just a few years before they were likely to identify with the more grown-up character, Barbie. By 2006, the princesses were available in over 90 countries and had captured over $3bn in worldwide sales.

## MULTIPLE PIPELINES

In some cases, success in new product launches requires development of more than one class of market resources. The fast-moving consumer brand from Chapter 4, for example, required development of both stores and consumers. The structure in that chapter assumed that both these resources could be simply switched from inactive to active, but the need to take consumers up the choice pipeline creates additional cost and delays. In practice, stores too will need to be developed. Buyers will need to be alerted to the forthcoming arrival of the new brand, and then alerted to its potential contribution to the stores' profits. Once informed in this manner, they may agree to feature the new brand, but not commit to continuing with it until they see evidence that it will be purchased in sufficient volume to fulfill their requirements.

A more complex case introduced in Chapter 1 concerns the launch by Roche of its new blood test meters for diabetics. People who have suffered the complaint for some time may be content with their existing meter, and not be aware of the new models. Since this population can be more difficult and costly to reach with marketing campaigns than larger potential markets, suppliers must rely to some extent on them discovering the new products in drugstores. With users typically replacing meters every 2–3 years, it will take a long time before the new model is widely used. This adoption rate may also be held back by users' contentment with their existing model. Simply withdrawing old products is a risky move, since it may annoy previously satisfied owners and drive them to purchase a competitor's product instead.

There is, though, another powerful constituency whose awareness, understanding and commitment will assist in the product's uptake—healthcare professionals (HCPs). The key group consists of the specialist staff in hospital diabetes units. Often, people only discover they have diabetes after some incident that leads them to be referred to these specialists, so their first exposure to blood meters is when those specialists supply or recommend a particular model. With the prevalence of diabetes rising rapidly in many countries, winning the inflow of first-time meter-users contributes substantially to growth in the installed base. Furthermore, with diabetes being a progressive disease, existing sufferers also need to consult HCPs from time to time, at which point they too become amenable to recommendations for a new model.

Figure 6.15 shows the complex multi-group structure that must be managed to drive the successful launch of a new blood meter model. The supplier has multiple decisions on where to target its marketing and sales efforts; not only which of the

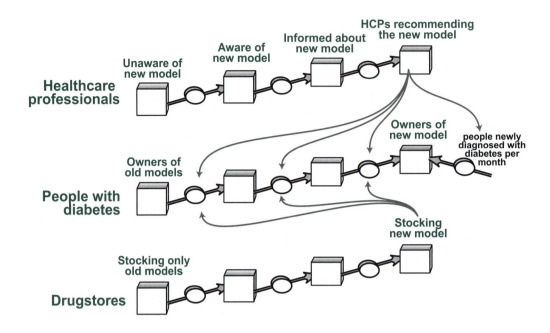

**Figure 6.15: Healthcare professionals and drugstores drive uptake for new blood test meters.**

three resources to develop, but also how to prioritize amongst the changing stages through which each is developing.

## REJECTORS

There is one other state into which customers can flow that is not as helpful as the positive states described thus far. Many situations feature a population of "rejectors," who hold explicitly negative feelings towards a product or service. Rejectors can arrive from multiple directions (Figure 6.16):

1.  "I have tried this product, and it's useless!"—perhaps the most obvious source of people who exhibit an active dislike.
2.  "I understand this product, and just know it's no good."
3.  "I've heard of this product, don't know anything about it, but am sure it can't be any good."

These rejectors are important, because they can significantly reduce the development of others with a positive attitude. If they engage with people who are already aware, their negative views might prevent those people becoming interested. If they engage with people who are interested, they might prevent them trying the

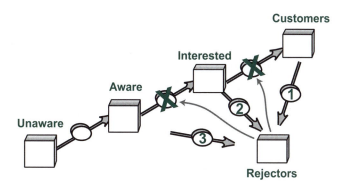

**Figure 6.16: Sources of rejectors for a product or service and the negative impact on customer development.**

product. They might even persuade already active customers of problems they had not considered, and thus encourage them to defect.

This phenomenon can be both detected and managed. One bank discovered that the probability of a customer leaving was strongly related to the number of incidents it termed "miserable moments" experienced in the few months prior to the departure (incorrect transactions, inaccurate charges, correspondence not dealt with, etc.). It put in place a system for highlighting the few such cases that arose and triggering an overcompensating response, such as an unexpected gift. Intriguingly, it then learned that customers who had been through this experience were not only less likely to leave, but actually *more* likely to recommend the bank to friends and family. They did not, so far as I am aware, go further and actually cause customers problems, just so they could overcompensate! This discovery did, however, lead to efforts to create good experiences ("magic moments") as a preventative measure against the risk that individual customers might become annoyed by occasional lapses in service.

## ORGANIZATIONAL CHANGE

An intriguing extension of the customer choice pipeline arises in cases where organizations are attempting to initiate substantial changes amongst their own staff. In essence, they face a problem of internal "marketing." One oil company wished to dismantle a culture of "command and control," in which decisions had to be referred up through several management levels. This culture was increasingly damaging in a competitive environment that required rapid responses. The culture was long-established, having remained essentially unchanged since the company's formation a century before.

The company faced the challenge of

- making management aware of the need for change
- helping them understand the new approach
- trying for themselves what is was like to take their own decisions
- getting them fully committed to the new style of management.

Awareness was raised through established communications channels—internal newsletters, regular department briefing meetings, and so on. Understanding was built through specially arranged discussion groups and workshops. Trial of the new style presented particular difficulties, since middle and junior executives had little confidence in their own ability to take decisions, so training played a key role. They were also reassured that errors would be tolerated, within reason, to reduce individuals' feeling of risk from taking more initiative.

The change program also featured two other mechanisms discussed above in relation to customer acquisition. First, the company identified successful and enthusiastic "early adopters" of the new decision-making freedom and involved them in spreading understanding and trial amongst their peers. Second, the company was alert to the emergence of "rejectors"—people whose feelings towards the change were so negative that they endangered the whole effort. Inevitably, not everyone could be carried through this quite fundamental change to the *modus operandi* of the organization, so rejectors were identified early on and means were found to prevent them undermining the forward progression of the majority.

In this application of the choice pipeline (Figure 6.17), as in others, it is not always essential that data and analysis be carried out—it can be helpful simply to be conscious of the structure, estimate roughly the way it is changing, and assess factors that are helping move the system in the desired direction or obstructing it.

## OTHER RESOURCES DEVELOPING OUTSIDE THE ORGANIZATION'S BOUNDARIES

Customers constitute the most obvious resources whose development may need to be both understood and influenced long before they become a part of the organization's substantive activities, but similar considerations also arise with other classes of resource. The case of Roche's blood meters extends the principle to other demand-side factors (healthcare professionals and drugstores), but development also occurs with supply-side resources.

This chapter started by looking at staff developing between levels of seniority within an organization—a medium-sized law firm. Since earlier chapters emphasized the

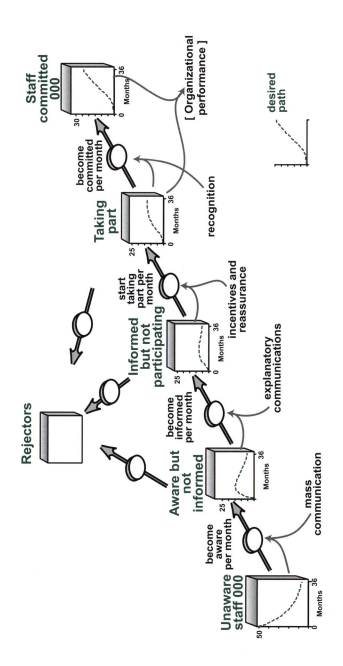

Figure 6.17: The "choice pipeline" in organizational change.

importance of winning resources from the outside world, the question arises as to where those staff came from originally. Like customers, staff do not spontaneously decide to join a particular organization, so this firm's staff were aware some years previously of organizations they might like to join. Furthermore, most had some understanding of those firms—the kind of legal work they do, the clients they serve, the possible career opportunities, and their chances of obtaining a position.

In essence, staff move through stages of awareness and understanding somewhat similar to customers before actually joining their chosen employer. Chapter 3 mentioned the case of one such firm whose annual applications from newly qualified lawyers fell by over 70 % simply because a merger led to a small change in its name. It had carelessly missed the mechanism that brought potential staff into awareness, and needed to work hard over the next two years to rebuild its visibility amongst students in the various institutions from which it hired.

The consequences of policy changes can be still more substantial and have ramifications that roll on for many years. The Shell oil company's 2005 drive to hire 1 000 experienced oil engineers, introduced in Chapter 4, demonstrates the point. Shell was not alone in experiencing this shortfall, as numerous press comments from oil firms and their contractors confirm, so it is instructive to see how this industry-wide situation came about.

Figure 6.18 shows the number of students enrolling and graduating from petroleum engineering degrees in the United States between 1975 and 2006.[17] Note the

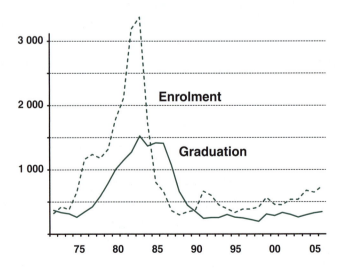

**Figure 6.18: Numbers of people enrolling and graduating in petroleum engineering in the US.**
Source: Reproduced by permission of Mukul M. Sharma.

exceptionally strong graduation rate during the 1980s. Intriguingly, the 1983 peak occurs four years after the second oil crisis of the 1970s triggered an unprecedented jump in world oil prices, and ends a similar number of years after oil prices fell back. Oil firms typically enjoy strong profitability when prices are high and have big incentives to find more oil, so that era also corresponded to high rates of hiring as companies raised their efforts to discover new reserves.

Employment surges of this kind can attract so many keen youngsters that many are unable to find jobs in the industry by the time they receive their degree. Similar experiences befell many Indian IT graduates when the technology boom of the late 1990s came to an end. As it becomes apparent that job prospects are not as strong as expected, many drop out before they would otherwise graduate. This is illustrated in Figure 6.18 by the considerably larger number enrolling in the 1980–1985 period than subsequently graduated. The problem in this case was exacerbated because the flood of graduates in the early 1980s coincided with much reduced hiring as the oil price fell back. The collapse in graduation rates from 1988 to 1991 can thus be traced back to a collapse in hiring between 1985 and 1988.

Why, though, are we concerned in 2006 with what happened in the late 1980s and early 1990s? First, this was not the first time, nor will it be the last, that an industry and those who would join its workforce have grossly misunderstood the big changes in supply and demand of appropriately trained labor over extended periods. Both employers and employees live to regret this misunderstanding after every such episode. It therefore pays to be conscious of how such a situation is developing, whether you are a young professional seeking to join an industry or an employer seeking to hire. A current safe bet for a mixup concerns the alternative energy industries. Many firms are growing and seeking to hire, and many keen young people are looking for jobs in the sector—there is every chance that shortages and surpluses will come and go over the coming years, with important implications for salary levels and job security.

The more direct reason to examine this long-ago episode is that the industry is still living with the consequences. Major oil companies traditionally hired young graduates in order to develop their own engineering talent, a process that takes 10 years or more of professional practice. Any company finding itself short of people in 2005, must have not hired those people during the early 1990s. Bright young school leavers in 1988 considering a career in the oil industry would have seen large numbers of their predecessors unable to get jobs, and looked elsewhere. If undergraduates did not start courses in 1988, they would not have been available to hire in 1991/2. Fortunately, the low oil price meant that companies had less pressure to find new oil, and in any case, they still had plenty of engineering capacity from the

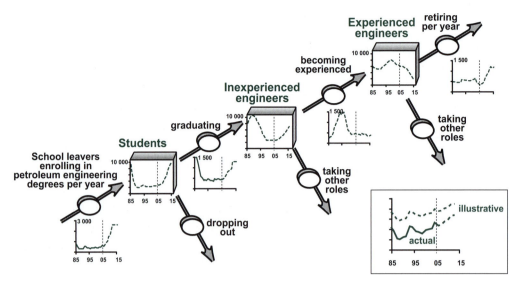

**Figure 6.19: Implications of graduation rates for industry experience in petroleum engineering.**

hiring boom of the mid 1980s. Hiring rates thus stayed low, only picking up again after a nine-year trough. Shell's shortage in 2005 of 1 000 people is thus directly traceable back to slow hiring, not only by Shell itself, but also its peers between 1990 and 1998.

Figure 6.19 illustrates how this particular issue will continue to pose challenges for the oil industry, because the next decade will see the retirement of that 1980s hiring bulge. During the 1970s and 1980s, many thousands of graduates joined the profession. (This total is nowhere near the roughly 15 000 who graduated, however, since most found no jobs in the industry and switched to other careers.) Yet graduation rates since the early 1990s have been just 200–300 per year. Note, incidentally, that Shell's 2005 aim of hiring 1 000 experienced staff corresponds to four years of the *entire* US output of new graduates! As Figure 6.19 shows, even if enrolment escalates immediately, this failure to back-fill the profession over the latest period means that the forthcoming retirement surge will decimate the industry's skills, unless rapid growth occurs in courses in other parts of the world.

Note that this model is only illustrative, since some important factors are unknown, for example rates of staff leaving the industry at each stage of their career.

Several issues complicate this situation.

- Domestic demand for petroleum engineers in the United States has almost certainly declined as reserves on United States' territory have progressively been developed. However, United States' and European oil firms are engaged in worldwide discovery and development, which continues to require these engineering skills.
- The United States is not the only source of suitable graduates, of course, with many hundreds emerging each year in Europe and other regions. But this global industry experienced the same boom and bust in oil prices, profitability and supply–demand as affected the United States, with similar results for graduate employment.
- The problem cannot be laid entirely at the door of oil company hiring policies. Since the early 1990s, there has been huge demand for talent by the IT and communications industries—undoubtedly a major attraction for numerate young school-leavers. However, oil firms' tolerance of such low graduate intake, for so many years has undoubtedly escalated the problem.

This challenge is not unique to the oil industry. One of Europe's largest power generation and distribution companies initiated a review of its physical assets in 2004, triggered by consideration of the model in Figure 6.4. It discovered that its asset maintenance and development strategy was in need of a major boost, and initiated plans to tackle the issue. To its alarm, it then learned that it was badly lacking in the technically skilled staff needed to carry out the program.

### The "bullwhip effect" in resource development

Earlier in this chapter it was noted that management needs to be aware of potentially severe disruptions in the product development process from changes in policy regarding the screening of ideas and products early in the process. As shown in this section, the employment chain can also generate highly disruptive consequences for strategy and performance.

This phenomenon of long-term, large-scale disruption of supply–demand balances along all stages of a supply system or other resource-development chain is known as the "bullwhip effect," from its similarity to the wave-form of a cracked whip. It was first specified in the 1960s when it was noted that small disturbances in final demand for a product had highly disruptive effects on product supply and inventories in the various stages of supply from production through distribution to the final customer.[18] For example, a small increase in final customer demand causes retailers to increase orders on their distributor, not only to meet the new demand rate, but also to cover further anticipated increases. Consequently, the distributor receives a greater increase in orders than actually arose from the end customers. The distributor now places orders on the supplier that are also exaggerated by its anticipation of higher future orders, so the producer has to raise production by a much higher proportion than the original increase in final demand. The anticipatory orders along the chain cause heavy overstocking, and a subsequent collapse in orders, even with no further change in final demand. The supply chain is then sent into repeated cycles of over- and underavailability of product.

Solutions to this problem include the Kanban system, which forces ordering to reflect *only* current demand, rather than uprating orders for anticipated future demand, and information systems that give the entire supply chain visibility of final customer demand.

The parallels with the employment story are clear—a small increase in final demand for petroleum engineers caused a shortage of graduates, so universities expanded capacity and promoted the courses, so potential students (anticipating plenty of jobs and attractive salaries) signed up in much larger numbers than the small increase in actual demand would have justified.

Like many of its peers, this company had responded to the regulatory pressure for low power prices and increased efficiency by limiting its operational costs, including maintenance. To contain its financing costs, it had also tightened its spending on new assets. With less maintenance and capital replacement work, the company did not need so many engineering staff, and was therefore able to reduce its operating costs still further by reducing its headcount. The need for a step-increase in its maintenance and capital replacement program triggered recognition of the staffing crisis. Although it quickly authorized the unavoidable increase in spending, the company then found that it had way too few staff to actually do the work.

Its first response was to try and outsource the solution to the companies that supply the industry's equipment. Although the suppliers were delighted to receive the orders, they too were unable to respond. When the generating and distribution industry had cut back their spending, the suppliers suffered a drop in orders for new equipment and parts, so they had reduced their own capacity and laid off engineering staff. The company in question therefore found that its suppliers were unable to respond when it called for their support. Regulators in the various markets concerned, it seemed, were blissfully unaware of the havoc their enthusiastic price-cutting efforts had caused.

Determined to establish a medium-term solution to this shortage of the essential technical talent it needed, the company approached a number of universities to sponsor a substantial increase in their electrical engineering programs.

## POLITICAL, ECONOMIC, SOCIAL AND TECHNOLOGICAL (PEST) FACTORS

The case of oil industry staffing is just one example of exogenous forces that often have substantial effects on resource development and strategy ("exogenous" meaning external to the situation). Such factors are conventionally divided into four categories—political, economic, social and technological—hence the use of the term PEST analysis to describe the process by which the impact of these items is assessed.[19] Some strategy writers add the influences of environmental and legal issues, extending the method's name to PESTEL analysis.[20] Whilst PEST factors are often considered in general terms by firms in evaluating business opportunities and threats, the framework developed here makes possible a rigorous, fact-based evaluation of the scale and pace at which they may drive change.

---

**Hidden assets?**

Publicly quoted companies in the US, Europe and other jurisdictions are increasingly expected to provide clear information about the true health of their business, so that investors can make well-informed judgments about their likely prospects. An example of the relevant regulations appears in the following extract from the UK government's 2004 draft regulations.[21]

*"An operating and financial review shall be a balanced and comprehensive analysis of –*

- *the development and performance of the business of the company and its subsidiary undertakings during the financial year,*
- *the position of the company ⋯ at the end of the year,*
- *the main trends and factors underlying the development, performance and position of the business ⋯ during the financial year, and*

- *the main trends and factors which are likely to affect their future development, performance and position, prepared so as to enable the members of the company [i.e. investors] to assess the strategies adopted by the company ··· and the potential for those strategies to succeed.*

*"The review shall include –*

- *a statement of the business, objectives and strategies of the company and its subsidiary undertakings;*
- *a description of the resources available to the company ···;*
- *a description of the principal risks and uncertainties facing the company and its subsidiary undertakings; and*
- *a description of the capital structure, treasury policies and objectives and liquidity of the company and its subsidiary undertakings."*

Similar sentiments lie behind the US Security and Exchange Commission's requirement for quoted companies to include "Management's Discussion and Analysis of Financial Condition and Results of Operations (MD&A)" in their statutory submissions.

Such requirements raise an interesting question. No quoted company reports information on the state of its human resources and fixed assets in a form that explains the dynamics illustrated in this chapter, nor are they required by these or other regulations to do so. Given the considerable impact these factors have on future performance, how then are investors to have any sense of such companies' likely future performance?

## POLITICAL FACTORS

These cover any influences that arise from the actions, policies or attitudes of governmental or nongovernmental entities or groups. The influence may be explicit and direct, such as legislation to open up competition in an industry. Today's US airline industry, for example, reflects considerable changes that arose when the administration of President Reagan "deregulated" the industry to make it easier for new airlines to start-up and compete with established carriers. Various markets in China and India have undergone considerable change following relaxation of regulations limiting foreign ownership of firms operating in those countries. The strategy of any nonlocal firm wishing to build a business in China or India clearly must adapt when such regulatory conditions change. A further case concerns the increasing approval of drugs for over-the-counter (OTC) sale, rather than by prescription only, a change that has already altered consumers' perceptions that they can purchase drugs directly rather than visiting their doctor. European markets are somewhat behind the United States in this particular trend, so drugs suppliers need to be alert to any similar changes in that region in case marketing plans need to be revised.

International trade agreements offer many further examples of political factors impacting on firms' strategies and performance. For example, January 2005 saw the ending of a 40-year quota system that protected the United States and European garment industries from cheap overseas producers, mostly Asian. Any company operating in that industry had no choice but to reassess its prospects, and many would have concluded that those prospects were so poor as to threaten their very existence.

Political influences may also be more subtle and indirect in their impact on firms and their strategy. Venezuelan President Hugo Chávez announced in January 2007 that the country's entire energy sector was to be nationalized, though he would permit foreign firms to hold minority stakes in energy deals. This announcement naturally had an immediate and direct effect on the plans of oil companies operating in that country. However, it also altered the mindset of other companies not currently involved in the Venezuelan oil industry. Any who were considering participating would likely reevaluate their plans. The announcement also raised the question as to whether other oil-producing nations might adopt a similarly assertive policy, leading to a still wider revision of strategy amongst independent oil firms. A second example concerns the 2006 entry of Google into the Chinese market. Critics with an interest in human rights and freedom of information felt the company had betrayed its own principles by agreeing to limit the functionality of its service to conform to Chinese government requirements. However, Google took the view that it would do more good than harm by offering its service in China, even with those constraints.

## ECONOMIC CHANGES

These have a variety of effects on business prospects and hence on strategy. Economic growth is generally understood to be helpful through the impact it has on growth of specific markets, enabling companies' sales and profits also to grow. Indeed, companies' strategy documents frequently start from projections of economic conditions and go on to work out likely market growth rates, before estimating increases in market share that the business may be able to capture.

As noted in Chapter 2, it is both possible and valuable to go beyond such simplistic, aggregate projections and assess the potential scale and development rate of specific opportunities. To illustrate how this can be done, the remainder of this section will build on the Bass model of new product diffusion introduced in Chapter 4. In that chapter, the model started with a fixed potential customer base for the product and went on to evaluate the way in which advertizing and word of mouth amongst actual and potential customers might drive sales over time. The potential market is rarely fixed, however, and economic changes can have a considerable impact on that potential.

Figure 6.20 introduces a new resource concept—the "ever-likely" market—that is, the population of people or organizations that would ever be likely to buy a product, however attractive its functionality or price. The ever-likely market for a home-improvement product, for example, would include only those people who had a home to improve, and the ever-likely markets for many consumer electronic devices exclude those who are too young to be able to use them, or too technically or culturally un-savvy to see the point of owning them. In Figure 6.20, there is an ever-likely population of 1 million consumers for such a product. It has a fixed price of $234, and is assumed to be adequately functional for most people's needs. The only change taking place is that average discretionary incomes are rising, starting at $400/month and growing at 1% per month (roughly 12.7% p.a.) over five years, or 60 months. This is greater than the growth in earnings, due to the cost of

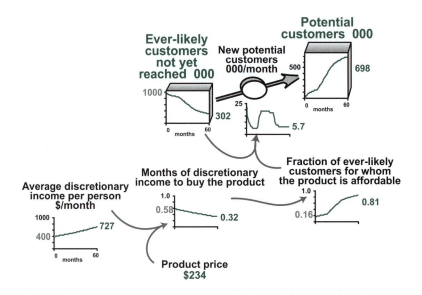

**Figure 6.20: Illustrating the impact of rising discretionary income on emergence of a potential market.**

necessities, like housing and food; for example, if your income is $800, and these items cost you $400, a 1% increase in total income results in a 2% increase in the income "left over" for nonessentials.

The product is initially affordable to a very small fraction of consumers, so there is a brief initial jump in potential customers, which quickly dies out because the product is not affordable to the vast majority. As monthly discretionary income rises, the fraction of the average person's monthly discretionary income required to purchase the product falls steadily. However, there is little change in the slow development rate for the potential market until a threshold is reached—very few people are willing to spend 70% of their monthly discretionary income on the product, but most will spend up to 50% (see notes on how lookup functions work in Chapter 2). When average incomes have grown to the point where most people find the product affordable, the rate at which customers become potentially available rises quickly to around 20000 per month. The rapid development rate continues to month 40, then slows because the easily-won majority have been encouraged into the market and only the lowest income segment remains. Note the highly nonlinear behavior in the customer development rate, in spite of the steady progression of average monthly income—an illustration both of a problematic source of "causal ambiguity" (see Chapter 3) and of a powerful "tipping-point" mechanism (Chapter 4).

## SOCIAL FACTORS

Social factors also drive change in market opportunity. The total ever-likely population may itself change in size due to population growth, age distribution and other demographic effects. Other social mechanisms reflect behavioral factors. This proved to be a problem for the United Kingdom's successful Internet bank, Egg PLC, when it tried to replicate in France the launch of its credit card that had been a great success in its home market. French consumers have a quite different attitude to the use of store cards, credit and debit cards than do the British. Convinced of the power of its business model, the company persisted in its business development efforts long after it was clear that the French ever-likely customer base would take many years to become genuinely reachable customers.

To avoid over-complicating the example, such changes are not included in Figure 6.20. However, the Bass model already includes an important social factor, namely the rate of interaction between potential customers and those who already buy or own the product. The higher is this interaction rate for any given level of price and functionality, the faster the potential market will develop. This mechanism, too, can vary widely between different markets. SMS text-messaging, for example,

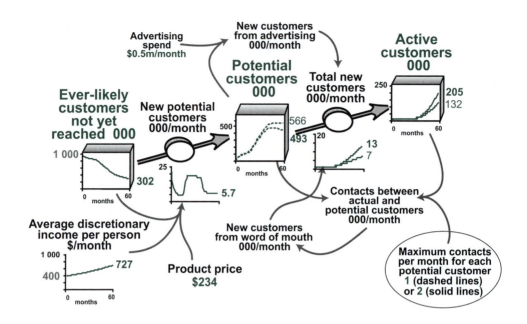

**Figure 6.21: Social contacts accelerate development of potential customers.**

took off particularly fast in Italy in the late 1990s because it matched perfectly with young Italians' needs for organizing their social life. Any young person lacking a cellphone with SMS capability missed out on important gatherings with friends—a powerful motivation driving word of mouth.

Figure 6.20 showed how economic growth alone brings ever-likely customers into the reachable potential population. By the end of the five years, 698 000 of the original 1 million population had become reachable. Figure 6.21 goes on to show how differences in the word-of-mouth social factor alter the development rate for those reachable customers. Given a fixed advertizing spend of $0.5m per month, an adequately functional product, and a fixed price, maximum contact rates for each potential customer with active customers of one occasion per month help the active customer base grow to 132 000 by month 60. A contact rate of two per month raises this total to 205 000. Note that both scenarios feature a long period of almost zero growth, due to the low numbers of consumers for whom the product is initially affordable.

Social factors also affect the development rate of potential and actual staff. Rising education standards create an increasing pool of potential trainees for many new industries. A notable case of political and social factors together stimulating an ever-likely pool of potential employees concerns the Chinese government's decision in 2003 to ensure that every school-leaver would be fluent in English. This is expected to result in the number of English-speaking Chinese exceeding the number of native English speakers in the rest of the world by 2025. Combined with widespread social enthusiasm for learning and personal advancement, this development has already initiated a rapid emergence of young professional Chinese capable of operating in international companies.

## TECHNOLOGICAL PROGRESS

This is largely manifest in two dynamics—the improving functionality of products and services that suppliers can offer, and the reducing unit cost of supplying them. Continuing the example of a consumer electronic product, industry-wide progress clearly gives rise to products that would not have been possible just a few years earlier, and at increasingly affordable prices. Technological progress is not always an exogenous factor. For manufacturers, much progress in both functionality and cost reduction is in their own hands, although it may well rely on similar improvements by suppliers of its components and raw materials. The retailer makes no significant contribution to these technologically driven improvements, other than to pressure manufacturers to pursue them.

Chapter 5 already introduced a framework for assessing how the functionality of a product improves as work is done to develop its performance. For this example, we will simply assume that the product starts at a low level of functionality, where it is acceptable only to a small fraction of consumers, and is progressively improved over the five years.

Changes in the product's cost are somewhat more complex. Unit costs reduce as cumulative output rises, following a mechanism known as the "experience curve" (see box below). The strategy dynamics approach allows this phenomenon to be captured explicitly. In Figure 6.22, unit costs start at $180 and reduce as sales start to occur. The producer sells the product directly to consumers, at a price that represents a mark-up of 30% over its production costs—initially $54, hence the starting price $234. As unit cost is driven down, competitive pressure continues to limit the mark-up achievable to 30%, so the product's price falls in parallel with reductions in unit cost. For simplicity, two issues are ignored:

1. There would in practice be substantial reductions in unit cost prior to the first sales, but we are assuming these merely bring the initial cost down to the launch cost of $180.

2. In practice, retailers would commonly sit between the producer and consumers of such products, taking their own profit margin out of the final price (see Chapter 2).

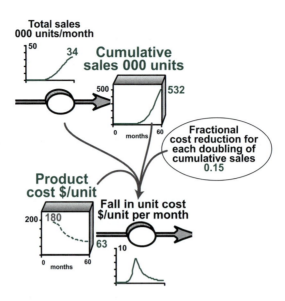

**Figure 6.22:** Cumulative sales reduce unit costs, due to experience curve effects.

### The experience curve

Building on the observation that a process takes less time to perform, the more it has been repeated (the "learning curve"), the experience curve is one of the few truly dynamic frameworks in the strategy field. Though widely acknowledged by management in qualitative terms—*"If we cut price and build sales, we can drive down the learning curve"* —the experience curve in its true form is a quantitative tool. It arose from observations by the Boston Consulting Group that the unit costs of production for many manufactured products fell by characteristic amounts as *cumulative* output (i.e. "experience") increased. Specifically, each time cumulative output doubles, unit costs fall by 10–20%, this percentage being lower in the early phase of prototype development, higher as mass production becomes established, then lower once more when the market matures and sales growth slows.[22]

The experience curve has arguably become so axiomatic for manufacturing firms in rapidly developing technology industries, and the dynamics of cost reduction so extensively exploited that it warrants little discussion.

However, its insights remain valid and significant, and must be taken into account when assessing how to develop strategic opportunities and to maximize value from doing so. Furthermore, not all firms that could benefit from understanding and exploiting the experience curve are aware of it or exploit it. It is especially important to note that the cost reductions from experience *must be worked at* to be achieved—they do not arise automatically.

Note that the arithmetic relationships in Figure 6.21 conform precisely to the rules of the strategy dynamics method, whilst also capturing the math of the experience curve. In any month, the reduction in unit cost can be calculated from the current unit cost, the proportion by which the current month's sales increase cumulative sales to date, and the fractional cost reduction that occurs with each doubling of cumulative sales. The framework does, however, simplify its treatment of unit cost. As noted in Chapter 2, sales and costs are not strictly resources, but are values that reflect the quantities of the true resources involved—in this case the production equipment and staff required to make the product. Figure 6.22 is implicitly encapsulating these resources in "unit cost." Any fall in unit cost is represented by an outflow from the unit cost resource. This is a simplified approach to reflecting the reality that total capacity and staffing costs would *increase* as production output rises, but at a slower rate, so that cost per unit reduces.

This reduction in unit cost as sales rise has a profound impact on the progress of this business, including mechanisms that reach right back to the development of ever-likely customers. These connections can be traced round the structure shown in Figure 6.23.

- Initially high unit costs (lower right) result in a price that is affordable only to a very small proportion of the population (lower middle).
- As incomes rise, the number of potentially reachable consumers rises (left), and advertizing starts to stimulate sales, albeit at a very slow rate (upper left and top).
- Even this slow sales rate, however, represents a substantial growth in cumulative production output (middle right). New sales of just 5000 units, for example, allow unit costs to fall by 15 % if cumulative sales to date have been only 5000 units.
- Consequently, unit cost and price fall significantly (lower right again), accelerating the rate at which ever-likely consumers find the product to be affordable.

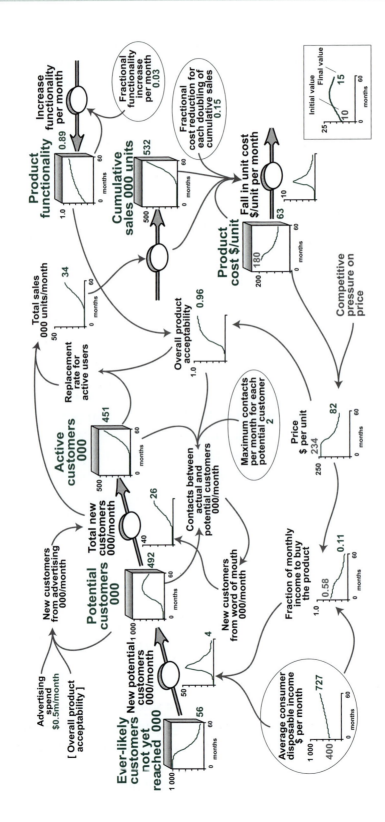

Figure 6.23: Combined impact of economic, social and technological factors on launch of a consumer electronic product.

The total number of potential customers then escalates more quickly than it did when price was fixed at $234.

- Escalating numbers of potential customers interact with the small number of already active customers (center), driving rapid increases in sales, and hence further falls in unit cost.

Note that the market's take-off is also held back by the product's functionality (top right), which only reaches acceptable levels during the middle of the five-year period.

This process continues until limited by four distinct mechanisms:

1. Progress on improved functionality slows down, as most of the possible improvements are identified and implemented.
2. Growth in active customer numbers slows, as the ever-likely population becomes reachable and the resulting potential customers are won to the product.
3. The scope for reduction in unit costs runs out as actual costs fall—15% saving on the year-five cost of $63 is less than it was on the original cost of $180.
4. It takes progressively longer for each doubling of cumulative output to occur—cumulative sales doubled from 5000 to 10000 in less than two months, but doubling from 250000 to 500000 takes nine months.

(Online learning materials are available to support this example, see p.xxi.)

### Lessons from the dot-com bust

In today's fast-moving economies, it is easy for important lessons to be lost, and few more important lessons are available than arose from the spectacular collapse of the dot-com boom in 2001. This did great damage not only to the multitudinous e-businesses themselves, but also to the vast number of enterprises supplying technology and services to the sector. Estimates put the financial cost of the downturn at over $2 trillion.

If there is a single phenomenon that encapsulates the central failure of strategy amongst corporations involved in this debacle it can be seen in the chart of 'New potential customers' in Figure 6.23. Note that this rate exhibits a sharp reversal a *very* long time before there is any sign of a slow-down in sales growth, let alone any decline in sales.

Strong growth in demand during the late 1990s led many kinds of organization to anticipate huge—and quite implausible—continued growth into the future. Following the same principles as the "bullwhip effect" described in an earlier box, they "placed demand" not only for equipment and services but also for people on a scale vastly in excess of their current needs (as briefly noted in Chapter 1 for the now extinct web site hosting firm Exodus Inc.). When final demand failed to grow as anticipated, this overhang of unnecessary physical and human capacity had to unwind, with downsizing of supply capacity and people, and the bankruptcy of many otherwise perfectly sound businesses.

This was not misfortune, nor the result of market conditions turned suddenly hostile. It was a gross failure of strategic management amongst many of the largest and most professional organizations around. It even afflicted some of the most expert of organizations, the strategy consultants, who overhired only to have to withdraw job offers when the inevitable collapse occurred. This is precisely the kind of situation where the strategic capability to "look over the hill" and see the future coming towards us is most critical. Such situations *will* arise again in future, even if not on the scale of the dot-com collapse.

It remains to be seen whether management and investors understood and learned the mechanisms that brought those troubles about. If an organization at the time had put Figure 6.23 on the wall of its executive suite, complete with the information relating to their specific case, it would likely have anticipated well ahead of time when demand growth would slow, then reverse, and planned its own expansion more cautiously.

Management of firms in industries that exhibit experience curve effects need to recognize the issue of market stimulation and development rates on their pricing and marketing strategies. It is especially tempting in the early phase of the strategy to limit the price, even to below current cost, in order to stimulate demand and hope that later reductions in unit cost will reestablish positive profit margins. Figure 6.24 compares the base case outcome from Figure 6.23, when price is always a 30 % mark-up over product cost with a simple policy of limiting the launch price to $150 or $100 respectively, regardless of the product's cost.

Limiting the launch price to $150 (solid green line) brings forward sales by some three months, compared with the base case of a constant price mark-up (gray line), because the price is accessible by the ever-likely population rather sooner. Note that

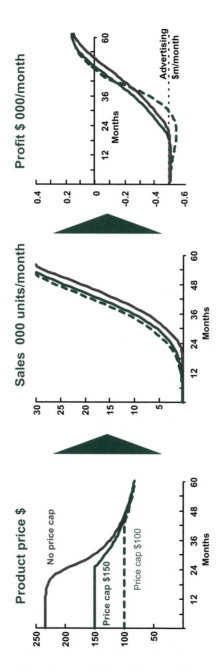

**Figure 6.24: Impact of low-price launch on product sales and monthly profit for the consumer electronic product.**

the price also starts falling below $150 earlier than in the base case, due to the following sequence of events:

- the lower launch price brings customers into the market sooner
- which initiates significant sales growth earlier
- which allows the experience-curve effect to reduce unit costs more quickly
- which allows the product cost to hit $115 (corresponding to a price of $150 after the 30% mark-up)
- after which the price continues to fall, as it tracks the continuing reductions in cost.

With the price capped at $150, the product spends very little time being sold below cost, so in spite of the price cap, losses are not significantly worse than in the base case.

### Product/service innovation, strategic innovation and transformation

The illustration developed in Figures 6.20–6.24 gives a general high-level approach to understanding and managing, quantitatively, the dynamics of product or service innovation. The principles thus offer a means of implementing the concepts discussed in Chapter 5 regarding disruptive technologies. To be mature, a technology must find itself towards or beyond the right-hand end of all the charts in Figure 6.23. If, at the same time, a disruptive technology emerges that finds itself at the early point on those same curves, then it will face plenty of opportunity to progress whilst the mature technology is stalled. The old technology's potential and active customer population therefore constitutes the minimum "ever-likely customers" for the new technology. If the new technology is sufficiently superior to the old, it may add still more people to that ever-likely population, e.g. more people are "ever-likely" to find the iPod appealing than were ever captured by portable CD players.

Combining the market emergence model for the new technology with that for the old is complex, but feasible, and the potential value it offers in terms of enabling successful diffusion of innovation may often justify the full analysis and simulation effort required.

This process should not be confused with "strategic innovation," which refers to fundamental changes in the products or services offered, the customer groups served, or how the business goes about getting its products or services to its chosen customers. Historically, innovation largely focused on the first two of these issues, urging firms whose growth was stalling to seek either new customers for existing products or new products that could be offered to existing customers (Figure 6.25). It is generally reckoned to be inadvisable to attempt to develop both new products and new customers at the same time, due to a probable lack of sufficient capabilities to accomplish both tasks.

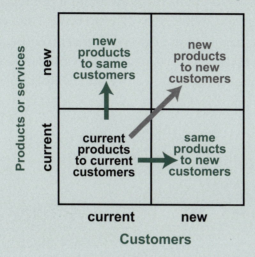

**Figure 6.25:** Strategic innovation—new customers or new products.

There is an important linkage between this question of new products or services versus new customers to the issue of "substitutes" that can threaten the profitability of existing industries (see discussion of competitive forces in Chapter 2). A substitute is a product or service that provides the same benefits to customers as existing offerings, whilst being fundamentally different in nature, e.g. videoconferencing as a substitute for business air travel. From the point of view of the established provider (the airline), the substitute is a new product offered to existing customers that they have no capability to provide, whilst from the point of view of the innovator (the telecoms and equipment suppliers) the substitute is a new product offered to existing customers that is easily within their capability.

Figure 6.25, however, misses the third innovation option, of changing *how* products or services are brought to customers.[23] Simple examples include Dell's innovation of selling the same products as its competitors (PCs) to the same end customers (consumers and businesses), but by using direct sales channels rather than retailers and resellers, or Netflix's supply of the same service (DVD rental) to the same customers (consumers), but via postal delivery rather than retail rental stores.

Whichever of these three dimensions are pursued, strategic innovation by an established company represents the addition of a fundamentally new class of resource to the strategic architecture (Figure 6.26). For a new entrant such as Amazon or Netflix, it may involve the creation of an entire architecture, which includes one or more classes of resource that are fundamentally different from those already involved in the architecture of incumbent firms.

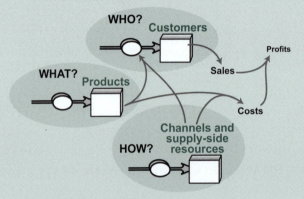

**Figure 6.26:** **Strategic innovation as the creation of a new strategic architecture.**

Whilst the new product/new customer/new approach framework is a neat simplification of the major choice dimensions available to a would-be innovator, it is important not to trivialize the challenge. It may be easy enough for a team to have a day's workshop to debate its options and agree on a desired direction for its innovation efforts—it is quite another challenge to quantify the scale of the opportunity and the resources that must be developed if it is to be taken, and confirm the feasibility of that initiative. Then the strategy actually has to be implemented. Products have to be taken through the development process of Figure 6.3; customers have to be taken up the pipeline of Figure 6.7, and the necessary supply-side resources and processes put in place.

The ultimate level to which strategic change can in principle be taken is known as "strategic transformation." Given the exciting title of this concept, it is no surprise that numerous books and articles have been published on the topic. It should be treated with extreme caution. Most of the cases cited concern major changes in organizational culture, processes and structure. They may also involve discontinuing certain business activities and increasing efforts on others. However, "transformation" implies a total change in most of the dimensions above—who to serve, with what, and how. There are few examples of such transformation attempts, and virtually no successful ones.

The company could consider driving sales forward still faster with the $100 launch price (dashed green line in Figure 6.24). This pulls customers into the market about one month earlier than the $150 launch price. However, this results in significant sales taking place during a period when the price is still well below cost, so losses are significantly greater than with the $150 launch-price case. These losses on each unit sold continue well into the period when substantial sales occur, to about month 30. Even from month 30 to 48 the margin made on each unit, multiplied by the number of units sold, is not sufficient to cover the continuing costs of advertising. Consequently, the product becomes profitable at about the same time as when it was launched with a $150 minimum price—the difference being that it has lost much more money in the earlier months.

The principle demonstrated here is that:

> **Launching products at prices below cost can bring forward sales,**
> **but if low prices give away too much value during the product's**
> **sales growth, total profits can be damaged for no purpose.**

Note that the constant advertising spend rate in all three cases of Figure 6.24 is far from optimal. As in the basic Bass model described in Chapter 4, it is preferable to spend more in the early period when the product has become affordable to consumers, and spend less later on. However, this should not be taken as a general rule—optimal advertising phasing will depend on factors not included in this model, such as:

- additional customer development stages, as explained with the choice pipeline earlier in this chapter
- the arrival of new potential customers, due to demographic effects
- the loss of customers from all stages of the chain
- the sequential release of improved versions of the product, each with higher functionality and launched at a new price.

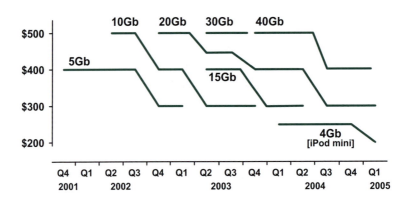

**Figure 6.27:** Early progress in capacity and pricing of iPod.

In addition, competitors have powerful impacts on both sales and profits. Figure 6.23 effectively portrays market development for a company with a unique product, such as the early period of the iPod's launch (see Figure 6.27). When multiple competitors are involved, their combined efforts can accelerate the emergence of the potential market, but they can also increase the pressure to improve functionality and to reduce cost and price. The history of USB memory sticks offers an example of intense pressure driving up functionality and driving down price amongst a number of competing suppliers.

Use of SMS text-messaging, mentioned above as one example of how social factors operate, also demonstrates interactions between technologically driven differences in the dynamics of price and functionality. Americans share with the French a relative lack of enthusiasm for the service. Incompatible wireless technologies in the United States held back the usefulness of the service for some time, and lower voice-call prices offered little incentive for subscribers to make use of the text-based alternative. Texting in the United States was also often an add-on service that had to be enabled, at a price, rather than being a built-in facility as in Europe. This badly undermined the social mechanism that drove rapid growth mentioned above in the Italian market, since an American text user could not be sure that the desired recipient had enabled the service unless explicitly informed of the fact.

## ENVIRONMENTAL AND LEGAL ISSUES

These are sometimes considered under the broader heading of political factors, but it is often useful to break them out for separate consideration. Generally, the impact of many political, regulatory, legal and environmental issues on strategy development is captured by the way in which they either enable or constrain the acquisition and retention of tangible resources—firms' freedom to hire and fire staff, to hold on to customers who would otherwise prefer to switch to competitors and so on. Depending on the nature of the issue and the activity and status of the business, the change may be beneficial or negative. Legislative changes that regulate industry practice in order to make it easier for new competitors to enter the market are a problem for established companies, but an opportunity for those who wish to start a new enterprise. Environmental concerns that impose limits on waste are a problem for the more wasteful companies, but an opportunity for the most efficient, as well as for suppliers of equipment that helps reduce waste.

Firms in many sectors are currently struggling to come to terms with societal concern regarding carbon emissions and global warming. This is arguably a mix of political, social and legal factors—public concern may put pressure directly on companies, but also leads to political pressure on firms to change policy and to legal regulations on their behavior. Oil companies face a particularly severe challenge, since they effectively make their living out of selling carbon for consumers, businesses and public organizations to burn. They have a range of options. Exxon, for example, devoted its efforts for many years to refuting the claim that carbon emissions were driving global warming, presumably in the hope of both winning the loyalty of consumers who shared their skepticism, and stalling the advent of political and legal pressure. (This example demonstrates that, just because influences are "external" this does not mean that they cannot themselves be influenced.) Meanwhile, BP adopted the motto "Beyond Petroleum," perhaps in the hope of winning customers who felt some concern about carbon emissions, but again seeking to defer political and regulatory pressure.

Aside from working on these pressures from external stakeholders, there are technological steps such companies can pursue to sustain their business whilst limiting somewhat the carbon emissions that so threaten their business. They have long invested in alternative energy sources, for example, although it is not clear that they would likely enjoy significant future cash flows, even if such investments were successful. Other types of business are better placed to benefit from success with these alternatives, because they already possess relevant resources, such as firms from the power generation and micro-electronics industries. Within their own field of expertise, oil firms have limited options, though efforts to develop liquefied petroleum gas (LPG) supplies, for example, could help somewhat, since LPG offers a lower carbon-to-hydrogen ratio than other hydrocarbons for a given energy output. Arguably, the rapid development of natural gas resources since the 1970s has for the same reason already contributed to slowing the growth in carbon emissions, compared with what would have happened had the same energy consumption been supplied solely with coal or petroleum.

Many other kinds of environmental pressure affect firms and have to be taken into account when assessing future prospects. Use of timber for construction, furniture, paper production, and so on, attracts the concern of environmentalists, and like carbon emissions can lead to regulatory changes. Many kinds of product result in considerable quantities of waste, either as a byproduct of their production, in their packaging, or in their own ultimate demise when they are no longer fit for purpose. European directives, for example, require car manufacturers to recycle vehicles at the end of their lives, and similar obligations relate to waste electrical and electronic products (affectionately referred to as "WEE"). In most cases, such factors impact on companies' costs, though it is sometimes possible to leverage them to build resource-based advantages. A company that can credibly claim reduced environmental harm compared with competitors can attract more customers, which may explain the current rush of companies keen to prove that their operations are "carbon neutral"; that is, not emitting more carbon than they absorb.

Legal pressures come in many forms. First, there are the simple obligations to comply with general regulatory rules on a wide range of issues, from the health and safety of employees, the avoidance of harm to customers, employment conditions for staff, and so on. Then there are specific regulations defining the conduct of certain kinds of business, such as the sale of financial products to consumers. A particularly important form of legislative influence concerns competition policy—the rules and regulations that constrain how companies can behave when competing with each other, and dealing with customers, suppliers and intermediaries (see Chapter 5).

Regulations may have a more substantial impact than simply imposing requirements on firms—they may fundamentally distort competitive conditions. Many European Union countries, for example, feature heavy taxation on employers to fund social costs, and also impose tough regulations on employment conditions such as working hours, holidays, redundancy and retirement. Whilst substantial companies cannot avoid these costly requirements, many small family businesses simply ignore them. As a result, markets such as hotels and catering feature a much larger fraction of independent operations than is common in the United States or United Kingdom. It is even likely that the high cost and risk of employing staff is responsible for long-term high rates of unemployment in some countries.

## NEGATIVE IMPACTS OF PEST FACTORS

These legal and environmental pressures are not the only exogenous factors that can undermine a business resource system. It has already been noted that demographic factors may slow the arrival of potential customers or staff. However, they can also accelerate the loss of already developed resources. A decline in the birth rate in a given year may lead to the loss of customers for children's products in later years, and then for a series of different categories of products and services as the reduced age-cohort becomes ever older.

Negative PEST factors can also give rise to unhelpful thresholds and tipping points. A dramatic example concerned the markets for new motor vehicles in Asian "tiger" nations in the late 1990s when those economies suffered a reversal in what had previously appeared to be inexorable growth. In the case of Indonesia, the economy shrank by 13% in 1998, but monthly new car sales fell by over 90% as the collapse in disposable income dropped a disproportionate number of people below the affordability threshold and destroyed confidence, even amongst those to whom a new car was still affordable.

Certain industries are subject to a different kind of unhelpful external influence—cyclicality. The sectors concerned include shipping, petrochemicals, construction and computer memory chips. What they have in common is that capacity comes in large lumps—a new plant or ship, for example. For a certain level of capacity, increasing demand leads to rising profitability, which causes many firms to believe that new capacity will be a profitable investment. Unfortunately, many firms take the same view at the same time, so large amounts of new capacity are initiated. There is a delay until this new capacity comes on-stream, at which point excess capacity leads to over-supply and collapsing prices and profits. Although not strictly an external force as far as the industry as a whole is concerned—the cyclicality is largely caused by the collective behavior of the firms themselves—it is certainly an external factor for any individual firm to deal with.

## RESOURCES REMAINING VALUABLE AFTER THEY LEAVE THE ORGANIZATION

Resources often continue to be significant to organizations' performance even after they have ceased to be directly involved. Former customers may recommend a company's products or services to new potential customers—or may, if dissatisfied, warn those prospects off. Former staff may recommend an employer, or again advise friends or relations to steer clear if their own work experience was unsatisfactory.

One of the clearest cases concerns university alumni. Most universities now have substantial programs in place to keep in touch with former students, predominantly with the aim of raising money from them, but also to attract future students and commercial partners. Figure 6.28 shows the mechanism by which future students may be made aware, informed and enrolled by the influence of alumni (for

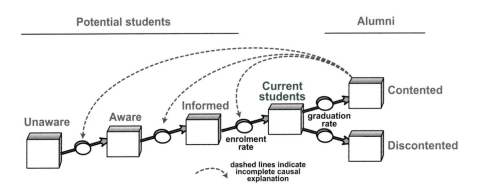

**Figure 6.28: The mechanisms by which university alumni contribute to future student enrolment.**

simplicity, excluding other linkages needed to estimate actual rates for these flows). In extreme cases, those future students may even be the daughters or sons, even granddaughters and grandsons, of alumni. Whilst this alumni-recommendation process is widely understood in qualitative terms, few institutions go to the trouble of tracking quantitatively the significance of its contribution to enrolment. Nor is the cost–benefit balance of these programs generally evaluated in comparison with other student acquisition strategies.

A derivation of this mechanism is used to great effect by many professional firms, especially the major management consultancies such as McKinsey and Bain & Co. For these firms, "alumni" are former consultants and partners of the firm who, for various reasons, have departed. Rather than lose this valuable resource, these companies take the opportunity to continue making use of them, and go to substantial efforts to place them in client organizations. From these positions, the consultant-alumni are ideally placed to engage their alma mater if ever they find themselves in need of consulting services—occasions that are sometimes surprisingly frequent. (See Figure 6.29.)

The principle of good strategy practice that this widespread policy illustrates is the value of staying in touch with former employees—a principle that can even extend to staff who switch to competitors. Often, organizations reassure themselves that departing staff were not actually all that good, and that they are certainly not welcome back if they joined a rival. But in an era where talent of all levels is scarce, this view can be badly misguided. One public relations agency adopted two policies that are quite contrary to this philosophy. First, when any staff member resigned they were told "*Sorry you have decided to leave us, but we wish you well in your new situation. If it doesn't work out, please do get in touch and we would be delighted to have you back.*"

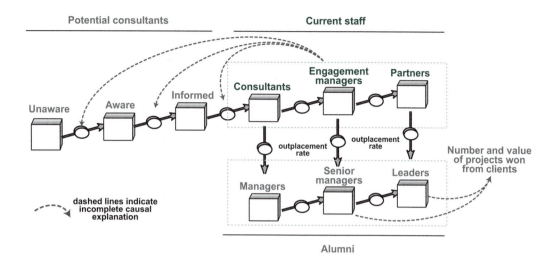

**Figure 6.29:** The contribution of consulting firm alumni in client-firms to future project work.

(They could say this to every departing employee because, by definition, if they had not wanted rid of them in the first place, they must have been valued.) Second, they organized half-yearly reunions with former employees, at which they discussed the exciting developments in their own firm, and asked how their erstwhile colleagues were getting on.

The result was a surprisingly high rate of returning employees. People often leave believing that "the grass is greener" in another organization, only to discover this to be untrue, whereupon they may feel too embarrassed to ask if they can return to their old job. By making departure-and-return a phenomenon to be encouraged and celebrated, this company enjoyed considerable benefits:

- They reduced considerably the rate at which they had to hire and train new staff, only to see that investment wasted.
- The returning staff generally brought back valuable experience—even intimate knowledge about competitors or clients.
- Returning staff were often much more contented and committed to the organization than those who had never left.

Even your lost customers can be valuable. Provided that they were previously satisfied and have left merely because their needs or circumstances have changed, they may still advocate your company's products or services to others. Suppliers of major durable items can benefit particularly from this resource. One supplier of solar-heating systems for domestic hot water—a product purchase that is unlikely to be repeated—leaves every customer with recommendation cards for friends, each worth $50 if it leads to an enquiry and $200 if it leads to a sale. This high value is well justified by profitability of sales that come from this effective word-of-mouth feedback mechanism.

## DORMANT CUSTOMERS

One category of former customers deserves special attention—namely those who may not recently have bought, but who nevertheless remain in touch or are merely known to a business. Banks have many such dormant accounts, held by customers who may have left some cash on deposit but not transacted through the account for many months or years. Many other kinds of business have customers who once bought from them but who have not done so recently, without explicitly saying that they will never do so again.

"Mining" such dormant customers or clients can often be highly profitable. One marketing agency discovered that its client database included large numbers of clients who had not used its services for many quarters or even years. For most of these clients, the firm had not done bad work or otherwise failed—it had simply not been in touch and consequently had fallen from the client's mind. It discovered a rich seam of new work from simply reconnecting with former clients it had ignored. Some clients even expressed surprise that the firm had not been in contact before, given how happy they had been with its work!

Figure 6.30 shows a more challenging example of this phenomenon. The case concerns a specialist investment company that managed high-risk/high-return investment funds for relatively wealthy investors. The company had grown strongly up to early 2004, but since suffered a serious reversal. Its products were sold through brokers, either independent individuals with their own client list or wealth-management advisors in major banks. The firm had a good database of brokers, who it believed numbered about 230. It put its recent loss of success down to general distrust amongst the broker community following a serious performance problem with one of its investment products early in 2004—the fund had lost most of its value, wiping out a great deal of wealth for many investors. The firm's strategy at the time focused on increased selling efforts to new brokers, supported by more attractive commissions to brokers who brought in client-investments.

Whilst its decline did indeed date from the bad performance event, closer examination revealed some misunderstandings and incorrect strategy. Management believed that any increase in investment receipts required winning new brokers.

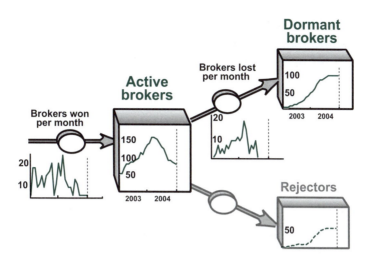

**Figure 6.30**: The potential to recapture dormant clients for an investment company.

However, resource flow analysis proved this interpretation to be flawed. First, they had won few new clients after the performance incident, in spite of their sales efforts and the better commission terms they were offering to brokers. They had previously traded with most of the brokers in their region with appropriate client lists, so the new brokers they approached felt the company's funds to be ill-suited to their clients' needs. Second, they were continuing to receive investment flows from many of their long standing brokers, in spite of the performance issue, which had after all only hit one of the company's funds.

The solution became clear when the broker database was examined more carefully. About half of the brokers brought at least some rate of investment receipts each month, though with occasional gaps. Others had sent their last investment many months ago, and had not been heard from since. A broker who had been out of touch for three months almost never reappeared on the sales list thereafter. Classifying all brokers on the database who had not traded with the firm for three months or more revealed the true picture (Figure 6.30). In reality, the firm had only about 80 active brokers, and the remaining 150 had apparently been lost. The team could see no reason why some two-thirds of this "lost" population would not deal with them again—their client profile was appropriate and they had not suffered especially from the earlier poor performance event. The only reason they could see for this group not dealing with them was that the firm's sales effort had been directed to new brokers instead!

Regrettably, the lapsed brokers did include a substantial number who were known to be actively hostile to the firm and its products, sometimes furiously so. (A few had instructed their reception staff to eject any of the firm's sales people who showed up—a rather dramatic definition of extreme "rejectors.") Nevertheless, a program of sales initiatives directed at the dormant brokers reactivated a large fraction and led to a recovery in sales and profits. Moreover, this did not require either costly marketing activities or higher broker commissions—savings that boosted profits still further.

# RESOURCE DEVELOPMENT IN NONCOMMERCIAL CASES

Resource development arises frequently in public service, voluntary and other noncommercial situations. As for the business cases, much of what is important is going on outside the direct involvement of the organizations involved. Many potential beneficiaries of charitable organizations move through stages of need before coming to their attention. Today's criminals may have moved through increasingly serious levels of antisocial and illegal activity, often at a young age, before becoming known to police. Political parties struggle to move voters through levels of apathy, interest and support, and in between elections the media and political groups alike pore over every detail of voters' awareness and support.

## DIABETES

A case that well illustrates resource development is the increasing prevalence of Type 2 (formerly called "adult-onset") diabetes, introduced in Chapter 1. The disease does not just strike overnight, but arises after individuals have spent some time in a prediabetes state, when blood glucose levels exceed normal but do not climb high enough to warrant a diagnosis of diabetes. Genetic factors play a large role in determining who develops prediabetes, but obesity is also an important risk factor. It is possible with weight loss to recover from prediabetes and move back to a situation where glucose is again in the normal range. Excess weight has also been shown to speed the progression from prediabetes to diabetes.

Diabetes marks the point at which the progression of the disease becomes irreversible, and damage to small blood vessels starts to occur. Nonetheless, diabetes can be effectively managed and controlled with proper medicines and monitoring, and with improved diet and exercise. At some point in this progression it may

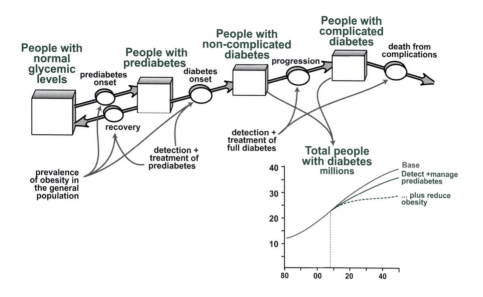

**Figure 6.31: Impacts of (1) prediabetes detection and management and (2) obesity reduction on the number of people with diabetes in the United States.**
Source: Reproduced by permission of Andrew Jones and Jack Homer.

become necessary to visit the doctor more frequently and to inject insulin. Many people with diabetes develop secondary health complications, owing to degradation of important blood vessels in the body, which may ultimately lead to heart disease, kidney failure, blindness or amputation.

Figure 6.31 shows a four-stage chain of this progress, together with historical and projected information for the number of people with diabetes in the United States. The chain is somewhat simplified, for example, by not separating out diabetics who do not yet know of their condition from those who do. The structure also leaves out, for simplicity, population inflows of birth, aging, immigration, and population outflows of emigration and death unrelated to diabetes.

The prevalence of diabetes has grown substantially since 1980. Policy options for responding to this growing health problem include the improved treatment of those with complicated diabetes, who can reap immediate benefits in terms of improved health and productivity, fewer hospitalizations, and a net reduction in costs. Additional options include the following:

● Increased efforts to detect and better manage people with uncomplicated diabetes, many of whom are either unaware of their condition or are not being as intensively managed as they should be. From a budgetary point of view, this may be problematic, since it implies an immediate expenditure but no immediate benefit. The expenditures must therefore be viewed as an investment with their pay-off coming in later years, with reduced disease progression and therefore lower medical and productivity costs.

● Efforts to detect and manage prediabetes, because at this stage simpler and cheaper interventions, with the emphasis on improved diet and exercise, may prevent onset of diabetes and its associated costs. Again, this gives rise to immediate costs that must be traded off against potential later savings.

● Efforts to reduce the general prevalence of obesity in society, and thereby reduce the onset of prediabetes and of diabetes.

Figure 6.31 summarizes the likely outcomes from combining two policy responses—greater detection and management of prediabetes, and reduction in obesity. The upper timeline labeled "Base" shows the expected numbers of people with diabetes if neither of these responses is implemented. The solid green line below it shows the reduction that could be achieved by management of about one-third of pre-diabetes cases, but no reduction in obesity from its assumed current level of 34%. This policy response reduces prevalence of full diabetes only by about 9% by 2050, due to the continued role of obesity driving people into the system. Below the solid green line is a dashed green line, which shows the much greater success that can be achieved when, in addition to prediabetes management, health and social policies manage to reduce population obesity to 25%.[24]

This case is a powerful example of the influence of exogenous factors. First, the total projected number of sufferers is amplified by simple population growth—as the total population grows, a constant prevalence (i.e. the fraction with the disease) would lead to increasing numbers of sufferers, even with no other changes taking place. Increasing life expectancy adds further to the total. Put somewhat starkly, if people do not die from other complaints, they remain available to contract diabetes. Then there are the numerous changes to lifestyle and socioeconomic factors that have taken place, from falling real prices of food to increasingly sedentary lifestyles. Such factors have together created a substantial impact, both on levels of obesity and the prevalence of diabetes, and will continue to do so. However, there are so many mechanisms and their interactions so complex, that unravelling them all remains a major challenge.

This case provides an interesting example of counterintuitive policy implications. Some public health agencies have declared ambitious goals for reducing diabetes prevalence, by an order of 20–40%. About 90% of the money in diabetes currently goes on detection and management of the full disease. Such efforts have brought great success in improving quality of life and reducing costs of complications. Paradoxically, they have also contributed to *increasing* prevalence, by reducing the death rate of people with complicated diabetes—people live longer and so the final group in the chain increases relative to what it would have been otherwise. The better the public health agencies do, the more they miss their goal. This is a common dilemma in public service and voluntary sectors:

**Success in tackling health and social issues can raise, rather than lower, the prevalence of the problem.**

Figure 6.31 suggests strongly that early detection and prevention can substantially reduce the prevalence of this costly chronic disease. However, the incentives and pressures on management can easily give rise to perverse choices. During 1999, four New York hospitals set up centers to help early stage diabetics manage their condition. Seven years later, with nearly double the number of diabetics in the city, the centers were shutting down because they were not making money. Insurers would typically not reimburse the small cost of a patient's visit to a nutritionist, but would happily pay many times the cost for every dialysis treatment—repeatedly over long periods—after the patient's disease had become serious.[25]

Taking a broader view of costs, it is not obvious that prevention is cheaper than treatment overall, even if it is cheaper per program recipient, because the number of potential recipients for prevention is greater than the number for treatment. In the US, the estimated number of people with prediabetes is about 50 million, compared with diabetics of about 20 million, of whom about 15 million are diagnosed. Intensive prediabetes management on all 50 million, at a cost of $1 000 per year, as suggested by the Diabetes Prevention Program (DPP) trial—$700 for a diet-plus-exercise program, plus $300 average additional medication—would cost $50 billion per year. Model simulations suggest it would take many decades before a prediabetes prevention program generated savings, if direct costs alone are considered.[26] The only hope for selling such a program to employers and taxpayers is on the basis of *total* savings, which include the indirect costs of productivity loss for patients and their relatives who stay home as caregivers.

## US WELFARE-TO-WORK

Chapter 3 introduced another noncommercial case with important social consequences—the impact of the 1996 *Personal Responsibility and Work Opportunity Reconciliation Act* (see Figure 3.11) that reformed the US social welfare system

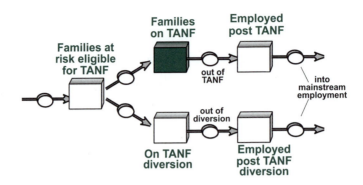

**Figure 6.32:** The principal family situations of concern regarding dependency and welfare.

between 1997 and 2002. Support shifted from a federally funded program of monetary assistance, called Aid to Families with Dependent Children (AFDC) to services designed to promote work and avoid dependency, called Temporary Assistance to Needy Families (TANF). The Act limited benefits to a cumulative five-year period per family—after which the family would lose eligibility to the federally funded program. The changes also moved responsibility for welfare support to state and local governments.

Figure 3.11 showed how changes occurred nationally to the single "resource" of families on welfare. However, behind this aggregate number lies a complex structure of different situations in which families can find themselves. Figure 6.32 shows the principal states involved, developed from a study carried out in New York State.[27] Families join TANF from some state of risk, and leave TANF when they obtain gainful employment. In addition, families can be diverted onto alternative support programs, which is advantageous because time spent in these programs does not use up time from their five years' cumulative entitlement. Although the highlighted upper middle stock—families on TANF— represents the state of principal concern, policy has to take into account the other states in which families may reside before, after and alongside this stock, since a variety of programs exist both to help welfare recipients avoid dependency, and to maintain gainful employment after they received TANF services. Any strategy for alleviating poverty and dependency *must* therefore take those policies into account and thus encompass the other situations in which families find themselves.

Unlike the diabetes case, where people largely flow forwards along the chain towards more serious problems, save for some possible recovery in the early stages, this situation is characterized by a large number of possible flows between different

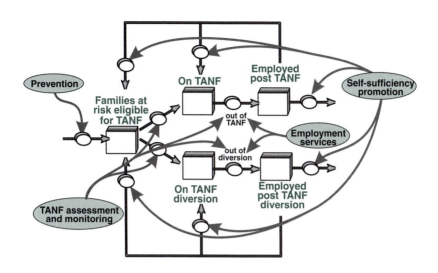

**Figure 6.33:** Some of the flows of families amongst various states of support, and some policies and programs impinging on those flows.
Source: Reproduced by permission of Aldo A. Zagonel-Santos.

states. These multiple flows, and some of the policies and programs that impinge on the situation (Figure 6.33) make its understanding and development of a strategy particularly challenging. Note that some of the policy influences are aimed at *reducing* flows that are problematic, e.g. self-sufficiency promotion slows the flow of employed people back to a state of risk. Additional influences not shown include, for example, child support and drug-dependency programs.

The situation is also extremely rich in the number and variety of aims and objectives—some complementary and others conflicting—that the various stakeholders might pursue:

- objectives relating to the numbers of people in the system, e.g. the number on TANF itself and the total number of families throughout the system
- objectives concerning improved flows of families, e.g. families flowing into employment, or back into risk
- objectives concerning the financing of the system, and who pays for it.

Added to these multiple objectives is the issue of timing, especially whether to spend more in the short term in order both to save costs and to bring other improvements in the longer term.

One important finding of the study was that emphasizing the middle of the system—that is, TANF assessment and monitoring—is best at pumping clients out

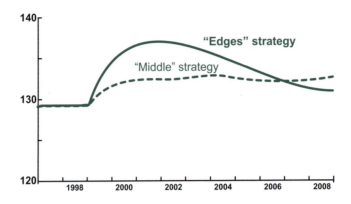

**Figure 6.34:** **Total costs of alternative strategies for managing welfare in one county.**

of the welfare roll and into jobs, and initially best at reducing the size of the TANF caseload, thus minimizing the loss of TANF eligibility for families in the short term. This strategy also results in the lowest share of costs being picked up at the state and local level. However, the community-wide approach that focuses on the "edges" of the system is best at preventing families coming out of the mainstream economy into the welfare system and best at helping families transition back into the main-stream economy. Consequently, this focus results in more families staying out of the system permanently and thus deflates the welfare system and produces the best long-term reduction in the size of the entire sector.

Finally, working at the edges is the better choice in terms of both the long-term reduction of local expenditures and the local share of costs. This "edges" strategy results in the worst performance for job finding, though for a good reason—there are fewer families *needing* jobs. It is also worst for overall total costs in the short term, though note from Figure 6.34 that total costs would still be increasing some seven years later under a strategy that concentrates on managing the heart of the TANF system, rather than seeking to stop families entering the system and keeping them out.

# RESOURCE DEVELOPMENT IN RYANAIR AND OTHER AIRLINES

Chapters 1–5 have built up a strategy dynamics analysis of the low-fare airline Ryanair and shown, for example, how its future business growth will be sensitive to the quality of routes it opens and the frequency of customer journeys.

The airline also features resource development structures. The customer choice pipeline clearly applies—potential customers must be made aware of the airline, understand what it offers, be persuaded to use it, and preferably become loyal repeat customers.

Like other businesses of its type, Ryanair has adopted interesting policies to mark itself out from the crowd of other airlines. Whilst similar firms may emphasize the fun of flying with them, or the special team culture they have, this company employs a relentless focus on being the cheapest possible provider—almost no matter what they have to do to achieve this position. In effect, it promotes price as the single overriding consideration on the value curve (see Chapters 2 and 3). This has the merit of turning customer annoyance against others who stand in the way of this goal, especially politicians and government agencies.

The PEST factors explained earlier in this chapter are of major significance to Ryanair and its industry. For decades now, increasing consumer incomes and social changes have boosted demand for travel. The industry has also benefited from powerful scale and experience effects, giving rise to dynamics analogous to the self-reinforcing growth illustrated in Figure 6.23. Remarkably, all these positive forces have not resulted in a universally profitable industry—rather the reverse, with most firms struggling to achieve profitability in most periods of time. This has in large part been due to the multiplicity of competitors and constant new entry discussed in generic terms towards the end of Chapter 5.

The industry may now be facing an era of new challenges. Whilst it accounts for only a very small fraction of global carbon emissions, these are growing quickly. Furthermore, those emissions occur at high altitudes, where the impact on atmospheric warming is greater. The industry can therefore expect rising public and governmental concern at the contribution it is making to the damage of the world's climate. This threatens substantial changes to various resource development rates in the industry's version of Figure 6.23. Although the factors driving the conversion of "ever-likely" customers into real potential users of airlines will likely continue, regulatory constraints may hold back the industry's ability to turn that potential into active customers. Governments have already started using taxation to slow that growth, and may be expected to do so increasingly in future. On the social front, sheer public concern may reduce consumers' frequency of travel, or even encourage others to leave altogether.

Taken together, these pressures will likely raise further the industry's already considerable efforts to reduce cost and improve technology, so as to reduce the carbon emissions that are giving rise to those pressures and enable it to keep reducing the low prices that encourage travel.

# RELATING RESOURCE DEVELOPMENT TO THE STRATEGIC ARCHITECTURE

## SEPARATE ANALYSIS OF RESOURCE DEVELOPMENT

Chapter 5 ended by showing how analysis of resource attributes can be carried out in isolation and only the summary information from that analysis carried over into the high level strategic architecture for the organization and its performance. The same principle applies to the analysis of resource development. The fast-moving consumer product company in Chapter 4, for example, would need extensive analysis of consumer flows along its choice pipeline, including the detailed examination of consumers in different segments. However, it need only bring the total number of consumers and their purchase rate into the summary architecture of Figures 4.20 and 4.21.

Figure 6.35 shows how this principle applies to a professional firm. The summary architecture from Figure 4.35 simply showed, for example, the total number of professional staff and the capacity of those staff to carry out work from clients. In reality, that capacity reflects the numbers and experience of staff at different levels of experience—partners to oversee the project and manage the client relationship, senior project managers to control the research and analysis, and junior consultants to do that work. The firm could be constrained in its capacity to handle projects if shortages

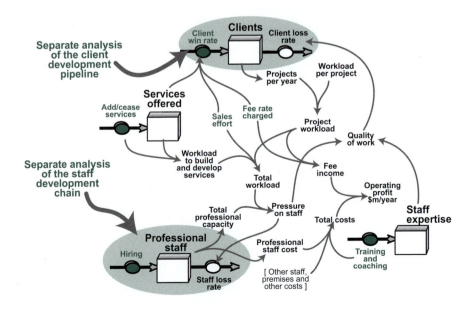

**Figure 6.35:** Bringing summary resource-development data on clients and staff into the professional firm architecture.

were to arise in any of these levels, so would benefit from the combining of historic and forward-looking staff development introduced in Figures 6.1 and 6.5. It would also be valuable to understand and plan its client development using an appropriate choice pipeline, but bring the summary information on client numbers and project rates into the summary architecture. Again, it may be necessary for these resource-development pictures to be replicated for distinct segments of customers or staff.

> ### Exploring the professional services architecture
>
> You can explore some of the challenges that arise from the staff development chain in a consulting-type firm in the Professional Services Microworld, available from www.strategydynamics.com. Decisions on hiring and promotion must be balanced to ensure sufficient staff in different levels of seniority to both win clients and perform well the work those clients bring (see Figure 6.36). Attempts to grow the firm make staff development particularly challenging, and the game also shows how an "up-or-out" policy can work. Along with the simple numbers of staff, experience levels in each grade change as people develop, and clients respond to service quality and reputation by staying with the firm or providing more work. The game also offers a simple balanced scorecard of performance (see Chapter 4). Like the other Microworld learning games mentioned in previous chapters, the Professional Services Microworld offers a number of different management challenges, in which teams can take on a variety of situations.

## BOUNDARIES OF THE FIRM

Figure 6.37 brings together in summary form the key resource-development chains discussed in this Chapter. Three observations stand out:

1. The business or organization is only using the active resources highlighted—products are in development, but not contributing to sales, and capacity is on order, but not providing output for sale.
2. Former customers and staff exist, and may still be known, but are not (generally) contributing to sales (former staff working for customers who bring you business being the exception).
3. The organization has some interest in, and some influence over, potential resources that are in development, but not yet contributing to the business.

This last point creates difficulties in defining where exactly the boundaries of the organization lie. If these are defined in terms of what the firm actually possesses, then

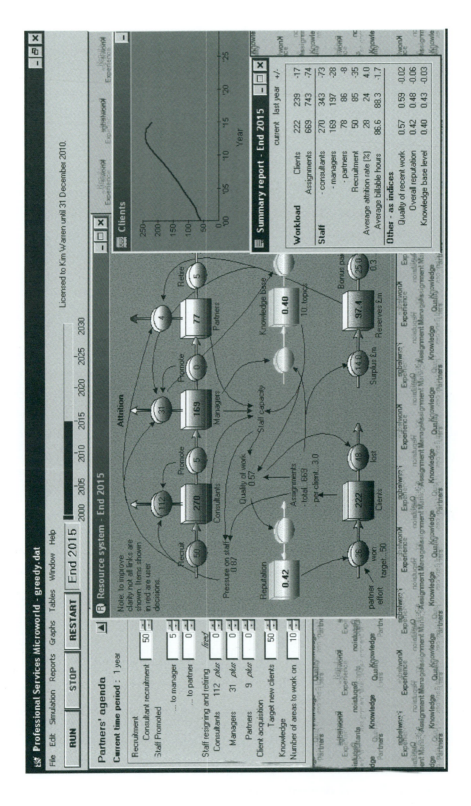

Figure 6.36: Screenshot of the Professional Services Microworld.

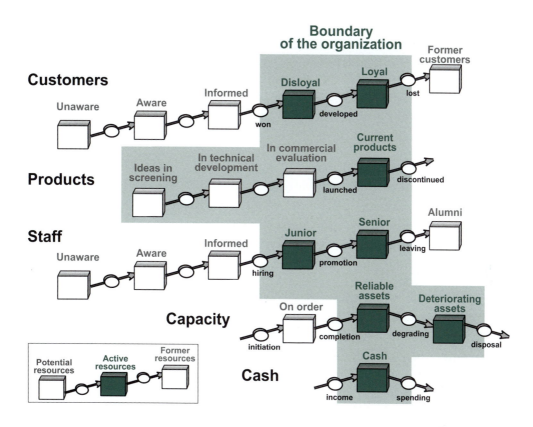

**Figure 6.37:** The multiple resource-development chains that make-up the overall business system.

only current cash and capacity, and the entire product pipeline are included. If it is defined in terms of ownership *and* what contributes to current sales, costs and profits, then active customers and staff must be added. If boundaries encompass all resources that affect current and future performance, then everything in Figure 6.37 is relevant, along with other factors such as intangible items. There is no set of general rules as to what must be treated as being "inside" the organization, and what is outside.

Organizations may also choose to place certain resources outside their own boundaries, buying in their contribution to the business system from outside suppliers. This is very common in the case of outsourced IT systems capacity, distribution capacity and the staff that go with them, for example. Some companies, such as Nike Inc., go further and buy in their product itself from outsourced providers of manufacturing capacity.

As repeatedly shown in this chapter, management frequently can, and must, understand and influence resources that are in development towards being an active part of the business system, or that have left it.

## Summary of Chapter 6

Many resources develop through stages, and their contribution to the organization's performance changes as they move between those stages—customers who were disloyal become loyal, staff move from junior to senior levels, products move through stages of development before being launched, and so on.

The development stages through which many kinds of resource move generally represent an improvement of their contribution to the business, but equipment and other fixed assets deteriorate, often from reliable to unreliable states. Strategy in asset-intensive cases must therefore include a substantial focus on developing sound policies to sustain their performance, balancing this objective against the substantial costs involved.

Customers must be moved through stages of awareness and understanding of a product or service before actively purchasing from a company. Since customers contribute no sales in these early stages, the marketing investment required can result in heavily negative cash flows before any profits are seen.

Potential employees may also need to be made aware and informed about an organization long before they become available to hire, for example during their later years of education. This long lead time, combined with the long periods of staff progression through levels of experience can cause very serious imbalances in staff availability, not only within a single organization but across entire industries.

Political, economic, social and technological influences from outside the organization or its sector can enable or constrain the development and retention of resources. Such changes can give rise to threshold effects where apparently small external changes cause disproportionately large effects on business development.

The impact of these external influences can combine with internal processes of product improvement and cost reduction to radically alter the pace of business development. This complicates decision making about issues such as the level and timing of pricing and marketing when management is trying to capture opportunities quickly, but profitably.

Certain resources can continue to contribute to performance, both positively and negatively, even after they have ceased to be directly involved, e.g. former staff (or alumni) and customers.

The development of resources through sequential stages is also common in many noncommercial situations, and additional complications arise when multiple organizations are involved in different parts of the system.

It is usually advisable to map out the development stages for any resource separately from the other resources involved in the organization's core business architecture, together with the policies and other factors influencing its development. Only the time charts for the key factors from that development picture need then be incorporated back into the core architecture.

## SUGGESTED QUESTIONS AND EXERCISES

Why is it important to identify the stages through which resources flow as they develop [e.g. customers becoming aware, informed, active and loyal; staff moving from junior to senior levels] ?

1. What is the critical rule concerning the relationship between the quantities of a resource in the differing stages along its development?
2. Give an example of a resource that deteriorates, rather than improves, as they move from state to state.
3. Why is it often important to identify certain stages of a resource's development *before* they make an active contribution to the organization?
4. Why can the resource-development process have very long-term implications for organizations' performance?
5. What are the four main categories of factor, aside from the direct actions of businesses and their competitors, which drive the emergence of potential customers and other resources? Give examples of each. Name other external factors sometimes identified separately from these four.
6. Explain how the experience curve reduces the unit cost of manufactured products, and how this works with market development to accelerate the emergence of a market.
7. Give examples of resource development in non-commercial cases.
8. Use one of Worksheets 7a to 7d to lay out the development chain for resources in a case of your choice.
9. Identify any resource-development chains likely to be found in one or more of the four examples introduced in chapter 4, Exercise 10.
   a. a retail chain, such as Starbucks

  b. a company manufacturing and servicing elevators

  c. an on-line dating agency

  d. a voluntary organization providing medical centres in locations that have no alternative provision.

10. Explain the implications of resource-development for how the boundaries of an organization are defined.

# USING WORKSHEETS 7a–7d, 8 AND 9 (NEXT PAGES)

The following pages provide a set of worksheets for:

- mapping out the development of different kinds of resource (7a–7d)
- working out the impact of politicial, economic, social and technological (PEST) factors (8)
- working out the impact of accumulating output on unit costs, the experience curve (9).

These worksheets can be used alone, in order to understand and make decisions about the development of a particular resource. Alternatively, they may be useful for examining in more detail what is happening to particular resources in the core architecture developed in Chapter 4.

These worksheets and their math are most easily handled with the **my**strategy software versions, see p.xxi.

# WORKSHEETS 7a–7d: RESOURCE DEVELOPMENT

These worksheets provide templates for the development of (a) staff, (b) customers (c) products and (d) equipment and other assets. The same principles apply to the use of each:

- specify the timescale and frequency over which the situation is to be examined, e.g. two years back and three years forward in months, and the scale for all variables
- identify and name the key stages through which the resource develops and put these titles on the stocks in the diagrams (see Figures 6.1 to 6.7 for examples)
- add a timescale and value scale to each stock, and insert data or estimates for how those quantities have changed in the past and might change in the future

- name the flows that move the resource from one stage to the next, remembering the rule that these flows must be expressed in terms of "units per period," e.g. customers becoming loyal per month, or staff promoted to top levels per year
- sketch what has happened to each flow rate over time, making sure that the numbers reconcile with the stocks that they are affecting (see Table 6.1)—you should end up with diagrams similar to Figures 6.2 or 6.3
- for the customer pipeline, where individual customers can move both forwards and backwards along the chain, it may be important to identify these two flows separately
- starting with a single resource flow, follow the discipline of working back through the logic of what is causing that flow, e.g. 50 customers move from aware to understanding our product each month because we give two presentations at industry conferences; five people out of 25 leave our senior management each year because that is the fraction who reach retirement age.

Repeat the last stage of this process for each resource flow, remembering to:

- recognize when a resource level can affect its own flow rates (e.g. only informed customers will start to buy from us; the number of middle managers limits the rate at which we can promote people to senior positions)
- identify external influences that are outside management control (e.g. graduation rates of potential employees; competitors' falling prices making customers disloyal)
- identify the factors on which management is able to make decisions that influence the development rates of the resources, either directly (we can promote five people) or indirectly (we can double advertizing in the hope of winning active customers 50% more quickly)—you should end up with diagrams such as Figures 6.4 and 6.7.

Having laid out what is happening to the development of your resource, and the factors driving that development, you can discuss and assess with colleagues the impact of external effects and alternative policies. For example:

a. In staff development, you might work out the consequences of a doubling in the loss rate of middle managers, perhaps due to intense poaching by competitors, and how much hiring and promotion of juniors would be needed to maintain the number of middle managers you need.

b. In customer development, you might evaluate by how much an improved product would slow the loss of active customers, how much new marketing and of what type would double the rate at which customers become informed about the product's improved performance, and by how much a doubling of sales effort could accelerate the winning of new customers. (Note that it may be necessary to examine separately the forward development and backward loss of customers, e.g. new customers interested per month, and customers losing interest per month; see Figure 6.8.)

c. In product development, you could consider whether the product pipeline contains too many potential products for the technical people to develop at an acceptable rate, and the likely impact on the product launch rate from removing a certain fraction from each development stage.

d. If you are looking at maintaining the quality or performance of some equipment or assets, you might identify that the current spending rate and its allocation will lead to inevitable deterioration, and compare the impact of a one-off replacement program with an increase in routine maintenance and repair.

# WORKSHEET 8: IMPACT OF POLITICAL, ECONOMIC, SOCIAL AND TECHNOLOGICAL (PEST) FACTORS

This worksheet provides a template that may be suitable for many situations, both business-to-consumer (B2C) and business-to-business (B2B). However, the considerable variety between business sectors makes it unlikely to suit all cases. If this applies to your case, it will be necessary to develop the architecture from first principles.

This template can also be considered at the "industry" level; that is, capturing the development of all customers across the market (rather than just for a single firm), and the functionality and cost reduction of leading suppliers.

To use this template:

- Specify the timescale and frequency over which the situation is to be examined, e.g. two years back and three years forward in quarters, and the scale for all variables.
- Identify the current "ever-likely" population of customers (this concept applies in many markets, though it may be necessary in some B2B cases to consider

customers on a smaller scale than thousands—in which case simply delete the "000" units on each stock and flow on the worksheet).

- If there are demographic or other factors that will likely bring new ever-likely customers into existence, list these at bottom left, and sketch the flow rate in the chart at far left—sketch what this would do to the total stock of ever-likely customers, assuming none are actually developed into potential or active customers.

- Define the initial functionality, unit cost and unit price of the product or service—for functionality, follow the principles introduced in Chapter 5.

- List the economies of scale, and competitive and technological factors that will improve functionality and reduce unit costs and prices over time, and sketch estimates of how these variables are likely to change in the lower charts.

- Estimate the rate at which improved functionality and lower price would develop potential customers from the ever-likely population by sketching the chart for "new potential customers 000 per ⋯."

- Revise downwards the sketch for "ever-likely customers" to reflect the fact that functionality and price have now moved them into the "potential" stock—sketch a chart for the stock of "potential customers," assuming that none of these become active.

- Estimate the rate at which improved functionality and lower price—plus word-of-mouth effects—would create active customers by sketching the chart for "total new customers 000 per ⋯" (note that word-of-mouth effects can drive B2B markets, as well as consumer sectors—businesses notice what others are doing and copy them if it seems to be useful, a process that B2B suppliers seek to encourage).

- Revise downwards the sketch for "potential customers" to reflect the fact that functionality, price and word of mouth have now moved them into the "active" stock—sketch a chart for the stock of "active customers."

- If relevant, identify PEST factors that may be working to drive customers away, e.g. demographic changes reducing numbers of people in the target age-range, or web-based alternatives taking customers out of the market for a non-web-based service.

Having completed this analysis, examine how it can be exploited or changed by your organization, for example whether pricing lower in early periods could bring forward growth in customers without too great a loss of profits, and result in faster subsequent growth in sales and profits.

# WORKSHEET 9: EXPERIENCE CURVE COST REDUCTION

This template allows analysis of the interaction between growing sales and the cost reduction that can be achieved as those sales grow. Like Worksheet 8, it may be completed from the perspective of an entire market if more than one firm is involved in the product's production and supply. To use the template:

- Specify the timescale and frequency over which the situation is to be examined, e.g. 10 years forward in quarters, and the scale for all variables.
- Estimate the current numbers of ever-likely customers in the left-hand stock, and the history of this quantity if the market is already part-way through its development.
- Enter the current functionality and unit cost of the product and its price in the lower charts, with any history if relevant.
- Estimate the fraction by which unit costs may fall each time cumulative sales double, e.g. if you have sold 10000 units to date and unit costs are $100, what will unit costs be by the time you have sold in total 20000 units?
- Estimate the initial number of potential customers and active customers, with any history.
- Estimate the flow of "new potential customers per ⋯." and the flow of "total new customers per ⋯."
- Enter the current (and historic) rate of sales to first-time and repeat customers in the upper charts, and the resulting "total sales 000 units per ⋯."
- If the product has already been launched and there is some history of cumulative sales, enter this in the stock at far right.

To project forward the likely trajectory of customers, sales, and so on:

- Update the stocks of ever-likely, potential and active customers to the next period, using the current rates at which potential customers are being developed and made active.
- Calculate the new rate of sales to first-time and repeat customers, and the total sales rate next period.
- Calculate the fraction by which these sales add to the cumulative total to date, e.g. if cumulative sales have been 100000 units, and next quarter's sales are likely to be 20000 units, then the fraction by which the cumulative total will increase is 0.2.

- Calculate the fraction by which this will reduce unit costs, e.g. if unit costs are expected to fall by 15 % for each doubling of cumulative sales, then a 0.2 growth in this cumulative total will reduce unit costs by roughly 3 %.
- Estimate the change in unit price, given this fall in unit costs and competitive pressures driving prices downwards, e.g. if there are no competitors, price may remain unchanged, and the cost savings simply taken as extra profit margin, whilst if there are many aggressive competitors, price may fall by more than your business's cost reduction rate.
- Estimate what change this reduction in price will make to the rates of customer development, taking account of likely increases in functionality.

For simplicity, this template assumes a constant fixed number of total ever-likely customers, ignoring the contribution of PEST factors that would change that total. To include these effects, use Worksheet 8 and 9 together by copying the "Active customers" charts from Worksheet 8 into Worksheet 9, and taking the "unit cost" values from Worksheet 9 back to Worksheet 8.

(Online learning materials are available to support this example, see p.xxi.)

# WORKSHEET 7a: STAFF DEVELOPMENT

NOTE: specify the time period for hiring, promotion and leaving rates: per month, quarter or year.

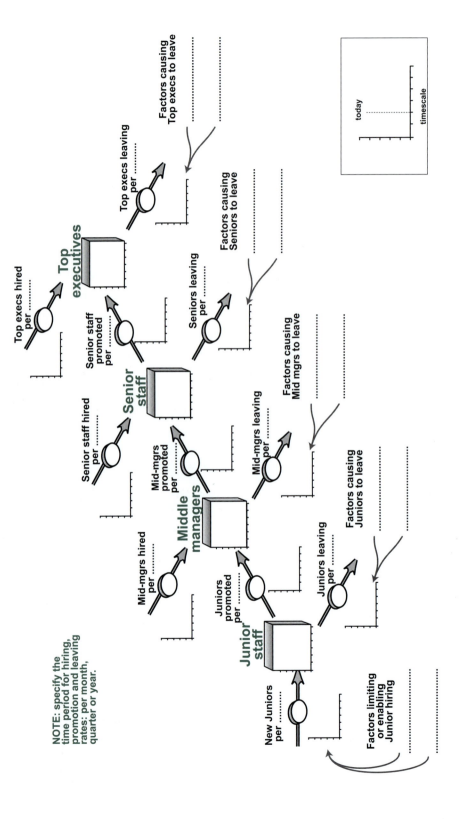

# WORKSHEET 7b: CUSTOMER DEVELOPMENT

NOTE: specify the time period for each flow rate [e.g. per month, quarter or year] and spending rate [e.g. $millions per month]

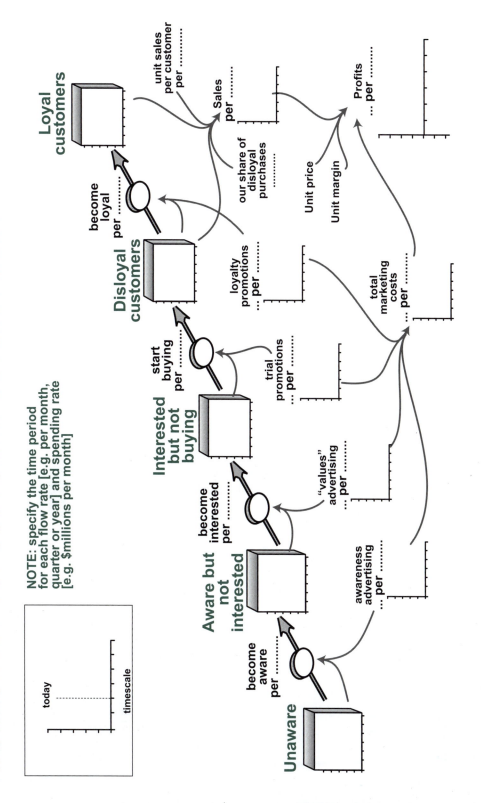

# WORKSHEET 7c: PRODUCT DEVELOPMENT

NOTE: specify the time period for each flow rate [e.g. per month, quarter or year]

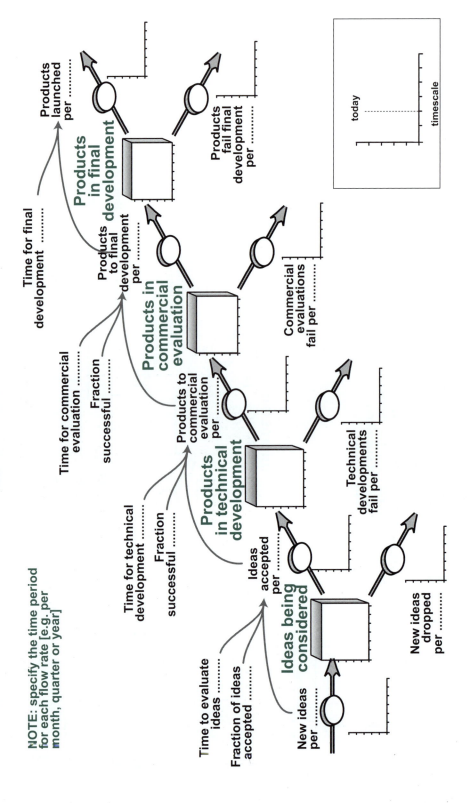

# WORKSHEET 7d: ASSET LIFE CYCLE

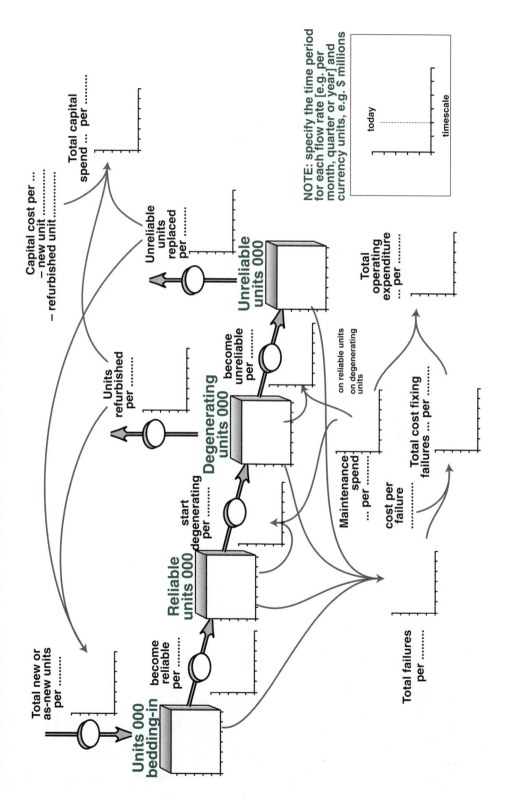

# WORKSHEET 8: IMPACT OF POLITICAL, ECONOMIC, SOCIAL AND TECHNOLOGICAL FACTORS (PEST)

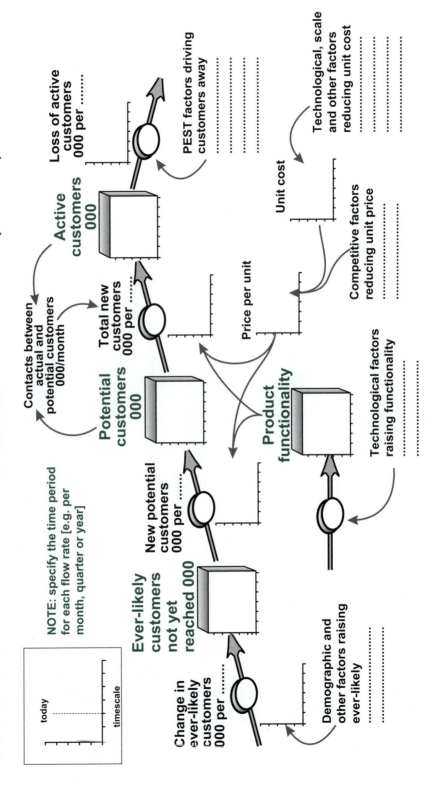

NOTE: specify the time period for each flow rate [e.g. per month, quarter or year]

today

timescale

Ever-likely customers not yet reached 000

Change in ever-likely customers 000 per ........

Demographic and other factors raising ever-likely ........

New potential customers 000 per ........

Potential customers 000

Contacts between actual and potential customers 000/month

Total new customers 000 per ........

Active customers 000

Loss of active customers 000 per ........

PEST factors driving customers away ........

Product functionality

Technological factors raising functionality ........

Price per unit

Unit cost

Competitive factors reducing unit price ........

Technological, scale and other factors reducing unit cost ........

# WORKSHEET 9: EXPERIENCE CURVE COST REDUCTION

NOTE: specify the time period for each flow rate [e.g. per month, quarter or year]

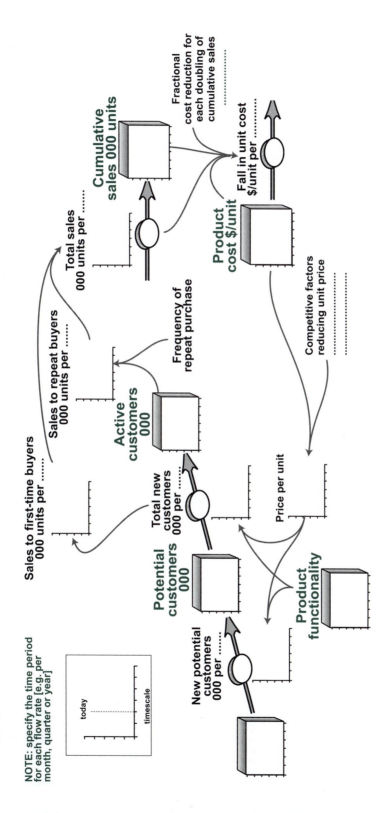

# NOTES

1.  The dynamics of new product development are explained in some detail in textbooks on the subject, such as Ulrich, K.T. and Eppinger, S.D. (2007) *Product Design and Development*, McGraw-Hill, New York. In addition, numerous studies have been carried out on the dynamics of new product development and the resulting implications for strategy in specific contexts, see for example Ford, D.N. and Sterman, J.D. (1998) Dynamic modeling of product development processes, *System Dynamics Review*, **14**(1), 31–68.

2.  See Eppinger, S.D. and Chitkara, A.R. (2006) The new practice of global product development. *Sloan Management Review*, **47**(4), 22–30; Gupta, A.K. and Wilemon, D. (1996) Changing patterns in industrial R&D management. *Journal of Product Innovation Management*, **13**(6), 497–511.

3.  Boer, F.P. (1999) *The Valuation of Technology: Business and Financial Issues in R&D*, John Wiley & Sons, Ltd, Chichester.

4.  *Fortune* (2006) Big Pharma's new R&D center: the trash-bin, 25 December, p.28.

5.  Toyota's approach to innovation is described in many articles, for example www.jpb.com/creative/article_littleideas.php. A more extensive description of the company's entire management philosophy, in which process innovation is a dominant feature, can be found in Liker, J.K. (2004) *The Toyota Way: 14 Management Principles from the World's Greatest Manufacturer*, McGraw-Hill, New York.

6.  A complete, professional maintenance strategy requires considerably greater detail and analysis than offered in this high-level summary of some of the issues involved. See, for example, Jardine, A.K.S. and Tsang, A.H.C. (2006) *Maintenance, Replacement & Reliability: Theory and Applications*, CRC/Taylor & Francis, London.

7.  I am indebted to Robert Thurlby of BT plc for bringing this case to my attention and for his insights on this widespread issue.

8.  See, for example, Kotler, P. and Keller, K. (2006) *Marketing Management* (12th edn), Prentice Hall, Upper Saddle River, NJ, Chapter 6. Extensive information on alternative customer development models is also available online from the American Marketing Association: www.marketingpower.com/mg-dictionary.php.

9.  Palda, K.S. (1966) The hypothesis of a hierarchy of effects: A partial evaluation. *Journal of Marketing Research*, **3**(1), 13–24.

10. Smith, R.E. and Swinyard, W.R. (1982) Information response models: An integrated approach. *Journal of Marketing*, **46**(1), 81–93.

11. Finskud, L. (2002) *Competing for Choice*, Vola Press, London. Available at www.vanguardstrategy.com/choice.

12. Extensive explanation of how marketing communications are defined and how they operate can be found in standard marketing textbooks, such as Kotler and Keller (2006)—note 7 above.

13. Guidance on customer/needs segmentation can be found in any good marketing textbook, as well as from many online sources, such as www.netmba.com/marketing/market/segmentation/

14. See for example www.mindtools.com/pages/article/newLDR_94.htm

15. Rogers, E. (2005) *The Diffusion of Innovations* (5th edn), Free Press, New York.

16. Moore, G. (1999) *Crossing the Chasm*, Harper Business, New York.

17. I am most grateful to Professor Mukul Sharma of the University of Texas for his extensive research on training and employment of petroleum engineers.

18. See http://en.wikipedia.org/wiki/Bullwhip_effect; Forrester, J.W. (1961) *Industrial Dynamics*, MIT Press, Cambridge, MA; Lee, H.L, Padmanabhan, V. and Whang, S. (1997) The bullwhip effect in supply chains, *Sloan Management Review*, **38**(3), 93–102; Bean, M. (2006) Bullwhips and Beer: Why Supply Chain Management is so Difficult, available from www.forio.com/resources/category/article. An excellent team-based exercise called the Beer Game, ideal for both students and groups, is available from the System Dynamics Society. www.systemdynamics.org/beer

19. Narayanan, V.K. and Fahey, L. (2001) Macroenvironmental analysis: Understanding the environment outside the industry, in *The Portable MBA in Strategy* (2nd edn) (Eds Fahey, L. and Randall, R.M.), John Wiley & Sons, Ltd, Chichester, pp. 189–214.

20. See Haberberg, A. and Rieple, A. (2001) *The Strategic Management of Organizations*, Prentice Hall, Harlow, pp. 133–139 and Fleisher, C.S. and Bensoussan, B.E. (2003), *Strategic and Competitive Analysis*, Pearson, Upper Saddle River, NJ, Chapter 17.

21. Details of the UK Department of Trade and Industry (2005) "Draft Regulations on the Operating and Financial Review and Directors' Report" can be found at www.opsi.gov.uk/si/si2005/draft/20051592.htm, especially Schedule 7ZA, pp.44–45. Explanation of the US Securities and Exchange Commission's equivalent regulations can be found at www.sec.gov/rules/other/33-8056.htm.

22. Hirschmann, W. (1964) Profit from the learning curve. *Harvard Business Review*, **42**(1), January–February; Boston Consulting Group (1972) *Perspectives on Experience*, Boston Consulting Group, Boston, MA; Hax, A.C. and Majluf,

N.S. (1982) Competitive cost dynamics: the experience curve. *Interfaces*, **12**, 50–61

23. An extensive explanation of strategic innovation as consideration of *who* to serve, with *what*, and *how* can be found in Markides, C. (2000) *All the Right Moves*, Harvard Business School Press, Boston, MA.

24. I am grateful to Drew Jones of the Sustainability Institute and Jack Homer of Homer Consulting for their assistance on this case. The team that created the project and model that supports this section includes Jones, Homer, Joyce Essien of Emory University, and Dara Murphy and Bobby Milstein, both of the Centers for Disease Control and Prevention (CDC). More information on the model is available at www.sustainabilityinstitute.org

25. Urbina, I. (2006) Bad blood, *New York Times*, 11 January.

26. Jones, A.P., Homer, J.B., Murphy, D.L., Essien, J.D.K., Milstein, B. and Seville, D.A. (2006) Understanding diabetes population dynamics through simulation modeling and experimentation, *American Journal of Public Health*, **96**(3), 488–494.

27. The Welfare Reform Project was led and directed by Dr John Rohrbaugh at the University at Albany, working closely with the NY State agency liaison, Robert Johnson. The group modeling effort was facilitated by Dr David Andersen and Dr George Richardson, with input from social welfare expert Dr Irene Lurie. Then doctoral students Naiyi Hsiao, Tsuey-Ping Lee and Aldo Zagonel provided support in data gathering, model building and testing, and interface development. For further information on the analysis, see Zagonel, A.A. and Rohrbaugh, J. (2007) Using group model building to inform public policy making and implementation, in *Complex Decision Making: Theory and Practice* (Eds Qudrat-Ullah, H., Spector, M. and Davidson, P.), Springer-Verlag, New York and Zagonel, A.A., Rohrbaugh, J., Richardson, G.P. and Andersen, D.F. (2004) Using simulation models to address "what if" questions about welfare reform, *Journal for Policy Analysis and Management*, **23**(4), 890–901.

# CHAPTER 7

# THE DYNAMICS OF RIVALRY

## KEY ISSUES

- ✪ Type-1 rivalry—capturing new customers, especially in growing markets.
- ✪ Type-2 rivalry—stealing customers from competitors, especially in mature markets.
- ✪ Type-3 rivalry—fighting for share of sales to nonexclusive customers.
- ✪ How the three types of rivalry may operate together.
- ✪ How rivalry accelerates development of emerging markets, and how product generations renew the competitive process.
- ✪ Rivalry for other resources, such as projects, staff, intermediaries and suppliers.
- ✪ How limited rationality and delays make competitive outcomes dependent on the sequence and timing of events.
- ✪ Dealing with multiple customer segments.
- ✪ Relevance of competition in noncommercial cases.
- ✪ Dealing with multiple competitors and grouping competitors according to similarities to simplify complicated cases.
- ✪ Rivalry for routes and passengers in the low-fare airline sector.

Worksheet 10a: Type-1 Rivalry

Worksheet 10b: Type-1 Rivalry (with increasing market potential)

Worksheet 11: Type-2 Rivalry

Worksheet 12: Type-3 Rivalry

This chapter makes connections to the following concepts: elasticity of demand, first-mover advantage, switching costs, competitor analysis, blue ocean strategy, game theory and strategic groups.

Chapters 1–6 have shown how organizations face a constant challenge to build and retain resources over time if they are to deliver continually improving earnings or other performance objectives. They are generally not alone in this effort, though, and struggle to accomplish these aims against others who are just as determined. This perspective on rivalry for resources makes competition as relevant to nonprofit organizations as it is to commercial firms—charities must win donors, just as airlines must win passengers.

All rivalry processes can be captured by just three dynamic structures, each applying not only to customers, but also to other resources that may be scarce and fought over, such as staff and sources of supply. The three forms of rivalry are:

1. **the race to develop potential resources**; e.g. winning first-time buyers, or hiring newly qualified staff
2. **the continuing battle to capture resources away from competitors and to prevent the reverse**; e.g. keeping customers or staff from switching to competitors
3. **the struggle for share of activity from nonexclusive customers and other resources**; e.g. voluntary groups capturing a larger share of donors' total giving, or consumer goods firms winning the largest share of retailers' shelf space.

These three mechanisms frequently operate simultaneously. For example, in fast-moving consumer goods, competitors rush to win new consumers whenever a new type of product is introduced, and strive to have competitors' products removed from stores and replaced with their own. Since they cannot ensure that either consumers or stores buy exclusively their own product, they then must try to capture more share of purchase than their rivals.

Two further issues deserve attention in competitive dynamics:

1. The three main types of rivalry all involve competitors interacting in some way—what one wins, another loses or fails to win. But on some issues competition involves no interaction—we might term these cases "type-zero" rivalry. Common examples concern the development of new technologies, products or services. Microsoft's success in developing a new version of the xBox games console does not prevent or slow Nintendo's or Sony's progress in developing their own new machines of similar performance. One pharmaceutical company's success in developing a drug for a particular disease does not hinder the progress of a competitor seeking their own product. There may possibly be competition for some related resources—the games machine companies need to win game developers' efforts to write software for their particular device, and the drugs companies may compete for scientific talent—but the product development race itself is not contestable.

2.  A further form of rivalry also arises in certain special situations—namely the effort to wreck rivals' strategic architectures (which was discussed in Chapter 5). If one firm can build its own performance by assembling an architecture of strongly integrated resources, the same understanding of a rival's business makes it possible to inflict damage on the competitor by unpicking that system. In extreme cases, firms may launch such wrecking attacks with no particular expectation of gaining resources themselves—for example, to weaken the competitor's ability to do battle in another market where the two firms *do* compete. These special circumstances are rare, however—organizations nearly always have scope to benefit positively from competitors' failures, and strive to do so.

The three mechanisms are most clearly evident for consumable products and services, whether in business-to-consumer (B2C) or business-to-business (B2B) cases (see Table 7.1).

The distinctions become less clear in other circumstances, however, and the appropriate competitive mechanisms may need specifying carefully. For durable and semidurable products, such as running shoes or cars, each purchase occasion may operate as a one-off type-1 competition—should I buy Nike or Adidas this time? Honda or Ford? Once the purchase has been made, there is no opportunity to get customers to switch until the product is to be replaced, and no meaningful way of capturing "share" of purchases. A bank account, on the other hand, may seem to be a "durable" purchase, but banks may lose customers who switch to competitors (type-2 rivalry) or even need to fight for share of transactions, deposits or lending to customers who have accounts with more than one bank.

---

### TABLE 7.1: THE THREE RIVALRY MECHANISMS IN COMMERCIAL SITUATIONS

|               | Business-to-consumer (B2C)                       | Business-to-business (B2B)                                          |
| ------------- | ------------------------------------------------ | ------------------------------------------------------------------- |
| Example       | Soft drink                                       | Business banking                                                    |
| Type-1 rivalry | Winning kids' first-time choice                 | Winning a new business's first requirement for banking             |
| Type-2 rivalry | Persuading consumers to switch brand            | Capturing business customers from a rival bank                      |
| Type-3 rivalry | Winning more share of choice by disloyal consumers | Winning more share of banking needs for businesses using more than one bank |

Services are just as likely as products to exhibit rivalry dynamics. Travellers may be captured for the first time when rival airlines start operating on the same new route. They may also be persuaded to switch from always using one airline to always using a competitor, or of course may be disloyal when rival airlines compete for more share of their journeys. Business services, too, can exhibit all three mechanisms. Large organizations may take all their consultancy advice from one provider, may switch to a competing consulting firm, or may use more than one advisor.

Competition for staff can typically exhibit only type-1 and type-2 rivalry. Law firms and oil companies compete to hire graduating lawyers or engineers (type-1). They also try to hire experienced professionals from competitors (type-2). An extra dimension in rivalry for staff is that a would-be employer may be competing with all kinds of other organizations. Shopfloor staff for Wal-Mart might equally seek work with McDonalds, the local hotel, or many other possible employers. Rivalry for staff is equally important in noncommercial cases. People who like to work in caring roles may choose teaching or nursing, and their behavioral characteristics may make them ideally suited to service businesses, such as airlines or restaurants.

# ILLUSTRATING THE THREE TYPES OF RIVALRY: COFFEE STORES

The three forms of rivalry can be clarified by a simple illustration. We and our rival each open a coffee store on the same day in a town that previously had none. The town has 5 000 potential customers.

1. Some customers passing our store choose to come in and continue to use it regularly, whereas others start using our competitor. The fraction choosing each store depends on its value for money—a balance between the typical price of the coffee and snacks versus the service, product-quality and store environment. This is type-1 rivalry.
2. Established customers of our store may become dissatisfied with the value we offer and switch to our competitor. Other customers may become dissatisfied with our competitor and switch to us. This is type-2 rivalry.
3. Some customers may choose to use both stores, so we and our rival each try to capture a greater fraction of the store visits made by these disloyal customers. This is type-3 rivalry.

Note that the customer development in this case differs from the steps in the choice pipeline discussed in Chapter 6. That framework showed people first becoming disloyal consumers of the product they start to buy, and only becoming loyal after extended good experience. In this case, customers choose one store and remain loyal to it until they have some reason to try its competitor.

Some simplifications will help make the behavior and strategy implications clear:

- The 5 000 customers are equally accessible to the two stores; i.e. the stores' locations are of identical quality.
- Each customer normally uses a coffee store twice per week, unless value for money raises or lowers their usage.
- Each customer normally spends an average of $5.00 per visit, including both the coffee and snack foods, unless value for money raises or lowers their spending.
- The quality of products, service and environment are all good, both in our store and in our rival's.
- Customers are won at the highest possible rate and do not leave, provided that value for money is "OK," i.e. the price matches what they expect. At any lower level of perceived value—i.e. higher price—customers are won more slowly.
- Customers are lost back to the potential pool increasingly quickly as the price escalates.

The price for a typical coffee is $2.95, the corresponding cost of raw materials is $0.90, and an equivalent gross profit margin is made on all products. Any change in the typical price of a coffee applies proportionately to all products. Since the cost of raw materials is fixed, any increase (decrease) in price raises (lowers) the gross profit by the same cash amount. The store's staff and overheads cost $9 000 per week.

## TYPE-1 RIVALRY: DEVELOPING POTENTIAL CUSTOMERS

Figure 7.1 shows the first year of each store's growth, when potential customers are being captured either by our store, or by the competitor. Both stores start by charging the expected price of $2.95 for their typical coffee and capture about 2 000 customers after six months. At that point, our competitor raises their typical price to $3.15, and we cut ours to $2.80. From that point in time:

- We start to win customers more quickly, whilst the competitor's win rate drops. They also start to lose customers more quickly than they win them, so their customer base starts to fall.

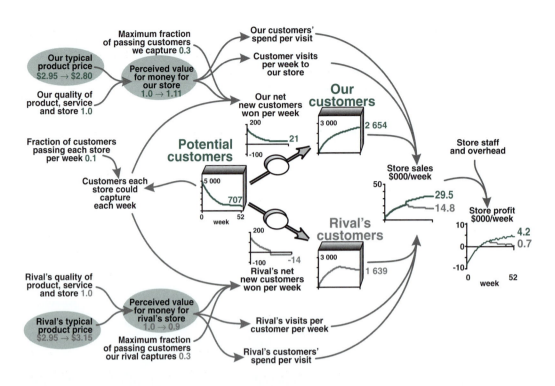

**Figure 7.1: Competing coffee stores capture potential customers in a previously unserved town.**

● Our customers visit more often (2.2 times per week), and spend more per visit ($5.56), whereas their customers visit less frequently (1.8 times per week), and spend less on each occasion ($4.50).

● Our sales jump somewhat, with the higher number of customer visits and spend, and then continue to rise. Their sales drop slightly, and start to decline, pushing their profits back down towards zero. Our profits would be still higher, except that we need to take on more staff to handle the greater number of customer visits. (Note: this is *not* a general rule that raising price loses customers so much as to reduce profits, either in this industry or others! The consequences of such an action depend on the specific responses of customers on each of the issues involved; that is, becoming and remaining customers, purchase frequency, spend per occasion, and so on.)

This illustration raises certain general points. The first of these is the rather simple observation that our successful capture of a new customer does not just come at the expense of our rival's win rate in the same week—it also denies them the possibility of winning that same new customer at any future time. This is a simple illustration of a "first-mover advantage" because our store has preempted strategically valuable resources—in this case customers. However, note that this is unlikely to be a *sustained* advantage, due to the ease with which customers may subsequently switch. More sustainable advantage might be achieved if, for example, there was only one good store location and we acquired that before our competitor. Other sources of first-mover advantage may arise from technological leadership (see Chapter 6 on product development) or from building the switching costs that make it hard for customers to move. Whilst it is hard for coffee stores to create switching costs, it is common in some other markets, both B2C (e.g. the contractual and inconvenience costs of switching between cellphone suppliers) and B2B (e.g. the costs of replacing the enterprise-resource-planning (ERP) systems that many larger organizations use to manage their operations).[1]

Secondly, note that customer capture is a two-way street—if either we or our competitor disappoint our customers, they may return to the potential pool where they become available once more to the other store. The customer is effectively saying "I didn't like that coffee store, but may still go to the other one if I happen to pass by and its offer is attractive to me." Alternatively, of course, they might say "I didn't like that store, but do like coffee stores, so will switch straight to the alternative next time I feel like a coffee"—this is the type-2 rivalry that we will look at next. Also note that both stores' success in capturing new customers depends not just on price—the only factor being changed in this case—but also on the quality of the products, service and environment we each offer; that is, other factors on the customers' value curve (see Chapters 2 and 3). We could equally have depicted here a differential customer win rate driven by a superior store environment, for example.

### Beware "elasticity of demand"

Some businesses try to work out pricing decisions by estimating the "price elasticity of demand" in their market; that is, the fraction by which demand changes for any fractional change in price.[2] In practice, this relationship is complicated by dynamic effects. In the rivalry structure of Figure 7.1, demand more or less stabilizes after 52 weeks for any given level of price charged by the two stores. If *both* stores charge higher prices, fewer customers are captured in total, more slowly; they visit less often and spend less on each occasion, resulting in lower overall sales volume. Conversely, a lower price by both stores captures more customers more quickly, and persuades them to visit more often and spend more, resulting in higher sales volume.

Figure 7.2 shows the year-end total demand volume for a range of prices between $2.50 and $3.50—what is known as the "long-run demand curve," because this is the level at which demand settles down after customers have fully adjusted their behavior. Note that the relationship is neither a straight line nor a smooth curve because of the particular behaviors of consumers in this model regarding whether to join or leave the market, how frequently to participate, and how much to spend on each occasion.

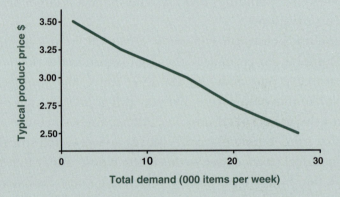

**Figure 7.2: The long-run relationship between demand and price for the two coffee stores.**

Next, consider what happens if both stores in this example change price by the same amount half-way through the year. Each initially charges the "expected" price, leading to 3936 customers being developed and a sales rate of 13340 units per week in total, split equally between the two stores. The market is still growing by that time, but rather slowly.

Figure 7.3 shows what happens when both stores then cut their price in week 26 from $2.95 to $2.50. There is an immediate increase in total demand as existing customers visit more often and spend more on each occasion. However, there is also a further increase in demand in subsequent weeks, as additional consumers are captured by the more attractive price. Note that demand is not even on the long-run demand curve in week 26 because by that time the two stores have still not captured all consumers who might find the product attractive at the initial price.

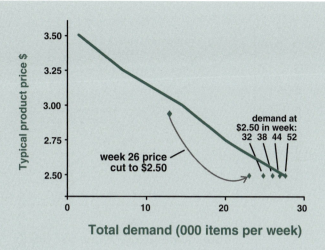

**Figure 7.3: Impact on total demand over time if both stores cut price in week 26.**

If the two stores raise price in week 26 rather than lower it, the converse happens—demand immediately drops, but then continues to fall as the higher price deters more and more consumers from using the stores at all.

If management were able to identify the immediate and long-term impact of both stores raising or lowering their prices, they would discover the two outcomes shown in Figure 7.4. However, neither result is safe for making pricing decisions; even if they could be sure the competing store would exactly match any price they set. If they use the estimate of the immediate impact to cut price to $2.50, they will understate the benefit to future cash flows because they will be ignoring the additional numbers of consumers who will gradually start using the stores. If they know, and use the long-run outcome they will overstate future cash flows because during the first six months they will not get all the extra sales that customers arriving later will bring. The difference is substantial, being worth over $5 000 per week in sales and more than $3 500 per week in operating profit to each store.

In this illustration the impact of price changes on weekly consumer spending is high, relative to the effect on consumers being won or lost completely. Consequently, most of the long-run change in demand takes place immediately. In other cases, the adjustment process can be more substantial and take a longer time. Increases in fuel prices, for example, make relatively little difference to

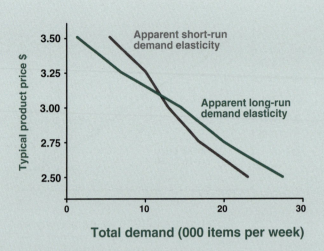

**Figure 7.4:** Short-term and long-term demand for a range of price changes by both coffee stores.

immediate demand for gasoline, because much of that demand is not discretionary—people still must get to work and immediate adjustments such as car sharing are inconvenient. However, as consumers replace their vehicles, they favor more fuel-efficient models, leading to a more substantial long-run drop in demand for fuel.

Ideally, then, it is preferable to understand the distinct impacts of price and other factors on specific behaviors—how frequently to purchase, how much to spend on each occasion, and most importantly, at what rate people (or business customers) will decide to become a customer at all, or to leave.

## TYPE-2 RIVALRY: CAPTURING A COMPETITOR'S CUSTOMERS

Type-2 rivalry can be demonstrated by taking the coffee store example forward in time to a point where all potential customers have been captured; that is, when the market is mature. The two stores have charged the same expected price of $2.95 for a typical product and each has half of the market's total of 5 000 customers.

Halfway through the year, the two stores make the same decisions as above: we lower our price to $2.80 and our competitor raises its price to $3.15. Figure 7.5 shows the impact on customers' choice to switch stores. There is a small immediate

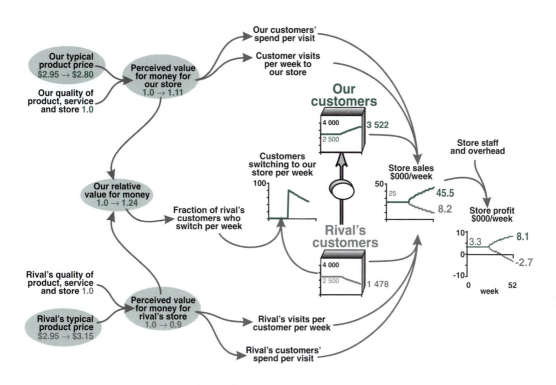

**Figure 7.5:** **Type-2 rivalry—customer switching between rival coffee stores.**

jump in our sales, as the visit frequency and average spend per customer increase, though this is not sufficient to increase our profits because of the cost of cutting price on each purchase. However, at the same time, customers start to switch from the competitor's store to our own at the rate of nearly 100 per week. Our customer base grows whilst our competitor's falls, leading to a rise in our weekly sales and profits and a fall in theirs.

A key assumption in this customer switching is that a constant fraction of the competitor's customer base switches each week; that is, some will tolerate the competitor's higher price for a longer time than others. Indeed, the scenario shown implies that customers are very patient—26 weeks after the price changes, less than half of the rival's customers have switched to our store, in spite of a $0.35 cheaper typical price. Different behavioral assumptions would result in different dynamics. For example, if customers concerned about price were to switch immediately, but the fraction of customers concerned varied with the size of the price gap, then there would be a pulse of "customers switching to our store per week," rather than the continuing flow shown in the center of Figure 7.5. The pulse would be small for a narrow price differential, and large for a greater one.

**Shifting the territory of type-2 rivalry—becoming a new entrant**

One factor that keeps firms from pushing hard to win customers in mature industries where type-2 rivalry is strong arises from the risk of escalating retaliation. This is of less concern for a new entrant, who has no current business to lose.

The airline industry offers examples of this, but at the other end from where SouthWest, Ryanair, and their low-cost rivals operate. As travel volumes generally have grown, it is becoming possible on some routes to offer flights that are exclusively business class; that is, expected business travelers are sufficiently numerous that they could fill an aircraft entirely, with no need to offer economy seating in addition. EOS, Silverjet and other new entrants started such services between the United Kingdom and United States in 2005/6, and such services are growing fast. This has considerable operational advantages, compared with the first/business/economy mixed services offered by the major airlines. It makes good profits possible with a 150-seat aircraft that has been adjusted to provide just 50 lie-flat seats, and still undercuts incumbent airline business fares.

So how is an incumbent to react? If it offers similar services itself, it damages the profitability of its major mixed-class services—unless, that is, it does so on new routes. This explains why British Airways in May 2007 announced the launch of business-class-only services to the United States from major European cities, but *not* from the United Kingdom. On those European routes, it is a new entrant, with no current business or profit streams to lose.

## WHEN TYPE-1 AND TYPE-2 RIVALRY OPERATE TOGETHER

Figure 7.5 featured type-2 rivalry alone—no customers would be won or lost in total, whatever pricing choices the two stores had made. This is clearly unrealistic—both stores could for example have doubled the price, with no loss of customers (though visit frequency and spend per visit would have suffered). We therefore need to allow both type-1 and type-2 rivalry to operate together, so that customers are won by each store from the potential population if their price is attractive, lost back again if not, *and* switch between the stores at a rate that depends on the differential in price.

**TABLE 7.2: COMPETING COFFEE STORE PRICE LEVELS DURING THE FIRST AND SECOND SIX-MONTH PERIODS**

|  | Our price | Rival's price |
|---|---|---|
| First half-year | $2.95 | $2.80 |
| Second half-year | $2.80 | $3.15 |

Table 7.2 summarizes the price levels for a scenario in which the rival store launches with a lower price in an effort to capture customers before we do. After the first half year, our concern with limited customer numbers causes us to drop our price, while the competitor raises price in the belief that higher margins can be captured with little loss of customers or sales volume.

Figure 7.6 shows the consequences of this pricing scenario, when both type-1 and type-2 rivalry are operating. During the first 26 weeks, our rival's more attractive price enables them to capture customers more quickly than we do—2 618 versus

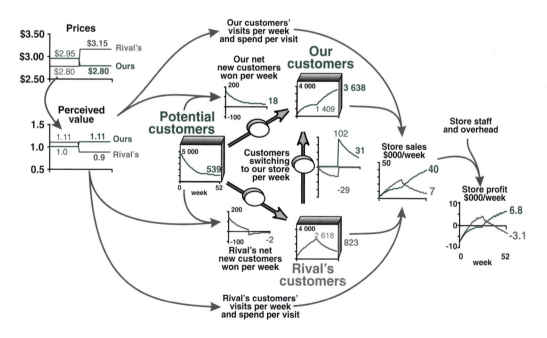

**Figure 7.6: Impact of changing price levels for type-1 and type-2 rivalry between coffee stores.**

our 1409. Importantly, we not only win customers more slowly, but also many of those that we *do* win switch to our competitor. This can be seen in the first half of the time chart for "customers switching to our store per week" (center), where a negative number indicates customer losses from our store. Despite the competitor's lower price and therefore gross margin, this is more than sufficient to give it higher sales and profits. Indeed, we have still not broken into profit at all.

The second half-year sees this situation reversed. Although few undeveloped potential customers remain by week 26, our new lower price allows us to continue capturing those who remain. Our rival's higher price actually causes some customers to stop using their store and return to the potential stock (the negative flow of "rival's net new customers won per week"). Those customers then become available for us to capture. At the same time, our wide price advantage leads to rapid switching of customers directly from their store to ours (the high positive flow of "customers switching to our store per week"). Driven by these two mechanisms, our sales grow strongly, push profits into positive territory, whilst our competitor loses sales and profitability.

Once again, different behavioral responses by customers would generate different trajectories than shown in Figure 7.6 for customer numbers, sales and profits. In practice, then, it is important to understand the nature and scale of those responses. It would not be sufficient, for example, for the competitor in about week 28 to observe simply that weekly sales had fallen. They should identify to what extent that loss is due to each of the four consequences—customers ceasing to use their store, switching to our store, visiting less often, or spending less on each occasion. In this illustration, the second of these mechanisms is powerful, whereas the third and fourth are modest. Consequently, the competitor would know that its immediate loss of sales was likely to get still worse. If, on the other hand, the early drop in sales were caused mostly by fewer, lower spend visits, rather than by customer switching, they could expect sales and profits not to fall much further.

## TYPE-3 RIVALRY

Many coffee store customers do not use a single store exclusively, but use two or more interchangeably. These people constitute a fourth population in addition to the three shown thus far—disloyal customers. They may reach that state from the start, following the sequence of behaviors described in the choice pipeline of Chapter 6, from where it may be possible for a store to capture their loyalty. Alternatively, they may be so satisfied with the first store they use that at first they remain loyal, only

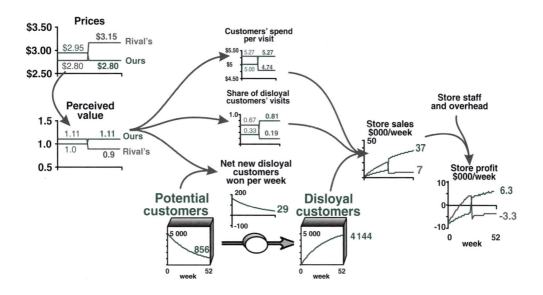

**Figure 7.7:** **Type-3 rivalry for visits and spend by disloyal customers of coffee stores.**

to be lost into the disloyal state at a later time. Competitors face a tough challenge with disloyal customers because their habit of frequent switching means that their choice must be competed for on every purchase occasion.

In Figure 7.7, the two stores again follow the pricing levels in Table 7.2. Customers *only* become disloyal and do so at a rate that reflects the best value for money offered by either of the two stores. The competitor's price is $2.80 for the first half of the year, and ours is $2.80 for the second half, so one store or other offers good value throughout the year. Consequently, the number of active customers grows strongly. For the first half-year, the competitor offers better value, so although our price of $2.95 is acceptable we only receive one-third of customer visits, although those customers do spend the normal amount of $5.00. However, this is not enough, even with the growth of total demand, to generate sufficient sales for our store to become profitable. Our rival enjoys two-thirds of customer visits and their better than acceptable price of $2.80 drives sales of $5.27 per visit. Consequently they break into profit after just a few months.

For the second half year, the situation reverses as our competitor raises its price to $3.15 and we drop ours to $2.80. It is unlikely in reality for a competitor to be so foolish as to persist with such a pricing policy if the consequences for customer visits and spend were so clearly harmful. Note also that if we had gone along with the competitor from week 26 and also charged $3.15, customer development would have stopped completely, and any higher price would have seen many customers leave the market altogether.

(Online learning materials are available to support this example, see p.xxi.)

### The value curve and blue ocean strategy

For simplicity, the examples offered above assume that competition takes place on only one factor—price. The value curve, introduced in Chapter 2 offers a more extensive framework for understanding the capture of both customers and their purchases. Competitors' relative success in these aims may be more clearly explained if their respective products or services are assessed on the multiple dimensions of a value curve. This comparison can then be used to identify opportunities to outcompete rivals by better meeting the complex needs of one or more customer segments.

All three rivalry mechanisms described above assume that competitors exist and that they are pursuing the same opportunity in ways that are similar to our own. Many executives would prefer to operate in an environment in which competition is limited or non-existent. This is the essence of "blue ocean" strategy,[3] which describes the discovery and exploitation of some novel proposition that is a leap in value for customers, compared with existing alternatives. It contrasts with "red ocean" strategy, in which firms continually seek to outperform competitors by incremental improvements in existing value curve factors—just a little more product performance, or just a little lower price, for example.

As noted by the authors, blue ocean strategies have always occurred, from the introduction of the Model-T Ford that brought affordable motoring to the general public, to Apple's first personal computer, to multiplex movie theaters. What these and other transformational strategies accomplish is the creation of a substantial new "potential" customer market, along with a value proposition so compelling that it both exploits that potential rapidly and establishes a lead that competitors can only pursue after many years of effort. As a result, blue ocean strategies can give firms long periods of highly profitable growth before any of the rivalry mechanisms above start to challenge them.

The search for blue ocean opportunities can offer substantial additional opportunities for established firms, as well as breakthrough opportunities for new entrants. Whilst it is valuable for established firms also to search for blue ocean opportunities, and advantageous if they can be found, it does not make the pursuit of competitive rivalry on existing dimensions irrelevant. Toyota, for example, could not safely ease up in its relentless progress on performance, reliability and cost for the broad mass of its motor vehicles, nor could Dell ease up in its efforts to improve the performance and value of its laptop computers and servers.

# FURTHER ISSUES IN TYPE-1 RIVALRY

Between them, the three types of rivalry provide the basis for understanding competitive dynamics in any situation, and for any kind of resource that may be fought over by rival organizations. However, some further mechanisms must be added in order to deal with various common features of real-world competition.

## RIVALRY IN EMERGING MARKETS

The coffee store example above assumed that a fixed population of potential customers already existed, and needed only to be offered stores to visit in order to express the demand they felt for the service. As Chapter 6 explained, markets are often in a process of emergence, when new potential customers develop. This development may be driven by product and/or price improvements offered by suppliers, as well as by wider external mechanisms of political, economic, social or technological change ("PEST" factors). This customer development process has important implications, especially for type-1 rivalry.

In Figures 6.20 and 6.21, potential customers developed in response to the functionality of the product and its price relative to their discretionary income. Although it was not disclosed in Chapter 6, it took only a short time—three months on average—for those people whose income crossed the threshold where the product was affordable to become genuinely available by moving into the potential pool. To illustrate, this means that for every 100 individuals who find they could for the first time afford the product in any month, one-third actually consider buying it immediately. In the following month, one-third of the remainder start considering the product, and so on. Even this, though, would be optimistic if suppliers did nothing to bring the appeal and affordability of the new product to the attention of ever-likely customers.

## Adoption costs

In certain markets, emergence and development of customers may be held back, even when the product or service is functionally and economically attractive, due to adoption costs. Chapter 6 described how rising incomes overtaking falling prices for a new product would bring new consumers into a market for a durable product (Figure 6.23). Adoption costs effectively move the threshold of affordability to a higher price level, so that although customers may be able to afford the regular costs of *owning* a product, they cannot afford to *acquire* it. Cellphone services have been a widespread example, with the initial cost of handsets being a substantial barrier to the rates at which new subscribers can be won. Service providers therefore decided very early on to cut the adoption-cost barrier by subsidizing the handset in return for higher monthly charges. A further example concerns cars—many of us would like to own a Lexus or BMW, and could perhaps afford to run such desirable vehicles but cannot afford the capital cost of purchase. In this case and similar situations, finance plans are commonly offered as a means of reducing or eliminating the adoption cost barrier.

Some companies go so far as to make adoption costs negative, effectively bribing customers to take their product. Banks, for example, have been known to offer cash to customers opening new types of account that they are keen to promote.

Companies in such markets would clearly benefit if all customers who could afford the product started considering it immediately. Their marketing communications therefore serve not only to win customers from the potential population but to speed the development of that potential itself. When competing suppliers are involved, their collective advertizing combines to accelerate this growth of the potential market. For example, a number of companies producing high-definition televisions (HDTVs) were advertizing their products in 2005. Many consumers in developed economies had sufficient income to afford these products, even at the relatively high price, but were not actively planning to buy one. The collective advertizing of the suppliers therefore had the effect of bringing those consumers into stores to investigate HDTVs generally, as well as to look at a particular supplier's models.

Figure 7.8 shows the market development for the consumer electronic device illustrated in Figure 6.23; that is, a durable product that customers upgrade or

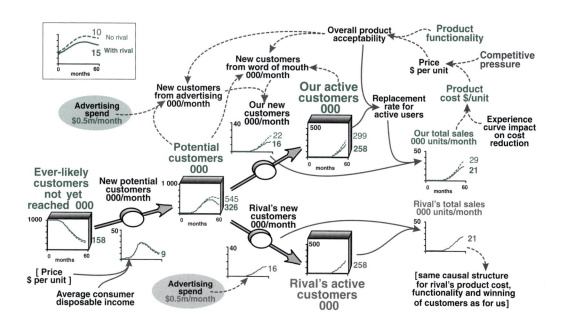

**Figure 7.8: Adding type-1 rivalry for a consumer electronic product.**

replace at a significant rate—with or without a competitor. (*The dashed causal links indicate that the structure is summarized, rather than being accurate in detail.*) This scenario assumes that advertizing has no impact on bringing ever-likely customers into the market, so it takes an average of 12 months for ever-likely customers who could afford the product to start taking an interest in it and become genuine potential customers. When building the market on our own, we capture nearly 300 000 customers after five years, and enjoy monthly sales of 29 000 units per months. If we have a competitor chasing the same market with exactly the same business model and advertizing rate, we each try to capture the same growing population of potential customers, so drain this pool more quickly. Together the two firms develop over 500 000 customers, and each reaches 21 000 units per month in sales. We are somewhat worse off with a competitor than without.

It is not realistic, however, that suppliers' advertizing would have no effect on bringing potential customers into the market. Even if they intend to target people already interested in the product, marketing efforts will certainly build awareness amongst the ever-likely customers who each month find they can afford the product. Figure 7.9 shows what happens if suppliers' advertizing has this additional effect, again comparing scenarios without (dashed lines) versus with (solid lines) a competitor.

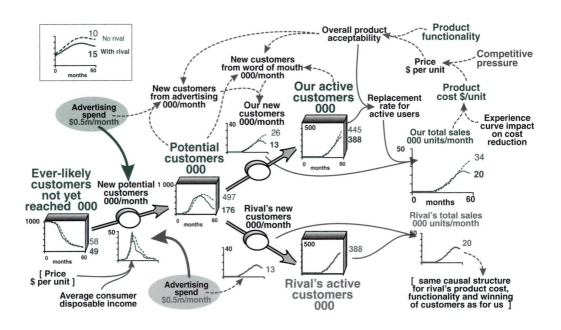

**Figure 7.9:** Impact on type-1 rivalry of advertizing bringing new customers more quickly into a market.

Our own advertizing alone is sufficient to bring forward the development of new potential customers as compared with Figure 7.8 (dashed lines), so that our customers and sales build sooner and more strongly. Adding a competitor brings forward the development of potential customers still earlier, allowing the two suppliers to capture over 75 % of the available market by the end of year five. Our sales rate finishes at 20 000 units per month, rather than 34 000 when no rival is present. However, note that the presence of a competitor actually *increases* our sales during much of the period, compared with what sales would have been without a rival. Our sales only fall below the no-rival case in year five, when the remaining potential is mostly used up. The mid-term strength of our sales, even when a competitor is chasing the same market, results from their help in bringing forward the development of potential customers for both companies to exploit.

> **Competitors can *raise* a company's sales by accelerating growth of a market in total.**

The interaction between competitors in type-1 rivalry for developing markets has further important implications.

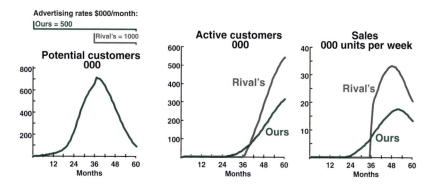

**Figure 7.10: One firm's early marketing builds the potential market for its competitor to capture.**

- **The risk of building the market for your competitors.** Given the customer development process above, it is entirely possible that early marketing efforts by one company will largely go to bringing new potential customers into a market, but be insufficient to capture that potential as actual sales. Figure 7.10 shows this effect for the consumer electronic product above. We spend $0.5m per month from the start which, along with improvements in the product's unit cost and functionality, develops over 600 000 potential customers by month 36. We also capture actual sales, which have grown to about 8 000 units per month, enabling our unit costs to fall somewhat. At this point, the competitor starts marketing also, spending at twice our rate. Note that, with no accumulated sales to this point, their unit cost is higher than ours, but their price is still acceptable to many customers. Their heavy marketing means they quickly overtake our sales rate, which helps bring their costs down and largely eliminates our early cost advantage.

- **The balance between first-mover and second-mover advantage.** The marketing-driven development of potential customers in Figure 7.10 is just one reason why firms who first develop a market may not ultimately win the competitive battle for supremacy in the longer term, despite their "first-mover advantage." Another common reason for second movers to win is their ability to learn from the early efforts of the first mover and introduce a product or service that is significantly better. In Figure 7.11, our firm introduces a product, as before, when its functionality is still not especially high. This time, however, we are slow to improve the product, so fail to develop much of the potential market, despite higher marketing efforts. By the time the competitor enters the market

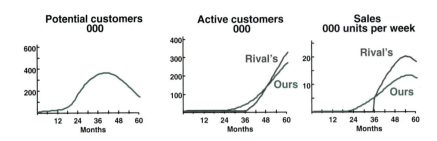

**Figure 7.11:** **Failure of first mover to capture the emerging market, due to slow product improvement.**

in month 36, their product is significantly better than ours, and they soon start to capture customers more quickly. This translates into faster monthly sales, which are boosted further by the more frequent replacement rate that their superior product encourages.

Both Figures 7.10 and 7.11 somewhat understate our poor sales performance relative to the competitor, since they allow only type-1 rivalry to operate. Once a customer has bought our product, they continue to buy our product whenever they replace or upgrade. Our sales performance in later months would be still more disappointing if type-2 rivalry was operating, so that owners also switch to the competitor for their later purchases.

### Progress of rivalry through sequences of product generations

A phenomenon that arises in many industries is the repeated replacement of one generation of product or service with another. In the cellphone industry, for example, the early analogue handsets and networks achieved some penetration of the potential market, but were then replaced by the early digital services, which in turn were replaced by today's 3G offerings. This generational progress of an industry has already been introduced with the discussion of disruptive technologies in Chapter 5. It is helpful to understand how rivalry is affected by this phenomenon.

In essence, for every generation of product or service after the first, the existing population of customers or users becomes a major part of the potential customer base for the next generation. In addition, because the new product generation offers significant increases in functionality or value over the previous one, it can accelerate both the development and capture of new potential customers (see Figure 7.12).

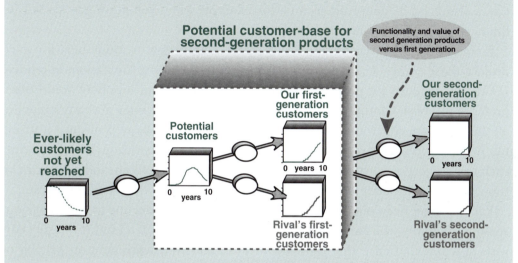

**Figure 7.12:** The development and capture of customers with new-generation products.

This succession of product generations brings new opportunities and challenges, by reinitializing the basis for type-1 rivalry. All of the previous generation's active and potential customers become available for capture with the new product or service, and strategy needs to be conscious of which new customer flows will start and at what rate. It may be easiest, for example, to ensure the business captures all of its existing first-generation customers or users with its second-generation offer. This focus, however, creates the risk that the business may cannibalize sales and profits from those existing customers. It may therefore prefer to focus on stealing competitors' first-generation customers with its superior second-generation offer, or perhaps target potential customers who have not yet found the first-generation sufficiently appealing or affordable to become active customers.

# RIVALRY IN PROJECT-BASED INDUSTRIES

Type-1 rivalry commonly persists in industries where customers buy substantial projects, rather than either individual products or continuing services. Examples include construction projects in civil engineering or process industries, large consultancy studies, and finance advice for firms wishing to acquire other businesses.[4] Cases also arise in nonprofit sectors, for example when voluntary groups bid for financial grants from funding providers.

Frequently, project customers ask possible suppliers to submit bids for each project, these events being known by various terms including "invitations to tender" (ITTs) or "requests for proposal" (RFPs). Although project suppliers would often prefer to establish continuing relationships, and thus guarantee a steady stream of all the project needs from each customer, the high cost of large projects is a strong motive for customers to seek the best bid on each separate occasion. In the extreme, each new project opportunity must be competed for from scratch, and hence can be thought of as equivalent to a new "potential customer" in other kinds of market.

Each supplier need not respond to every ITT. They may decline to bid for various reasons, including the fact that a particular project is not of a kind they especially wish to win, experience that the customer is excessively aggressive on pricing or otherwise difficult to do business with, or that the firm is already overloaded with work. A key issue for project suppliers therefore concerns how many of the possible ITTs to accept or reject, and how much effort to devote to preparing bids. Many organizations find it hard to say "no" to potential work, even if they are unlikely to be able to fulfill the resulting demands. It is therefore common for project suppliers to respond to many more ITTs than they could possibly deal with in the knowledge that they will only ever win a small fraction of the opportunities that arise.

In Figure 7.13, we compete with various rivals for a steady stream of 50 potential large projects per quarter, each of which takes four quarters to complete. Better quality bids win us more projects, and this quality depends on putting enough staff time onto preparing each bid. One particular competitor is virtually identical to our business, with the same staff of 40 on bid preparation, the same price and cost per project of $10m and $9m respectively, the same overhead, and the same performance when it comes to actually completing projects.

Some three quarters before the end point shown in Figure 7.13, our firm experienced a sharp reduction in the total number of projects won each quarter. Furthermore, we seemed to lose every bid that we contested with the main competitor, although we won slightly more of those where this rival was not bidding. As a result, our stock of active projects is falling, as the larger numbers won previously work

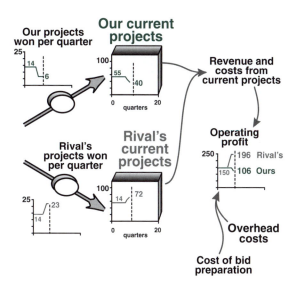

**Figure 7.13:** Falling win rate for new projects versus one main rival amongst others.

through the system, to be only partially replaced by the new projects we are winning. Operating profits are therefore falling and likely to continue doing so until the stock of active projects bottoms out.

It seems evident that we need to increase the number of new projects won per quarter, so we decide to increase the fraction of opportunities on which we bid. Unfortunately, the result is that we actually win fewer of those where the main competitor is not bidding and we continue to win none of those where we are up against that rival.

Figure 7.14 explains why this unsatisfactory outcome arises. Initially, we and our rival were bidding on 60 % of all possible projects, so we came up against each other on about 36 % of cases. Since we each put the same, limited effort into bidding for these opportunities, our bids were equally inadequate. We therefore each won 14 per quarter, nine from each other and five others. In the fourth quarter, our competitor decided it was losing too many bids through the poor quality of its proposals, and decided to focus its efforts on producing better bids for fewer projects. The quality of its bids increased substantially, allowing it to win every bid against us, and most of its other bids.

Our response was precisely the opposite of what was needed. In going for a larger fraction of project opportunities, our bid-preparation staff had still less time to give to each proposal, so quality fell further. This led to the failure to win any new projects from our main competitor and also led to us losing more bids to other rivals.

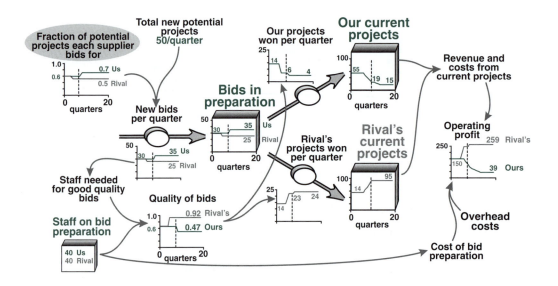

**Figure 7.14:** Increasing the number of project bids damages the quality of our proposals and cuts our win rate.

This illustration demonstrates just one of the many strategy issues that organizations in project-based industries must deal with. There would in practice be several other dimensions on which the success of these competitors would depend, including:

- the consequences of increasing the number of bid-preparation staff—although the tight pressure on margins in many such industries often makes management reluctant to do so
- the pricing of bids
- selection of specific *types* of projects to bid on, rather than just a fraction of all possible projects
- commitment of larger resources in the actual delivery of projects, both to speed their completion and enhance quality, consequences that can increase firm's reputation in the market and lead to a higher win rate on new project proposals.

Note also that the finding in this case—that we should have cut the fraction of projects on which we bid—is *not* to be taken as a general recommendation in all cases where bidding success is disappointing. As in other cases discussed throughout this book, the optimum response will depend on the specifics of each situation.

(Online learning materials are available to support this example, see p.xxi.)

# EXTENDING TYPE-2 RIVALRY
## SWITCHING COSTS LIMIT THE CAPTURE OF RIVALS' CUSTOMERS

The principal addition required for type-2 rivalry to be widely applicable is to include switching costs.[5] In the coffee store example above, customers of one store could prefer at any moment the value offered by the other and simply walk in through a different door. In other cases, customers face some costs in switching to a new competitor, so fail to switch even when offered better value, a phenomenon known as lock-in. They therefore stay with the existing supplier unless the better value on offer exceeds those switching costs.

In some cases, the costs are real, financial expenses. These can be very substantial. The owner of a Windows-based PC who feels that a Mac might be preferable would have to spend considerably on new software in order to make the switch. A company using one kind of software for managing its accounts would also incur considerable costs in switching to an alternative package—retraining staff, adapting other systems to work with the new software, and so on. Explicit financial switching costs are not especially common in consumer markets—there are rarely significant financial costs, for example, for a consumer wishing to switch to a different hairdresser, phone service or bank. However, even where financial costs are negligible, there may be other implicit costs:

- Switching can require time and effort. Consumers in many deregulated electricity markets, for example, could switch to lower price suppliers, but do not do so because the potential savings are not sufficient to justify the effort of contacting both the existing and new supplier to arrange for the switch. In cellphones, the effort involved for phone users to advise all their contacts of a new phone number would be a major deterrent against switching. This is why regulators in many markets have imposed on cellphone operators a requirement that subscribers be allowed to take their number with them— so-called "number-portability"—in order to ensure active price competition between competitors.

- A further nonfinancial barrier to switching concerns the uncertainty involved in changing supplier. We may be told by friends that a different bank offers excellent customer service, but we cannot be certain that it will serve us better than our current bank. A business-to-business case illustrating the same issue concerns organizations using a contract catering service for their staff. They may be offered a better price by a competing supplier, but worry that the new supplier's food would not be popular with their staff and thus put staff satisfaction at risk—one reason why suppliers in this industry commonly retain over 90 % of their contracts that come up for renewal.

Firms commonly try to create switching costs for their customers, to reduce their inclination to switch. Cellphone operators subsidize the cost of handsets for subscribers, but cannot afford these costs if subscribers soon switch to another provider. They therefore require users to take contracts for periods long enough to recover those subsidies from the monthly service charge. Providers of mortgages for house purchases impose cost penalties for homeowners who want to redeem their mortgages before the end of the contracted period, reducing the temptation for people to switch to lower cost mortgages that may be offered by competitors. Loyalty schemes of various kinds, such as airlines' frequent-flyer programs or retail loyalty cards serve to create partly financial switching costs for customers.

As explained earlier, companies may offer financing or other means of reducing adoption costs that would otherwise hold back customers from starting to use a product or service. Similarly, companies also try to eliminate or reduce the costs for customers to switch from competitors, or even make those costs negative. The subsidies offered by many cellphone operators in order to reduce the barrier for new subscribers continue to be used to steal customers from other operators. Such subsidies also help counter the nonfinancial switching costs, such as the effort involved for a user to become familiar with a new handset.

Intense and dynamic competitive conditions can arise when multiple competitors seek to eliminate switching costs for customers switching from their rivals. These cases effectively become "switching cost wars" in which escalating offers by several firms to persuade customers to switch leads to escalating switching barriers imposed by those same providers. In some markets, for example, credit card companies have sought to capture new card users by offering periods of zero interest charges on outstanding credit balances. Others have gone further, also offering zero charges on the credit balances from their previous card; that is, if you have $1 000 of debt on your existing card and take a competitor's card instead, you can pay-off the debt on the first card by using the second and pay no interest on that debt for an introductory period. Since heavy switching subsidies are costly, such cases can lead to competitors introducing ever higher switching *barriers* to make sure they recover those costs—for example, minimum contract periods for cellphones get longer and mortgage providers impose greater penalties for borrowers who wish to redeem the mortgage early.

Switching cost is a familiar phenomenon, and is included in simple economic models of markets, but a realistic treatment is needed if management is to make decisions that reflect the true nature of their particular situation. This realism should include:

- the limited rationality with which customers make decisions (see box); that is, some will switch when it is not rationally best for them to do so, whereas others will not switch when it is
- the delays that may arise between changes in functionality and/or price and customers' awareness of the change and decision to act on it
- the variation amongst customers in their rate of demand and response to functionality and price

### Limitations to rational choices

Economic models often assume that human behavior is rational; that is, that people behave as if they have perfect knowledge of functionality and prices and make choices on what is rationally in their best interests. A car is bought, for example, because it offers exactly the right amount of space, performance, fuel economy and other known factors that the customer wants for the price being charged. It is not purchased, on the rational view, because it's a nice shade of blue nor because it has cup holders that will never be used. It may be argued that blueness and cup holders also have some monetary value in the minds of the buyer, but it soon becomes implausible to argue that customers both know the value of all these features and balance their total value against the price.

Apart from the limited cognitive capacity of people to evaluate and compare so many details about a product or service, customers first need to be both aware of and understand the better value on offer from alternative suppliers if they are to switch. There are costs in finding out such information, if only in terms of time that must be spent The financial services industry features a number of sectors in which many customers could enjoy considerably better value than they do from their existing provider, but are either not aware of the alternatives or do not appreciate the scale of benefit available. Interest charges on credit cards vary widely and most consumers at most times could find cheaper alternatives to the card they commonly use. They choose not to investigate the possibility and may even deliberately avoid information that may encourage them to do so, for example by not opening statements that show the cost of their debt.

Although it is more realistic to recognize the limited rationality of customers and others making simple decisions, this requires research into real-world behavior that perfect rationality can avoid and is significantly more complex to work with. Nevertheless, for the purposes of understanding business perform-ance and making decisions to improve that performance, the additional effort is frequently worthwhile. Indeed, assumptions of perfect rationality can be so far wide of reality as to be highly dangerous for such purposes.

Executives who manage organizations also struggle to make rational deci-sions. In addition to the difficulties facing customers making simple buying choices, organizations present the further challenges that multiple decisions interact with each other, and are often fragmented amongst different parts of the organization. These obstacles to rational decision making in organizations have given rise to the notion of "bounded rationality." This notion recognizes that people adopt certain tactics to cope with the limited feasibility of making rational decisions—they use only a limited number of criteria in making their choices, favor information that is concrete and certain rather than abstract and ambiguous and decide on some balance between those criteria by using simple rules of thumb ("heuristics").[6] (The concept of bounded rationality will be discussed further in Chapter 8.)

Take, for example, the arrival of a competitor in a newly deregulated regional market for power supply, assumed for simplicity to consist of domestic users only. As the established monopoly competitor, we start with all one million customers and charge them a price that results in a bill of $400 per quarter, given average consumption rates per household. Consumers incur switching costs of $10 due to the monetary costs, time and risk they feel in making a switch.

Initially assume that all consumers are perfectly rational, act immediately to take any available savings, have the same demand for electricity and are equally price-sensitive; that is, ignore the requirements above for a realistic model. Their rational evaluation is that these costs are worth incurring if they can save the switching cost over four quarters; that is, if their quarterly saving is $2.50. (Although we will define this as "rational" they should really compare the switching cost against the discounted value of all future savings, but few consumers behave that way.)

The new supplier enters the market in quarter four, charging prices that give customers quarterly costs of $380; that is, a saving of $20. This is more than sufficient to recover their $10 switching cost over four quarters so, if perfectly rational, all one million customers switch immediately. If we respond in quarter eight with a price of $360, all customers again see a saving of $20 and switch back to us. Both events would be somewhat challenging for the two suppliers to manage in practice, of course. In some markets this challenge is eased by regulations allowing competing suppliers to offer power over the same electricity network. All a new competitor need do, then, is to obtain a source of generated power and sell it through the shared network.

## IMPACT OF LIMITED RATIONALITY

There are various ways in which customers' limited rationality could operate. This example takes the simple likelihood that an increasing fraction of customers switch as their possible savings rise, even at the lowest level of rational behavior (see Table 7.3, shaded column). If, for example, our new competitor offers a price that costs customers $10/quarter less than our price *and* covers their switching costs, then we immediately lose 18% of our one million customers. As the potential savings rise,

**TABLE 7.3: FRACTION OF CUSTOMERS SWITCHING POWER SUPPLIERS AS POTENTIAL SAVINGS INCREASE, FOR INCREASING LEVELS OF RATIONALITY**

| Saving per quarter over switching threshold | Implied competitor price $/qtr | Fraction of customers who switch from the higher-priced supplier | | | |
|:---:|:---:|:---:|:---:|:---:|:---:|
| | | Rationality level > | 0 | 0.3 | 0.6 | 1.0 |
| $0.10 | $2.60 | | 0 | 0.3 | 0.6 | 1.0 |
| $10 | $12.50 | | 0.18 | 0.43 | 0.67 | 1.0 |
| $20 | $22.50 | | 0.50 | 0.65 | 0.80 | 1.0 |
| $30 | $32.50 | | 0.76 | 0.83 | 0.90 | 1.0 |
| $40 | $42.50 | | 0.96 | 0.97 | 0.98 | 1.0 |
| $50 | $52.50 | | 1.0 | 1.0 | 1.0 | 1.0 |

we lose larger fractions of customers, until at a saving of $50/quarter even the least rational customer switches.

The effect of increasingly rational behavior is to raise the fraction of customers who switch for any given level of savings, until at perfect rationality (rightmost column) all customers switch for any net positive saving no matter how small. This feature alone is sufficient to create the need for careful choices by management. Since it is hard to charge different prices to similar customers, the only way the competitor can increase its penetration of the market is to offer lower prices to all. At a price that saves customers $30 after switching costs, they can expect to capture 760 000 customers, but must drop the price a further $10 if they are to capture nearly all (96%). Depending on the cost of generating or acquiring the power that customers require, this additional price cut could wipe out the profit they make on the now larger number of customers.

Figure 7.15 shows what happens to each supplier's customer base at each of these levels of rational behavior by customers if the competitor enters with a price of $390; that is, a saving of $7.50 after customers have allowed for recovering their switching costs over four quarters. With all customers motivated to switch immediately, our customer base drops to a new level the quarter after the competitor enters.

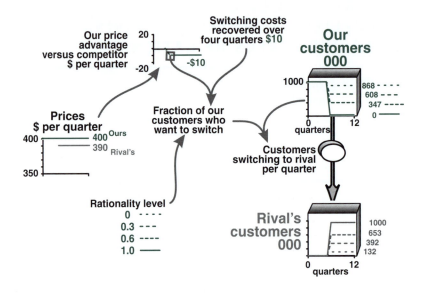

**Figure 7.15:** Customers switching for $10/quarter saving on domestic power as rational behavior rises.

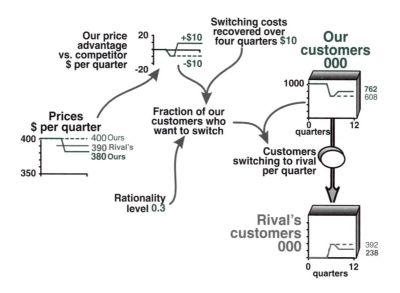

**Figure 7.16:** Customers recaptured by a second $10/quarter saving with limited rationality.

Perhaps less obvious is what happens if we subsequently respond by offering customers the same saving again by dropping our price to $380. Figure 7.16 shows the result of our responding with this price cut two quarters after the competitor enters, with customers exhibiting a rationality level of 0.3, as defined in Table 7.3. As in the second case of Figure 7.15, this limited rationality means we lose only 302 000 customers when the competitor enters, rather than all one million if they were entirely rational. However, we also win back only a small fraction of those customers we lost when we offer customers the same saving once again.

This puzzling result arises because all customers are assumed to be equally rational in their switching decisions, so those we lose are just as likely to be irrational when we offer them a saving as they were when the competitor did so. In reality, it is likely that first-time switchers will be more rational than those who choose to stay put, so that we could expect to win back with our price cut a larger fraction of the customers we originally lost than is shown in Figure 7.16. Nevertheless, with limited customer rationality, we should not expect to win back all of them. This phenomenon corresponds to the experience of many firms who lose business to lower cost competitors, only to discover that similar price cuts of their own fail to win back the customers they lost.

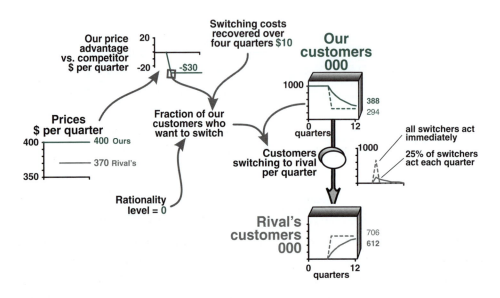

**Figure 7.17: Impact of behavioral delays on customer switching between power suppliers.**[*]

## DELAYS IN CUSTOMER RESPONSE

To the challenge of limited rationality amongst customers must be added the problems caused by their delayed responses. Figures 7.15 and 7.16 already include a short delay for the practical process of switching—customers must be sent the new price offer from our competitor, receive a bill from the existing supplier that shows they could save, apply to switch, and have their account transferred. In addition to these processing times, there can be behavioral delays—some customers act immediately on noticing they could save money, whereas others may not act until they have received several marketing communications from our competitor and several bills from us. Figure 7.17 compares the rate of customer switching for a $30/quarter saving with the lowest level of rational behavior, when only a quarter of customers who will eventually switch do so each quarter. (Note that with no delay only 706 000 customers switch, rather than the 760 000 implied by the shaded column in Table 7.3 due to the switching costs.)

---

[*] To capture this phenomenon correctly, customers move in response to a new saving opportunity into a state of "wanting to switch" from which a fraction actually switches in each subsequent quarter. Whilst in that state, they remain our customers.

## Path dependency

If customers are perfectly rational and respond instantly, conditions generally move between alternative states predictably, regardless of what happened previously. In the power-market case, for example, all customers are either with us or with the competitor. An important consequence of limited rationality and delays is that the eventual outcome of changes in a competitive market depends on where it started and on the sequence of events.

If we and our competitor in the electricity market each started with 0.5 million customers, for example, rather than our opening monopoly, we would only have half the number of customers for our competitor to capture. With limited rationality a competitor price that saved customers $30 after switching costs would steal 76 % of our customers; that is, 380 000, leaving us with 120 000, rather than the 240 000 that we would have kept had we started with one million customers.

With no delays in customer reaction, the timing of multiple events does not matter to the situations that arise after each. If we reacted to the competitor's price cut with a further cut of our own, perhaps saving customers a further $20, we would end up with the same number of customers whether we made that cut one quarter later or a year later. Time-delays in customer behavior break this certainty. If we respond quickly, the competitor will only have captured a fraction of those customers who would eventually switch. Our response then stops those customers who would have switched later from doing so.

In Figure 7.18, the competitor enters with a price $20 below ours so, with perfectly rational evaluation, all customers want to switch. However, they do not act immediately—each quarter thereafter, 25 % of those still wanting to switch do so. If we act the following quarter with a price cut to $20 less than our competitor (solid lines), we only lose the first quarter's group of 250 000 customers before we start to recapture them. On the other hand, if we do not act for another four quarters (dashed line), most of those who might want to switch will have done so. We start to recapture customers quite fast, simply because our competitor has so many, but we are still a long way from recapturing all those we lost after a further four quarters.

Where the market ends up after any set of events therefore depends on where it started, how rational customers are in their behavior, how quickly they respond to new information *and* on the timing and sequence of those events.

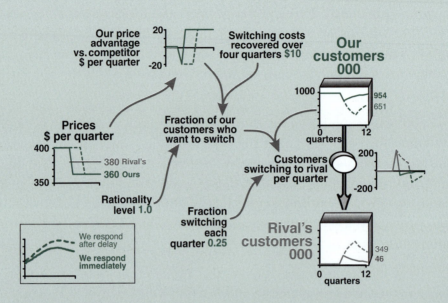

**Figure 7.18:** Path dependency arising from delays in customer response to price changes in electricity supply.

## VARYING CUSTOMER CHARACTERISTICS

The last element of realism to add to the limited rationality and delays in customer behavior concerns the various differences that may exist between customers. They will likely differ on many factors in this situation—usage rates, price sensitivity, switching costs, rationality of response, and time to respond to available savings. Table 7.4 gives some illustrative characteristics for two distinct customer groups in this electricity market.

Figure 7.19 shows the implications for customer switching by each group resulting from a competitor's entry worth $20 saving to low users ($30 to high users), followed by our response four quarters later with a price cut worth the same amount to each group. The rational and instantaneous response of low users results in us losing them all in quarter four when the competitor enters, but we recapture them all

**TABLE 7.4: DIFFERING CHARACTERISTICS OF LOW-USE AND HIGH-USE CUSTOMERS IN THE ELECTRICITY MARKET**

| | Low users | High users |
|---|---|---|
| Fraction of customers in each group | 0.7 | 0.3 |
| Quarterly usage cost | $400 | $600 |
| Price sensitivity (*price difference for all customers to switch if not rational*) | $50 | $100 |
| Switching cost | $10 | $50 |
| Rationality | 1.0 | 0.5 |
| Fraction acting each quarter on potential savings | 1.0 | 0.25 |

again when we cut price in quarter eight. Amongst high-use customers, in contrast, only a fraction is motivated to switch by the competitor's entry, and their slow response results in most of that group still being with us when we cut price in quarter eight. Thereafter, we slowly recapture some high users.

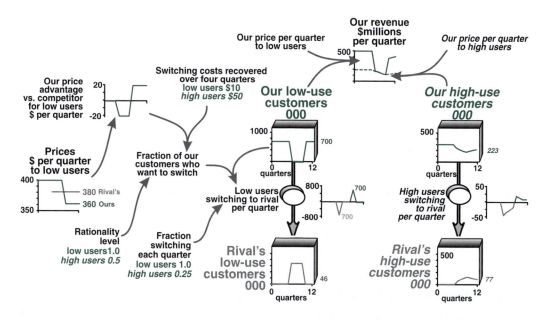

**Figure 7.19: Impact of price changes on two groups of electricity consumers with differing characteristics.**

This principle could be repeated for more than one group of customers to give a more exact view of behavior in a market of diverse customers. If necessary, the full variety of customers' varying characteristics would be captured by means of the attribute principles described in Chapter 5. However, there are important practical limits to extending the analysis to such a degree. First, the causal structure encompassing multiple attributes would be complex, risking the introduction of errors into the model and making its results hard to understand. Second, such detailed complexity would need to be populated with realistic information across the whole spectrum of behavioral responses of customers. These are unlikely to be knowable with much certainty. It is therefore more feasible in practice to carry out careful, simplified customer segmentation than to attempt to capture the detailed profiling of all attributes amongst the customer population.

(Online learning materials are available to support this example, see p.xxi.)

# EXTENDING TYPE-3 RIVALRY

Limited rationality is already implicit in the type-3 rivalry concerning the battle between rivals for share of customers' purchase decisions. After all, if customers are fully rational and there is a detectable difference between the price and/or functionality of competing products then all would choose only the best alternative on every purchase occasion.

In business-to-business cases, one common constraint that limits this all-or-nothing choice by customers is the possible risk that may arise from putting all of the firm's purchases with one supplier. First, large organizations often cannot afford the damage that would be done to their own business if some difficulty arose with the supply of raw materials or other bought-in products from a single supplier. They may therefore prefer to keep buying from at least two suppliers to ensure they have an alternative source available for such eventualities. Second, it is often important to maintain competition between suppliers in order to keep up pressure on price, product performance and service; in other words, to reduce "supplier power" in the competitive forces framework described in Chapter 2. This need to reduce supply risk and sustain active rivalry between suppliers can lead large customers to have both a first-line supplier who receives most of their purchases, and one or two second-line suppliers who receive the rest. Just how much of the customer's purchases each supplier receives varies widely, depending on the importance of the bought-in product to the customer, the ease with which customers can switch to other suppliers, the number and quality of suppliers available, and so on.

From the point of view of a supplier to such business customers, the challenge therefore falls into two stages:

1. getting onto the customer's list of suppliers
2. once on the customer's list, winning the status of favored supplier with the largest share of the customer's purchases.

One situation in which this kind of rivalry features is in business banking. Many small organizations take all of their financial services from a single bank, but larger organizations commonly look at the total cost of those services and seek out better terms for some of those services from competing suppliers. They might, for example, arrange large loans with a bank that does not deal with most of their financial needs. Competing banks are constantly on the look out for opportunities to win this kind of initial deal, in the hope of capturing a second and third piece of business. Switching between banks is a costly, inconvenient and risky decision for a large organization, so the ultimate prize for a supplier—to win the main banking relationship—will only be possible after a long period of good performance to build trust with the customer, plus a significantly superior proposition regarding the utility or price of its services.

Figure 7.20 shows how a bank's total sales to larger business customers arises from the sum of three elements; the whole of the banking needs of customers with whom it has the sole relationship, the share it can retain of customer business where

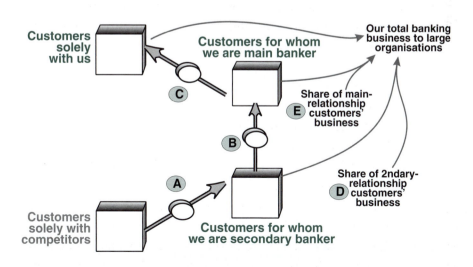

**Figure 7.20:** How type-3 rivalry applies to primary and secondary customers, e.g. in business banking.

it is the main (but not exclusive) banker, and the share it can capture of customers' needs where it is a secondary supplier. This structure causes some difficulty in deciding on the priorities for the customer-relationship executives who seek to win, retain and develop such customers. They have a number of alternatives:

A.   winning completely new relationships
B.   persuading customers to give the bank the main relationship
C.   persuading customers to give the bank all of their business
D.   increasing share of secondary business with customers (in the hope of leading to change B above)
E.   increasing share of business with main-relationship customers (i.e. taking business from the customers' secondary bankers).

Choosing the balance of effort between these distinct priorities is complex, increasing since time spent on any one of them has to come from others. A focus on winning completely new relationships (A), for example, could leave existing main-relationship customers vulnerable to attack by competitors, risking loss of valuable business to those customers or even the loss of that relationship.

## COMPETING WHEN INTERMEDIARIES ARE INVOLVED

The presence of intermediaries can give rise to powerful type-3 rivalry mechanisms, both in B2C and B2B cases. Often, a key objective for suppliers is to capture more share of the intermediaries' attention, so they promote the supplier's product more strongly to the end-customer. That "attention" can come in a variety of forms, for example:

- a consumer-goods company would like retailers to allocate a larger share of shelf space to its product than to rival products in the same category
- business supplies companies would like their products to be given more pages in distributors' catalogues than competitors' products
- insurance companies would like brokers to spend more time selling their policies to customers than those of their competitor
- Intel would like PC manufacturers to feature Intel processors in more of the models in their product ranges, rather than AMD processors
- suppliers of many kinds would like Web-based services to give more prominence to their products than to those of their competitors.

Not only is the quantity of space or attention important in such cases, so too is the quality. Stores' shelf space can be high quality (near the entrance, at eye level) or low (back of the store, at floor level). Space on a Web site can be prominent, or buried away below other more visible pages. Insurance brokers may focus their best sales people on a product or less capable people. However, this is an additional complication to a mechanism that provides important insights in its simple form. In essence, the intermediary's attention—whatever form it takes—is a further resource over which rivals compete. Where customers are not loyal and choose from amongst two or more products in a type-3 manner, suppliers who can only reach them through intermediaries are engaged in a type-2 rivalry for the attention of those intermediaries. Fast-moving consumer goods—breakfast cereals, cleaning products, crackers, margarines, and so on—provide a familiar situation where this can be observed.

Figure 7.21 shows (to the right) a basic type-3 rivalry structure for consumers of such a product. This is exactly the same as in the coffee store rivalry for disloyal customers shown in Figure 7.7. That structure is only sufficient on its own, however, in situations where suppliers have direct access to customers. (Coffee stores generally sell only their own brands in their own stores.) In this new case, however, our share of total sales is itself dependent on the outcome of type-2 rivalry for stores' shelf space (to the left). Sales per unit area of floor space (dollars per sq. foot or sq. metre) is a critical performance indicator for retailers, but within this broad perspective stores often focus closely on the profitability of each foot (metre) of shelf.

This competition for shelf space has important implications for rivalry amongst competing suppliers of any single product category. If one product in a category

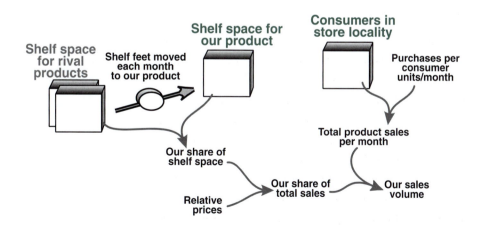

**Figure 7.21: How type-2 rivalry for retailer shelf space contributes to type-3 rivalry for share of consumer purchases.**

generates less gross profit per foot than rival products, whether due to lower sales, smaller retail margin or both, the store will give more shelf space to competing products on which it makes more profit. There will be limits to this shelf allocation, however. Stores may be reluctant to give any one product too large a share of space, both to ensure that loyal consumers of competing products can find the brands they want and to ensure continuing competitive efforts amongst suppliers.

Figure 7.22 shows a situation in which we and a single competitor have equally appealing products for a market of 5 000 entirely disloyal (but not entirely rational) consumers in the locality surrounding a store. We and our rival charge a wholesale price of $1.50 (bottom-left), to which the store adds a 25 % mark-up—38 cents—resulting in a retail price of $1.88 per unit. The store has 20 feet (just over 6 metres) in total for the product category, and this is initially allocated equally between the two products. Total sales of 30 000 units per month give the store a gross profit of $11 250/month, or $562.50 for each foot of shelf space. (There are some small rounding differences in the values shown in Figure 7.22.)

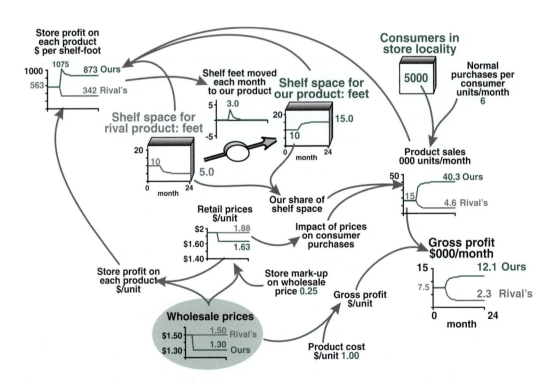

**Figure 7.22: A wholesale price reduction captures retailer shelf space from rival products.**

In an effort to boost our sales and profitability, we reduce the wholesale price from month 6 to $1.30, with the following consequences:

- The store keeps the same percentage margin on our product, so reduces the retail price by the same fraction as we cut the wholesale price. The store thus makes less *cash* margin per unit.
- The lower retail price enables our product immediately to capture a larger share of consumers' purchases.
- If this were all that changed, the store would not be happy, as it would be making less cash margin on the same total sales. However, the lower retail price also leads to an increase in consumers' total purchases.
- With higher total sales, and a big increase in our product's share, the store makes substantially more cash per foot on our product than before ($377), and rather less on the rival product (top left).
- The store therefore allocates 3 feet more shelf space to our product, and takes this amount from the rival product.
- The following month, the store still makes more cash per foot on our product, and moves still more space away from the competitor. We achieve greater sales volume and make more profit, despite the lower price.
- In each subsequent month our product is given still more shelf space, until it has gained 5 feet from the rival product. Although the store could still make more cash from our product with further reallocations, it is reluctant to do so for the reasons given above.

(Online learning materials are available to support this example, see p.xxi.)

The competitor is not likely to accept the outcome in Figure 7.22, and may respond with price reductions of its own. If it does so, total product sales will increase again and the store will reallocate shelf space away from our product. Figure 7.23 shows the outcome if the competitor cuts price to $1.20 six months after our price cut— shelf space is reallocated back to their product, consumer purchases rise once more *and* they switch to the competitor.

If rivals continue this tit-for-tat price cutting, the eventual outcome will be a progressive reduction in wholesale price towards the minimum that we and our competitor can tolerate and a considerable loss of total suppliers' gross profit. The store's total profit from the products may increase, despite the reduced cash margin per unit, provided that consumer demand rises substantially with lower prices.

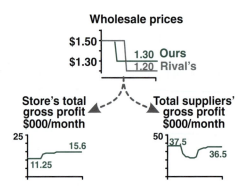

**Figure 7.23:** Consequences of retaliatory price cut for rival product suppliers to a store.

As noted above, similar causal structures and competitive implications arise in many other situations, both B2C and B2B, so the structure in Figure 7.23 is readily modified to capture rivalry in such cases. Figures 7.24a–7.24c summarize some examples.

Note that competition for supply of manufactured components (Figure 7.24b) includes an important simplification—manufacturers may not directly switch end-products from incorporating one supplier's components to those of a competing supplier. It is more common for *new* products to be designed around a choice of suppliers' components. Suppliers therefore raise their share of manufacturers' product ranges by winning their inclusion in these new products and lose share when

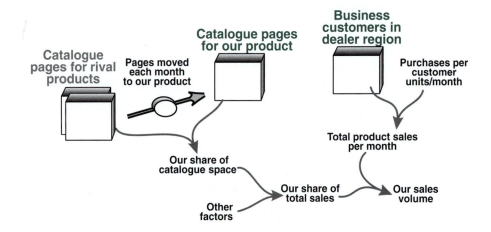

**Figure 7.24a:** Rivalry for supply of consumable business products through prominence in dealer catalogues.

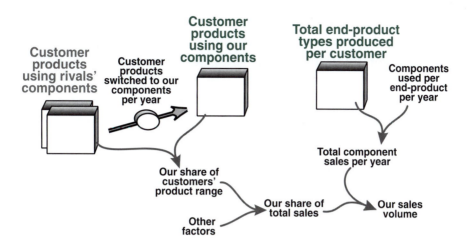

**Figure 7.24b:** Rivalry for supply of manufactured components through share of customers' end-product range.

older products are discontinued. For example, Intel once enjoyed exclusive supply of microprocessors to the whole of Dell's range of PCs and servers. However, in May 2006, Dell announced that it would for the first time use AMD processors in its high-end servers—the last of the major server manufacturers to do so. Intel then started to lose share of Dell's product range as each Intel-based product was discontinued and each AMD-based product was added. Thereafter Intel would be fighting AMD for each new Dell product, a battle that it had previously been in little doubt of winning.

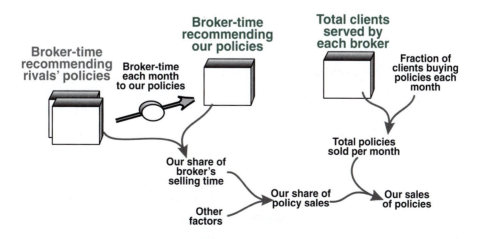

**Figure 7.24c:** Rivalry for sales of insurance policies through share of brokers' selling time.

Note also that in the third case—insurance companies' rivalry to capture brokers' sales attention—time is not strictly a resource, although it can be used as a good proxy for attention in this and similar cases. Such a situation arises in other cases where sales people compete for buyers' time. Where pharmaceuticals producers sell direct to doctors, for example, there is a limited amount of time that those doctors are willing to give to listening to those sales people rather than seeing their patients, so sales people plan carefully how to catch the maximum share of doctors' attention.

## GAME THEORY AND COMPETITIVE DYNAMICS

Game theory is a way of understanding situations in which multiple players make decisions on a certain issue or issues, in an attempt to maximize their returns. It can therefore be used to help decision makers select competitive actions, and choose how to react to competitors' actions; for example, changing prices, spending on marketing, or expanding capacity.[7]

The situation in Figure 7.22 offers the choice of leaving the price at $1.50 or cutting it to $1.30. Many other possibilities exist of course, including an increase in the price. If we cut the price, the competitor might react, or not—again a wide range of reactions is possible, but matching our price cut is one simple possibility.

- If we cut the price and the competitor does not react, we can expect to win more shelf space, attract a higher purchase rate from consumers, and therefore make a higher rate of cash gross profit each month, in spite of the reduction in gross profit margin. This will, though, come partly at the expense of our competitor, who will lose shelf space and consumer purchases, leading to a drop in their monthly gross profit.
- If the competitor *does* react, by matching our price cut, neither of us gain any shelf space, but may enjoy some increase in consumer purchases. In this case, since this increase in sales volume is small, relative to the price reduction, both of us suffer a fall in gross profit.

A third possibility is that we leave the price at $1.50 and instead our competitor reduces their price. Figure 7.25, shows what is known as the "pay-off matrix," with these three possibilities compared with the base case where neither company cuts price. The gross profit of $7 100/month for both companies arises if either company responds immediately to a price cut by its rival of a matching amount. (Strictly, the "pay-off" in each case should be calculated as the present value of future cash flows in each case, rather than the equilibrium profit—see Chapter 1.)

**Our price**

|  | $1.50 | $1.30 |  |
|---|---|---|---|
| **Competitor price $1.50** | 7.5<br>7.5 | 12.1<br>2.3 | **Gross profit**<br>**$000/month**<br><br>**Ours**<br><br>**Rival's** |
| **$1.30** | 2.3<br>12.1 | 7.1<br>7.1 |  |

**Figure 7.25:** **Pay-off matrix for price reductions in supply of consumer product to a store.**

In Figure 7.25 both firms are worse off from a mutual price cut to $1.30, but equal pain need not always be the outcome. If we start with a smaller price cut from $1.50 to $1.40 and our competitor reacts immediately, both suppliers enjoy an increase in gross profit, to $8 330 each. This attractive outcome arises because increased purchases by consumers in that price range outweigh the loss of margin. Indeed, it is possible (though not with the particular parameters in this case), for suppliers to do best by following each other in *raising* prices rather than cutting them. This can give rise to what looks like collusion amongst suppliers to raise prices; that is, direct agreement between suppliers to push prices up, a practice of which competition authorities strongly disapprove and work hard to stamp out. However, collusion need not be involved, merely the transparent observation by suppliers of the consequence of each others' decisions.

## SEQUENTIAL VERSUS SIMULTANEOUS COMPETITIVE RESPONSE

Game theory recognizes that outcomes differ when one competitor waits to see what its rival does before deciding whether to respond, rather than making its decision at the same time. In the case above, the store's policy of rebalancing shelf space results in no difference in long-term outcomes, regardless of whether the competitor responds immediately, or after one, three or six months. This rebalancing ensures that the two products eventually occupy the same space. However the outcomes of simultaneous versus sequential pricing decisions by the suppliers are not the same if the store has no rebalancing policy. If we cut price and our competitor does not respond immediately, we capture shelf space that we keep, even after the competitor responds, because of the store's indifference to one product dominating its shelves.

## COMPETING VERSUS COOPERATING

The outcomes of games change if competitors can both benefit from certain decisions. If there is no mutual benefit to be had, competition is likely to be more aggressive. This is known as a zero-sum situation, because each competitor's gains must come at the expense of the other. That is not the situation in Figure 7.25, because of the impact that lower prices have on raising total consumer demand. Our initial price cut raises demand for our product, as well as switching demand from the competitor, and their response raises demand for their product, as well as taking demand from ours.

If consumers' demand for this product were not increased at all by any reduction in price, the gain for the company that cuts price alone is much less than in Figure 7.25 at only $9 000/month rather than $12 100, and the competitor's profit is eliminated altogether. If both suppliers cut price, each ends up with profits of just $4 500/month. Conversely, if much greater elasticity of consumer demand occurs (i.e. consumers buy considerably more of either product at lower prices) both companies could enjoy higher profits from a price cut. Cooperation is therefore more prevalent when total returns to all competitors can be increased by their pursuit of similar strategies. This is most likely to occur when there is unexploited potential in a market, so that price cuts, advertizing increases, product improvements and so on may all accelerate total demand. This has already been shown to be possible with the addition of a competitor to the launch of a consumer electronic product in Figure 7.9.

## REPEATED GAMES

From each new position, it is possible that the game will be repeated, making it necessary to estimate pay-offs from further pricing decisions. Starting from the position in Figure 7.25, for example, either supplier is again better off if it cuts price by 10 cents to $1.20 and the competitor does not react, but is worse off if its rival also cuts the price. However, the result is quite different if we make a price cut of 20 cents (Figure 7.26). In this case, the increase in consumer demand is not sufficient to offset the loss of gross margin from our price cut, even if the competitor does not respond. Their gross profit, meanwhile, is hit by the switch of consumer purchases to our product. If the competitor *does* respond, we are both worse off than if we had held the price at $1.30.

**Our price**

|  | $1.30 | $1.10 |
|---|---|---|
| **Competitor price $1.30** | 7.1 <br> 7.1 | 4.7 <br> 2.2 |
| **$1.10** | 2.2 <br> 4.7 | 2.8 <br> 2.8 |

Gross profit
$000/month
**Ours**

Rival's

**Figure 7.26: Pay-off matrix for a further price reduction in supply of consumer product to a store.**

## THE USE OF GAME THEORY IN STRATEGY

Game theory recognizes that strategy is conducted in a wider system in which it is not possible to make unilateral decisions. Rather, decisions must be made in the expectation that others will respond. In spite of the profusion of material on the topic, and its undoubted theoretical strength and analytical sophistication, few managerial articles describe how game theory can be incorporated in strategic planning and management.[8] The principle is not widely used in practice, nor familiar to most executives except in the most general terms.

A number of explanations have been offered for this, notably that game theory is able only to focus on very limited numbers of factors, often only one at a time (price in the case above), that it does not deal realistically, if at all, with most of the strategic choices available to management and that it requires an impractical degree of rationality.[9] In essence, the last of these points can be summarized thus: for game theory to be useful, *management must be able to estimate the pay-offs from their decisions.* As has been demonstrated throughout earlier chapters, the dynamic performance consequences arising from the interdependent resource-systems of real organizations make this requirement almost impossible to fulfill, unless that system is made explicit. To these difficulties can be added others that arise from a truly dynamic treatment of business performance:

- there are highly nonlinear relationships between decisions of differing degree; for example, whether the price cut decision above is from $1.50 to $1.40, $1.30 or $1.10 gives rise to entirely different results

- competitors have many more options on the same factor than whether simply to match the move—they could respond to a price cut to $1.30 with any price change, ranging from a reduction to zero margin ($1.00) to a price *increase*
- the consequences of a competitive response may depend strongly on the timing of that response; not just whether the rival waits to see what we do before reacting, but whether that reaction follows after one week, one month, or many months—in the case above, since the store waits to see the result of moving some shelf space between products before deciding on further reallocations, an early response by the competitor can reduce its loss of sales compared with waiting several months to see the long-term outcome.

Game theory is, however, increasingly used by business purchasers to set up 'bidding wars' amongst suppliers. A major cellphone network operator seeking bids from rival providers of equipment, for example, can create an open online auction in which not only the price of competing bids but other terms of supply are entirely transparent. The buyer can then sit back and watch the competing suppliers fight to win the business by making ever better offers. Such bidding wars can be so destructive of value to suppliers that some refuse to participate.

A dramatic example of the use of game theory in a bidding situation occurred when telecommunications authorities offered licenses for cellphone operators to build third generation (3G) services. Industry hype in the late 1990s, and enthusiasm for 3G were considerable, so in spring 2000, the British government auctioned five licences for the 3G radio spectrum using game-theory principles to ensure the highest possible offers from competing bidders. The auction raised a colossal £22.5 billion. Germany's subsequent auction raised even more, £31 billion, and the resulting huge financing costs dragged down profitability amongst the operators for several years. The industry then learned it could not sustain such aggressive bidding wars, and the later auction of Italy's spectrum raised just £7.5 billion, rather than the expected £13 billion, when overstretched bidders pulled out completely.

## Competitor analysis

Given the numerous issues on which competitors can act, and the multiplicity of considerations they can take into account when doing so, it is often recommended that firms carry out analysis of specific rivals in order to anticipate their likely behavior. Figure 7.27 provides a simple check-list of issues to consider in such a review.

To assess a competitor's likely behavior one should understand the objectives it seems to be pursuing—whether it is tryng to improve profitability, gain market share, or simply trying to survive. Different objectives imply different responses. A firm trying to improve profitability, for example, is less likely to start a price war, and may be reluctant to spend on important items such as service support. Pursuit of increased market share, on the other hand, may well encourage aggressive pricing behavior.

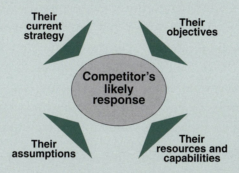

**Figure 7.27:** **Factors to consider when assessing how a competitor may behave.**

People inevitably make assumptions about issues and executives are no exception. They make assumptions about the market, for example that strong demand growth will continue or that customers value certain factors, even in the face of contrary evidence or unsupportable reasoning. They make assumptions about us and their other competitors, believing for example that we always undercut their pricing. They make assumptions about their own organization, such as that their costs are lower than ours, or that their service support is excellent. All such assumptions affect their decision making.

Competitors are as dependent as us on the resources and capabilities they have. They may be reluctant to develop a new business if they don't have the people. Alternatively, their assumptions may override this consideration and they may initiate the new development but then be unable to push it through because the required staff are not available.

Finally, the competitor's current strategy can provide strong evidence about how it may behave. A company that has for some years been first to market with strong new products is not likely suddenly to reduce its product development effort and just milk the profitability of products previously introduced. We can also expect a company with a track record of aggressive retaliation against rivals who target its best customers to ignore us if we decide to do so.

Whilst these are useful issues to consider when trying to anticipate competitors' responses to strategies we might pursue, a qualitative discussion around the management team's opinions on these matters hardly deserves to be termed "analysis." Ideally, we need evidence that can be substantiated on the issues within each of these four categories, and some method of assessing the scale of impact involved. If we believe them to be pursuing market share by keen pricing, and targeting what we know to be strong sales people at our best customers, for example, by how much might this threaten our profit margins, and what number of customers are vulnerable, accounting for what fraction of our sales?

Assessing properly the impact of objectives, assumptions, resources and capabilities on an organization's strategy and likely responses requires an understanding of how decision making works on the strategic architecture—a topic that will be addressed further in Chapter 8.

# EXTENDING RIVALRY TO RESOURCES OTHER THAN CUSTOMERS

As noted at the start of this chapter, the three rivalry mechanisms may arise in relation to resources other than customers. Competition for staff is widespread, especially for people with scarce and valuable skills. Generally, only type-1 (competing to win new potential employees) and type-2 (trying to win existing employees from rivals) mechanisms apply to staff—it is unusual for people to work simultaneously for two employers who then have to compete in a type-3 manner for a share of their time. Type-3 rivalry may arise, however, with contractors who have agreed to work for two or more clients and share the available time between them. People seeking construction work for domestic housing may be familiar with this phenomenon in the building industry.

Competition between clients for their contractors' time is more accurately described as competing for *supply*, and other supplier cases may also give rise to rivalry. Firms may compete for access to sources of raw materials, as occurs when oil and minerals companies bid for the right to prospect for new reserves in certain geographic areas. When a strongly anticipated new product is introduced, customers may compete with each other for a share of the product's early limited availability. This occurs in situations as diverse as the introduction of a new PC processor chip, a new consumer electronic device, or luxury designer fashion goods.

Competition for supply often features win-lose outcomes—we either get what we want or do not. Television channels frequently compete for the right to broadcast popular programs—another scarce "supply" without which their business will struggle. Each such product is competed for anew. Oil companies either win the right to explore in certain regions or lose out and, as explained above, construction companies either win or lose each new project opportunity. Nevertheless, there can still be accumulating effects that give firms advantage from occasion to occasion. A broadcaster who wins large numbers of viewers for a TV series, for example, will be able to make a strong bid for future series, and a construction company with a good record of completing projects on time and to budget will be favored by project clients.

We have already looked at the way in which rivalry can play out for intermediaries in supply of consumer goods and other cases, but other types of resource that provide access to markets may also be fought over. Airlines compete for access to airport landing slots. Broadcast companies and cellphone operators often compete for licenses to use sections of the radio spectrum. Such resources again operate in a win-lose manner—as far as the firm's strategic architecture is concerned, they either have a value of "1," in which case the business can operate, or "0," in which case it cannot.

## RIVALRY FOR STAFF

Since competition for staff is so widespread, this section illustrates how the principles of type-1 and type-2 rivalry work, taking the example of two organizations wishing to grow a call center operation in a town with a limited number of potential employees. In Figure 7.28, it can be seen that the town has a total of 500 people who might be ever-likely to work in a call center. We need to grow our operation to 250 people within 12 months, and offer pay rates of $10/hour. This is sufficient to motivate increasing numbers of people to consider working for us, and numbers of staff start to rise.

After three months, a competitor starts a similar operation, also aiming to take on 250 staff by the end of the year. Since they need to grow faster, they offer pay rates of $11 per hour. This has three effects:

1.  the competitor stimulates people to start considering this employment opportunity at a faster rate (left of Figure 7.28)
2.  in a type-1 rivalry mechanism, they also start to capture the potential employees who were already considering working in our call center, but now have a better offer (bottom-center)
3.  in a type-2 process, the competitor starts taking people who are already working for us (right).

If this were to continue (dashed lines), the competitor would nearly reach their goal, capturing 215 staff by the end of the year. Of these, about 30 will have been stolen directly from us and the rest both stimulated and captured from the ever-likely population. Halfway through the year, therefore, we raise our pay rates to $12. This stimulates still more people in the town to consider the job opportunities in call centers (the third peak on the chart of "new potential staff per month") and nearly doubles the rate at which we can hire those potential staff. It also allows us to steal staff from our competitor, with the net flow of staff (right) reversing in our favor.

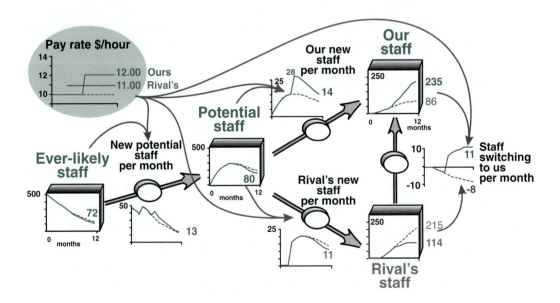

**Figure 7.28:** **Rivalry with pay rates for new call center staff in a locallty.**

Naturally, other factors would feature in people's decision to take job opportunities of this kind, such as working conditions and the recommendations of friends. However, these issues too will operate by impacting on the flows of staff around this structure of type-1 and type-2 rivalry. There will also be people leaving employment in either of these organizations; in other words flowing out to the right of the structure, from where they may return to the potential population once more or leave the system altogether—in effect taking the view that they will not consider working in either call center again.

## WHEN COMPETITION MOVES TO A BATTLE FOR EXPERIENCED STAFF

Some firms are faced with a rather challenging extension of this rivalry structure for staff. These organizations hire successfully from the emerging population of potential employees, often hiring young people from colleges and universities because they are well known and have a good reputation. Effectively, they have been successful in creating an "employer brand," following principles of the choice pipeline discussed in Chapter 6. The staff they take on work for them for a few years, gaining skills and experience. Other organizations then steal those staff with better job offers, whether in terms of pay rates, better promotion prospects, or more interesting work. What the second employer has done is to treat the first organization as its potential hiring ground, saving itself the trouble and expense of training people and giving them experience, becoming what is known as a "free rider" in the employment market.

One such case appeared to present a quite intractable problem for the first employer, and gave rise to a surprising and counterintuitive strategy. This case concerned a company in the aerospace industry who needed a strong team of highly skilled systems engineers (aerospace products depend just as much on sophisticated software as they do on cutting metal!). The company was a longstanding recruiter at the best technical universities, taking only the top-grade graduates by offering the best salaries and the opportunity to gain experience with some of the most sophisticated technology around. The problem that arose came from firms in the finance industry, who saw the people this firm had trained as outstandingly capable and, with just a little retraining, highly suited to help them with the sophisticated systems on which their business relied. These firms employed recruitment consultants to target the aerospace and other high-tech engineering sectors. Typically when one of the best employees in those industries got the headhunter's phone call offering a considerable increase in salary, it was most probable that that individual would take the offer and leave (Figure 7.29).

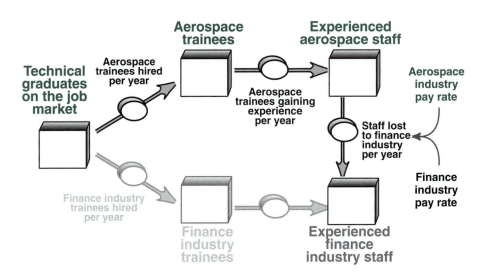

**Figure 7.29:** Capture of systems specialists from an aerospace firm by the finance industry.

The aerospace firm was in serious trouble. It was heavily dependent on the skills and experience of these specialists, but could not afford to match the high pay rates offered by the finance employers because of the tight profit margins in their own industry. Nor could the firm find any other way of holding on to the staff that it had so expensively developed.

A solution emerged when it was recognized that a significant number of staff (though not enough) had *not* left the company—indeed they had not even been approached with attractive job offers to join finance companies. They were entirely competent and apparently contented in their jobs, so the puzzle was how these people differed from those that had been lost. Although the company had always tried to hire the best technical graduates, it had not always been able to find all the trainees it needed from those sources, and had been forced to take on people with what seemed to be lower qualifications from second-tier universities. Although these young employees were in theory not quite up to the company's hiring standards, most turned out to have considerable aptitude for the job that did not show up in their paper qualifications. They were not treated to the same accelerated job development as the alleged "stars," so typically took a couple more years to get promoted to the level at which the headhunters were hunting. Furthermore, the simple screening system headhunters used for targeting the best staff missed these other people altogether. This group also did not have the high opinions of themselves shared by the stars and were generally somewhat older, with families and strong connections in the local community.

The aerospace company concluded that its hiring policy had been misguided. It did not need people with the high levels of theoretical capability indicated by the top-rate degrees from the top-rate universities—it needed people with strong aptitudes for the special kind of work involved in its industry. The firm concluded that it should *lower* its hiring criteria, which paradoxically both increased its hiring success and lowered its salary costs, but add to its hiring process some new aptitude testing.

Similar challenges arose in a rather different context and for somewhat different reasons. United States firms providing IT-based and other services saw a strong growth in demand for their services arising from increases in the United States homeland security needs following the 9/11 tragedy. In order to work on such services, staff must be security cleared, a process that at the time could take many months. It was common, therefore, for these companies to make job offers to new staff, but not actually take them on until after the security clearance process had completed. Not surprisingly, competition switched towards attempts by these firms to steal from each other staff who had already been cleared.

# RIVALRY IN NONCOMMERCIAL SITUATIONS

Competition is widespread in public services and voluntary organizations, and may sometimes be similar to the rivalry for customers in business situations. Voluntary organizations must be clearly helpful to the beneficiaries of their services if they are to attract funding from donors, so any such organization with few such "customers" will lose out in the fundraising market. Other customer-like rivalry arises for political parties who compete for voters, and Churches who compete for followers.

Rivalry for staff is ubiquitous amongst public services, and the framework in Figure 7.28 is directly applicable to competition over staff in such cases as well as other noncommercial situations. Competition for staff can become international in scope, such as when nursing staff are attracted from low-pay economies to work in the health services of richer nations. It is even helpful to regard terrorism as a "career path" for people that competes against alternative occupations that are benign.

Rivalry certainly occurs between voluntary organizations for attracting donors and the giving they bring, and can readily take any of the three forms discussed in this chapter—capturing new donors, winning donors from other organizations, and capturing more share of the giving from donors who support more than one organization. As for businesses competing for customers and sales, voluntary organizations may need to be conscious of which form of competition they are engaged in, and

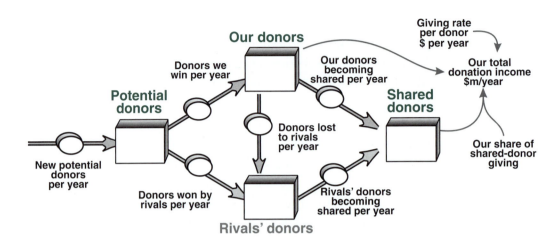

**Figure 7.30:** The three rivalry mechanisms for donors to voluntary organizations.

where their efforts should focus. Depending on the scale of the challenge, it may be valuable to go further and make the effort to estimate the numbers and value of donors involved and the rate at which they are moving around the structure in Figure 7.30.

This framework, like those for customer-based rivalry discussed earlier in this chapter may need to be segmented to differentiate between high-giving donors and others, or extended to deal in more detail with the varying attributes of the donor population explained in Chapter 5.

# DEALING WITH MULTIPLE COMPETITORS

Few companies are so fortunate as to have only one competitor to deal with, so it is often necessary to extend the principles discussed in this chapter to handle multiple rivals. It is relatively straightforward to adapt the three standard rivalry structures to capture several competitors. Figure 7.31, for example, shows the structure for three coffee stores—ours plus two competitors—seeking to win potential customers in the local market described in Figure 7.1.

In the original scenario for this case, two stores started up, each charging $2.95. Then in month 6, we cut the price to $2.80, and our rival raised its price to $3.15. In Figure 7.31, a third store opens at the start, and follows our pricing strategy, reducing price in month six. It captures a fraction of new consumers who would otherwise have come to our store and to the first competitor. However, it also speeds

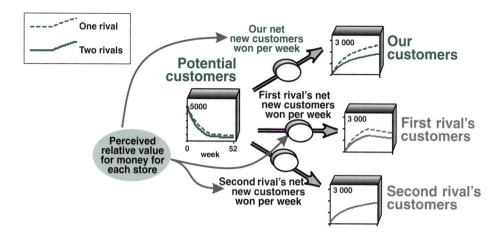

**Figure 7.31:** A second coffee store competitor speeds market development and captures new customers.

the capture of new customers, so that the total market grows faster and to a higher level than with just the two rivals.

Figure 7.5 showed type-2 customer switching in a mature coffee store market when there were just two competitors. Figure 7.32 extends this case to three competitors, so each starts with a smaller number of customers. The pricing scenario

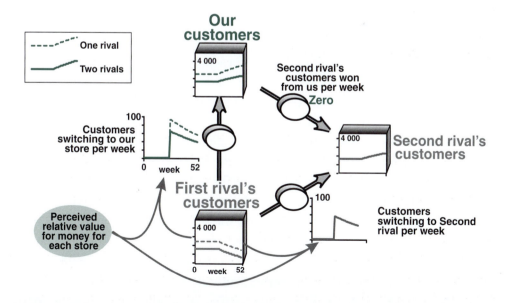

**Figure 7.32:** Rivalry between three coffee stores in a mature market.

is the same as above, with our store and the second rival lowering price from $2.95 to $2.80 in month six and the first competitor raising price at the same time from $2.95 to $3.15. The first rival now loses customers both to us and the new competitor, and because there are two lower priced options, it loses a larger proportion (though not a larger total number) of its customers.

The type-3 rivalry case in Figure 7.7 can also be modified to show customers' total purchases being shared amongst three rival stores rather than two.

---

### Doing it right: simplifying the display of multiple competitors

Extending the rivalry frameworks from two firms to just three, as shown in Figure 7.31 and 7.32, adds further complexity to diagrams that are already complicated, so extending to four, five or more quickly makes the figures too messy to work with. There are three ways of dealing with this:

1. *Focus on key competitors only.* Even when many competitors exist, the main competitive threat or opportunity is often focused on just a small number. Indeed, as explained in Chapter 5, an important skill in setting competitive strategy is the choice of which rival offers the best chance for our firm to attack, so selecting that target reduces the problem of analysis back to one of the one-on-one structures already discussed. If this choice is made, it is of course advisable to remain alert to the activities of other rivals, even if the details of rivalry dynamics with each are not assessed in detail.

2. *Show several competitors on the same charts.* Simplifying to just a single competitor is often inadequate for assessing competitive dynamics, so you may need to examine customer movements and purchase rates versus a few specific rivals. In the car industry, for example, Mercedes is especially concerned with how it is performing against BMW and Lexus, but may feel it can largely ignore both the threat and opportunity from Ford, Renault or Nissan. It is not necessary, however, to add separate customer resource and flow rate icons for every rival—simply show charts for two or three competitors on a simpler picture with just "us" versus "rivals." For example, rather than add the third customer stock to the right of Figure 7.31—simply put the time charts for both competitors into the second stock, using different colours or line styles. It is certainly possible to handle up to three competitors that way with relative ease. You can do the same with the flow rates

into each rival's customer base by putting a single flow rate into the stock for the multiple rivals and again show separate time charts for each.

Type-2 rivalry can be handled similarly, by sticking with two customer stocks rather than three as shown in Figure 7.33. Note, however that this loses the flows of customers that do not involve us, such as those customers moving between rival 1 and rival 2.

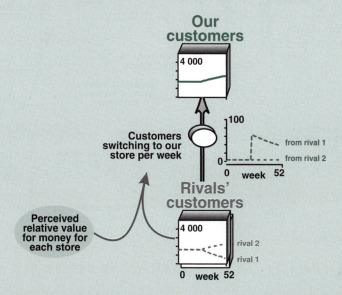

**Figure 7.33: Two rivals in a single stock for type-2 rivalry in coffee stores.**

3.  *Treat competitors in groups.* If several rivals are somewhat similar, they can be grouped and effectively treated as one larger combined competitor, although with appropriately modified assessment of the strength of their overall business. This treatment of several competitors as a "strategic group" is already established as an important principle in strategy and will be developed further in this chapter (see p.491).

Figure 7.34 shows the competition for shelf space amongst consumer goods suppliers from Figure 7.22 adapted to show us competing with four rivals rather than one. The store's locality contains the same number of consumers but their purchases are now split amongst five possible products. It is assumed that the store starts by

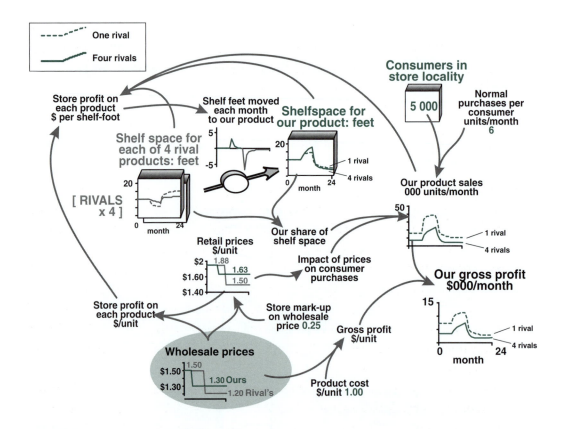

**Figure 7.34:** Rivalry for store shelf space versus one competitor or four.

offering the same shelf space to each rival, regardless of whether there are two or five competitors; in other words, with five suppliers there is 2.5 times the amount of shelf space in total. This is not likely in practice, as the store would not expect 2.5 times the volume of sales with five products versus two, but is chosen to simplify comparison.

When competing against four rival products, our price cut and the resulting increase in the store's profit per foot again causes us to win shelf space from the competing products. The store now continues giving our product more shelf space because, as we now do not dominate its shelves to the same degree, its policy of rebalancing space does not hold our product back. Sharing the same base demand with four rivals rather than one means that we (and each rival) start with only 40% of the sales rate we received with only one competitor. With four products to win from rather than one, we now receive a proportionately greater increase in sales when we are given more shelf space.

Unfortunately, we also suffer more when all four competitors cut price in the later period. With the store making more cash margin per foot on all four rival products than on ours, it takes more space from us than with only one rival product to spread around the larger number of alternatives.

## ASSESSING CUSTOMER CHOICES AMONGST MULTIPLE COMPETITORS

The display of multiple competitors is problematic but the more substantive challenge concerns how to understand customers' responses, now that they have the choice of more than two alternatives. Chapters 2 and 3 introduced the value curve framework and explained that it is a simplification of a sophisticated tool in market research known as conjoint analysis. It seeks to explain how customers trade-off different benefits offered by a product or service, and compare them with the benefits they would prefer. With multiple competitors, customers now have a choice between the unique sets of benefits provided by each alternative, and their trade-off now determines the rate at which they decide to move between more possible states and/or alter their rate of purchase.

Figure 7.35 illustrates how this value curve assessment links to the win rates of customers for new coffee stores in Figure 7.31. It would explain how strongly customers rate our store against rival 1 and against rival 2, and how they rate rival 1 versus rival 2. In the second period of Figure 7.31, we and the second rival have lowered our prices, so have moved to a position where we exceed customers' expectation for "low price." The first rival increased its price, believing that its superior rating on choice and quality of environment would still win customers in spite of the higher price. However, its poor rating on quality of service wiped out these two advantages, so the choice came back to being predominantly driven by price.

Similar analyses will explain customers' decisions to *switch between* rivals in type-2 rivalry, and to *allocate their purchases* in type-3 rivalry. As noted in earlier chapters, customer research typically examines the state in which customers reside (being loyal to us or disloyal to both us and rival 1, for example), and their rate of purchase. Rarely does research address the critical question determining how performance will change into the future, namely the rate at which customers are changing between states; for example, potential customers becoming loyal to us each month, or switching from us to a competitor.

In practice, the customer research to address these questions accurately is complex and requires careful design. It is further complicated in many cases by

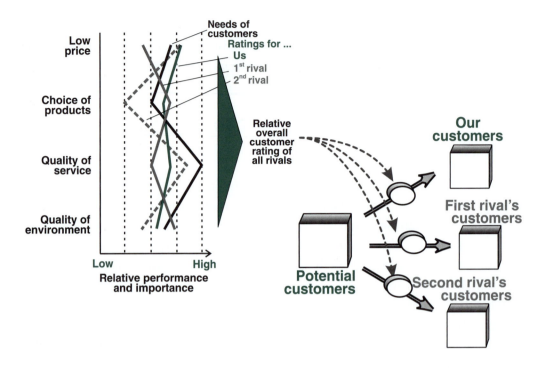

**Figure 7.35: How consumer research and value curve analysis informs customer win rates in type-1 rivalry for coffee stores.**

the need to explain not just how average customers behave but also how distinct *groups* of customers make decisions. The cost and effort of such complex research may be justifiable for large organizations with large revenues and potential profits at stake but will be beyond the reach of small or mid-size organizations. In these circumstances, it is nevertheless valuable to have a clear picture in principle of what is driving relative performance versus competitors, as shown in Figure 7.35, and to seek indicative evidence as to what rivals are offering and how customers are responding. Such evidence can be assembled from our own estimation of competitors' products and services, from informal feedback via sales people or customer service staff, or from small-scale efforts simply to ask customers their opinion. The CEO of one small clothing supplier, for example, made a point of visiting its largest customer's main stores whenever a new product line was introduced to watch consumers' responses and ask their opinion. Armed with this informal assessment, he returned to his business to make modifications to the product's design and inform his team for the design of future products—far preferable to relying on the product's weekly sales figures alone.

The principles for dealing with multi-rival competition are directly applicable to B2B cases, and can also be used in noncommercial cases. The principles also apply to the winning and retention of staff. People seek different things from their jobs and careers, and balance them in different ways. As remarked on earlier in this chapter, choosing to join and stay with an employer, or switch to alternative employment is closely analogous to the choices made by customers, so Figure 7.35 is readily adapted to dealing with situations where several organizations are competing to win and retain people from a large group of potential or existing staff.

## SIMPLIFYING MULTI-COMPETITOR DYNAMICS WITH STRATEGIC GROUPS

It is generally important for management to focus attention on their rivalry with specific competitors, be they old, new or potential entrants. However, it is sometimes necessary to look more widely. Returning to the car industry example, Mercedes gains new customers who graduate from less-premium vehicles as a result of increases in their personal income. The company may therefore want to assess the extent to which manufacturers of those vehicles are succeeding in retaining customers by offering more sophisticated models of their own. For this purpose, it may be sufficient to track only how a group of lesser manufacturers is adding to its product range in this way, and the rate at which they are collectively enjoying sales of those vehicles—sales that might otherwise have come to Mercedes.

As explained in Chapter 5, it is sometimes helpful to understand how an entire industry has developed and how it will likely evolve in future (see Figure 5.27). In cases involving many competitors it is quite impractical—and unnecessary—to evaluate customer and sales dynamics amongst all unique rivals.

To deal with these two needs, multicompetitor industries can often be simplified by adding similar rivals together into what are known as "strategic groups." Individual firms in a strategic group are similar to each other on various important dimensions, such as the market segment they serve, the channels to market they use, the range, performance and/or price position of their products, and so on, but differ significantly from other firms or groups on those same issues. We can then track how well we are competing against the whole group. We too may be part of a strategic group of our own. If the insight we need is not too detailed, we could then treat our close rivals too as a group. Alternatively, we could analyse how competition is working *both* with each close rival *and* with one or more other groups. So Mercedes might track its competitive interactions with (1) BMW and Lexus specifically, (2) with a group including other premium brands, and (3) with a third group consisting of those less-premium producers who are trying to retain higher-value customers by offering more sophisticated models.

Whilst much work has been done to refine exactly what is meant by a strategic group, a useful start-point comes from an early definition of the term:

> **... a group of firms in an industry following the same or a similar strategy along strategic dimensions.**[10]

The strategic dimensions referred to include a wide range of factors, covering sources of competitive advantage (e.g. relative cost position, product differentiation, technological lead), policies (e.g. pricing, service support, choice of distribution channel), as well as wider considerations, such as whether the firm is part of a larger corporation and whether it is vertically integrated; that is, owns its own sources of supply or sales channels.

The important consideration for choosing the dimensions on which groups differ is whether these dimensions constitute a "mobility barrier," preventing a firm in one group trying to compete directly with firms in another group. Many full-service airlines, for example, have found that the complex and costly resources of their business model, such as prime-time take-off slots at major airport hubs, make it impossible for them to move their business into the low-fare segment. The few successful efforts have required these firms to create a new business quite separate from the full-service parent company, effectively starting up as a new entrant in the low-fare strategic group. In the brewing industry, successful local producers in many countries face a major mobility barrier to joining the group of global brands in the form of the brand recognition that those major products have built over many years.

An extensive investigation of strategic groups dating from 1986 identified three broad categories of mobility barriers that may arise (Table 7.5), and these remain broadly useful to this day, though the arrival of the Internet and the Web-based strategies this has made possible have undoubtedly altered the relative influence of these factors to varying degrees in different industries.[11]

By seeking systematic differences between firms on factors such as those in Table 7.5, it is often possible to clarify exactly how groups of firms differ, and produce an *industry segmentation*. Though there is a connection between this concept and "market segmentation," the two should not be confused. Market segmentation seeks differences between the characteristics and needs of subgroups of customers and channels. Industry segmentation, in contrast, seeks differences between firms

TABLE 7.5: **SOURCES OF MOBILITY BARRIERS AGAINST THE MOVEMENT OF FIRMS BETWEEN STRATEGIC GROUPS**

| Market-related strategies | Supply and cost characteristics | Characteristics of the firms themselves |
|---|---|---|
| Product range | Economies of scale in production, marketing and administration | Ownerships |
| User technologies | | Organization structure |
| Market segmentation | Manufacturing processes R&D capability | Control systems |
| Distribution channels | | Management skills |
| Brand names | Marketing and distribution systems | Firm boundaries (diversification and vertical integration) |
| Geographic coverage | | Firm size |
| Selling systems | | Relationships with influence groups |

serving that market. Those differences include the quantities and types of resources they employ and how these are structured, capabilities they have developed, and a wide variety of policies they adopt, including of course the choice of which market segments to serve.

The concept of strategic groups has developed somewhat since it emerged in the strategy field, and discussion and examples of the concept can be found in many strategy texts.[12] Some uncertainty remains about the importance of strategic groups, and even about whether they exist at all.[13] Much of the research effort seeking evidence to confirm or deny the existence of strategic groups focuses on analysis of differences in financial performance. However, it is not clear that this line of enquiry would detect strategic groups of similar firms, even if they existed. It is quite plausible, for example, that two firms could achieve very similar financial returns, even if their operating model or policies are quite different. Indeed, firms choose to operate in one group or another precisely because profitability can be obtained in each. It is also plausible that two firms could be committing similar fractions of revenue to marketing or R&D, for example, whilst using that expenditure in quite different ways. Conversely, it is equally possible for two firms possessing similar sets of resources and pursuing similar policies—which would put them in the same strategic group—to achieve very different financial performance despite these strategic similarities. Many low-fare airlines have struggled or failed financially, even though operating near-identical business models to those of the well-known success cases.

Regardless of this theoretical debate, industry executives are often clear that groups of firms exist that differ from each other significantly in what their member firms possess and how they behave. Furthermore, it seems that perceptions of these differences are widely shared between executives from different firms in the industry.[14] For the practical purpose of developing and directing strategy over time, then it is undoubtedly useful to group firms in ways that are reasonably reliable and stable, using the principles outlined above. If this grouping is accurate, groups of firms will likely differ in ways that affect the competition between them for building and retaining resource.

- *Different resources may be involved in the architectures.* A clear example concerns Dell's architecture for competing in the PC market, which does not include retailers whilst Hewlett Packard's does, and Amazon.com operates no stores whilst Barnes & Noble does. Some banks' product ranges include their own noncore banking products, such as investment funds, whilst others only resell products from other providers.

- *There may be significant differences in the quantity or attributes of resources at their disposal.* Mercedes differs significantly from, say, Honda in both the number and affluence of the consumers who own its cars, as well as in the number and location-quality of its dealer outlets. Southwest Airlines, AirAsia and Ryanair differ from American Airlines, Singapore Airlines and Lufthansa in the quality of airports between which they fly (even if they operated between similar *numbers* of airports). Exxon-Mobil and Royal Dutch/Shell differ from Petronas and Petrobras, the Malaysian and Brazilian national oil companies respectively, in both the scale and geographical spread of their oil production sources, refining plants and downstream distribution and sales channels.

- *They will likely differ in the policies that they pursue.* In the newspaper and other media sectors, some firms focus on content to win viewers or readers, whilst others are advertizing-led. The extreme cases are TV shopping channels and some free papers, which win their audience largely due to the advertizing they carry. The holiday industry features firms who offer apparently similar styles of holidays, aimed at similar groups of tourists, but whereas some firms advertize intensively, and maintain a price premium to sustain this cost, others consistently price more cheaply and rely on tourists to discover the better value on offer.

These three considerations help to clarify both the similarities between firms within an industry segment and the key differences they exhibit when compared with competitors in other groups. The three distinctions may overlap in many cases—for example, you can't have a policy towards distributor incentives if, by selling directly, your architecture does not include distributors.

The principles of rivalry dynamics discussed earlier in this chapter are readily adapted to deal with strategic groups, as well as or instead of individual competitors. The firms in a group can be treated as a collective "competitor," and their resources shown in aggregate. For example, all the customers of a group's member firms can be displayed on the architecture as a single stock and flows of customers into and out of that stock can also be aggregated. Similarly, all of the group's staff of some type can be shown as a single stock, and our firm's success or failure in winning and retaining staff versus that group can be captured in just the same way as for individual competitors.

# RIVALRY IN THE LOW-FARE AIRLINE INDUSTRY

Earlier chapters have built up the strategic architecture for a low-fare airline (Chapter 4) and shown how attributes of key resources in such a business operate (Chapter 5). The airline industry is intensely competitive of course, especially in regard to winning and keeping customers and capturing the largest possible amount of their travel needs. The transparency of fares and the ease with which customers can often switch between rival airlines exacerbate the intensity of competition and explain why so many firms in the industry struggle for profitability. The main characteristic of the market that limits this otherwise frictionless movement of customers' choice is the limited number of services that less busy travel routes can support.

The frameworks for customer rivalry introduced at the start of this chapter are therefore directly applicable to airlines. In the full-service sector, some genuine loyalty to specific airlines is common, driven by frequent-flyer programs as well as by customers' experience of reliability and service with specific firms. Loyalty is hard to achieve in the low-fare sector, where customer choice is so strongly motivated by price. This makes it especially important for airlines to win the competitive battle for the major scarce resource—routes.

Competition for air-travel routes also features all three of the rivalry mechanisms, though with particular adjustments characteristic of the issue in this industry.

Unlike customers, routes do not "decide" which airline to deal with, so if access to airports were unconstrained, rivalry would simply be a matter of which routes each airline chose to operate. Airport access is, however, often limited by their capacity to handle aircraft departures and landings, so those close to important travel destinations often have some power to levy substantial charges for airlines that wish to use them. In the case of major hubs, such as New York JFK and London Heathrow, the attraction of the airport to travelers is so strong that many airlines are desperate to win take-off slots, especially those at the busiest times of the week. Airport slots are therefore a special case of rivalry for supply of a scarce resource.

Many low-fare airlines have limited this difficulty of airport access by two means. First, on busy routes, they deliberately choose secondary airports rather than the major hubs. Even if these airports are inconvenient to travelers, the big savings on fares compared with full service competitors means that large numbers of customers still choose the service. Furthermore, the secondary airports are often so anxious to win passenger traffic to boost their own income that they offer very good terms to airlines that choose to use them—in some cases even subsidizing a popular airline that is considering services through that location. This of course helps the airline drive down its own costs and therefore keep passenger fares as low as possible.

The second way in which low-fare airlines mitigate the problem of limited access to popular airports is by starting operations on routes that have previously been unserved. This is a powerful example of firms creating the very market that they themselves then serve, rather than waiting for "market demand" to grow until it is viable for them to provide for it. The histories of all successful low-fare airlines have featured continual and rapid expansion onto routes that previously had no direct airline service. Once again, the airports on these newly served routes are keen to welcome the starting up of services into their facility. Indeed, this welcome often extends beyond the airport to encompass the entire local economy—many towns and cities see the arrival of a low-fare airline as a major catalyst for their communities, especially for sectors such as construction, retailing and leisure.

Figure 7.36 shows a 15-year scenario for competition between two major low-fare airlines to open routes in a fast-developing regional market. The competitor started operating before our airline, at a time when there was estimated to be 50 potential routes that could support a low-fare service. The competitor grew rapidly over the first few years, growing to about 30 routes on its own, at which time we started operating in the same market, but on different routes ("sole" routes are those on which the airline is the only low-fare provider operating, although full-service airlines may be present). We started opening routes relatively slowly, then, as

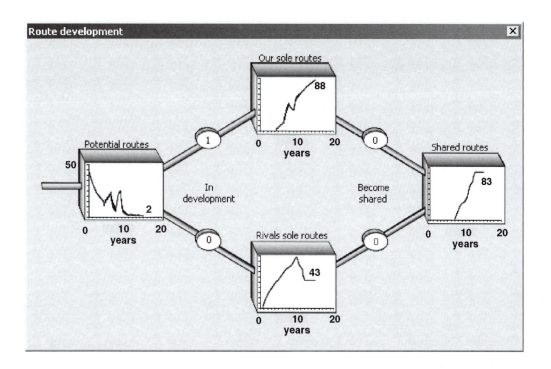

**Figure 7.36: Rivalry by low-fare airlines to open routes in a major regional market.\***

confidence grew, opened a large number of routes in quick succession. By the end of year eight we were operating 44 routes versus the competitor's 64.

As the two airlines grew, the appeal of their services stimulated demand to create more potential new routes, a clear case of the key mechanism mentioned earlier in this chapter, namely the emergence of new potential resources. However, our rapid growth in year eight depleted this potential significantly, forcing the competitor to start operations on routes that we previously served alone and converting *our sole routes* into *shared routes*. By the end of that year, we were competing directly on 20 routes. By year 15, both firms have grown strongly and used up all the new opportunities they can find, so neither airline is able to grow except by invading each others' routes—a strategy each seems reluctant to pursue.

Figure 7.37 shows the state of our business at the end of year eight, when this head-on rivalry was at its most aggressive. Having enjoyed a few years of growing

---

\* The LoFare Airline Microworld from which Figures 7.36–7.38 were taken is a PC-based simulation, in which individuals or groups can experience strategy in this intensely competitive industry. Information on how to obtain this software is available at www.strategydynamics.com.

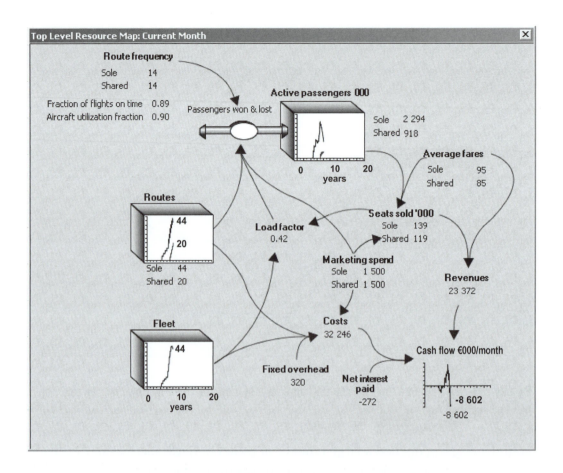

**Figure 7.37:** Summary strategic architecture and performance for our airline after 8 years of the market's development.

revenues and cash flows from operating large numbers of routes with no low-fare rivals, the main competitor's arrival on 20 of our routes had stolen substantial numbers of passengers from our airline. We suffered this loss of business despite having reduced our average fare to €85 per flight. Taken together, the loss of passenger traffic and lower price have badly damaged our cash flow.

From year eight onwards, competition was fierce, and we were forced to reduce price levels substantially, especially on shared routes (Figure 7.38). We also reduced prices on the routes we served alone, to deter the competitor's entry.

This intense rivalry for route expansion is highly evident in the low-fare sector, and has progressed well beyond the development described in the figures above. In Europe, for example, the situation between the two largest competitors in early 2007 was as follows:

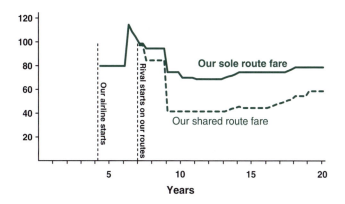

**Figure 7.38: Our airline's pricing levels on sole and shared routes.**

- easyJet's network covered 292 routes and 75 airports in 20 countries.
- Ryanair operated 381 routes, serving 130 destinations, also in 20 countries.

## RELATED RIVALRY FOR ROUTES AND PASSENGERS

As mentioned above, routes do not really "choose" whether to be served by one or other of these airlines, or by both. Nevertheless, each competitor is undoubtedly engaged in a race to serve new routes and to enter successfully into routes already served by other airlines. When this second stage of competition starts, it initiates further competition, this time for passengers. Chapter 5 already explained how the opening of routes for airlines brings with it access to potential passengers via a "co-flow" mechanism, with those potential passengers being an attribute of each new route (Figure 5.19).

Figure 7.39 shows the rivalry structure for the competition to win passengers and journeys on shared routes alone. Even though we may share these routes with rivals, there will be passengers who favor our airline over the competitor, whether because of convenient flight times, their experience of our service or for other reasons. Other passengers will favor the competitors. A further group will not be loyal to either airline. Our total sales on shared routes will therefore be the sum of the total journeys made by our loyal customers, plus our share of the journeys taken by disloyal users.

Note that, whenever we open a new route on which competitors already operate, we effectively dump into our system the potential to access the current number of passengers flying with the competitors (i.e. people in the lower stock in Figure 7.39), plus any inactive potential passengers (people in the leftmost stock). We also give

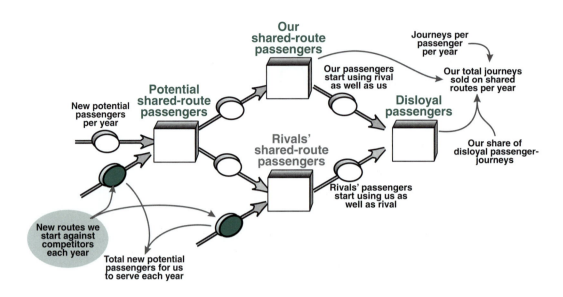

**Figure 7.39:** Starting services on competitors' routes gives us access to their current and potential passengers.

ourselves access to the stream of totally new potential passengers who emerge each year, whether these arise for demographic or economic reasons, or because of the increasing attractiveness of the competing services.

**Summary of Chapter 7**

Three distinct mechanisms explain how competing firms win and lose customers and sales. These mechanisms may also apply to other resources, including staff, intermediaries, and sources of supply. They also apply in many public service and voluntary organizations, even though these may not be competing in a commercial sense, for example in relation to staff and sources of funding.

Type-1 rivalry explains how rivalry works when firms try to capture potential new customers. This mechanism dominates in growing markets. The process also continues in mature markets if new customers emerge to replace those who leave the market, due for example to demographic effects.

In emerging markets, competitors' efforts may substantially accelerate the development of potential customers, and can even cause our sales to grow faster than if we were serving the market alone. There is also the risk that our efforts may create potential demand that is then taken by rivals. Type-1 rivalry can also be renewed whenever a new generation of products is introduced, at which point customers or users of existing products form an important part of the new potential. In project-based industries, efforts to win business from the stream of new opportunities effectively becomes a constant type-1 challenge.

Type-2 rivalry explains how existing customers are captured from rival firms. It applies most strongly in mature markets, but can start as soon as more than one competitor has won some customers. Switching costs may slow down or prevent customers being won from competitors, even if they would otherwise prefer our product or service, so the benefits need to be sufficient to overcome this barrier. Competitors often try to put up barriers to prevent customers leaving them and to overcome barriers erected by rivals.

Type-3 rivalry concerns how rivals fight for share of sales to customers who buy from more than one firm. It is therefore most significant when most customers are disloyal in their purchases, and may not be significant in markets where this is not easily possible, such as cell-phone services and power supply. Type-3 rivalry for staff is very unusual, as most people work only for a single employer.

It may be ideal if management can find ways of offering customers products or services whose benefits are so different from competitors that it would take a long time before competitors can replicate those benefits—what is known as a "blue ocean" strategy. So long as this is not possible, however, management continue to face the challenge of handling more head-on rivalry.

Game theory offers some insight into the consequences of how we interact with competitors on certain key decisions, such as pricing or marketing spend, but to make effective use of the method requires a clear understanding of the likely pay-off, given alternative competitive responses. It is precisely the estimation of that pay-off that is complex, reflecting as it does the dynamics of customer behavior across multiple choice factors from multiple competitors.

The three types of rivalry frequently operate together, with new customers being won, existing customers being tempted to switch, and disloyal customers' business being fought for. These processes concern different decisions being made by different people, so competitive efforts need to be made with a conscious choice about which decisions we want to be made by which customers—are we hoping to persuade new customers to join us, existing customers to stay with us, or disloyal customers to buy more from us?

Customers are rarely rational in how they choose amongst alternative products or suppliers. There may also be considerable delays between events that should trigger their response, such as a change in price or product performance, and their acting on that event. These factors can cause consequences that continue long after a decision or action on the part of ourselves or our competitors. They also imply that great caution should be used when estimating demand elasticity. Finally, they can give rise to path dependency, in which the consequences of decisions or actions by competing firms depend on the sequence, scale and timing of those events.

Real-world competition usually involves more than one competitor, which complicates both the display and analysis of competitive dynamics. First, it is important to identify whether it may be appropriate and safe to focus analysis on just one competitor, even if several others exist. If that is not adequate, it may still be possible to focus analysis on a small number of key rivals. If that is still insufficiently precise, other competitors can be clustered into strategic groups, where firms with similar resources and behaviors can be treated as a single class of rival.

In the low-fare airline industry, rivalry focuses on the race to develop new routes with the potential to serve significant numbers of customers, or else on the question of whether to start operations on routes already served by others. When offering services on the same routes as rivals, one then needs to examine rivalry for passengers in detail.

# SUGGESTED QUESTIONS AND EXERCISES

1. Describe the three main mechanisms by which competition works. In what circumstances is each most likely to be found?

2. Apart from customers, for what other types of resource may rivals compete? Which can apply to not-for-profit cases?

3. Why must care be taken when using estimates for elasticity of demand to make decisions?

4. Describe a situation in which type-1 and type-2 competition are both taking place and explain whether their relative importance is changing and why.

5. Use the worksheets at the end of this chapter to lay out the rivalry structures that will be likely for one or more of the following examples (continued from the exercises at the end of Chapter 4):

   a. a retail chain, such as Starbucks
   b. a company manufacturing and servicing elevators
   c. an online dating agency
   d. a voluntary organization providing medical centers in locations that have no alternative provision (include competition for resources other than "customers").

6. What makes it possible for a competitor's presence in a market to accelerate our own sales growth? Why might the same mechanism lead to us helping our competitor capture sales faster than we do ourselves?

7. Describe what happens to the type-1 rivalry mechanism when a new generation of products is introduced by all competitors.

8. What role do switching costs play in type-2 rivalry cases? What impact do they have on the rate at which competitors can steal customers from each other?

9. Why are customers not entirely rational in their purchase decisions? What impact does this have on customer switching and competitors' sales over time?

10. Describe and sketch the rivalry mechanism that operates when competitors try to capture sales from end-customers who can only be reached through intermediaries such as stores, wholesalers or distributors.

11. What factors may account for the limited use of game theory by management to assist in competitive decision making?

12. In what ways can the three rivalry mechanisms be simplified when there are many competitors involved? Give an example of each, choosing a market in each case that would make the simplification appropriate.

13.  What characteristics may firms in a strategic group share that distinguishes them from other firms in the same industry?

14.  What are the key resources over which airlines compete, and which rivalry mechanisms apply? How do these mechanisms affect the decisions that rival airlines must take in developing their business?

# USING WORKSHEETS 10–12

The worksheets on the following pages can be used to sketch out the following rivalry mechanisms:

- type-1 rivalry (Worksheets 10a and 10b)
- type-2 rivalry (Worksheet 11)
- type-3 rivalry (Worksheet 12).

For combinations of rivalry mechanisms, e.g. type-1 and type-2 rivalry operating together, or rivalry involving intermediaries, copy elements from these worksheets and follow the principles explained in the relevant section of this chapter to assemble the structure appropriate to the situation you are investigating.

These worksheets can be used either (1) with current-period numbers only, to assess today's situation and immediate decisions, or (2) with historic and future time-path data to identify how competitive performance is changing over time and how decisions should be made as the situation develops.

The following steps should be taken first, whichever worksheet is being used:

- specify the timescale and frequency over which the situation is to be examined, for example two years back and three years forward in months, and the scale for all variables (this step is not required if the worksheets are only to be used to examine the current period)
- identify and name the resource that is being competed for and put the appropriate label on each resource-stock in the worksheet
- add a timescale and value scale to each stock, and insert data or estimates for how those quantities have changed in the past and might change in the future
- name the flows that move the resource from potential to each competitor, or between competitors, remembering the rule that these flows *must* be expressed in terms of "units per period," for example customers won *per month*, or customers lost to rival *per year*
- if using the worksheet for examining how competition has played out in the past and may develop in future (rather than just a snapshot of

the current situation), sketch what has happened to each flow rate over time, making sure that the numbers reconcile with the stocks that they are affecting—look back to the figures in this chapter to check that your diagrams are correct.

## NOTES ON THE WORKSHEETS

1. Throughout these worksheets, "product" implies product or service.
2. To use the worksheets with rivalry for staff or other resources, the resource-stocks themselves need to be renamed and the factors driving resource movements will also need revising; for example, *staff hired from rival per year* may depend on *our salaries* and *rival salaries*, instead of customer movements depending on prices.
3. If working with a durable or semi-durable product or service, the stocks of *our customers* and *rivals customers'* will capture the number of owners of the product, so should be renamed for example *our owners* and *rivals' owners*. Note also that *sales* will be driven by both the flow of new owners per period, plus the stock of owners multiplied by the replacement rate (see Chapter 4, Figure 4.11).
4. For simplicity, a single variable is shown for *our marketing* and for *rival marketing*. It may be necessary to show more elements of marketing and sales, such as sales calls per period.
5. If dealing with more than one competitor, follow the advice in this chapter for keeping the diagrams simple:

   — put information for each competitor on a single chart, using different colours or line styles for each
   — if necessary, redraw the worksheet to display two or more competitors
   — group similar competitors together and show their total customers, etc. in the charts.

Additional instructions for each specific worksheet follow.

## WORKSHEETS 10A AND 10B: TYPE-1 RIVALRY

Worksheet 10a is sufficient if the potential market is not increasing. If the potential *is* increasing, it is likely that the products, pricing, etc. of competitors will be affecting its growth, and Worksheet 10b will be needed.

After specifying the timescale of the challenge, the resources involved and the flow rates:

- enter the current number for potential customers, our customers and rival's customers in the resource-stocks
- enter or estimate the rate at which you and your competitor(s) are winning customers from the potential population
- enter the product performance, price, marketing and other factors relating to both your firm and your competitor(s), and explain clearly the relationship between these items and the customer win rate; for example, "we are winning customers twice as fast as our competitor, and since our products are similar, this seems to be due to our price being 5% lower, and our 30% greater rate of marketing"
- use the worksheet to explore alternatives; for example, what would happen if your competitor improved its product so that customers rated it 10% superior to yours? What would then happen if you reduced the price by a further 10%?

## WORKSHEET 11: TYPE-2 RIVALRY

After specifying the timescale of the challenge, the resources involved and the flow rates:

- enter the current number for our customers and rival's customers in the resource-stocks
- enter or estimate the rate at which you are winning customers from your competitor, and/or it is winning customers from you (note that it is quite possible for some customers to move from you to the competitor at the same time as others move from the competitor to you, so show both rates on the chart if you believe this to be happening)
- enter the product performance, price, marketing and other factors relating to both your firm and your competitor(s), and explain clearly the relationship between these items and the customer switch rate; for example, "we are winning 20 customers per month from our competitor, because we are making 50 calls per month on their customers, and the product and price are significantly better" (replace *marketing* with *sales calls* in this case)
- use the worksheet to explore alternatives; for example, what would happen if your competitor switched its own sales effort away from trying to win your customers and back on to defending its existing customers?

## WORKSHEET 12: TYPE-3 RIVALRY

After specifying the timescale of the challenge, the resources involved and the flow rates:

- enter the current number of nonexclusive, or disloyal, customers that you share with your competitor(s)
- enter or estimate the rate at which this number of shared customers is changing over time, for example because the overall market is growing, or because loyal customers are starting to buy from competitors
- enter the product performance, price, marketing and other factors relating to both your firm and your competitor(s), and explain clearly the relationship between these items and the customers' purchase rate; for example, "we are winning 65% of shared customers' business, because our competitor's price is 7% higher than ours for a comparable product"
- use the worksheet to explore alternatives; for example, what would happen if your competitor matched your price or if it undercut your price by 5%?

# WORKSHEET 10A: TYPE-1 RIVALRY

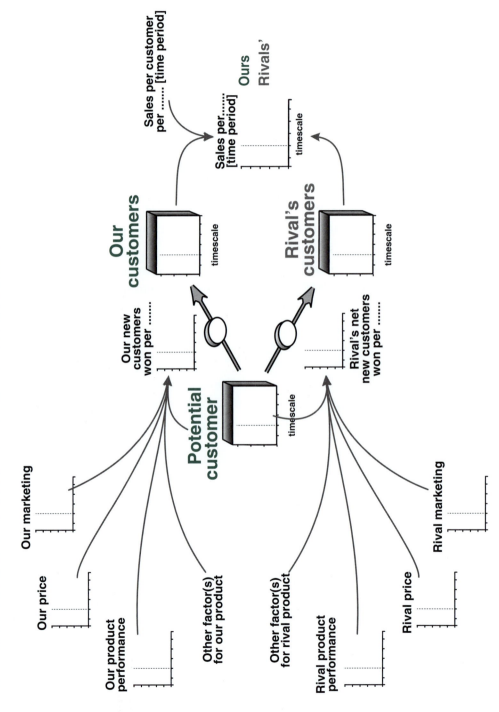

# WORKSHEET 10B: TYPE-1 RIVALRY (WITH INCREASING MARKET POTENTIAL)

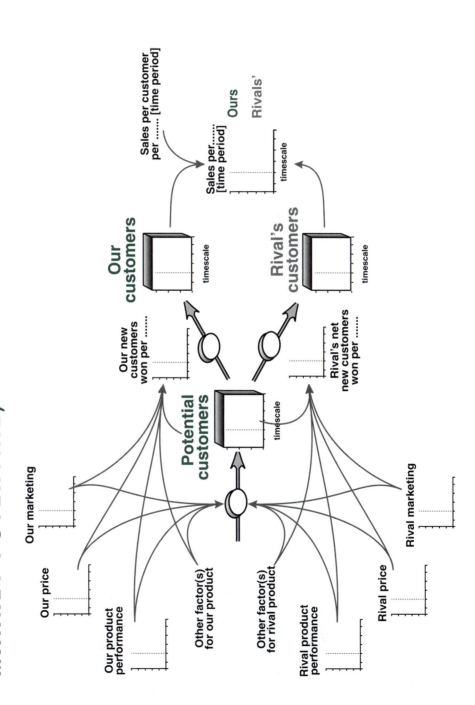

# WORKSHEET 11: TYPE-2 RIVALRY

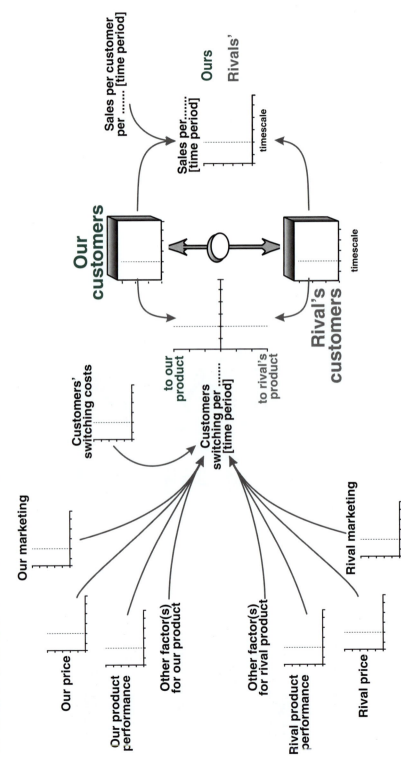

# WORKSHEET 12: TYPE-3 RIVALRY

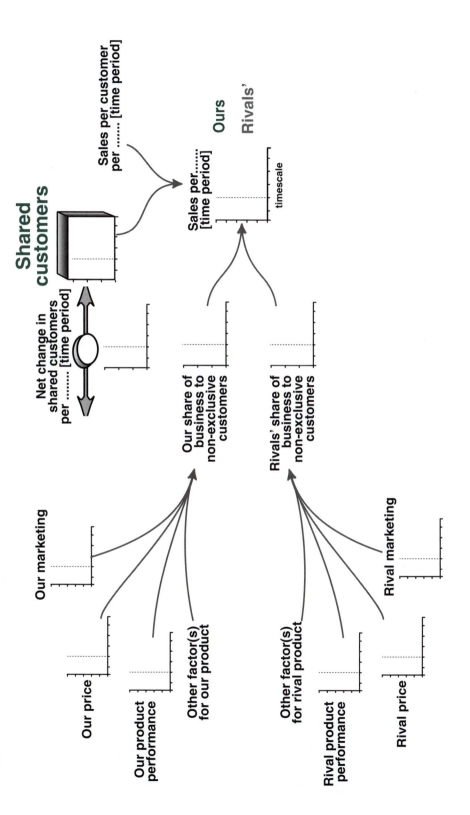

# NOTES

1.  For more on first-mover advantage, see Barney, J. (2007) *Gaining and Sustaining Competitive Advantage*, 3rd edn, Pearson, Upper Saddle River, NJ, pp. 90–93 and Markides, C. and Geroski, P. (2005) *Fast Second*, John Wiley & Sons, Ltd, Chichester. A theoretical discussion of the principles of first-mover advantages, along with their disadvantages and the advantages of followers, can be found in Lieberman, M.B. and Montgomery, D.B. (1998) First-mover (dis)advantages: retrospective and link with the resource-based view, *Strategic Management Journal*, **19**(12), 1111–1125.

2.  Explanations of price elasticity of demand are given in all good economics textbooks. Its relevance to strategy and the relationship with other basic principles of microeconomics are explained in Besanko, D., Dranove, D., Shanley, M. and Schaefer, S. (2004) *The Economics of Strategy*, 3rd edn, John Wiley & Sons, Ltd, Chichester, Introduction.

3.  Chan Kim, W. and Mauborgne, R. (2004) Blue Ocean Strategy, *Harvard Business Review*, **82**(10), October, 76–85; and Chan Kim, W. and Mauborgne, R. (2004) *Blue Ocean Strategy: How to Create Uncontested Market Space and Make the Competition Irrelevant*, Harvard Business School Press, Boston.

4.  For more on dynamic issues in project-based firms see for example Bayer, S. and Gann, D. (2006), Balancing work: bidding strategies and workload dynamics in a project-based professional service organisation, *System Dynamics Review*, **22**(3), 185–211.

5.  See Besanko, D., Darnove, D., Shanley, M. and Schaefer, S. (2004) *Economics of Strategy*, 3rd edn, John Wiley & Sons, Ltd, Chichester, Chapter 12; Farrell, J. and Shapiro, C. (1988) Dynamic competition and switching costs, *RAND Journal of Economics*, **19**, 123–137.

6.  An early description of bounded rationality was given by Herbert Simon 1955, 'A behavioral model of rational choice', *The Quarterly Journal of Economics*, Vol. 69, No. 1, pp. 99–118. For a more recent discussion of the phenomenon, see Gigerenzer, G. and Selten, R. (2002) *Bounded Rationality*, The MIT Press, Cambridge, MA.

7.  Numerous books provide information and examples of how game theory works and how it can be applied. See for example Dutta, P. (2000) *Strategies and Games: Theory and Practice*, MIT Press, Boston, MA; Miller, J. (2003) *Game Theory At Work*, McGraw-Hill, Boston, MA.

8.  Articles that discuss the contribution of game theory to business include Brandenburger, A. and Nalebuff, B. (1995) The right game: use game theory to

shape strategy, *Harvard Business Review*, **73**(4), July-August, 57–74; Courtney, H., Kirkland, J. and Viguerie, P. (1997) Strategy under uncertainty, *Harvard Business Review*, **75**(6), November-December, 66–81 and Courtney, H. (2000) Games managers should play, *McKinsey Quarterly Strategy Anthology*, Vol. 1, pp. 91–96.

9. A summary of some critiques of game theory's value to strategy is given by Powell, J.H. (2003) Game theory in strategy, in *The Oxford Handbook of Strategy (Volume II)* (Eds Faulkner, D. and Campbell, A.), Blackwell, Oxford, pp. 383–415.

10. Porter, M. (1980) *Competitive Strategy*, Free Press, New York, Chapter 7.

11. McGee, J. and Thomas, H. (1986) Strategic groups: theory, research and taxonomy, *Strategic Management Journal*, **7**(2), 141–160.

12. Some discussion and examples of strategic groups can be found in Grant, R.M. (2005) *Contemporary Strategy Analysis*, 5th edn, Blackwell, Oxford, Chapter 4; McGee, J., Thomas, H. and Wilson, D. (2005) *Strategy: Analysis and Practice*, McGraw-Hill, Maidenhead, Chapter 6; Johnson, G., Scholes, K. and Whittington, R. (2005) *Exploring Corporate Strategy*, 7th edn, Prentice Hall, Harlow, Chapter 2.

13. Dranove, D., Peteraf, M. and Shanley, M. (1998) Do strategic groups exist? An economic framework for analysis, *Strategic Management Journal*, **19**(11), 1029–1044.

14. Reger, R. and Huff, A. (1993) Strategic groups: a cognitive perspective, *Strategic Management Journal*, **14**(2), 103–124; Daniels, K., Johnson, G. and De Chernatony, L. (1994) Differences in managerial cognitions of competition, *British Journal of Management*, **5**(s1), 21–s29.

# GOALS AND CONTROLS

## DIFFERENT TYPES OF STRATEGIC DECISION

Strategic decision-making covers such a wide range of issues confronting management that it is important to organize these in some way, to see where they arise and how they are connected. A logical approach is to follow a more or less chronological sequence, although it will not be possible to treat these questions in complete isolation from each other:

1. *Whether to take part.* Following through the life cycle of a business concept, the first likely question is whether it is a good idea even to get involved at all. This question naturally arises for every new business idea that enthusiastic entrepreneurs come up with, but applies equally to new business opportunities

discovered by established firms. As explained in Chapter 2, competitive conditions in an industry can conspire to make profitable participation, or even survival, extremely difficult, so it is advisable at least to identify whether any viable business might be possible. It is not so simple, however, that we can merely examine the soundness of similar enterprises already in existence, or write out a plausible model for how a putative enterprise might operate—we have to see a path from start-up *to* that future state.

2. *Choosing a strategy for taking part.* The first question cannot in practice be separated from this second issue. The question of whether to compete in a market can only be answered in the context of some concept of what that business actually looks like. This is where the two broad questions of strategy choice mentioned in earlier chapters arise—*where* to compete? (which breaks down further into who to serve, with what products and services) and *how* to compete? Only when the options under these two headings have been defined and evaluated is it possible to answer with confidence the first question of whether to take part at all.

   It is all very well to have identified that a viable business opportunity could in principle exist, but a further question at this point is whether the people involved with that idea are actually capable of bringing it about. This depends on issues of managerial and leadership talent that are beyond the scope of this book, but nevertheless are of vital importance. It is widely accepted amongst venture capital providers that it is safer to back people with a weak business idea but strong managerial ability, leadership qualities and personal commitment, rather than investing in a great business idea pursued by people lacking those qualities. Nevertheless, the high failure rate amongst new ventures suggests there is still room for better evaluation of business ideas themselves, as well as of the people who would lead them.

3. *Designing a likely path to success.* Whilst it may be possible to describe, even in some detail, a future business operation that could operate successfully, there remains a substantial challenge in defining a realistic path by which that business could be started, developed and grown to create that ultimate vision. When a business venture fails to fulfill the hopes of its backers and managers, there is no reliable and objective means for knowing with certainty to what extent that failure arose because the business vision was never feasible, because the organization was poorly led, or because its development was badly planned and implemented. However, given the dynamic complexities we have previously seen for even simple business systems, it is likely that both non-feasibility and erroneous implementation feature significantly in many failures.

4. *Steering strategy through time.* This is a continuation of the previous issue, except that rather than focusing on the effectiveness of business development, we are now concerned with on-going guidance of an existing enterprise as challenges it faces alter. The competitive conditions in which a business operates, as described in Chapter 2, are rarely stable, being subject to numerous changes initiated by other participants in the industry as well as the exogenous factors described in Chapter 6. Strategic management must therefore encompass the full range of significant decisions that continue to require attention, and the policies that guide those decisions.

5. *Whether to extend or revise the strategy.* This is in essence a repeat of the first two—whether to compete and if so with what strategy—except that now we are looking at adding to an already existing enterprise. Should we enter a new market, extend our product range, develop a service offer alongside our product sales, and so on? This issue covers all kinds of possible changes to the business system currently in existence. It therefore includes any changes to the three principal elements of strategy choice—who to serve, with what products and services, and how. For clarity, we will leave changes to policies and decisions under the heading of "steering strategy," although these two issues may well arise together.

As has been the case in previous chapters, many of the issues in this list apply, with little modification, to strategic challenges in public services and voluntary organizations. A public service initiative may, for example, prove both to be feasible to operate and to possess a viable strategy for bringing it about. The case of zero-tolerance policing first brought to prominence in New York City offers such an example, where acting strongly against minor infringements brought down the rates of more serious crimes. Replicating the policy in other cities has sometimes worked, but sometimes failed, either because the structure of the crime "industry" did not possess the same characteristics as in New York, or else because the policy was not implemented correctly.

Voluntary organizations too may be started with good motives and optimism amongst their founders, and either succeed or fail, depending on whether there is a feasible model for winning the necessary funding, finding the right staff, and capturing enough uptake by the organization's hoped-for beneficiaries. Failure is often not as apparent as in corporate settings, with voluntary groups struggling on through the goodwill of its participants, in spite of there being no prospect of meaningful success.

## EVALUATING STRATEGIC OPPORTUNITIES

Most of the illustrations and cases discussed in earlier chapters have implicitly concerned situations in which a working business exists, or can be created. However, we need a way of testing whether a business is actually feasible.

Chapters 1–7 of this book laid out a rigorous, logical description of an organization as a collection of tangible resources that enable pursuit of its purpose by supporting each others' development. The strategic architecture is, if you like, "the machine" designed for that purpose, so this first question is effectively whether it is possible for that machine to exist at all. For that to be true, its resources must be capable of generating sufficient cash flow to fuel their own existence, plus sufficient surplus to justify creating it in the first place. Two inter-related problems could cause this requirement to be missed:

- there could be insufficient potential customers and other demand-side resources to generate adequate cash flows, and/or
- it could be too costly, or require too many supply-side resources to win and sustain those customers.

This principle can be demonstrated with the basic consumer brand model from Chapter 4, though other business models examined previously would do equally well. In that model, the potential market offered 3 million possible consumers, each willing to buy 0.8 units per month at a retail price of $11.25—higher prices reduce this purchase rate and lower prices raise it.

Figure 8.1 shows the same architecture of stores, salesforce and consumers, but compares the outcome of there being only 2 million or 1 million potential consumers, rather than the 3 million expected.

This illustration makes the rather simple point that a smaller potential market will offer lower potential sales, and thus make it harder to build a profitable business. In fact, since the fraction of consumers reached by advertizing is the same in each case, sales volumes are reduced in direct proportion to the number of potential consumers initially available. With less gross profit from the lower sales rate, the brand struggles to become profitable, and with only 1 million potential consumers fails to do so within four years of its launch.

Consider, though, how the 1 million consumer scenario would seem to the management concerned. They might conclude that the slow early sales rate is *not* due to the smaller potential market, but to insufficient advertizing spend. A reasonable response, then, would be to quickly increase advertizing spend. Figure 8.2 shows that this does indeed increase early sales substantially, but because the ultimate

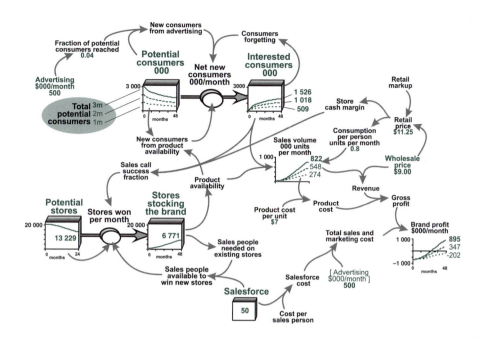

**Figure 8.1: Reduced sales and profits from a brand launch into a smaller than expected market.**

potential is way too small, the product still fails to become profitable. (Dashed lines indicate incomplete causal relationships.) This example shows once again the critical importance of understanding the underlying reasons for performance, in particular the level of resources and their flow rates, rather than relying solely on outcome measures.

## INTERDEPENDENCE IN THE STRATEGIC ARCHITECTURE

The smaller than expected market potential has further implications. This example was chosen originally because it demonstrates a simple case of interdependence between resources—consumers are won more quickly because of increasing product availability in stores, and stores are won more quickly because of growing demand from consumers. In Figure 8.1, this interdependence is not accounted for—store win rates are the same for any given fraction of interested consumers, whether that fraction is of 3 million consumers or fewer. This is clearly unrealistic. Stores will only stock the product if the *quantity* of consumers is enough to generate retail sales and profitability.

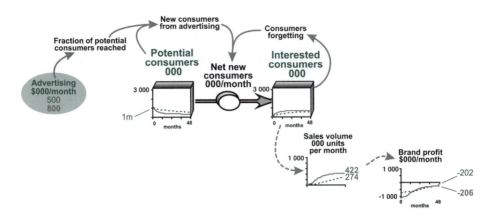

**Figure 8.2: Greater advertizing fails to create a successful product launch in a too-small potential market.**

Figure 8.3 shows how with 2 million consumers this interdependence causes a far more serious under-performance. In Figure 8.1, sales were simply reduced in proportion to the size of the potential consumer market. Now, though, the reduced demand from consumers slows the success of sales calls on stores. Not only does this reduce sales volume directly, it also slows still further the growth in consumer interest, so that sales are reduced not by one third, but by nearly two thirds as compared with the case with 3 million potential consumers. The consequences for profitability are also dire, with the brand failing to become profitable after four years. This example makes an important general point about assessing the viability of a new strategic opportunity:

**Interdependence amongst resources substantially amplifies the consequences of either over- or under-estimating the scale of a strategic opportunity.**

**Sensitivity analysis for new business opportunities**

It is common good practice when evaluating the case for a new business opportunity to include a sensitivity analysis. This is useful whether the opportunity comes from an entrepreneur seeking funding for a new venture, or a corporate executive seeking approval to develop a new line of business. Typically, such a business case will justify the estimated potential market and likely sales, lay out the resources and costs needed to develop the opportunity, and show a "central forecast" for the expected profit outcomes. It will also include some analysis of the sensitivity of this forecast to uncertainties in the underlying assumptions, e.g. what if sales turn out to be $+/- 20\%$ vs. the central estimate, or costs required are 10% higher or lower than expected. Such sensitivities are easy to test with the spreadsheet models on which business cases are usually evaluated.

The interdependence in the strategic architecture suggests that such simplistic sensitivities can be badly inadequate. As Figure 8.3 demonstrates, the impact on performance of an error in estimating one resource in the system can be multiplied substantially by interactions with other resources. Sensitivity analysis should therefore be explicit both about the assumptions regarding underlying resources *and* about the interdependence between them.

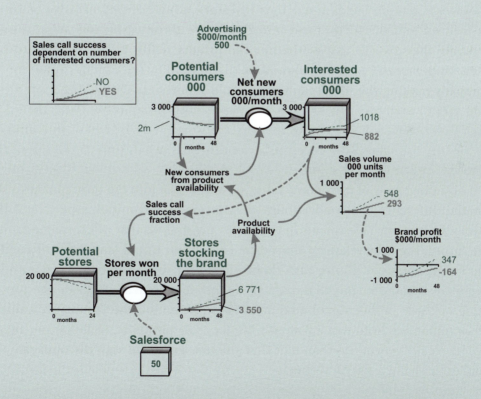

**Figure 8.3: Interdependence between resources worsens the impact of a lower than expected potential market.**

An important implication of this principle is that new venture prospects are unlikely to be somewhere around the point at which they are just about viable. They will more likely be either highly attractive, or else deeply inadequate. This phenomenon is familiar in the venture capital field, where most investments fail, only to be more than made up for by a few spectacular successes.

## NET PRESENT VALUE OF OPPORTUNITIES

It may seem self-evident that, with a potential market of 3 million consumers, the brand launch shown in Figure 8.1 is a good investment. The brand is profitable after just two years, is strongly profitable after four, and appears almost to have made back the negative cash flow it incurred during the launch period. However, Chapter 1 explained that investors value the *present value* of future cash flows, and the further out into the future those cash flows arise, the less valuable they are. To assess whether the project really should be undertaken, then, each month's cash flow should be discounted by the cost of capital for the company making the investment decision, a process known as "discounted cash flow (DCF) analysis."[1] If, say, the company's cost of capital is 10%, then $100 cash flow received at the end of month 12 is worth only 1/ 1.10 of that amount, or $90.91, the same $100 received at month 24 is worth only 1/ 1.10^2 of that amount, or $82.64, and so on.

This fading away of cash flows' value as they recede into the future makes a substantial difference to the advisability of strategic opportunities, especially if they involve heavy early investments in the hope of cash flows that will continue far into the future. Even the relatively short-term case of our brand launch is impacted by the reduced value of future cash flows. Figure 8.4 shows the brand profit and its cumulative total over the 48 months of the product launch, alongside the present value of those profits, discounted at 20% per year, and the cumulative value of those amounts.* Note that by month 48, monthly profits of $895 000 per month will be "really" worth less than half that amount, given the high discount rate that applies to what is a risky investment.

---

* This illustration takes the brand's monthly profit to be the same as the cash flow it generates. To evaluate the project's net present value accurately in practice would require adjustments to be made for changes in working capital, taxation and other factors, assumed here for simplicity to be zero.

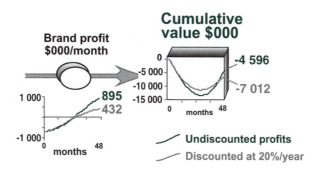

**Figure 8.4: The discounted present value of the brand launch with 3 million consumers and advertizing of $0.5m per month.**

## CHOOSING A STRATEGY

This brand case is implicitly about a single, clearly identifiable customer group with an equally clear set of requirements for products in the brand's category. Strategic opportunities frequently arise because of the variety of potential customer groups that may be available and the richly varying mix of needs they have of the products and services within a broad category. One only has to look at the diversity of offerings available in the restaurant market for an example of just how extensive that variety can be.

The question of "whether to take part" must therefore nearly always be extended with the question "take part in what, exactly?" Segmentation of customers and their needs offers a basis for answering this question (see Chapters 2 and 3). In essence, the evaluation of strategy outlined above needs to be repeated for each promising alternative. The outcome of this process need not be a single, exclusive focus, though this has the advantage of providing clarity of purpose and simplicity of execution.

It is nevertheless possible, indeed rather common, for firms to pursue multiple segments simultaneously. The major car manufacturers all serve diverse customer groups with a variety of product types, some hotel companies operate chains with different positioning in the market, utilities serve consumers and business customers simultaneously, and so on. For any such organization, choosing a strategy is not the exclusive choice that the phrase implies. They evaluate a range of alternatives, and may conclude that there is a strong case for pursuing more than one of these.

## DESIGNING A PATH TO SUCCESS

Thus far, our brand launch looks just about worth pursuing, given the choices we have made about how to undertake it. But maybe this is not the best strategy. The broad choices of strategy in this case have already been made. We know *who* we want to serve—the market of about 3 million people with their particular characteristics and preferences. We know *what* we want to serve them with—a product with some value curve of benefits that has been proven in test research to appeal to that target group. And we know *how* we wish to serve them—by capturing their interest in the product and making it available through sales effort into retail stores.

But these high level selections are not the end of the issue. "Choosing a strategy" must also include deciding on:

## What to do, when and how much?

There are three factors on which these choices must be made in this case. We must decide how much to spend on advertising each month, how much sales effort to deploy, and what wholesale price to charge. Chapter 4 already examined the impact of some variations in these decisions, e.g. the poor consequences of spending just $0.3m/month on advertising. But a "strategy" for the launch implies a coordinated set of choices on all available decision levers. The scenario shown in Figure 8.1 makes simple, static choices on each decision—advertising of $0.5 million per month, sales effort of 50 people, and a wholesale price of $9.00. But is this a good choice of strategy? We cannot answer this question without some further information, not disclosed in Figure 8.1.

First, the advertising spend of $0.5m/month is enough to reach just 4% of the potential consumers. "Reach" here implies not just that people are exposed to the advertising, but actually notice it sufficiently to become interested, so there is a highly non-linear impact of our spending—$1.0m/month reaches just over 20% of the market, and $1.5m reaches over 60%. The implication is that our launch advertising was so low that it would take a very long time for the interest of most consumers to be captured.

Secondly, the 50 sales people can each make 50 calls per month, so with 20 000 stores it will take some 8 months to visit them all. We also know, however, that their calls will not be successful if no consumers are interested in the product, so is there any point in making sales calls until consumers are interested? (In practice, sales effort in such cases focuses on the consumer demand that *will* arise once advertising has had its effect, but this simple case does not allow that possibility). Since this product is just one of many that our company sells, we can simply reallocate sales effort back and forth between other products and this one, so perhaps our best choice would be to delay sales effort until consumer interest is significant, then throw a lot of sales calls at the stores, and cut that effort later to a maintenance level after most of the stores have been captured.

Lastly, the wholesale price determines the retail price through the addition of the stores' mark-up, and this affects consumers' purchase rate through a simple

TABLE 8.1: AN IMPROVED STRATEGY FOR THE BRAND LAUNCH

| Month | Advertizing | Sales people | Wholesale price |
|-------|-------------|--------------|-----------------|
| 1–6   | $1.2m       | 0            | 8.00            |
| 7–12  | $1.2m       | 100          | 8.00            |
| 13–18 | $1.2m       | 100          | 10.00           |
| 19–48 | $0.5m       | 50           | 10.00           |

price elasticity—a higher price reduces consumption and a lower price increases it. And the more profit the stores are likely to make from the product, the more successful our sales people will be when they try to sell the product. If consumers are sufficiently price sensitive, then, a lower initial price might increase consumption and potential store profits and improve the success of our salesforce.

Given these considerations, perhaps a better launch strategy might look something like Table 8.1. Start by spending heavily to win consumer interest, delay selling to stores until there is enough interest for stores to take the product, and price low to grow volume and stores' commitment. Next, keep advertizing strongly to capture most of the potential market as quickly as possible, and sell heavily to grow distribution. Lastly, raise price and cut sales and marketing to extract profitability. (In practice, increasing the achieved price is more likely to result from reducing discounts and promotions, rather than by a real increase in headline prices, and would not typically occur on the scale suggested here).

The result of this strategy, compared with the simple, static set of policies above is shown in Figure 8.5 (dashed lines again indicate incomplete structure). As can be seen, it is not just somewhat better than the original plan—it is radically better, achieving much larger and more rapid uptake by consumers and stores, breaking into profit after just 12 months, and driving high rates of profit thereafter.

This is a common feature of strategic initiatives:

**The difference between poor strategies and better ones for exploiting a single opportunity can be vast.**

It is also common for organizations to under-invest in strategic initiatives, and to be unaware of how much stronger their performance could have been, had they

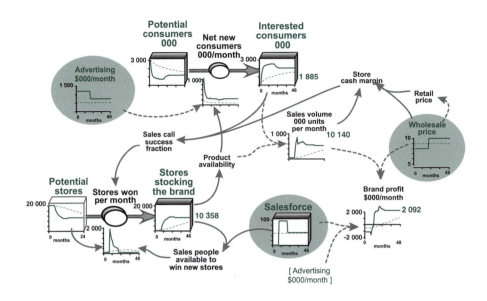

**Figure 8.5: How the improved strategy for the brand launch plays out.**

chosen otherwise. Note too the importance of certain critical information items in informing this strategy. As each month passes, management can be confident of the advisability of its strategy, even before strong sales and profits have arisen, because key flow rates are running rapidly—consumers becoming interested and stores adopting the product. Conversely, had these flow rates not been so strong, management could have reviewed the plausible performance outcomes early on, and if necessary abandoned the project before wasting millions of dollars on trying to make it work.

It can now be seen why the first two questions—whether to embark on a new initiative, and what strategy to adopt in doing so—cannot in practice be disentangled. Given this latest approach to the strategy, the product launch is a good move to pursue; under the original policies it was not.

**Doing it right! Make sure to evaluate the correct strategy**

We have seen repeatedly the scope for strategy to vary in its success, depending on how it is implemented. Strategy evaluations often start with some forecast of market growth, assumptions about the firm's ability to capture market share, estimates of prices and costs, to arrive at some "straight-line" projection of profits if the strategy is or is not pursued. (Chapter 2 included an extensive explanation of the flaws in this approach.)

Before evaluating whether a strategy investment or initiative should be pursued, then, it is useful just to check that the strategy being assessed is actually as strong as it could be.

## STEERING STRATEGY

Although it is common to distinguish strategy development from strategy implementation, it is not now generally recommended that management develop strategy first, then switch to implementing it. Not only is it impossible to know everything in advance but conditions continue to change as events unfold. Our strategy will also cause competitors and customers to respond, giving rise to new challenges and opportunities, so the chosen strategy will inevitably need constant review.

This steering and adjustment of strategy should be handled with care, though. Whilst it is a good principle to keep alert to the possible need for revisions, most strategy frameworks provide guidance at too general a level to assist in this adjustment process. It is rarely advisable to make different choices next year on where to compete and how from those you made last year. It is certainly unlikely that altering those choices from quarter to quarter would be advisable. Similarly, having used the value curve to identify a set of benefits for target customers that should win substantial, profitable business, it is not likely that a repeat of that analysis next quarter will come up with different answers from those it came up with last quarter. Indeed, contrary to popular wisdom, strongly performing organizations do not constantly reinvent themselves. Rather they relentlessly pursue broad strategic choices that have been proved to work, with incremental extensions and adjustments that are modest relative to the scale of their overall operations. The recommended "continual updating" of strategy therefore needs an approach that supports policy and decision-making at a more detailed level than popular strategy frameworks allow.

Strategic decision-making thus encompasses the entire stream of decisions that follow initial high-level choices. Indeed, it is entirely possible for a promising set of initial choices to be entirely destroyed by poor choice of the subsequent strategy implementation. Recall from Chapter 1 that the term "strategic" simply means "capable of having a significant impact on the medium- to long-term performance of the organization." On this view, many decisions on a wide variety of issues are genuinely strategic and continue to be so throughout the life of the organization.

## EXAMPLES OF DECISION IMPACTS FROM EARLIER CHAPTERS

Throughout previous chapters it has been rather taken for granted that management makes decisions to keep an organization working well and pursuing its purpose. Strategic decision-making is no simple matter, however. Various examples have shown the substantial improvements that are possible from better decisions and the damage that poor decisions can inflict (Table 8.2).

### TABLE 8.2: IMPACT OF DECISIONS ON PERFORMANCE OUTCOMES IN EXAMPLES FROM EARLIER CHAPTERS

| Chapter | Figure | Example |
|---------|--------|---------|
| 4 | 4.21 | drop in performance for the simple consumer brand resulting from decisions to cut advertizing and sales effort |
| 5 | 5.6 | the drop in staff skills and loss of customers resulting from under-investment in training for a call center |
| 5 | 5.9 | recovery in reliability and performance from changed policies towards equipment maintenance |
| 5 | 5.14 | profit decline from over-expansion of a retail store-chain |
| 5 | 5.20 | improved rate of donor-giving to a voluntary organization from re-targeting its fundraising efforts |
| 6 | 6.2 | changing promotion rates at a bank to increase the fraction of minority staff at senior levels |
| 6 | 6.3 | raising the number of new product ideas, and tighter screening, to increase the rate of new product launches |
| 6 | 6.4 | changing maintenance, refurbishment and replacement decisions to improve reliability and performance for assets at a utility company |
| 6 | 6.7 | phasing of marketing spend priorities to accelerate profit growth for a consumer brand |

TABLE 8.2: (*CONTINUED*)

| Chapter | Figure | Example |
|---------|--------|---------|
| 6 | 6.24 | market uptake for a new consumer electronic product arising from choice of launch-price levels as unit costs fall |
| 6 | 6.34 | consequences for total costs of welfare support over time arising from alternative spending choices |
| 7 | 7.1–7.5 | impact of competing coffee stores' pricing on customers, sales and profits under differing rivalry conditions |
| 7 | 7.9–7.10 | accelerating sales growth for a consumer electronic product, and competitor's share of sales, due to alternative advertizing spend |
| 7 | 7.14 | changes in the number of large projects won against rivals by raising the fraction of initial opportunities that are bid for |
| 7 | 7.16–7.19 | customer switching in response to electricity prices offered by competing suppliers |
| 7 | 7.22 | capture of retail store space and sales volume for a consumer brand resulting from choice of wholesale prices vs. competitors |
| 7 | 7.28 | staff win rate for competing call centers due to differing pay rates offered |
| 7 | 7.36–7.37 | consequences for growth in passenger volumes and profits arising from competing low-fare airlines' choice of route-development rates |

A number of observations emerge from these examples.

- *Potentially large impacts on performance.* As in the consumer brand example in Figure 8.5, the differences in performance between alternative decisions are often vast, for example:
  - The drop in skills at the call center due to limited training time (Figure 5.6) crosses a threshold between adequate and inadequate customer service that hits customer numbers by 15% after just 12 months. If the scenario is extended, customer numbers are devastated.
  - The changed targeting of the voluntary organization's fundraising efforts does not just increase donor giving by a few percent, but more than doubles that rate—a substantial effect, especially considering that it requires no change in the actual *amount* of effort involved.

This considerable difference between decisions that are better or worse should not really be so surprising. Since decisions affect resource-building, their effects must be cumulative, so small differences build up considerable strengths or problems as time passes.

- *Big changes to decisions.* Note the often substantial movements in decision-levels that are indicated if performance is to be improved. The utility firm's fixing of its equipment reliability in Figure 6.4 would not have occurred within a decade by mere percentage changes in capital spend and maintenance—it required more than twice the rate of equipment replacement and a doubling of maintenance spend. Conversely, we failed badly in our efforts to capture sales of the consumer electronic product in Figures 7.9 and 7.10 because our competitor spent on advertizing at twice our rate. This contrasts strongly with common practice, where management rarely makes large scale changes in decision factors, and competitors often match each others' policies closely.

- *Delays between decisions and outcomes.* We have observed before that resources' accumulating behavior can result in long periods elapsing between decisions that are made and the consequences of those decisions being evident. This is a real problem for decision-making for two reasons.

  - It can appear that a decision is not working when in fact it is, so management reverses the decision before its benefit is apparent. In Figure 6.3, many quarters pass between the decision to seek more ideas for new products and the eventual change in actual new products reaching the market. In Figure 6.7, the advertizing for a consumer brand results in little apparent growth in demand for many quarters, so management could easily drop the initiative altogether, even though awareness and interest are rising.

  - Alternatively, management can press on with policies that are seriously wrong because they cannot see problems building up. The over-expansion of retail stores in Figure 5.14 appeared to be well-justified by continuing sales growth, long after it started hitting operating profits due to the dilution of average sales per store.

- *Counter-intuitive recommendations.* Sometimes the interaction of resources has implications for decision-making that are quite opposite to what seems best. The project-based firm in Figure 7.14 quite reasonably believed that it must accept more invitations to tender for projects if it were to increase its revenue and profits, whereas the opposite was in fact the case. The aerospace firm in Figure 7.29 had long believed that it needed to pay the best salaries to systems graduates from the best universities to build its capability, whereas its best policy was the reverse of this.

> **Doing it right! A stable strategy does not imply unchanging decisions**
>
> Since the market and competitive situation against which strategy is being steered is constantly changing, it is most unlikely that an unchanging set of choices on important decision factors will lead to anywhere near the best long term outcome. This should not be confused with making constant changes to the strategy itself.

- *Changing decisions over time.* Unless the organization and its environment are both very stable, it is highly unlikely that management's best policy option will be to pursue a stable set of decisions from period to period. The rescue of the utility firm with unreliable assets in Figure 6.4, the strong reallocation of marketing and sales support for the consumer brand in Figure 6.7, and the customer switching between electricity suppliers in Figure 7.19 all demonstrate that outcomes can be substantially improved if decisions are adjusted, often to a considerable degree, in response to the changing opportunities and challenges as a situation develops. Care is needed with this principle, however. Well-informed, programmatic changes in decisions are not the same as constant reaction to short-term results.

- *No visibility of "the path not chosen."* A more subtle implication arising from some of these examples is that it is easy for management to continue with policies and decisions that are sub-optimal, because they simply are not aware of how things might have been, had they chosen otherwise. Had welfare spending in Figure 6.34 focused on direct support for families in need, it may never have been known that substantial reductions in the numbers of needy families would have been possible. The airline in Figure 7.38 would never know what might have happened during the last 5 years of its history, had it chosen to keep prices down rather than gradually raise them. Would its competitor have matched those low prices, depressing their own profit margins, or would they have resisted lower pricing and allowed our airline to capture more sales? Would either of these options have made life so difficult for rivals that they would have failed to keep up with the company's route-expansion, or would they perhaps have failed altogether?

- *Satisficing decision-making.* A widespread consequence of this failure to consider what might otherwise have occurred is incremental decision-making leading to performance that, whilst not too bad, could be substantially better. We try to achieve 10% annual profit growth because it already looks tough to hit

5%, and 5% looks tough because that is the best we get by pursuing more or less what we did last year. Decision rules that allocate fixed proportions of revenue to certain costs and spending budgets that are set at last year's rate plus or minus a small fraction lock in this kind of satisficing behavior and condemn organizations to underperforming their potential, often by a wide margin.

## Where strategy is managed

The path that strategy takes is not, as might be expected, always determined by big decisions made by the most senior people. Gone are the days when, for example, the CEO of a major hotel chain reserved the authority for every decision, right down to the choice of carpet for his hotels. Modern business life is just too complex and fast-moving for organizations to accept the delays caused be such command-and-control decision systems. Consequently, many organizations have chosen to devolve authority to people at lower levels.

Whilst devolved decision-making should be quicker and more responsive to local changes than systems that rely on hierarchical decision-processes, it clearly poses risks. Decisions may not be consistent, so one executive makes what looks like a perfectly reasonable decision in ignorance of other decisions that make his own inappropriate. And though it is now accepted that people are more capable of intelligent decision-making than they were once given credit for, there is still the risk that decision authority may be granted that is beyond their skills or experience.

Organizations try to reduce the risk of devolved decision-making, whilst retaining the benefits it offers, by providing guidelines. Essentially, they are saying to individuals "Yes, we want you to make your own decisions, provided they conform to the following principles." Rules that guide strategy choices, for example, may define[2]:

- boundaries; things that can be pursued and others that cannot.
- priorities; how to choose between alternatives.
- exit rules: when to drop something that is not working

Other classes of rule provide guidance on how things should be done, and when. Further controls on the risks arising from devolved decision-making can be imposed by limiting the scope for individuals to make decisions, by setting the resources at their disposal, the items for which they are accountable, the issues over which they are allowed to exert influence, and the range of support they can call on from elsewhere in the organization.[3]

### Emergent vs. deliberate strategy

An important consequence of devolved decision-making about issues of strategic choice is that strategy can cease to be an intentional, deliberate process. Instead, strategy "emerges" from the stream of initiatives that are started, and then survive both the internal competition for attention and resources and the external competitive marketplace. Indeed, it has been suggested that emergence is a widespread mechanism by which organizations develop their strategies through a process of building on successes and learning from failures in a progressively incremental manner.[4] Care is needed, however, in adopting this approach to strategy. Whilst it may well describe how many organizations *actually* develop strategy, it does not necessarily follow that they do better as a result compared with how they would have done had they adopted a more organized and deliberate approach.

# POLICY TO CONTROL STRATEGY

Given the considerable implications arising from the numerous examples of alternative decisions we have already seen, a disciplined approach to decision-making is clearly valuable. We introduced earlier in this chapter the idea of the strategic architecture of interdependent resources as "the machine" designed to fulfill the organization's purpose, and like any machine, this one too needs a control system if it is to perform well.

The machine analogy is made more complex when human behaviors are involved, because unlike the physics of mechanical systems those responses are not entirely certain—issues that will be clarified in the final two chapters. However that is no reason to abandon any attempt at managing logically those parts of the system that are more predictable, or indeed to make use of what limited degree of predictability can be found in the behavioral parts of the system. Indeed, history shows an increasing penetration of organized control systems into more and more parts of the business system. We gave up long ago any attempt to control oil refineries by having operators look at read-outs of the thousands of performance measures involved and then use just their skill to decide whether to open or close valves, start or stop pumps, and so on. Logistics systems that were once managed by the skilled intuition of senior distribution managers are now largely computer-controlled. Customer service that was once left to the skill of service department managers is now directed by customer-relationship-management systems (CRM). Systematic decision-making is even encroaching on issues with substantial behavioral dimensions, such as the lending decisions for banks that were once made on the basis of individual managers' personal assessment of each loan applicant, but now rely almost entirely on credit-scoring systems.

Human beings operate many kinds of system, from the temperature control on their shower to the more complex challenge of flying an aircraft. Recognizing that some skill is needed to do these tasks successfully, we help ourselves with automated mechanisms to do some or all of the controlling for us. A thermostatic valve keeps the temperature of our shower just right, and whilst pilots may know how to fly a plane, it is more convenient and reliable to have an autopilot do much of that task for them.

Some automated systems are utterly simple. Take for example that thermostatic control of your shower. All it needs is to be told the temperature you want and the current temperature, plus a simple rule—if the actual temperature is less than desired, swing the valve towards the hot inlet, otherwise towards the cold. A car's cruise-control system is similarly simple—if the vehicle speed is less than desired, step on the gas; if faster, ease up.

The examples from earlier chapters summarized in Table 8.2 show the consequences of different decisions made over time in a variety of cases. But it is not especially helpful for management merely to be told the best decision to make under a specific set of circumstances at a certain time. Rather, they need to know *how* to make that best decision under a wide variety of situations. This needs some kind of guideline or rule, into which information about the situation is entered and out of which a decision emerges.

*Fixed decision rules.* Some rules are utterly simple, e.g. "Keep the price at $100, whatever the situation"—indeed it is hardly a decision-rule at all, since it takes no account of anything about the situation. Although this may seem an unlikely kind of rule, it is sometimes adopted. Organizations often operate a head-count limit for certain departments, for example, such as "You may not employ more than 50 sales staff, under any circumstances." Financial versions of such rules are actually quite common—a budget is effectively a rule saying "You may not spend more than $X 000 next quarter on activity Y [under any circumstances]."

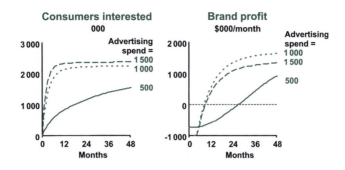

**Figure 8.6: Fixed advertizing rates for the brand launch (salesforce and price also fixed).**

Given the range of better or worse decisions illustrated in Table 8.2, it seems unlikely that a rule of that kind would ever be close to optimal. In reality, such rules are rarely quite so naïve. Although a fixed number has been chosen, that number itself arises from knowledge about what is likely to work well. The limit to salesforce numbers has arisen because experience has shown that adding additional people does not result in sufficient extra sales to justify the expense. The budget limit for spending has been chosen for similar reasons. However, these are very crude reasons for choosing such simplistic rules.

Figure 8.6 gives an example of how the simplest decision rule plays out with the consumer brand launch. The salesforce size is fixed at 50, and the wholesale price is fixed at $9.00.

- In the base case (solid line), advertizing is fixed at $0.5m per month. Consumer interest grows slowly, due to the limited reach of this low expenditure rate, but profits eventually become positive and continue to grow. However, profit growth is slowing after 48 months, and more or less peaks out three years later at a profit rate of $1.4m per month.
- With higher spending of $1.0m per month, consumer interest is captured much more quickly, and the rapidly increasing sales soon repay this cost and drive profits into positive territory in under 12 months.
- Spending at a still higher rate of $1.5m per month makes little further improvement on the $1.0m case, due to limits on the possible fraction of potential consumers that advertizing can ever reach. Note that we do not capture all of the 3 million potentially available because a fraction of consumers are constantly losing interest. The higher spending cannot drive enough additional sales to pay for itself, so profits are actually lower than in the second case.

**Figure 8.7: Spending a fraction of sales revenue on the brand launch, but at least $0.5/month.**

A rule that spends a fixed fraction of sales revenue on advertizing hits an immediate problem—when we have no customers we have no sales, so spend nothing on advertizing. This rule therefore has to be supplemented by spending at least at a minimum rate, say $0.5m per month. Otherwise, this rule seems reasonable enough, since the more revenue we make the more we can "afford" to spend in order to drive still greater revenue and hence grow profits. However Figure 8.7 shows the rule to be rather dysfunctional. Setting the fraction at 5% never leads to any spending above the minimum of $0.5m/month. A fraction of 10% eventually exceeds the minimum and starts to grow consumer interest faster from about month 36. Higher fractions of revenue accelerate the capture of the remaining consumers, once the base spending rate is exceeded. But in spite of this benefit, profits are actually reduced because the gross margin on any extra sales is more than wiped out by the additional advertizing needed to generate it. (The gross profit per unit is $2 on a price of $9, so giving 20% of revenue to advertizing implies spending $1.80 of that gross profit, leaving virtually nothing to cover the cost of the salesforce.)

Whilst it should *not* be taken as a general rule that spending larger fractions of revenue on marketing or any other item inevitably reduces profits, it is not uncommon to find that this is the case. One pharmaceuticals firm adopted a similar rule for deciding on the size of its salesforce in a large European market for a mature product.

Pharmaceuticals firms often track an indicator known as "share of voice" which refers to the fraction of sales effort in a market sector that each firm is committing. So if one firm has 70 sales people selling into a certain market, and all the competing firms together are deploying 200, the firm's share of voice is 35%. If a particular firm's desired share of voice is determined by the share of the product market that it commands, the result is effectively the same as a share-of-revenue rule. If the company sells more, its market share rises, so it spends a larger amount on sales effort and thus raises its share of voice to reflect its market share. In this particular case, since the product market was mature, the sales people were making no difference to the capture of new customers, the retention of existing customers or the rate of sales to those customers. Effectively, then, the entire salesforce cost of over €10m/year was pointless, and simply reduced the product's net profit.

## A GENERIC STRUCTURE FOR DECISION-MAKING POLICY

The rules just described may be very simple, but they illustrate the key elements involved in making decisions to control strategy:

- a target value for some measure in the system
- the current value of that measure
- a rule for choosing a value for the decision item, using the information on the target and current value of the measure
- the actual value chosen for the decision
- various consequences for other items in the system caused by the decision

The relationship between these elements is shown in Figure 8.8. The two simple rules discussed in relation to Figures 8.6 and 8.7 both conform to this pattern. The value chosen is $X 000/month of advertizing spend, and the other items this value affects are the rate at which consumers are won and the next period's profit. In Figure 8.6, the measure to be targeted is simply the advertizing spend rate itself, and the rule is "Set spending to be $X 000 per month." In Figure 8.7, the measure

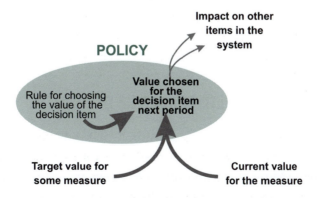

**Figure 8.8:** Generic structure of a policy for making a decision on some item.

to be targeted is the fraction of revenue spent on advertizing, and the rule is "Set spending to be Y% of this month's sales revenue."

Figure 8.8 clarifies exactly what a "policy" is.

### A policy is a rule for making a decision[5]

The policy is informed by data about the situation, and the decision that emerges from the policy works by affecting one or more other items in the system. Each policy is therefore an integral part of the strategic architecture itself. Figure 8.5 already shows where policies are located in our brand launch, although it does not show the measures that feed into each policy.

Some further details should be clarified at this point.

1. It is not possible to base a decision for the current period on information in this same period. Rather the decision is always for some future period of time. The period concerned may be very short. For example, a manufacturing company may order goods for delivery tomorrow based on its inventory and production rate today. It may even be ultra-short, as when an airline's systems set the price for the next ticket to be sold on the basis of the latest availability of seats on a flight. Nevertheless, the decision for "now" still has to rely on information from the past.

2. To overcome problems that may arise from this delay, decisions may well be based on forecasts for some measure, rather than the current value. A store selling ice cream, for example, might set its orders according to a forecast of next week's weather.

3. It is not in fact possible for management to make decisions about the level of a resource, as is implied in the salesforce decision in the lower part of Figure 8.5. Since the level of a resource can only be altered by its inflow or outflow, it is these items that the decision must actually affect. In that case, management decided to *add* 100 sales people at the end of month 6 and to *reduce* the number by 50 at the end of month 18.

## BASING DECISIONS ON PERFORMANCE OUTCOMES

We clearly need better policies than the simplistic kinds illustrated in Figures 8.6 and 8.7, so what exactly is wrong with these? Chapter 1 made a strong case that management's overriding objective is to build performance over time, and that the principal performance measure of concern in commercial settings should be cash flow. It might be thought, then, that this cash flow should be the "measure" used to inform decisions. For our consumer brand, profit is effectively the same as cash flow, so perhaps our policy on advertizing spend should be based on that measure? Neither of the two simplistic policies above takes any account of profit, so they are not likely to be especially effective.

Defining a policy that adjusts advertizing spend according to its impact on profits is not overly complex. One example is:

- If we previously increased advertizing and profits went up, it may be advisable to repeat the increase, and keep doing so until profits stop rising. An increase in advertizing might also seem best if a previous cut in advertizing led to a fall in profits.
- If, on the other hand we previously reduced advertizing and profits increased (or *vice versa*), a further reduction should be best.

Figure 8.9 shows the disappointing results of this policy, starting with advertizing spend of $0.5m per month and increasing (decreasing) this by $50 000/month if profit increased (decreased) in the previous month. The "∥" symbol indicates the unavoidable delay between evaluating information from *last* month in order to make the decision for *this* month.

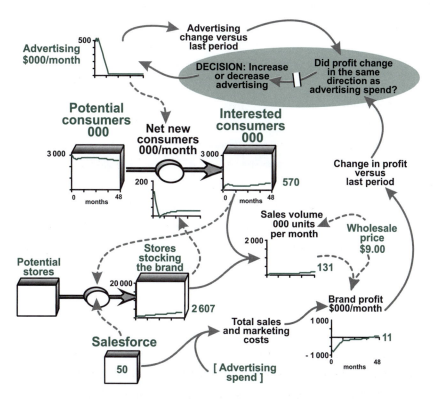

**Figure 8.9:** Results of a policy to adjust advertizing spend based on the change in last month's profit.

The policy did not work too well. A reduction in advertizing spend today raises profit immediately, simply by reducing the amount of this cost in the income statement, but the low spend *still* brings in new consumers, albeit more slowly. Even when advertizing is so small that more consumers forget the brand each month than are captured by the advertizing (month 6), the savings in cost still outweigh the small profit contribution from lost sales opportunity. Note, incidentally, that we continue to capture consumers during the last 30 months or so, even though we are not advertizing at all, thanks to the efforts of the salesforce making the product increasingly visible in the stores.

We really need to give advertizing enough time to bring in new consumers and sales before deciding whether the spending was useful, but how long should we wait? If we evaluate the profit impact of a $50 000 increase after three months rather than one, it still has not captured enough consumers to justify its cost, so the policy again results in a continuing cut in spending, and sales and profits disappoint once more. If we give it six months, however, the results are quite different (Figure 8.10).

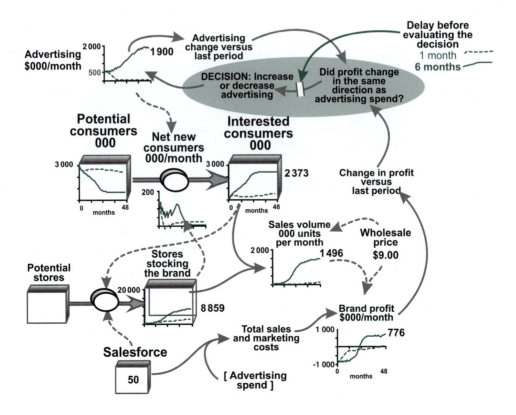

Figure 8.10: Results of a policy to change advertizing spend based on change in profit six months earlier.

The first six month's advertizing spend wins enough new consumers that the first month's decision to spend more achieves a real increase in profits by month 6. The decision in month seven is therefore to increase spending again. This decision is then repeated continually until month 36 because every month sees an increase in profits compared with six months before. By that time, advertizing is running at $1.9 million per month. From then on, it becomes more difficult for advertizing to capture enough new consumers to pay for itself, because the remaining potential is too small, so spending hovers at about the same rate.

Note that we have fixed two important parameters of our decision in this case. First, we decided to start by spending $0.5m per month. We could have started at a higher rate, in which case consumers are won more quickly and a further increase of $50000 proves to be worthwhile after just three months. Conversely, we could have started at a lower rate—at especially low spending rates it may never seem that an increase is justified. We also decided to change spending up or down by $50000 in any month, rather than say twice as much or half as much. Again, the resulting changes in profit may or may not indicate whether further increases or cuts are advisable.

There is a further problem with this policy. Although it can result in appropriately high rates of advertising spending and build a strong and profitable business, that situation is unstable. For example, starting with $1.0m spending and evaluating any changes after three months results in rapid growth and continued increases in spending until most of the opportunity is captured. However, continued scrutiny of the relationship between increased advertising and changes in profit eventually results in a coincidence of monthly decisions that appear to show *lower* spending to be advisable. Thereafter spending is continually reduced and profits progressively raised until few consumers remain—whereupon it once again seems that increased spending is correct.

This is rather disappointing. We have a policy that is explicitly linked to the performance outcome we are pursuing, yet it appears very difficult to define that policy in a way that gives something like the best outcome with much confidence. This disappointment is a direct reflection of the point highlighted in Chapter 3—that it is not possible to extract a reliable relationship directly between a causal item (advertising) and a dependent outcome (profit) when one or more accumulating factors exist between the two.

## BASING POLICY ON DIRECT EFFECTS

It is possible to improve on the reliability of individual decisions by using information on the factors to which that decision is directly linked. In this example, advertizing is being spent in order to capture potential consumers, so it makes sense to use information on its success in this purpose to guide the decision.

There are various ways in which this could be done. Spending could be set in relation to the number of potential consumers remaining, for example by spending a lot when that number is high, and less when it is low. That would require a confident estimate of the remaining potential, and we would have to guess what the range of actual spending rates should be. Spending could also be set according to the proportion of potential consumers that the spending rate could reach, for example spending enough to reach 25 % of the potential market. Again, we would need a good estimate of the potential, and good information on the reach achieved by various spending rates. Versions of this rule are commonly used in practice, encouraged by advertizing agencies and marketing channels. This may be because information on reach is something they can provide to advertizers, rather than because it is the best information on which to make the decision.

Another way in which the advertizing rate could respond to its success in developing potential consumers is to link the decision to the consumer win rate itself. This promises to be a strong and reliable policy, and illustrates a useful principle:

> ### Since resource flows determine performance improvements, decisions should take strong account of their affects on those flows.

This principle can rarely be used on its own. For example, increasing the spending rate on some important resource-building activity also has a direct impact on current profits. Nevertheless, it should certainly be *part* of policy whenever decisions affect resource flows. We will examine later how to deal with the conflict that can arise between different aims.

Two factors might interfere with how this principle can be applied in this case. First, a fraction of currently active consumers leave the product each month, flowing back into the potential population. Second, new consumers are also won by the visibility of the product in the stores. Ideally, we would want to know just the actual number of new consumers won by advertizing alone, that is, removing these other two effects. However, that requires more detailed evidence than practical market research can reliably provide.

A further benefit of linking decisions to the resource flows they control is that there is no need to wait for their effects to work all through the system, as we had to do when using profit to inform the advertizing decision. As soon as we know whether more advertizing spend caused an increase in the consumer win rate, we can decide whether to spend more or less next period. Since we are now more

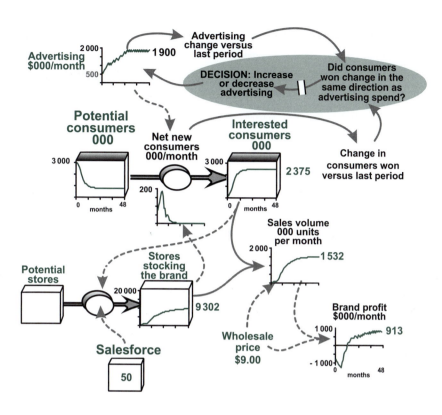

**Figure 8.11:** Results of a policy to change advertizing spend based on change in the consumer win rate.

confident in the policy, we can also move the decision by greater amounts, so Figure 8.11 shows the result of starting with spend of $0.5 million per month, and raising (lowering) that spend by $100 000 each month if it resulted in an increase (decrease) of the consumer win rate. Remember that this is the *net* consumer win rate, including gains from product visibility and the back-flow of consumer losses, but since we want advertizing to ensure a positive rate overall, the policy should still work.

(Online learning materials are available to support this example, see p.xxi.)

Figure 8.11 suggests this new policy has worked well. The number of consumers interested in the product has risen quickly to near its maximum level, given the tendency of some consumers to lose interest each month. This occurred because the advertizing rose relatively fast to a rate that just ensured a net consumer win rate that was positive, if near-zero.

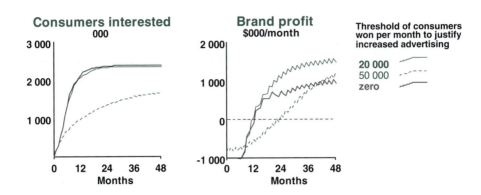

**Figure 8.12:** The effect on profits of a minimum threshold for the brand's consumer win rate before raising advertising spend.

There is one last adjustment we could make to this policy. As it stands, the guideline calls for more advertising for any net positive change in interested consumers. It could therefore might push us to spend another $100 000, just to win one more consumer, which is clearly not sensible. We can modify the rule so that the net consumer win rate must exceed some threshold of affordability. Since changes in spending are made in large steps, the threshold too needs to be substantial, so Figure 8.12 shows the consequences of setting a threshold of zero, 20 000 and 50 000 new consumers before an increase in spending is indicated.

With no threshold (gray line) profits reach a maximum of just under $1.0m per month, as shown in Figure 8.11. Setting a minimum of 20 000 additional consumers per month reduces the number of advertising increases substantially, allowing profits to grow to $1.5m per month. Advertising spend under these conditions never rises above $1.3m per month, although this is still sufficient to capture nearly the same number of consumers overall as when no threshold was set. A threshold of 50 000 new consumers won, however, is too severe—it never permits any increase in advertising, which remains stuck at $0.5m per month, sufficient only to allow a very slow growth in business and profits.

The simple decision rule demonstrated in Figure 8.11 hides certain issues that may make the policy somewhat more complex to apply in practice. For example, if the spending rate is rather low, and customers lose interest quickly, an increase in spending could appear to have too little impact to be worthwhile. Management may then feel "Well, we tried more advertising and it didn't work, so let's cut back again," simply because they spent nowhere near the rate needed to reach enough of the potential market to make any difference.

The existence of multiple customer segments also complicates the picture. Advertising may appear to win new consumers at a rapid rate, but as explained in

Chapter 3, this could reflect the existence of a particularly responsive but small segment. Further increases in spending could then have disappointing results as the less responsive segment increasingly dominates the remaining market potential.

## POLICY AND RESOURCE DEVELOPMENT

The consumer brand model above ignores for simplicity the important phenomenon of resource development discussed in Chapter 6, in particular the choice pipeline that moves customers through stages such as awareness, interest in the product, purchase and loyalty. In reality, therefore, decisions are needed regarding how much should be spent on each stage of this development process. The principle identified above—that decisions are best based upon the part of the system that they seek to influence—applies once more. Spending money and effort to increase awareness may have absolutely no effect, for example, on the number of loyal customers, if customers are not moving forwards in the upper stages of the pipeline. Consequently, it will be best to base specific decisions on the flow rates at each stage of the development process (Figure 8.13).

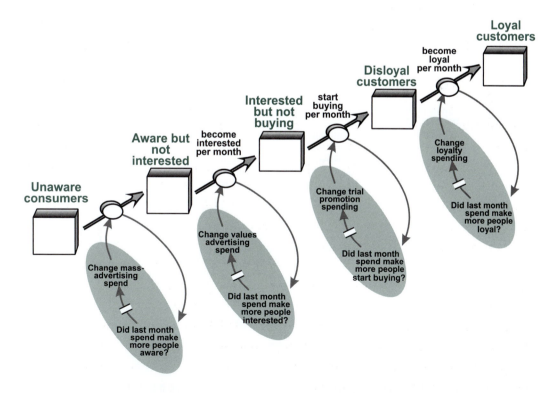

**Figure 8.13: Basing detailed marketing spend decisions on customer flows along the choice pipeline.**

**Doing it right! Deciding *how much* is needed, not how to allocate**

Note we did not say in discussing Figure 8.13 that management should use the process to *allocate* the total marketing spend. It should inform the *actual* amount of spending needed to make customers move at the desired rate through each stage. The required overall marketing spend should then be the total of these amounts. Commonly, this investigation results in spending rates that are very different from existing policy. Money is often being spent with little or no effect on the customer-flow it is expected to drive, while in other cases far too little is being spent to have any significant benefit. Of course, spending decisions will also need to recognize what is affordable. However, if the affordable spending rate cannot drive customer development along the pipeline sufficiently to generate worthwhile future sales and profits, then management should question whether the business is worthwhile at all.

Similar principles apply to other policies that concern resources moving through more than one stage. Chapter 6 also looked, for example, at a strategy to improve reliability of equipment assets (Figure 6.4). In this structure, the decision to spend money on maintenance slows the rate at which individual items of equipment deteriorate (Figure 8.14). The two specific decisions in this case concern how much to spend on reliable units to slow the rate at which they degenerate, and how much to

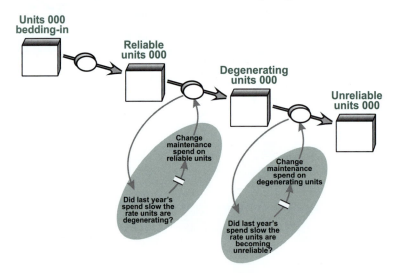

**Figure 8.14: Basing maintenance spend decisions on rates of equipment degeneration.**

spend on degenerating units to stop them becoming unreliable. Both of these decisions may reach a point at which maintenance has achieved all that it can to slow the rate of deterioration, so further spending will be pointless.

# STRATEGY, POLICY AND COMPETITION

A major complicating factor in developing policy to steer strategy, of course, is the reaction of competitors. Chapter 7 outlined the three mechanisms by which rivalry operates, and gave a number of examples in which a sequence of decisions by competing firms played out to determine their contrasting performance results. These responses would in practice be guided by policies. They may be explicit or implicit, simplistic or sophisticated, stable or adapting, but they are nevertheless policies—rules for making decisions.

The presence of competitors introduces an additional factor outside our control that may alter our own performance, so their actions must be reflected in the policy in some way. It could be included directly, for example "We match our competitor, whatever price they charge (within reason!)" or "We maintain a $10 lower price than our competitor." Such rules may come about from experience of tangling with particular competitors over many years. However, they do not observe our guiding principle of good practice—tracking how customer numbers or other resources are moving. It is therefore hard to know for sure whether they are adequate or not.

Figure 8.15 shows customer movements in the simple case of competitive electricity supply from Chapter 7. In the scenarios that follow, there is only a

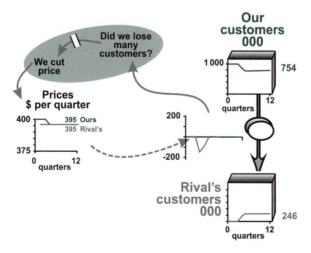

**Figure 8.15:** Price changes in electricity supply respond to customer losses.

single customer segment. They are only partly rational in their decision to switch suppliers, and do so only slowly. The competitor's entry with a price that saves the average household $5 per quarter causes 320 000 people to consider switching, of whom 160 000 do so immediately. This is more than we are willing to tolerate, so we cut our price by $5 to $395, too late to prevent a further 80 000 people switching. We would cut our price again, but we need to see if the first cut stopped the losses. In the next quarter, our price cut does indeed stop more customers leaving so we take no further action.

There are two important and related elements of the policy we have just followed. The first is the number of lost customers we will tolerate before responding. We would not cut $5 from the profit we make on each of our one million customers simply to prevent the loss of a single household, so we must have some threshold of customer losses up to which we will not react. We make a gross profit of $230 per consumer (the price of $400 minus the variable cost of $170), so losing 160 000 would hit our profits by nearly $40m per quarter. On the other hand, cutting our price by $5 for all our customers in order to hold on to this minority group will cost us $5 million per quarter. A $5 price cut would seem to be justified if we fear losing about 20 000 customers.

The second element of the policy is the size of the price cut with which we respond. $5 is chosen simply because it is the amount of the competitor's differential when they entered, but it may not be the best value.

Our competitor would likely not be satisfied with the small victory in Figure 8.15, so can be expected to make a further cut if we match their price. The math looks very different from their point of view. If they have 240 000 customers before our response stops them winning more, a further $5 price cut will cost them $1.2m per quarter on their sales to this group. However, if it allowed them to win a further 240 000 customers, the gross profit they will still make on each one would give them just over $50m in additional gross profit. It is worthwhile, then, for them to cut price by $5 if they expect to win roughly 6 000 customers.

Figure 8.16 shows the consequences if the competitor cuts its price whenever it fails to win the number of customers that would be justified by a cut, and we cut price whenever we lose enough customers that it is worth a price cut to prevent further losses.

- Our first matching of the competitor's price of $395 prevents us losing any customers in quarter five, so the competitor cuts its price to $390. We have already lost 240 000 by that time, so this further cut by the competitor captures fewer customers from us than on the first occasion.

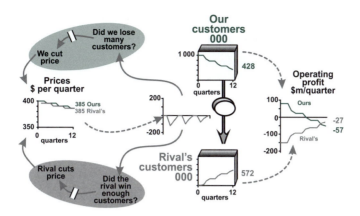

**Figure 8.16:** **Evolution of electricity customers and profits as competitors react to price cuts**

- Our second price response prevents this loss continuing also, so the competitor cuts again, and so on.

Note that the two firms' policies are not initially identical. The rival cuts price if they fail to win customers, while we cut price if we lose customers—ours is defensive whilst the rival is aggressive. However, as the competitor wins customers, they become increasingly concerned to hold on to those they have won, whilst we become interested in winning back customers we have lost.

The consequences for the profits of both suppliers are disastrous. Each company's decision on each occasion appears justified by comparing the gross profit made on customers won or lost with the smaller change in gross margin across the whole business. However, the other party's response wipes out the expected benefits from winning or retaining customers, and leaves both making less profit overall.

The two companies have other options for price changes, rather than simply to cut price by $5. We might, for example, respond with smaller price cuts of say $3, in an effort to preserve gross profit on our remaining customers whilst slowing their defection to the competitor. Unfortunately, our competitor still wants to capture customers, and continues to cut price by $5 whenever this does not occur. Although their price cuts are less frequent, the resulting customer losses continue for longer on each occasion, and we end up in a very similar position to Figure 8.16 above.

Alternatively, we could react with larger price cuts, say $7, hoping to win back some of the customers we lost. If the competitor continues to cut prices only by $5 each time, we do indeed recapture some customers and end the three years with

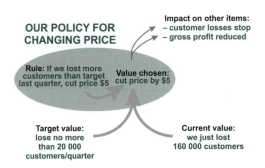

**Figure 8.17:** **Formal display of our policy for changing electricity prices.**

667 000; just sufficient to break even in profit, even though our price has fallen to $386. If the rival reacts with the same $7 price steps, however, we drive each other to still lower prices of $379, leaving us both in losses once again.

It is useful at this point to reflect once more on the distinction between "decisions" and "policies." When this example was introduced in Chapter 7, the scenarios shown simply displayed the result of a sequence of specific decisions—a change in price of a certain amount at a certain time by one firm or the other. Although the rationale for each decision was explained, the principle guiding each decision was unique to each occasion. What we have in Figures 8.15 and 8.16 in contrast are *stable* rules that live through time, even though they lead to decisions that alter repeatedly from quarter to quarter.

Figure 8.17 shows the rule for our firm in the generic policy structure from Figure 8.8, and showing the information for quarter three in Figure 8.16. The loss of $4.2m in gross profit arises because our price cut of $5 applies to the 840 000 customers we are left with after the first quarter in which households switched to the competitor. There will be a further loss of gross profit in the next quarter before our price cut deters more customers from switching.

# CONFLICTING OBJECTIVES

Although the pricing policies just explained for the two electricity suppliers are nicely linked to the immediate effect on the flow of customers, their effect on the profitability of both companies is ultimately disastrous. Neither company would in practice continue pursuing their one-dimensional policy indefinitely, and would add some consideration of how profits were changing. This could be done in

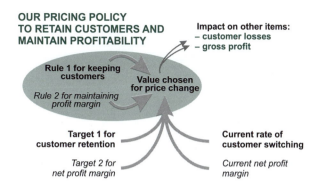

**Figure 8.18: Composite display for changing electricity prices when pursuing customers and profitability.**

various ways. For example, a company could set a target for quarterly profits, or for the operating profit margin (operating profit divided by sales revenue).

As the established supplier in this case, we will likely lose profits from the start as the new entrant takes our customers, and the cuts in price that we follow add to this pain. We therefore face a serious conflict between the objectives of keeping customers, which requires price cuts, and maintaining profits which requires holding prices up.

Our rival initially has a simpler aim—merely to win our customers. They know they will not be profitable, so set prices sufficiently below ours to keep winning customers. This cannot continue indefinitely, however, and at some point they have to try and become profitable.

What both firms need now is a "composite" policy that compares current values for customer switching *and* profitability with the targets for each, and arrives at a single decision for price that is a good compromise between these conflicting aims. This is set out in Figure 8.18. Both companies once again cut price by $5 whenever they lose too many customers, or fail to win enough. But in addition, we raise prices (or cut them by less) if our operating profit margin drops below 10%, and the larger the shortfall, the more we raise prices. Our rival starts with no objective for profitability, but from quarter six they too seek to get their net margin up to 10% by raising prices.

In Figure 8.19, the competitor again enters with a price cut worth $5/quarter for a typical customer. We are driven to respond to the threat with a price reduction of our own, and our strong profitability means we need not moderate this response. The competitor's second price cut again steals customers from us, but this time we

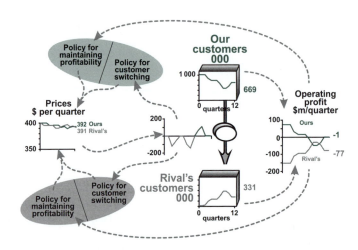

**Figure 8.19:** Composite policies aimed at customer switching and profitability in electricity supply.

are barely profitable, so cut price by rather less than $5. Meanwhile, the competitor is forced to start considering their profitability, which pushes them into raising prices rather strongly. This puts us in the unexpected position of having a lower price than our rival, leading to the recapture of more than 200 000 customers, nearly enough to cover our fixed costs and make us profitable once again.

(Online learning materials are available to support this example, see p.xxi.)

---

**Doing it right! Ensuring policy includes all possibilities**

Policy-design is a complex matter, as the examples to this point have already shown, and it is tempting to limit the rules that constitute policy to deal with just a few of the most important likely situations. However, this raises the risk of blinding management to issues they really should be considering. The pharmaceutical firm mentioned above that set its sales effort by a share-of-voice rule simply never considered the possibility that this effort was almost entirely wasted.

It is important, then, always to question whether policy is open to considering the full range of possible changes, rather than being stuck with guidelines that work fine under some conditions, but not all.

Given the numerous parameters involved in this case and the interactions between them, the scenario shown here is just one of a wide variety of outcomes that differ considerably in both scale and speed of customer movements, and in long-run profit rates for each firm. For example, if the rival is timid with its pricing and moves only by $2 each time, they do not build a significant business before they are driven to seek profitability, and both companies' prices end up well above $400.

In reality, when regulations allow new entry into a market previously served by a single monopoly supplier, the whole point of the change is to stimulate price competition and drive down prices. This would not appear to be feasible in the scenario illustrated in Figure 8.19, because the same amount of business is fought out between two organizations with the same, unchanging cost base. This is not usually what happens in such cases. First, the new entrant may have much lower overheads than the incumbent, who may not previously have had much incentive to hold down costs. The newcomer could therefore reach a profitable position both sooner than shown here and on a lower scale of business. Secondly, the competitive process itself spurs both suppliers to reduce costs further, allowing prices to fall, often substantially, even while both competitors become profitable.

## GOALS AND POLICY IN NONCOMMERCIAL CASES

The principles of developing policy to steer strategy are readily applicable to voluntary and public service situations. It is rarely advisable to link policy on most decisions to the overall performance outcome because so many resources and other influences intervene between those decisions and outcomes that a well-intended change can easily make matters worse. A voluntary organization concerned with fundraising, for example, would gain little information to help decide on its efforts from monitoring simply its flow of cash. It would be well advised to track instead the inflow of new donors, the donation rate of donors, and the rate at which previously loyal donors were lapsing. Each of these indicators implies quite different policy responses, as the illustration in Figure 5.20 shows.

Another simple example of the need to connect policy to the key flows in a situation concerns many cities' efforts to deal with homelessness. Voluntary organizations often responded to the suffering by offering food and drink to rough sleepers on the street. The unintended consequence was to discourage the homeless from seeking help to escape from their situation, so with a continuing inflow of new people, the numbers sleeping rough escalated. Policy in many major cities now focuses on slowing the arrival of the newly homeless, and making it easy for people already in that situation to access services supportive of their needs, such as sheltered accommodation and drug treatment. The responses to the changes in US welfare policy in Chapter 6 make a similar point about focusing attention on the key flow rates.

*Multiple agencies*   The US Welfare reforms case also illustrates a further challenge in many social policy issues not found in most commercial cases—the involvement of multiple agencies in different parts of the system. Often, groups who appear to be far removed from the expressed problem nevertheless have a role to play in its solution. In the UK, for example, it was discovered that many homeless people had previously been in the armed forces. This link was not visible to the military because people retiring seemed to move into reasonable employment. This has led to more attention being paid to ensuring that people retiring from the military are better set up to cope with the unfamiliar challenges of civilian life[6].

*Zero-goals*   A further feature of noncommercial cases, introduced in Chapter 1, is that the goal is often to move an indicator towards zero; no crime, no diabetes, no homelessness, and so on. It is perfectly possible to include such an "aim for zero" goal into the standard policy framework of Figure 8.17.

*Conflicting goals*   Public services and voluntary organizations will also recognize the challenge of conflicting goals, analogous to the example in Figure 8.18. The challenge of "How do we balance a drive for business growth with the need to increase short-term profit?" translates into "How do we drive to provide more service or make faster progress on fixing the problem we exist to achieve, whilst containing the cost of doing so?"

The aim of limiting the number of people with type-2 diabetes explained in Chapter 6 raises a further complication. There is clearly a conflict between the goal of detecting and preventing the advancement of the disease, and the need to limit the costs involved. Added to this, however, is the conflict between seeking to maintain the greatest quality of life for people with the disease and the wish to minimize the number of sufferers. As previously noted, success in the first objective results in failure on the second, due to increased life-expectancy, although it would clearly be inhumane to drive health policy by a goal that resulted in more, earlier deaths.

# WHEN MULTIPLE DECISIONS AFFECT THE SAME RESOURCE

The examples so far have assumed for simplicity that one decision affects one part of the system and others affect different parts. The consumer brand, for example, allows marketing spend only to affect consumers' purchase rates, and price to affect only their consumption rate. It would be convenient if this was realistic, but it is often not so. Price would probably also affect the gain and loss of consumers' interest, and marketing would influence their purchase rate. Other cases we have considered also feature factors whose levels are affected by more than one decision.

- In the staffing challenge for the law firm in Figure 6.1, both hiring and promotion change the number of lawyers below partner level that the firm will have in the next quarter. In this case, co-ordinating the two decisions is not too difficult. The firm would probably want to assess the rate at which it will upgrade lawyers to partners, allow for likely losses of lawyers, anticipate the number of lawyers it will need, then hire to fill the shortfall.
- The flow of products in the first part of the product development pipeline in Figure 6.3 depended both upon the number of new ideas the business sought, and the fraction that were screened out as being most promising. In that case, the two decisions were balanced by reference to the limited capacity of later parts of the development process.[7]
- The equipment reliability problem in Figure 6.4 requires four spending decisions—maintenance on reliable and degenerating units, and the rate of refurbishment and replacement. Maintenance spend and the refurbishment rate both affect the stock of degenerating units and the rate at which these become unreliable. So if there are too many degenerating units (and hence too fast a rise in unreliable units), how should maintenance and refurbishment be balanced? This balance is again not too difficult, since there is a maximum useful maintenance rate that optimizes the time that units can be kept from becoming unreliable (10 years). Any aim the business may have to cut numbers of degenerating units still further can only be met by refurbishing those extra units. How much should be spent on this in each year simply depends on the period of time management is prepared to wait to see the problem fixed and any constraints they may face on available capital.

One of the most common pairs of decisions to interfere with each other is price and marketing. As noted above, both may affect customer flows, and both may affect purchase rates. In addition, price directly affects gross profit, and marketing spend is a significant cost, so together the two decisions immediately affect operating profit.

This conflict between marketing and price can be explored by modifying and extending the model of new-product adoption from Chapter 4 (Figure 4.10). In Figure 8.20, a consumer electronic product is launched into a market with an

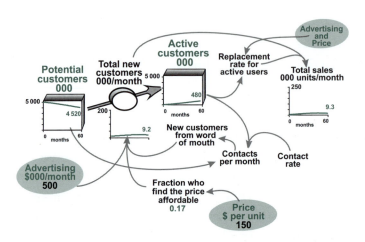

**Figure 8.20:** Constant, cautious decision on advertizing and pricing for a consumer electronic product.

estimated 5 million users. As in Chapter 4, increasing advertizing spend raises the fraction of consumers reached, a process that is assisted by word-of-mouth contact between potential and actual customers. The product is assumed to fully meet customers' needs for functionality. Price determines the fraction of would-be customers who find the product affordable, so moderates the number of first- time customers buying, whether due to advertizing or to word of mouth. Advertizing reach and price also limit the fraction of existing customers who replace the product each month.

The scenario shown has no policy whatever—advertizing is a constant $0.5m per month, and price is fixed at $150 per unit. The outcome is not exactly exciting either. Few potential customers are reached by the advertizing, and the price is attractive to only a small fraction of them. Consequently, too few active customers develop to drive any significant word-of-mouth growth, and even those few customers who come into contact with existing users mostly find the product too expensive. Consequently, sales never become significant. Clearly some policies are needed that will move price to a level that is affordable to a significant fraction of customers and to move advertizing spend to a rate that will reach enough potential customers to get sales going. Bear in mind that, though we can see clearly all the important information in this case, especially the number of potential customers and the affordability of the product, such information would in reality be only roughly known as the initiative starts, if at all.

## A POLICY FOR ADVERTIZING ALONE

We do not know how effective advertizing spend actually is, so it would be reasonable to set an initial spending rate that is similar to comparable products, which we discover is up to $4m per month. However, since we do not know the product's potential, it might also be wise to set this at the more cautious end of the range, say $0.5 m per month. What we then need is a policy that checks whether advertizing is working, and raises spending if so, or lowers it if not. Since the product sector moves rather rapidly, we also need this policy to change our advertizing rate quickly, rather than waiting for long periods or making relatively small adjustments.

One approach would be to check if the monthly sales to new users are worth more than the monthly advertizing cost, and if so, implement a substantial fractional increase in advertizing. As the spending rate increases, subsequent increases in spending will also be greater, reflecting increasing confidence that advertizing is indeed working. This could drive our spending to very high rates, very fast, so we may also need the policy to include a mechanism for limiting the spending rate when further increases serve no purpose.

Although we did not know initially how much advertizing would reach how many people, by the time we have been advertizing for a few months this information will be known. It is therefore easy to add a limit that stops any further increases once research tells us that most of the target market is being reached.

Finally, the policy needs to start reducing the advertizing spend when it is no longer being effective. This could start to happen once most of the potential market has been captured. Unfortunately, since we do not know what that number is, we will have to use some other information. The using-up of the potential market has one particular effect, namely the slow-down in the rate at which new customers are captured. At some point, the amount we are spending will not be justified by the gross profit on sales to the declining number of new customers. At that point, we might be well-advised to start reducing the rate of spending. This cutback should not be too severe, in case we misjudge what is happening, but the longer the decline in customer capture continues, the more it is likely that advertizing is not achieving any benefit and can safely be cut.

The policy then is:

- start with a modest rate of advertizing ($0.5m per month)
- increase by a large fraction each month (up to 50%) if advertizing seems to be winning new customers, the fraction being larger if the apparent value is higher
- stop any increases when advertizing is reaching all of the potential market

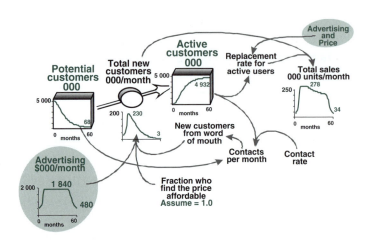

**Figure 8.21:** **Effect of a policy for advertizing rates on uptake and sales for the consumer electronic product (assuming it is affordable).**

- cut advertizing by a fraction each month (10%) when it seems to have stopped being worthwhile.

Figure 8.21 shows the consequences of this policy, given the specific characteristics of this product market. Early sales to new users justify increased spending (assuming the price is affordable), which quickly rises to a rate at which all the potential customers are being reached. This, and the significant word-of-mouth effect drive a rapid capture of new customers until, after four years, there is so little remaining potential that advertising is cut back again. Note that unit sales continue at a high rate, even when the customer win rate falls back, because of repurchases by the customer-base. However, sales too later drop, when the advertising policy—which was geared to capturing new customers—leads to a fall in spending.

This example shows once again the distinction between decisions and policy. Whereas in previous chapters we worked out what decisions might be best from time to time as the various scenarios progressed, we needed to repeat this every period. Now, we have a single *rule* for making a decision that survives through time. In effect, we could write this rule down, give it to a clerk (or a computer) and leave, confident in the knowledge that it would do the decision-making for us! This may seem shocking, but as remarked earlier in the chapter, it is no more than a continuation of a process that has gone on for over a century—seeking ways of optimizing and then automating decision-making processes that would otherwise have been unreliable.

Fortunately, there is still a role for management. Most of the parameters in this example are known and fixed, and there are no shocks to the system, brought about for example by the arrival of new competitors or other external forces. Just as we still need aircraft pilots in case of unexpected events that are beyond what the auto-pilot can handle, we need management to be alert for exceptional circumstances and if these occur to either adjust the policies or take over hands-on control.

A further point to note about the structure in Figure 8.21, as well as earlier examples in this chapter, concerns exactly the decision that is being made. Except for the initial decision, it is *not* "What advertizing rate should we set?" Rather, it is "By how much should we change the advertizing rate?" This is a common feature of strategy:

**Policies frequently concern *changes* to decision parameters, rather than choice of the next decision-value.**

There are good reasons for this use of "policy by adjustment," as well as risks. First, the most reliable information available often concerns the recent past, which will include recent values of the decisions that were taken. Secondly, the information needed to construct the ideal decision from first principles is rarely available. The "best" decision for advertizing in this case, for example, would require good information on the number of remaining potential customers, the market reach that different rates of advertizing would achieve, and the fractional response of those customers the advertizing did in fact reach. None of this is available with much reliability, whereas we do (or can) know the latest monthly sales rate to new customers.

The risks, however, are also significant. The current choice of decision may be so far from a good range that no information is available to indicate a move in the right direction. Second, the adjustment rate may be so slow as to provide no clear conclusion as to the true impact of any change in decision—hence the common stagnation of policy and performance caused by annual budgeting processes based on "last year $+/-$ X%" rules.

This approach to decision-making reflects a principle known as "anchoring and adjustment," a widely prevalent feature of human behavior (see box below).

### Anchoring and adjustment in decision-making

Anchoring and adjustment is a psychological phenomenon that influences the way people assess probabilities. Following a rule of thumb, or heuristic, defined by the anchor-and-adjust principle, people start with an implied reference point (the "anchor") and make adjustments to it to reach their estimate.[8]

For example, people asked if they think the population of Shangai is more or less than 10 million will on average make higher estimates of the actual number than those asked if it is more or less than 5 million. The phenomenon has now been so widely observed and replicated in experimentation that it is widely regarded as axiomatic of the way in which people make judgments.

It is a small step to see how this principle gets built into decision-making. Given the need to work out the best decision for something today, people reasonably anchor their thinking with recent decision values. This implies that the mechanics of the anchoring and adjustment decision process can be made explicit. It requires past decisions to be stored, and then some rule of thumb or heuristic applied to the scale and direction of the adjustment that must be made to that stored value to arrive at the new decision. But we already know how things get stored and adjusted—with the stock and flow structure.

Figure 8.22 shows what is really happening when the advertizing policy in Figure 8.21 is operating. The stock contains the anchor for the decision—last month's decision-value. This and the rate of customer capture are compared and, inside the flow, the policy computes what change should be made to the decision-value for this period. The stock and flow are shown in dashed lines because they do not conform to our definition from Chapter 2 of what constitutes a "resource" in the strategic architecture. Nevertheless, the decision - value genuinely *is* stored, and is adjusted up or down by the flow rate that is the change in decision value.

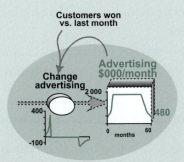

**Figure 8.22: The stock-and-flow view of the anchor-and-adjustment principle for advertizing spend.**

The policy for changes in advertizing rate given above is already quite complex. Indeed, management may take the view that it is unrealistically so. However, the alternative is to fall back on "judgment" which is just another word for an implicit policy that no-one can see or evaluate. Whilst not wishing to under-value the excellent judgment that many experienced executives make constantly about a wide range of strategically vital issues, there remains a substantial opportunity to improve on that judgment by making it explicit and testing it against evidence, just as has been done for many other instances of human decision-making.

That being said, our policy in Figure 8.21 has limitations of its own. Most seriously, it relies on information about a factor—the customer win rate—that is subject to other important influences besides that of the decision variable we are changing. Customers are also being won by word of mouth, so it is possible that the policy would continue to recommend high rates of spending, due to strong customer growth, when in fact most of that growth is arising for other reasons. Secondly, the customer win rate is moderated by the product's price, so it is also possible for that rate to be low, and hence lead to a cut in spending, when in fact the advertizing is doing its job just fine but is being held back by a too-high price.

There is a further problem with the advertizing policy based solely on its impact on the customer win rate—it allows spending to be reduced, even though it supports continued repurchasing by existing owners of the product. So one further useful adjustment would be to slow down or stop the later reduction in spending if there are signs that it is reducing this repurchase rate. This should be straightforward to achieve, since by that stage there will be a large population of existing users for the product whose behavior can be researched. A suitable policy might be:

- increase advertizing by $100000 per month if sales to existing owners fall by so much as to lose this amount of gross profit, up to a limit of $2m per month

## ADDING A POLICY FOR PRICE

Now we have a policy for advertizing that appears to work, provided that the product is affordable, it is possible to add a policy that adjusts the product price. Once again, since this is a new kind of product, the initial price may need to be estimated from looking at the price of any nearly comparable products that may exist, or else from customer research as to what people might be willing to pay, given the benefits the product offers. The more novel the product, the less exact this process will be. In that case, it is worth noting that price reductions are often easier to justify to the market than price increases, which implies starting with a price at the higher end of the likely acceptable range.

In this case, that initial price is chosen to be $150, which research suggests should be affordable to about a quarter of the potential market. This compares with an initial production cost of $120, giving a small gross profit of just $30 per unit. This unit cost will fall, though, as experience curve effects drive substantial improvements in efficiency (see Chapter 6). In this case, each doubling of cumulative sales volume is expected to cut unit costs by 15%.

At this point, the first conflict with the advertizing policy becomes apparent. With a margin of just $30 per unit, advertizing of $0.5m/month must capture about 7000 new customers to be justified. With the low advertizing rate having a limited reach into the market, few potential customers are encouraged to consider the product, and with only a small fraction of those finding the price affordable, the rate of 7000 new customers per month is missed, so unit sales do not generate enough gross profit to justify continuing with the advertizing. Spending is therefore cut, which reaches still fewer customers, and the firm abandons the product because "there was not sufficient market demand."

There might, however, be sufficient market demand if advertizing could be sustained until the price can be reduced. The advertizing policy is therefore modified with a further piece of the rule stating that:

● advertizing will not be cut during the first 12 months

This is a perfectly common policy element for new initiatives. Management readily recognizes that it may take some time before marketing, price cuts and other efforts produce enough response in the market to be worthwhile, so suspend spending cuts, price increases and other policies to boost profitability until a reasonable time has elapsed for the initiative to show whether it may be viable.

With initial advertizing rate sustained for the first few months, the firm can now set about a policy for pricing aimed at helping the capture of new customers. Although it believed that the price of $150 would capture a quarter of potential customers, early research suggests that only 17% found the price affordable. The company therefore decides to reduce the price. Three questions then arise. First, how often should this price review be repeated? Second, by how much should the price be cut? Third, should the price continue to be cut until every last customer finds it affordable, or should there be some floor below which price will not be reduced?

Even in fast moving markets, it can be hard to know whether information on customer responses in just a short period is reliable, so this firm reviews the price level every three months, rather than monthly. With such a low fraction of customers finding the product affordable, the firm would likely consider reasonably substantial price moves so as to make a significant shift in this key parameter, say 20% rather than 5–10%. The first price cut would therefore be from $150 to $120. Management can, however, be reasonably confident that unit costs will have dropped substantially by that stage, so gross margin may be sustained.

To answer the third question, management will eventually have good information on the fraction of customers who find the price affordable, and could develop a rather sophisticated rule to identify if a further price reduction is justified. For example, they could compare the cost of a further $1 across all the sales they would receive with the likely gross profit they would add from capturing the small extra fraction of customers that the price cut would win. (This is a similar principle to the price-cut evaluation in the electricity market, earlier in this chapter.) Such a policy is complicated in this case by the repeat sales made by existing customers, so for simplicity, we will stop cutting price when 85% of potential customers find the price affordable.

The pricing policy is therefore:

● set an initial price of $150
● every three months, cut price by 20% if the fraction of customers who find the product affordable is less than 85%

The result of adopting this policy—and the modified policy for advertizing spend, is shown in Figure 8.23. The advertizing policy ensures that spending continues

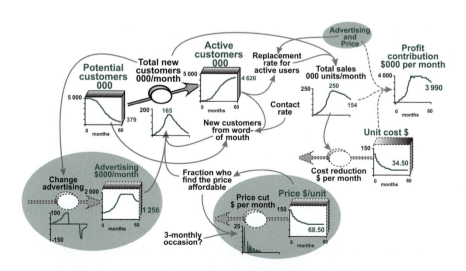

**Figure 8.23: Coordinated policies for advertizing and pricing for the consumer electronic product.**

while the product's price is brought to an affordable level, at which point sales to new customers start to grow. After six months, the profit contribution on new sales justifies testing significant increases in advertizing expenditure. This works increasingly well, so causes still further spending increases until research shows that the entire potential market is being reached by the advertizing spend. Meanwhile, checking on the product's affordability has led to progressive price cuts, but the escalating sales have driven unit costs down, so the product remains profitable.

By half way through the period, the product is cheap enough to be affordable for enough of the potential market to stop reducing prices further, and by the end of year four, the full exploitation of the market leads to advertizing being cut back, but no so much as to allow a serious fall in repeat sales.

Just one further policy element would be needed to complete this picture, namely some check that prices do not fall too far towards the level of unit cost, which would destroy gross margin. With that last addition, we would have a policy set for steering this product's strategy that *both* builds sales and profitability quickly, *and* sustains them in the longer term.

(Online learning materials are available to support this example, see p.xxi.)

## POLICY, DECISION-MAKING AND THE BALANCED SCORECARD AND VALUE-BASED MANAGEMENT

Chapter 4 ended with a brief description of how the balanced scorecards (BSCs) now increasingly used by organizations can be populated with information from the strategic architecture of an organization. What was missing, however, was an explanation of how exactly the organization should respond to any disparities that arise between the actual value for a variable and its target value at a particular point in time. The policy framework developed in this chapter goes some way to providing that missing item. Such a "gap" between actual and target for a performance measure is precisely the input that a policy-function requires. Given that gap and a decision-rule, the policy leads to a change in decision that is designed specifically to close the gap.

Chapter 4 also offered some warning about the difficulty in attributing value to any particular element in a business, because of the mutual interdependence between resources. Figure 8.23 adds to this warning. There is simply no such thing as "a value" for any particular choice of advertizing or price because the enterprise value is the outcome of a complex, dynamic interaction between each of these items. The actual value that will eventually emerge from a particular choice at a particular time depends on the history of the case up to that point, and the future choices that will be made on both items. Given these problems in this simple case, the difficulties in more complex real-world situations can well be imagined.

## GOALS, POLICIES AND DECISIONS IN LOW-FARE AIRLINES

Companies such as Southwest, Ryanair and AirAsia offer a quite transparent view of strategy and policy making, because so much of what they do is highly public; from the opening of new routes and ordering of aircraft to changes in pricing levels.

The first observation to make goes back to the first kind of strategic decision discussed at the start of this chapter, that is whether to get involved by starting a new business in the industry at all. The global airline market has a long history of destroying value, going way back to the earliest days of commercial service. Yet somehow the industry continues to attract hopeful new entrants, most of whom will fail outright, or fail to become significant, viable operators.

This question of whether to participate, specifically in the low-fare sector of the industry, has changed substantially over the years. When deregulation of the US domestic market threw open the doors to new operators during the 1980s, a number of hopeful new businesses started up, Southwest airlines among them. That era also demonstrates, however, the powerful connection between the question of *whether* to take part and *how*. Another entrant at the time, People Express, got off to a meteoric start, but then collapsed in a still more spectacular fashion.[9] The answer to the question as to whether to enter the industry was therefore "Yes, if you follow a strategy like Southwest," but "No, if you plan to develop like People Express."

As the industry segment has opened up and developed in various regions around the world, the same division between new entrants with sound strategies and others with weaker alternatives has played out repeatedly. Some early entrants, such as AirAsia, Ryanair and easyJet have found a powerful strategy and grown, while others have not, and failed.

Key to the successes has been some subtle choices, such as the choice of which airport to choose in a general locality. Some airlines are happy to start operations from major city airports—an expensive option—in the knowledge that their otherwise low costs will enable them to under-price and capture passengers from the full-service operators. Others, such as Ryanair, go to great lengths to find the cheapest possible airport somewhere within range of the target city, so they can price way lower than competitors.

Both kinds of strategy towards choice of airport have proved successful for some airlines, and unsuccessful for others. The successes must therefore also have discovered sound policies for *steering* the strategy once it had been started. These include both the rate of adding new airports and routes, selection of the flight frequency and schedule, and the rate of expansion both of the fleet and staff numbers.

One policy for steering these firms is a good example of complex decision-making on an issue of strategic importance becoming automated, even when it concerns complex behavioral responses. Setting prices for airline tickets was once a decision taken by human management, and revised rather infrequently. Today, systems for yield management, or revenue management, constantly adjust prices for the next ticket to be sold on a particular flight in response to demand and the remaining number of seats available, as the date and time of the flight approaches. Similar systems are also deployed for making reservations in hotels and car rental.[10]

The subtle differences in strategy choices and on-going management of strategy may go some way to explain the wide variety of outcomes amongst airlines, from the astonishing success of some to the regular failure of others. However, difference in strategy choices and policy alone may not be sufficient to account for these differential results. An important additional factor concerns the development of *capability* in those firms. Several low-fare airlines, for example, may have identical criteria for choice of airport in a locality, and identical approaches to minimizing costs to enable them to offer the lowest possible fares. One firm, however (in Europe, Ryanair), has simply become much better at doing these things, an issue that will be examined in Chapter 10.

## BEHAVIORAL DECISION-MAKING AND BOUNDED RATIONALITY[11]

Chapter 7 already raised the issue of human beings' limited capacity to make rational choices. At that point, attention was given to customers' choice of which product to choose, or which supplier to buy from. When these considerations impact on management decision-making, it gives rise to the "bounded rationality" which infects the decisions that executives take in order to pursue their strategy.

It has long been known that bounded rationality causes organizations as a whole to behave in an "adaptively" rational manner,[12] in which:

- there exist a number of states of the system, some of which are preferred to others, depending on circumstances
- the system is subject to uncontrollable shocks from the outside world

- the system contains a number of decision variables, whose values are chosen according to certain decision rules
- the combination of external events and internal decisions trigger changes in the system and thus move it to a new state (which connects closely to the limited set of equations defining the strategic architecture of the firm, given at the start of Chapter 4)
- any decision rule that leads to a preferred state is more likely to be used in future.

The illustrations given in this chapter show clearly the principal features of bounded rationality:

- they use only a limited number of criteria in making choices: the advertizing policy in Figure 8.23 could have used a number of alternative or additional criteria, such as its market reach, but it gets too complex to use this criterion as well as the new customer win rate, so the alternative is ignored
- they favor information that is concrete and certain rather than abstract and ambiguous: the number of new customers won per month is relatively easy to discover, and can be known with a good degree of confidence, rather than say the remaining number of potential customers, which could only be very roughly estimated
- they use simple rules of thumb to decide on the balance between competing criteria: for example, advertizing would be cut if the customer capture in Figure 8.23 fell to a low rate, but not if it resulted in a reduction in repeat sales.

The second of these issues is worth considering in a little more detail. Confronted with the need to make a decision, an individual must inevitably select amongst the wide range of information items that might be relevant. The policy framework in Figure 8.8 therefore includes some "filters" that screen out only those few items that the decision-maker can cope with.[13] In organizations large enough to be beyond the scope of a single individual's control, these considerations give rise to a "factored decision-making"; the tendency for the many necessary decisions to be divided out, or factored, amongst a number of people or groups.[14] This too is evident in the illustration in Figure 8.23, since the separate, self-contained rules for pricing and advertizing could readily be issued to two quite different parts of the organization and pursued independently, with little danger of inconsistency between them.

Whilst factored decision-making is a pragmatic solution to an organization's problem of making choices continuously on numerous decisions, it clearly comes with some dangers. It would be just perfect if each of the "factored" decisions could anticipate all the eventualities that may arise from choices on other decisions, but as has just been established, it is not possible for people or teams who are not omniscient to include all possible values of all possibly-relevant criteria. There remains, then, a very real possibility that decisions taken in one part of an organization may run into conflict with decisions taken in good faith elsewhere. This is especially likely when the delays caused by accumulation effects give rise to a separation in time between decisions and their consequences.

### Summary of Chapter 8

"Strategic decisions" cover a wide range of choices that management must make, starting with whether to pursue an opportunity, and if so how. There can be considerable variance in the likely outcome, depending on the choices made along that path, which can result in perfectly attractive opportunities being missed.

Strategic decision-making does not stop when the choice has been made of who to serve, with what, and how, but continues to include any choices that have the potential to make a significant impact on medium- to long-term performance, at any time.

A "policy" is a rule for working out a decision's value for the next period. It requires a target of some kind for one or more performance indicators, and information for the latest period on the actual value of those indicators. The rule is a procedure for computing the decision from the gap between these target and actual values. The policy may include other parameters, such as the scale of any change that is to be made to the decision in any period.

Competitors also make decisions, guided by their own objectives and policies, and these will have consequences for our own performance that must be factored into our own policies.

Policy often defines any *change* that should be made to a decision, rather than the absolute level of the decision, a process known as "anchoring and adjustment." This has the advantage of avoiding frequent, radical revisions, but can also slow down movement to better decisions.

Policy often has to include procedures for resolving conflicts between two or more objectives, and for balancing the impact of a single decision on more than one part of the business system.

# SUGGESTED QUESTIONS AND EXERCISES

1.  Describe different kinds of "strategic" decisions and explain the connections between them.

2.  Why are decisions that continue to be made from period to period throughout the life of the organization nevertheless of "strategic" importance?

3.  Define a "policy." What is the difference between a policy and a decision? What are the key elements of a policy and how are they related?

4.  Identify a few of the most important decisions that management must continue to make in order to steer strategy for the organization you chose to look at in Chapters 2–4. Make sure that your choices include decisions that can guide the growth and retention of each of the key resources. Alternatively, carry out the same exercise using the outline architectures you developed after Chapter 4 for one or more of the following examples:
    a.  a retail chain, such as Starbucks
    b.  a company manufacturing and servicing elevators
    c.  an online dating agency
    d.  a voluntary organization providing medical centers in locations that have no alternative provision.

5.  For one or more of the decisions you identified in answer to question 4, specify a policy for guiding that decision, following the principles defined in this chapter (especially Figures 8.8 and 8.22). You should end up with a series of statements similar to those given for the advertizing policy for the consumer electronic product on pages 557 and 558.

6.  Use Worksheet 13 to lay out the connections involved in one of the policies specified in answer to question 5.

7.  Continuing with the example from question 4, identify one or more performance indicators that will be affected by competitors' decisions. How will your own policy need to be adapted to take account of this competitive impact?

8.  Continuing with the example from question 4, identify any decision that will impact on more than one important performance measure. Again, develop a list of statements that define a policy for this decision, ensuring that those statements reflect all of the decision's potential effects.

# USING WORKSHEET 13

Before using this Worksheet the following steps should be taken:

- specify the timescale and frequency over which the situation is to be examined, e.g. two years back and three years forward in months, and the scale for all variables
- identify and specify the decision value that the policy is intended to guide.
- identify and name the resource affected by the decision variable
- add a timescale and value scale to each item, and insert data or estimates for how those quantities have changed in the past and might change in the future

(In common with other worksheets, this one can also be used to examine just the current situation and implications of alternative choices for the next period. In this case, it is not necessary to specify the timescale to be studied, nor to sketch the time charts as suggested below. Simply enter numerical values instead. In that case, though, it is important to beware of the sometimes surprising implications for performance in future periods arising from choices that are apparently sound on a short-term view.)

Write out a verbal statement of the policy, similar to that given for the advertizing policy for the consumer electronic product on pages 557 and 558.

Identify the measures that will inform the policy, and link these to the "Change in decision" item. (In Figure 8.23, for example, the flow of new customers drives the decision for "change advertizing.")

Link the decision item to any other variable in the structure that it may affect. (In Figure 8.23, the advertizing rate affects the repurchase rate and profit contribution, as well as the new customer win rate.)

Connect the resource and remaining items into a causal explanation for the performance indicator at lower-right, following the principles specified in Chapter 2. This need not be a complete explanation, but note any incomplete links.

To use the completed worksheet, start with the change you intend to make to the decision variable in the next period:

- follow the links from the decision to estimate what difference it will make to the resource flow and other items it affects
- continue to follow the causal linkages to estimate the effects of the next-period decision
- trace the feedback from the consequences of this decision back into the policy itself (for example, the link from "new customers" to "change advertizing" in Figure 8.23)
- following your written statement of the policy, estimate the next period's change in the decision.

Repeat this procedure to trace out the likely change in the decision and its consequences over future periods.

This worksheet is most easily worked using the **my**strategy software version, see paragraph about online learning materials on p.xxi.

# WORKSHEET 13: POLICY STRUCTURE

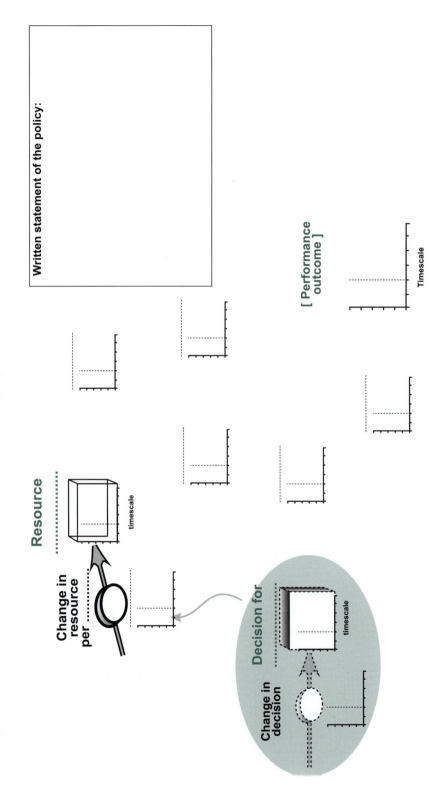

Written statement of the policy:

Resource

Change in resource per ........

timescale

Decision for

timescale

Change in decision

[ Performance outcome ]

Timescale

# NOTES

1. Calculating this cost of capital is a complex matter, detailed explanation of which can be found in any good finance reference book. See for example Copeland, T., Koller, T. and J. Murrin, *Valuation – Measuring and Managing the Value of Companies*, 4th edn, (2005) John Wiley & Sons, Ltd, Chichester, Chapter 10. This source or similar should also be studied for more extensive explanation of how to value strategies and firms.

2. Eisenhardt K. and Sull, D. (2001) Strategy as Simple Rules, *Harvard Business Review*, (January), 107–116.

3. Simons, R. (2005) Desiging High-Performance Jobs, *Harvard Business Review*, (July-August), 54–63

4. See Minzberg, H. (1985) Of Strategies Deliberate and Emergent, *Strategic Management Journal*, **6**, 257–272 Quinn, J.B.(1978) Strategic Change: Logical Incrementalism, *Sloan Management Review*, (Fall volume), 1–21, Mintzberg, H., Lampel, J., Quinn, J.B. and Ghoshal, S. (2003) *The Strategy Process* (4th edn), Prentice Hall, Hemel Hempstead, Chapters 3 and 5.

5. More can be found on formulating policy for guiding decisions in Sterman, J. (2000) *Business Dynamics: Systems Thinking and Modeling for a Complex World*, McGraw-Hill, New York, Chapter 13.

6. Extensive work has been done on the development of strategy and policy for tackling dynamically complex societal problems involving multiple agencies. Homer, J.B. (1993) A system dynamics model of national cocaine prevalence, *System Dynamics Review*, **9**(1), 49–78; a number of articles on policy in Health Care, *System Dynamics Review*, **15**(3), 1999; Rouwette, E.A.J.A., Jongebreur, W., van Hooff, P., Heijmen, T., Vennix, J.A.M. (2004) Modeling Crime Control in the Netherlands, *Proceedings of the 22nd International Conference of the System Dynamics Society*, Oxford, UK.

7. For an example of policy implications arising from the dynamics of new product introductions see Milling, P.M. (1996) Modeling innovation processes for decision support and management simulation, *System Dynamics Review*, **12**(3), 211–234.

8. The concept of anchoring and adjustment was developed in Amos Tversky 1 and Daniel Kahneman 1, 1974, Judgment under Uncertainty: Heuristics and Biases *Science*, **185**(4157), 112–1131. An example of its application in a marketing context is given in Wansink, B., Kent, R.J., Hoch, S.J. (1998) An Anchoring and Adjustment Model of Purchase Quantity Decisions, *Journal of Marketing Research*, **35**(1), 71–81.

9. See the case study (1980) Holland, P. *People Express Airlines: Rise and Decline*, Case 9-490-012, Harvard Business School Publishing, Boston MA.

10. Much information on how yield management systems work is available from The Institute for Operations Research and the Management Sciences (INFORMS), at http://revenue-mgt.section.informs.org/index.html.

11. More can be found on modeling human behavior and bounded rationality in Sterman, J. (2000) see note 5 above, Chapter 15.

12. An early exploration of how bounded rationality is manifest in the way that organizations behave appeared with Cyert, R.M. and March, R.M. (1963) *A behavioural theory of the firm*, Prentice Hall, Engelwood Cliffs.

13. An explanation of this filtering of information and its links to decision-making can be found in Morecroft, J.D.W. (1985) The feedback view of business and strategy. *System Dynamics Review*, **1**, 4–19. The implications for strategic control of business systems are discussed and illustrated in Sterman, J. (2000) *Business Dynamics*, McGraw-Hill: Boston, Chapter 15.

14. Some of the dangers that arise from factored decision-making are discussed in Bower, J.L. and Gilbert, C.G. (2007) How Managers' Everyday Decisions Create—or Destroy—Your Company's Strategy, *Harvard Business Review*, **85**(2), February, 72–79.

# CHAPTER 9

# INTANGIBLE RESOURCES*

## KEY ISSUES

✪ Classifying resources and capabilities to give a clear specification of intangible resources

✪ Three main classes of intangibles affecting the tangible heart of the strategic architecture: psychological factors, information-based resources, and quality-related items

✪ The distinction between current quality driving behavior for current customers vs. reputation influencing potential customers

✪ Perceptions that build up to threshold levels where they trigger big changes in behavior

✪ Problems with intangibles that bring the system back into balance, though not for good reasons

✪ The decay of information-related intangibles, causing a need to rebuild, and the key role of information systems strategy

✪ Knowledge as a higher-level concept than data or information, requiring effort to develop and maintain, but with important effects for many firms

✪ How quality factors, not all of which are strictly "resources" contribute to strategic performance

This chapter makes connections to the following concepts: the general classification of resources, capabilities and other asset-stocks in the resource-based view of strategy, quality management, and information and knowledge systems.

---

* This term when used in relation to strategic management should not be confused with the accounting concept of "intangible assets"—see comments later in the chapter.

It is widely accepted that intangible or soft factors have a substantial impact on organizational performance—a damaged reputation can destroy a business, strong staff motivation can drive powerful growth, proprietary knowledge can give rise to market-leading products, and so on. But there is a considerable challenge in making practical use of this general understanding to steer strategy, because of terminology that is overly wide-ranging, ambiguous and inconsistent. The following explanations from various printed sources illustrate the difficulty:

- A firm's intangible resources and capabilities are productive assets that are difficult to observe, describe and value, but that nevertheless can have a significant effect on a firm's performance. Intangible resources and capabilities such as "close relationships with customers", "close cooperation amongst managers", a sense of loyalty to the firm", and "brand awareness" are difficult to measure yet are often important determinants of firm success.[1]

- Sustainable advantage ... appears to reside in large part with intangible organizational resources–capabilities and their ilk. These are the processes, systems and structures that are at the core of the firm. ... They are tacit; that is they cannot be fully described, and they are embedded in the firm and cannot be taken out of it with any individual. These unique processes comprise what have been called intangible or "invisible" assets'[2]

- The expression "intangible" is being applied more and more frequently to resources and to capabilities. For our purposes, it refers to the following: intellectual property rights ..., trade secrets, contracts and licences, information in the public domain, personal and organizational networks, the know-how of employees, advisers, suppliers and distributors, the reputation of products and of the company, and the culture of the organization. .. and later ... [The resource-based view, RBV] identifies a range of intangible assets, including technology, patents, skills, etc. which, when combined with human and organizational resources, define the firm's core dynamic capabilities. A key set of intangible assets are the firm's reputational assets and these include the company name, its identity, brands, brand image and customer loyalty, the reputation of the firm's products and services, and the integrity of its relationships with the complex web of customers, suppliers, communities and governments.[3]

- Intangible resources cannot be touched, but are largely carried within the people in the organization. In general, tangible resources need to be purchased, while intangible resources need to be developed. ... Within the category of intangible resources, relational resources and competences can be distinguished. ... The firm can cultivate specific relationships with individuals and organizations in the environment, such as buyers, suppliers, competitors and government agencies. ... Besides direct relationships, a firm's reputation among other parties can also be an important resource. Competence, on the other hand, refers to the firm's fitness to perform in a particular field.[4]

- Intangible resources include assets that are rooted deeply in the firm's history and that have accumulated over time. Because they are embedded in unique patterns offroutines, intangible resources are relatively difficult for competitors to understand and imitate. Knowledge, trust between managers and employees or associates, ideas, the capacity for innovation, managerial capabilities, organizational routines, scientific capabilities and the firm's reputation for its goods or services and the ways it interacts with people (e.g. employees, customers, and suppliers) are examples of intangible resources.[5]

It is not feasible to find a single analytical method that deals with such diverse factors whilst accurately describing their role and behavior, and several of the comments above are open to challenge. Strategy writers acknowledge the limitations of the current confusing nomenclature and analytical treatment of intangible resources. Efforts continue to be made to resolve these problems,[6] although much of this work is directed at making RBV a useful perspective for research into strategic management, rather than at developing terminology and methods of practical value for management, advisors and analysts. This chapter therefore starts with an attempt to distinguish and specify the main groups of factors involved in strategic performance.

There is no definitively correct approach to carving out and defining distinct categories from the wide diversity of intangible issues. The following reasoning is therefore offered as a well-intentioned effort to deal with the problem, whose worth should be judged on whether the result is fit for purpose, rather than on whether it conforms with current academic treatment of the issue.

Several of the intangible factors mentioned in the sources quoted above have already been dealt with in earlier chapters, or will be tackled in Chapter 10:

- *Relationships with customers* are simply captured by the existence in the strategic architecture of a customer-base resource. That this asset-stock persists from period to period is itself representative of the fact that there is a relationship between the firm and its customers, not simply a series of isolated transactions. Indeed, this is amongst the most dominant elements of every case we have considered. It is also entirely justified by everyday business reality—virtually no business in any sector, whether product- or service-based, has to create a new relationship with each customer each day. Indeed it was previously remarked that for many enterprises, customers are a more reliable resource than their staff, that is they are more likely to remain available in future periods.

- *Staff skills* were already dealt with in detail with the principle of resource attributes covered in Chapter 5. However, skills are undoubtedly intangible, so are perhaps best described as an "intangible attribute." It was noted at the time that organizational capabilities are at a level above and beyond the sum of individuals' skills.

- *Capabilities*, as noted in Chapter 2 are activities that organizations, or groups within them, are good at doing, as distinct from resources that are things organizations have. Capabilities may well be intangible, but they deserve a category of their own, so can be removed from the lists above. They will be examined in Chapter 10.

- *Routines and processes* describe what takes place when organizations or teams get things done, such as developing new products, finding and hiring good people, dealing with customers' needs for service and support, and so on. These too will be examined in the next chapter.

- There is one notable omission from the examples of intangibles generally offered, namely the firm's *product range.* This is intangible in the sense that, although the physical product itself may be touched, the product range is a descriptive list of differing items. This too has already been dealt with, for example in relation to its appeal to customers (see Chapter 5).

- Some aspects of *reputation* have also been covered previously. The choice pipeline in Chapter 6 captures the intangible notion of "awareness" in terms of the more tangible measure of the number of people who are aware. It can depict reputation in a similar manner, that is the number of people, or fraction, who believe a product to be of high quality or who think that a company is a reliable supplier. Nevertheless, it may still be helpful to treat reputation as an intangible resource whilst recognizing that it is backed by some more tangible factor.

"Brand" deserves separate discussion. It is widely accepted that a brand is a critical kind of intangible asset, simply because of the considerable impact it has on economic value. Numerous studies have confirmed that companies with strong brands outperform their peers on several criteria.[7] Nevertheless, we argue that a brand itself is not a single resource, but a complete system of resources. If it were possible, for example, for you to buy the Coca-Cola brand from its corporate owner, its value would immediately collapse. That is because the brand is more than just a name and logo. Its continuing sales and ability to command a good price persist because of all the *other* resources of which it is a part, many of them tangible. This would include, for example, all the distributors who promote it, all the shelf space in stores that it occupies, all the consumers who are aware of, informed about, and desirous of the product, and so on. Transferring the brand from Coca-Cola Inc. to you immediately threatens the growth and sustainability of all these and other resources. This reality is certainly recognized when firms buy and sell brands, as occasionally occurs. The seller may well estimate the value of the brand to its business by some means similar to that promoted by specialist advisors such as Interbrand (see note 7), but the buyer will ask themselves by how much they can improve future sales and profits by integrating the brand they are buying into their existing system of resources—their salesforce, distributors, and so on. Only if the answer to this question is significantly positive should the transaction take place.

Given the arguments above, this book *excludes* the following factors from the definition of intangible resources:

- customer relationships
- capabilities and competences
- processes and routines
- brand

It also leaves some intangible items, such as staff skills, to be covered within the topic of attributes (see Chapter 5). Attributes that are carried by tangible resources can only be dealt with by the co-flow structures explained in Chapter 5, whether those attributes are themselves tangible (e.g. the potential customers brought by the opening of a new retail store) or intangible such as the skills brought by staff, the risk of default brought by a bank's new loan customer, or the probability of failure brought by a new piece of equipment.

This still leaves some elements to deal with from the above descriptions of intangibles:

- *Customer loyalty* is already captured in the strategic architecture in the fractional likelihood that a customer will leave in any given period. However, customers do not just stay or leave a firm because of objectively measurable features of products or services and their price. True loyalty must therefore stand one level behind this customer-flow, and reduce customers' tendency to leave, in spite of those objective factors that might otherwise motivate them to do so. It would appear to reflect their state of mind, so will be included in the treatment of intangibles.
- Similar reasoning applies to *staff loyalty*. Zero staff turnover is rare (and not necessarily a good thing), so people are continually leaving organizations for various reasons, from pay rate to career opportunities. An extra ingredient of loyalty should therefore account for the difference between how quickly staff actually respond to those motivations and the rate that they would do so if they had no feeling of loyalty. Staff turnover may reflect how loyal staff feel towards the organization, but it is a consequence of that loyalty, not the thing itself—the

feeling that staff have in their minds. The loss of staff, like that of customers, also requires that some realistic alternative exists. Low turnover does not reflect loyalty if staff are staying with you only because there is no other reasonable job to move to.

- It is debatable whether *technology* is intangible at all. To the extent that it is a written specification of how to make certain components or products, it can be (and often is) traded and licensed to others. Patents are a particular form of codified technology, also tradable. To be useful in driving firm performance, however, documented technology relies on other knowledge and capability, much of which is tacit. An illustration of this phenomenon concerns a discovery by Intel early in its experience of manufacturing microprocessors. When it wanted to expand capacity by building a new Silicon Fab manufacturing plant, it always seemed better to blindly copy every detail of an existing plant, right down to the type of screws used and the layout of the route to the washrooms. Doing so rapidly increased the speed at which each new plant reached its expected output. Although no-one could document exactly why, all the small changes introduced when engineers tried to improve the new plants' design introduced unanticipated errors that damaged performance.

- *Knowledge* is similarly manifest in organizations' records, whether on paper or in information systems. This is certainly the case insofar as it concerns *what* the organization knows, and may apply also to knowledge about *how* to do things. Sometimes know-how too is codified, as for example in the franchise manuals of McDonald's. It is therefore possible for both forms of knowledge to be traded, which rather suggests it can be treated in the same way as tangible resources. Similar arguments apply to information systems. That being said, finding a way to quantify such factors is not straightforward. Counting the pages in the franchise manual does not define the contribution it makes to business performance, nor does counting the number of case files in a consulting firm's knowledge base or the number of data records in a firm's information systems.

- Also excluded from most common explanations of intangible resources are the various manifestations of *quality*. As will be explained, many examples of quality do not fulfill the criteria of being a resource in that they do not accumulate or deplete over time. For example, quality of service is low if there are too few people to deal with customer enquiries today. If enough people could be added tomorrow, quality of service may be fine. Since the quality itself can be changed immediately, it cannot be an accumulating asset-stock and is therefore not a resource. Since staff can in most cases be added only gradually, quality may appear to take time to fix, but it is the staff that is the accumulating resource, not the quality itself.

Nevertheless, in cases such as the performance or reliability of manufactured products, quality is most easily understood as a resource in its own right. Quality reflects an unknowable number of factors causing problems that need to be worked on by skilled people and gradually eliminated.

*Not "intangible assets"*

Some further terms used in relation to resources and capabilities include the word "assets." One hierarchy suggested for these assets is that they range from "make-or-buy" assets, which can as the name implies be simply bought, through "complementary assets" that work together with "strategic assets" to generate sustained competitive advantage.[8] As often used, then, the term "assets" encompasses all resources and capabilities. There is a good technical reason for adopting this word in that all the factors discussed above show bathtub behavior of filling and draining over time, a process defined as "asset-stock accumulation" (see Chapter 3). However, there are two reasons for *not* using "assets" when assessing resources and capabilities in practice. First is the problem we started with above, namely that a term encompassing such an extensive variety of factors will be confusing when also used to define any particular category of those factors. Second, the term "assets" also has a specific and widely accepted meaning relating to items in a company's accounting statements. The term "intangible assets," too, has a specific meaning in that context, referring to the value of such items as patents and brands. To avoid confusion with use of the term in financial accounting, this chapter will therefore not refer to "intangible assets."

Whilst financial values in companies' reports are directly ascribed to particular intangible factors, we are concerned here with the intangible elements themselves, not with their financial value. As several of the sources quoted at the start of this chapter suggest, those financial values do not provide a useful basis for analysing the contribution made by intangible resources to firms' performance. For the same reason, we will avoid the term "invisible assets," even though this too has been used to describe many resources and capabilities.[9]

## A CLASSIFICATION OF RESOURCES AND CAPABILITIES

The reasoning above leaves us with just a few categories of truly intangible resources that are not caught by other definitions.

1. *Psychological factors* concerning the state of mind of key groups, especially customers and staff, but also investors and other stakeholders
2. *Information-based resources*, such as data, technology, knowledge
3. Certain *quality factors* that must be built up and sustained over time

These categories are still somewhat diverse, but if likely intangibles in a given context are properly defined and the role they play carefully investigated, it is generally possible to clarify the key items. For example, when seeking to understand why staff remain with an organization when better opportunities are easily available, loyalty will be an important feature. If concerned with improving customer service, availability of data about those customers will likely be important. For a company whose customers are experiencing high failure rates of its products, effort will need to be expended for some time to work away at the causes of those failures.

This effort to clarify terminology is not being made out of intellectual curiosity, but with the aim of improving business performance. The intention is that, having defined the intangibles involved in a situation, the level of these factors can be estimated or measured, and their impact on the rest of the system assessed. With this information available, it is then possible to design actions to improve matters, and put in place procedures for ensuring they stay that way. In many cases, it is not possible to go as far as we have done in earlier chapters in quantifying every item. However, much can often be achieved with estimation supported by relatively informal efforts to check those estimates.

The discussion above implies a classification (Figure 9.1) for most of the asset-stocks to be found in an organization.

- The tangible resources listed at left have largely dominated the early chapters of this book, and constitute the core of an organization's strategic architecture. Not all will apply to every case, and some situations require specific additional items of their own, such as "projects" in contract-based firms.

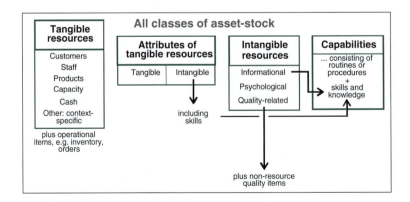

Figure 9.1: A classification of resources and capabilities.

- Note the existence of certain other tangible factors that observe asset-stock behavior, but are not sufficiently significant in most cases to be relevant to strategic performance. Few firms, for example, can claim that their inventory level makes a significant difference to their medium- to long-term performance, even though it observes the bathtub behavior of all asset-stocks.

- The attributes of those tangible resources form the second category of resources. The extra clarification added here is that some of those attributes are intangible.

- The reasoning above leads to the three principal groups of intangible resources in the third column: psychological, information-based and quality-related. As noted above, some such items do not accumulate, so lie outside the domain of asset-stocks.

- This leaves capabilities, which combine the skills of individuals and teams with knowledge that may have been captured, and routines and procedures. This will be further explained in Chapter 10.

Having made some progress in sorting out the jungle of concepts covered by the term "intangible resources," certain issues of importance to strategic performance nevertheless remain out of reach.

"Dynamic capabilities" has become an accepted term for the ability of management to respond to changes in the external environment and adapt the organization's strategy and its regular capabilities to ensure strong performance under these emerging conditions. Further comment on dynamic capabilities will be offered in Chapter 10.

"Leadership" is undoubtedly of critical importance, but it is simply not possible to put a definitive measure on leadership for the purpose of analysing its quantitative impact on organizations' performance over time. Nor can we specify what to do, when and how much to cause what degree of change to this intangible resource, nor quantify by how much a certain change in leadership quality will improve exactly which elements of business performance.

It is also not possible to deal analytically with all "relationships"—by how much it helps a business to have relationships with certain politicians, for example. The same goes for the networks of relationships amongst staff both within and beyond an organization. It is certainly the case that individuals vary in the number and type of people with whom they have connections, and the quality of those relationships varies significantly.[10] Equally certainly, those networks enhance people's performance and that of the organizations they work for, but exactly how, and by how much remains to be well understood.

# INTANGIBLES CONCERNING STATE OF MIND

Intangible resources reflecting the state of mind of key groups can be illustrated by the case of a computer support firm that provides assistance and advice to small and medium sized enterprises (SMEs). It recommends choices of hardware and software, installs these for clients, and provides continuing maintenance, support, upgrades and training. Two years before the time in question, the company served some 90 clients who required about 75 hours per month of service. Its founder and CEO was signing up just under two new clients per month, and none were leaving. Each new client also needed about 200 hours of initial work to get them set up on a sound basis. The company was delivering good service to its clients, and had a solid reputation that helped the CEO sign up more new clients.

The staffing situation two years before the study had seen the company employing 70 technical staff, of whom 15 were relatively new. It was taking on two or three new people per month to cope with growing demand, and losing only about one person per month. Experienced staff had 120 hours per month available to serve clients, after allowing for administrative tasks, holidays, and so on. New staff were not so effective, taking about three times as long as experienced people to do typical tasks. In addition, each new staff member needed about 10 hours per month of supervisory time from an experienced employee. It took three months for new staff to become fully productive, though initially only on a limited range of tasks. Staff morale back then had been high, reflecting the company's stable situation and the interesting variety of work. Staff had been busy, but not overloaded, having to work at about 95 % of their top rate to ensure good client service.

About 18 months previously, the CEO found himself needing to spend too much time managing the growing operations of the business, to continue his selling efforts, so brought in an experienced business development executive to take on the task of winning new customers. With the company's strong reputation, the efforts of this new executive were successful and soon he was bringing in about five new clients per month instead of two (see Figure 9.2). Work and sales streamed in, and all seemed well until about nine months later. Staff were increasingly busy, and the CEO noticed from the payroll information that on average they were putting in 15 % more time than normal. There had also been an increase in complaints from clients about service quality.

Then after a further three months, that is six months before the time of the study, things really started to fall apart. Staff pressure got still worse, although numbers

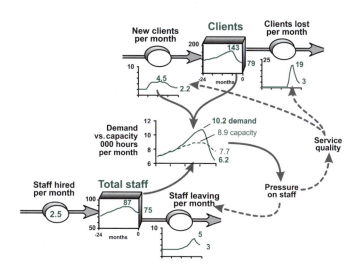

**Figure 9.2: Growth and decline at a computer service provider (dashed lines = incomplete causality).**

had grown to 87, and complaints from the clients, by now numbering 143, escalated sharply. For the first time, some clients actually left the business to find service support from other providers, and the business development executive was having less success in bringing in new clients to replace them. Still worse, staff were starting to leave more quickly than ever before, apparently due to the pressure they were under. Over the latest few months, clients and staff both left in increasing numbers, and the new client win rate more than halved.

By the time of the study, client numbers had fallen to only 79, staff losses had cut their numbers to just 75, and the few new clients being won were more than matched by continuing departures. The only good news was that customer complaints were down and staff did not seem to be so overloaded. In fact, the work logs suggested that they were only 80% utilized.

The story is rather simple to explain, and clearly reflects some problems with the organization's intangibles—work pressure rising, and service quality falling—leading to loss of staff and clients respectively. But this generalized statement of what caused what is not sufficient for our purpose. We need to know not only why things happened, but why they happened *to that degree* and *on that timescale*. Without that understanding, it is not possible to know by how much the organization should have acted to avert the problem. Nor is it possible to know what to do when and how much, to put the organization back on a strong path. Avoiding a repeat of the problem is easy—don't chase business again—but that will leave the business way short of the potential it could achieve if it put in place procedures for ensuring reliable growth.

Probing deeper into the story, some puzzles become apparent. For instance, staff were overloaded from month −15, so why was it not until month −9 that customers started complaining? Then why was it a further few months before clients actually left? And why did staff losses only pick up some three months after the overload started, and grow only slowly over the next few months? Next, if the worst point reached was an overload of about 20 %, how come the firm subsequently lost nearly half of its clients? This number clearly matters a great deal, not only because it implies that revenue nearly halved, threatening to hit profitability badly, but also because management needs to know what their staffing plans should be.

The difficulty in answering these questions arises for several reasons. First, the intangibles involved are exactly that—difficult to touch or see, and therefore hard to measure. Next, even if the intangibles were known with complete accuracy, the impact they have on the tangible resources of clients and staff cannot be known with any certainty. Some of the intangibles accumulate, that is they build up over time, and may also drain away. And it is difficult to know how quickly these proc-esses are happening. Lastly, there may be threshold effects, where nothing appears to go wrong until a problem has built up to a level that triggers a sudden change.

Figure 9.3 pulls apart just one of the mechanisms operating in this case. Start-ing from the bottom of the diagram the staff are just able to sustain good service quality until the pressure gets too high—pressure defined as the ratio between the

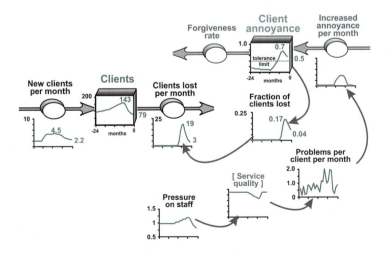

**Figure 9.3: Staff pressure hits service quality, annoys clients and causes some to leave.**

amount of work to be done and the capacity of staff to do the work. Service quality then falls. This is not easily observed or measured, consisting as it does of various issues, from delays in answering the phone, to incorrect advice to users, to faulty installations. But one measure is the number of problems reported by customers. This is not a nice smooth data series, but fluctuates substantially from month to month. Nevertheless, there was clearly an increase in the problem rate during the time that staff pressure escalated.

The section at the top of Figure 9.3 is quite invisible to management, but is a reasonable description of what is going on. Every problem incident makes the client who experienced it just a little more annoyed with the service provider than they were before. Few such firms can promise never to make any kind of mistake, but the problems in the early months happen so seldom that the last one is forgotten or forgiven before the next arises. The more frequently failures occur, the more customers' annoyance builds up, and now this is not forgiven before the next problem occurs. (This will be a familiar feeling for consumers in many markets, such as air travel and banking).

It is at this point that an important threshold effect occurs. Switching to a new service provider is risky. Clients cannot be sure that another provider will give better service, and there may be some inconvenience—searching for, assessing and briefing another supplier will take time and effort. Consequently, annoyance must build up to some significant level before it triggers clients to leave. This is why some five to six months elapse between service quality starting to cause clients increasing problems and the first clients actually leaving. By this time, annoyance is so high and so widespread amongst clients that it is not just a few who leave, but a large fraction every month. This explains why the total losses are so great. Note also that losses continue long after the time that service quality recovers and the reported rate of problems drops back. For an already-angry customer, even a small additional problem may be enough to tip them over the edge. The dominant consequence of client annoyance, then, is that it triggers a catastrophic episode of customer losses.[11]

The quantification in Figure 9.3 suggests a degree of exactness in the causality that would be hard to confirm in reality. The use of lighter outlines and gray text acknowledges the somewhat approximate nature of the intangible factors. However, the phenomena it portrays are very real. The clients must have left for *some* reason, and it is entirely likely that, had they been asked at the time why they were leaving, they would have answered "Because I am very annoyed with this supplier." Asked why *that* was, we would be pretty certain to get the answer "Because I have had more and more problems over many months." The number of problems reported is not speculative at all, but actual data. And though the figure shows service quality as an unknown variable, many organizations in fact measure this item in some detail.

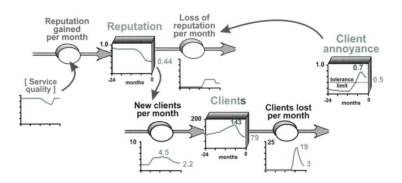

**Figure 9.4: Annoyance amongst clients damages reputation, and cuts the client win rate.**

Of course, it is not possible to know all of these items accurately. It is difficult, for example, to find out just how "annoyed" clients actually are—at least not without making them even more so! Nor can we be certain what level of annoyance will trigger their decision to leave. But difficulty of measurement does not refute the likelihood that this is what is happening.

Figure 9.4 expands on a further part of the system, and examines why the business development executive found increasing difficulty in winning new clients for the firm. Current customers talk to other people, and organizations needing service ask others about their experiences. Until about month −15, those conversations were largely positive. Continuous experience of good service quality by existing clients led them to sustain the firm's reputation. More recently, the increasing annoyance amongst clients caused them to undermine this reputation—"Well I have had really bad problems with this firm recently, so I could not possibly recommend you to use them." It takes time for this reputation to spread, so note that it has barely started to recover by the end of the period, even though the actual service quality has been OK for some time.

The practical consequences are clear. When reputation was high, the business development executive was successful with nearly all his approaches to new clients. As reputation fell, most of those organizations he approached refused, citing the bad things they had heard about the firm's service.

Once again, the quantification shown here is not knowable with any precision, but reflects answers that might be given if potential clients in the region were asked "What have you heard about how people rate this firm for service?" It is important to note that they do not have any direct experience of service themselves, so cannot be directly influenced by that factor. In other cases, current service quality may be made public, for example by various research agencies, but even then it is more likely to report client's recent experiences with some delay, rather than current reality.

## Quality and reputation: a common structure

The connection between quality and reputation implied by Figures 9.3 and 9.4 turns out to be extremely widespread. The common principle that it reflects is that "quality affects current customers: reputation affects potential customers" (see Figure 9.5). It is important to note that active and potential customers are different groups, and that our concern is with different behaviors from each group—we want potential customers to join us, and we want active customers to stay with us and buy more from us.

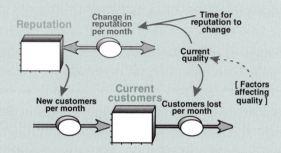

**Figure 9.5:** A widespread relationship between quality, reputation and customer movements.

The reason this structure is so common is that current customers have direct experience of current quality factors, at least to the degree determined by the frequency with which they transact with the supplier. Potential customers, on the other hand, have no such direct experience, so can only go on what they hear indirectly about quality. The speed with which reputation changes depends on various factors. It may be fast if, for example, research organizations assess the views of current customers frequently and in detail, but will be slow if word is spread only by infrequent contact between current and potential customers.

Similar mechanisms operate in the case of employees who know first-hand what it is like to work for an employer, and prospective employees who can only go on what they come to believe from speaking to others.

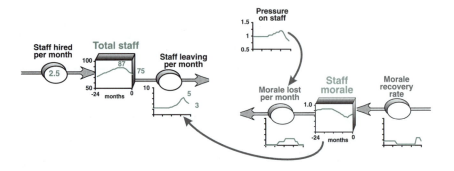

**Figure 9.6: Pressure on staff undermines morale, raising the rate people leave.**

The last piece of this story to explain is the behavior of the staff (Figure 9.6). Once again, there is no immediate link from the underlying cause—pressure on staff—to the rate at which people leave. Instead, it has to go through a process that changes their state of mind. Initially, with work and service demand more or less in balance, people are busy but not over-stressed and morale continues to strengthen. Increasing work pressure then damages morale, but this is a gradual process; overwork is at first tolerable, but the longer it goes on, and the more heavily overloaded people are, the more the stock of morale is drained. The lower morale becomes, the larger the fraction of staff who leave each month. There could again be a trigger level similar to that which drives clients away—"I have put up with the stress for long enough, so I'm off."—but some staff turnover is normal as people find other opportunities or just move on in their lives. The declining morale just accelerates this process.

### An unthinkable strategy response: stop selling!

An apparently obvious response for this firm, once the service quality problems start, is to hire more staff. Unfortunately, this just will not work—at least not fast enough. It takes time for established staff to interview and select new people, and then support them once they have arrived. The last thing overstressed professionals need is the extra burden of hiring and training newcomers.

Given that the firm can't boost the supply side of its business, there is only one other alternative—cut the demand side. At one level, this implies a stop to new selling efforts; at a more serious level it may even mean dropping existing customers. This of course is utterly unthinkable! When business is in trouble, surely the last thing you need is to stop selling? And surely you would be mad to cut customers off when in such trouble.

Remarkably, there are situations when both of these responses are exactly what should be done. In this case, the sales message is implicitly "Come join us, so we can do a really bad job for you," and that is not a message anyone would want to give. Even dropping customers could be useful. As explained in Chapter 5, some customers will contribute little profitability, and they or others will demand disproportionate amounts of support.

It is now axiomatic that keeping existing customers is much easier than winning new ones, but this is not necessarily the case when existing customers know how badly you are doing, and new ones do not. Also, the slogan "It costs X times more to win a customer than to keep one" is meaningless—keeping a customer has to be done continually, whereas winning one is a one-off event.

So—if service quality is a problem and supply cannot be quickly raised, cutting demand may well be advisable.

(Online learning materials are available to support this example, see p.xxi.)

As with the reputation issue above, the level of morale is in principle researchable. Indeed many organizations carry out morale surveys as a matter of course. Rarely, though, do they check on staff feelings often enough to detect the kinds of changes shown in this case. This may not be necessary, when skilled team leaders and managers take trouble to keep themselves well in touch with how their people are feeling. However, this is not always the case, so it is often helpful, especially in larger organizations, to have systems in place for tracking this important issue.

This company's experience demonstrates some common features of how psychological intangibles feature in the strategic performance of organizations:

- *State of mind drives behavior.* The fact that clients left this company because of their annoyance, that others did not join because of the impressions they had gained from others and that staff left more quickly because of their low morale are simple examples of a very widespread phenomenon—people act because of how they feel. This is hardly news to the field of psychology, but we are making explicit the link between some simple measures of how people feel and the rate at which they exhibit behaviors that are important to how the wider business system performs. Extremely detailed and tightly controlled experimentation is of course required for scientific proof of these links, exactly how they work, and how they relate to other influences. But this framework is adequate for a high-level understanding of what is happening.

- *Intangibles have considerable influence.* The performance of the case above is not merely *somewhat* influenced by the intangibles involved; it is *heavily* determined by them. There is no possibility whatever of explaining the outcome without taking account of those issues. Equally, had the client growth initiative not been started, the outcomes would have been radically different, not just marginally better. Well known cases in the public domain also illustrate this principle. Amongst the most dramatic of these is the total collapse in 2002 of accounting firm Arthur Andersen, following its involvement in the demise of Enron Inc.[12] On a more positive note, there is evidence that strong reputation can show up in real business value.[13]

- *Intangibles are influenced by, as well as influencing the tangible system.* The problems here are not caused by staff disrespecting the clients, by management failing to promote a good reputation for the firm, or by leaders behaving unreasonably towards their staff. They are caused by the simple physics of the relationships between the tangible factors involved; client numbers, staff, workload and capacity. If those negative behaviors were to occur, of course, they would also cause problems, but they are not the explanation here, nor in many real situations. People are doing their best, but poor strategy makes it impossible to do well.

- *Intangibles are manageable.* A senior partner in one of the major strategy consulting firms once remarked that their firm's work for clients ignored intangibles because they are undetectable, unmeasurable and unmanageable. All three of these assertions are untrue. Sales people can certainly detect when customers are annoyed, and managers know when their staff are unhappy. These and other intangible factors can be measured, and often are. Finally, skilled managers in all kinds of situations work successfully to turn round low morale in teams and whole organizations, and can drive high levels of commitment and motivation. Chapter 6 mentioned the case of the bank whose detection of "miserable moments" experienced by their customers was matched to a deliberate policy of giving them "magic moments" in order to reset their feelings of annoyance. Intangibles are also manageable indirectly by acting to fix the tangible system that is driving them.

- *Managing the system can manage intangibles.* The problems above were created by management, and could be fixed by them. Had the organization not attempted to increase its growth in the first place, but continued on the sound trajectory with which it started, it would have ended with about 130 very happy clients, and some 80 contented staff. Even after the problem started, the situation could have been rescued. Had the firm stopped chasing new clients as soon as the work overload hit 10%, the growth in staff coming through the system would have brought down the client problems. After a few months, more cautious growth could have been resumed. The firm could even have made it possible to cope with the growth it sought, had it raised its hiring rate some months prior to taking on the business development executive.

- *Problems "fix themselves"*—though not necessarily as we would like. In Figure 9.3, most of the problems have disappeared by the time of the study. Workload and client service are no longer at critical levels, client annoyance is dropping, staff morale is recovering, and even reputation will start to build again once clients have experienced good service for some months. The problem is, the medicine that fixed the problem is very unpleasant—a 45% drop in business! Chapter 4 introduced the idea of feedback amongst resources and explained how balancing feedback can obstruct growth. This explains what is happening in this case, where the mechanism that brings things back into balance is the departure of unhappy clients.

- *Persistent bad performance.* Though not shown in this case, this self-fixing of the problem can readily become a persistent state. We win more customers than we can handle, so serve them badly, so they leave, to be replaced with more new customers we will disappoint. Given the sometimes obsessive concern with improved efficiency, this phenomenon of organizations seeking growth they cannot serve, only to be continually disappointed that it is not sustained appears to be widespread. To prevent such chronic difficulty requires some degree of organizational "slack"—a little more capacity than you strictly need, just to make sure it never becomes a constraint. If concerned at the costly inefficiency of such a policy, it is worth recalling the reasoning offered at the start of Chapter 1. Would you prefer to make a return on sales of 15% and for ever struggle to cope, or make 12% and be able to develop strongly?

- *Negative factors vs. absences of positives.* Not all of peoples' feelings are positive. As shown in this case, annoyance is a realistic description of customers' state of mind that drives behavior that we would prefer did not occur. It is quite different from the absence of a positive emotion, such as "customer satisfaction," which may result in indifference but not explicit hostility.

- *Thresholds and tipping points.* This case again shows the problems caused when factors move towards a threshold that triggers new behavior. As explained in chapter 4, the resulting tipping point is not caused by feedback, but simply by the crossing of two lines. Here, service quality is fine until pressure of work exceeds what the staff can do well, and clients do not actually leave until annoyance crosses their tolerance limit. The impact of morale on staff turnover is less clear-cut, but is nevertheless highly non-linear in its behavior.

- *When success on the balanced scorecard is really failure.* During the early months of this episode, management may reasonably have been pleased with their success. Not only did client numbers grow more strongly for at least six months, but productivity reached new high levels, as a result of which profitability on the growing revenues would have been outstanding. Had these measures all appeared on the firm's balanced scorecard, green lights would have been flashing continuously. However, the reality would have been that high staff utilization should have been flashing a *negatived* red, and even the high client win rate should have been highlighted as a problem, not a success. In spite of the unavoidable implications of these observations, balanced scorecards rarely highlight high rates of sales success as a problem!

## INTANGIBLE FACTORS VS. INTANGIBLE RESOURCES

This situation above features several intangible factors: work pressure, service quality, client annoyance, reputation and staff morale. But not all of these are resources; that is, accumulating stocks. The telling feature that marks out those non-resource items is whether they could feasibly be instantly fixed. Work pressure would instantly drop if work demand fell, and in this case service quality would instantly recover if work pressure were to drop. Neither of these items, then, can be resources. There can be cases where quality shows resource-like behavior, for example in manufactured products where an intangible stock of problems that damage quality must be worked away over some time. But that is not the case here.

## MEASURES FOR STATE-OF-MIND INTANGIBLES

If intangible resources concerning the state of mind of important groups is to be useful in assessing and managing strategic performance, it will be necessary to find measures for them that are reliable. A full exploration of research methods is beyond the scope of this discussion, but since the aim is to understand how strongly people are feeling on an issue, scales that in some way indicate a range from "empty" to "full" will often be appropriate. A common example is the Likert scale, which seeks ratings on (usually) a 5-point scale from "strongly disagree" to "strongly agree."[14]

---

**TABLE 9.1: EXAMPLES OF PSYCHOLOGICAL INTANGIBLE RESOURCES**

| State-of-mind intangible resources | Measure | Resource flows that may be affected |
|---|---|---|
| Satisfaction level | 0–1.0 | Customer purchase rate |
| Annoyance level | 0–1.0 | Customer loss rate |
| Reputation | 0–1.0 | Customer acquisition rate |
| Morale | 0–1.0 | Work rate<br>Attrition rate |
| Investor confidence | 0–1.0 | Additional finance raised |

---

For the purpose of assessing dynamically how the factors that drive changes in feelings operate, it is useful to adopt a zero-to-one scale, where zero implies no feeling and 1.0 implies the strongest possible feeling. This approach is useful when assessing dynamics because it is self-balancing at both ends of the scale—if there is little feeling in place, then there is little that can happen to reduce that feeling still further; if the feeling is nearly full, then there is little potential to add any more to that emotion (Table 9.1). It also allows the factors that depend on the intangible to be "looked up" in a consistent manner. How hard will staff work, for example, if their morale is at the highest possible level, or how quickly will customers leave if their annoyance is at a level of 0.5?

### Think of neurones firing

An imaginary device may help picture how state-of-mind factors such as those shown in this section are working. Imagine you could peer inside people's brains and actually count how many neurones are firing off instructions, such as "look for a new job" or "fire that supplier." Whilst all is well, those neurones are largely quiet, not urging the brain's owner to do anything at all. When something bad happens, some of those neurones start firing away, but others are also at work, telling the person not to act—maybe due to the employee having been well-treated, or that supplier having done well in the past. If nothing bad happens for a time, a fraction of those neurones urging action will quiet down, and the longer the period of no bad news, the fewer neurones continue to fire away.

The more frequently bad experiences arrive however, and the more serious they are, the more neurones can be seen firing off instructions to act. If this goes on long enough, the number urging action outnumber those urging in-action, and the person makes their move. Some of our efforts are aimed at preventing the events that start this negative brain activity, while others aim, almost literally, to calm it down.

A similar analogy may help visualize positive states of mind, only this time we are trying to get neurones firing that urge their owner to work harder or to recommend a product to friends. For both positive and negative states of mind, there is a limit to just how strongly we can feel about a wide range of issues—we can't stay angry about everything bad that ever happened, or enthusiastic about everything good. So it is only to be expected that both kinds of feeling fade away over time unless stimulated once more.

## REPUTATION, PERCEPTIONS AND THE VALUE CURVE

In Figure 9.4, the computer service organization was only able to win new clients if its reputation for good service was strong. As noted earlier, that reputation is a *perception* amongst potential clients, rather than the reality of the service currently being experienced by active customers. In other cases, several perceptions may be involved in the decisions made by customers, staff or other groups. Few cases show this more dramatically than do luxury brands, most of which have no functional superiority over a large number of equivalent products, but nevertheless enjoy a perception amongst many consumers as to their desirability. The expected admira-tion of others that this group expects to gain by being seen with the branded item is enough to persuade them to seek the product out and to pay more—often many times more—than they would for perfectly functional alternatives.

Business-to-business marketing and sales situations exhibit similar perceptual biases, though rarely on a similar scale. The phrase "nobody got fired for buying IBM" dates back decades to a time when the company dominated the market for large corporate computer systems, and reflected the perception that the company's products and service were substantially superior to those of competitors. However, the people responsible for recommending large IT investments rarely had any objective evidence as to the true reliability of competing suppliers. Even where such information was available for specific pieces of equipment, this might not be sufficiently persuasive on its own to counter the overall confidence in the company's general offering. Very similar phenomena continue today, for example when companies purchase outsourced services such as recruitment, catering or information systems. They almost certainly do not know for sure that Sodexho or one of its rivals such as Compass Group is better at providing catering, or that CSC is better than EDS in information systems services, so must rely on their perceptions.

Whether in consumer or B2B markets, firms naturally go to some effort to change how potential and active customers perceive performance on various issues concerning quality and service. Changing perceptions of business customers regarding objectively measurable factors such as quality may be more difficult, but managing perceptions of service can be possible and important. For example, outsourcing contracts often last many years, and providers pay special attention to service quality as contracts come up for renewal, to ensure that any customer perceptions of poor service in earlier years are forgotten or forgiven.

Managing customer perceptions is a complex task. Since customer behavior is affected by several factors, we may need to make efforts to influence the perception of each factor. Figure 9.7 shows the situation facing a certain European drinks brand with a long heritage, but now facing declining popularity. Once seen as a sophisticated drink, whose distinctive taste had been an advantage, it was now perceived to be too rough on the palate, and not the kind of product that young people drink. This was a growing problem, since even its older consumers preferred to associate themselves with more youth-oriented products.

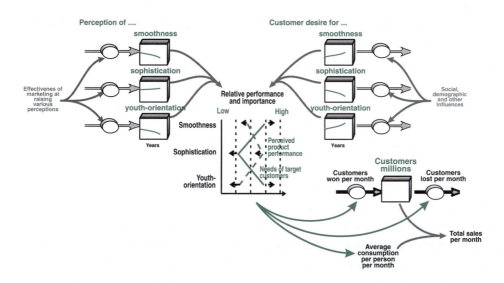

**Figure 9.7: Widening gap between requirements and perceptions of a drinks brand.**

**Doing it right! Reputation: with whom, for what?**

Reputation is widely recognized to be important, but if it is to be understood, managed and actively used to improve performance, it is important to be clear about exactly what reputation is involved. This involves asking two questions:

*With whom* does the reputation exist? The purpose of understanding the phenomenon is to enable desirable changes to occur in the behavior of specific individuals or groups. It is therefore important to specify carefully which audience is of concern. This may be the population of potential customers—in which case it may be necessary to focus in more closely on particular segments. Reputation amongst existing customers may also be relevant. For example, a customer unhappy with a product or service may nevertheless stick with it if reputation amongst other active customers is strong. Reputation can also arise amongst potential employees. Accounting firm PwC, for example, enjoys a strong reputation as a first career choice for new graduates, which enhances its ability to hire from each new year's emerging cohort.

*For what* does the reputation relate? Amazon.com may have a reputation amongst many consumers for being the cheapest supplier of books and other products, whether or not that is true for any particular product segment or individual item. Its reputation for reliable delivery is a quite separate issue, but important nonetheless to customers' purchase decisions.

All this implies that reputation may need to be tracked on several dimensions in any particular context, if its impact on behavior of customers, employees, distributors, investors and other groups is to be understood and managed.

The product's brand manager had information going back over several years, showing how both consumers' overall needs were changing and how their perceptions of the product were being altered by its advertizing. The value curve compared the two and showed clearly the nature and scale of the problem. Not only did the product miss the most positive needs of target customers, but its main strength was with a perception that no longer mattered to people.

After some deliberation, it was decided that the likelihood of closing the gap between perceptions and requirements were so low that it was not worth making the effort. Instead, the brand's advertizing was re-oriented towards consolidating its perceptions amongst a smaller group, but one whose needs it more closely reflected.

Two further points arise in relation to the structure operating in this case. First, the brand's difficulties had been exacerbated by changes in the expectations of its target customers. Whilst its demise on those measures was problematic, it would not have been so severe had consumers' requirements on those same measures not moved against it.

Secondly, not all brands are passive in this issue and merely accept whatever changes in customer requirements may occur. Instead, they drive changes in customers' needs towards a state that suits the firm's positioning. Coca-Cola's advertizing long focused on international friendship values, implying not only that the brand was living those values, but that those were the values that consumers *ought* to identify with. BMW promoted its vehicles as "the ultimate driving machine," suggesting not only that those vehicles conformed with that description, but that this was the criterion on which sophisticated car buyers should make their choices. More recently, IBM's advertizing has been emphasizing the importance of enabling people to collaborate globally on any issue, and implying of course that IBM solutions would make this possible. Even for organizations with no international presence, this marketing-driven perception of the company's ability to help people work together was likely to be appealing.

So in Figure 9.7, marketing is not just shifting brand perceptions on the left side of the diagram, it is also driving change in customers' expectations on the right. This is a powerful source of competitive advantage if it can be achieved. It is tough enough to compete with a strong competitor that does an outstanding job of meeting customer needs, but taking on one that is itself driving the agenda of those needs is particularly challenging!

## TIME TO ADJUST PERCEPTIONS

A complication that affects differences between perception and objective measures is the time it takes for people to adjust those perceptions. If you regularly experience delays of about five minutes in a regular train journey that you take, you may adjust other activities to take account of this expectation, for example by arranging meetings to start five minutes later than you would if the train arrived at its destination on time. If the train then starts arriving typically ten minutes late, you may regard the first few occasions as exceptional, and make no further changes to your habits. If the increased delays continue for some time, however, your expectation will gradually move towards the new reality (Figure 9.8).

Depending on your observation and patience, the time it takes for you to adjust this perception may be short or long. If the adjustment time is long enough, the reality may have changed back again before you have fully become used to the longer average delays.

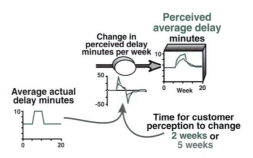

**Figure 9.8: Perceptions take time to adjust to reality for train service delays.**

Various additional issues arise from these kinds of perceptual gap.

- There is no certainty that perceptions *ever* match reality. A no doubt apocryphal tale concerns a hotel beset with frequent complaints from guests that the elevators always took over three minutes to arrive. Faced with the danger that this annoyance would put customers off deciding to visit the hotel in future, management considered having the elevators renovated, at considerable cost. A simpler and cheaper solution was suggested—installing mirrors near the elevators. This gave guests something else to think about, namely their appearance, rather than the delays in the elevator's arrival. Complaints dropped sharply, even though no change had occurred to the elevators' promptness.

- There can be big differences in the time for perceptions to adjust, depending on the direction and scale of change. You may more quickly decide that the train service really *will* be twenty minutes late if that happens for a few days, but not alter your feeling that it will be five minutes late if the average increases to seven minutes. More seriously in many cases, customers will change their perceptions sharply when a situation deteriorates, but only slowly recogize real improvements that occur. In some cases, the delays can be quite considerable. Many car buyers "know" for example that diesel-engined vehicles are slow, dirty and noisy, even though the reality has been quite different for some twenty years.

- It is not always the case that an objective measure actually exists. In the case of the drinks brand above, for example, there were some objective measures of "smoothness," such as levels of acidity or tannin. On the other hand an objective measure of "sophistication" was much less plausible. This does not however prevent marketing efforts from attempting to change perceptions by implying some reality even though none exists.

Similar processes apply to other situations and other groups. An employer may have a perception about the timeliness of their employees, and those employees may have perceptions about the amount of work they are asked to do. It is even possible for investors to have perceptions about the financial performance of a company in which they invest that clearly does not match the realities of that company's track record.

Incidentally, the slogan sometimes vigorously promoted that "perception *is* reality" is quite unhelpful. Whilst travelers on the train service above may well adjust their behavior to reflect their perception of its delays, it does not remove the need for management to know what those delays are in reality or to work to eliminate them. Similarly, the computer service company mentioned earlier needs to ensure its clients are well served, whatever their current perception. Persuasive communication to change perceptions may be important as well, but does not remove the need to manage the objective reality.

Indeed, there can be risks in paying too much attention to shifting people's perceptions rather than changing the real situation. For example, many professional firms today face pressure to offer employees a better balance between work and the rest of their lives—the so-called work–life balance. Several such organizations have got into difficulty by promising that they were indeed offering a better balance when in fact little had changed. This can give rise to "cognitive dissonance," a psychological discomfort that arises when a difference is discovered between actual experience and expectations. The principle is widely recognized in marketing, in the difference between buyers' expectation of a product or service they have purchased and the reality of what they receive.[15]

## INTANGIBLES DRIVEN BY SPORADIC EVENTS

The perception of delays for a train service brings out an important feature of many intangibles. It has rather been implied that resource flows are driven by factors that continue steadily—our hiring success reflects our pay rates, customer losses reflect a general level of service quality, and so on. However, some factors that trigger changes in intangibles are sporadic. Our perception that the train will be late is boosted on each occasion that it happens, but not otherwise, and the more late it is on any day, the larger the increase in the perception.

Annoyance with service quality can exhibit a similar mechanism. Experience of service occurs only on each occasion that some support is required, so annoyance is boosted by each disappointing service incident, rather than by a continuous stream of experience.

A similar phenomenon affects certain states of mind amongst employees. While work pressure or pay rates tend to be experienced continuously, other factors are not. An important state of mind amongst employees, for example, concerns trust;

trust that others will do as they have promised, that they are good at their job, or that they will support you rather than find ways to benefit at your expense. It clearly has a reciprocal character, with evidence of trustworthy behavior by one person encouraging similar behavior by those with whom they interact. Trust may exist between colleagues of the same level, becoming an important component of effective teamwork, between managers and the people they manage, or between staff in general and the leadership of the organization.[16] Trust will often be changed by sporadic incidents, rather than by continuous conditions. Each time a person does something they promised that is not trivial or does a noticeably good job on some important task, others' trust in them will increase.

Sporadic events also drive outflows, both for positive and negative perceptions. An apologetic phone call from the CEO of a supplier that has let us down is an incident intended to reset our perception of their poor service. Similarly, any time a colleague fails to deliver on something important they promised to do is a sporadic incident that drops our trust in them.

So important are such sporadic factors that many organizations try to establish norms to make sure that positive states of mind are built and sustained, and negative ones prevented from arising. One train operator, for example, faced with frequent minor delays on its services noticed that these were repeating because an initial delay to one service disrupted those that followed. To prevent this escalation, they instituted a policy of cancelling altogether any service that was late enough to disrupt others, taking the view that a single substantial disappointment to a minority of travelers was preferable to a large number of small disappointments to many that might be experienced repeatedly over successive days and weeks. Some organizations go so far as to build required behaviors into their corporate "values," setting out what is expected in the way staff relate to each other, to customers and to other third parties. When successfully embedded, there is no danger of trust between colleagues falling from a high level, for example, because it is just not done to let others down.[17]

# INFORMATION-BASED INTANGIBLE RESOURCES

The inclusion of data, knowledge, and so on in the strategic architecture explaining firm performance reflects the existence of two classes of entity—the "material" factors that have been dealt with as tangible resources, and various "informational" factors that also can be collected, lost, stored and used.

The simplest informational factor is just data—specific pieces of information about something of importance. This can be illustrated by extending the example

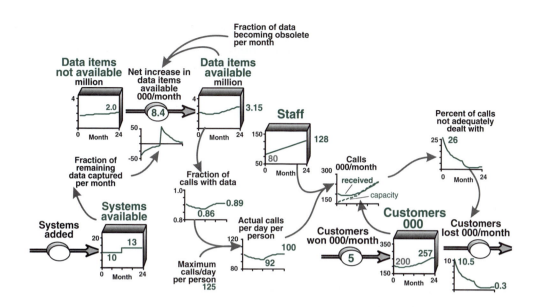

**Figure 9.9:** Adding systems to capture data allows growth in call center activity.

from Chapter 5 concerning the performance of a call center providing customer service. At that point, we were concerned with whether staff in that call center had the skills required to serve customers well. Now we will look at the importance of having the *data* needed to do so (see Figure 9.9).

The call center started with 200 000 customers making on average one call per month. The 80 staff could each take 125 calls per day, or 2 500 per month if fully trained, so were just able to handle all the calls received. However, in order to respond to customers' enquiries, these staff need information about customers and their activity, that is, data. Some of that data is long-lived, such as name, address and other personal details, whilst other data is transitory, such as the customer's recent transactions or enquiries. It used to require much effort and cost to collect and maintain such data, although these have been radically reduced by advances in information technology over the last couple of decades.

Assume in this case that 20 items of data are required in order to answer every enquiry customers might raise, but only 60 % of that data is actually available. This is sufficient to deal with nearly 90 % of customer enquiries. Lacking all the necessary data increases the time that staff have to spend on the average enquiry, so instead of being able to respond to 125 calls per month, each person can only answer 99. The call center therefore has too few staff, simply because of the lack of data. Over a quarter of calls go unanswered, causing the loss of about 5% of customers each month. (This example does not include the notion of accumulating annoyance discussed above.)

As each month passes, more of the call center's data becomes obsolete—old transactions become irrelevant to current enquiries, customers' details change without being updated, and so on. The company therefore continues to spend some $20 000 per month updating and maintaining the data. However, this is not sufficient to keep even the limited data up to date, so this fraction of adequate data continues to decline, reducing staff productivity still more.

By about month 12, the system comes into balance, but only through the same kind of bad mechanism we saw earlier for the computer service firm—losing customers brings pressure back to a level that the center's capacity can deal with. This is helped by the continuing increase in staff numbers, so although each person can only respond to 92 calls per day, there are by this time enough staff to manage all the incoming calls.

Realizing from the start that the lack of data is damaging customer service and holding back staff productivity, the call center decides to invest in improved systems for data collection. This takes the first 12 months to complete, but when those systems come online, the flow of data items available swings strongly positive and the database starts to fill. Staff productivity rises strongly over months 12–18, so that the center's capacity is easily able to handle the larger number of calls from the increasing customer base. Note, incidentally, that the total quantity of data to be captured is itself rising in the later months, due to the growing number of customers.

(Online learning materials are available to support this example, see p.xxi.)

New systems can do more than merely improve the availability of data, of course. They can also automate business processes, and thus directly raise productivity. The call center could also have decided to invest in some further systems designed with that purpose in mind (Figure 9.10). These become available from month 18, and raise the maximum rate at which each person can deal with calls from 125 per hour to 140. Note, however, that the number they can actually handle still depends on the availability of customer data.

This situation illustrates a common issue in systems investment—interdependence between systems. This poses challenges for senior management trying to assess the value of IT investments.[18] In the call center case, there is clearly a business benefit of investing in data capture systems. There is also a benefit from investing in the call support systems. However, the benefit of both initiatives in combination is not a simple addition of the two. The investment in improved call-handling will be devalued if not accompanied by efforts to improve the availability of data,

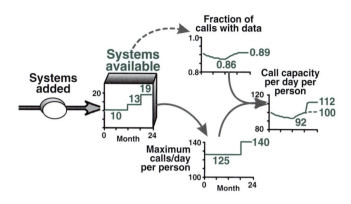

**Figure 9.10:** Systems investment also enables increase in staff productivity.

and more data will be of limited help if it still has to be used with slow, manual processes.

This interdependence amongst IT projects can make it meaningless to attempt to put a value on any single investment. The case above shows just two such projects in one isolated business department. Any substantial organization will at any time be pursuing a portfolio of investments, for multiple purposes in multiple functions. Given this extensive impact, valuing the whole program is as complex as estimating the value of the organization's strategy. Further complexity arises from additional considerations:

- The contribution of information systems is taking place against a background of overall degradation. The call center case shows a simple mechanism for this decay, in the obsolescence of data. But decay arises for other reasons. The business processes that an IT system supports will change, so that the system's contribution becomes increasingly ineffective at supporting those processes. The organization's needs may increase in scope and complexity, so that an unchanging system again becomes less effective.

- Systems investments may help improve the organization's overall performance both by improving efficiency and increasing effectiveness, and any single project may contribute to each to some degree. These two contributions will operate on the firm's strategic architecture to deliver some mix of cost reduction and business growth.

- Systems investments are rarely just about data and the processing of that data. Often they involve significant changes to the business processes themselves, and changing or raising the skills of the people using them. A credit-scoring system for a bank, for example, relieves executives of the need to be skilled at assessing a customer's risk. On the other hand, increasingly sophisticated advice-support systems for customer service staff may make it possible for them to handle a large fraction of enquiries that they would previously have needed to refer to others. This, however, will require those staff to be trained in understanding services that were previously provided by others.

Although a full examination of how systems investments contribute to improving business performance through time is beyond the scope of this book, the essence of the mechanisms is summarized in Figure 9.11. Any particular investment makes some contribution to improving skills, data, the systems themselves, or business processes, or to some mix of these. All of those intangible resources are undergoing decay, so investing nothing will ultimately undermine the business. If correctly prioritized and phased, the improved skills, data, systems and processes operate on the tangible resources of the organization's strategic architecture—customer retention, product development, staff productivity, capacity, etc.—to improve its performance. The mechanisms by which any individual initiative operates on the strategic architecture can be assessed by extending the principles illustrated in Figure 9.9 above, which will allow judgments to be made regarding the scale and make-up of the whole investment program.

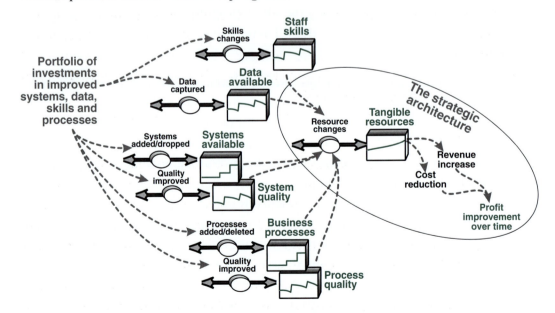

**Figure 9.11: Overview of systems investments' impact on the strategic architecture and performance.**

# KNOWLEDGE

Taking a higher-level view of data and information, "knowledge" has, as explained in Chapter 2, become an important concept in efforts to understand business performance to the extent that it has become a sub-field within the resource-based view of strategy. The role of information technology in enabling organizations to capture, synthesize, disseminate and leverage knowledge is now seen as increasingly important.[19]

Technology-rich industries clearly rely on large quantities of technical knowledge, accumulated over many years, and protected by secrecy and sometimes by patents. The importance of such knowledge is not limited to businesses that make physical products, and may be found in firms across many sectors, from retailers who use knowledge about customer behavior to the likes of Amazon.com and eBay, who voraciously gather information and insight about the best approach to many aspects of their business operations.

Consulting firms belong to a class of organizations that are especially dependent on building, maintaining and leveraging a wide range of knowledge domains. They must understand the markets and segments their potential clients serve, the structure of supply and competition in those industries, and the operating models and economics of various kinds of firms involved. Ideally, they would also have access to as much operational, financial and strategic information as possible about many of the individual firms in the industry, so that they can identify practices that appear to be advantageous and incorporate these in recommendations to specific clients.[20] So important is knowledge recognized to be in such firms that staff appraisal and promotion systems frequently balance three contributions that each professional must make: developing clients, developing people and developing knowledge.

Figure 9.12 shows just some of the benefits of adding knowledge management systems to such a firm.

- Knowledge enables new services to be created. Having extensive insight into current issues confronting potential clients in an industry allows the firm to develop and test new services. This is exactly what occurred with the choice pipeline model described in Chapter 6. One firm possessed information on the pipeline data for many clients across several industries. This knowledge was developed into a sophisticated advisory service, well beyond the capabilities of organizations in those industries, and tested out with one of the firm's most trusted clients. Having demonstrated the method's value and codified how the process could be applied, the firm was then in a position to take the new service to many potential clients across a wide range of industries.

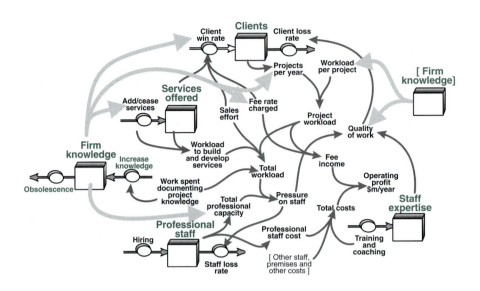

**Figure 9.12:** Contribution of firm knowledge to performance for consulting firms.

- Naturally, being able to demonstrate in-depth knowledge of a potential client's industry, markets and competitors greatly improves the ability to win clients.
- With more widespread knowledge of the issues confronting their clients, the firm can also sell them more projects
- … and charge higher fees, since the projects will be more valuable to the client.
- Knowledge brings large increases in productivity of professional staff and hence raises their capacity—both directly, by showing individuals how best to approach a certain problem, and indirectly, by providing access to others in the firm with prior experience of the issue.
- In addition to improving staff productivity, knowledge reduces the workload needed to complete each project simply by making available information that would otherwise have to be looked for.
- Finally, the knowledge base can enhance the quality of work done for clients, both by demonstrating how well similar problems were previously tackled, and by providing benchmarks for performance.

The power of such knowledge systems should not be underestimated. Leading consulting firms have vastly more knowledge about numerous industries and firms within them than any of those firms could usually find and manage for themselves. Consequently, even industry-leading firms frequently seek the advice of top consulting companies. It is important to recognize that this is not because the client firms could not, if they wished, assemble equivalent knowledge, but the potential contribution to the performance of their strategic architecture cannot match the equivalent benefit that a consulting organization can obtain by leveraging the same knowledge across multiple situations. Often, the only constraint on this leverage is the conflicts of interest that can arise when a single consultancy offers advice to more than one firm in the same industry.

Some further points are worth noting:

- Such a knowledge base is not a "free lunch." It takes significant time and effort on the part of consultants and managers in the firm to collect, organize, submit and update information in the knowledge base—time that is not directly chargeable to current client projects. Nevertheless, the contribution to project sales and fee rates can be considerable, and therefore justify the effort involved.
- High-level knowledge of this kind decays, in just the same way as the data discussed with the call center firm above. Quite simply, it becomes out of date, and less relevant to the new issues constantly arising for potential clients.
- There are diminishing returns to knowledge building. On the one hand, it would be great to have access to the latest information on every conceivable issue that every potential client in every industry might raise. On the other hand, it would use up more and more of the firm's professional capacity to collect all that information; capacity that would not be available to charge to clients.
- Furthermore, there are implications for staff morale arising from over-ambitious knowledge gathering. These professionals want to be spending time working on real client problems, rather than being shut in the office writing up what they have learned. The more they try to capture, the less likely it is that the knowledge will ever be utilized by their colleagues, which is a demoralizing experience.

Major consulting firms have largely mastered the management of their knowledge, and similar processes are to be found in most other kinds of professional firm; lawyers, marketing agencies, recruitment consultants, and so on. Few feel a need to quantify in detail the knowledge they hold, or to analyse rigorously exactly how much difference it makes to each of the elements of the strategic architecture in Figure 9.12. The benefits are so large that it is self-evidently a good thing to do, and to do well.

The case is often less clear-cut for other kinds of organization. Especially when embarking on knowledge capture for the first time, the effort to establish the information systems and persuade people to contribute to the knowledge base may well be daunting. It is therefore common for such initiatives to fail, with management and staff alike withdrawing their support before the benefits are realized. This risk can be reduced if at least some attention is given before starting out to assessing just what kinds and what quantities of information should be gathered, what effort this will require from whom, the uses to which the knowledge will be put, what benefits will arise for performance of different parts of the business system, and the continuing effort that will be needed to maintain the system.[21]

# QUALITY-BASED INTANGIBLES

There is an extensive and rich literature on the development of quality management,[22] and it has undoubtedly been central to the effective operation of many of the world's most admired companies.[23] However, the focus on quality over recent decades has been of considerably more importance than merely to make firms cost-efficient and reliable in their day-to-day operations. As the small example of the computer service company's problems described earlier in this chapter demonstrate, quality related issues are of critical importance to the *strategic* progress of organizations. That is to say, quality has a substantial impact on the medium- to long-term development of performance.

## NON-RESOURCE QUALITIES

In the classification of resources in Figure 9.1, it was pointed out that certain quality measures can move immediately, depending on the values of factors on which they depend. If a retail store offering good service quality finds that five of the 20 staff it normally needs do not show up for work one day, its service quality will instantly suffer. If those same employees show up again on the following day, service quality will jump back to its normal level. Similar observations arise in relation to service quality in many contexts:

- an airline suffering a serious breakdown on one of its aircraft may find that its on-time performance instantly drops, but recovers when the breakdown is fixed
- a football team suffering injuries to three of its key players can expect its performance to drop immediately, but perform well once more when their injuries recover
- a law firm winning a major engagement that pushes workloads well above the capacity of its staff will deliver poor work, either to this project or more likely to others—client enquiries will go unanswered, paperwork will be delayed, and so on—but quality will recover when that engagement ends

None of these examples is surprising, but a number of observations arise. First, and most importantly:

**Quality is key to strategic performance, so should feature in the business architecture if it is not guaranteed to be OK.**

Many firms manage quality so well that it has become utterly reliable, and so can be safely ignored for the purposes of assessing its strategic prospects. However, for most organizations this is not the case.

- *Quantification is important.* There is a big difference for the customers of the retail store if its staff shortage leads to queues of five minutes or 15. The aircraft shortage is more serious if it leads to cancellations rather than merely short delays. The football team's injuries may lead to just one lost game or a sequence of losses. And the law firm's overload will be more serious if it leads to clients losing cases, rather than just experiencing delays. The differences between these contrasting outcomes are a consequence of *how much* the factors accounting for quality have moved. It is therefore important to assess when the factors determining quality will hit values that may cause problems, even if it is not easy to estimate exactly the scale of the problem that will result.

- *Quality may be manifest in multiple measures.* In many situations, there can be multiple measures of quality. An interesting case concerned the delivery performance of an office furniture supplier. The company had been experiencing problems with this issue since deciding to expand its product range from a simple choice of durable but unexciting items to a wider range of designer-products with various customer options to customize their furniture choices. Delivery performance suffered, but on what measure? Delivery lead-time, measured in days, is an obvious measure, but in fact is less important, since office refits are mostly planned well in advance. On-time delivery on the other hand, that is delivering on the day and time promised, is vital. Nor is it helpful to arrive before the expected date. Delivery completeness is also important, since missing items cause inconvenience. This posed a dilemma for the warehouse dispatcher faced with an incomplete order—should he send it out and hit the on-time objective, or hold on until it is complete? Given the more substantial inconvenience of missing the promised delivery time, the decision was usually to send the incomplete load, rather than wait for it to be completed.

- *Track the quality drivers, not just the quality itself.* The computer service case shows how situations can progress towards a crisis, while exhibiting no actual problems until the factors driving it have moved into critical territory. Had the company tracked workload and staff capacity, it would have seen the quality problem approaching, rather than waiting to hear of the problem when it was manifest.

- *The customer's viewpoint is the key consideration.* The office furniture case illustrates a simple situation in which several quality measures may arise, but some are of more importance than others. This is why quality initiatives place heavy emphasis on the "voice of the customer" (VoC). Indeed, VoC is now the term used for the stated and unstated needs of customers. These can be captured in various ways: Direct discussion or interviews, surveys, complaint logs, focus groups, observation, warranty data, and so on. Note that a similar process can be utilized for new product development, as well as for ensuring continuing quality.[24] The essential point here is the need to track what matters to customers, rather than information that happens to be conveniently available, a fundamental principle within the Six Sigma approach to quality.[25]

- *Internal quality matters too.* Sustaining high quality performance is not just important to external customers, but is also of concern within the organization. Many activities are carried out by one department or function in a business for the benefit of other internal customers. The call center's information systems described above directly affect the call center staff themselves, even though their ultimate purpose is to deliver good service to external customers. A call handler faced with a system that makes it hard to answer certain enquiries may nevertheless be able to do so, but the system's quality is not sufficiently high. Unless the problem is severe, the internal IT department will never hear of problems from external customers, but would do well to track quality from the point of view of the internal customer.

## QUALITY RELATED RESOURCES

Although many quality measures respond more or less instantly to the factors that drive them, others clearly accumulate. We have already dealt with certain forms of quality resource under the discussion of functionality in Chapter 5. Product development efforts progressively increase that performance towards the best that customers could want. In essence, the measure of quality being assessed at that point was how much of the users' requirement is fulfilled, *assuming* that it is produced 100% to specification. That, then, was the critical, positive dimension of quality

Other positive quality indicators include various forms of efficiency, as for example with fuel-efficiency in motor vehicles and aircraft, or the fraction of incident energy captured by solar cells. However, important indicators that run alongside product functionality and performance are not so much "quality" as "lack of quality." The quality of the deteriorating equipment examples in Chapters 5 and 6, was experienced as the rate at which units fail. Other examples include:

- manufactured quality in microprocessors, memory chips and so on which shows up in the fraction of components that are rejected
- quality in chemicals and pharmaceuticals, measures in terms of purity
- quality for many manufactured products, which shows up as the fraction of units sold that result in warranty claims or customer-reported flaws
- software quality, experienced by users as the lack of bugs

In contrast with the zero-to-one scales that were appropriate for many psychological intangibles earlier in this chapter, appropriate measures for such items will be more specific (Table 9.2).

Note that some of these quality indicators may not be knowable accurately without unrealistic efforts being made over unrealistically long periods. Every aero engine that comes off the production lines comes with a significant number of manufacturing faults. (Do not be too alarmed; these are not a threat to safety, but consist of small deviations from specification that may marginally affect performance or reliability.) Similarly, every software package includes bugs of some kind, an example that illustrates the tricky trade-off suppliers face. Users might prefer the software to be worked on until the probability that they personally will experience any bug at all is infinitesimal. Unfortunately, that would take so much effort and take so long that the software would never actually be launched.

This phenomenon shows up in manufactured products too. We might prefer that a new car we purchase is entirely free of faults, but manufacturers would have to work for many years to achieve an absolute guarantee of zero defects. In spite of the

## TABLE 9.2: MEASURES FOR INTANGIBLE QUALITY RESOURCES AND NON-RESOURCE QUALITY FACTORS

| Intangible quality resource | Common measure | Units |
|---|---|---|
| manufactured production yield | reject rate | fraction rejected |
| chemicals quality | purity | fraction of impurities |
| manufactured product quality | reported faults | average faults per 000 units |
| software quality | bugs | total bugs |

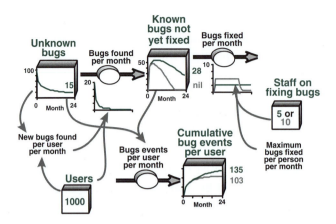

**Figure 9.13: Working off bugs discovered in a piece of software.**

considerable impact that Six Sigma and other approaches to quality have had over recent decades, it is still not possible to eliminate entirely the possibility of faults in all kinds of manufactured goods.[26]

To illustrate the link between the kind of negative quality measure and user-experienced quality, Figure 9.13 illustrates progress in quality improvement for a very simple software application, tailor made for a group of just 1 000 users. The software is released to the users with 100 bugs, although that number is not known either to the users or developers. As the software starts to be used, users discover the bugs and report them to be fixed. The bugs are gradually fixed by a small team who work to resolve them. However, these bugs continue to be experienced by users until such time as the fix is made and deployed.

In both scenarios, the initially high discovery rate of unknown bugs falls very sharply because of the large number of user-days to which the software is exposed. Nevertheless, this does not eliminate the unknown bugs entirely, even after many months of use, because the probability of any particular user making use of the feature in exactly the way that gives rise to a bug event falls to a very low value.

In the first case (green lines and text) a team of five staff struggle to work off the known bugs, and have failed to reduce that number significantly even after 12 months. In the second case (gray lines and text), a larger team manages to work off the known bugs more quickly. Surprisingly, however, this considerable reduction overall in known bugs is not reflected to the same degree in the total bug-events that users experience over the two-year episode, due to the large number of new bug events that continue to be found by users.

This example illustrates some features that may arise in other cases where fault-based quality is involved.

- The problem experienced by the customer or user is different in nature from the fault itself that generates the problem. In this case, while the underlying problem is an error in the software code, the problem experienced could be anything from an error in the result that the software generates, to a messy screen format to a complete system crash. In car production, a problem with the physical manufacture of the transmission system could show up as excessive noise, high fuel consumption, or a road-side breakdown.
- Many problems continue to exist, unknown either to the producer or the customer, simply because of a low probability that the combination of events which make the problem show up will actually arise.
- There is a trade-off between the desire to release the product as soon as possible, and the aim to release it with the fewest number of problems.
- Discovered problems require time and effort to be worked off, so there is a balance to be made between the cost of providing sufficient resources to fix all the discovered problems as soon as possible, and the costs that arise from allowing problems to persist.

## INTANGIBLES IN NONCOMMERCIAL CASES

The principles outlined in this chapter are readily observable in public service and voluntary organizations, and subject to very similar change mechanisms.

Public funding constraints often cause public services to display problems analogous to that of the computer service firm in Figure 9.2. A shortfall of staff capacity relative to demand makes good service impossible to deliver. Annoyance amongst the public follows, leading some, if they can, to give up on the service and either seek private provision or else become resigned to the fact that they are not going to get the service they hope for. The pressure on staff also builds up causing many to leave for less stressful employment.

One such case concerned pressure on the Canadian armed forces arising from their popularity for assignments to support United Nations initiatives. The more such calls they received, the shorter was the period of recuperation for the average soldier between one deployment and the next. The pressure led to increasing levels of sickness, as well as family stress, causing both a reduction in availability of people to be deployed and a more rapid departure of those same people for other jobs.

Intangibles can play a positive role too in public service settings. The zero-tolerance of minor misdemeanours is a well-known case where policy seeks deliberately to drive an increase in an important perception—that damaging or criminal behavior is not acceptable—a changed state of mind that drives changes in behavior in the form of less criminal activity. Many communities have enabled a substantial improvement in tidiness and cleanliness by a similar intolerance of garbage. Any occurrence is immediately removed, building a perception that the neighborhood *is* clean and tidy, and instilling a state of mind amongst its population that is less inclined to drop garbage.

Similar phenomena arise for voluntary organizations. Many voluntary groups enjoy strong public support and thus are successful in fundraising as a result of building up perceptions of the value of their work. Some even utilize the impact of sporadic incidents to boost these important perceptions, such as the stunts carried out by some environmental campaign groups. A problematic example was given in Chapter 2, which described the imbalance at the Motor Neurone Disease Association between the capacity of its volunteers to provide the promised support to people living with the disease and the rate of demand for that service. The disappointment amongst the organization's beneficiaries led to the equivalent of low sales rates for a business—they did not call the Association for help as often as they needed.

The contribution of information-related intangibles is also widely observable in public service and voluntary organizations. Adequate data, sufficiently up to date is clearly essential for health services, social services and others to perform their role effectively, as are effective and efficient systems. Large voluntary organizations, too, rely on good data and effective systems to perform their role well. The campaign group Amnesty International, for example, has a large amount of detailed data, constantly updated, on the human rights abuses that they seek to publicize and hence deter.

## INTANGIBLE FACTORS IN LOW-FARE AIRLINES

The low-fare airline case developed through earlier parts of the book features some clear examples of the kinds of intangible resources discussed in this chapter.

First, there is clear potential for linkages to exist between service quality, customer annoyance and reputation that closely resemble the computer service case at the start of this chapter (Figure 9.14). As in that case, problems can potentially arise from the simple physics of the system, rather than any attitudinal or behavioral causes of poor service or reputation. Service quality will be poor if there are too

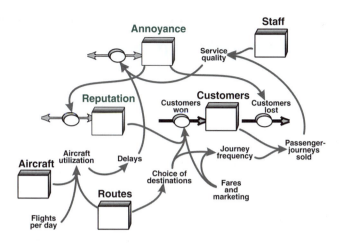

**Figure 9.14:** Service quality, delays, customer annoyance and reputation in airline performance.

few staff to handle the number of journeys customers wish to make, an issue that can arise in relation to both flight crew and ground staff. There is a second potential cause of trouble in this case, in the delays that would arise from a shortage of aircraft relative to the number required to fulfill the routes and flight frequency offered.

Both these quality factors will generate sporadic problem incidents for particular passengers, and if these are sufficiently frequent and serious, they can raise levels of annoyance to the point that customers will choose to avoid this airline in favor of alternatives. Rising annoyance levels risk damage to the airline's reputation with other travelers for on-time performance and service quality, cutting its ability to win new customers.

The structure in Figure 9.14 offers other possibilities discussed before. First, an airline could readily create its own trouble, for example by offering routes and flights that are beyond the capacity of its fleet and/or its staff to fulfill. The system also has the potential to rebalance itself in an undesirable manner—if poor service drives customers away, or causes them to fly less frequently, then limited numbers of staff will be better able to cope, and service quality can recover. However, this does not apply to the same degree to the delays caused by having too few aircraft. Whilst a drop in passenger-journeys may help somewhat with aircraft turn round times, a more serious shortage of aircraft would lead to delays, even if load factors were low.

# INTEGRATING INTANGIBLE RESOURCES INTO THE STRATEGIC ARCHITECTURE

As for the attribute frameworks in Chapter 5, resource development in Chapter 6 and rivalry in Chapter 7, it is not generally practical or helpful to add every intangible item to a strategic architecture with the aim of producing a comprehensive map of the entire system. When considering how intangibles affect a particular issue, it is often safe to limit consideration only to those factors that are located close to that issue, as was the case for the computer service firm and call center data examples earlier in this chapter.

When taking a wider view of the overall strategy and prospects for an organization, it may also be possible to minimize the effort directed to dealing with intangibles. The strategic architecture can first be developed with tangible resources alone. From this foundation:

- The architecture can be reviewed for resource flows that are sensitive to intangibles that could become problematic, and the policies for developing the tangibles checked to ensure that they do not risk compromizing the integrity of the system and hence damage future performance.
- On a more positive note, the core business can also be inspected for opportunities where exceptional performance on one or more intangibles could give rise to resource-development above expectations, such as exceptional customer acquisition.
- There may in particular be scope for intensive knowledge building to drive market-leading products or services, and hence customer growth, revenue and profits.

### Summary of Chapter 9

It is important to adopt a well specified terminology for intangible resources, distinguishing them in particular from tangible factors, attributes, capabilities, routines and processes. The items that remain within the definition of intangibles come in three broad categories; state-of-mind factors, information-related and quality issues. Certain important quality issues do not exhibit the behavior required of resources, but should nevertheless feature in any professional analysis and development of strategy.

Psychological factors can have powerful effects on the tangible resources of the organization's strategic architecture because state of mind drives behavior of customers, staff and other groups. Quality issues frequently cause changes in levels of these psychological resources, and these often reflect numerical imbalances in tangible elements of the business. A common consequence of intangible factors becoming problematic is to force the business back into a state of balance, although this may arise through mechanisms that are undesirable, such as loss of customers.

Not all states of mind are positive, and issues such as irritation or annoyance can trigger major shifts in behavior when they pass tolerance thresholds. Reputation and perception levels often respond only slowly to changes in the underlying drivers, obstructing efforts to make improvements in those levels.

Data, information and knowledge are important in enabling staff to do key activities effectively and efficiently. They have a tendency to decay, making it necessary to maintain, update or replace any elements that become obsolete. Investment in information systems is often of strategic importance, and achieves its contribution by raising or maintaining the organization's data, processes and skills, in addition to the functionality of the systems themselves.

Knowledge is a higher-level resource than simple data, and can make a powerful contribution to an organization's products and services, performance in delivering those products and services, its acquisition and retention of customers, and productivity and performance of staff.

Quality has become increasingly important, not only to operational effectiveness and efficiency but also to strategic performance. Multiple indicators of quality may be influential in any particular case, including positive measure of product performance and negative measures, such as absence of failures.

# SUGGESTED QUESTIONS AND EXERCISES

1.  Explain the different categories of resources and capabilities involved in organizations' strategic performance. In particular, how are "intangible resources," as narrowly defined for the purposes of assessing dynamic performance, distinguished from other asset-stocks.

2.  What are the three main groups of intangible resource? Give examples of each.

3.  Identify intangible resources that may be influential for the organization you chose to look at in Chapters 2 – 4. Look for examples in each of the three main categories of intangibles. Alternatively, carry out the same exercise using the outline architectures you developed after Chapter 4 for one or more of the following examples:

    a.   a retail chain, such as Starbucks

    b.   a company manufacturing and servicing elevators

    c.   an online dating agency

    d.   a voluntary organization providing medical centers in locations that have no alternative provision.

4.  What feature of intangible resources gives rise to "tipping points," that is sudden changes in behavior? Give an example that could arise in the case you considered for question 3.

5.  Review the intangibles you identified in answer to question 3, and give a practical measurement that could be used to quantify each one. Explain how management might go about finding this information.

6.  Use Worksheet 14 to lay out the connections between one or more intangibles you identified in answer to question 3 and the tangible resources involved. Describe a scenario in which these intangibles become problematic, show the kind of impact they could have on the business performance.

## USING WORKSHEET 14

This Worksheet offers a template for the common structure involving the widespread relationship between quality, reputation and customer gains and losses. Before using this Worksheet, the following steps should be taken:

●   specify the timescale and frequency over which the situation is to be examined, e.g. two years back and three years forward in months, and the scale for all variables

- identify and name the resources involved, and other variables
- add a timescale and value scale to each item, and insert data or estimates for how those quantities have changed in the past and might change in the future

(In common with other worksheets, this one can also be used to examine just the current situation and implications of alternative choices for the next period. In this case, it is not necessary to specify the timescale to be studied, nor to sketch the time charts as suggested below. Simply enter numerical values instead. In that case, though, it is important to beware of the sometimes surprising implications for performance in future periods arising from choices that are apparently sound on a short term view.)

Given the intangible nature of the issues this worksheet covers, it is possible that accurate data is not available for many of the elements they include. This is not, however, a good reason to abandon efforts to assess what is happening and work out ways to improve the situation. Involving people with real experience of the issues, effort can be given to estimating what may have been happening to the unknown elements. This requires those items to be clearly specified and the appropriate measurement defined. Using estimated information in this way may be sufficient to work out what needs to be done, by how much over what time, to make how much difference to the situation. It may also suggest practical and useful ways to identify and track factual information that will enable the situation to be more clearly analysed in future.

To make use of this worksheet (after following the setup steps above), the following sequence is suggested:

1. Enter the historical values for the actual quality indicator and the factors that are causing the quality to change over time (see Figure 9.2 for an example), and project how that indicator might change in the future.
2. Enter estimates for how customers' feelings about the quality issue have been changing (see numbered items in the worksheet). Ask how quickly their feelings would decline if the source of their concern ceased (i.e. the outflow from their concern), and how that concern might build up if your projected quality problem level in (1) were to happen.
3. Estimate the consequences for customer losses if your projection of the problem and customers' perception were to come about.
4. Estimate what has happened to your organization's reputation for quality with the potential target customers, and how your projection of quality changes would likely alter that reputation (see Figures 9.3 and 9.4).

5.  Estimate what impact reputation has had historically on customer acquisition, and what impact it may have in future, given the changes in quality and reputation identified above.

From this assessment of the history and likely future of the situation, the worksheet can be used to assess what might be done to tackle the quality problem itself (bottom-left), and what impact this may have on customer perceptions and reputation. Recognizing that perceptions themselves can be influenced, seek ways in which customers' perception of quality can be more rapidly improved, and ways of enhancing reputation. Beware, though, the risk of causing hostility (or "dissonance") if efforts to improve perceptions and reputation are not matched by the reality.

This worksheet is more easily worked using the **my**strategy software version, see paragraph about online learning materials on p.xxi.

# WORKSHEET 14: QUALITY AND REPUTATION

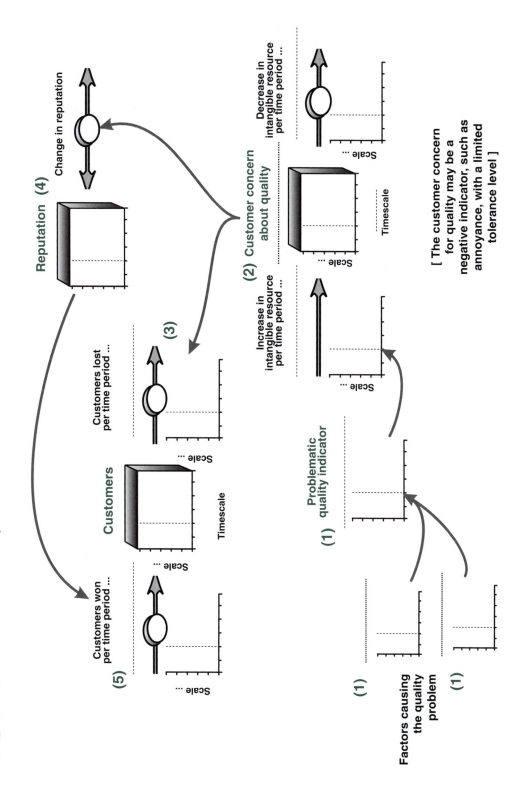

# NOTES

1. Barney, J. (2007) *Gaining and Sustaining Competitive Advantage* (3rd edn), Prentice Hall Upper Saddle River, NJ, p.24.

2. Tallman, S. (2003) *Dynamic Capailities*, in David Faulkner and Andrew Campbell (Eds), *The Oxford Handbook of Strategy (Volume I)*, p.375.

3. McGee, J., Thomas, H. and Wilson, D. (2005) *Strategy: Analysis and Practice*, McGraw-Hill, Maidenhead, p.263 and p.789.

4. de Wit B. and Meyer, R. (2004) *Strategy: Process, Content, Context* 3rd edn, Thomson, London, p.243.

5. Hitt, M., Ireland D. and Hoskisson, R. (2001) *Strategic Management: Competitiveness and Globalization*, 4th edn, South-Western/Thomson, Cincinatti, p.106.

6. Johnson, G. Scholes, K. and Whittington, R. (2005) *Exploring Corporate Strategy* (7th edn), Prentice Hall, Harlow, p.155.

7. See for example Stobart, P. and Perrier, R. (1997) *Brand Valuation*, Premier books, London. Considerable information on the topic of brand valuation and its contribution to corporate performance is provided by Interbrand (www.interbrand.com), including a range of books and papers. An example of empirical evidence supporting the contribution of brands to corporate value can be found in Madden, T. J., Fehle, F. and Fournier, S. (2006) Brands Matter: An Empirical Demonstration of the Creation of Shareholder Value Through Branding, *Journal of the Academy of Marketing Science*, **34**(2), 224–235.

8. A definition of strategic assets is given in Amit, R. and Schoemaker, P. (1993) Strategic assets and organizational rent, *Strategic Management Journal*, **14**(1) 33–46.

9. Itami, H. (1987) *Mobilizing Invisible Assets*, Harvard University Press, Boston, MA.

10. See Nohria, N. and Eccles, R. (1994) *Networks in Organizations*. 2nd edn Harvard Business School Press, Boston.

11. Mathematicians have long known of tipping points, which are dealt with by catastrophe theory. Originated by René Thom in the 1960s, the idea was taken up and popularized by Christopher Zeeman, especially as applied to the field of biology and behavioural science (see Zeeman, E. C. (1977) *Catastrophe Theory-Selected Papers 1972–1977*. Addison-Wesley, Reading, MA). However, the theory has found little application in management.

12. See Squires, S., Smith, C., Yeack, W. and McDougall, L. (2003) *Inside Arthur Andersen: Shifting Values, Unexpected Consequences*, Prentice Hall, Harlow' UK.

13. Fombrun, C. J. (1996) *Reputation: Realizing Value from the Corporate Image*, Harvard Business School Press, Boston, MA.

14. Barnett, V. (2002) *Sample Survey principles and methods*, Hodder & Staughton, London.

15. The phenomenon of cognitive dissonance is widespread in settings other than the management of organizations. More information on the theory's relevance to marketing contexts, including connections to "buyer's remorse" (the anxiety that may arise having made a purchase decision) and post-purchase evaluation, can be found at the American Marketing Association; www.marketingpower.com/mg-dictionary-view594.php.

16. Lane, C., Bachmann, R. (Eds), (2000) *Trust Within and Between Organizations: Conceptual Issues and Empirical Applications*, Oxford University Press, Oxford; Currall, S.C., Epstein, M.J. (2003) The Fragility of Organizational Trust: Lessons from the Rise and Fall of Enron. *Organizational Dynamics*, **32**(2), 193–206; Collins, J. C. and Porras, J. I. (1996) Building your company's Vision, *Harvard Business Review*, **74**(5) September-October, 64–77.

17. Lencioni, P. M. (2002) Make your values mean something. *Harvard Business Review*, **80**(7), July, 113–117.

18. Valuing investments in information systems was a popular issue of research in the 1980s and 1990s; see for example Porter, M. and Millar, V. 1985, How information gives you a competitive advantage, *Harvard Business Review*, **63**(4) July/August, 149–161 and Hitt, L. M., Brynjolfsson, E. (1996) Productivity, Business Profitability, and Consumer Surplus: Three Different Measures of Information Technology Value, *MIS Quarterly*, **20**(2), 121–142. It remains a significant challenge for senior management, for which a number of helpful books are available, such as Lutchen, M. (2004) *Managing IT as a Business: A Survival Guide for CEO's*, Wiley & Sons, Ltd., Hoboken, NJ.

19. In addition to the references noted in Chapter 2, see Alavi, M. and Leidner, D. (2001) Knowledge Management Systems: issues, challenges and benefits, *Communications of the Association for Information Systems*, **1**(7), 1–37 and Spender, J. (1996) Making Knowledge the Basis of a Dynamic Theory of the Firm, *Strategic Management Journal*, **17** (Special Issues), 45–62.

20. An illuminating description of how one consulting firm gathers, disseminates and uses knowledge can be found in the case study by Bartlett, C. (1996) *McKinsey & Company: Managing Knowledge and Learning*, Case 9-396-357, Harvard Business School, Cambridge, MA

21. Numerous publications offer advice on how successful knowledge management can be initiated and maintained, including for example Collison, C.

and Parcell, G. (2004) *Learning to Fly: Practical Knowledge Management from Leading and Learning Organizations,* John Wiley & Sons, Ltd, Chichester and Davenport, T. and Prusak, L. (2000) *Working Knowledge: How Organizations Manage What They Know,* Harvard Business School Press, Cambridge, MA.

22. See Dale, B. (2003) *Managing Quality* (4th edn), Blackwell, Oxford, Chapter 3; Reponning, N. and Sterman, J. (2001), Nobody Ever Gets Credit for Fixing Problems that Never Happened, *California Management Review* **43**(4), 64–88; Keating, Oliva, E.R. Repenning, N. Rockart, S. and Sterman, J. (1999), Overcoming the Improvement Paradox, *European Management Journal,* **17**(2), 120–134.

23. Eckes, G. (2001) *The Six Sigma Revolution: How General Electric and Others Turned Process into Profits,* John Wiley &Sons, Ltd, Chichester.

24. Ulwick, A. (2002) Turn Customer Input into Innovation. *Harvard Business Review,* **80**(1) (January), 91–97; Griffin, A. and Hauser, J. (1993) The Voice of the Customer. *Marketing Science,* **12**(1): pp. 1–27.

25. For a practical explanation of how voice of the customer is used in the Six Sigma method, see Maxey, J., Rowlands, D., George M. and Upton, M. (2005) *The Lean Six Sigma Pocket Toolbook: A Quick Reference Guide to 70 Tools for Improving Quality and Speed,* McGraw-Hill, New York, Chapter 4.

26. For more on the dynamics of quality during product development processes see for example Black L.J. and Repenning, N.P. (2001) Why fire-fighting is never enough: preserving high quality product development, *System Dynamics Review,* **17**(1), 33–62.

# CHAPTER 10

# CAPABILITIES

## KEY ISSUES

- ✪ Capabilities as activities groups are good at doing, that can be and often are deliberately identified and developed
- ✪ The importance of clear terminology and specification for capabilities
- ✪ Most important capabilities concern acquiring, developing or retaining resources, so can be found at each resource flow in the strategic architecture
- ✪ … and three detailed capabilities are often required; to get things done quickly, with good quality and at low cost
- ✪ Small differences in capability explain large differences in performance, with no need to invoke complex, abstract concepts
- ✪ The dividing out of capabilities amongst teams with particular responsibilities
- ✪ Contrasting the stock-and-flow view of how capabilities develop resources vs. the activity flow of business process mapping
- ✪ The self-reinforcing link between resource flows and building capability as the basis for learning
- ✪ Capabilities as composite asset-stocks, combining people, skills, processes and information systems
- ✪ Certain capabilities that are not linked to resource flows
- ✪ Capabilities in noncommercial settings
- ✪ Learning mechanisms incorporate limits to growth and the forgetting of capabilities
- ✪ The powerful consequences arising from capabilities working together
- ✪ Learning from games

The chapter makes connections to the concepts of the value chain, business process mapping and redesign, tacit vs. explicit knowledge and evolutionary views on capability development

Firms with few resources are not necessarily doomed to weak, low growth competitive positions in their industries. If they do not possess or have access to important resources, they can develop those they need. For this purpose, they need the capability to build and sustain resources. Whilst this much is clear in principle, making use of capabilities to design and deliver strong strategic performance faces the same difficulties as those encountered with intangible resources in Chapter 9; namely a terminology that is wide-ranging, inconsistent and abstract, as the following explanations from various printed sources demonstrate.

> … Resources include [a firm's] fundamental financial, physical, individual and organizational capital attributes. "Capabilities" in contrast include only those internal firm attributes that enable a firm to coordinate and exploit its other resources. … Although these distinctions among resources, capabilities and competencies can be drawn in theory, it is likely that they will become badly blurred in practice. In particular, it seems unlikely that a debate about whether a particular firm attribute is a resource, and capability or competence will be of much value to managers or firm.[1]
>
> … capabilities and competencies arise through interaction of the firm, as a bundle of physical, human and organizational resources, with its competitive environment. Only through application in a specific environment do the capabilities and resources generate competitive advantage and rents. In addition, capabilities and other intangible resources develop through evolutionary processes of variation, selection and retention of new processes within a specific environment. Capabilities contain an inherent learning aspect. They cannot be bought and are too complex and unspecified to be built intentionally.[2]
>
> A capability is the ability to perform a task or activity that involves complex patterns of coordination and co-operation between people and other resources. Capabilities would include research and development expertise, customer service and high-quality manufacturing. Skills, by contrast, are more specific, relating to narrowly defined activities such as typing, machine maintenance and book-keeping.[3]
>
> … resources are the productive assets owned by the firm; capabilities are what the firm can do. … Creating certain resources … may be difficult, costly and time consuming, but at least the challenge can be comprehended and planned. Creating organizational capability poses a much higher level of difficulty. We know that capabilities involve teams of resources working together, but even with the tools of business process mapping, we typically have sketchy understanding of how people, machines, technology and organizational culture fit together to achieve a particular level of performance. … Organizational capability is path dependent—a company's capabilities today are the result of its history.[4]

Initiatives to enhance market sensing and customer linking capabilities are integral to broader efforts to build a market-driven organization. The overall objective is to demonstrate a pervasive commitment to a set of processes, beliefs, and values, reflecting the philosophy that all decisions start with the customer and are guided by a deep and shared understanding of the customer's needs and behavior ...[5]

Capabilities are the firm's capacity to deploy resources that have been purposely integrated to achieve a desired end state. As the glue that binds the organization together, capabilities emerge over time through complex interactions among tangible and intangible resources. Capabilities enable the firm to create and exploit external opportunities and develop sustained advantages when used with insight and adroitness. ... capabilities are often based on developing, carrying, and exchanging information and knowledge through the firm's human capital.[6]

[The experiences of] successful companies suggest four basic principles of capabilities-based competition [1] the building blocks of strategy are not products and markets but business processes [2] competitive success depends on transforming these key processes into strategic capabilities that consistently provide superior value to the customer [3] companies create these capabilities by making strategic investments in a support infrastructure that links together and transcends traditional business units [4] because capabilities necessarily cross functions the champion of a capabilities-based strategy is the CEO.[7]

As for the specification of intangibles given at the start of Chapter 9, there is no definitively correct resolution of the diverse explanations offered above, so the following argument should again be judged on whether it enables management and their advisors to undertake reliable analysis, as the basis for designing and steering strategy to raise performance over time. That is, is it fit for purpose?

First, it is not in fact difficult to distinguish a capability from a resource, at least as the latter term is defined in previous chapters. Note in particular that we specifically defined the term "resources" to *exclude* capabilities, in contrast to the treatment in other sources. As Grant observes (see note 4), resources are things a firm has, while capabilities are things it is good at doing. Common English usage too implies that a capability is about getting something done, while a resource is some useful thing (whether tangible or intangible) that can help to get those things done, but is not the activity itself. In simple grammatical terms, since a capability is about doing something, it can be expressed as the present participle of a verb—market*ing*, hir*ing*, serv*ing* customers, develop*ing* products—or the noun describing such a process, for example product develop*ment*, recruit*ment*, and so on.

This distinction between resources and capabilities challenges another inconsistency between discussion in the strategy literature and common English usage, namely that resources somehow create or lead to capabilities. Cash, products, skills or reputation don't actually "do" anything unless people work with them, so the dependency is actually the other way round—many of the most important capabilities drive the creation, development and sustaining of resources. It will however be shown that growth in a capability is driven by the *flows* of an associated resource, rather than by its existence. Simply having a good product, for example, tells you little about how to develop one well, and having a good employee tells you little about how to develop others.

Whilst some capabilities may develop through exploratory learning, many—perhaps most—are deliberately designed. The effective logistics systems at Wal-Mart and Dell, Tesco's relentless development of retail stores, CapitalOne's customer-segment targeting for credit cards, Ryanair's yield management of ticket sales, and Amazon.com's identification of customer-needs are neither accidents of history, nor the result of undirected experimentation. Each has been purposefully designed to perform specific functions with great effectiveness and efficiency, and each continues to be enhanced. Business process mapping plays a key role in this design of capabilities and, as will be shown, gives a clear picture of how many capabilities operate.

Even when strong capabilities have indeed emerged through experimentation, it is quite possible that they would have emerged stronger and faster if deliberately designed. This is not to argue that learning is unimportant. Indeed, effective capability building often includes formal processes to capture learning, sometimes with deliberate rather than undirected experimentation.

It was previously explained (see Chapter 2) that resources need not, in fact, be owned; the organization only requires somewhat reliable access to them. The same applies to capabilities, many of which can be bought or accessed through partner organizations. CRM systems can be purchased, along with the processes and training to use them, as can knowledge management systems. A vast industry has grown up, involving accounting, consulting and information systems firms to help organizations of all kinds implement enterprise-resource-planning (ERP) solutions. Numerous organizations outsource capabilities to third-party suppliers; provision of IT, recruitment, logistics, even product development and manufacture of the firm's products. Nor can it be argued that only "non-strategic" capabilities can be outsourced. The ability to hire the right people, or to deliver goods rapidly and conveniently to customers, undoubtedly have a significant effect on firms' medium- to long-term performance. Yet even these capabilities are often sourced from other providers.

Not all capabilities are or should be customer-focused. The capability of Wal-Mart to find good store locations of course includes the ability to pick exactly the right spot to ensure the best access to the largest number of target customers.

However, it also includes the ability to pay the minimum price for the real-estate, to acquire and develop it quickly, and even to make the building energy efficient, none of which directly impact on customers' experience. Negotiating good payment terms with suppliers is not customer-facing either. The speed and effectiveness of its logistics systems to ensure the shelves always display the goods that should be there is of course important to satisfying customers' needs, but it can hardly be argued that a hallmark of a customer-focused company is to actually have available the products they know customers want. If we do define such capabilities as being customer-focused, then so is everything the firm does and there is no distinct set of capabilities that especially conform to that description.

Capabilities need not be dependent on the specifics of the organization's culture, beyond the observation that people need to work together to get things done. Some organizations accomplish outstanding customer service through command-and-control styles of management, while others do so through empowerment. Whilst encouraging cooperation between people would seem to be essential, there are even examples of organizations that have built powerful capabilities in spite of a culture that encourages internal conflict between individuals and teams.

Most capabilities reside largely within functional boundaries, so do not serve to hold the organization together. Sales capability often sits largely with the sales team, and whilst it may use information from other departments, it does not involve complex collaboration. Maintenance of fixed assets resides within a technical service team, and the capability to run delivery systems that are efficient and effective is owned by the logistics department. Some capabilities, however, do require collaboration between groups. Product development capability, for example, relies on the involvement of marketing, sales, and engineering to be effective.

Incorporating these observations to resolve the ambiguity and confusion surrounding capabilities starts from the specification of tangible, intangible and attribute resources in Chapter 9 (see Table 9.1).

- *Capabilities are asset-stocks, but not resources.* They therefore accumulate and deplete, and exhibit many of the characteristics of asset-stocks established in Chapter 3. Their present level reflects the history of those factors that caused their development, so they are certainly path-dependent. Growth of capabilities, that is their inflow rate, depends on rates of change in the resources with which most are associated—we get better at hiring people by doing it. Capabilities can also be lost, i.e. they have an outflow.
- *Capabilities differ from skills.* As explained in Chapter 5, skills are attributes of individuals, and move with the people who hold them. That it not to say they are

merely simple tasks, such as typing, or generic skills like book-keeping. Complex skills such as actuarial analysis and maintenance of sophisticated equipment are also held by individuals—move them to another situation offering the same challenge, with the same basic tools and information, and they will perform to the same level. The key distinction adopted here is that individuals cannot take capability with them to a new situation, because it relies on the existence of other significant resources, many of which are intangible and somewhat specific to the organization. Whilst organizations may have very similar resources, even small differences can have a big impact on an individual's ability to perform in a different environment.

- *Capabilities are composite asset-stocks.* The implication of the previous point is that capabilities must inevitably be composite factors, arising from the combination of several elements. This means that any properly specified capability could be reliably disaggregated into the elements that make it up. That is, two skilled business analysts picking apart the same capability would arrive at the same list and definitions of elements making it up. Nevertheless, it will prove both possible and helpful to formulate a specific capability as a single factor.

- *Capabilities are indistinguishable from competences.* The term "competences" is often used in discussion of capabilities within the strategy field.[8] When applied to a single business, there is no clear and agreed difference between capabilities and competences. Therefore, we will adopt the convention of referring only to capabilities when discussing things that need to be done well within an organization.

- *Core competences are different.* The catchy phrase "core competence" is now in widespread use, though its meaning has become blurred to the point that it is referred to indiscriminately in managerial discussions and in articles and books. The phrase was originally used to describe the powerful underlying technologies developed in multi-business firms that find their expression in products and services sold into diverse end-markets. Examples given in the original article include Honda's mastery of four-stroke engine technology, which enabled them to compete in motor-cycles, cars and ski-mobiles, or Canon's laser technology which lay at the heart of its ranges of scanners and printers.[9] It should be pointed out that a core competence alone is not sufficient for success if the organization lacks basic capabilities in other functions (see note 7). Honda struggled in the car industry during the 1990s, for example, because of weaknesses in design, marketing and production engineering.

  We will limit use of the phrase core competences to its original definition, and otherwise refer only to "capability."

- *Capabilities need not be core, distinctive, strategic or organizational.* To add to the confusion, phrases such as "core capability" are also used, one definition of the phrase being " ... *the knowledge set that distinguishes and provides a competitive advantage. ... Its content is embodied in [1] employee knowledge and skills and embedded in [2] technical systems. The processes of knowledge creation and control are guided by [3] managerial systems. The fourth dimension is [4] the values and norms associated with the various types of embodied and embedded knowledge and with the processes of knowledge creation and control.*[10]

Much discussion of capabilities seems to discount the possibility that anything easily specified could feasibly contribute to competitive advantage, by the logic that if it *could* be so specified then others would copy it and the advantage would disappear. This has led to a rich variety of phrases for the more special capabilities thought to explain competitive advantage—in addition to core capabilities, the literature mentions distinctive capabilities, strategic capabilities, firm-specific competence, organizational competence and many other adjective–noun combinations.

As argued previously when defining resources, it is not safe to dismiss mundane capabilities as being irrelevant to competitive advantage. Even if everyone knows what a specific, simple capability *is*, there can be significant differences in the level of that capability between competitors. Firms vary widely in the effort and investment they devote to building a particular capability, and in their success at doing so. There can also be considerable costs and lead-times in building capabilities, just as there are for many resources, both tangible and intangible. Furthermore, as explained previously, it is the *system* that generates performance, not a simple sum of separate elements.

### Ockham's Razor

Ockham's razor is a principle attributed to the 14th-century friar William of Ockham. In essence it states that the simplest explanation for any phenomenon is likely to be the best. This implies that, in the search for scientific theories, it is advisable to seek explanations that are economical or "parsimonious" (requiring the minimum number of factors), and involve the smallest number of hypothetical or abstract factors and mechanisms. This principle is worth bearing in mind when considering the likely usefulness and reliability of strategy theories and frameworks.

We will therefore drop all qualifiers, such as "core," "distinctive," "strategic" and "organizational" and use the single term "capabilities." Most of these are not at all distinctive from those possessed by competitors, though they may well differ in scale. Borders and Barnes & Noble, for example, are both highly capable at negotiating good terms with book suppliers, designing and opening appealing stores, merchandizing their ranges of books, and so on. As will be shown, which competitor performs better depends on their *relative* capability on each of these and other issues, the *relative* scale and quality of their tangible and intangible resources, and how effectively the whole system of each firm functions.

The explanation of intangible resources in Chapter 9 admitted a limit to just how far it is possible to go for a rigorous definition and measurement of those factors. The same will apply here. There are undoubtedly complex, subtle and sophisticated capabilities that play an important role in helping firms perform. However, their incremental contribution should not distract from efforts to understand and assess the very substantial impact that can arise from identifying, developing and using much simpler capabilities.

# EXAMPLE OF CAPABILITY EFFECTS

To illustrate how capabilities affect the performance of a firm's strategic architecture Figure 10.1 reconsiders the retailer from Chapter 5 (Figure 5.14), though now with a more detailed timescale covering its first 20 quarters of operation.

The firm tries to open stores quickly in order to capture the new customers available around each location. The fastest it could possibly open any particular new store, having made the decision to start-up in a locality, is three quarters (dashed lines and light text). However, being a new company, with little experience of finding, acquiring and developing stores, the best it can do is open each store after a process taking six quarters. This puts back substantially its capture of customers (solid lines and bold text), noting as in Chapter 5 that not all potential customers are captured immediately.

This first model already demonstrates a principle that will recur as the role of capabilities is explored further:

**Most capabilities are concerned with**
**building and retaining resources.**

There are exceptions, which will be examined later, but very many of the most important capabilities are clearly located at the flow rates in the strategic architecture. Since it has been shown throughout earlier chapters that flow rates determine the growth of resources, and are where management act to drive performance, it is only to be expected that this is where capabilities will be found.

## MULTIPLE CAPABILITY IMPACTS

There is more to getting stores open than simply doing so quickly. Further concerns include:

- finding good quality locations that can attract as many potential customers, as possible in each area
- acquiring and developing stores for a low cost

In Figure 10.1, the capability's value is an easy metric to arrive at. The lead-time is actually six quarters, but should be three, so it can be assigned a capability level of 3/6, or 0.5. It might be possible to continue with this value, and look up what it implies for the quality and cost of new stores locations. However, it makes more sense to apply appropriate metrics directly to each of these items. Furthermore, these capabilities are genuinely distinct. The organization may be good at negotiating a good price and at finding the best location to reach all potential customers, but poor at managing the process quickly.

The capability to acquire and develop stores at a good price can be defined as the ratio between the best possible cost and the cost actually incurred. The capability to find good quality store locations can be given by the fraction of potential customers in an area that each store actually captures. (This will turn out to interact with another capability in the marketing of each store, which also aims to capture potential customers.)

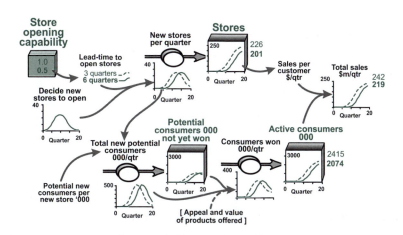

**Figure 10.1:** Low capability delays the store opening rate for a retailer.

**TABLE 10.1:  CAPABILITY METRICS FOR STORE OPENING**

| Detailed capability | Success factor | Capability indicator | Low value |
|---|---|---|---|
| Opening stores quickly | Lead-time: quarters | Actual lead-time vs. shortest | 0.5 |
| Finding good locations | Fraction of potential customers reached | Actual customers reached vs. total potential | 0.7 |
| Minimizing cost of new stores | Total cost of opening each store $millions | Actual cost vs. lowest possible cost | 0.8 |

Adopting this style of measurement for capabilities will often result in capabilities that are near to 1.0, rather than varying widely across a zero-to-one range. For example, a less capable retailer may open stores that are easily reached by only 90 % of the potential customers in an area, but is unlikely to be so incompetent as to choose locations that no one can find at all. Similarly, they may well spend 20 % more than the best purchaser could achieve, but will not likely spend two or three times that amount.

Table 10.1 summarizes the metrics for each capability, and Figure 10.2 shows the performance consequences that arise from the low capability levels shown in the table. The original low capability for lead-time (middle left) delays both the

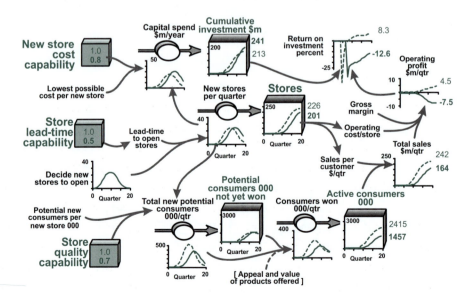

**Figure 10.2: Impact of low capabilities for store opening speed, quality and cost.**

store openings and the spending of capital investment, but the poor capability for opening at low cost means that cumulative investment overtakes the high-capability case. The slow capture of customers is worsened by the poor quality of store locations opened, cutting still further the sales revenue the stores achieve. Since stores still incur full operating costs, the chain cannot become profitable and losses increase, leading to a negative return on investment.* The business is clearly not doing well, relying as it does on these poor store-opening capabilities.

(Online learning materials are available to support this example, see p.xxi.)

It was argued earlier that the search for special or distinctive capabilities had distracted researchers from trying to understand the influence of capabilities that are entirely transparent. Figure 10.2 illustrates the point. It requires only a partial increase in each capability to allow sales to grow and the operating losses to be entirely eliminated.

And this is only *one* domain in which capabilities will arise. Others, concerning management of product range, logistics, staff hiring and training, marketing and pricing will all have significant impacts on their own part of the strategic architecture and on the performance of the business as a whole. Any significant company operating in the sector will be fully aware of the nature and importance of each capability, and will strive to improve it. It is not necessary to invoke complex, abstract, cross-organizational capabilities to explain extreme performance differences between competitors. The real puzzle is not so much why firms in the same sector differ in performance, as why they do not differ considerably more than they often do.

# CAPABILITIES AND BUSINESS PROCESSES

The mapping and deliberate design of effective business processes has become almost ubiquitous amongst larger organizations since business process reengineering (BPR) first came to prominence in the 1990s. The key observation at the time was that many businesses were using information technology to automate activities that were pointless, rather than redesigning processes to incur the minimum amount of essential activity.[11] One bank, for example, automated a process that had involved one employee checking the work of another as a protection against fraud, with the result that it developed two computer systems, each of which checked that the other was not attempting to defraud the company. This insight regarding widespread automation of wasteful activity then quickly developed into an approach that management

---

\* This is a much simplified indicator of return on investment, with no recognition of depreciation, working capital, tax and other issues.

could adopt, or employ consultants to apply for them, to fundamentally redesign or "re-engineer" processes throughout their business. The result would often be a considerable improvement in speed, reliability and cost efficiency.[12]

In summary, the core of BPR is, first, to identify the activities involved in current processes and the problems to which these give rise. From this understanding of how things currently operate, a revised (and usually reduced) set of activities is developed, together with new HR and IT systems as appropriate. Finally, the revised process is introduced, its effectiveness monitored, and any necessary adjustments made. Around these central elements, extensive attention should be given to management and leadership issues, such as obtaining backing and investment from senior executives, engaging with the teams concerned, canvassing opinion and feedback, and so on.[13] Redesign of processes continues to be an important element when organizations out-source their information systems support to third-party suppliers, who of course have a powerful incentive to make the processes they look after for clients as efficient as possible. Arguably, the most egregious examples of bad business processes to be found in the early 1990s have by now been redesigned, or else the firms that held on to them declined or died, so attention currently focuses on designing business processes correctly in the first place.

It is not the purpose here to discuss the details of process mapping or redesign. However, some examples of business processes clearly show an important connection to the frameworks developed in earlier chapters, and hence to capabilities. In Table 10.2, for example, the first column clearly lists activities that have been identified before as *resource flows*. In the strategy dynamics language, hiring is a flow of people into the staff resource, but it is also a process that some part of the organization must undertake. That process consists of several activities, such as specifying the job, placing advertizements, screening applicants, interviewing, selection and making offers. The second column, whilst not concerning factors we have specified as resources, nevertheless concern operational asset-stocks of various kinds, that is items that display bathtub behavior. For example, distribution moves finished goods to customer premises, production moves raw materials into

### TABLE 10.2: EXAMPLES OF BUSINESS PROCESSES

| | | |
|---|---|---|
| Marketing | Distribution | Credit control |
| Product development | Production | Payroll |
| Hiring | Order processing | Budgeting |
| Information-systems development | Purchasing | |

work-in-progress, and so on. Note that some of these processes concern movement of information, such as orders, rather than physical materials. The third column concerns details of processes by which cash is moved and its flows controlled.

It soon becomes clear that every resource flow in an organization's strategic architecture is a *process*, whether consisting of just a few steps or several. In order to be effective, the organization (or its outsource providers) must have a strong enough *capability* to enable it to acquire, develop and retain each resource. Furthermore, each capability often needs to be adequate on at least three dimensions:

- sufficient *speed*: customer win rate, product-development rate, hiring rate
- good *quality*: valuable customers, appealing products, skilled people
- adequate *efficiency*, whether in terms of financial cost or effort, marketing spend per acquired customer, product development effort, cost per new hire

The resource development perspective in Chapter 6 breaks down large-scale and multi-stage resource-building domains into distinct, subordinate, but nevertheless substantial resource flows, each of which is again a process performed with some capability. Examples include growing the number of aware customers, promotion of staff, product testing, and refurbishment of equipment.

Figure 10.3 shows (green text) some of the principal locations where strong capability may be needed, and where key processes therefore take place. Whilst most of these capabilities concern enabling desirable resource development, some focus on slowing undesirable flows, such as customer losses or equipment deterioration.

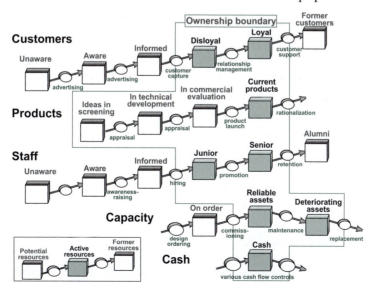

**Figure 10.3: The location of capabilities and processes at major resource flow rates.**

Whilst not an entirely adequate picture—processes are happening to products whilst *within* the stocks of the product development chain, for example, not just at the flows—it nevertheless demonstrates the close coincidence of capabilities and processes at the principal resource flows of the organization.

### Locating capabilities within the value chain

One technique sometimes used for guiding the search for capabilities is to investigate each part of the value chain (see Chapters 2 and 3) for activities that teams must do well for the enterprise overall to perform strongly.[14] Figure 10.4 illustrates some of the function-based capabilities that may be identified in the main domains of the value chain for a manufacturing firm.

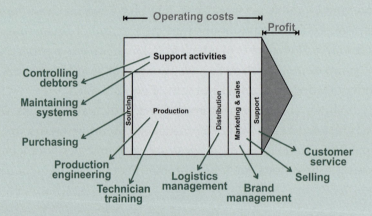

**Figure 10.4: Locating capabilities in the value chain of a business.**

Note that the relative size of each element in the diagram is proportional to the cost of that activity. This therefore indicates the scale of opportunity that may exist for capabilities in each domain to reduce the organization's overall cost. However it does not offer any guidance as to their potential to help drive business growth.

## "FACTORED" CAPABILITIES

Although the opening of new stores by the retail firm has so far been portrayed as a single activity, albeit with distinct capabilities for speed, quality and cost, it is in fact a multi-stage process, as shown in Figure 10.5. The diversity of activities along this

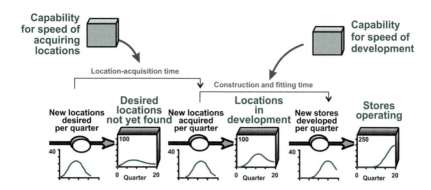

**Figure 10.5: Dividing store opening capability between acquisition and development.**

chain is too broad to be mastered by a single individual or team, so is broken down into two stages: site acquisition and store development.

One team of experts handles the first part of the process, looking for locations that could be purchased on which a store will later be constructed. They need capabilities in searching for, assessing and negotiating real-estate. A second team handles the construction and fitting out of a building on that location. This group needs capabilities in design and construction, or at least in the management of external developers to do those tasks. Figure 10.5 shows that each team would have some capability for doing their task quickly. Each would also need the capability to complete their stage of the process at low cost. So, if the new opening rate is too delayed or too costly, it could be due either to poor capability in real-estate acquisition, or in construction, or both. The third criterion—that the site be of good quality so as to attract the maximum proportion of potential customers—lies more in the hands of the real-estate team.

Note incidentally that the two first resource-stocks are largely undesirable, since they represent unfulfilled wishes and unproductive capital assets respectively. However, whilst they can be minimized, they cannot be eliminated. The real-estate team will try to get localities out of the "desired" stock and into the "in development" stock as quickly as they can. But if they are too good at this relative to the development group, the middle stock will fill up, leaving the company with a large number of undeveloped sites. Conversely, if the development team is much more effective than the acquisition team, they will empty the middle stock and be waiting around for the first team to catch up. (In practice, many retailers have a bank of real-estate locations awaiting development, since growth in their capital value reduces the penalty of holding unproductive sites).

Just as Chapter 8 discussed the needs for decision-making to be broken down, or "factored," between different parts of the organization, Figure 10.5 shows that capabilities too are commonly sub-divided. Similar factoring of capabilities may be found in various resource-development activities:

- in product development, different teams are responsible for technical development and commercial evaluation
- in hiring, HR staff may deal with initial advertizing and screening of applicants, leaving line management the final tasks of interviewing and selection
- in customer development, the marketing team may work on building awareness and understanding amongst potential customers, while the sales team works to convert these interested people to active customers
- a further team such as a telephone-sales group may pick up the task of growing sales to those customers, and yet another group may be responsible for service to ensure customers are retained

### Doing it right! Finding capabilities

Capabilities can be identified in broad terms by asking what needs to happen well in each stage of the value chain (see previous box). However, this does not identify capabilities with sufficient precision to enable quantified analysis and planning and thus to work out what to do and by how much to make known improvements to the firm's resource development rates.

To make a start on identifying important capabilities, look at each flow rate for each tangible resource in the strategic architecture and ask "What is it that the organization needs to be good at doing to perform well on this flow?" For example, in building a strong staff resource, the main flows are hiring, promotion and retention (Figure 10.6). For hiring, we are probably concerned with achieving the process quickly, and hiring people fast enough in total for our needs, but not spending too much on doing it. For staff development, we would want to promote people fast enough to meet our needs (and theirs!), but also ensure that the quality of people promoted is high enough. For staff retention, the key capability is to avoid loss rates becoming too rapid, and to retain in particular the best people at each stage.

To make the connection with business processes, the resource flow chain may need to be subdivided still further, although more than one of these sub-stages may be handled by a single group. The flow for store opening above can be seen in

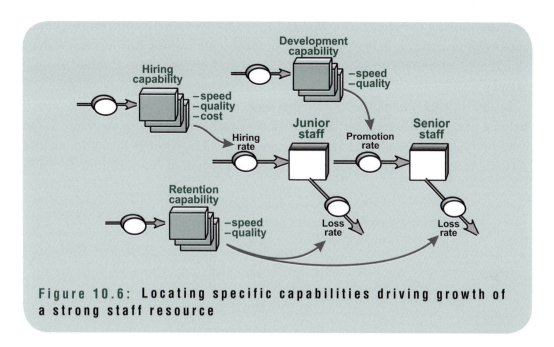

**Figure 10.6: Locating specific capabilities driving growth of a strong staff resource**

Figure 10.7 to consist of individual store locations moving from stage to stage along a chain. At each stage, the locations are having something different done to them; they are being assessed, negotiated for, and so on. The stock-and-flow view shows how many individual entities exist in each state at any time, and the rate at which

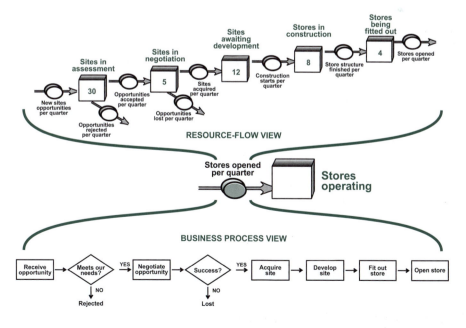

**Figure 10.7: Contrasting business process vs. stock-and-flow views of a major resource flow—opening retail stores.**

they are moving between them. The business process view, in contrast, highlights the activities that are being performed on each entity whilst it is in each state. It would also quantify the amount of work, cost and elapsed time involved in each activity.

Business process mapping and design serve an extremely important purpose in helping organizations improve their efficiency and effectiveness. It therefore makes a substantial contribution to strategic performance. The strategy dynamics method serves a quite different purpose, and is not to be thought of as a substitute for BPR.

> **Doing it right! Business processes vs. resource flows**
>
> These two views can be confused with each other, but are quite distinct. Business process mapping traces the sequence of activities that happen in order to get something done. It therefore quantifies how much *activity* takes place. Strategy dynamics tracks the location and movements of resources as they arrive, are developed and leave the enterprise. It therefore focuses on quantifying how much *resource* exists at each stage of this development, and how much is moving between states in each period.

Figure 10.8 offers a similar translation of the staff hiring rate into the detailed stocks and flows of applicants, and the corresponding detail of the process involved. As with the store opening example, we are not generally concerned from a strategic point of view with the details of either perspective. Nevertheless, Figures 10.6 and 10.7 clarify some useful points:

- Delays arise between wishing something to occur ("Hire more staff please") and the delivery of that desire, due to the stages through which resources must move, and the corresponding time taken by each element of the process—hence the importance of BPR in speeding the acquisition and development of resources.
- We do not always get all of what we want. There is scope for resources to be lost along the chain, both for reasons outside our control, and because of process activities designed to ensure quality of those resources, such as assessing the retail locations and screening initial job applications.

The hiring example also illustrates some activities captured by the BPR perspective that is not visible in the stock-and-flow view. For example, specifying the job and placing advertizements happen before any applications arrive in the stock-and-flow structure. The BPR perspective additionally clarifies where work and costs arise,

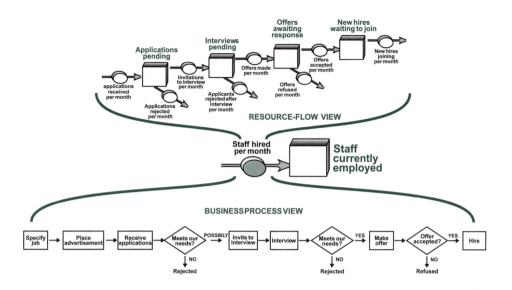

**Figure 10.8:** Contrasting business process vs. stock-and-flow views of a major resource flow—hiring staff.

and therefore contributes powerfully to our three strategic concerns regarding resource development; speed, quality and low cost. This gives rise to a further contrast between the operational focus of BPR and the strategic focus on resource building:

> **Business process redesign helps minimize *unproductive* stocks.**
> **Strategy dynamics focuses on acquiring and retaining**
> ***desirable* stocks (resources).**

# DEVELOPING CAPABILITIES: LEARNING

Going back to the very start of the retail business above, management would likely know from the start that finding locations for new stores would be an important capability, and hire someone with relevant experience for the task. At that point, the firm's capability would consist solely of the individual's skill. Since capabilities, like resources, are asset-stocks, they must accumulate and deplete—phenomena recognizable respectively as learning and forgetting. In order to complete the picture of how resources drive performance, and how capabilities arise to grow resources, it is therefore necessary to formulate a model for how learning occurs.

For the retail company struggling to grow a profitable business because of its poor store-opening capabilities, management might reasonably hope that their people will gradually learn to do the job better on all three dimensions; opening better stores, faster and cheaper. The following events describe the development of capability for one particular retailer in the restaurant sector over a period of some five years.

- Their first site acquisition expert had some initial success in finding promising locations for new stores, and taking them through the first half of the process in Figure 10.7 before handing them over to colleagues responsible for the construction phase.

- He was soon extremely busy, traveling long distances to visit promising locations, evaluating their suitability, rejecting a large fraction as unsuitable, making offers and negotiating the acquisition of good opportunities (many of which failed), and following through the purchase itself.

- The company's ambitions would later require an increased rate of site acquisition, growing to almost two per week at its peak—way beyond the capacity of this individual to cope. So the company hired a second expert and a third. Still, its capability was no more than the sum of these experts' skills. A particular location was chosen because it seemed to one of the team to meet the company's needs.

- By this point, the group was getting information on which factors were most important to the performance of its stores—visibility, high rates of passing traffic, ease of access from highways, proximity to similar retailers, and so on. To improve their success, the group wrote out this specification and issued it to real-estate agents in their search areas. They started to receive fewer opportunities, but much better ones—so they had fewer locations to inspect but an increased acceptance rate in the first stage.

- The team also discussed how successful they were with each purchase negotiation, and shared with each other tips for achieving the lowest possible price.

- The analysis required for new opportunities was by now better understood, so the team hired an analyst. To support this person, they had some computer systems set up to automate parts of the assessment, for example calculation of the socio-demographic profile of the surrounding population. This allowed a quick desk-top appraisal of each new opportunity, cutting the number of locations the experts had to visit still further.

- Meanwhile, more staff were being added, but now they could bring in people with less experience, quickly coach them in how their processes worked and support them with the information and systems that had been developed.

New individuals' skills therefore rose rapidly. Throughout this time, the team's success was increasingly valued by the company's management, to the extent that almost anything they asked for was granted; more staff or better IT systems, for example.

● Some two years into its development, the company was becoming well known amongst agents. Not only were its needs widely understood, but agents also knew they would get a quick decision on any opportunity, and the company was known to be effective at completing purchases. Consequently, the company started to be the first buyer to be informed of a new opportunity, often before the site had actually been offered for sale. Indeed, agents started pursuing sites on their behalf, even though the present owners had not put them on the market.

As a result of these events, the company was by years four and five acquiring much better locations, more quickly and at lower prices than competitors in its sector.

Taking a high-level view of this story offers a simple architecture for capturing how a capability develops. The small initial capability drives an inflow of the target resource—sites in this case—and the flow itself drives the increase in capability. The next period's increased capability drives a faster, better, cheaper inflow of further resource. This leads to the generic architecture for learning mechanisms in Figure 10.9. The "R" symbol indicates self-reinforcing feedback between resource acquisition and the growing capability (see Chapter 4 on feedback).

This additional structure can also be translated into an extension of the three equations explaining firm performance offered in Chapter 4:

The change in quantity of resource $R_i$ between time $t-1$ and time $t$ is a function of the quantity of resources $R_1$ to $R_n$ at time $t-1$, including that of resource $R_i$ itself, on management choices, $M$, on exogenous factors $E$ at that time, *and on the related capability* $C_i$.

$$\Delta R_i(t - 1 .. t) = f[R_1(t-1), .. R_n(t-1), M(t-1), E(t-1), C_i (t-1)] \qquad (3)$$

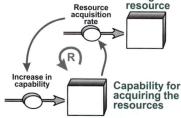

**Figure 10.9: Generic architecture of learning: building capability mutually reinforces resource-building.**

The current quantity of capability $C_i$ at time $t$ is its level at time $t-1$ plus or minus any flows into or out of that capability that have occurred between $t-1$ and $t$.

$$C_i(t) = C_i (t-1) +/- \Delta(C_i(t-1 .. t)) \qquad (4)$$

The change in quantity of capability $C_i$ between time $t-1$ and time $t$ is a function of the change that occurs to the quantity of the associated resource $R_i$ during that same period.

$$\Delta C_i(t-1 .. t) = f[\Delta R_i(t-1 .. t)] \qquad (5)$$

Even at this aggregate level, it is both possible and useful in many cases to populate the structure with factual information and use the resulting insight to focus efforts. To take the retail store example, the company knows the rate at which it is acquiring locations, the quality and the cost. Each of these indicators can be compared with what it believes to be the best possible speed, quality and cost, and thus the current level of these capability elements can be assessed. The scope for improvement in each can be estimated, along with the effort required; for example "If we learn effectively from the ten locations we expect to acquire in the next quarter, by how many days could we shorten the process for future quarters?"

We can illustrate the impact of learning by allowing the retail business in Figure 10.2 to improve its capabilities as experience of acquiring sites builds up over its first five years. Figure 10.10 shows how learning speeds up the firm's site acquisition rate. With no learning, lead-time capability remains stuck at 0.5, but learning enables capability to grow over about one year.

If the firm waited until the whole process had completed for the first new stores before making improvements, those acquisitions that were initiated during the first six quarters would take just as long as the first one. However, because the firm works to raise its capability along the whole process right from the start, and

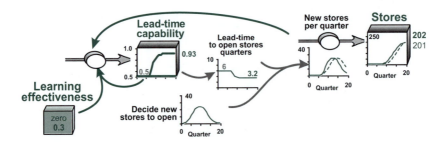

**Figure 10.10: Learning raises the retailer's site-acquisition capability.**

because it starts so poorly, there is much opportunity to improve, and lead-times drop sharply as soon as the full process has completed for the first few stores. The business actually ends up with virtually the same number of stores by the end of year five, but only because its growth program has by that time slowed considerably. In earlier periods, the total size of the chain is substantially greater than with no learning.

Learning is still not totally effective; if it were, lead times would drop instantly from six quarters to three. But over the first year or so after the team has completed its first acquisitions, the lead-time drops near to this shortest possible time. Note the feedback from the rate of store acquisition to growth of capability, which implies that the more stores are opened, the more is to be learned. The link from the existing capability level back to its own growth rate indicates that the stronger the capability is, the less opportunity there is to improve further.

Capturing the same mechanism for all three of the team's capabilities—for speed, quality and cost—leads to substantial improvements in performance, sufficient to move the business into profits over the final year (Figure 10.11). Not only does the more rapid opening of stores enable customers to be captured more quickly, but the improving quality of new stores gives access to a larger proportion of potential customers.

(Online learning materials are available to support this example, see p.xxi.)

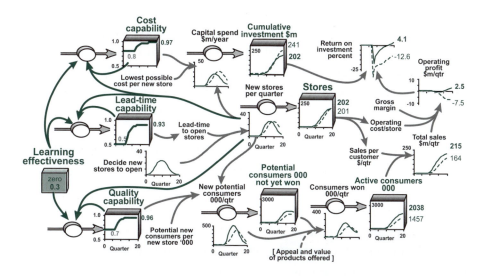

**Figure 10.11: The impact of learning on each of the retailer's site-acquisition capabilities.**

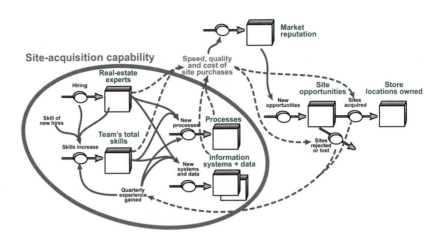

**Figure 10.12: The elements contributing to the retailer's composite site-acquisition capability.**

As was signalled in the classification of resources and capabilities in Figure 9.1, and argued earlier in this chapter, capabilities are composite factors, combining people, skills, processes and intangible factors. Each of these is clearly demonstrated in the story of this company's learning (Figure 10.12). The first expert brought just a little skill that allowed some sites to be acquired with modest speed, quality and cost. This experience allowed him to increase his skill, and further hiring added capacity and hence increased the group's capability as measured in terms of its maximum rate of acquisition. The early sharing between the team led to adoption of simple processes to improve the speed, quality and cost, raising further the rate of site acquisition and providing further experience. Adding the analyst and computer systems raised capability still further. To this was added the benefit of data, both about the real-estate market itself and regarding the attributes of previous successful acquisitions. Finally, this whole process was accelerated by the development of the company's reputation in the real-estate market.

This further detail enables still more specific assessment and decision-making about the building of capability for this company. Should it, for example, add a particular new information system? This is answered by assessing the impact the system will have, given the team's size, skill, available data and other processes, on the speed, quality or cost of future site acquisitions. Could its processes be improved? A standard business-process mapping study would clarify exactly the stages involved in the process, identify any shortcomings and improvements, and if these were significant lead to a redesign to make the process more effective to a known extent.

The organization has exactly what it needs to accomplish these improvements in the form of its own experience of previous activity. Every new store they open tells them something about how to cut the time, find better locations and cut cost from the process. Like most learning processes, the more experience teams have, the better they will become, but there are some important details concerning the scope for such learning and the speed at which it can occur.

- Early experience can make the greatest fractional impact. First, since the initial capability is low, there is a large opportunity for improvement. Second, each new experience in the beginning is a large fractional increase in total experience. (See equivalent discussion for the impact of cumulative manufactured output via the experience curve in Chapter 6.)
- Conversely, there will be diminishing returns to learning from experience. Not only will capability eventually be high, leaving little scope for further improvement, but each new event will provide little that has not been experienced before. There will be practical limits to just how quickly a new store could be opened, or its costs reduced, no matter how capable the team becomes.
- Learning does not happen automatically. For example, if one member of the team discovers a better way of contacting real-estate agents to improve the flow of good quality opportunities, that learning will be merely an increase in the individual's skill unless they explain it the rest of the team. Their discovery will have further impact if it is deliberately embedded in the process by which the entire team goes about their task.

## CAPABILITIES NOT ASSOCIATED WITH RESOURCE-BUILDING

Figure 10.3 showed that critical capabilities are linked to the acquisition, development and retention of the main tangible resources for most organizations. However, certain capabilities focus on intermediate factors that are not resources.

One example concerns the teams of sales people that some newspapers and magazines employ to sell advertizing space by phone to known advertizers. Other sales staff are responsible for winning those advertizers in the first place. This is a common practice in other organizations too, where winning and retaining customers is the main responsibility of sales people who call on customers, leaving continuing sales capture to telephone-based sales groups. Chapter 3 showed how sales performance in many situations depends on winning and keeping customers, *and* on growing sales to existing customers. It is therefore to be expected

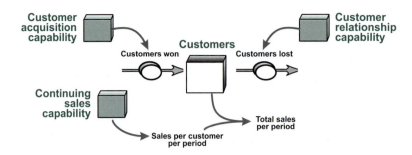

**Figure 10.13:** Distinct capabilities linked to winning, retaining and selling to customers.

that we will find a capability associated with each of these three elements (Figure 10.13).

These distinct capabilities are also reflected in a common sales management approach known as the "hunter/farmer model." Some sales people have a particular talent for finding and capturing new customers, that is the top left capability in Figure 10.13, while others are particularly skilled at maintaining relationships, covering the top-right capability in that diagram, plus the continuing sales capability where that is not the responsibility of a separate group.

Elevator companies have service teams with a strong capability to keep customers' elevators running and fix any breakdowns quickly and reliably. As for the computer service firm in chapter 9, service quality will ultimately affect customer losses, but the capability of the team has a more immediate focus on ensuring high quality service, rather than a more general aim of "retaining customers" (Figure 10.14).

**Figure 10.14:** Service quality capability for elevator maintenance and similar companies.

### Doing it right! Measuring capabilities

The example discussed earlier gives each of the detailed capabilities within the retailer's site-finding group a measure directly related to the objective it is pursuing—speed, quality or cost. If capabilities are to be usable for strategy analysis and planning, it is important that they be given measures that are accurately expressed and unambiguous. As for intangible resources, it is often appropriate to start with the extremes of a zero-to-one scale:

- Zero capability implies that, no matter how much other useful resource the team is given, it would not succeed in building the resource for which it is responsible. If their task is to retain a resource against loss, then its outflow continues at the rapid rate that would occur if the team did not exist.
- Capability of 1.0 is the maximum performance that can be imagined, or that is possible, given absolute limits.

As noted earlier, this zero-to-one range often leads to capability levels that are nearer the 1.0 end of the scale, since organizations with especially low capabilities on important processes will not likely survive. Three common reference points some precision to these measures:

1. A maximum rate of resource-building—a sales team's capability would be 1.0, for example, if every sales call won a new customer.
2. The resource-building rate of outstanding groups within the firm itself—e.g. "If all our plant management teams were as effective as those running the French factory, how high would our production yields be?" This benchmark may not be 1.0, if we can imagine productivity being still higher than this team is achieving, but gives us a sense of how close to 1.0 each team might be.
3. The resource-building rate of an exemplary firm in a comparable sector— e.g. if we believe that no marketing team could do a better job than the people at Coca-Cola, we could ask how fast *they* would build consumer awareness if they had our product and marketing budgets to work with.

Our team's capability is then defined as the ratio between the rate at which they are actually building the resource, and the best rate that can be imagined, given one of the benchmarks above.

**Figure 10.15: Learning structures for sales and service capabilities not linked to resource flows.**

Other examples of capabilities not directly focused on resource flows include distribution capabilities to ensure on-time delivery to customers and product range selection to maximize customer purchase rates. The generic capability/resource structure from Figure 10.9 is easily modified to deal with such cases, simply substituting the sales rate, service quality or other performance metric for the resource flow rate (Figure 10.15).

These capabilities also share other commonalities with those linked to resource-building:

- they rely on developing sufficient staff, of adequate skill, provided with effective procedures, and supported by efficient systems and data (as in Figure 10.12)
- the capability can have three principal components; speed (do the sales people sell quickly, and the service people fix the elevators fast), quality (do the sales people win valuable sales, are the elevators fixed well), and low cost (is it cheap to finalize each sale, and to fix each elevator)

## CAPABILITIES IN LOW-FAIR AIRLINES

Ryanair and similar low-fare airlines demonstrate well many of the principles regarding capabilities. Following the principle that capabilities will be found at the major resource flows in the strategic architecture, and with certain non-resource performance measures, Table 10.3 lists the main capabilities, and Figure 10.16 shows the location of each (green resource flows and text).

Each of these capabilities can then be examined in detail, following the principle illustrated previously. The opening of operations at new airports is a particularly close match for the site-acquisition capability of the retail store chain. Figure 10.17 shows how elements of this particular capability at Ryanair have combined with the capability to identify and add new travel routes and to market those services in

## TABLE 10.3: PRINCIPAL CAPABILITIES FOR LOW-FARE AIRLINES

| Resources needed | Capability | Criteria | Measures |
|---|---|---|---|
| Airports | Opening new airports | Speed<br>Number of potential customers reached<br>Cost of operating from each airport<br>Cost of access and starting operations | Months from decision<br>000 people<br><br>€ 000 per year<br><br>€ 000 |
| Routes | Starting services on new routes | Speed<br>Number of passengers using the route | Months from decision<br>000 people |
| Aircraft | Acquiring and commissioning new aircraft | Speed<br>Cost | Months from decision<br>€000 |
| Staff [repeated for each function] | Hiring, training and retention | Speed of hiring<br>[Low] rate of loss<br>Staff performance<br>Cost | Time to full productivity<br>Fractional turnover<br>Rating on job tasks<br>Cost per person hired |
| Customers | Marketing | New customer win rate<br>Retention<br>Customer quality<br>Cost | 000 people per month<br>000 lost per month<br>Travel frequency<br>Cost per new customer |

| Capabilities not related to resources | Criteria | Measures |
|---|---|---|
| Flight operations | Reliability<br>Service quality | On-time performance<br>Customer rating |
| Sales and pricing | Load factor | Fraction of seats sold |
| Operating efficiency [repeated for each function] | Cost per activity | € per passenger flight |

order to build customer numbers and passenger-journeys over the company's history to date. It also shows (dashed lines) the pace of future resource development that those capabilities will need to drive in order to hit the prospective performance described in Chapter 4.

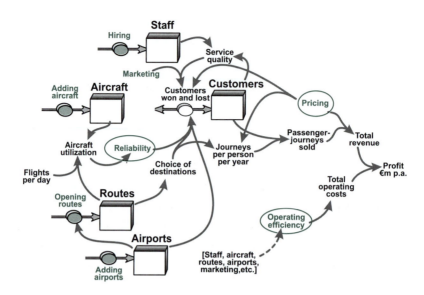

**Figure 10.16:** Locating the main capabilities for a low-fare airline on its strategic architecture.

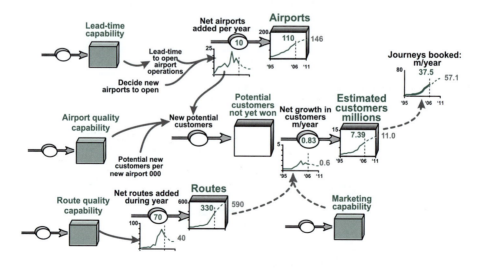

**Figure 10.17:** How Ryanair's capability for opening new airport operations and routes has driven growth of customers and sales.

# CAPABILITIES IN PUBLIC SECTOR AND VOLUNTARY ORGANIZATIONS

The frameworks for linking capabilities to resource-development are directly applicable to noncommercial organizations. Chapter 5 demonstrated the challenge for a voluntary organization seeking to improve its income from donors by balancing its efforts between winning new donors, retaining existing donors and raising more money from those donors it currently had. Figure 10.18 shows the structure of the composite capability for identifying and winning new donors. Just as for the retailer's site-acquisition team, the group starts by needing some individuals with fundraising skills. As the team's experience grows, they share good ideas about how to win the particular kinds of new donors this organization is seeking. They can then go on to develop processes and information systems to make the process more reliable and still more effective.

Public services and voluntary organizations also have in common with business cases a focus on some intermediate performance measure, rather than on resource-building, such as the quality of support for groups they serve. The Motor Neurone Disease Association discussed in Chapter 2 relied on visitors and care advisors to provide effective support for members living with the disease. The Association's difficulties arose at various points along the knowledge development chain. The low frequency of calls to members made by most of its visitors gave few opportunities for individuals to learn. The wide geographic dispersion of these individuals made

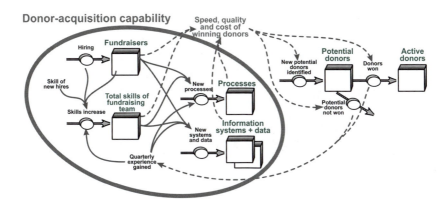

**Figure 10.18:** **Donor-acquisition capability for a voluntary organization.**

it hard to share tacit knowledge. Finally, heavy work on the care advisors gave little spare capacity for anyone to record effective processes, to disseminate them to visitors or to encourage their use.

# CAPABILITIES AND ORGANIZATIONAL LEARNING

The observations that arose above from the retailer's capability-building suggest that four further features need to be added to the standard architecture of learning dynamics in Figure 10.9:

*1. Limits to learning*
Like many asset-stocks, there is a limit to how far most capabilities can be improved, even if everything went perfectly, and all internal processes were instantaneous and 100% reliable.

*2. Learning from failure*
There can be plenty of opportunity to learn from failure, both on acquisition and retention of resources. Examples of the first include product launches that did not work, bids for projects that failed and marketing campaigns that did not capture the additional customers hoped for. Regarding resource losses, companies increasingly carry out exit interviews with departing staff in order to find out how they can do better at retaining their people. Some even interview customers to find out why they left, so as to improve service levels, product quality, and so on.

*3. Loss of capability: forgetting*
Also in common with other asset-stocks, capabilities may be depleted. One mechanism was already explained in Chapter 5, with the departure of skills when individuals leave the organization. Other mechanisms for capability depletion were mentioned in Chapter 9, such as the obsolescence of data, systems and processes. However, the mutual reinforcement between people's skills, processes and information systems can make capabilities robust against minor losses of staff.

*4. Learning effectiveness*
Some building of capability may occur naturally, as individuals and teams learn from experience and informally share their growing understanding. However,

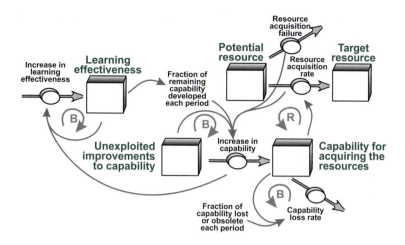

**Figure 10.19:** Extending the generic picture of capability-building dynamics.

this is unlikely to generate the rate of learning that might be possible if the team deliberately designed processes for reviewing recent experience to seek new insight, and using that review for improving processes, systems and their own skills. The team's learning effectiveness is then the rate at which they are actually increasing capability relative to the best rate at which they could conceivably do so.

These four additional mechanisms are shown in the expanded diagram of generic capability development in Figure 10.19. The "B" symbols indicate self-limiting, or balancing, feedback structures, as explained in Chapter 4.

To illustrate the third of these points, there is an interesting epilogue to the site-acquisition story above. During the company's fifth year, a competitor seeking to grow in the same market hired away the company's first and most experienced expert, hoping to emulate their success. In spite of this loss, the original company experienced no disruption whatever to its growth plans. His expertise had become embedded in the systems, processes and routines of the team, and the small loss of his capacity was soon replaced by rising younger staff. One mechanism for organizational forgetting in this case—loss of people—was therefore ineffective. This is not to say that the capability would survive a larger scale of defection. It is common in some industries for firms to target and hire not individuals, but entire teams, in the expectation that the firm will be able to jump almost instantly from a low capability to a higher level. Some further investment may still be needed, for example in the systems the team needs to function at its peak, but the major delay will have been overcome.

The second outcome of this episode is that the competitor still failed to match the first company's success. Their controls on staff hiring and "non-essential" spending meant that their new hire was unable to build either the team or the systems that he had assembled in his first company. Furthermore, the original company continued to get the favored treatment by real-estate agents.

## CAPABILITIES AND TACIT KNOWLEDGE

Chapter 9 explained the importance of the intangible resource of knowledge to the performance of a firm's tangible resource-system, and signaled that knowledge would feature again in this chapter's discussion of capabilities. For effective learning, knowledge must be captured. Since we are concerned here with the ability to get things done, this discussion is about know-*how* (how to do things), rather than the know-*what* of factual information.

A framework for understanding better the effectiveness of group learning starts with a distinction between tacit and explicit knowledge. The discussion of the retailer's building of a site-acquisition capability above rather implies that all the activities in the process came to be defined, written down, and followed in detail. However, this was not the reality in that situation, nor is it generally the case, even in the most regimented process-driven teams.

Early in the retailer's growth, the first few experts discovered problems in how they were doing the job, worked out better approaches, and discussed them with each other. Their discussion shared what is known as "tacit knowledge"—things that group members know how to do without recording them as "explicit knowledge" or rigorously observing them.

Organizations constantly move many small pieces of knowledge from tacit to explicit, either in a deliberately planned manner or because it seems to make sense. The "spiral of knowledge" model[15] describes how knowledge moves from individuals to groups to organizations as a whole and thence to other organizations, whilst at the same time moving from tacit to explicit forms. How well this process works is of considerable importance to the effectiveness with which groups and organizations learn.

To make this phenomenon concrete and therefore amenable to analysis and deliberate management intervention, it is possible to survey a group at a point in time and have them record:

- things individuals know but have not shared
- things people know and have shared, but not recorded

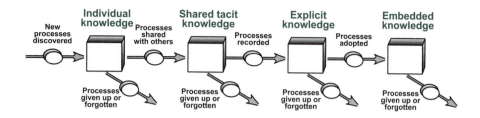

**Figure 10.20: Know-how moving from tacit to explicit and from individual to shared.**

- things the group has recorded, but do not use
- things that are recorded and regularly used

This is a resource-development chain similar to others explained in Chapter 6. Figure 10.20 offers one possibility for how knowledge progresses, starting with individuals discovering good ways of doing things.

The store-acquisition knowledge above was first shared with the other individuals, but not recorded, that is it flowed from being held by individuals to being shared, but still tacit. Next certain know-how that seemed worthwhile to document was recorded, that is made explicit. There is no guarantee that know-how about how best to do things will be adopted by everyone, even if it is highly effective, so finally some explicit knowledge moves to being adopted.

It is assumed in Figure 10.20 that individuals and groups make use of the tacit knowledge early in the chain, but this is not necessarily the case, so a complete model would need additional stocks of unused, tacit knowledge. As for many of the resources discussed in earlier chapters, two further things can happen to these knowledge items. First, they can move backwards as well as forwards along the chain. Embedded knowledge can fall into disuse, or shared, tacit knowledge can be forgotten by the team but not by a particular individual. Secondly, knowledge can fall out of the chain altogether, with know-how being lost because individuals or groups forget about it, because people leave, because knowledge becomes obsolete, or for other reasons.

There is no presumption here that all knowledge necessarily *should* move forward along the chain. It is costly in both effort and money to share, record and disseminate knowledge, and much knowledge is not of sufficient impact to be worth this investment. On the other hand, organizations have found some remarkably effective ways of disseminating know-how. At the extremely simple end of the scale is a solution discovered by one law-firm, concerned that different groups of lawyers were not sufficiently aware of each others' knowledge. Their solution was monthly "speed-dating" sessions, at which people moved from partner to partner every five minutes, during which time each had to tell the other important know-how about both legal practice and client development. At the more sophisticated level, organizations with a strong technology base, such as 3M Inc and CSC operate internal technology "shows" where groups show off their knowledge to others who may then combine what they find with other knowledge they possess to move further forward.

## WHEN LEARNING BUILDS MULTIPLE CAPABILITIES

Previously it has been argued that organizational performance arises from the complementary development of resources reinforcing each others' growth, leading to outcomes that reflect the power of the entire system, rather than the sum of individual elements (see Chapter 4). Figure 10.11 shows the scope for complementarity between resources and their related capabilities to add to this system-performance. However, that picture was looking only at the impact of capabilities around growth of a single resource—retail stores.

A retail firm, or any other, will possess capabilities linked to all the main resources of the business (see Figure 10.3). It is therefore to be expected that learning on several of these would add still further to performance. Figure 10.21 shows the impact for the retailer if it also improves its merchandizing capability—the ability to identify the best product range to attract consumers and display them in the most appealing manner. At first this capability is modest, at 0.5, implying

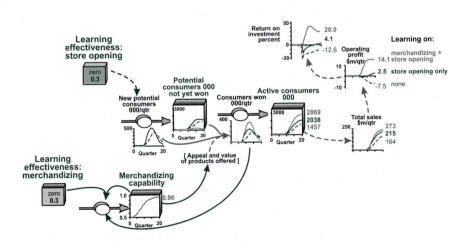

**Figure 10.21: Adding further to the retailer's performance with increasing merchandizing capability.**

that the business is winning potential consumers at only half the rate it could if it were totally capable. Its experience with new stores allows its merchandizing team to improve their capability until, by year five, the capability is near total. The consequences of this are that whenever a new store is opened, virtually all potential consumers are captured immediately. (This is in fact what leading retailers often expect to accomplish, with newly opened stores moving straight to high levels of penetration in their local market.)

The further improvement in performance is considerable, but entirely explicable. Although customer numbers and sales only grow to some 30% more than when relying on low levels of merchandizing capability, the resulting increase in gross profit is added to the stores' largely fixed cost base, so operating profits and return on investment both rise sharply. This further justifies the suggestion offered previously that small differences in capabilities and learning can explain exceedingly wide differences in performance of rival firms, with no need to hypothesize the existence of complex, abstract and cross-organizational capabilities.

## ORGANIZATIONAL LEARNING

Organizational learning has attracted considerable attention, both in the academic and managerial journals, and has understandably led to many companies making efforts to ensure that learning is encouraged and enabled. We have already distinguished between individual learning (Chapter 5 on skills attributes) and team learning that builds capability for key parts of the organization system to improve its performance and hence raise that of the entire enterprise. However a still further level of learning has been identified, concerning change in learning itself.

An early conceptualization of this idea distinguished "single-loop" learning from "double-loop" learning.[16] Single-loop learning was explained in terms of individuals or groups modifying their actions according to the difference between expected outcomes and actual outcomes. In double-loop learning, people have the additional ability to question the assumptions that led to the actions in the first place, and make further changes. In effect, double-loop learning is about "learning to learn." This becomes particularly important when changes occur in just what the organization *needs* to be good at. For example, it was once of great importance for music publishers to excel at promoting their artists' music via CD sales through stores. With growth of online access to music, that capability has declined sharply in relevance, to the point that its

### Learning from games

Many fields of human endeavor now recognize that if it is too costly, time-consuming or simply impossible to learn about complex processes by working with the real-world itself, then it may be both effective and efficient to use simulations instead. Pharmaceuticals companies model the biochemical behavior of new drugs, plane makers model aerodynamics of new wings, pilots train on simulators, and armies use war games, both physical and computer-based, to prepare for combat.

Games for management learning come in a wide variety of styles, from role-play exercises and board games, through to complex, computer-based, multi-team competitive games that run over many days. Experienced executives develop an intuitive understanding for many of the phenomena described in this book, simply by working in their industries for some years. Working together, they also develop collective understanding, much of which is tacit. Whilst this approach to learning may eventually be somewhat effective, it takes many years and may not be entirely reliable, allowing poor strategy and policy to arise rather more frequently than we might prefer.

This unreliable learning arises from the "dynamic complexity" of strategy challenges. (Dynamic complexity implies complications arising from how things interact and change over time, in contrast to "detail complexity" which describes the problems caused by very large amounts of information that may need to be considered.) Some management problems have analytical solutions. Examples include the impact on unit cost of raising production rates, the net present value of an investment with known future cash flows, or the impact of price changes on demand when only direct demand elasticity can take place. Most strategy challenges, and many functional, operational problems, on the other hand, feature a combination of accumulation and feedback mechanisms for which no analytical solution exists.

For these dynamically complex problems, it is simply not possible to learn which interventions will produce what outcomes by reading about the mechanisms at work—the only route to learning is by repeated experimentation.[17] The models and microworlds featured throughout this book are designed to provide exactly that opportunity for individuals and teams to accelerate their understanding of these dynamics. See p.xxi and further information at www.strategydynamics.com.

It is possible to take the principle further. First, simulating the real history of business issues or entire companies can allow testing of strategy and policy options for the future. Such models can be constantly updated with live data to become living, and truly dynamic balanced scorecards. Second, competitive situations can be modeled and used in gaming mode to learn about the consequences of alternative strategies and competitive responses, following some of the principles outlined in Chapter 7. Lastly, industry situations can be modeled, generating alternative scenarios for the future that allow management to "visit the future" and test out the success of alternative strategies in these differing possible worlds.

For more on the value of dynamic modeling for strategy and policy, see the wide range of resources available from the International System Dynamics Society at www.systemdynamics.org.

value is threatened with extinction. They still need to promote their artists, but now as a means of capturing ticket sales for live shows and the resulting sales of related products.

This is a more serious case of obsolescence than discussed in Chapter 9, when procedures and systems needed to be updated so as to remain relevant—in these new cases, no amount of updating can keep the capability relevant. This has led to the suggestion that established capabilities can in fact become obstacles that prevent organizations adopting the new capabilities they require, in effect becoming "rigidities," that need to be dismantled.[18] A related concept is that of "dominant logic"; the tendency for management to become accustomed to one way of understanding how the business works and thus adopting ways of making decisions that come to dominate strategy and policy.[19] Although introduced in the context of how multi-business corporations tend to apply similar mental models to business units that function somewhat differently, it is clear that a similar dominant logic could prevent a single activity organization initiating changes away from capabilities that have supported previous success.

If current capabilities risk becoming obsolete, or even obstructive, management may need to anticipate changes in their environment in order to consider how their strategies might have to change and what new capabilities may be required. Given uncertainties about many of the exogenous forces at work (see Chapter 6 on PEST anlaysis), there may be several directions in which that environment could develop. Management can either wait and see what happens and try to learn as they go, or else explore what those alternative futures might hold and work out what they may need to be good at in each. A powerful approach now widely adopted among some larger firms is "scenario planning," in which management seeks contrasting stories of how the future might play out, often with outside advice to avoid the problems arising from dominant logic.[20]

There is an extensive literature on the many concepts involved in organizational learning, scenario planning and related issues, both academic[21] and managerial.[22] Whilst the phenomena are both real and important, they are as yet not sufficiently definitive and quantifiable as to be amenable to rigorous analysis. It is not possible to specify how much organizational learning capability any enterprise possesses, how much difference this makes to the performance they deliver over time, how input of what effort will make what difference to that capability, or what improvements in performance will result. Nevertheless, our inability to specify and quantify these factors does not in any way imply that they are unimportant. Many organizations gain considerable benefit from considering qualitatively how to enhance their learning. Many also sustain strong competitive performance by assessing their plans against qualitative scenarios for the future.

### Summary of Chapter 10

Capabilities (or competences) are activities that groups and organizations are good at doing, as distinct from the resources, both tangible and intangible, to which organizations have access. Most capabilities can be simply expressed as activities concerned with acquiring, developing or retaining resources. To perform well the organization will need a capability linked to each significant resource flow in its architecture.

It is not necessary to invoke complex, abstract, cross-organizational capabilities in order to explain large differences in performance, because small differences in simple capabilities have an accumulating impact on resources.

It is easiest to work with capabilities when three more specific elements are distinguished—getting things done quickly, with high quality and at low cost. This makes it possible to put quantitative measures on a capability, and on its impact on performance. From this start-point management can identify specifically what scope exists to improve the capability, what to do to make that happen, and the likely impact on performance that will result.

Capabilities are composite asset-stocks, consisting of the people associated with the activity, the sum of their individual and shared skills, the business processes they follow to get the activity done, and the information systems and data available to help them. Nevertheless, it can be sufficient to formulate any capability as a single asset-stock. Broad capabilities, such as product development or hiring are often sub-divided amongst teams with particular responsibilities; HR staff attract and screen job applicants while line management interview and select, for example.

Business process mapping and redesign focuses on simplifying and eliminating activities to speed up and cut the cost for each entity that flows through the process. As a result BPR often reduces or eliminates unproductive asset-stocks, such as products in market testing but not yet launched, or orders received but not yet despatched. Strategy dynamics, in contrast, focuses on the rate of acquiring, developing and retaining *desirable* asset-stocks. Each approach serves its own important purpose.

Whilst most capabilities are located at the resource flows in an organization's strategic architecture, certain capabilities are not linked to flows, but aim to raise performance on other important measures, such as delivering service quality or growing sales to existing customers. Capabilities are often easily measured as the ratio between how well an activity is actually done (speed, quality and cost), compared wit the best possible performance that could be imagined.

The capability framework is directly applicable to public sector and voluntary organizations, along with all the additional considerations above concerning speed, quality and cost, business process design, and so on.

Capabilities grow as a result of feedback from the activity they support—the more we do, the more we discover how to do it well—and this self-reinforcing process is the principal mechanism that drives learning. Organizations can, and do, set out deliberately to capture such learning and hence grow capability as strongly as possible. Much knowledge may be tacit, rather than explicit and held by individuals, so learning involves seeking out such knowledge and making it explicit, shared and utilized by whole groups, often by documenting and embedding it in group processes.

While there are diminishing opportunities for further improvement to already-strong capabilities, the marginal impact of even small increases in resource-building on performance justifies constant efforts to raise capability still further. Capabilities, like resources, may be lost or become obsolete—loss of capabilities can be thought of as organizational forgetting, driven by staff turnover or simply by lack of attention to retaining important capabilities.

If small differences in isolated capabilities can have a substantial impact on resource-building and overall performance, the potential impact of strong capabilities working together is considerable. The puzzle, then, is not so much why apparently similar organizations differ in their performance, but why performance differences are not much wider than observed in many industries.

There is a limit to how much codification can be applied to capabilities and learning, and complex, subtle capabilities undoubtedly play a role in addition to the simple capabilities defined in this chapter. Furthermore, capabilities need to be changed as competitive and other external factors change the detail of what organizations need to be good at doing. This exploration of the future can be accomplished with scenario-based planning, and strategy can be usefully explored and learned about by the use of simulation-based games.

# SUGGESTED QUESTIONS AND EXERCISES

1.  Explain how a capability differs from a resource. The most important capabilities in an organization contribute to performance in a specific way—what is that?
2.  Many capabilities help the organization do something well on three distinct criteria—what are these? That is, what does doing it "well" actually mean?
3.  Where would you start to look in a firm's strategic architecture to find capabilities that may be important?
4.  Identify capabilities that may be influential for the organization you chose to look at in Chapters 2–4. Alternatively, carry out the same exercise using the outline architectures you developed after Chapter 4 for one or more of the following examples:
    a.  a retail chain, such as Starbucks
    b.  a company manufacturing and servicing elevators
    c.  an online dating agency
    d.  a voluntary organization providing medical centers in locations that have no alternative provision.
5.  Use Worksheet 15a to show the relationship between one or more of the capabilities identified in answer to question 4 and the resource flow that it enables. What exactly is it that the organization learns about the resource flow that enables its capability to increase?
6.  Looking in more detail at the capabilities in your example, identify any that require distinct capabilities for the speed, quality and cost of building the resource, and give measures for those three separate elements.
7.  Looking in more detail at your chosen example, identify whether distinct capabilities exist for [a] acquiring [b] developing and [c] retaining any particular resource

# USING WORKSHEETS 15A AND 15B

These Worksheets offer templates for the widespread relationship between capability and resource-building. Before using them, the following steps should be taken:

*   specify the timescale and frequency over which the situation is to be examined, e.g. two years back and three years forward in months, and the scale for all variables
*   identify and name the resources involved, and other variables

- add a timescale and value scale to each item, and insert data or estimates for how those quantities have changed in the past and might change in the future

(In common with other worksheets, this one can also be used to examine just the current situation and implications of alternative choices for the next period. In this case, it is not necessary to specify the timescale to be studied, nor to sketch the time charts as suggested below. Simply enter numerical values instead. In that case, though, it is important to beware of the sometimes surprizing implications for performance in future periods arising from choices that are apparently sound on a short-term view.)

Worksheet 15a deals only with the simplest relationship between a single aggregate measure for a capability and the rate of growth of the resource it enables (see for example Figure 10.10). If the issue of concern is the capability to develop or retain a resource rather than acquire it, simply redraw the upper section of the diagram to connect the capability to the appropriate resource flow (see Figure 10.6). To use this worksheet:

- enter the historical rate of resource-growth and the level of the resource itself in the upper section
- specify the highest rate of resource-growth that would be feasible, that is if the organization possessed the highest capability imaginable
- comparing the actual rate of resource-growth with the highest rate achievable, estimate how the capability level has been changing

Having completed this assessment of the organization's historic capability on this resource-growth issue, estimate the rate of increase in capability that may be possible, and the impact this will have on future resource-growth.

Worksheet 15b examines separately the capabilities for acquiring resources rapidly, of good quality and at low cost. Repeat the steps above for each of these sub-capabilities (see for example Figure 10.2)

These worksheets are easier to work with using the **my**strategy software versions, see paragraph about online learning materials on p.xxi.

# WORKSHEET 15A: CAPABILITY AND RESOURCE-BUILDING

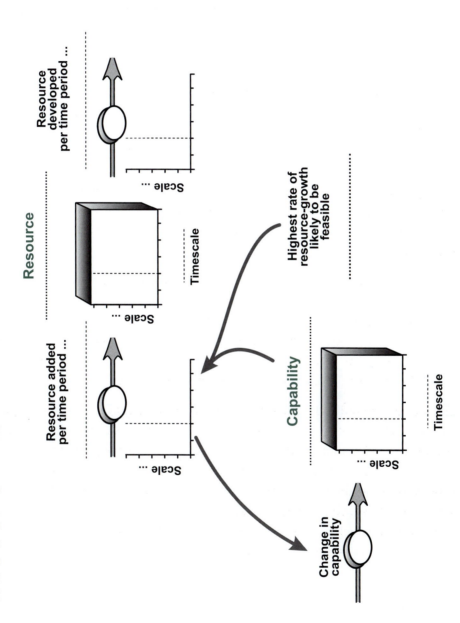

# WORKSHEET 15B: CAPABILITY FOR SPEED, QUALITY AND COST

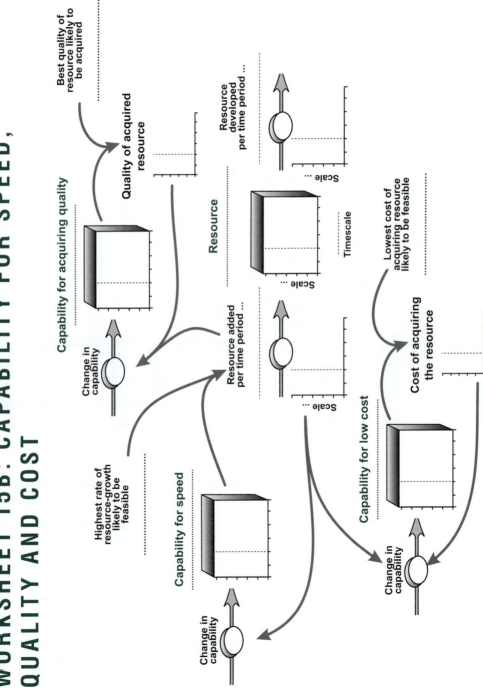

# NOTES

1. Barney, J. (2007) *Gaining and Sustaining Competitive Advantage* (3rd edn), Prentice Hall, Upper Saddle River, NJ, p. 24.

2. Stephen Tallman, *Dynamic Capabilities*, in Faulkner, D. and Campbell, A. (Eds) (2003) *The Oxford Handbook of Strategy (Volume I)*, p. 380. The evolutionary view of capabilities came into focus in Nelson, R. and Winter, S. (1982) *An evolutionary theory of economic change.* Harvard University Press, Cambridge, MA.

3. McGee, J. Thomas, H. and Wilson, D. (2005) *Strategy: Analysis and Practice*, McGraw-Hill, Maidenhead, p. 252.

4. Grant, R. *Contemporary Strategy Analysis*, (2005), Blackwell, Oxford, pp. 105–151.

5. de Wit, B. and Meyer, R. *Strategy: Process, Content, Context* 3rd edn, (2004), Thomson, London, p. 284.

6. Hitt, M., Ireland, D. and Hoskisson, R. (2001) *Strategic Management: Competitiveness and Globalization*, 4th edn, South-Western/Thomson, Cincinatti, p. 108.

7. Stalk, G., Evans, P. and Shulman, L. (1992) Competing on Capabilities, *Harvard Business Review*, **70**(2) (March/April), 57–69

8. See Hamel, G. and Heene, A. (Eds) (1994) Competence-based Competition, John Wiley & Sons, Ltd, Chichester.

9. Prahalad, C.K. and Hamel, G. (1990), The Core Competence of the Corporation, *Harvard Busienss Review*, **68**(3), May-June, 79–91.

10. Leonard-Barton, D. (1992) Core Capabilities and Core Rigidities; a Paradox in Managing New Product Development, *Strategic Management Journal*, **13** (Special Summer Issue), 111–125. The phrase also appears in managerial articles, such as Schoemaker, P.J.H. (1992) How to Link Strategic Vision to Core Capabilities, *Sloan Management Review*, **34**(1), 67–81.

11. Hammer, M. (1990) Reengineering Work: Don't automate, obliterate, *Harvard Business Review*, **68**(4), (July/August), 104–112; Davenport, T.H. and Short, J.E., The New Industrial Engineering: Information Technology and Business Process Redesign, *Sloan Management Review*, **31**(4), 11–27.

12. Hammer, M. and Champney, J. (1993) *Reengineering the Corporation: a Manifesto for Business Revolution*, Harper Collins, New York; Davenport, T. (1993) *Process Innovation: Reengineering work through Information Technology*, Harvard Business School Press, Boston, MA.

13. There is now a vast array of resources explaining business process mapping and redesign. An accessible explanation can be found in Hunt, D. V. (1996)

*Process Mapping: How to Reengineer your Business Processes*, John Wiley & Sons, Ltd, New York.

14.   Johnson, G., Scholes, K. and Whittington, R. *Exploring Corporate Strategy*, 7th edn (2005), Prentice Hall, Harlow, p. 137.

15.   Nonaka, I. (1994) A dynamics theory of knowledge creation, *Organizational Science*, **5**(1), 14–35; von Krogh, G. Ichijo, K. Nonaka, I. (2000) *Enabling Knowledge Creation: How to Unlock the Mystery of Tacit Knowledge and Release the Power of Innovation*, Oxford University Press, Oxford.

16.   Argyris, C. and Schön, D. (1978) *Organizational Learning: a theory of action perspective*, Addison-Wesley, Reading, MA.

17.   See for example Schrage, M. (2000) *Serious Play*, Harvard Business School Press, Boston, MA.

18.   See Leonard-Barton, D. (1992) note 10 above. Other sources that discuss factors slowing or obstructing organizational learning include Rumelt, R. (1995) Inertia and Transformation, in Cynthia Montgomery (Ed), *Resource-based and evolutionary theories of the firm*, Kluwer, Boston; Argyris, C. (1990) *Overcoming organizational defenses; facilitating organizational learning*, Allyn and Bacon, Needham, MA; Baden-Fuller, C. and Stopford, J. (1994) *Rejuvenating the mature business*, Harvard Business School Press, Boston, MA.

19.   Prahalad, C.K. and Bettis, R.A. (1986) The dominant logic: a new linkage between diversity and performance, *Strategic Management Journal*, **7**, 485–501; Bettis, R. A. and Prahalad, C. K. (1995) The dominant logic: retrospective and extension, *Strategic Management Journal*, **16**, 5–14.

20.   de Geus, A. (1988) Planning as Learning, *Harvard Business Review*, **66**(2), March-April, 70–74.; van der Heijden, K. (1996) *Scenarios: the art of strategic conversation*, John Wiley & Sons, Ltd, Chichester.

21.   Teece, D.J., Pisano, G. and Shuen, A. (1997) Dynamic Capabilities and Strategic Management, *Strategic Management Journal*, **18**(7), 509–533; Eisenhardt, K.M. and Martin, J.A. (2000) Dynamic Capabilities: What are they?, *Strategic Management Journal*, **21**(11), 1105–1121; Zollo, M. and Winter, S.G. (2002) Deliberate learning and the evolution of dynamic capabilities, *Organization Science*, **13**(3), pp. 339–351; Winter, S. G. (2000) The satisficing principle in capability learning, *Strategic Management Journal*, **21**(10), 981–986; March, J.G. (1991) Exploration and exploitation in organizational learning, *Organization Science*, **2**, 71–87.

22.   See articles such as Garvin, D.A. (1993) Building a Learning Organization, *Harvard Business Review*, **71**(4), July-August, 78–91; Senge, P. (1990) The Leader's New Work: Building Learning Organizations, *Sloan Management*

*Review*, **32** (Fall), 7–23; Wenger, E.C. and Snydet, W.M. (2000) Communities of Practice: the organizational frontier, *Harvard Business Review*, **78** (1), January–February, 139–145. Books include Nonaka, I. and Takeuchi, H. (1995) *The Knowledge Creating Company*, Oxford University Press, New York, Senge, P. (1996) *The Fifth Discipline* (Revised edn), Random House, Sydney; Argyris, C. (1999) *On Organizational Learning* (2nd edn), Blackwell, Oxford.

# INDEX